The History of Florida

UNIVERSITY PRESS OF FLORIDA

Florida A&M University, Tallahassee
Florida Atlantic University, Boca Raton
Florida Gulf coast University, Ft. Myers
Florida International University, Miami
Florida State University, Tallahassee
New College of Florida, Sarasota
University of Central Florida, Orlando
University of Florida, Gainesville
University of North Florida, Jacksonville
University of South Florida, Tampa
University of West Florida, Pensacola

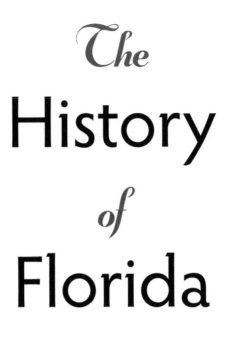

The
History
of
Florida

~

Edited by
Michael Gannon

University Press of Florida
Gainesville · Tallahassee · Tampa · Boca Raton
Pensacola · Orlando · Miami · Jacksonville · Ft. Myers · Sarasota

A Florida Quincentennial Book

Frontispiece: Lois Duncan Steinmetz admiring the scenery of the Suwannee River, 1949. Photo by Joseph Janney Steinmetz. State Archives of Florida, *Florida Memory*, http://floridamemory.com/items/show/245397.

Library of Congress Cataloging-in-Publication Data
The history of Florida / edited by Michael Gannon.
p. cm.
Includes bibliographical references and index.
"A Florida Quincentennial Book"
"Previously published as The New History of Florida."
ISBN 978-0-8130-4464-4 (alk. paper)
1. Florida—History. I. Gannon, Michael, 1927– II. New history of Florida.
F311.5.N49 2013
975.9—dc23
2013021903

The University Press of Florida is the scholarly publishing agency for the State University System of Florida, comprising Florida A&M University, Florida Atlantic University, Florida Gulf Coast University, Florida International University, Florida State University, New College of Florida, University of Central Florida, University of Florida, University of North Florida, University of South Florida, and University of West Florida.

University Press of Florida
15 Northwest 15th Street
Gainesville, FL 32611-2079
http://www.upf.com

The editor dedicates this volume to that gentle band of Franciscan friars, nearly 200-strong, who over 130 years of ministry in the hinterlands ensured that Florida's written history began with narratives of education, social justice, and benevolent service.

Contents

Introduction 1
Michael Gannon

1. Original Inhabitants 3
Jerald T. Milanich

2. First European Contacts 18
Michael Gannon

3. The Land They Found 41
Paul E. Hoffman

4. Settlement and Survival 55
Eugene Lyon

5. Republic of Spaniards, Republic of Indians 76
Amy Turner Bushnell

6. The Missions of Spanish Florida 91
John H. Hann

7. Raids, Sieges, and International Wars 112
Daniel L. Schafer

8. Pensacola, 1686–1763 128
William S. Coker

9. British Rule in the Floridas 144
Robin F. A. Fabel and Daniel L. Schafer

10. The Second Spanish Period in the Two Floridas . . . 162
Susan Richbourg Parker and William S. Coker

11. Free and Enslaved 179
Jane Landers

12. Florida's Seminole and Miccosukee Peoples 195
Brent R. Weisman

13. U.S. Territory and State 220
   Daniel L. Schafer

14. The Civil War, 1861–1865 244
   Robert A. Taylor

15. Reconstruction and Renewal, 1865–1877 260
   Jerrell H. Shofner

16. The First Developers 276
   Thomas Graham

17. Fortune and Misfortune: The Paradoxical 1920s 296
   William W. Rogers

18. The Great Depression 313
   William W. Rogers

19. World War II 332
   Gary R. Mormino

20. Florida by Nature: A Survey of Extrahuman
   Historical Agency 353
   Jack E. Davis

21. The Maritime Heritage of Florida 389
   Della A. Scott-Ireton and Amy M. Mitchell-Cook

22. Florida Politics: The State Evolves into One of
   the Nation's Premier Political Battlegrounds 415
   Susan A. MacManus and David R. Colburn

23. Florida's African American Experience:
   The Twentieth Century and Beyond 444
   Larry Eugene Rivers

24. Immigration and Ethnicity in Florida History 470
   Raymond A. Mohl and George E. Pozzetta

25. Boom, Bust, and Uncertainty: A Social History
   of Modern Florida 497
   Raymond A. Mohl and Gary R. Mormino

List of Contributors 529
Index 533

Introduction

MICHAEL GANNON

It is a happy coincidence of history that within three years' time, Florida celebrates two major historical moments. The first, occurring in 2013, is the 500th anniversary of the documented discovery of the peninsula by Juan Ponce de León. The second, to take place in 2015, is the 450th birthday of St. Augustine, the oldest permanent European community in what are now the United States and Canada, antedating Jamestown in Virginia and Plymouth in Massachusetts by forty-two and fifty-five years, respectively. Consider the age of St. Augustine: founded in 1565, it appeared on the scene one year after the death of Michelangelo and the birth of William Shakespeare.

To tell the long recorded history of this state, the University Press of Florida in 1993 commissioned twenty-three historians, all leading authorities in their fields, to collaborate on a joint history. Published in 1996, *The New History of Florida* has had a consoling success. Now that volume has been updated and enlarged by three new chapters and is offered as *The History of Florida*.

Readers will observe that most of the twenty-five chapters of this book follow upon each other chronologically, that is, "Fortune and Misfortune: The Paradoxical 1920s" (chapter 17) is followed by "The Great Depression" (chapter 18), which in turn is followed by "World War II" (chapter 19). Certain subject areas, however, overlap several or numerous time periods, and these are treated thematically. Thus, chapter 11, "Free and Enslaved," treats African societies in Florida from the sixteenth century to the middle of the nineteenth century. Similarly, chapter 12, "Florida's Seminole and Miccosukee Peoples," follows those peoples from their first arrival in Florida during the early eighteenth century as far as the 1900s. In this way, certain subjects of special interest are not broken up into segmented time periods but are presented as studies in one continuous, connected form.

The editor thanks Meredith Babb for her leadership in sparking this revised edition, his fellow authors for their exceptional chapters, and his spouse, Genevieve Haugen, who was a true coeditor.

1

Original Inhabitants

JERALD T. MILANICH

What is now the state of Florida was first settled by humans whose ancestors had entered North America from eastern Asia during the Pleistocene era, the Great Ice Age, about 12,000 years ago. Sea levels—as much as 350 feet lower than at present because of huge amounts of water tied up in Ice Age glaciers—exposed a large land bridge between Siberia and Alaska across what is now the Bering Strait. Hunter-gatherers in search of game and other foods easily crossed this land bridge which connected Asia and North America and was at least as wide as the distance from Orlando to New York City.

These early hunter-gatherers are called Paleoindians, and they entered Florida around 10,000 B.C., about the same time that they moved into other parts of what is now the United States. Evidently their nonsedentary lifestyle and a new world filled with plant and animal foods never encountered previously by humans enabled—perhaps encouraged—them to colonize the Americas quickly. Campsites of the Paleoindians are found across North America from Alaska to south Florida.

Some archaeologists argue that the Paleoindian migration was preceded by even earlier movements of people from Asia across the Siberia-Alaska land bridge into the Americas. But as yet the evidence for such a pre-Paleoindian presence in North America is tenuous. Certainly in Florida, the Paleoindians were the first human residents.

At the time of the Florida Paleoindians, the same lowered seas that created a transcontinental bridge across the Bering Strait gave Florida a total landmass about twice what it is today. The Gulf of Mexico shoreline, for instance, was more than 100 miles west of its present location. During the Paleoindian period, Florida also was much drier than it is today. Many of our present rivers, springs, and lakes were not here, and even groundwater levels were significantly lower. Plants that survived were those that could grow in the dry, cool conditions. Scrub vegetation, open grassy prairies, and savannahs were common.

Sources of surface water, so important to Paleoindians and to the animals they hunted for food, were limited. The Paleoindians sought water in deep springs, like Little Salt Spring in Sarasota County, or at watering holes or shallow lakes or prairies where limestone strata near the surface provided catchment basins. Such limestone deposits are found from the Hillsborough River drainage north through peninsular Florida into the Panhandle. Paleoindians hunted, butchered, and consumed animals at these watering holes, leaving behind their refuse, artifacts that can be studied and interpreted by modern archaeologists.

Today, with higher water levels, many of these catchment basins are flowing rivers, like the Ichetucknee, Wacissa, Aucilla, and Chipola. Paleoindian camps with bone and stone weapons and tools, including distinctive lanceolate stone spear points, are found in deposits at the bottoms of these rivers, as well as at land sites nearby. With the stone tools are found bones of the animals the Paleoindians hunted, some exhibiting butchering marks. A number of the animal species hunted by Paleoindians became extinct shortly after the end of the Pleistocene epoch, perhaps in part because of human predation. They include mastodon, mammoth, horse, camel, bison, and giant land tortoise. Other of the animals that provided meat for the Paleoindian diet—deer, rabbits, raccoons, and many more—continue to inhabit Florida today.

After about 9000 B.C., as glaciers melted and sea levels rose, Florida's climate generally became wetter than it had been, providing more water sources around which the Paleoindians could camp. But as the sea rose, coastal areas were flooded and the Florida landmass was reduced. Less land and larger human populations may have influenced the later Paleoindians to follow a less nomadic way of life. They moved between water sources less frequently, and their camps were occupied for longer periods of time. Archaeological sites corresponding to these larger late Paleoindian camps have been found in the Hillsborough River drainage near Tampa, around Paynes Prairie south of Gainesville, near Silver Springs, and at other locations in northern Florida.

Paleoindian sites, relatively common in the northern half of the state in the region of surface limestone strata, also occur in smaller numbers in southern Florida. Paleoindian artifacts have been found as far south as Dade County.

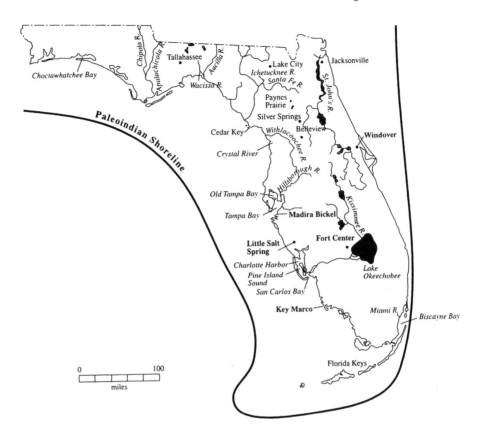

Archaeological sites (*in bold*) and other Florida locations mentioned in chapter 1.

Over time the tool kits of the Paleoindians changed as people altered their lifeways to adjust to the new environmental conditions that confronted them. They began to use a wider variety of stone tools, and many of the stone points originally used to hunt the large Pleistocene animals were no longer made. These changes were sufficient by 7500 B.C. for archaeologists to delineate a new culture, the early Archaic.

The environment of the early Archaic peoples was still drier than our modern climate, but it was wetter than it had been in earlier times. Early Archaic peoples continued to live next to wetlands and water sources and to hunt and gather wild foods.

One remarkable early Archaic period site is the Windover Pond site in Brevard County, which contains peat deposits in which early Archaic people interred their dead. Careful excavations by Glen Doran and David Dickel of Florida State University revealed that during the period between 6000 and 5000 B.C., human burials were placed in the peat in the bottom of the shallow pond. The peat helped to preserve an array of normally perishable artifacts and human tissues, including brains, from which scientists have recovered and studied genetic material.

Artifacts recovered by the excavation team included shark teeth and dog or wolf teeth which had been attached with pitch to wooden handles for use as tools. Other tools were made from deer bone and antler, from manatee and either panther or bobcat bone, and from bird bone. Bone pins, barbed points, and awls were found preserved in the peat, along with throwing stick weights made from deer antler. The weights were used with a handheld shaft to help launch spears; the earlier Paleoindians probably also used throwing sticks.

Animal bones found in the pond, presumably from animals eaten by the people who lived there, were from otter, rat, squirrel, rabbit, opossum, duck and wading birds, alligator, turtle, snake, frog, and fish. Remains of plants, including prickly pear and a wild gourd fashioned into a dipper, were also preserved.

A well-developed and sophisticated array of cordage and fiber fabrics and matting lay in the Windover Pond peat. Fibers taken from Sable palms, saw palmettos, and other plants were used in twining and weaving. The early Archaic people of Florida, like the people that preceded them and those that would follow, had an assemblage of material items—tools, woven fabrics, and the like—well suited to life in Florida.

After 5000 B.C., the climate of Florida began to ameliorate, becoming more like modern conditions, which were reached by about 3000 B.C. The time between 5000 and 3000 B.C. is known as the middle Archaic period. Middle Archaic sites are found in a variety of settings, some very different from those of the Paleoindians and early Archaic periods, including, for the first time, some along the St. Johns River and the Atlantic coastal strand. Middle Archaic peoples also were living in the Hillsborough River drainage northeast of Tampa Bay, along the southwest Florida coast, and in a few south Florida locales. And middle Archaic sites are found in large numbers in interior northern Florida. The presence of a larger number of surface water sites than had been available in earlier times provided many more locales for people to inhabit.

It is clear that during the middle Archaic period Florida natives took advantage of the increased number of hospitable areas. Populations increased significantly. The people practiced a more settled way of life and utilized a larger variety of specialized tools than their ancestors had done.

By 3000 B.C., the onset of the late Archaic period, essentially modern environmental conditions were reached in Florida, and expanding populations occupied almost every part of the state. Wetland locales were heavily settled. Numerous late Archaic sites have been found in coastal regions in northwest, southwest, and northeast Florida and in the St. Johns River drainage. Such sites, representing the remains of villages, are characterized by extensive deposits of mollusks—snails and mussels at freshwater locations and oysters along the coasts—which represent the remains of thousands of precolumbian meals. At both marine and freshwater settlements, fish and shellfish were dietary staples, as they were for many generations of later native Floridians.

Late Archaic groups probably lived along most if not all of Florida's coasts, but many of their sites have been inundated by the sea rise that continued throughout the Archaic period as Pleistocene glaciers melted. This is certainly true around Tampa Bay, where dredging has revealed extensive shell middens that today are underwater. It is also likely that Paleoindian and early and middle Archaic sites have been covered by the rising sea.

Slightly before 2000 B.C., the late Archaic villagers learned to make fired clay pottery, tempering it with Spanish moss or palmetto fibers. Sites with fiber-tempered pottery, some associated with massive shell middens, are distributed throughout the entire state down to the Florida Keys.

By the end of the late Archaic period at 500 B.C., many new types of fired clay pottery were being made by regional groups. Because different groups made their ceramic vessels in specific shapes and decorated them with distinctive designs, archaeologists can use pottery as a tool to define and study specific cultures. Often those cultures are named for the modern geographical landmarks where their remains were first recognized. In some instances we can trace, albeit incompletely, the evolution of these regional cultures from 500 B.C. into the sixteenth and seventeenth centuries, when European powers sought to colonize Florida. We can correlate the precolumbian archaeological cultures with native American groups described in colonial-period European documents.

Each regional culture with its distinctive style of pottery tended to live within one major environmental or physiographic zone. Each developed an economic base and other cultural practices that were well suited to that particular region and its various habitats and resources.

Like their Archaic and Paleoindian ancestors, the people associated with these post–500 B.C. regional cultures made a variety of stone tools as well. Today examples of those tools are found throughout Florida, although they are more numerous in regions where chert—a flintlike stone—was mined from limestone deposits and fashioned into spear and arrow points, knives, scrapers, and a variety of other tools.

East Florida—including the St. Johns River drainage from Brevard County north to Jacksonville, the adjacent Atlantic coastal region, and the many lakes of central Florida—was the region of the St. Johns culture. Like the late Archaic groups that preceded them, the St. Johns people made extensive use of fish and shellfish and other wild foods. They hunted and collected the foods that could be found in the natural environment where they lived.

By 100 B.C. or shortly after, the St. Johns people were constructing sand burial mounds in which to inter their dead. Each village had a leader or leaders who helped coordinate activities, such as communal ceremonies. Villagers most likely were organized into a number of lineages or other kin-based groups, each of which probably had a name and distinctive paraphernalia or other symbols of membership.

When a village grew too large for its residents to be supported easily by local economic resources, one or more lineages broke away, establishing a new village nearby. Traditions and shared kinship and origins served to tie old and new villages together. Such a social system probably was present in nearly all of Florida at this same time.

Although squashes and gourds probably were grown in gardens even in the late Archaic period, it was not until A.D. 750 or even later that some of the northerly St. Johns peoples began to cultivate corn. Food production, in conjunction with hunting, collecting, and fishing, could support larger human populations. Many more post–A.D. 750 St. Johns villages are known than earlier sites, reflecting this population increase.

Agriculture, important to native groups in the central portion of peninsular Florida and the eastern Panhandle, led to changes in lifeways. After about A.D. 1000, some of the St. Johns groups living along the northern St. Johns River constructed large sand mounds to serve as bases for temples or for residences in which their leaders lived. Larger populations, a desire to understand and try to control such things as agricultural fertility and rainfall, and the need for more social cooperation in order to maintain fields and protect territory stimulated the development of more complex forms of political organization and new beliefs and ceremonial practices.

With the coming of agriculture, village leaders were replaced by chiefs and religious figures, who exercised control over the people and sought to bridge the gap between the villagers and the supernatural. Often these chiefly and religious officials were associated with special objects and symbols, visible reminders of their power. Through alliances or the threat of military force, some chiefs sought to extend their political power and increase the territory under their aegis. At times such leaders controlled outlying villages and their chiefs, receiving respect and tribute from those chiefs as symbols of their allegiance.

Many villages of the St. Johns region, some with large mounds, were inhabited in the early sixteenth century when Europeans first entered the interior of east Florida and traveled up the St. Johns River. From that period on, we have written records left by those Europeans which offer firsthand descriptions of the early colonial-period descendants of the St. Johns people. Those descendants include many eastern groups speaking the Timucuan language who lived along and near the St. Johns River and its tributaries, groups with names like Saturiwa, Utina, and Acuera.

In northwest Florida and the interior of northern Florida and along the Gulf coast from Cedar Key north, the earliest post–500 B.C. regional culture was called Deptford. Especially numerous in locales adjacent to the salt marshes and tidal streams of the Gulf coast are village sites and fishing camps characterized by the distinctive Deptford pottery (decorated with check-stamped and grooved surface designs applied by using carved wooden or clay paddles to malleate the surface of the ceramic vessels before they were fired). Smaller hunting camps are found inland.

In the Panhandle after about A.D. 100, increased use of interior wetland and forest resources, especially the rivers and lakes in Gadsden, Leon, and Jefferson Counties, led to the development of the Swift Creek culture out of the Deptford culture. Swift Creek, with its distinctive pottery stamped with geometric designs, was related to the Santa Rosa–Swift Creek culture that followed Deptford in the western Panhandle at about the same time. Influenced by cultures to the north of Florida, the ideology of the late Deptford and Swift Creek cultures was associated with a rich variety of ceramic, shell, stone, and even copper items, some traded into the state from the north. Many of these objects display stylized animal motifs representing the same species important to later native Floridians as well.

Like the Deptford people who preceded them, the Swift Creek and Santa Rosa–Swift Creek built sand mounds in which they interred their deceased relatives. Swift Creek villages are found in the interior of eastern northwest Florida, evidence that people were moving into that region, perhaps a result of continuing population increase.

The Weeden Island culture and its coastal and inland regional variants

A late-sixteenth-century engraving offers a European view of Florida Indian chief Saturiwa and his wife going for a walk by their village on the south bank of the St. Johns River near its mouth. The chief and his wife are both tattooed, a sign of their high status, and they are wearing shell beads. Feather cloaks and tanned and painted animal hides also were worn. Male villagers typically wore breechcloths, and women dressed in skirts skillfully woven from Spanish moss. The men's hair was pulled up and tied.

appeared after about A.D. 300 from Sarasota County north along the Gulf coast to Alabama as well as in the interior of north and northwest Florida. Weeden Island, named for a site on Old Tampa Bay in Pinellas County excavated in the early 1920s, emerged out of local Deptford, Swift Creek, Santa Rosa–Swift Creek, and related cultures that were present in that large area.

Weeden Island villages, often with burial mounds and other mounds in association, are found in a variety of environments and geographical locations from Crystal River to near Lake City to Tallahassee and beyond to Pensacola. In each area, villagers practiced distinctive lifeways, but they shared many aspects of Weeden Island ideology and social and political organization.

One Weeden Island variant culture was the Cades Pond culture of Alachua County and the western portion of Putnam County. Cades Pond peoples lived in villages adjacent to extensive wetlands—lakes, wet prairies, marshes, and the like—where they could fish and gather waterbirds and a wide variety of other wetland-dwelling animals. They also hunted in the adjacent forests and collected acorns, hickory nuts, and persimmons. Numerous Cades Pond mounds are known, some with Weeden Island pottery. Like the Swift Creek people in northwest Florida, Cades Pond villages took advantage of the resources in the interior away from the coast to establish settlements.

Weeden Island variant cultures also are found around Tampa Bay (the Manasota culture) and along the north peninsular Gulf coast. In those regions, people continued to practice the same patterns of subsistence as did their late Archaic ancestors. Like the villagers in other Weeden Island cultures, they built mounds and manufactured and traded for ornate ceramic vessels and other objects displaying a rich array of symbols important to their beliefs. The ceramic complex associated with mounds is the defining characteristic of these cultures.

Cultivation of corn appeared among the northern Weeden Island cultures after about A.D. 800, about the same time it did in the St. Johns region. In the eastern portion of northwest Florida, maize agriculture became particularly important to aboriginal subsistence, providing—after A.D. 100—the economic base for the development and elaboration of the Fort Walton culture, which eventually stretched from the Aucilla River west through the Panhandle. Fertile inland locales—especially the Tallahassee Hills zone of Leon and Jefferson Counties and the upper Apalachicola River Valley—supported a number of large Fort Walton villages, some with mounds built as platforms on which to erect the temples and residences of chiefs and religious leaders. The Lake Jackson Mounds, in a state park near Tallahassee, is one such site.

Fort Walton was the largest and most politically complex precolumbian culture in Florida. Separate political units—each consisting of a number of villages, village chiefs, and other officials, and outlying agricultural homesteads, all united under a paramount chief—vied with one another for power and territory. The Apalachee natives encountered by Spanish expeditions in the early colonial period were the descendants of precolumbian Fort Walton populations. West of the Fort Walton region in the western Panhandle, influences from the north, from cultures in Alabama, provided the impetus for the development of the Pensacola culture. Pensacola villages and mounds are found clustered around the coastal bays from Choctawhatchee Bay west. The Pensacola people probably practiced agriculture, but it was not as extensive as the cleared-field farming of the Fort Walton culture.

Agriculture also was added to the economic system of the late Weeden

Line drawing of a copper breastplate excavated at Lake Jackson, a Fort Walton archaeological site in Leon County. The figure depicted is probably a person dressed in the costume of a bird.

Island–period culture of north Florida, which occupied the region east of the Aucilla River, north of the Santa Fe River, and west of the St. Johns River drainage. Named the Suwannee Valley culture, the people of this post–A.D. 750 culture also never practiced agriculture as extensively as did Fort Walton farmers. The descendants of Suwannee Valley populations are the various western Timucua-speaking groups of Madison, Suwannee, Hamilton, and Columbia Counties who witnessed the passage of the Hernando de Soto expedition in 1539. They include, among others, the Aguacaleyquen, Napituca, and Uzachile.

Farther south in north central Florida from the Santa Fe River down to Belleview in Marion County, another culture replaced the Weeden Island–period Cades Pond culture around A.D. 600. The Alachua culture represents a migration of a new population into Alachua and western Marion Counties from the river valleys of southern Georgia. It is uncertain if this intrusive culture was associated with farming when it first appeared in north central Florida, but by about A.D. 1250, if not before, we are certain that maize was being cultivated.

Early in their history in Florida, the Alachua villages expanded westward into Levy and Dixie Counties, although they apparently did not live on the coast itself, where villagers continued to make their livelihood from the marine environments. The Potano Indians, a Timucua-speaking native group, are the descendants of the Alachua population.

Around Tampa Bay, a huge estuary capable of supporting large populations, the Weeden Island–period culture developed into the Safety Harbor culture after about A.D. 900. Safety Harbor sites are found along the Gulf coast from Charlotte Harbor north to the Withlacoochee River in Citrus County. The Safety Harbor people on Tampa Bay probably were not farmers, but the villagers just north of Tampa Bay did grow corn, though it was not as important to their diet as it was in northwest Florida.

Safety Harbor sites, some with huge heaps of shellfish as well as mounds and village areas, once dotted the shoreline of Tampa Bay, but many were destroyed around the turn of the twentieth century when the shell was mined to build roads. Today only a few of these large sites exist, such as the one at the Madira Bickel Mound State Archaeological Site.

Small, triangular stone points were used by the Safety Harbor people to tip arrows. Similar points—suggesting bow and arrow use—are common in the contemporary Fort Walton, Suwannee Valley, and Alachua cultures in northern Florida.

The colonial-period Uzita, Mocoso, Pohoy, Tocobaga, and possibly the Ocale Indians all were Safety Harbor groups, and at least some of them— those living from Tampa Bay north—spoke Timucua. Like other north Florida native societies, all of these people of the Tampa Bay region were in contact with Spanish expeditions in the sixteenth century.

The lifeways of the various regional cultures of southern Florida also were well established by 500 B.C., the end of the late Archaic period. Although some beliefs and symbols were shared with the agricultural cultures farther north in Florida, the nature of the south Florida precolumbian cultures reflects their reliance on coastal and freshwater wetlands for their subsistence.

The vast savannah around Lake Okeechobee, called by Florida natives Lake Mayaimi, was the home of the Belle Glade culture. By as early as 400 B.C., shortly after the end of the late Archaic period, the Belle Glade peoples evidently grew small amounts of maize. But the practice seems to have been abandoned by A.D. 500 or so, possibly because of increasingly wet conditions. The Belle Glade peoples built a remarkable series of villages, each containing mounds and earthen embankments and other earthworks, some in geometric shapes. They also dug ditches and canals. One such complex site is Fort Center in Glades County, where numerous wooden carvings of animals were found preserved in a pond.

Belle Glade villagers continued to live around the lake and in the Kissimmee River drainage into early colonial times. The wetlands and savannahs provided them with a rich assortment of fish, birds, turtles, alligator, and other animals, as well as plants. The Belle Glade culture was one of the most distinctive in all of Florida.

Along the mangrove coasts and estuaries of southeast Florida, the coasts of the Ten Thousand Island region, and the coast of Monroe County north of the Florida keys, a distinctive regional culture developed. Hunter-gatherers, these Glades culture people lived by fishing, gathering shellfish, and collecting plants and other animals. Numerous Glades sites also are found in the Everglades and other areas of interior Florida south of the Okeechobee Basin.

Glades archaeological sites once blanketed the shores of the Florida Gold Coast; where huge precolumbian shell heaps once dotted Biscayne Bay, today there are high-rise buildings. Scattered sites are still visible in a few places, such as along the Miami River.

At Key Marco, a site on Marco Island excavated in the late nineteenth century, archaeologists recovered nets, net floats, and other fishing gear along with beautifully carved and painted wooden masks and animal figurines and depictions, providing us with a glimpse into the rich culture of these precolumbian coastal dwellers. These southern Florida native peoples used bows and arrows along with a variety of other tools made of shell and wood. Stone is not as common in southern Florida as it is farther north, and the precolumbian peoples used other raw materials for their artifacts.

In Dade County, the colonial-period descendants of the Glades populations were the Tequesta natives. To the north were groups like the Boca Ratones and Santaluces, names given the natives by the Spaniards.

Another coastal-oriented culture, the Caloosahatchee, occupied the southwest coast from Charlotte Harbor south into Collier County. The largest shell mounds in Florida are found there today, as well as large and small shell heaps on nearly every coastal island and the adjacent mainland, especially in Charlotte Harbor, Pine Island Sound, and San Carlos Bay.

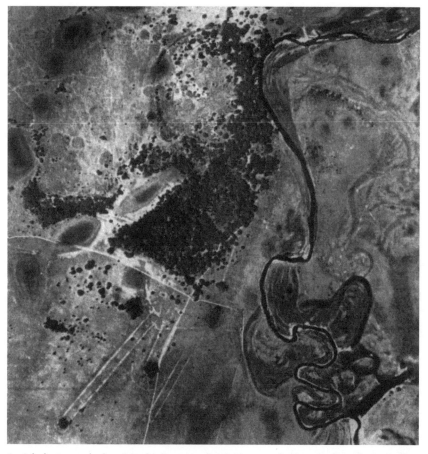

Aerial photograph showing the linear embankments and other earthworks, including a circular ditch, at Fort Center, a Belle Glade culture archaeological site in the Lake Okeechobee Basin. The site covers approximately one mile along the creek bank (*north is to the right*).

The extensive shell middens contain the remains of hundreds of thousands of native meals: fish, sharks, oysters, *Busycons,* and other mollusks. The size and contents of the mounds attest to the antiquity of the Indian cultures of the region and their reliance on marine resources.

The Caloosahatchee peoples, ancestors of the Calusa Indians, also built mounds of shell and earth to serve as the bases for temples. They dug ditches and canals similar to those of the Lake Okeechobee Basin, a region to which they were connected by the Caloosahatchee River, a canoe highway.

These were the major native cultures of precolumbian Florida. When Juan Ponce de León sailed the coastline in 1513, the native population numbered 350,000, including 50,000 Apalachee, 150,000 Timucua speakers, and 150,000 other people in the western Panhandle and central and southern Florida. But as we shall see in subsequent chapters, the European presence brought diseases and slaving raids that severely reduced and ultimately destroyed Florida's original inhabitants. By the late eighteenth century, they were no more.

Bibliography

Carr, Robert S., and John G. Beriault. "Prehistoric Man in South Florida." In *Environments of South Florida: Present and Past,* 2d ed., edited by P. J. Gleason, pp. 1–14. Miami Geological Society Memoir 2. Coral Gables, 1984.

Daniel, I. Randolph, Jr., and Michael Wisenbaker. *Harney Flats: A Florida Paleo-Indian Site.* Farmingdale, N.Y.: Baywood Publishing, 1987.

Doran, Glen H., and David N. Dickel. "Multidisciplinary Investigations at the Windover Site." In *Wet Site Archaeology,* edited by B. A. Purdy, pp. 263–89. Caldwell, N.J.: Telford Press, 1988.

Dunbar, James S. "Resource Orientation of Clovis and Suwannee Age Paleoindian Sites in Florida." In *Clovis: Origins and Adaptations,* edited by R. Bonnichsen and K. Turnmier, pp. 185–213. Corvallis: Center for the First Americans, Oregon State University, 1991.

Gilliland, Marion S. *The Material Culture of Key Marco, Florida.* Gainesville: University of Florida Press, 1975.

Goggin, John M. *Space and Time Perspectives in Northern St. Johns Archeology, Florida.* Yale University Publications in Anthropology No. 47. New Haven, 1952.

Griffin, John W., Sue B. Richardson, Mary Pohl, Carl D. McMurray, C. Margaret Scarry, Suzanne K. Fish, Elizabeth S. Wing, L. Jill Loucks, and Marcia K. Welch. *Excavations at the Granada Site.* Vol. 1 of *Archaeology and History of the Granada Site.* Tallahassee: Florida Division of Archives, History and Records Management, 1985.

Jones, B. Calvin. "Southern Cult Manifestations at the Lake Jackson Site, Leon County, Florida: Salvage Excavation of Mound 3." *Midcontinental Journal of Archaeology* 7 (1982):3–44.

Marquardt, William H., ed. *Culture and Environment in the Domain of the Calusa.* Institute of Archaeology and Paleoenvironmental Studies, Monograph 1. Gainesville: Florida Museum of Natural History, 1992.

Milanich, Jerald T. *Archaeology of Precolumbian Florida.* Gainesville: University Press of Florida, 1994.

———. *Florida Indians and the Invasion from Europe.* Gainesville: University Press of Florida, 1995.

Milanich, Jerald T., Ann S. Cordell, Vernon J. Knight, Jr., Timothy A. Kohler, and Brenda J. Sigler-Lavelle. *McKeithen Weeden Island: The Culture of Northern Florida, A.D. 200–900.* Orlando: Academic Press, 1984.

Purdy, Barbara A. *The Art and Archaeology of Florida's Wetlands*. Boca Raton: CRC Press, 1991.

———. *Florida's Prehistoric Stone Tool Technology*. Gainesville: University of Florida Press, 1981.

Sears, William H. *Fort Center: An Archaeological Site in the Lake Okeechobee Basin*. Gainesville: University Presses of Florida, 1982.

Widmer, Randolph E. *The Evolution of the Calusa: A Nonagricultural Chiefdom on the Southwest Florida Coast*. Tuscaloosa and London: University of Alabama Press, 1988.

Willey, Gordon R. *Archeology of the Florida Gulf coast*. Smithsonian Miscellaneous Collections No. 113. Washington, 1949.

2

First European Contacts

MICHAEL GANNON

The first encounters between the indigenous peoples of Florida and the Europeans who traveled the Atlantic in the wake of Christopher Columbus occurred over five centuries ago. The documents and maps are unclear on the point, but it appears that the initial contacts preceded the famous voyage of Juan Ponce de León in 1513 by a number of years. After the turn of the sixteenth century, Spain launched an ever-widening circle of voyages from bases in the Caribbean Sea. Some of those were slaving expeditions in search of island natives to replace the native laborers of La Española and, later, the Isla de Cuba, where, owing to the Spaniards' introduction of harsh work practices and European diseases, indigenous populations were rapidly collapsing. Probably one or more of those expeditions happened upon the Florida peninsula, which may account for the hostility that the natives demonstrated toward Juan Ponce upon his arrival there, as well as for his discovery on the lower Gulf coast of "an Indian who understood the Spaniards." In any event, the historian can speculate what must have been the wonderment, perhaps terror, that passed through the original Floridians' minds when they beheld the ultimate artifact of European technology, the sailing ship, with its huge hull, masts and shrouds, spread canvas sails, and white, bearded seamen.

Tantalizing suggestions of those first contacts appear in maps and charts as early as 1502, the date of a Portuguese world map known by the name of its owner, Italian nobleman Alberto Cantino. Where it depicted the Spanish Caribbean discoveries, there appears a narrow landmass that is possibly the Florida peninsula but is more likely the coast of Central America. More striking, a map of the islands and shores of the New World was published in 1511 by Peter Martyr (Pietro Martire d'Anghiera), an Italian priest-humanist in the Spanish court of Fernando II of Aragón. Drawn from oral and written reports of navigators, this map shows a long shoreline "to the north" of Cuba which he labeled "Isla de beimeni parte" (Island of Bimini). With the Grand Bahama Bank directly abutting them, the land features of Bimini, and what appear to be keys descending from them, could be Florida.

It was this island of Bimini that Juan Ponce de León was authorized to seek in an *asiento* (charter) issued him by the Spanish Crown on 23 February 1512. Born to a noble family in Valladolid, Juan Ponce at age nineteen shipped to the Caribbean on Columbus's second voyage in 1493, and, after New World seasoning, he conducted the conquest of Puerto Rico in 1506–7, becoming its governor in 1509. In 1512 he was deposed on a technicality by Columbus's older son, Diego Colon, and, finding himself wealthy and with time on his hands, he accepted an asiento to discover and conquer the land "to the north" called Bimini. According to legend, Bimini contained a fountain of waters that rejuvenated old men, the so-called Fountain of Youth. It should be emphasized that those mythical waters were not mentioned in Juan Ponce's charter from Fernando II, which was meticulously detailed in its specification of the expedition's purpose and goals. Nor were they mentioned in any firsthand report or narrative, including Juan Ponce's own correspondence, although the one extant detailed source for Juan Ponce's voyage of 1513—historian Antonio de Herrera y Tordesillas, who in 1601–15 published a chronicle of Spanish New World explorations—states that on the return end of that voyage, Juan Ponce sent one of his ships into the Lucayan, or Bahama, chain to search for "that celebrated fountain which the Indians said turned men from old men [into] youths."[1] This probably was a gloss by Herrera based on an unsubstantiated account by Peter Martyr. Probably more important to Juan Ponce were gold and the glory of conquest, the lust for which drove all conquistadors of the period.

On 3 March 1513, Juan Ponce left Añasco Bay on the western side of Puerto Rico with two caravels and a bergantina. Notable among the crews and passenger list were thirty-eight-year-old Antón de Alaminos, the most experienced pilot in the islands; two women, Beatriz and Juana Jiménez, who probably were related; two African freemen, Juan Gárrido and Juan González [Ponce] de León; and two unnamed native Taíno seafarer-guides from Puerto Rico.

Alaminos set a course of northwest a quarter by north that took the three ships seaward up the eastern edge of the Lucayans as far as the northernmost charted island of San Salvador (the Lucayan Guanahaní that was Columbus's first landfall in 1492), which they reached after eleven days. They were at sea again on the same base compass heading, but in unknown waters,

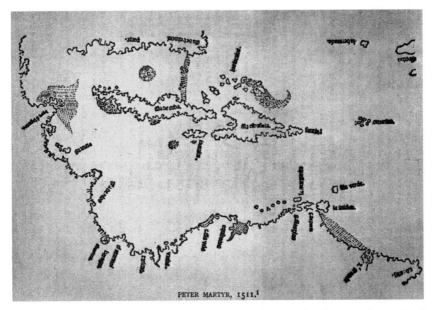

PETER MARTYR, 1511.[1]

Map of the Caribbean published by Peter Martyr in 1511. The landmass to the north of Cuba is named *isla de beimeni parte*. Its placement, and what appear to be keys descending from it, have led some historians to speculate that it is a depiction of Florida, drawn from navigators' reports, two years before the voyage of Juan Ponce de León.

on Sunday, 27 March, when the crews and passengers observed the feast of Easter. That day, too, they sighted an island, which probably was Eleuthera. From that point, as indicated by a recent resailing of the route to test the prevailing winds and currents, Alaminos took a new heading of west-northwest through the New Providence Channel and passed well below the southern cape of Great Abaco and the whole of Grand Bahama. This course placed the vessels out of the sight of land for the next six days. When they crossed the three-knot Gulf Stream, the Spanish hulls were carried north faster than they shouldered west, with the result that on 2 April they made landfall on what turned out to be the Florida shoreline. The most recent study contends that they were at a point just south of Cape Canaveral, probably near Melbourne Beach, where they anchored in eight *brazas* (forty-four feet) of water.[2]

Herrera describes what followed: "And thinking that this land was an island, they called it *La Florida*, because it was very pretty to behold with many and refreshing trees, and it was flat, and even: and also because they discovered it in the time of Flowery Easter [Pascua Florida], Juan Ponce wanted to agree in the name, with these two reasons."[3]

Juan Ponce went ashore to take formal possession of the "island," but there is no indication in the record that he encountered people indigenous to the site. After remaining in the region for six days, he raised anchor on 8 April and sailed south along a featureless coastline. On 21 April, he made his second great discovery, though it is doubtful that he and Alaminos realized its dimensions at the time: the Florida Current, or Gulf Stream. That current had made itself felt when the three ships crossed it going west in the first days of April, but now, at a cape north of Lake Worth Inlet, which Juan Ponce named Cabo de las Corrientes (Cape of the Currents), it faced him head-on and with such force that his ships were propelled backward even though they had wind abaft the beam. One, the bergantina, was swept out to deep water. Anchoring north of the cape, Juan Ponce and some of his men rowed ashore in a longboat to make contact with natives they sighted on shore. The encounter did not go well. The native party assaulted the Spaniards with clubs and arrows, rendering one seaman unconscious and wounding two others. Herrera states that Juan Ponce had not wished to do the natives harm but was forced to fight in order to save both his men's lives and their boat, oars, and weapons, which their assailants sought to seize. No cause for the natives' violence is given in the record, whether it was provoked by earlier visits of slaving expeditions, or by the natives' own long tradition of intertribal warfare, or by simple fear of these strange creatures from another world.

Regaining his ships, Juan Ponce put in at Jupiter Inlet to take on firewood and water, only to be attacked again by a larger party of sixty men. This time he seized a warrior for use as a guide. He would remain anchored in the river until rejoined by the bergantina. And somewhere along this river, which he named La Cruz (The Cross), he planted a quarry-stone cross, inscribed, with what words we do not know, in the manner of other Spanish or Portuguese explorers of the period who erected a stone *patrón*, or standard, to identify their claims.

Finally navigating the Cape of the Currents by hugging the shore, Alaminos navigated southward to Key Biscayne, which Juan Ponce named Santa Marta, and, on Friday, 13 May, to one of the Keys, possibly Key Largo, which he named Pola, its derivation and meaning unclear. Rounding the Keys as a body, Juan Ponce named them Los Mártires (Martyrs), "because viewed from afar the rocks as they rose up seemed like men who are suffering."[4] From Key West he sailed west a short distance and then proceeded north to explore the reverse side of his "island," making a Gulf coast landfall, it is thought, at San Carlos Bay, off the deep mouth of the Caloosahatchee River, and anchoring near the southeast tip of Sanibel Island. There he found fire-wood and freshwater, careened one of his ships, and had two belligerent encounters with natives of the Calusa nation, whose chief, Carlos (as the Spaniards pronounced and wrote his name), resided on Estero Island. The Calusa attacked the anchored ships in canoes. One Spaniard and at least four natives died in these actions, leading Juan Ponce to give Sanibel its first European name, Matanzas (Massacre). After nine days in the vicinity, a decision was made to return to Puerto Rico. Accordingly, Alaminos laid a course that took the ships south-southwest, which caused them, on 21 June, to come upon waterless keys that Juan Ponce named Las Tortugas (Turtles), where the crews provisioned the vessels with, among other land and sea species, 160 loggerhead turtles. Following a brief reconnaissance of the Cuban coastline west of Havana, the expedition made for Puerto Rico. Two of the three ships reached it in mid-October. The third ship, with chief pilot Alaminos aboard, Juan Ponce had dispatched into the Lucayans to search again for the elusive Bimini; that ship would arrive in Añasco Bay four months later.

In 1514, Juan Ponce sailed to Spain, where he secured a revised royal asiento naming him *adelantado* (self-financing conqueror and direct representative of the king) and governor of the islands of Bimini and Florida. He was delayed for seven years in executing the contract by the death of his wife and his need to raise their two young daughters. During that interim, however, La Florida did not lack for Spanish visitors, including slavers, such as Pedro de Salazar during a voyage of 1514–16. In 1517, Alaminos, now chief pilot for Francisco Hernández de Córdoba, took refuge in San Carlos Bay when Córdoba's expedition returned eastward from its voyage to Yucatán. And two years later, Alaminos again, this time for Alonzo Alvarez de Pineda, put into the same bay for its firewood and drinking water during an expedition that established that Florida was not an island after all but a peninsula attached to a huge continent. Pineda fixed its western juncture to the mainland at a feature he named after the Holy Spirit—Río de Espíritu Santo; this could have been either the Mobile River and Bay, the Mississippi River, or Vermillion Bay, Louisiana.

His own interest in Florida no doubt requickened by news of Hernán Cortés's astonishing discoveries in Mexico, Juan Ponce wrote to the emperor Carlos V (Carlos I, king of Spain) on 10 February 1521 expressing his intention to establish a permanent town, a fort, and missions in the Florida he still thought was an island. On 26 February, he sailed out of Puerto Rico in two ships loaded down with 200 male and female settlers, parish priests and

Juan Ponce de León (ca. 1460–1521). The left side of this seventeenth-century engraving represents Juan Ponce and his expedition of 1521 in combat with the Calusa natives at Florida's San Carlos Bay.

missionary friars, horses and domestic animals, seeds, cuttings, and agricultural implements. The site of his landing in Florida is not known with any certainty, though it has been widely assumed it was in the same San Carlos Bay region that twice had brought back his former pilot, Alaminos. In any event, the natives of that site were no more receptive to strangers than were those Juan Ponce had encountered eight years before. They attacked the Spaniards as they debarked, as they erected buildings, and as they planted their crops and tended their cattle. When Juan Ponce himself received a painful, suppurating arrow wound in his thigh, he ordered the frustrated and fearful colonists to withdraw to Cuba. There, in July, he died from his infection.

By the mid-1520s, La Florida was the name given by Spain to the southeastern quarter of what is now the United States. Much of its Atlantic coastline was probed by slaving expeditions during the decade, and one loquacious captive from Winyah Bay, South Carolina, came into the hands of Lucas Vázquez de Ayllón, a royal judge in La Española. Persuaded by the captive, who was given the name Francisco de Chicora, that South Carolina was a land of almonds, olives, and figs—a new Andalucía?—Ayllón sought and received a charter to settle the "Land of Chicora," as he called it. In 1526 he sailed from La Española in six ships carrying 600 colonists, including women and children, three Dominican friars, African slaves, and a number of Carolina captives, including Chicora. After pausing for a short time on the Carolina shore, which, it turned out, bore little resemblance to Andalucía, Ayllón led the party south to the more inhabitable Georgia coast, probably to Sapelo Sound, where on 29 September he established a town named San Miguel de Gualdape (St. Michael of Gualdape, the latter half of the name being the native appellation for the site). It was the first named European settlement in what is now the United States, antedating Pensacola (1559), Fort Caroline (1564), and St. Augustine (1565), though the last-named would be the first permanent settlement. San Miguel lasted fewer than two months, owing to famine, disease, and cold temperatures. Taking advantage of a mutiny among the Spaniards, black slaves deserted and some found freedom in nearby native societies. About 150 survivors, including the Dominican friar Antonio de Montesinos, first priest in the hemisphere to defend the human rights of America's indigenous people, made their way by ship to various ports in the Antilles. Ayllón was not among the survivors.

Next in line to test himself against La Florida was the red-bearded, one-eyed, deep-voiced Pánfilo de Narváez, whose last official mission, in 1520, was to arrest the rogue conquistador Cortés in México. He failed in that, as he would also fail in Florida, where he arrived from Spain on 14 April 1528, near Tampa Bay, with a license to settle and govern a vast principality that ranged along the Gulf littoral from coastal northern México (Amichel) to the Florida peninsula and as far inland as he could control. Carlos V had conferred on him the lofty titles adelantado, governor, and captain general, but no mortal could confer on him common good sense. Foolishly, on landing he dispatched his ships that carried all his food, wine, and supplies, not to mention ten wives destined never to see their spouses again, with the order to rendezvous with him at an indeterminately defined harbor to the north. Though the ships' masters found a harbor that corresponded to Narváez's description, they did not locate the land party, and they cruised in search of them for nearly a year before, finally, sailing to New Spain (México) with their (one supposes) grieving women and depleted cargoes.

Meanwhile, Narváez with 300 men and 40 horses marched northward up the peninsula, toward the chiefdom of Apalachee, around present-day Tallahassee, which, the Tampa Bay natives had assured Narváez, possessed "gold and plenty of everything we wanted." These are the words of surely the most notable member of the party, Alvar Núñez Cabeza de Vaca, treasurer and provost marshal. Fourteen years later, as one of only four survivors of this ill-starred expedition, he would publish a lengthy account of the adventure, thus allowing us to know what happened to the doomed procession.[5]

Cabeza de Vaca's description of the Florida interior is the first we have. The land was flat and sandy, he wrote, with numerous lakes and trees fallen into them. Together with tall stands of pine, there were cypress, oaks, cedars, and other varieties of trees. Animals sighted included deer, bears, and panthers. Wildfowl were abundant. In Apalachee, which the army reached after fifty-six days of marching, there was native-planted maize in the fields ready for harvest.

Although the army encountered Timucua speakers at various points along their route, and were sometimes trailed by them at a distance, it was in Apalachee that they had their first prolonged contacts, most of them violent. The hostility of the Apalachee should not have surprised the Spaniards since Narváez had seized a principal village with its maize stores and held their chief hostage. Cabeza de Vaca paid tribute to their warrior skills, particularly in archery. The men were wonderfully built, he recorded: "Tall and naked, at a distance they appear giants"—an understandable observation since the Spaniards were a good three to four inches shorter in stature—but skeletal remains indicate that six-footers were rare. "Their bows," he wrote, "are as thick as an arm, seven feet long, shooting an arrow at 200 paces with unerring aim." After a day of battle with the Apalachee, some of the soldiers "swore they had seen two oak trees, each as thick as the calf of a leg, shot through and through by arrows, which is not surprising if we consider the force and dexterity with which they shoot. I myself saw an arrow that had penetrated the base of a [hardwood] tree for half a foot in length."[6]

After a month in the region, despairing of finding their ships, enfeebled by illness, down to the last food rations, and continually harried by Apalachee archers, Narváez's men followed their leader to a bay on the Gulf (probably in the vicinity of present-day St. Marks) where they began construction of barges on which to effect an escape by following the coast to refuge in the Spanish settlement at Río Pánuco in México. Although no one among them knew anything about ship construction, desperation lent invention. Killing a horse every third day for food, they fashioned the flayed and tanned leg hides into freshwater bags and used deerskins and hollowed logs to make a bellows with which they operated a forge for melting down their swords, stirrups, spurs, and crossbow iron into saws, axes, and nails. The horses' manes and tails became ropes. Yellow pine trees were split into planks, and pitch for caulking them was drawn from longleaf pine and mixed with palmetto oakum. The men sewed their shirts together to make patchwork sails and shaped cypress logs into oars. On 22 September, after six weeks of work, 242 survivors of the original land party of 300 boarded five rough-hewn thirty-foot-long craft and set out to sea. As a final gesture they christened their embarkation site Bahía de Caballos, Bay of the Horses.

Cabeza de Vaca related the sad consequences. After passing the coasts of Florida, Alabama, Mississippi, and Louisiana, the barges capsized in a violent storm in November and eighty survivors were cast up on an island, either Galveston, Follet's, or Matagorda, off the coast of Texas. As they learned later, Narváez perished in a separate incident. By the following spring, having made it to the mainland, their number was reduced by illness, exposure, and starvation to fifteen. Eventually, there were only four, who managed to eke out an existence as healers, traders, and slaves among the tribes indigenous to southern Texas. In September 1534, those four set out on foot across Texas toward the Sonora Valley. Their two-year-long convoluted trek, in which they crossed the continent from the Gulf to the Pacific, brought them eventually to Mexico City on 24 June 1536, where Cabeza de Vaca related his incredible story to the Spanish viceroy. His three companions were Alonso del Castillo Maldonado, Andrés Dorantes, and the latter's black Moorish servant, Estévan. Behind them the wilderness of La Florida had returned to the private use of its original inhabitants nearly eight years before.

Next to Ponce de León's, the name most closely associated in the public's mind with Florida's early contact period is that of Hernando de Soto. He arrived on Florida's Gulf coast in 1539 and set out on an overland reconnaissance that would penetrate Florida and nine other states of the American South, covering nearly 4,000 miles over four years' time. Nothing about de Soto, from his landing site, to his treatment of the natives, to his route of march, has escaped controversy, down to and including the present.

Born in the barren Spanish province of Extremadura, whence many New World conquistadors came, de Soto went to Central America in 1513–14 under the ruthless Pedro Arias de Ávila (Pedrárias Dávila). He received further schooling in the grim arts of subjugation as a lieutenant to his fellow Extremaduran Francisco Pizarro during the looting of Incan Peru in 1532–35. Returning to Spain in 1536, immensely rich, he married Isabel de Bobadilla, third daughter of Pedrárias Dávila, and sought permission from Carlos V to become a conquistador in his own right. As for territory, his preferences were for what later became Ecuador and Guatemala. Instead, Carlos V awarded him La Florida, the vast geographical region previously awarded Narváez and Ayllón, with the titles of adelantado, captain general, and governor over any 200 leagues of coast he could "conquer, pacify and

Hernando de Soto (1497?–1542). An engraving from *Retratos de los Españoles Ilustres con un Epitome de sus Vidas* (Madrid: Imprenta real, 1791).

populate." At the same time, the king made him governor of Cuba, where he would establish a base, requisition additional supplies, and organize his expedition. In the elaborate terms of his asiento, dated 20 April 1537, de Soto was enjoined to recruit, arm, supply, and transport the Florida army entirely at his own cost, which he did so well that, by his departure from Seville on 7 April 1538, he had spent his entire fortune and was heavily in debt. But no matter: the gold he was certain to find in Florida would replenish the chests.

De Soto spent half a year at Havana in prudent preparation for the Florida campaign, determined to avoid the mistakes of Narváez about which he had learned from Cabeza de Vaca. Thus, he insisted on adequate provisioning and reliable intelligence. In pursuit of the latter, he sent a trusted aide, Juan de Añasco, with fifty men in three small ships to reconnoiter the

Florida Gulf coast. A guide for navigators, compiled by Alonso de Chaves at Seville, probably in 1537, indicated that there were two favorable harbors, Bahía de Juan Ponce to the south, and Bahía Honda (Deep Harbor) to the north.[7] When de Soto made his landing it would be at Bahía Honda, according to one of the expedition's chroniclers. Añasco returned with four native captives to serve as guides and interpreters.

The expedition set out from Havana on 18 May 1539 in five large and four smaller vessels. On board were more than 600 soldiers, twelve priests, two women, servants and slaves, 223 horses, numerous mules and war dogs, and a herd of swine. About half the force was from Extremadura; fifteen were Portuguese. The ships made landfall on 25 May and five days later disembarked all of their horses and most of their men. Where was this done? Of all the questions raised by students of the Florida discovery period, none has been more argued for the past half century than this one. In 1939, a U.S. De Soto Expedition Commission chaired by Dr. John R. Swanton determined that the de Soto landing site was Tampa Bay.[8] Numerous other studies since have concluded that the descriptions given in the documents, as well as de Soto's route of march, favored either Charlotte Harbor[9] or Pine Island Sound–Caloosahatchee River, or San Carlos Bay, all to the south. In 1989, a State of Florida de Soto Trail Committee, relying on the recently republished Chaves guide, on the accounts given by the original de Soto chroniclers, and on correlations of the expedition narratives with an archaeological list of known native encampments greatly expanded since 1939, decided that a Tampa Bay landing best fit the evidence.[10]

According to this last view, which remains provisional, de Soto made his initial landing at Piney Point and finally made camp at a native village, Uzita, which the 1989 findings place at the northern side of the mouth of the Little Manatee River. A cavalry patrol from that site into the interior flushed out a Spanish survivor of an expedition sent from Cuba eleven years earlier to discover, if possible, what had happened to Pánfilo de Narváez. Juan Ortíz by name, he had lived as a tribal native in the region for years. Now his providential rescue provided de Soto with an interpreter who spoke indigenous tongues and Spanish, but as the army encountered different linguistic groups on its march, his facility as a translator and as a geographer would diminish.

The march into the interior began on 15 July. Mindful of Narváez's fateful error, de Soto left all his supplies on board four ships in the harbor, guarded by forty cavalry and sixty infantry, with firm orders not to sail until he sent men to guide the vessels to a precisely known anchorage to the north. The long overland procession of people, horses, mules, and long-legged Spanish range pigs then entered the vastness of Florida's forests, rivers, bogs, and sandhills. The last feature was discovered just three days into the march, in the vicinity of Zephyrhills and Lumberton, where one man died of thirst and others barely survived the absence of springs, streams, or standing water. The next day, near Dade City, the army found its first cornfields. Though he had crossed a smaller river, the Alafia, by constructing a bridge, and had successfully though painfully negotiated the wetlands of the Cove of the Withlacoochee in eastern Citrus County, on 26 July de Soto met his first serious test at the strong currents of the Withlacoochee River itself, not far from Inverness. There the army stretched a rope from bank to bank and managed to wade across, losing one horse to the currents.

On 29 July, the army found itself in the major Timucuan province of Ocale, believed to have occupied what now is southwest Marion County. Here and at the province of Acuera, north of Leesburg on or near the Ocklawaha River, the Spaniards commandeered the natives' standing crops and food stores. Then, leaving the main body of the army at Ocale, de Soto led a reconnaissance force through Levy and Alachua Counties, passing on Gainesville's west side (the native Potano) and reaching the Santa Fe River, which the advance party bridged on 17 August. Here the unity of the force was rent by disagreements of some kind, not recorded, but perhaps rising out of plain frustration: the El Dorado of their dreams must never have seemed less real than it did among the swamps and pines of Florida. The soldiers named the river Santa Fe de las Discordias, the River of Discords.

De Soto camped across the river at a moderately sized village named Aguacaleyquen and dispatched eight horsemen to lead forward the main body still in Ocale. At Aguacaleyquen, abandoned by its inhabitants, de Soto found their hidden maize stores. Later, he captured seventeen natives, seized their chief, and held his daughter hostage. To this behavior may be added other, worse, violations that characterized de Soto's peregrinations through the Florida chiefdoms, all of them in direct violation of the king's ordinance to observe "good treatment and conversion" of the natives: some natives he summarily executed for offenses real or perceived; others he mutilated (e.g., cutting off noses or hands) as a warning of what would be done to all if he was not granted free passage through a village or a province; still others he enslaved and shackled to serve the marching army as bearers. By such actions he showed that he had not forgotten the intimidating and violent approach to indigenous societies learned under Pedrárias in Panama and Nicaragua. Ostensibly the actions were authorized by a formal theological

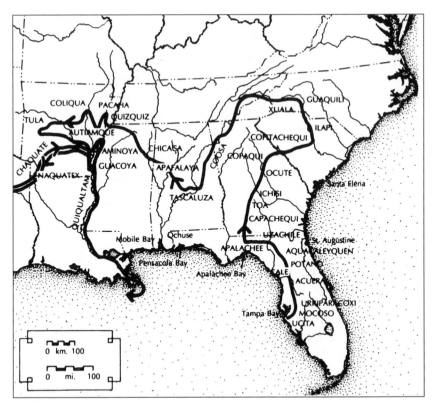

The route of Hernando de Soto's expedition through La Florida, which at the time embraced the entire region shown here. Place-names along the march are the principal native chiefdoms encountered. Also shown here are the future settlements of Tristán de Luna (Ochuse) and of Pedro Menéndez de Avilés (St. Augustine and Santa Elena).

proclamation, the *Requirimiento*, which was read aloud in Spanish to the uncomprehending natives. Some probable cultural explanations can be offered for this harsh conduct. First, the Spanish captains' actions to control New World natives were to a large measure an extension of the Reconquista, the struggle to regain control of Iberia from the Muslims, concluded in 1492. A cult of military violence nourished over many centuries carried over into the circum-Caribbean, of which Florida was a part. Second, Roman Catholic theology in Spain was still uncertain about the moral standing of the native Americans, whose existence was not accounted for in holy scripture. Were they fully developed human beings with souls? Or were they a lower species that might justifiably be exploited and enslaved? The question would not be resolved in the natives' favor until Carlos V's promulgation of the so-called New Laws in 1542, the year of de Soto's death. It may be added that, though de Soto's entourage included twelve priests, none appears to have had the vision and moral courage of Ayllón's friar Montesinos where treatment of the natives was concerned.

In their turn, the Florida natives gave back as good as they got, from Tampa Bay, where the aborigines raked the army with cane arrows tipped with fishbones, crab claws, or stone points, until de Soto's withdrawal northward into Georgia from Apalachee. All along the line of march, native archers, darting from woodland cover, killed Spanish dispatch riders or stragglers, set ambushes, or fired volleys into nighttime bivouacs. Brave native hostage-guides coolly led the army into ambushes, though it meant certain death for the hostage, probably at the jaws of war dogs. The Spaniards marveled at the velocity and accuracy of the arrows discharged against them by the natives' tall, stiff bows. This would be particularly so in Apalachee, where the projectiles were said to have penetrated horses lengthwise nearly from chest to tail, and de Soto watched one captured archer place an arrow through two coats of Milan chain steel from eighty feet back. The best defense, the Spaniards eventually learned, for their horses as well as for themselves, was to wear quilted fabric three or four fingers thick under their chain mail.

From Tampa Bay through Apalachee, de Soto enjoyed only one stand-up fight in open country where the massed cavalry charge for which he was equipped held the advantage. It took place at Napituca, near Live Oak, in mid-September. Anticipating an ambush, de Soto stationed his cavalry in woods surrounding two flooded limestone sinkholes and charged the warriors of the district when they betrayed their intent. Many natives were lanced in the field. Others threw themselves into the ponds where they treaded water until exhausted. Eventually captured, these and other natives of the region later rose up against their captors, which caused de Soto to execute all the mature warriors among them.

From Napituca the Spaniards traveled almost due west, seeking the province of Apalachee, where Narváez's men had found abundant crops. On 25 September they bridged the River of the Deer, as they named the Suwannee, and six days later, they came to Agile, the first town that was subject to the Apalachee. It was not until 3 October, when they made a difficult crossing of the flooded Aucilla River, that they encountered the Apalachee proper. The natives put up a fierce armed resistance and burned their crops and villages as they drew back before the foreigners' advance. Thirty-eight miles farther west, on 6 October, de Soto entered Anhaica, the main town of Apalachee, where he decided to make his winter camp. Near the coast on Apalachee

Bay his men found the remains, including horse skulls, of Narváez's camp of eleven years before. With a known anchorage, de Soto sent a party of cavalrymen south to lead forward the ships, supplies, and men left at Tampa Bay. On 25 December the camp celebrated the first Christmas in what is now the United States.

The Anhaica encampment site was discovered in 1987 by archaeologist B. Calvin Jones, who, while excavating a short distance east of the Capitol in Tallahassee, turned up a pig mandible (de Soto had introduced the pig to this country), an iron crossbow point, iron nails, chain mail still linked together, and dated copper coins. (In 2012 a landowner named Ashley White in north Marion County unearthed on his property a pig mandible, chain mail, medieval coins, and glass beads, all apparently lost earlier from uniform pockets or saddlebags along de Soto's line of march.) The Spaniards' stay at Anhaica was beset by almost constant guerilla warfare, with the result that, by the date of their departure north into Georgia, on 3 March 1540, numerous bones of man and horse alike remained behind under the Apalachee sun.

It would be tedious to detail the remainder of the expedition outside present-day Florida, which seems to the reader of the surviving chronicles to be an aimless, feckless wandering in search of the same gold, silver, and gems that de Soto had found in Peru. No known attempt was made to map the interior, to record flora and fauna, to understand the polities and cultures of the native societies encountered, to evangelize, or to forge alliances. Suffice it to say that the Spaniards marched northeast through Georgia into South and North Carolina, turned west through a corner of Tennessee, then south through the northwest corner of Georgia, finding plentiful corn and game at Coosa (east of Carters, Georgia) but just missing the gold fields at Dahlonega. They passed southwest into Alabama where the army's supplies were ravaged in a day-long battle, disastrous for both sides, with the warriors of Chief Tascaluza at Mabila; the Mabila lost perhaps as many as 3,000 men. In the aftermath of the battle, de Soto made a fateful decision not to avail himself of provisions awaiting him by prearrangement on ships at Pensacola Bay lest his dispirited men seize the ships and desert the enterprise.

"From that day," wrote one of the chroniclers, who interviewed survivors, "as a disillusioned man whose own people have betrayed his hopes . . . he went about thereafter wasting his time and life without any gain, always traveling from one place to another without order or purpose."[11] Those subsequent meanderings took the army northwest into Mississippi, where they wintered in 1540–41 among the hostile Chickasaw near Tupelo, to whom they lost more men, horses, and more than 300 pigs. Sometime in May 1541 they discovered the great river Mississippi, crossing it on flatboats a few miles south of Memphis on 19 June. Another difficult winter (1541–42) was spent in Arkansas, where the men suffered greatly from cold temperatures, sickness, and malnutrition; several died, including the interpreter Juan Ortíz.

In March 1542, de Soto led the survivors back through southern Arkansas to the Mississippi, where, on 21 May, the would-be conquistador himself died of an unidentified disease and was secretly interred in the bed of the river. Campmaster Luis Moscoso de Alvarado succeeded to command and led the army in an overland attempt to reach New Spain, but by October they had gotten no farther than the Trinity River in eastern Texas. There, with no further signs of maize-cultivating natives, they were forced back to the Mississippi, which they reached in December. They constructed seven keeled boats and boarded them on 2 July in an attempt to escape downriver to the Gulf. A sail and seven oars on each vessel provided propulsion, which was desperately needed on two occasions when riverbank warriors in canoes pursued them with arrows. After successfully reaching the mouth of the Father of Waters, the tiny fleet pressed westward along the Gulf beaches and headlands toward the Spanish settlement at Río Pánuco, where they landed on 10 September 1543.

Fully four years and four months since setting out from the port of Havana, and after 3,700 miles of travel by land and water, 311 survivors clambered ashore to the embrace of their countrymen. Behind them, they had left the whitened bones of half their original number, including de Soto's; all their horses and pigs; their only plunder, poor-quality freshwater pearls they had found at Camden, South Carolina, but had lost to fire at Mabila; and all their dreams of Incan gold and Mexican magnificence. None of the chartered goals established by the king had been met: behind them stood no settlement or hospital, no mine or farm, no presidio or mission, no flag, no cross. The most significant practical result of what may be called that extended armed raid was the damage inflicted on the southeastern native populations. Dozens of chiefdoms, overstressed and humiliated by de Soto, went into decline or collapsed. And in the wake of the *entrada*, thousands of native people lay dead and dying, not from the sword but from the introduction of Old World pathogens against which the aborigines had no acquired immunities—smallpox, measles, and typhoid fever, among others.

That "microbial invasion" had begun many years before with the first slavers or with the crews of Juan Ponce, but de Soto's men unwittingly reinforced it on their long, doubly tragic death march through the interior of La Florida.

Then, six years later, there came a Dominican friar's brief humanitarian intervention that startles with its courage and magnanimity. In the spring of 1549, Fray Luis Cáncer de Barbastro set sail in an unarmed vessel from Veracruz, México, bound for the same La Florida in order to win the friendship of its native people by peaceful means alone. Cast in much the same mold as Montesinos and the other, current, great Dominican "defender of the Indians," Fray Bartolomé de las Casas, Cáncer had earlier participated in the pacification and conversion of the seemingly intractable inhabitants of Guatemala, causing that former "province of war" now to be called by his Mexican countrymen the "province of true peace." With Cáncer sailed three other Dominican friars, a Spanish lay brother, a captured Florida native woman interpreter named Magdalena, sailors, and a pilot, Juan de Arana, who had been given strict orders to avoid any harbor where Spaniards had earlier spread the terror of their arms. Whether through perversity or ignorance, Arana delivered his passengers to Tampa Bay.

Contact with the natives was almost immediate. Cáncer made several friendly entreaties to them, and his touching references to the aborigines in a journal he kept on board ship display a genuine concern for their welfare. But news soon arrived by the surprising agency of one Juan Muñoz, one of de Soto's soldiers who had been captured in that locale ten years before, that one of the priests and the lay brother had been killed, that a ship's sailor was being held captive, and that Magdalena, having divested herself of Christian clothing, had deserted to her people. On 26 June, Cáncer took a boat from the ship to the beach where, with a crucifix in hand, he fell on his knees in prayer. A group of natives approached. One of them took away his hat. Another crushed his head with a club.

The province of Florida would remain for now a province of war. But at one shining moment in 1549 it witnessed the spiritual gallantry of a guileless messenger of peace, whose name should be writ large in the pantheon of Floridian and American heroes. Culturally and politically what was most significant about Cáncer's sacrifice was that it demonstrated Spain's commitment in Florida to the New Laws of 1542, a commitment that would be played out on a larger scale in the next Spanish undertaking.

After yet another decade passed without a permanent Iberian presence in La Florida, which by that date was the name given to coastal territory that ranged from the Florida Keys to Newfoundland, Spain was determined to launch another settlement effort. The reasons were various. The Gulf shore and the Atlantic coast of Spanish-claimed Florida were vulnerable to French or English interlopers. Indeed France was advancing its own claim to the Atlantic coast: French fishermen were already going ashore along the Carolina coast to smoke their fish and mend their nets. And pirate ships, French and English alike, were threatening the Gulf and Atlantic trade, particularly the routes of the treasure ships, which departed Mexican ports twice each year heavily laden with gold, silver, and gems and sailed via Havana up the Canal de Bahama (Strait of Florida) as far as Bermuda, where they followed the westerlies to Sevilla in Spain. For the protection of the plate fleets it was decided that Spain needed effective occupation of two anchor sites, Pensacola Bay, with its deep harbor, on the Gulf and what was then called Punta de Santa Elena (Point of St. Helen, probably Tybee Island, Georgia), on the Atlantic. The latter was to be the principal settlement, with town lots, a plaza, church, and stronghouse.

Among the other concerns of Spain at the time were protection of shipwrecked sailors along the Gulf and Atlantic shores and missionary evangelization, now long delayed, of the aborigines. The bishop of Cuba weighed in with still another concern: so few native Cuban women remained as eligible wives for Spanish soldiers that a male on that island was lucky if he could find a wife eighty years old, and Florida, he argued, ought to be an excellent source of young brides.

The new King Felipe II ordered a large Florida expedition to be mounted out of México. To lead it, Luis de Velasco, viceroy of New Spain, chose an army colonel, Don Tristán de Luna y Arellano, veteran of the Francisco Vázquez de Coronado expedition into the southwestern corner of the North American continent that had been conducted contemporaneously with de Soto's entrada (the two expeditions being at one point only 300 miles apart in the winter of 1541–42). Three Florida sites now were to be occupied: Pensacola Bay, known as native Ochuse or Spanish Polanco; de Soto's Coosa in northwest Georgia; and Santa Elena, which was thought, erroneously, to be only 120 miles east from Coosa overland. Eventually, it was envisioned, a string of Spanish settlements would link the three sites. Besides their primary mission of preempting French designs on the region, Velasco and Luna hoped to convert the natives to Christianity—for which purpose five Dominican priests and one lay brother joined the expedition—and to find gold, silver, mercury, and precious gems, an aspiration never far from the Spanish mind. To assist Luna in his travels, Velasco provided him with a map of the de Soto march.

On 11 June 1559, Luna departed San Juan de Ulúa on the Mexican Gulf coast in thirteen ships of varying tonnage. His expedition numbered 200 foot soldiers, 200 cavalrymen with 240 horses in slings, 100 craftsmen and tradesmen, a number of de Soto campaigners who knew the Florida interior, a native woman interpreter from Coosa whom the de Soto survivors had brought to México with them, 100 Mexican warriors, and about 900 colonists, including married men, wives, and children. The last category of passengers would prove to be more a burden than an advantage, since the land toward which they headed had too little food and too much hardship for untested civilians. The bishop of Cuba would later comment that, instead of indolent and undisciplined men from New Spain, the expedition should have recruited hardworking peasants from the mountains of León in Old Spain.

After an unexpectedly long voyage, during which about 100 horses died, and after several false sightings, the fleet entered Pensacola Bay (Ochuse) on 14 August. Luna named the bay Bahía Filipina del Puerto Santa María, after Felipe II and the Virgin Mary, and immediately set to work laying out a settlement; exactly where it is not known, although two recent estimates are Gulf Breeze or Tartar Point. We know that there were few natives in the region, which meant few food crops, and that Luna dispatched two search parties, one by land and one by the Escambia River, to hunt for villages and food to the north. The patrols returned empty-handed.

Disaster struck on 19 September in the form of a hurricane that, besides killing an unknown number of colonists, sank or ran aground all but three of the expedition's ships. Half the supplies, including personal belongings, were lost. Worse, most of the food was still on board one of the ships that went down, and what food had already been unloaded was spoiled by the storm's downpour. The lot of nearly 1,500 people was now desperate.

In this extremity Luna had the wit to send two surviving frigates to Havana for food, and another overland patrol north for the same reason, before experiencing the first of a number of physical and mental breakdowns that would afflict him throughout his Florida command. When he recovered, he acted on a promising report from the northern patrol and, except for fifty men, moved his starving coastal colony inland to the eighty-hut native town of Nanipacana, about 100 miles up the Alabama River. There the Spaniards found that the inhabitants had decamped with most of their food stores. A 100-man patrol sent north from Nanipacana, to which Luna appended the name Santa Cruz (Holy Cross), found no better prospects. Meanwhile, the settlers were reduced to eating acorns, tree leaves, and wild roots. Remembering the de Soto survivors' tales of Coosa and its fertile fields, Luna then dispatched 150 foot soldiers and 50 cavalrymen to find that bountiful chiefdom. After three months, during which they subsisted on blackberries, acorns, and the leather of their shoes, while their horses became so famished they could hardly walk three miles a day, the travelers came upon the principal town of Coosa.

It was not the Coosa described by de Soto's men who were in the party. Those men were astonished to find that the populous and wealthy society they had encountered twenty years before had declined to a comparatively few huts and fields. The demographic collapse was attributed to the dep-redations of "a certain captain," i.e., de Soto; even so, the natives who remained willingly shared their food with the new invaders. During the three months the Spanish detachment remained in the region, the Coosa asked them to assist their forces in subjugating a nearby troublesome tribe, the Napoochie. The Spaniards agreed to cooperate. Except for that single act of warfare, the behavior of Luna's men toward the aborigines of La Florida was pacific and correct, in keeping with the spirit of the New Laws.

Meanwhile, three supply ships from México put in at Ochuse, and the famished colonists at Nanipacana fled south to claim the provisions, leaving behind a note to that effect for the Coosa command, which returned to Nanipacana in October 1560. From Ochuse, a number of women, children, and invalids returned to México on the supply ships. Besides food and clothing those ships had brought urgent royal and viceregal orders for Luna to establish a presence at Santa Elena without further delay. Accordingly, in July or August 1560, Luna directed sixty soldiers and three Dominicans to sail around the peninsula to that Atlantic coastal site. On the voyage the ships encountered foul weather, and the attempt was abandoned. At Ochuse the remaining colonists soon exhausted their new rations and were reduced to eating their leather, grass, and shellfish. Mutinous in mood, they engaged in endless wrangling and insubordination, a situation that was aggravated by Luna's occasional mental seizures and deliriums. The inevitable rebellion was averted by the skillful intervention of two Dominican friars and by the arrival, in April 1561, of a new governor to relieve Luna, the alcalde mayor of Veracruz, Ángel de Villafañe. Luna sailed to Spain by way of Havana to answer charges of dereliction. The commander of the fleet on which he took passage was Pedro Menéndez de Avilés (see chapter 4).

Villafañe bore orders identical to those last given to Luna: settle Santa Elena at once. Leaving seventy or eighty men behind at Ochuse, he sailed first to Havana to pick up horses and additional supplies. There, not surprisingly, about half his force deserted. With the remainder he followed the Florida current north to what his pilots believed to be Santa Elena. The four extant documents on the voyage are unclear, even contradictory, on what happened at that site, wherever it was. They agree, however, in stating that Villafañe made no settlement there. Instead, he continued north by ship exploring capes, inlets, and rivers as far as 35° north, or Cape Lookout, North Carolina; he lost two small ships and twenty-five men in a storm and, discouraged, returned to Havana, where more of his men disappeared into the local population. In the bitter denouement of the Luna-Villafañe undertaking, the detachment left at Ochuse was rescued and brought home to México.

At the viceregal capital, a "pained and saddened" Velasco pondered a communication from Felipe II reporting the opinion of Menéndez de Avilés that La Florida's shoreline was too low and sandy, her countryside too poor in resources, and her harbors too barred and shallow to permit practicable settlement. For that reason, the report concluded, there was no cause to fear that the French would establish themselves there or attempt to take possession.[12]

Notes

1. Antonio de Herrera y Tordesillas, *Historia general de los hechos de los Castellanos en las Islas y tierra firme del mar Océano,* 4 vols. in quarto (Madrid, 1601–15), 1:249. [*Note:* The diminutive form Juan Ponce was used by the first Spanish chroniclers of the period of exploration.—M. G.]

2. Douglas T. Peck, "Reconstruction and Analysis of the 1513 Discovery Voyage of Juan Ponce de León," *Florida Historical Quarterly* 71, no. 2 (October 1992):133–54; Peck, *Ponce de León and the Discovery of Florida: The Man, the Myth, and the Truth* (St. Paul, Minn.: Pogo Press, 1993), pp. 36–39.

3. This is the translation by James E. Kelley Jr. in his "Juan Ponce de León's Discovery of Florida: Herrera's Narrative Revisited," *Revista de Historia de América* 111 (January–June 1991):42. I have altered Kelley's rendering of Pascua as "Passover" to "Easter."

4. Ibid.

5. Alvar Núñez Cabeza de Vaca, *La "Relación" o "Naufragios" de Alvar Núñez Cabeza de Vaca,* ed. Martin A. Favata and José B. Fernández (Potomac, Md.: Scripta Humanística, 1986). See also new translations in Charles Hudson and Carmen McClendon, eds., *Forgotten Centuries* (Athens: University of Georgia Press, 1994), and in John H. Hann, "Translation of the Florida Section of the Álvar Núñez Cabeza de Vaca Accounts of the 1528 Trek from South Florida to Apalachee led by Pánfilo de Narváez," manuscript, Florida Bureau of Archaeological Research, Tallahassee.

6. John Francis Bannon, introduction to *The Narrative of Alvar Núñez Cabeza de Vaca,*

trans. Fanny Bandelier, with Oviedo's version of the lost joint report translated by Gerald Theisen (Barre, Mass.: Imprint Society, 1972), p. 27.

7. Alonso de Chaves, *Quatri Partitu en Cosmographia practica, y por otro nombre Espejo de Navegantes* (Madrid, 1537; reprint, Madrid, 1983); Luys Hernández de Biedma, "Relation of the Island of Florida . . . 1539," ed. and trans. John E. Worth, in Lawrence A. Clayton, Vernon James Knight, Jr., and Edward C. Moore, eds., *The De Soto Chronicles: The Expedition of Hernando De Soto to North America in 1539–1543,* 2 vols. (Tuscaloosa: University of Alabama Press, 1993), 1:225.

8. John R. Swanton, ed., *Final Report of the United States De Soto Expedition Commission,* U.S. House of Representatives Doc. 71, 76th Cong., 1st sess. (Washington: Government Printing Office, 1939); reprint, with an introduction by Jeffrey P. Brain (Washington: Smithsonian Institution Press, 1985).

9. Louis D. Tesar, "The Case for Concluding That De Soto Landed Near Present-Day Fort Myers, Florida: The Conclusions Presented by Warren H. Wilkinson Reviewed," *Florida Anthropologist* 42, no. 4 (December 1989):276–79, and Lindsey Williams, "A Charlotte Harbor Perspective on de Soto's Landing Site," ibid., 280–94. See also Rolfe F. Schell, *De Soto Didn't Land at Tampa* (Ft. Myers Beach: Island Press, 1966).

10. Jerald T. Milanich and Charles Hudson, *Hernando de Soto and the Indians of Florida* (Gainesville: University Press of Florida, 1993).

11. Garcilaso de la Vega, the Inca, *La Florida,* trans. Charmion Shelby, in *The De Soto Chronicles,* ed. Clayton, Knight, Moore, 2:357–58.

12. See the transcript "Paracer que da a S.M. el Consejo de la Nueva España, en virtud de su Real Cédula [fecha en Madrid a 23 de Septiembre de 1561] que sigue, sobre la forma en que estava la costa de la Florida, y que no convenía aumentar la Población," Buckingham Smith Collection (New York Public Library), vol. 1561–93, p. 11.

Bibliography

Avellaneda, Ignacio. *Los Sobrevivientes de la Florida: The Survivors of the de Soto Expedition.* Edited by Bruce Chappell. Research Publications of the P. K. Yonge Library of Florida History, no. 2. Gainesville: University of Florida Libraries, 1990.

Badger, R. Reid, and Lawrence A. Clayton, eds. *Alabama and the Borderlands: From Prehistory to Statehood.* Tuscaloosa: University of Alabama Press, 1985.

Bishop, Morris. *The Odyssey of Cabeza de Vaca.* New York: Century Co., 1933.

Curren, Caleb, Keith J. Little, and Harry O. Holstein. "Aboriginal Societies Encountered by the Tristán de Luna Expedition." *Florida Anthropologist* 42, no. 4 (December 1989): 381–95.

Devereux, Anthony Q. *Juan Ponce de León, King Ferdinand and the Fountain of Youth.* Spartanburg, S.C.: Reprint Company, 1993.

Dobyns, Henry F. *Their Number Become Thinned: Native American Population Dynamics in Eastern North America.* Knoxville: University of Tennessee Press, 1983.

Eubanks, W. S., Jr. "Studying De Soto's Route: A Georgian House of Cards." *Florida Anthropologist* 42 (December 1989):369–80.

Gannon, Michael V. *The Cross in the Sand: The Early Catholic Church in Florida, 1513–1870.* Gainesville: University of Florida Press, 1965.

Hanke, Lewis. *The Spanish Struggle for Justice in the Conquest of America.* Philadelphia: University of Pennsylvania Press, 1949.

Henige, David. "The Context, Content, and Credibility of La Florida del Ynca." *The Americas* 43 (July 1986):1–23.

Hoffman, Paul E. "Nature and Sequence of the Spanish Borderlands." In *Native, European, and African Cultures in Mississippi, 1500–1800,* edited by Patricia K. Galloway. Jackson: Mississippi Department of Archives and History, 1991.

———. *A New Andalucía and a Way to the Orient: The American Southeast during the Sixteenth Century.* Baton Rouge: Louisiana State University Press, 1990.

Lyon, Eugene. "Spain's Sixteenth-Century North American Settlement Attempts: A Neglected Aspect." *Florida Historical Quarterly* 59, no. 3 (January 1981):275–91.

Milanich, Jerald T., and Susan Milbrath, eds. *First Encounters: Spanish Explorations in the Caribbean and the United States, 1492–1570.* Gainesville: University of Florida Press, 1989.

O'Daniel, V[ictor] F[rancis], O.P. *Dominicans in Early Florida.* New York: United States Catholic Historical Society, 1930.

Priestley, Herbert Ingram. *The Luna Papers: Documents Relating to the Expedition of Don Tristán de Luna y Arellano for the Conquest of La Florida in 1559–1561.* 2 vols. DeLand: Florida State Historical Society, 1928.

Quinn, David B. *North America from Earliest Discovery to First Settlements: The Norse Voyages to 1612.* New York: Harper & Row, 1977.

Sauer, Carl O. *Sixteenth Century North America: The Land and the People as Seen by the Europeans.* Berkeley: University of California Press, 1971.

Swagerty, William R. "Beyond Bimini: Indian Responses to European Incursions in the Spanish Borderlands, 1513–1600." Ph.D. diss., University of California, Santa Barbara (Ann Arbor, Mich.: University Microfilms International, 1982).

Thomas, David Hurst, ed. *Columbian Consequences: Archaeological and Historical Perspectives on the Spanish Borderlands East.* Washington: Smithsonian Institution Press, 1990.

Tío, Aurelio. "Número conmemorativo del cuadringentisexagésimo aniversario del descubrimiento de la Florida y Yucatan." *Boletín de la Academia Puertorriqueña de la Historia* 2, no. 8 (30 June 1972).

Weber, David J. *The Spanish Frontier in North America.* New Haven: Yale University Press, 1992.

Weddle, Robert S. *Spanish Sea: The Gulf of Mexico in North American Discovery, 1500–1685.* College Station: Texas A&M University Press, 1985.

3

The Land They Found

PAUL E. HOFFMAN

The ecology of the Floridas is the stage upon which the actors who figure in the chapters of this *History of Florida* played out their stories. Ecology did not *determine* those stories, it must be stressed, but it did influence them to varying degrees over time and helped people determine where to build their homes and economic enterprises. Until well into the twentieth century, the topography, soils, flora and fauna, and weather of the region profoundly shaped the livelihoods and thus lives of the Native Americans, Europeans, and Africans who inhabited what was at first a vast, ill-defined region in southeastern North America (La Florida) but which in time became just the area of the modern state. The influences of the peninsula's ecology on the lives of Florida's residents have become less pronounced since the mid-twentieth century because the economy has shifted away from a near total dependence on agriculture and because modern technologies have allowed at least a limited reshaping of aspects of that ecology. For example, drainage patterns and the characteristics of soils can be modified if not completely overcome. Heat and humidity do not trouble individuals living and work-ing in air-conditioning. Still other aspects of the region's ecology—notably floral and faunal diversity—have been profoundly altered when Old World peoples introduced, and continue to introduce, what Alfred Crosby has called their portmanteaux biota. Too, since Europeans and their enslaved, and later freed, African companions arrived, the Floridas have never been without trade with the world and thus means to overcome local ecologi-cally linked problems of subsistence and economic prosperity. And, since the late nineteenth century, peninsular Florida's generally warm dry win-ters have attracted persons from colder climes, creating tourism and retire-ment industries that capitalize on at least those aspects of the state's ecol-ogy. Even so, some characteristics of the region's ecology—notably periods of drought and tropical storms—are beyond modern control. This chapter explores the ecology of the Floridas, especially with regard to the colonial and early-nineteenth-century periods when it had the greatest impact on human lives.[1]

The late-sixteenth-century Spanish royal cartographer Juan Lopez de Velasco claimed as Spanish Florida (La Florida) the vast region running from the cod fisheries of Newfoundland, Nova Scotia, and northern New England to as far south as the Florida Keys and west along the Gulf coast to the Soto La Marina River in Mexico. Inland, it reached as far west as the undefined eastern edge of New Mexico. If this La Florida had a northwestern boundary, it was the supposed arm of the Pacific Ocean that was thought to reach deep into the continent to the north of New Mexico to an elusive point west of the Appalachian Mountains.

In sixteenth-century practice, those grand, vague boundaries shrank to encompass the coastal and piedmont zones of the modern states of Virginia, North and South Carolina, Georgia, and Alabama; the Appalachian Mountains of the Carolinas; southeastern Tennessee and northern Alabama; an undetermined part of the Gulf of Mexico's northern coast and the Mississippi Valley; and peninsular Florida. This definition arose from coastal explorations and the de Soto expedition's peregrination through the Southeast (see map on p. 30). In legal and diplomatic terms, it was a claim based on discovery and possession taking as well as the so-called Papal Donation and the Treaty of Tordesillas of 1494. Yet within this area, effective occupation and influence extended only as far as Spanish settlements or missions or active trade did, which in the sixteenth century effectively meant coastal areas of peninsular north Florida, Georgia, and South Carolina, and, briefly in the 1560s, the Carolinas' piedmont (see map on p. 97). During the seventeenth century, the area of active missions expanded into various parts of the interior of the peninsula (see map on p. 99). Trade via Native American intermediaries may have reached farther into the backcountry that is today western Georgia and Alabama, but we know little about it. That is, Spain's La Florida in reality was based on effective occupation of only a small part of the expansive land claims its diplomats sometimes made in negotiations in Europe or that its maps and geographers laid down.

As chapters 4, 5, 6, and 8 show, epidemics among the Native American populations (limiting the area of mission work and trade), wars, and European treaties slowly reduced La Florida's effective extent. When the British took over the colony in 1764, they decreed the northern limit of today's state (31° North and the course of the St. Marys River) but did not accept the

Franco-Spanish understanding of 1723 that the Perdido River marked the line between Spanish La Florida and French La Louisiane. Thirty-one years later, the United States accepted and then surveyed the 31° border under the Treaty of San Lorenzo of 1795 (Pinckney's Treaty). Finally, in 1822, when Congress organized the Territory of Florida, it used the Perdido River to mark its western boundary.

The Spanish mariners who first saw the shores of La Florida encountered what appeared to their untutored eyes to be unbroken forests of pines and mixed pines and hardwoods running from the sea to the great stands of fire-tolerant longleaf pine trees that marked the edges of the piedmont in the Carolinas and Georgia and covered the northern highlands of the peninsula. Along the shore and on the backs of coastal islands were hammocks of live oaks where soils were appropriate. The river valleys that ran to the sea were thickly grown with multiple hardwood species. On the piedmont, the oak-pine-hickory forest appeared, while on some slopes of the Appalachian Mountains the dominant forest was the oak-hickory-elm association now largely lost to Dutch elm disease. Appearing uniform, these vast bands of forest were in fact mosaics of many floristic communities, communities determined by soils, rainfall, drainage, temperature, and the shaping of the forests by lightning fires, insects, and Native American agricultural and hunting practices, including the use of fire. Faunal diversity accompanied this floral diversity, although most species were too small for use as food.[2]

Less clearly in peninsular Florida than farther north along the coastal plain, the rising and retreating of the Atlantic and the warping of the North American geologic plate have shaped as many as a dozen step-like, if discontinuous, "terraces" in what geologists classify as three sections (lower or outer, middle, and upper or inner) of the coastal plain. The soils on these coastal terraces were once back barrier marsh surfaces, bay bottoms, and/or areas of alluvial deposition and are generally acidic sands of low fertility and high moisture content during the rainy season. In general, they are classified as Aquults, although areas of Humaquepts occur along the Georgia coast.[3] Inland swamps, marshes, and low areas that flood during the rainy season reflect this geologic history. Hardpans (horizons of nearly impermeable clay) underlie some areas, notably on the east and west coasts of Florida where the soils are Aquods. These hardpans result in rainy-season flooding and the famous pine flatwoods that some British-era "planters" exploited for naval stores and that today support the pulpwood industry where subdivisions have not sprung up. Scarps or even sand hills (in Georgia and the Carolinas) mark the edges of the terraces and provide gradations in moisture from wetter (close to the water) to drier on the uplands, gradations that define ecotones where floral and faunal diversity is greater than on the terrace below or above. Ecotones can also be found around ponds and lakes and along stream beds, especially in central Florida.[4]

The Piedmont has a similar topography of terraces although the soils are more fertile and better drained by numerous small streams flowing into the rivers that drain to the east or south. In general, the soils are mostly reddish Udults. Native Americans and modern farmers used and use the friable, quality soils of the valley floodplains associated with the smaller streams. De Soto's men (1539–40) and Juan Pardo's soldiers (1566–68) recognized these areas as places suitable for Spanish agricultural settlement.[5] Historian Eugene Lyon believes that had Pedro Menéndez de Avilés lived long enough, he would have claimed the upper Wateree River Valley (explored by Pardo) as part of the marquisate Philip II had promised him if he successfully settled La Florida.[6] Had Spanish settlement developed in this area in the Carolinas, the history of Florida might have unfolded quite differently. Instead, the Spanish towns of Santa Elena (1566–87; Parris Island, South Carolina) and St. Augustine were built on the sands of the Atlantic coastal plain; that is, on soils with limited agricultural potentials, aside from running cattle in the pine woods, characteristics that, along with the absence of minerals, limited Spanish interest in the colony. Only Florida's strategic location on the Bahama Channel and the pleas of the Franciscan missionaries prevented its abandonment in the early seventeenth century.[7] For most of the rest of the first Spanish period, the colony depended on its *situado* (civil list or subsidy) as the main engine of its economy, although Apalachee is known to have exported deerskins and foods to Havana. During the British, second Spanish, and early American periods, a more diverse economy gradually built up based on the export of hides, oranges, naval stores and timbers, and cotton produced at various places mostly north of the I-4 corridor of today. Cuban fishermen developed that industry along the lower west coast, but it did not depend on the qualities of soils.

In peninsular Florida, geologists have identified sections of as many as five of the eight terraces of the lower coastal plain in the strip of land between the Atlantic Ocean and the 15-meter (50-foot) contour west of the St. Johns River and generally north of the Tampa–Daytona Beach line. The higher ground of the flatwoods of the upper St. Johns and Kissimmee River basins as well as the flatwoods between Sebring and Lake Okeechobee, and in southwest Florida along the Caloosahatchee River and between Fort Myers and Tampa Bay are also classified as parts of these coastal terraces. On the western side of Florida's central ridge north of Tampa Bay, some of the terraces also are evident, for example on State Highway 24 between Cedar Key and Gainesville. The terraces of the middle coastal plain that are notable features of Virginia and the Carolinas (three and four terraces, respectively) but less so in Georgia (two terraces) continue in Florida to form four identifiable terraces east of the Haines City Ridge in central Florida and west of the Trail Ridge feature (and 15-meter contour) of northern Florida and southeastern Georgia. Less certain is whether the highest elevations of Florida's central ridge should be classed as continuations of the upper coastal plain found in Virginia and the Carolinas.

Whatever the relationship of the central ridge to geologic features farther north, the western highlands and the Mariana, Tallahassee, and Madison Hills are part of the south and southeastward tilted "southern" or Tifton uplands that extend into adjacent parts of southwestern Georgia. Streams and rivers have carved this upland into hills and valleys with generally moderate (10–25°) slopes. The soils are mostly Udults, with red-yellow sands over clayey subsoils west of the Madison Hills and gray-brown sandy loams on those hills. Early-nineteenth-century atlas maps described these hills as having "good soils" because they, like similar soils on the central Florida ridge, have moderate to good fertility and generally excellent drainage. The Tallahassee Hills were home to the Apalachee Indians. In the nineteenth century, cotton plantations were established on all three sets of hills. Because of the slopes, these hills have as many as thirty-five species of trees per acre and generally support one of the more diverse ecological areas in the Southeast.

The central ridge and its outlying hills to the east and south are generally covered with gray-brown sandy soils (Quartzipsamments) of varying slope. The so-called Arredondo-Kendrick-Millhopper Association of red-yellow sandy loams (Udults) cuts across the ridge in a north to south pattern. Both regions or soil groups are moist to well drained and of moderate fertility. The natural climax forest varies with moisture but is generally various kinds of pines with scrub oaks (on drier soils), although areas of oak and hickory hardwoods occur on the Arredondo-Kendrick-Millhopper Association soils and on the more moist slopes. The central ridge was home to the majority of Florida's precolonial Timucuan speakers, the late-eighteenth-century home of the Seminole and Miccosukee, and is today an area of increasingly dense settlement.

North of a line from Fort Myers to the Fort Pierce Inlet, and south of the Central Ridge, are superficially gray, very acidic infertile soils (Aquods) that

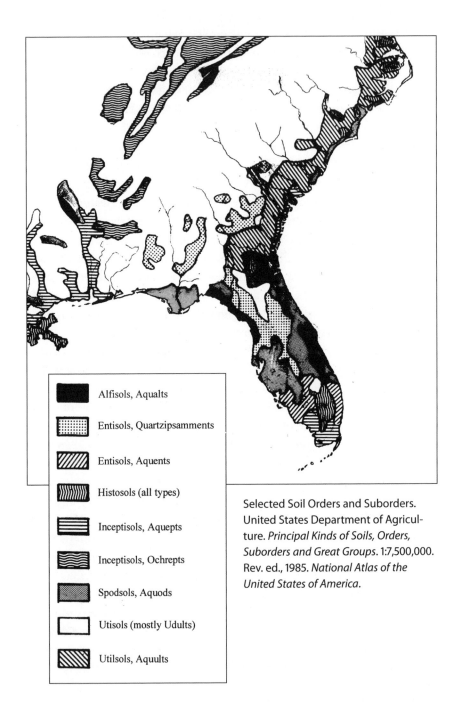

Alfisols, Aqualts

Entisols, Quartzipsamments

Entisols, Aquents

Histosols (all types)

Inceptisols, Aquepts

Inceptisols, Ochrepts

Spodsols, Aquods

Utisols (mostly Udults)

Utilsols, Aquults

Selected Soil Orders and Suborders. United States Department of Agriculture. *Principal Kinds of Soils, Orders, Suborders and Great Groups*. 1:7,500,000. Rev. ed., 1985. *National Atlas of the United States of America*.

flood seasonally because of high water tables and underlying hardpans or limestones that are close to the surface. Here are found flatwoods of pines and palmettos, areas used to run cattle beginning in the nineteenth century. Modern drainage and agricultural practices have allowed the cultivation of oranges and other crops. Swamps are common where no modern drainage has been built. In precontact times, maize cultivation extended to the Fort Myers–Fort Pierce Inlet line, but was confined to naturally higher, drained soils and man-made ridges.

South of the Fort Myers–Fort Pierce Inlet line, the soils are all of wet types (Aquents, Histosols, and Aquepts), and the original vegetation was wet—pine savannah, cypress swamps, and sawgrass or other types of marshes depending on location. Where hammocks rise above this wet environment, oaks and some tropical hardwoods grow. There is some evidence that Native Americans exploited these hammocks and the other potentials of south Florida well before the Seminole and Miccosukee made them a refuge during the nineteenth-century Seminole Wars. Twentieth-century drainage works reclaimed some of this area south of Lake Okeechobee and disrupted the natural flow of water into the Everglades. Sugarcane and some winter vegetables grow on these drained areas today.

The Pleistocene barrier islands of Georgia and the Carolinas and to a lesser degree those of Florida's east coast separate shallow bays and the mouths of rivers such as the Satilla, Altamaha, and St. Lucy from the Atlantic Ocean. Live-oak maritime forests on the landward sides of the islands and on the mainlands opposite, especially around river mouths, are associated with soils capable of growing maize, beans, squash, and other plants but in amounts limited by the small extent of those soils and the difficulties of clearing the oaks. These forests, and the marshes that fringe the bays, provide rich sources of protein in the form of turkey, deer, raccoons, turtles, and migratory birds. The bays and marshes shelter fish, shellfish, and, within the marsh, edible tuberous roots. Native Americans exploited all of these resources as did later European and African settlers.[8] After the United States took over Florida, the live-oak groves along its east coast were reserved for the U.S. Navy, which cut them to provide the naturally curved timbers needed for the ribs of wooden warships. As the cutters moved on, small farmers sometimes replaced them.

A few attempts have been made to correlate the locations of Native American settlements, especially on the central ridge and northern hills, with particular soil types, but so far the results are suggestive only.[9] More important for village sites in the peninsula (and some later European settlements) are sources of surface freshwater and the ecotones associated with them. In Georgia and the Carolinas, settlements other than those on the coast were sited where freshwater, floodplain soils, and adjacent uplands offered ideal combinations for agriculture and hunting and gathering.[10] In the peninsula, aside from the rather dense cluster of Timucuan-speaking villages on the lower St. Johns River and along the back bays and rivers to the north (into southern Georgia), Native American villages were strung at intervals along the central ridge and clustered in the Madison–Tallahassee Hills area. Around Tampa Bay, Sarasota Bay, and Charlotte Harbor were other clusters of villages supported primarily by maritime resources supplemented by some maize-bean-squash agriculture on the poor-quality gray-white sandy soils of the area and some hunting of deer and other animals and the gathering of nuts and berries. Modern home owners who try to maintain lush lawns in these areas know well that such soils demand high costs in water and fertilizers. Lacking the technologies that make such lawns possible, Native Americans and pre-twentieth-century European settlers had to make do with what the land would allow to grow. A consequence was frequent rotation of their plantings and the clearing of new fields as the old lost fertility. Not surprisingly, those pioneers mostly ran cattle and tended small gardens and groves and were few in number. South of the Fort Myers–Fort Pierce Inlet line, Native American villages wholly dependent on marine resources and wetland plants occupied coastal high ground locations and, as in the case of the Calusa, islands like Key Marcos.

While the qualities of the land for agricultural and other uses have been critical determinants of human settlement in the Floridas, the numerous rivers that flow through La Florida have also played a role. Large and small, all of La Florida's rivers are navigable in small boats and canoes deep into the land before the waters either narrow and become shallow to the point of being impassable or—as in the case of the Altamaha, the Savannah, and the Chattahoochee—encounter the fall line rapids at the foot of the piedmont. The rivers of the Carolinas and Georgia and the Chattahoochee and other rivers that flow from the piedmont were, before twentieth-century flood-control work, subject to flash flooding along their lower courses. Moreover, they were/are fringed by dense swamps and forests that made their banks unsuitable for human habitation, especially as they approach the coast. Nonetheless, they provided the freshwater that makes the coastal marshes so productive of exploitable marine life. Other rivers such as the St. Johns, St. Marys, Suwannee, St. Marks, Hillsborough, Peace, and Miami did not flash-flood, although they can flood some of their margins during periods of very heavy rains. Native American settlements were found along their courses and around their mouths where other factors such as soils were favorable. Shorter rivers arising on the upper coastal plain were less likely to flood and were often without heavy forests along their margins, but few Native American settlements occupied their banks. We know little of how Native Americans used these natural routes for commerce or exploited the fish, turtles, and birds that frequented these waters and the ecotones along their shores.

For Old World settlers, on the other hand, the rivers clearly were routes for communication and trade, allowing settlers to reach agricultural and other natural resources beyond those found along the coasts and to bring those products to market.[11] For the Spaniards, the St. Johns, the Suwannee, and the St. Marks were avenues for commerce at various times in the sixteenth and seventeenth centuries, joining the bays behind the Atlantic barrier islands (and the Atlantic and Gulf of Mexico) as parts of their communications system. That system tied the missions and garrisons together and allowed the transportation of the agricultural products of Guale (roughly modern coastal Georgia) and Apalachee and the hides from ranches in central Florida (near Paynes Prairie) to market and of supplies from the larger Atlantic world to missions and garrisons. The English during their control, and the Anglo-Americans entering Spanish Florida after 1784, mostly used the St. Johns and the St. Marys as routes into the interior, to wild orange groves (along the St. Johns), lands to be farmed, and forests to be tapped for naval stores. In the nineteenth century, small steamboats on the St. Johns were the preferred means to reach trails and then roads that gave access to the central ridge's healthful air around Brooksville, a refuge (like St. Augustine) for the tubercular. Only slowly did a few of the peninsula's other rivers (aside always from those that joined the bays behind the barrier islands) become avenues of commerce. But in time, the use of larger ships that drew more water than what was found in most of Florida's rivers, railroads, and paved highways moved commerce away from the water, leaving the rivers and bays largely to recreational fishermen and boaters.

One aspect of Florida's hydrography that remained a puzzle until the nineteenth century was what connections, if any, existed between the waters of the St. Johns and Kissimmee Rivers, the Everglades and the Peace and other rivers of southern Florida. Spanish and English maps reflect the *hope* that somehow all that water would allow a cross-peninsula route that might even be navigable by small sailing ships. But there is no such natural route.

The climate of the Southeast and the peninsula is, with soils, drainage, and the frequency of fires, another major component of the area's ecology. Average frost-free days range from 300 in central Florida to 270 to 210 over the Georgia-Carolinas coastal plain (according to elevation), to about 210 in the piedmont. This long growing season allows as many as two crops in Florida and fairly secure ones elsewhere if rainfall is adequate during the growing months and temperatures are not too high. In general, both summer rainfall and temperatures are modulated by the movement of the Bermuda High, which controls airflow from the south and southeast to the northwest over northern Florida and the Georgia-Carolinas area. When the High is "onshore," drought and very hot conditions can develop over the coastal plain and piedmont; when "offshore," rainfall can be adequate and temperatures somewhat reduced during July and August. South of the northern Florida hills, summer rainfall and temperatures are governed by the strength of the trade winds, daily patterns of evaporation and thunderstorm formation, and tropical storms.

Everywhere, but especially in northern Florida, lightning strikes from thunderstorms are common. Northern Florida has up to ninety days a year of lightning, making that part of the state one of the more active lightning areas in the world. Strikes are somewhat less common farther south.

Lightning-caused fires were essential for maintaining the longleaf pine forests of the northern hills. There and in some other areas those fires served to clear out accumulated understory plants. Native Americans who hunted deer and then the "cracker" settlers who ran cattle set fires for the same purpose when lightning fires did not do an adequate job. In these cases, the goal was to encourage the growth of grasses that fed deer and cattle.

The normal annual rainfall pattern is one of sometimes prolonged and heavy rains during the passage of cold fronts and Gulf of Mexico–generated lows during the winter months (November to March), followed by late afternoon and evening thunderstorms during the summer months (June–September) as evaporation provides moisture that condenses into thunderstorms. Annual totals range from about 40 inches along coastal areas, 50 inches over much of the interior of the peninsula, and 60 inches in the southern Appalachians.

Within this general weather pattern, spring rainfall is critical for agriculture. In the northern parts of the peninsula, spring rainfall seems to be influenced by the same large-scale climate fluctuations that tree-ring studies have shown operate over Georgia (especially) and the Carolinas. Chronologies derived from these studies show repeated alternations of below- and above-normal rainfall (that is, rainfall that is more than one standard deviation below or above the running mean), changes that imply crop failures, especially in years when rainfall is well below normal. Thus regarding the settling of Santa Elena and the first Jesuit mission (1566 and 1570, respectively), the "lost colony" on Roanoke Island (1587), and Jamestown (1606–1612), we know that rainfall was well below normal for periods of years associated with each event, a fact that helps to explain the added stress that the new European presence and demand for food placed on Native Americans in those areas and their usually hostile responses.[12] A correlation with below-normal rainfall over Georgia has also been found for some later years during the first Spanish period (1565–1763), when maize harvests at St. Augustine are recorded to have been well below expectations.[13] Further correlations of agricultural fortunes with rainfall patterns in northern Florida may be possible because the documentary record gets progressively better after the middle of the nineteenth century. As yet no proxy studies have determined historical rainfall patterns for the rest of the peninsula in the centuries before instruments were used to measure them. Historians studying topics other than agriculture have generally not taken weather events, or soils, and thus economic productivity, into account even though until the early twentieth century and the tourism and retirement booms, agricultural production was a key to state revenues and hence central to many political struggles.

A final component of the ecology of the Floridas is the tropical storm. Climate science has established that variability in the El Niño–La Niña Southern Oscillation (ENSO) phenomenon in the Pacific Ocean has important effects in the Caribbean and tropical Atlantic as well as over western and northern North America. When the El Niño is strong, upper-level winds shear storm clouds forming in the Caribbean and tropical Atlantic, thus reducing the number and severity of tropical storms. When La Niña is strong, the reverse is the case. A recent study of various physical proxy records has found a predominance of La Niña years (140 La Niñas, 110 El Niños in the 324 years in question) during the years 1525 to 1850, many of them strong (47 or 33.6 percent of La Niña years), very strong (27 or 19.3 percent), or even extreme (7 or 5 percent). Since 1850, El Niño years are slightly more numerous (79 vs. 72 in 152 years, to 2002).[14] Twentieth-century data suggest that during La Niña years there is a high annual probability (68 percent) of one or more hurricanes striking Florida, defined as the area south of Tarpon Springs on the west and all of the rest of the peninsula to the east. The stronger the La Niña, the stronger the probability of a hurricane landfall on the peninsula or on the Gulf coast (especially Texas and

Louisiana). Probabilities based on recent proxies and instrumental data do not, of course, indicate what happened in earlier times.[15] For those years, like the better-documented ones since about 1850, specific historical records are needed. What is presently known suggests that settlement in those years was seldom affected by tropical weather, primarily, one suspects, because it was clustered in the north and northeast of the present state, areas that do not now receive many tropical storm strikes. But there were some, notably one in 1599 whose storm surge swept over St. Augustine.

In sum, while we know a great deal about the general ecology of La Florida and peninsular Florida, historical knowledge is limited about how the many aspects of that ecology interacted with Native American and European and African peoples' attempts to wrest a living from the area in the years before modern technologies allowed at least limited alterations of the state's ecology, sometimes with harmful effects that were not anticipated when they were made. What is clear is that the general ecology of the peninsula shaped where people lived well into the twentieth century and continues to account for aspects of its history.

Notes

1. This chapter is drawn from Paul E. Hoffman, *Florida's Frontiers* (Bloomington: Indiana University Press, 2002), esp. pp. 2–17 and passim, and sources cited therein with the addition of materials on climate.

2. E[mma] Lucy Braun, *Deciduous Forests of North America* (New York: Macmillan, 1950), pp. 296, 260–65, 284–89, 296–98, 195–97; B. W. Wells, "Ecological Problems of the Southeastern United States Coastal Plain," *Botanical Review* 8 (1942):533–61, esp. 534; *North Carolina Atlas; Portrait of a Changing Southern State*, ed. James W. Clay, Douglas M. Orr Jr., and Alfred W. Stuart (Chapel Hill: University of North Carolina Press, 1975); Charles H. Wharton, *The Natural Environments of Georgia* (Atlanta: Georgia Department of Natural Resources, 1977), pp. 5–9; *Ecosystems of Florida*, ed. Ronald L. Myers and John J. Ewel (Orlando: University of Central Florida Press, 1990).

3. For simplicity, soil types noted herein generally are given by Great Groups from the map in U.S. Department of the Interior, U.S. Geological Survey, *The National Atlas of the United States* (Washington, D.C., 1970), p. 87. Within each Great Group, there are many subtypes based on the presence or absence of soil horizons, minerals present or absent, moisture regime, mechanical characteristics, and color. For peninsular Florida, some 400 different named subtypes of soils have been identified. For more details, see Randall B. Brown, Earl L. Stone, and Victor W. Carlisle, "Soils," in *Ecosystems of Florida*, pp. 42–53.

4. Donald J. Colquhoun et al., "Quaternary Geology of the Atlantic Coastal Plain," in *Quaternary Non-glacial Geology, Conterminous United States*, ed. Roger B. Morrison (Boulder, Colo.: Geological Society of America, 1991), pp. 629–50. Timothy Silver, *A New Face on the Countryside: Indians, Colonists and Slaves in the South Atlantic Forests,*

1500-1800 (New York: Cambridge University Press, 1990), pp. 9–13, offers a simplified explanation of this geology. For coastal soils as well as vegetation, see Norman L. Christensen, "Vegetation of the Southeastern Coastal Plain," in *North American Terrestrial Vegetation,* ed. Michael G. Barbour and W. D. Billings (New York: Cambridge University Press, 1988), pp. 321–22.

5. De Soto's surviving soldiers remembered Coosa (northwest Georgia) and Cofitachequi (near modern Camden, South Carolina), both places in the piedmont, as polities of abundant food and good general conditions (Paul E. Hoffman, *A New Andalucia and a Way to the Orient* [Baton Rouge: Louisiana State University, 1990], p. 97); Juan de la Bandera, "The 'Short' Bandera Relation," in Charles Hudson, *The Juan Pardo Expeditions,* rev. ed. (Tuscaloosa: University of Alabama Press, 2005), pp. 297–305.

6. Eugene Lyon, *The Enterprise of Florida; Pedro Menéndez de Avilés and the Spanish Conquest of 1565-1568* (Gainesville: University of Florida Press, 1976), pp. 51, 210, and personal communication.

7. Charles Arnade, *Florida on Trial, 1593-1602* (Coral Gables: University of Miami Press, 1959); Hoffman, *Florida's Frontiers,* pp. 91–92, 97–99.

8. Andrew Turnbull's ultimately unsuccessful indigo-producing colony at New Smyrna was built by clearing forests on the shores of the Indian River near Mosquito Inlet, a setting giving access to this sort of richness as well as the resources of the mainland.

9. Marion M. Almy, "The Archaeological Potential of Soil Survey Reports," *Florida Anthropologist* 31 (1978):75–91; Marion F. Smith Jr. and John F. Scarry, "Apalachee Settlement Distribution: The View from the Florida Master Site File," *Florida Anthropologist* 41 (1988):355–59.

10. Lewis H. Larson Jr., *Aboriginal Subsistence Technology on the Southeastern Coastal Plain during the Late Prehistoric Period* (Gainesville: University of Florida Press, 1980), is the general account of Native American subsistence practices, especially in Georgia.

11. The St. Johns, and even more the San Sebastian, Matanzas, and North Rivers, provided St. Augustine with natural moats against European and Indian enemies, although not to much effect, as the English sieges of the eighteenth century repeatedly showed. Santa Elena, although on the southeastern tip of Parris Island, gained little advantage from having the Broad River and Port Royal Sound and fringing marshes as "moats." The northwestern approaches to the island were too remote from the settlement and broad to be effectively guarded against Native American raiding parties, as events of 1576 showed.

12. David W. Stahle, Malcolm K. Cleaveland, Dennis B. Blanton, Matthew D. Terrell, and David A. Gay, "The Lost Colony and Jamestown Droughts," *Science,* n.s., 280, no. 5363 (1998):565.

13. Hoffman, *Florida's Frontiers,* pp. 86–87, 120, 142, 252–53, 265, 287.

14. Joëlle L. Gergis and Anthony M. Fowler, "A History of ENSO Events since A.D. 1525: Implications for Future Climate Change," *Climate Change* 92 (2009):367–72 (table 9). The number of proxies and the general quality of the data increase with time since 1525. The figures for ENSO events between 1525 and 1850 are given because Florida's exploration, colonial, and territorial periods all took place during the Little Ice Age (LIA), ca. 1400–ca. 1850. In Europe and the northern latitudes of what is now the United States, this period of cooling reduced crop yields by shortening the growing season, caused glaciers to advance down Alpine valleys, and produced a variety of what contemporaries viewed as unusual

weather events. At present, no evidence has been found to suggest that this cooling had any effect in the Floridas, nor has the LIA been linked to the ENSO-related events. Nonetheless, I have separated the LIA period from the years that follow in case such links are found in the future.

15. Philip J. Klotzbach, "El Niño–Southern Oscillation's Impact on Atlantic Basin Hurricanes and U.S. Landfalls," *Journal of Climate* 24 (2011):1252–63.

Bibliography

Braun, E[mma] Lucy. *Deciduous Forests of North America.* New York: Macmillan, 1950.

Brown, Randall B., Earl L. Stone, and Victor W. Carlisle. "Soils." In *Ecosystems of Florida,* edited by Ronald L. Myers and John L. Ewel, pp. 42–53. Orlando: University of Central Florida Press, 1990.

Christensen, Norman L. "Vegetation of the Southeastern Coastal Plain." In *North American Terrestrial Vegetation,* edited by Michael G. Barbour and W. D. Billings, pp. 317–63. New York: Cambridge University Press, 1988.

Colquhoun, Donald J., et al. "Quaternary Geology of the Atlantic Coastal Plain." In *Quaternary Non-glacial Geology, Conterminous United States,* edited by Roger B. Morrison, pp. 629–50. Boulder, Colo.: Geological Society of America, 1991.

Ecosystems of Florida, edited by Ronald L. Myers and John J. Ewel. Orlando: University of Central Florida Press, 1990.

Gergis, Joëlle L., and Anthony M. Fowler. "A History of ENSO Events since A.D. 1525: Implications for Future Climate Change." *Climate Change* 92 (2009):343–87.

Hoffman, Paul E. *Florida's Frontiers.* Bloomington: Indiana University Press, 2002.

Klotzbach, Philip J. "El Niño-Southern Oscillation's Impact on Atlantic Basin Hurricanes and U.S. Landfalls." *Journal of Climate* 24 (2011):1252–63.

Larson, Lewis H., Jr. *Aboriginal Subsistence Technology on the Southeastern Coastal Plain during the Late Prehistoric Period.* Gainesville: University of Florida Press, 1980.

North Carolina Atlas: Portrait of a Changing Southern State. Edited by James W. Clay, Douglas, M. Orr Jr., and Alfred W. Stuart. Chapel Hill: University of North Carolina Press, 1975.

Silver, Timothy. *A New Face on the Countryside: Indians, Colonists and Slaves in the South Atlantic Forests, 1500–1800.* New York: Cambridge University Press, 1990.

Stahle, David W., Malcolm K. Cleaveland, Dennis B. Blanton, Matthew D. Terrell, and David A. Gay. "The Lost Colony and Jamestown Drought." *Science,* n.s., 280, no. 5363 (1998):564–67.

U.S. Department of the Interior, U.S. Geological Survey. *The National Atlas of the United States* (Washington, D.C.: Government Printing Office, 1970).

Wells, B. W. "Ecological Problems of the Southeastern United States Coastal Plain." *Botanical Review* 8 (1942):533–61.

Wharton, Charles H. *The Natural Environments of Georgia.* Atlanta: Georgia Department of Natural Resources, 1977.

4

Settlement and Survival

EUGENE LYON

Despite the poor opinion of Florida held at the Spanish Court and the belief that the French were equally uninterested in settling there, the situation was about to change dramatically. A brief look at France in this period helps to explain why.

After the middle of the sixteenth century, France was rent by internal dissension between its Crown and groups of powerful nobles. Those conflicts, which had come to a head in 1560, were worsened by religious differences between Catholics and Protestants that often erupted into violence. The intervention of other nations such as Spain in these internal wars further destabilized France. Queen Catherine de Medicis, acting as regent for her minor sons, Francis and Charles, temporized with the various factions and married her daughter to King Felipe (Philip) II of Spain, but she was also influenced by Gaspard de Coligny, *seigneur* of Châtillon, a Protestant noble and admiral of France.

Despite internal troubles, France continued its Atlantic policy. When the Treaty of Cateau-Cambrésis (1559) ended the last war with Spain, the parties had not agreed upon the vital issue of the right of nations to settle in the Americas, leaving the matter in an ambiguous state. While Spain insisted that the papal donations gave her exclusive rights to North America, the French maintained that unsettled areas were free for anyone to sail to and colonize. Thus, beginning in 1562, with the support of the French Crown, Coligny dispatched three royal expeditions to what France called Nouvelle France (New France), on the southeast coast of what is now the United States. Like Coligny himself, many of the leaders and mariners on those voyages were Calvinist Protestants from the ports of Normandy and Brittany.

An able captain, Jean Ribaut, commanded the first expedition, which made landfall near the present site of St. Augustine in the spring of 1562 and erected a marble column bearing the French arms near the mouth of the St. Johns, which he called the River May. Proceeding northward, he discovered Port Royal harbor and planted a colony there, guarded by a fortification called Charlesfort. But when he returned to Europe, Ribaut was arrested and detained in England; that and continuing disturbances in France prevented the sending of reinforcements to Port Royal until April 1564. That year proved to be one of heavy European traffic to and from Florida.

The Spaniards had learned belatedly of Ribaut's settlement the year before, and Philip II licensed Lucas Vázquez de Ayllón the younger to settle Florida but he never sailed. Then the Cuban governor sent an expedition to probe the French base. Arriving at Port Royal in late May, the Spaniards found that the discouraged Frenchmen had already deserted the place, leaving behind among the Indians one young man, Guillaume Rouffi. They returned to Havana, bearing Rouffi and the news of the failed French colony.

Meanwhile, on 22 April 1564, René de Laudonnière sailed from Le Havre with a full-fledged expedition of colonization, and somehow his departure escaped immediate Spanish attention. The French ships were laden with livestock, supplies, and tools for husbandry and Indian trade. There were artisans, women and children, and Protestant nobles from France and Germany. Once in Florida, the Frenchmen did not settle again at Port Royal; instead, they built Fort Caroline inside the mouth of the St. Johns, overlooking the river. At first, the colony prospered as Laudonnière set out to explore the interior of New France. He established generally good relations with the Native Americans in the nearby Timucua and Mocama groupings. Believing that the great river was the highway to the exploitation of peninsular Florida, he dispatched an expedition upriver, perhaps as far as Lake George. Guillaume Brouhart, one of those who made the river voyage, reported that the Indians there were powerful warriors and skilled bowmen who lived in a fruitful land of maize and grapevines, rich in nuts, fruits, deer, and small game.

Supplies soon ran short in Fort Caroline, and not enough food could be obtained from the natives. A series of mutinies and desertions began. Eleven men fled in a small craft, and then in December 1564, seventy men captured Laudonnière and forced him to authorize their departure in two vessels. All the deserters headed for the booty they hoped to gain in the Spanish Caribbean. Instead, their adventure led to the capture of some of their number and the unmasking of the French colony. After corsairing and

The French Fort Caroline was founded in 1564 by René Goulaine de Laudonnière a short distance inside the mouth of the St. Johns River, which the French called "Rivière de Mai." This drawing, by Jacques le Moyne de Morgues, who accompanied Laudonnière, was published by Théodor de Bry in 1591. Laudonnière was relieved of command by Jean Ribaut in 1565. The fort was captured by Pedro Menéndez de Avilés in the same year and renamed San Mateo.

raiding in Cuba and Hispaniola, two groups of the Frenchmen were captured by the Spaniards; only one small ship returned to Fort Caroline. But word had now been sent to Madrid, and Philip II was made aware of the French settlement.

In the meantime, the French Crown had prepared to send Jean Ribaut to reinforce Fort Caroline with a sizable fleet. The report of a skilled Spanish spy, Dr. Gabriel de Enveja, gave Philip II a full account of the ships, soldiers, and supplies being readied in Dieppe for the Florida voyage. More than 500 arquebusiers and their munitions, together with many dismounted bronze cannons, were loaded aboard. Ribaut himself went armed with royal decrees making him "captain general and viceroy" of New France.

But by this time, Philip II had already granted a contract to a new Florida adelantado, Pedro Menéndez de Avilés. Even though the news of Laudonnière's fort impelled the Spanish king to add royal aid to Menéndez's effort, private motivations in the Florida conquest remained significant. Like other would-be Spanish conquerors, Pedro Menéndez had contracted with his king and had been promised the offices and titles of governor, captain general, and adelantado. Under his agreement, Menéndez was obliged to found two cities and was charged with seeing that the natives were converted to the Roman Catholic faith. If successful in his enterprise, Menéndez would receive a large land grant and the title of marquis to go with it. His jurisdiction was immense, extending from Newfoundland to the Florida Keys and, after 1573, westward to México.

In the days of Emperor Charles V, Menéndez had come to royal attention for his daring deeds in the Bay of Biscay against French corsairs. Thereafter, he advanced himself in royal favor while he fought Spain's enemies at sea and on land. The young seaman became renowned for his prompt and decisive actions. For his services to Mary Tudor and young King Philip, the Asturian was awarded a habit in the prestigious Order of Santiago.

Menéndez's exploits and his influence with the Crown aroused the jealousy of the Seville merchants and the associated Crown agency, the Casa de Contratación (House of Trade). He was jailed by Casa officials in 1563 for alleged smuggling but succeeded in having his case transferred to court. Thereafter, when the urgencies of the Florida matter came to the Crown's attention early in 1565, Menéndez was available to serve as adelantado. Before he learned of the existence of Fort Caroline, Menéndez disclosed his interest in the fabled Northwest Passage and the route to the riches of the Orient, when he told the king of his geographic and strategic beliefs about Florida:

> If the French or English should come to settle Florida . . . it would be the greatest inconvenience, as much for the mines and territories of New Spain as for the navigation and trade of China and Molucca, if that arm of the sea goes to the South Sea, as is certain. . . . By being masters of Newfoundland. . . . Your Majesty may proceed to master that land. . . . It is such a great land and [situated] at such a good juncture, that if some other nations go to settle it . . . it will afterwards be most difficult to take and master it.
>
> And they must go directly to Cape Santa Elena, and, with fast ships discover all the bays, rivers, sounds and shallows on the route to Newfoundland. And to provide settlers, in the largest number possible, for two or three towns in the places which seem best . . . and after seeking out the best ports, having first explored inland for four or five leagues, to see that it might have a good disposition of land for farming and livestock-raising. And each town would have its fort to defend against the Indians if they should come upon them, or against other nations.[1]

Menéndez expected the Florida enterprise to prove profitable to himself and to the Crown. He anticipated the development of agriculture, stock-raising, fisheries, and forest resources for naval stores and shipbuilding. Menéndez also hoped to profit from the ships' licenses granted to him. He planned to utilize waterways that he believed connected with the mines of New Spain and the Pacific and those he thought crossed Florida from the Atlantic to the Gulf.

In his Florida venture, the kinship alliance that supported the adelantado was made up of seventeen families from the north of Spain, closely tied by blood and marriage. Members of this coterie pledged their persons and their fortunes to sustain their leader's efforts, and they hoped to acquire town and country lands and civil and military offices in Florida. These partners in Menéndez's enterprise thus shared his vision of enlarged estate and advanced standing before their sovereign. The existence of this familial territorial elite explains much of the dynamism of the Florida enterprise; the adelantado was loyally if not always ably served by his lieutenants and other officials, who held such close connection with him.

At the end of June 1565, Menéndez sailed for Florida with ten ships and more than a thousand men. Other ships departed from the north of Spain, and Menéndez was to receive added support from Santo Domingo. His voyage was beset with storms; several ships were lost before he reached Puerto Rico. He decided to strike out for Florida with the reduced forces he had at hand.

The adelantado arrived at Cape Canaveral in late August 1565. He knew that Jean Ribaut had sailed from Dieppe at the end of May with reinforcements for Laudonnière. The Spaniards had pressed their voyage, hoping to arrive at Fort Caroline before Ribaut. In the event, Menéndez found the French fleet already anchored off the St. Johns bar. After a short but sharp battle, the French put out to sea and Menéndez sailed south to found St. Augustine.

To affirm his king's title to North America, Menéndez took formal possession of all Florida when he landed at St. Augustine on 8 September 1565, officially placing the land and its peoples under Philip II's authority. This action authorized Menéndez to dispense lands to his followers and to make treaties with the natives. The adelantado built his first fort in Florida around a longhouse given him by Seloy, a local leader of the numerous and powerful Eastern Timucua people.

After Ribaut failed in an attack on the new Spanish colony, a storm struck the French fleet. Sensing that Fort Caroline was weakly defended and that

Pedro Menéndez de Avilés (1519–74), Adelantado de la Florida, Comendador de Santa Cruz de la Zarza, Orden de Santiago. Engraving based on a painting, reproduced from Cesáreo Fernández Duro, *Armada Española* (Madrid, 1895–1903). It was Menéndez who, on 8 September 1565, founded Florida's and the country's first permanent European settlement, St. Augustine.

the storm prevented Ribaut from a quick return, Menéndez struck out overland to Fort Caroline. At dawn on 20 September, he attacked the fort, surprised the French defenders, and put most of them to the sword.

Renaming the captured fort San Mateo (St. Matthew), the adelantado left a Spanish garrison there and returned to St. Augustine. Meanwhile, Ribaut's ships had been wrecked along the coast as far south as Cape Canaveral. Two groups of shipwreck survivors, straggling northward along the beaches, reached an inlet of the sea south of St. Augustine. Apprised of this, Menéndez took a body of soldiers there and persuaded many of the Frenchmen, including Ribaut himself, to surrender. Except for a few captives he spared, Menéndez had Ribaut and the rest killed. Thereafter, the little inlet would be called Matanzas, meaning "place of slaughter." Menéndez's actions at Fort

Caroline and Matanzas would take their place in history and would tend to overshadow the whole complex story of Spain's colonizing effort in Florida.

Menéndez realized now that his supplies were critically short. He marched south to Cape Canaveral, destroyed a small fort built there by survivors from Ribaut's fleet, met the cacique of Ais, and appointed a Spanish governor for the area. Leaving a contingent of troops there, the adelantado took a small boat for Havana. Once in the Cuban port, he linked up with his forces from Asturias, meeting his nephew, Pedro Menéndez Marqués, and another key lieutenant, Esteban de las Alas. Next the adelantado arranged for supplies to be sent to Florida. Thereafter, meat, corn, cassava, squash, and livestock were regularly dispatched from Cuba and Yucatan to the peninsular garrisons.

Commandeering a ship, Menéndez next sailed for southwest Florida, seeking the outlet of his imagined cross-peninsular waterway. At the chief town of the Calusa, located on Mound Key in Estero Bay, the Spanish leader had an amicable meeting with the cacique Carlos and arranged for the freeing of several captives. Among those was a shipwrecked Spaniard from Cartagena, Hernando de Escalante Fontaneda, who became an interpreter for the Spaniards and later wrote a memoir about his Florida experiences.

Meanwhile, in the Florida garrisons, a harsh winter set in before Menéndez's supply network could begin to function. The garrison left on the east coast rebelled, moved southward, and founded Fort Santa Lucía. Conditions there deteriorated as Indian friendship turned to enmity. The mutinous spirit spread to San Mateo and St. Augustine; it was rooted in the semi-independent nature of the hired soldiers and their captains. By mid-February, mutineers from San Mateo and St. Augustine, looking for a means of escape from Florida, were actively working to complete a half-built ship the French had left on the way. Several of the captains and noncommissioned officers were also disaffected. After a supply ship entered the port of St. Augustine, the rebels struck. Seizing and confining Don Pedro de Valdés, the adelantado's son-in-law, they captured the ship and prepared to depart. Although Valdés managed to free himself and attacked the mutineers, they sailed away, as did the vessel from San Mateo. Altogether, more than 200 soldiers deserted Florida. Shortly afterward, Menéndez arrived in St. Augustine with the Santa Lucía mutineers, whom he had picked up at sea. Having restored order and reinforced the garrisons, he sailed northward in a small craft to explore farther.

He passed the sea islands of the Georgia coast, meeting their native inhabitants and taking possession of each area for the king. That coast looked

Sites of settlement and exploration during the period of Spanish expansion in La Florida, 1565–87, are shown here in bold. Spanish claims under the name La Florida extended north to Newfoundland and westward indefinitely from the Atlantic. Other sites in the Caribbean and Gulf of Mexico are shown for reference.

promising to Menéndez, as the people were numerous and seemed more pacific in nature than the Timucua or their neighbors, the Mocama. At Eastertide of 1566, Menéndez neared the Point of Santa Elena, a place of legendary fertility and plenty, and founded a city on present-day Parris Island. He appointed Esteban de las Alas as regional governor and departed once more for St. Augustine.

The adelantado returned to his first city to find that the fort had been burned by hostile natives and many of the supplies destroyed. He undertook yet another voyage to secure the Cuban supply line; while he was gone, the royal reinforcement fleet arrived in St. Augustine with shiploads of supplies and 1,500 soldiers. One of the companies of newly arrived troops was sent with its captain, Juan Pardo, to strengthen the garrison at Santa Elena.

A powerful incentive for Menéndez and his followers was nonmaterial: as fervent Catholics, they coveted the spiritual merit to be gained by successfully evangelizing Florida's native populations. To further that aim, the adelantado had arranged for members of the Society of Jesus (Jesuits), those noted "shock troops of the Counter-Reformation," to send missionaries to Florida. But the other side of the coin of Spanish–Native American relations was the Spaniards' expectations of native service, to be met through the *repartimientos* and *encomiendas* granted elsewhere in the Spanish Indies. None of these jointly cherished expectations could be realized without satisfactorily resolving the relationships with the present occupants of Florida, whom the Spaniards called Indios. Those diverse peoples, who represented long-established cultures and lived in ordered, hierarchical societies, were spread over the wide reaches of Menéndez's new domains.

By now, the Spaniards had met many of the peoples of Florida: Timucua, Surruque, Ais, Jeaga, Calusa, Tequesta, Mocama, Guale, and Orista. To Menéndez, Indian relations were all of a piece. He meant to establish a benevolent overlordship over them, bringing peace to warring groupings, eradicating heresy and unbelief, and spreading the gospel among them. He planned, conforming to the Jesuit modus operandi, to build a school in Havana to educate the children of their leaders. He also hoped to establish fort-missions in peninsular Florida and Guale and also westward on the route to México. It was for this perceived devotion to his church that the Guale called the adelantado Mico Santamaría, Holy Mary's Chief of Chiefs.

To overcome the language barriers between Europeans and Native Americans, the Spaniards employed interpreters. Those men, usually ransomed Spaniards or Frenchmen who had learned the native languages in captivity, acted also as cultural brokers. They made negotiations possible between the Europeans and the representatives of the diverse indigenous cultures in Florida. Thus it was possible for Menéndez and his lieutenants to negotiate treaties of fealty, tribute, and submission to Philip II. At times, in order to undergird negotiations, the Spaniards took or even exchanged hostages with the Indians. Still, there remained many mutual misunderstandings among the parties to these cultural exchanges.

An example of such misapprehensions was Menéndez's preoccupation with the relationship between the Timucua, who had collaborated in the time of Laudonnière and would again in the time of Dominique de Gourgues. The adelantado believed that the creed of the French Protestants, whom he termed "Lutheran heretics," was at many points similar to the "Satanic" beliefs of the Indians. For that reason, his suspicions continually affected his relationship with the Timucua.

Despite the treaties signed with Florida's native groups, troubles persisted and even multiplied. When the first group of Jesuit missionaries came to Florida in the supply ship *Pantecras,* the ship's pilot missed the St. Augustine harbor entrance, got lost, and put into the inlet near the St. Marys River, now Florida's northeast boundary. There the Jesuit priest Pedro Martínez went ashore in a small boat seeking directions. He and three crewmen were killed by the Mocama, and the Jesuits had their first New World martyr. The surviving missionaries were posted to missions at Tequesta, on the Miami River at Biscayne Bay, and at San Antonio de Padua, built at the main Calusa village at Mound Key on the Gulf. In both places the missionaries were accompanied by a small Spanish garrison. They dedicated themselves to learning the Indian languages and acquainting the Indians with the main symbols and basic beliefs of Christianity, the latter facilitated by the use of some cloth picture books of Christian doctrine developed in México.

But the Spaniards' attempts to impose the Christian religion upon the native people, their claimed right to interfere in native leadership succession, and their propensity to requisition food from Indian stores alienated the Indians, who began to fear for their own survival and for the survival of their cultural identity. Now warfare also broke out at many places in Timucua. Soldier-farmers were killed in cornfields near St. Augustine. Captain Pedro de Andrada and his company were ambushed near Potano in the north central peninsula; he and many of his soldiers were slain. On the west coast, at the Tampa Bay fort called Tocobaga, the whole Spanish garrison was massacred by natives and the fort was evacuated. To counter the Indians' rapid arrow fire, Menéndez had to change his war tactics; he ordered 500 crossbows for his soldiers and began to dress them in protective padded cotton armor, first used by Spaniards in the conquest of Yucatan and later by de Soto in Apalachee.

On Good Friday of 1568, a French nobleman, Dominique de Gourgues, arrived at the St. Johns River to take revenge upon the Spaniards for the deaths of Jean Ribaut and many of his followers. Guided by Timucua, the attacking Frenchmen and their Indian allies captured the Spanish blockhouses at the river mouth and then took and burned Fort San Mateo. Most of the defending Spaniards had already fled.

Meanwhile, tensions had mounted between Spaniards and the Calusa at Carlos. The attempts of the Europeans to impose their sovereignty and religion finally caused a complete break with the Calusa. Cacique Carlos, the Spaniards believed, planned to kill them all. Captain Francisco de Reinoso forestalled this by executing the Calusa leader and installing an Indian named Philip as his successor. The Tequesta mission on the lower Atlantic coast had already failed; the Jesuit there had been unable to convert more than one old dying woman to the Catholic faith, and a clash between the soldiers and the Indians led to the withdrawal of the Spaniards.

Painstakingly, on the lower Gulf coast, the Jesuit priest Juan Rogel gave daily instruction to cacique Philip, his principal people, their wives and children. Many of them learned the prayers, and some of the Christian doctrine coincided with Calusa beliefs, but when the Jesuit pressed the Indians to renounce their own rites, cut their long hair, and burn the images of their deities, they refused. The cacique rejected the proposal that he leave his sister-wife and dismiss his other wives. This dialogue continued, without notable success for the missionaries, until 1569, when both the garrison and the Jesuit mission were withdrawn, and the attempt to evangelize the Calusa ended.

The abandonment of the south Florida forts and missions foreshadowed a general northward relocation of Menéndez's Florida enterprise. Forsaking the effort to exploit the St. Johns River and other inland waterways, the Spaniards evacuated San Mateo and shifted the garrison to a new fort, San Pedro de Tacatacuru, on Cumberland Island. The new fort would anchor the route from St. Augustine to the colony's new center, Santa Elena. The Jesuits, in an attempt to evangelize the Guale and the Orista, moved north with the soldiers.

From Santa Elena the adelantado sent Captain Juan Pardo on two long expeditions westward to the Appalachian Mountains. Pardo's mission was to scout fertile lands for future economic development and to find the route to the silver mines of Guanajuato and Zacatecas in México. On his first journey in December 1566, Pardo proceeded into present-day North Carolina, then westward to the foot of the Blue Ridge. There, at a place called Joara, he founded the city of Cuenca and left a garrison in Fort San Juan under Sergeant Hernando Moyano. The lands there, said the Spanish captain, were "as pretty as . . . the best in Spain."[2] At Guatari, near today's Salisbury, North Carolina, Pardo noted a particularly fertile area, where he left four soldiers and a secular priest, the company's chaplain Sebastian Montero, to evangelize the Indians.

When he returned to Santa Elena, Pardo told Menéndez of his inland discoveries, and the adelantado fixed upon the area of Guatari for his own personal land grant, which would undergird his family's future prosperity and make him a marquis. Sent out a second time, in September 1567, Pardo took with him as interpreter the young Frenchman Guillaume Rouffi. He followed much the same route as before, finding rich bottomlands near present-day Asheville. He then went westward across the mountains into eastern Tennessee, to the populous town of Chiaha. After that, concerned about being attacked by powerful Indian groupings, Pardo did not press on to Coosa and Tascaluza, waypoints for him on the road to México. Instead, the Spaniards turned back and returned to Santa Elena.

Now, Menéndez concluded, in order to begin to populate the vast areas of coastal and inland Florida, it was time to begin its serious settlement. From the beginning of his enterprise, the adelantado had planned to import settler-farmers. One of the clauses in his contract required him to establish two towns, to bring livestock, and to carry 500 settlers to Florida. In his first expedition, 138 of his soldiers—carried at his own expense—were craftsmen who represented many of the trades of sixteenth-century Castile. Another 117 of his soldiers were farmers, and 26 brought their wives and children.

In their agreements with the adelantado, the soldier-farmers were promised by Menéndez that he would "give them rations in the said coast and land of Florida, and lands and estates for their planting, farming and stock-raising, and divisions of land, in accordance with their service and the quality which each one possesses."[3]

After he expelled the French, established his Florida supply lines, and put down the soldiers' mutinies, Menéndez contracted with one Hernán Pérez, a Portuguese, to bring farmers from the Azores. In his arrangements with this and other settler groups, the adelantado promised to "give them their passage and pay for their freight. Having arrived at this land, I will give them lands and estates for their farms and stockraising, and within two years a dozen cows with one bull, two oxen for plowing, twelve sheep, and the same number of goats, hogs and chickens, and two mares and one farmhand, and a house constructed, with its winepress, and a male and a female slave, and vineshoots to plant."[4] Menéndez then indicated that the settlers would sharecrop with him until the costs incurred were paid out. He added, "I do not have the capability to do this, but I believe that there will be merchants who, once they know how good this land is for cultivation, . . . might wish to put in a part of their wealth in that profitable agricultural enterprise—in order to settle themselves on large *haciendas* of sugar mills, livestock and farms of bread and wine."

This arrangement fell through, but in 1568 Menéndez had the funds in hand to put his plan in motion with settlers from the Iberian peninsula. The potential Florida settlers in Castile were mostly small farmers, *labradores.* Although it had a number of cities, Castile was an essentially agricultural and pastoral area. Most people worked the land, raising sheep and hogs for food; donkeys, mules, and horses to serve as work animals; and cattle. They cultivated gardens and orchards and had widespread wheat, vineyard, and olive plantings. Spanish agriculture was therefore both extensive and intensive. Except for a few fertile plains and the lush green Cantabrian north, Castilians were accustomed to marginal soils and a dry, harsh climate. Water was rare and precious; in the Castilian language, the words for *wealthy* and for *abundant waters* were the same: *caudaloso.* Castilian emigrants to the Americas sought rich and well-watered lands for their husbandry and hoped to find them in Florida.

In the provinces of Extremadura and upper Andalucía, Menéndez recruited a number of farmers who came with their wives and children to Cádiz, where Pedro del Castillo arranged for them to board ship for Florida. After a sharp skirmish with the Casa de Contratación over permission to set sail, Castillo obtained royal permission for two ships, the *Nuestra Señora de la Vitoria* and the *Nuestra Señora de la Concepción,* to depart. Many of the settlers aboard came from Mérida and the area of Guadalcanal.

In the spring of 1569, the ships reached Florida, and 273 settlers landed in St. Augustine; 193 of these were sent quickly to Santa Elena. Once established there, the settlers built houses, worked at their lands and livestock, engaged in trade, and involved themselves in the city government. On 1 August of that same year, thirty-six households were enumerated in Santa Elena, together with four houses for single men. By October, 327 persons, including the settlers and soldiers, lived there. The families that had come to build their hearths and futures in La Florida were participants in a major transfer of Hispanic culture.

Sixteenth-century Florida society was broadly representative of several regions of the Spanish homeland. It presented a cross section of the trades, crafts, professions, and social strata of early modern Castile. It was a deferential, hierarchical society; goods inventories disclose how real and personal property in Spanish Florida generally mirrored the stratification of the community. Ordinary soldiers and sailors had few possessions, although some had musical instruments and acted as moneylenders. The servant Juan Rodríguez slept on the floor outside his mistress's St. Augustine rooms. At the other end of the social scale, Adelantado Menéndez kept court like a viceroy, with noble retainers and liveried servants. When Menéndez and his wife, Doña María de Solis, moved to Santa Elena in 1571, they shipped

The surnames of many of the first European inhabitants of Florida are given in a four-page document dated 27 September 1568, the first page of which is shown. The document lists the names of 209 farmers, their wives, children, other relatives, and servants from the Spanish province of Extremadura who sailed for Florida in two caravels out of Cádiz in October 1568. The names given in the document are Sedeño, Martínez Salvatierra, González, Díaz, Martín, Perez, García, Ruyz Cavallero, Muñoz, Escudero, de Merlo, de Moya, Sánchez, Hernández, Ortíz, Martin Cumplido, Gómez, Oliveros, de Vía, Martín Texada, Olivares, de las Eras, Calvo, Asencio, de la Torre, Rodríguez, de Herrera, de Berrío, Domínguez, Pinto, Rueda, de Sellera Porra, de Segovia, González Dorado, Romero, Martín Silvestre, Serrano, Viejo, Gordillo, Mener, de la Rosa, Ruyz, Alonso, de Olmo, Sigüenza, Tristán, López, and Azaro.

luxurious household furnishings: ornate rugs and wall hangings, beds and bedding, and fine table linens and plate. The inventories also describe the sumptuous clothing and elegant accessories imported by the Menéndez family and other noble persons in Florida. The archaeologist Stanley South found the remnants of gold embroidery at Santa Elena, together with jewelry and a fragment from a costly Ming Dynasty porcelain wine ewer. The import lists also feature majolica tableware and food delicacies: dates, almonds, quince-paste, and marzipan. But the class lines evidenced by those goods were tempered by Spanish individualism and by the upward mobility many Florida citizens displayed.

This was, moreover, a corporate society. The Florida immigrants shared many unifying beliefs, traits, and customs, which included their Castilian language. All were communicants of the Tridentine Roman Catholic Church; many of the men belonged to one of the Florida confraternities, whose membership cut across social lines. Those laymen organized funerals, marched in processions, and supported their members' widows. The sacramental Mother Church dominated the daily life of Spanish Florida; the very hours and days were numbered by the church bells and the Christian calendar. An inventory of the parish church included a fine painted retable and gilded altar cross. Menéndez's deeds in expelling the French "Lutherans," as all Protestants were called, called forth praise from Pope Pius V. The adelantado then asked the pope for special indulgences for his colonists and soldiers who might die without confession during the events of the conquest.

For their part, the soldiers were the bearers of a long military tradition, formed since the time of Isabel and Fernando. They and their officers were the king's shield against his enemies, but the military had another, darker side; the mutinies of 1566 had been caused by Spanish veterans of wars in Italy and France, who were accustomed, as Menéndez said, to "banquets, booty, and wine."[5]

Qualifying as *vecinos,* or city electors, the citizens of St. Augustine and Santa Elena enjoyed the ancient Castilian municipal liberties. Everyday life was governed by the municipality, which determined prices, established weights and measures, controlled the local court for civil and criminal matters, and regulated the marketplaces.

The surviving body of Florida lawsuits depicts many of the realities of daily life and the prevailing sixteenth-century social climate there. One case, for instance, involved a litigious tailor named Alonso de Olmos, who sued the governor for libel. Olmos claimed that Governor Don Diego de

Velasco directed epithets at Olmos's daughter as he ejected her from a religious procession. Moreover, he contended, the governor had also insulted him with the taunt "See the Lutheran going to the synagogue!"[6] In another case, the settlers sued the governor for payment of the clothing, food, and rental owed them; prosperous with goods, the settlers had been extending credit to soldiers and wanted repayment. Velasco was authoritarian in his dealings with the Indians but took care to provide them with the usual gifts and presents.

Documents disclose the vigorous economic life of sixteenth-century Spanish Florida. The farmers from Spain learned to cultivate corn, which was at first imported or bought from the natives; it slowly replaced wheat and cassava as the staple carbohydrate in the colonists' diet. Later, wheat farms would be planted in West Florida. At Santa Elena, archaeologist Stanley South has uncovered ditches from vineyards. Said one witness, "I have planted with my own hands grapevines, pomegranates, orange trees and figs, wheat, barley, onions, garlic and many vegetables that grow in Spain."[7]

One Antonio de Carbajal, describing the richness of Guale and the easy access to inland areas from there, said that "the land of Guale is as fertile as the best land of Spain . . . because he has seen many fruits and plants produced in the said land, and livestock being produced, and the large number of grasslands for the raising of cattle and sheep."[8]

In the cities, peddlers, shoemakers, moneylenders, tavernkeepers, fishermen and hunters, prostitutes, smiths, and carpenters plied their trades. Soldiers' wives operated boardinghouses for unmarried men. Alonso de Olmos made suits of padded cotton armor for the garrison; others worked to make palmetto matchcord. Pedro Menéndez had two ships built in Florida, one near St. Augustine and one at Santa Elena. Silk culture and sugar production never succeeded, but there was substantial export of juniper, oak, and laurel-wood, together with sassafras root bark for medicinal purposes. The production of tar and pitch began. The fur trade with the Indians began, and deerskin boots and jackets were locally made. Commercial documents the very stuff of trade and business—abound in the Florida records.

In 1569 there occurred a general crisis in Menéndez's finances, strained by his efforts in Florida and worsened by the added costs of bringing in settlers. The adelantado had already filed a suit seeking recompense from the Crown for his ship losses in the Florida expedition and for additional expenses above and beyond those foreseen in his royal contract. Now Menéndez went to Madrid to make his plea before the Council of the Indies for a regular subsidy to support the Florida garrisons. When no immediate action was taken, Menéndez decided to force the issue. He ordered his lieutenants to denude the Florida garrisons of all but 150 men, the number the Crown had in principle agreed to support. In the meantime, difficulties arose with the Jesuit order over Menéndez's control over the missionaries.

Finally, Philip II convened four royal councils—State, Indies, War, and Treasury—and put the Florida matter to them. From that meeting resulted a royal decree, in November 1570, that established a subsidy to undergird the Florida garrisons. Meanwhile, the Jesuits agreed to one more attempt at the difficult Florida mission field: they sent Father Juan Bautista de Segura with other missionaries to the Chesapeake, known to the Spaniards as the Bay of Santa María. Pedro Menéndez Marqués had explored the coasts north of there, all the way to Newfoundland.

For some years, Adelantado Menéndez had been largely absent from Florida, carrying out various royal assignments. Because of stressful events, two of his principal lieutenants, Esteban de las Alas and Pedro de Valdés, had also left Florida. Moreover, after the murder of his favorite daughter, Ana, in Asturias, the adelantado was forced to rethink the succession to his Florida enterprise. His only son, Juan, had been lost at sea. Now Menéndez reconciled with his daughter, Catalina, and the man she had married, Hernando de Miranda. Menéndez also arranged a marriage between his illegitimate daughter, Maria, and Don Diego de Velasco, the legitimized grandson of the constable of Castile, a high nobleman, and made a dower contract with Velasco to encourage him to serve in Florida.

The new royal subsidy stimulated fresh private efforts. For his part, Menéndez moved his wife and ten other persons in his household to Santa Elena. Velasco also came there as governor with his wife. A new group of settlers came to augment the number of farmers. A list of the new colonists includes "Lorenzo García, native of Puebla del Prior in Badajoz, who has a thin face, is of medium stature, and is missing the little finger of his left hand; he is forty-two years of age."[9]

In February 1571, the Indians of Jacan killed the Jesuit missionaries at the Chesapeake. After word of this reached Santa Elena, Menéndez led a punitive expedition to the site, hanging several Jacan leaders and rescuing a Spanish boy, the son of Alonso de Olmos, who had survived the massacre. After he learned of the missionaries' death, the general of the Society of Jesus terminated their six-year Florida mission.

The tragic end of the Jesuits at the Chesapeake culminated a long list of Indian difficulties that had faced the Spaniards in Florida since 1565. In the Indian River area, at Tequesta, Carlos, and Tocobaga, and among the

Timucua peoples, there had been no sustained peace between the Native Americans and the Spanish leaders, soldiers, and settlers. So incensed was Menéndez at the failure of his Indian policies that in 1573 he asked the king's permission to capture rebellious Indians and to sell them as slaves. The king refused the request, but it was apparent that Menéndez's failure to reach a settled peace with many of Florida's indigenous people made it virtually impossible for Spaniards to work the land. In fact, the continual disturbances confined the settlers, and Menéndez himself, to the poorer coastal soils. The Spaniards could not safely reside in the interior, where the land was well suited to pastoral and agricultural enterprise. One by one, the inland garrisons were abandoned.

Back in Spain, while on assignment from the king to assemble a great fleet to reinforce Spanish forces in Flanders, Pedro Menéndez de Avilés fell ill, likely from a typhus outbreak which had swept his fleet. On 17 September 1574, at Santander, he died. His will divided the Florida inheritance: daughter Catalina received the title of adelantado, the Florida profits, and his entail; daughter María inherited his land grant and the title of marquis.

Catalina's husband hastened to claim his wife's Florida privileges and set sail from Spain late in 1575. Arriving at Santa Elena, Hernando de Miranda deposed Velasco and set to work to ensure his own profits from the enterprise. However, Miranda failed to attend properly to the Florida defenses, and he neglected to give gifts to the natives. He also permitted his lieutenants to abuse the Guale and Orista peoples. Angered, the Indians joined in confederation; by mid-1576, they had killed a number of Spanish officials and soldiers and surrounded Santa Elena itself. Miranda, no leader of men, panicked, evacuated the city, and fled from Florida.

The Council of the Indies removed Miranda as governor and vacated his title of adelantado; they appointed Pedro Menéndez Marqués as the new governor. Henceforth Florida would no longer be a proprietary colony but a Crown colony. Menéndez Marqués rebuilt Santa Elena, but after Sir Francis Drake's raid on St. Augustine in 1586 it was finally abandoned—ironically, just as John White, who led Sir Walter Raleigh's third colonizing expedition, landed at Roanoke Island. Thus the Spaniards were poorly positioned to forestall or to combat the English settlements that were later successfully planted to the north of Florida. Pedro Menéndez's dream of a viable colony based on agriculture and commerce had vanished forever.

One man's plaint summed up the experience in Spanish Florida since 1565. "I have served," said Bartolomé Martínez, "in these provinces of Florida . . . since the Adelantado brought me as a soldier, and in this time I have suffered hunger, nudity and much misery, not because the land is so bad as they hold it to be, but due to the poor government it has had, and because their resources were little to conquer so many people and such a great land. I have seen the greater part of the coast of these provinces and thirty leagues around the fort of Santa Elena. What I say to Your Majesty about this land of which all the world says ill, is that it is a marvel of good, because there are most rich lands for tillage and stock-farms, powerful rivers of sweet water, great fertile plains and mountains. . . . And I wish to beg Your Majesty that you might give me some land in it, where I might remain always."[10]

Florida's founding in 1565 was impelled by Hapsburg dynastic strategy and disputes among European powers. But it was also directly linked with the settlement impulse that drove sixteenth-century Spaniards to implant their rich and complex culture in the Americas. After an initial expansion, Spanish Florida became a shrinking empire, struggling with powerful England over the disputed lands to the north of the peninsula.

Only once was serious thought given to abandonment of the peninsula. In 1602 an official inquiry conducted by an administrative investigator from Cuba heard eighteen long-term residents of Florida on the question—soldiers, civilians, and Franciscan friars. Instead of dismantling St. Augustine and transferring the center of Spanish activity farther north on the Atlantic coast, as some in Florida were urging, the official decision was made to keep that center where it was.

The strong desire to settle the peninsula was never completely abandoned. It was revived in the eighteenth century, when farmers from the Canary Islands came to Florida. And St. Augustine, that quintessential survivor city founded by Pedro Menéndez de Avilés, remains today the oldest city of European origin in what is today the United States of America.

Notes

1. Pedro Menéndez de Avilés to the king, no place, no date (probably late February–early March, 1565), from Archives of the Indies, Seville (hereafter AGI), *Patronato* 19; reprinted in Eugenio Ruidíaz y Caravía, *La Florida: Su conquista per Pedro Menéndez de Avilés*, 2 vols. (Madrid, 1893), 2:320–26.

2. Narrative of Juan de la Vandera, from Archives of the Counts of Revillagigedo, *Canalejas* 46, reel 105 of microfilm at Flagler College, Center for Historic Research, image 561.

3. Pedro Menéndez to the Crown, St. Augustine, 20 October 1566, AGI *Santo Domingo* 115.

4. Ibid.

5. Ibid.

6. AGI *Escribanía de Cámara* 154-A, fol. 471vto.

7. Bartolomé Martínez to Crown, 17 February 1577, AGI *Santo Domingo* 125.

8. AGI *Escribanía de Cámara* 154-A, fol. 370.

9. Juan de Abalia to the Crown, 27 June 1573, AGI *Patronato* 257.

10. Bartolomé Martínez to the Crown, Havana, 17 February 1577, from AGI Santo Domingo 125.

Bibliography

Altman, Ida. *Emigrants and Society: Extremadura and America in the Sixteenth Century.* Berkeley: University of California Press, 1989.

Arnade, Charles W. "The Failure of Spanish Florida." *Americas* 16, no. 3 (January 1960):271–81.

———. *Florida on Trial, 1593–1602.* Coral Gables: University of Miami Press, 1959.

Bennett, Charles E. *Laudonnière and Fort Caroline: History and Documents.* Gainesville: University of Florida Press, 1964.

Bushnell, Amy Turner. *The King's Coffer: Proprietors of the Spanish Florida Treasury, 1565–1702.* Gainesville: University Presses of Florida, 1981.

Deagan, Kathleen. *Spanish St. Augustine: The Archaeology of a Colonial Creole Community.* New York: Academic Press, 1983.

Gaffarel, Paul. *Histoire de la floride Française.* Paris: Firman-Didot et Cie., 1875.

Gannon, Michael V. *The Cross in the Sand: The Early Catholic Church in Florida, 1513–1870.* Gainesville: University of Florida Press, 1965.

———. "The New Alliance of History and Archaeology in the Eastern Spanish Borderlands." *William and Mary Quarterly,* 3d ser., 49, no. 2 (April 1992):321–34.

———. "Sebastian Montero, Pioneer American Missionary, 1566–1572." *Catholic Historical Review* 51, no. 3 (October 1965):335–53.

Hoffman, Paul E. "Diplomacy and the Papal Donation." *Americas* 30, no. 2 (October 1973):151–83.

———. *A New Andalucía and a Way to the Orient: The American Southeast during the Sixteenth Century.* Baton Rouge: Louisiana State University Press, 1990.

Hudson, Charles. *The Juan Pardo Expeditions: Explorations of the Carolinas and Tennessee, 1566–1568.* Washington: Smithsonian Institution Press, 1990.

Lyon, Eugene. "The Control Structure of Spanish Florida, 1580." Manuscript, Center for Historic Research, Flagler College, 1977.

———. "Cultural Brokers in Sixteenth-Century Spanish Florida." Symposium, "The Provinces of Florida: Defining a Spanish-Indian Society in Colonial North America." Johns Hopkins University, 1987.

———. *The Enterprise of Florida: Pedro Menéndez de Avilés and the Spanish Conquest of 1565–1568.* Gainesville: University Presses of Florida, 1976.

———. "La Visita de 1576 y la Transformacion del Gobierno en la Florida. Espanola." *La Influencia de España en el Caribe, la Florida y la Luisiana.* Madrid: Ministero de Cultura, 1983.

———. *Pedro Menéndez de Avilés: A Sourcebook.* Hamden, Conn.: Spanish Borderland Sourcebooks, Garland Publishing Company, 1994.

———. "The Revolt of 1576 at Santa Elena: A Failure of Indian Policy." Paper. American Historical Association, Washington, 1987.

———. *Richer Than We Thought: The Material Culture of Sixteenth-Century St. Augustine.* St. Augustine: St. Augustine Historical Society, 1992.

———. *Santa Elena: A Brief History of the Colony.* Columbia: Institute of Archaeology and Anthropology, University of South Carolina, 1984.

———. "Spain's Sixteenth-Century North American Settlement Attempts: A Neglected Aspect." *Florida Historical Quarterly* 59, no. 3 (January 1981):275–91.

Milanich, Jerald T. "The Western Timuqua: Patterns of Acculturation and Change." In *Tacachale: Essays on the Indians of Florida and Southeastern Georgia during the Historic Period,* edited by Jerald T. Milanich and Samuel Proctor, pp. 59–88. Gainesville: University Presses of Florida, 1978.

Ribaut, Jean. *The Whole and True Discoverye of Terra Florida.* A Facsimile Reprint of the London Edition of 1563. Introduction by David L. Dowd. Gainesville: University of Florida Press, 1964.

5

Republic of Spaniards, Republic of Indians

AMY TURNER BUSHNELL

In 1573 and 1574, Philip II issued three sets of laws for the governing of Spain's empire in the Americas: the Ordinances of Pacification, of Patronage, and of The Laying Out of Towns. In eastern North America, they marked the end of the High Conquest, of would-be conquistadors such as Juan Ponce de León, Pánfilo de Narváez, and Hernando de Soto, and of *adelantados* like Lucas Vázquez de Ayllón, Tristan de Luna y Arellano, and Pedro Menéndez de Avilés. Future expansion would be Crown-controlled.

European fighting men were accustomed to band together under a captain for a limited military objective, after which the company would divide the spoils and disband to be free for other ventures. On the edges of the Spanish empire, however, captains of conquest had been prolonging the wars in order to sell their captives. A resolve to end this abuse lay behind the king's new policy of pacification through gifts and conversions. In future, it would not be the military's business to advance the frontier; its mandate was to defend the advancing missionary. As patron of the church, the king was equally determined to reestablish control over the preaching orders to whom Charles V had entrusted the spiritual conquest of the Indians. He would make pastors from the "regular" clergy answer to his bishops as other priests did. Both of these policies encouraged members of the Franciscan Order, especially, to strike out for fresh mission fields.

A third matter on the king's mind was the vital flow of silver from America, threatened by the wild Chichimeca Indians in northern New Spain and by foreign corsairs on the seaways of the Caribbean and the Gulf Stream. To guarantee the deliveries of silver, the king resorted to a presidial system of fortified outposts and ports. The soldiers and sailors stationed at a *presidio*, like those in a royal *armada*, were regular troops on wages. Unlike conquistadors, they were forbidden to take booty or captives; unlike *encomenderos*, the traditional guardians of newly conquered lands, they were denied the tribute and forced services of the conquered. In those places where the Indians accepted Christianity, presidios were reinforced by mission provinces and converts provided a buffer zone against invasion and a source of reinforcements, provisions, and labor. Where the Indians rejected Christianity, the frontier did not advance.

Spaniards posted to a "land renowned for active war," whether as fighting men, missionaries, or bureaucrats, were supported by a subvention known as the *situado*, a transfer of royal revenues from one royal treasury in the Indies to another, for purposes of defense. During the seventeenth century, Florida's situado came from Mexico City, capital of the viceroyalty of New Spain, which also supported presidios on the road to the silver mines of Zacatecas and in selected ports of the Caribbean and the Philippines.

Indians who could not be pacified by the sword, the gift, or the gospel shared certain characteristics. Typically, they were seasonal nomads, indifferent to the sacraments and unwilling to settle down in farming villages on the Mediterranean model. They had a high regard for individual liberty and were governed by consensus instead of coercion. Finally, they could not be quarantined from contact with Spain's European rivals.

Every condition that made a pacification difficult was present in Spanish Florida; the colony would never lose its character as a military outpost. Yet in the seventeenth century Florida enjoyed two periods of expansion and a hinterland of productive mission provinces. This was possible because the native societies were diverse. While some Florida peoples were seasonally nomadic, recognizing no power above the band, others were sedentary, with *caciques* and *cacicas* who exercised considerable authority. Through these "lords of the land," the Spaniards could implement a Conquest by Contract, establishing an autonomous Republic of Indians to share the land with the Republic of Spaniards, two castes united by their common allegiance to God and the king. The notarized treaties of peace or trade, acts of homage or submission, records of mission foundings, declarations of just war, and lists of chiefs presenting themselves to the governor are evidence of the legal side of pacification, the contracts, theoretically voluntary, that the Spaniards called into existence, recorded, and endeavored to enforce. But the success of the Conquest by Contract and the corollary Republics required a degree of isolation and a flow of gifts that a maritime periphery could not easily sustain.

Florida's transformation from an *adelantamiento* to a royal colony was gradual. Slowly, the situado was institutionalized, troops from the armadas were replaced by permanent garrisons, temporary treasury appointments gave way to lifetime offices, and governors began to govern in person rather than through lieutenants. When Santa Elena was abandoned in 1587, the adelantado's dream of a Greater Florida of transcontinental proportions was tabled for the more practical goal of consolidation. Promotional activities ceased, and settlement incentives to farmer families were discontinued.

If the new capital of St. Augustine was to be populated, the soldiers themselves would have to become family men, and Spanish women were scarce. The answer was mixed marriage. By the turn of the century, half of the wives in town were Indians, adding their genes to the pool of *floridanos*. Once an increased birthrate had brought the sex ratio closer to equilibrium, consensual unions between the Republic of Spaniards and the Republic of Indians became less common and efforts were made to enforce segregation. Indians could not come to St. Augustine without a pass, and non-Indians traveling on the king's business could stay no more than three days in a native town and must sleep in the council house. These restrictions did not apply to the Franciscans, who resided among the Indians and could not leave their posts without permission.

Persons of African origin added a third ethnic element to the colony. At one time, more than fifty black "slaves of the king" were at work on the wooden fortifications, and numerous families had African domestics. Taking advantage of lapses in security, many of the enslaved escaped to live among the Indians or in maroon communities. Free blacks and mulattoes occupied the lower social levels of the Spanish community, being Spanish in language, faith, and fealty.

Although Philip II would have preferred it otherwise, the Spanish empire was cosmopolitan and its borders were permeable. By the unwritten rule of "foreigners to the frontiers," St. Augustine was home to several nationalities. Many of the colony's ship captains, pilots, and merchants were Portuguese, who in the Indies were likely to be *conversos* of Jewish background, and other inhabitants might be Dutch or German artillerists, a French surgeon, or an English pirate turned carpenter. Like the Spanish presidios in North Africa, St. Augustine functioned as a penal colony, a place of exile for unruly officers, trouble-making friars, and sentenced criminals, or *forzados*. Many of the soldiers, too, were *involuntarios*, with records as debtors, petty thieves, vagrants, and rioters. Those from New Spain were further stigmatized, their mixed racial heritage being associated with illegitimacy.

Finally, St. Augustine was a seaside presidio, the only coast guard station along 600 miles of strategic sea lane. After a storm, its vessels scoured the

The oldest European document of North American origin preserved in the United States is this page of the surviving Parish Registers of St. Augustine, Florida. Dated 24 January 1594, the first entry records the marriage of Gabriel Hernándes, "a soldier of this presidio," and Catalina de Valdés. The officiating priest was the pastor of the parish church and chaplain of the garrison, Diego Escobar de Sambrana. The registers form a continuous record to the present day of Catholic life in the city. The fate of entries from 1565, when the parish was founded, to 1594 is not known.

coast for castaways, cargoes, and naval artillery. Their presence reassured voyagers in the Fleet of the Indies, sailing northward on the Gulf Stream 60 miles offshore. When not escorting the Fleet, frigates from the presidio sailed to Havana and Veracruz for supplies, to Spain with dispatches, or to show the flag and trade with the natives in Florida's deepwater harbors, along the inland waterway, and up the St. Johns River.

As advised in the Ordinances of Pacification, the Franciscans charged with the spiritual conquest of Florida took their "flying missions" directly to the Indians, raising crosses on town plazas, preaching, and inviting the chiefs to come and receive the king's gifts. Once in St. Augustine, the native leaders negotiated alliances of trade and mutual defense and registered a request for friars. In Spanish eyes, these acts made them and their vassals subjects of the king of Spain and neophyte Christians.

Churches and convents rose in *cabecera* towns, giving paramount chiefs access to exotic goods, influential allies, and new forms of spiritual power. From these mission centers, or *doctrinas*, missionaries called *doctrineros* serviced strings of outstations, or *visitas*, in towns of lesser importance. To maintain the "divine cult" in all these places, Franciscans relied on the sons of caciques, whom they trained to be sacristans, musicians, interpreters, catechists, and overseers, and on male orphans, whom they raised to be gardeners, grooms, and cooks.

The Florida situado underwrote the doctrinas much as it did the presidio. In St. Augustine's 300-man garrison, missionaries and soldiers were budgetarily interchangeable, costing the Crown 115 ducats a year apiece, and, until the number of *religiosos* on the rolls was capped at forty-three, every added friar meant one fewer soldier. Out of deference to a Franciscan's vow of poverty, his stipend was issued in the form of supplies, called "alms from the king." From other royal funds the friar received a vestment allowance called "habit and sandals" and, if he was an ordained priest, an altar allowance of wine, wheat, and wax. New churches, too, were subsidized. When a town achieved the status of a doctrina, the Crown made it a 1,000-peso baptismal gift of religious essentials: vestments, linens, images, vessels, parish registers, bells, and an altar stone. The natives prized this sacred treasure and sought to keep it whether or not they had a priest in residence to conduct services.

From 1587 through the 1620s, Spanish efforts created a tier of mission provinces along Florida's east coast and up the north-flowing St. Johns River, with its two districts of Mocamo (Saltwater) and Agua Dulce (Freshwater).

Mapa del Pueblo, Fuerte y Caño de San Agustín. . . . A bird's-eye view of St. Augustine and surrounding area drawn by an unknown cartographer, probably in 1593, shows the principal structures of the town, with vertical board walls and thatched roofs and a wharf extending into the Matanzas River (*left*); the town's seventh wooden fort (*right*); and the Indian mission and town of Nombre de Dios (*upper right*).

This first wave of expansion, the Nearer Pacifications, added an element of Indian tribute and labor to the support system.

The Timucuan chiefs near the presidio were the first to prove their loyalty. During the sixteenth-century wars, don Gaspar Marquez of the town of San Sebastián provided the Spaniards with scouts, porters, couriers, boatmen, and archers. When St. Augustine was temporarily overrun by castaways from the wrecks of five galleons, doña María Meléndez, cacica of Nombre de Dios and wife of a soldier, came to the rescue. The Crown rewarded her timely gift of provisions with 500 ducats worth of red cloth. By the turn of the century, Governor Gonzalo Méndez Canzo was drafting natives from Guale province in present-day Georgia to rebuild St. Augustine, which had been destroyed by fire and a flood. The laborers received a ration of maize and a daily wage in trade goods. Thereafter, unmarried Indian males came in relays from the provinces to cultivate the soldiers' fields, or *sabanas*, in a labor levy that historians call the *repartimiento*.

Spaniards also made themselves beneficiaries of the Sabana System, which was the native method of public finance. By custom, each planting season the commoners of an Indian town planted one sabana of maize for each of their caciques or cacicas and another for the community as a whole. Now, with their new iron adzes and hoes, they cleared and planted other sabanas for the "service of the convent" and the "service of the king." Nor was this their only contribution: often they were pressured to sell the surplus of their harvest to the presidio on credit, in what amounted to a forced loan. The colony became increasingly dependent on these transfers of labor and produce, sanctioned and brokered by the Hispanized chiefs. As a reward for their services, the rulers of the Republic of Indians were honored with ceremonial staves of office, entertained by the governor, and given gifts of European garments and weapons for themselves and of cloth, blankets, tools, and beads for their followers. The expense of "regaling" the Indians was the one open-ended fund in the situado.

A nation conquered by the gospel instead of the sword was not supposed to be subject to the labor levy, but all of the Florida pacifications seemed to turn into conquests. Years of Spanish steel, firepower, and scorched-earth campaigns were required to divide and conquer the natives of the east coast, and each chiefdom that rebelled against Spain's overlordship was reconquered and reintegrated under new terms. Meanwhile, undaunted by the Spanish presence, French corsairs continued to trade with the natives for ambergris, a perfume fixative, and sassafras and china root, popular specifics for syphilis. The regions they favored were Ais, above Cape Canaveral, and Guale, on the coast of present-day Georgia. In 1596, the Spaniards took action by treaty, turning both Ais and Guale into provinces.

The Guale Uprising of 1597, the best-known of the Florida revolts, began with the killing of five friars. The war lasted for six years, during which French corsairs came and went freely in Guale ports. At last, Governor Méndez Canzo defeated the rebel leader Juanillo and sentenced the people of his town, Tolomato, to service a portage near the capital. The province of Ais also rebelled in 1597, with more immediate consequences. A raid on the border town of Surruque yielded fifty captives, whom the governor condemned to terms of slavery and distributed among his men. Set free by royal order, the Surruques were relocated where they, too, could make themselves useful to the presidio, but unlike Guale, Ais did not return to the fold. The Eastern Timucuans did their share of rebelling. In 1629, in a spontaneous

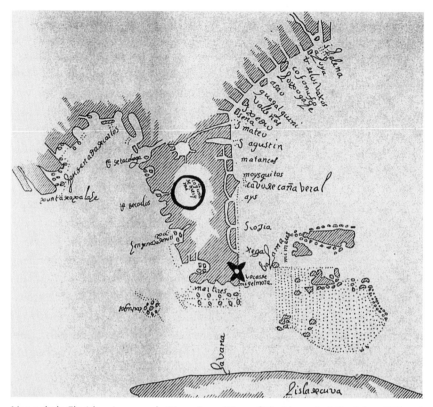

Mapa de la Florida y Laguna de Maymi. . . . (Map of Florida and of the lake of Maymi [Okeechobee]) drawn by an unknown Spanish cartographer during the period 1595–1600, depicts a somewhat squared-off peninsula with a misplaced Okeechobee. It is valuable for its list of place-names, from Santa Elena in the northeast around to Punta de Apalache in the west.

uprising at the ferry town of San Juan del Puerto, a cacica and her vassals freed her brother from soldiers who were taking him, bound, to St. Augustine. Governor Luis de Rojas y Borja sentenced the cacica to be hanged and her confederates to exile and hard labor in Havana, with their ears docked.

War and disease worked in tandem to empty the eastern doctrinas. Between 1613 and 1617, half of the 16,000 converted Indians in Florida and an unknown number of other natives died of a "plague," and other epidemics followed. The colony was further beset by hurricanes and pirates. The great storm of 1622 was responsible for the loss of many ships between the Keys and Bermuda. For years afterward, salvagers from St. Augustine haunted the wreck sites, while Dutch and English corsairs lurked near Cape Canaveral to chase their vessels onto the shoals. More than one supply ship trying to escape these enemies ran aground on the St. Augustine sandbar. Coastal Indians traded with the interlopers as they came ashore for wood and water. No help came from the Crown. Instead, the presidio found its reinforcements and matériel diverted to other garrisons. The situado fell years behind. It was a time of short rations and missing wages. The low point was reached in 1628, when the corsair Piet Heyn captured the Fleet of the Indies off the coast of Cuba, with the subsidies for all of the Caribbean, including Florida, on board. Nor did a peace treaty in Europe end hostilities in the Americas, where hundreds of unemployed soldiers and seamen turned to piracy.

Harassed by seaborne enemies and with dwindling resources in capital and labor, the colonists turned their energies inland. Franciscans made dramatic expeditions into new territory, with banners flying and escorts of Indian arquebusiers. There was even a resurgence of interest in Menéndez's Greater Florida. Governor Rojas y Borja alone sent three parties of Indians and soldiers to investigate the stories of gold mines, diamonds, and freshwater pearls told by veterans of the Juan Pardo expeditions. Two parties turned back; the third reached fabled Cofitachequi, looted by Soto more than eighty years earlier. But the Crown refused to countenance a conquest that would push the northern boundary high into the Appalachian Mountains.

The impulse for the second wave of expansion—the Farther Pacifications, lasting from the 1630s to around 1670—was not a royal initiative but came from within the colony. In the Gulf, floridanos scented opportunities for private trade as well as fresh sources of provisions and labor. Their first step was to "pacify" the Pohoy, Tocobaga, and Calusa who had long dominated the peninsula's Gulf coast and rivers. Captain Juan Rodríguez de Cartaya made the western watershed safe for Christianity with a gunboat, and the result was the new mission province of Timucua, of which the northern part was sometimes called Timucua Alta, or Yustaga.

In 1633, at long last, Governor Luis de Horruytiner was ready to let the Franciscans carry the Evangel into fertile and populous Apalache, in the Red Hills surrounding present-day Tallahassee. That province's port, he assured the Council of the Indies, would provide the Fleet with a haven from storms and corsairs, serve as a supply depot for the western missions, and guarantee the food supply for St. Augustine's 500 inhabitants. Boatloads of maize would leave the Apalache port of San Marcos and follow the curving coast to the Timucuan port on the San Martín River (combining the Suwannee and the Santa Fe), where the maize could be transferred to pack animals and taken overland to the capital. Something the governor did not mention was the rapidly growing city of Havana, a short week's sail from the fields of Apalache.

The populous new provinces replenished the number of peasant farmers and repartimiento laborers in Florida. At the same time, the new ports on Gulf rivers offered outlets for a flourishing coastal trade with Havana in cured deerskins, dried maize and beans, chickens, hogs, and ranch products and drew Caribbean buccaneers into Gulf waters. That the traffic with Cuba was untaxed and unlawful and that foreign vessels were entering the western ports did not trouble caciques or floridanos. Even the friars participated, raising hogs and increasing the size of their sabanas with the object of adorning their churches and bringing comfort to their convents.

In the mid-seventeenth century, royal support for soldiers, friars, and caciques became increasingly irregular. Deeply involved in European wars and peninsular rebellions, Spain could barely maintain the centers, much less the peripheries. The situado was stolen by pirates, lost at sea, swamped in red tape, or sequestered by the king's command for more urgent needs. For years at a time it was not paid at all. Although eventually most of the funds would be replaced, their arrival was so unpredictable that the colonists learned to rely less on the metropolis and more on their own devices.

During periods of wavering royal support, the demands on Christian Indians rose. When the situado failed to materialize, chiefs who had not received the gifts that reinforced their authority were pressed all the more urgently to have their vassals feed the Spanish. Secondary garrisons were stationed in the provincial capitals of San Luis de Apalache, San Francisco de Potano (in Timucua), and Santa Catalina de Guale. Settlements of floridano traders and ranchers grew up around these garrisons, and these settlers, too, demanded an allotment of Indian labor. Natives in the provinces now had not only caciques and friars to feed, but soldiers and "people of quality." Juana Caterina de Florencia, wife of the deputy governor of Apalache, expected to be supplied with fish, milk, and six women to grind maize.

Because the waters around the peninsula were dangerous and the journey by sea was long, and because cart roads were nonexistent and pack animals scarce, most of the freight between St. Augustine and San Luis was carried on Indian backs. The yearly ration for a Franciscan weighed no less than 1,800 pounds. As the number of friars increased and the supply lines to the western doctrinas lengthened to seventy leagues and longer, more and more burdener-days were required to deliver religious rations, and the packs did not travel back to St. Augustine empty but full of products from the provinces. Two mid-seventeenth-century west coast Indian rebellions would be blamed on burdening, with the friars pointing at the governors and the governors at the friars.

Governor Benito Ruíz de Salazar y Vallecilla, who secured the governorship of Florida in 1645 by promising to build a galleon, marshaled the colony's resources and embarked on a program of economic development. While the king's galleon took shape in the shipyards of Campeche, Yucatan, Salazar y Vallecilla sent the soldiers of the San Luis garrison north into Apalachicola with trade goods to exchange for deerskins. To remedy the shortage of beasts of burden he began to breed mules, and on the border between Yustaga and Apalache he started a wheat farm.

These enterprises received a series of setbacks. The first was the Apalache Rebellion of 1647, a kind of civil war between Christian and non-Christian chiefs. No sooner was that suppressed than the colony was stricken with the yellow fever that was sweeping through Caribbean ports. The "black vomit" killed indiscriminately—whites and blacks as well as Indians—and among the many who died was the governor. Development was interrupted a third time by the Timucua Rebellion of 1656, triggered by Governor Diego de Rebolledo's mobilization of the Indian militia after the English capture of Jamaica. Disease, famine, and fugitivism wreaked demographic havoc in central Florida. Outside of Yustaga, Timucua Province had too few inhabitants even to service the transportation network.

St. Augustine itself was badly shaken in 1668 when the privateer Robert Searles, with a patent issued by the Jamaican governor, sacked the city, reportedly killing more than a hundred people in the streets and rounding up everyone who looked African or Indian to be sold as a slave. The colony was too strategic to be abandoned to the English, as many thought that it must. Queen Regent Mariana ordered the viceroy of New Spain to make Florida a priority, bring its situado up to date, increase the Franciscan fund enough to replace the forty-three friars on the rolls with soldiers, and begin sending the Florida treasury an extra 10,000 pesos yearly with which to construct a lasting fort of stone. In 1670, the founding of Charleston by settlers from Barbados underscored the urgency of defense measures, and the queen increased the garrison from 300 to 350 men.

Floridanos, who regarded militia service as something for Indians, appropriated a tenth of the billets in the garrison as reserve officers, or *reformados*, who received the pay of a soldier but were exempt from guard duty. They had already naturalized the benefice and lesser positions of the parish, the office of public notary, the two proprietary offices of the treasury—offices so important that those who held them doubled as a municipal council, or *cabildo*, to advise the governor—and its clerkships, and the position of defender of the Indians, which they were seeking to make permanent and salaried.

Among Florida's notable families, the Menéndez Marquezes stood out for their able family strategy. Descended from Juan Menéndez Marquez and María Menéndez y Posada, two close relatives of the sixteenth-century governor Pedro Menéndez Marquez, himself a nephew of Pedro Menéndez de Avilés, the family maintained its position and fortunes for 150 years through marriage, treasury offices, military offices, Cuban commerce, unofficial borrowing from the situado, and cattle ranching. Don Thomás Menéndez Marquez was typical. From his ranch at La Chua in the depopulated savannahs of central Florida, he shipped tallow, hides, and dried beef out the San Martín and down to Havana. Although his brother, father, and grandfather had all been royal officials of the treasury, and he, his son, and his grandson would follow their lead, don Thomás had no compunction about avoiding customs duties. Floridanos honored the king's person, not his regulations.

All told, the building of St. Augustine's stone fort, the Castillo de San Marcos, took twenty-four years and cost the Crown more than 138,000 pesos, much of it going for Indian labor in the coquina quarries on Anastasia Island. Twice as many native workmen were stationed at the capital as formerly; many brought their families and settled down. The influx of money and people caused prices to rise, stimulating agriculture and ranches like La Chua. Even so, there were times when the royal storehouses stood empty and governors were forced to seize the stores of private individuals. It was dangerous to do this to friars or priests, who could quickly close ranks against anyone who threatened their prerogatives.

Governor Juan Marquez Cabrera alienated the religious establishment throughout the course of his administration (1680–1687). In one typical instance, he ordered Captain Francisco de Fuentes, lieutenant governor of Guale, to requisition some maize belonging to Father Juan de Uzeda, doctrinero of San José de Zapala, in order to provide rations for refugees from Santa Catalina de Guale who had been asked to build a fort on Sapelo Island. When, at last, no priest would give him the sacraments, the governor deserted his post. Governor Diego de Quiroga y Losada similarly made an enemy of parish priest Alonso de Leturiondo by exercising eminent domain over his granary. The priest responded by padlocking the parish church on the Feastday of St. Mark and doing his part to ruin Quiroga in the lengthy judicial review, or *residencia*, that followed every governor's term of office.

In the late seventeenth century, Florida regained its sixteenth-century reputation as a land of war. The provinces came under attack seasonally by pirates and by slave-raiding Indians armed with English firearms in the southeastern version of the proxy war. Yet the new royal funds for fortifications were absorbed by the castillo, with little to spare for the defense of the provinces. When the viceroy of New Spain sent an extra 6,000 pesos with which to build a stone tower on Cumberland Island for the protection of the Guale, Governor Laureano de Torres y Ayala spent it on a seawall for St. Augustine, which ended up costing three-fourths as much as the castillo itself.

North of Apalache, in the province of Apalachicola, traders from Charleston were replacing the Spanish as buyers of deerskins. Although the Apalachicolos were not Christians, as allies and trading partners they had fallen within the Spanish sphere of influence since the 1640s. Florida governors tried to counter the Anglo advance with gifts, warnings, hastily founded missions, and a blockhouse to serve as a trading post, but the lure of English manufactures proved too strong. The Apalachicolos moved out of the Spanish orbit and into the English one, to reenter history as the Lower Creeks.

Between 1680 and 1706, a major part of the Indians in the provinces also withdrew their allegiance, silently deserting their doctrinas for a life of liberty without friars, soldiers, or chiefs who were more Spanish than Indian. The first to defect were the Guale, whose towns on the sea islands had become magnets for pirates and other predators. The Guale's declining numbers were temporarily masked by a contrary influx of Yamasee moving down the Atlantic coast. By 1696, when the Quaker Jonathan Dickinson passed through Florida, three towns of refugees on Amelia Island were all that remained of Guale province. The last to leave were the Apalaches, who forsook their province after it was invaded by Creeks and Carolinians in 1704 during Queen Anne's War. Some of them fled to Pensacola, refounded in 1698 to counter French influence in the Gulf. Some, under don Patricio de Hinachuba, chief of Ivitachuco, migrated to Timucua, then to the environs of St. Augustine, where they hoped to find safety under the guns of the fort. Others left Apalache for parts unknown, saying that they would not remain to die with Spaniards.

The kings of Spain had seen themselves as patrons of the Florida Indians and the Indians as wards of the Crown. Royal alms supported their missionaries, royal subsidies regaled their chiefs, and a royal defender of the Indians represented their interests. But wars in Europe, spilling into the Americas, strained the royal revenues and patrimony to the limit. The Spanish elite survived the war years by demanding advances of goods and services from people who were in no position to refuse. At such times, the colony survived because it was ideologically reinforced. The "cult of the king" threw a mantle of duty about forced loans and labor, while the "divine cult" taught Indians that they were natural inferiors.

To many Spaniards, Florida must have seemed a native Utopia. In this maritime periphery of strategic rather than economic importance, the goals of peaceful evangelism were largely met. Indians were not enslaved; their lands were not alienated; their lives were not shortened in mines or workhouses. Territorial expansion observed the forms of the Conquest by Contract. The rulers of the Republic of Indians, mission-educated, channeled the labor and products of Indian peasants to the priests, fighting men, and merchants of the Republic of Spaniards. In exchange, the natives were offered an afterlife in heaven, a sanctuary on earth, and useful tools, plants, and animals.

But pacification, Spain's idealistic design for the mastery of North America, depended on enduring hierarchies and exclusive relationships. The isolation on which it depended was repeatedly breached, giving common Indians a chance to show how little they cared for lords of any kind. When, in the last quarter of the seventeenth century, increasing royal investments and increasing demands on native commoners strengthened the colony's center at the expense of its peripheries, the mission hinterland—source of food, labor, and export products—sloughed away, and with it went the comparatively enlightened system of the Two Republics.

Bibliography

Arana, Luis Rafael, and Albert Manucy. *The Building of Castillo de San Marcos*. Eastern National Park & Monument Association, 1977.

Bushnell, Amy Turner. "Escape of the Nickaleers: European-Indian Relations on the Wild Coast of Florida in 1696, from Jonathan Dickinson's Journal." In *Coastal Encounters: The Transformation of the Gulf South in the Eighteenth Century*, edited by Richmond Brown, 31–58. Lincoln: University of Nebraska Press, 2007.

———. "The First Southerners: Indians of the Early South." In *A Companion to the American South*, rev. ed., edited by John B. Boles, 3–23. Oxford: Basil Blackwell, 2004.

———. "'Gastos de Indios': The Crown and the Chiefdom-Presidio Compact in Florida." In *El Gran Norte Mexicano: Indios, misioneros y pobladores entre el mito y la historia*, edited by Salvador Bernabéu Albert, 137–63. Sevilla: Consejo Superior de Investigaciones Científicas, 2009.

———. "How to Fight a Pirate: Provincials, Royalists, and the Raiding of San Marcos de Apalache." In *Pirates, Jack Tar, and Memory: New Directions in American Maritime History*, edited by Paul A. Gilje and William Pencak, 11–25. Mystic, Conn.: Mystic Seaport, 2007.

———. *The King's Coffer: Proprietors of the Spanish Florida Treasury, 1565–1702*. Gainesville: University Presses of Florida, 1981.

———. "A Requiem for Lesser Conquerors: Honor and Oblivion on a Maritime Periphery." In *Beyond Books and Borders: Garcilaso de la Vega and La Florida del Inca*, edited by Raquel Chang-Rodríguez, 66–74. Lewisburg, Penn.: Bucknell University Press, 2006.

———. "Ruling the Republic of Indians in Seventeenth-Century Florida." In *Powhatan's Mantle: Indians in the Colonial Southeast*, rev. ed., edited by Gregory A. Waselkov, Peter H. Wood, and Tom Hatley, 195–21. Lincoln: University of Nebraska Press, 2006.

———. *Situado and Sabana: Spain's Support System for the Presidio and Mission Provinces of Florida*. Anthropological Papers of the American Museum of Natural History, no. 74 (1994).

———. "Spain's Conquest by Contract: Pacification and the Mission System in Eastern North America." In *The World Turned Upside Down: The State of Eighteenth-Century American Studies at the Beginning of the Twenty-First Century*, edited by Michael V. Kennedy and William G. Shade, 289–320. Bethlehem, Penn.: Lehigh University Press, 2001.

Francis, J. Michael, and Kathleen M. Kole. *Murder and Martyrdom in Spanish Florida: Don Juan and the Guale Uprising of 1597*. Anthropological Papers of the American Museum of Natural History, no. 95 (2011).

Hall, Joseph M., Jr. *Zamumo's Gifts: Indian-European Exchange in the Colonial Southeast*. Philadelphia: University of Pennsylvania Press, 2009.

Hann, John H. *Indians of Central and South Florida, 1513–1763*. Gainesville: University Press of Florida, 2003.

———. *The Native American World beyond Apalachee: West Florida and the Chattahoochee Valley*. Gainesville: University Press of Florida, 2006.

Hoffman, Paul E. *Florida's Frontiers*. Bloomington: Indiana University Press, 2002.

———. *A New Andalucia and a Way to the Orient: The American Southeast during the Sixteenth Century*. Baton Rouge: Louisiana State University Press, 1990.

———. *The Spanish Crown and the Defense of the Caribbean, 1535–1585*. Baton Rouge: Louisiana State University Press, 1980.

Hudson, Charles. *The Juan Pardo Expeditions: Exploration of the Carolinas and Tennessee, 1566–1568*, with documents relating to the Pardo expeditions, transcribed, translated, and annotated by Paul E. Hoffman. Washington, D.C.: Smithsonian Institution Press, 1990.

Milanich, Jerald T. *Laboring in the Fields of the Lord: Spanish Missions and Southeastern Indians*. Washington, D.C.: Smithsonian Institution Press, 1999.

Waselkov, Gregory A. "Seventeenth-Century Trade in the Colonial Southeast." *Southeastern Archaeology* 8, no. 2 (1989):117–60.

Worth, John E. *The Struggle for the Georgia Coast: An Eighteenth-Century Spanish Retrospective on Guale and Mocama*. Anthropological Papers of the American Museum of Natural History, no. 75 (1995).

———. *Timucuan Chiefdoms of Spanish Florida*, 2 vols. Volume 1: *Assimilation*, Volume 2: *Resistance and Destruction*. Gainesville: University Press of Florida, 1998.

6

The Missions of Spanish Florida

JOHN H. HANN

Missions in Florida, as in other parts of the Spanish New World, sought to spread the knowledge and message of Christ to native peoples. Their goal was to persuade the natives to accept Catholicism and allegiance to the king of Spain. Establishment of missions assumed special importance in the Spanish New World under Pope Alexander VI's grant of exclusive dominion in the New World to Spain's monarchs because the grant was justified by the Crown's assumption of the obligation of preaching Christ's teachings to the natives. The royal contract given to Florida's founder, Menéndez de Avilés, clearly included the obligation to bring clergymen to instruct the natives in the Christian faith.

People may not associate missions with Spanish Florida as readily as they link them with the early Spanish experience from Texas through California. But missions played no less a role in Florida than they did elsewhere in the establishment of Spanish control. During the 138 years of Florida's mission era, 1567 to 1705, missions were attempted or established among at least eleven distinct Indian peoples at about eighty mission centers that served a far greater number of individual villages and hamlets. Almost all of this was the work of Spanish Franciscans. The missions existing simultaneously numbered forty-four by the mid-1630s and probably increased by a few more over the next ten years as new missions appeared among the Apalachee of the Tallahassee region. The number may have begun to contract by 1650, if not before. Twenty thousand Indians had been baptized by 1630, and more than 50,000 others catechized. Only twenty-seven Franciscans were then available to staff the thirty-two missions, which served more than two hundred settlements, sixty of which had churches. Thirty-five Franciscans served 30,000 Christian Indians by 1635. Contraction had definitely set in by 1655, when there were about forty missions. The thirty-six that had friars held only 26,000 Christian Indians by then. A 1656 revolt, the turmoil that followed, and the spread of diseases further hastened the decline.

The relatively successful missions stretched from just south of St. Augustine northward along the coast through Georgia almost to the Savannah River. They reached westward across north Florida to the Apalachicola and extended into parts of south Georgia west of the Okefenokee Swamp. They penetrated central Florida along the St. Johns River for an undefined distance south of Lake George, possibly reached farther south along the Oklawaha, and probably went farthest south in Marion County to the vicinity of the Cove of the Withlacoochee. Apalachee, Guale of the north Georgia coast, and various Timucua-speaking groups constituted the majority of the missionized natives. The Apalachee lived between the Aucilla and Ochlockonee Rivers. Timucua-speakers occupied all of north Florida east of Jefferson County, much of the eastern half of Georgia below the Altamaha River, coastal Florida southward to the vicinity of Daytona Beach, and central Florida southward along the rivers for an undefined distance. Tama-Yamasee, Chine, Amacano, Pacara, and Chacato, Mayaca-speakers, and a few Sabacola comprised the remainder. The Tama, from north central Georgia, migrated to Apalachee to be missionized. Yamasee, also from north central Georgia, migrated to Apalachee, to coastal Georgia, and to Mayaca-speaking territory along the upper St. Johns River. The Sabacola lived along the Chattahoochee River. The Chine and Chacato migrated to Apalachee from the Florida Panhandle. The Amacano and Pacara, linguistic brothers of the Chine, were living with the Chine on Apalachee Bay's Spring Creek when the Chine mission was established in 1674.

In general, Florida's mission experience paralleled that of other frontier territories of the Iberian New World, but its experience was unique in a number of ways because of various interrelated factors. First, and foremost, soldiers rather than settlers remained the core of most of Florida's Spanish families, even though historian Eugene Lyon has recently revised our image of early Spanish Florida as little more than a bleak and often starving garrison town. The relative lack of settlers and the Crown's close supervision of developments in Florida spared its natives from some of Spain's most exploitative economic institutions. The Crown checked the several attempts to introduce enslavement of the natives. Tribute was not a regular part of the formal Spanish regime in Florida. Spaniards introduced tribute to a degree in an informal sense. In areas where soldiers were introduced some time after the establishment of missions, natives were expected to contribute some of the food those soldiers consumed, although there was no uniform policy in this matter. Similarly, natives carried soldiers' bedding from post to post without pay as a service to the king. The paid labor draft known as the repartimiento was the sole formalized, economically exploitative institution imposed on Florida's natives in general.

Although economic considerations were a factor motivating establishment of missions in Florida, none is known to have become an economic enterprise dominated by friars in the way of the typical California mission. Except for the earliest approaches to coastal natives in the 1560s, missionaries began their work unaccompanied by soldiers and, with few exceptions, at the invitation of elements among the native leaders rather than by thrusting themselves uninvited upon the indigenous societies. By the last years of the sixteenth century, leaders from interior provinces, where no Spanish conquest of the Indians preceded establishment of the mission, began to render obedience to Spain's king and to ask for missionaries.

On the other hand, missions were not the major feature in Spain's initial approaches to Florida's natives that they were in the Spanish domination of Texas and California. The first missionaries were overshadowed by the adelantado, Menéndez de Avilés, and his soldiers or by his governor-successors and their soldiers. With the possible exception of some coastal missions and a few tribes from distant hinterland frontiers, the practice of bringing natives to mission centers at places chosen by the missionaries was not employed in Florida as it was in California. Florida Franciscans established their missions in preexisting villages. In contrast to the Franciscans who established the first missions in New Mexico and Alta or Upper California, Florida's Franciscans did not bring large herds of cattle, horses, or sheep to strengthen their hand in convincing natives to accept their tutelage. There is no evidence that the Spanish authorities induced Florida's Indians to adopt a Spanish-type roster of governor, lieutenant governor, alcalde, or mayor, and *alguacil,* or peace officer, for their villages as was done in New Mexico. Except for the installation of the Spanish governor or his lieutenants as supreme authority over each native polity, a traditional roster of native political officials remained largely unchanged and unchallenged. Such differences doubtless were among the reasons that the new faith seemingly held stronger sway over Florida's natives than it did over New Mexico's Pueblo during an equivalent span of time, that Florida's mission structures retained their original simplicity, and that the natives' council house continued to be the mission villages' most impressive and most frequented building.

Members of the Society of Jesus (Jesuits), who made the first mission efforts in Florida, uniformly met resistance, even though the missionaries were accompanied by soldiers. Jesuits are members of a religious society founded in 1534 and devoted to missionary and educational work. They worked briefly at single sites among southwest Florida's Calusa, the Miami area's Tequesta, the Escamacu in the region of Beaufort, South Carolina, and at Tupiqui and one or more other places in Guale. Some of the resistance was doubtless a legacy of de Soto's brutal passage through Florida or was influenced by the natives' contact with the French just before the Jesuits' arrival. But, more fundamentally, the Jesuits met resistance to their message everywhere as soon as they spoke ill of the natives' deities or when they revealed that the natives would have to abandon polygyny, sororal marriage, and other customs on becoming Christians. Soldiers' demands for food and friction with natives also handicapped the Jesuits' efforts. The soldiers' killing of two successive head chiefs and other nobles at Calusa precipitated flight by the rest of the inhabitants, which ended the mission effort among them until late in the seventeenth century. The Jesuits viewed friction or hostilities between soldiers and natives as insuperable obstacles, responsible for their failure.

In reality, from Calusa and Tequesta to Guale and Escamacu, the Jesuits dealt with natives whose confidence in their own value system and worldview had not been shaken sufficiently to make them susceptible to the European Christian message. However much Jesuits might browbeat the Indians with their superior training in rhetoric and logic, they could not move them to abandon their beliefs. Everywhere in Florida, Jesuits made their efforts before the time was right. For the Calusa and other nonagricultural Indians of south Florida, the time would never be right. The Indians' killing of Jesuits who had gone to the Chesapeake Bay region caused the withdrawal of the society from Florida in 1572. But their work among the natives had ceased prior to their leaving.

Down to 1595, little is known about the activity of the first Franciscans, who came in 1573. Franciscans were members of the religious community formally called the Order of Friars Minor, founded in Italy by St. Francis of Assisi in 1209. They dedicated themselves especially to preaching in the growing cities of medieval Europe, to missions among non-Christians, and to charitable work. They emphasized humility and were usually referred to as friars, a term derived from the French word for "brother."

In Florida the friars had their earliest success among Saltwater and Freshwater Timucua living near St. Augustine and on the St. Johns River in the latter part of the 1570s. Surprisingly, Jesuits appear to have made no effort in those regions despite the Freshwater Timucua's friendship with Menéndez de Avilés from the beginning and despite his friendly relations with some Saltwater Timucua as well. At the start, as Eugene Lyon has noted, a language barrier, a lack of trained missionaries, and unsettled relations with Saltwater Timucua limited religious contact. The Jesuits may have passed over the St. Augustine region initially because one of the first three to arrive was killed by Timucua-speaking Mocama just to the north of the mouth of the St. Johns River when he was stranded on shore with some sailors.

Nombre de Dios is considered the oldest of Florida's enduring missions. Work among its people and the Freshwater Timucua of San Sebastian, just to the south of St. Augustine, appears to have begun around 1577. But people of both villages attended Mass in St. Augustine until 1587, when the first formal missions, known as doctrinas, appear to have been established in both villages. San Juan del Puerto, at the mouth of the St. Johns River, was also founded by 1587. A bridgehead represented by the Franciscans' conversion of a Guale head chief disappeared quickly when that chief was killed by a nephew of another chief whom he had confronted over disrespect for his authority. The Spanish governor's reluctant hanging of the nephew at the insistence of the deceased chief's wife precipitated revolt from Guale north to South Carolina's Escamacu-Orista. The revolt precluded missionary work in that region at least until 1588, when San Pedro Mocama was founded on Georgia's Cumberland Island. Family ties between chiefs of Nombre de Dios, San Juan, and San Pedro may have facilitated mission activity at this date, as had arrival of a new band of friars in 1587. By 1588 at least five missions and a number of outstations, or visitas, existed among Freshwater and Saltwater Timucua.

Arrival of more friars in 1594 permitted a major effort among the Guale. Six friars were working there by 1597. By then friars were making sorties into hinterland Timucua villages whose chiefs had responded favorably to a new governor's invitation to render obedience to his king and to receive gifts the king had sent to those ready to give that obedience. But later that same year, a general uprising of the Guale interrupted the mission effort, as they killed five of their six friars and carried off the sixth one to an inland town to serve his captors as a slave. An imprudent friar's effort to block the rise to head chieftainship of a young Christianized chief who refused to abandon polygyny precipitated the trouble, but the support given the uprising suggests that the discontent involved more than the sexual mores of one individual. The friars' baptism of natives before telling them clearly about the scope of the obligations they were assuming in accepting baptism and about the tribute and labor demands of Spanish civil authorities were factors as well. In the uprising's wake, the governor reduced the maize tribute for the Mocamas to a symbolic six ears for each married Indian. A young Spaniard shipwrecked on Guale's coast in 1595 placed part of the blame on earlier atrocities committed by soldiers on punitive expeditions. The governor's sustained campaign of fire and blood eventually broke the solidarity of the Guales. A majority, coalescing behind a new leader, sued for peace and agreed to capture or kill the rebellion's initial leaders in the inland region where they had taken refuge to escape Spanish retaliation.

Rapid growth resumed in 1607, when arrival of a few new friars made it possible to capitalize on the interest in Christianization shown by some among the hinterland tribes ten years earlier. In that year the friars established the first new missions among Timucua-speakers known as Potano living in the vicinity of Gainesville. Within several years, a friar descending the Santa Fe to the Suwannee established a mission on the Gulf in a village named Cofa at the mouth of the Suwannee. From Potano, friars moved into Columbia County to work among Timucua-speakers identified as Utina. In 1623 friars began to work among other Timucua-speakers known as Yustaga, living between the Suwannee and Aucilla Rivers. Friars also resurrected the Guale missions and began work in the remaining Timucua-speaking provinces of mainland south Georgia's coast and hinterland, Acuera along the Oklawaha, and Ocale south of Potano. Two friars began formal missionization of Apalachee in 1633. It was the last of the major mission provinces to be established until late in the century. A mission at Mayaca on the St. Johns River south of Lake George consolidated work done by visiting friars prior to 1602.

Evidence to account for the change of heart that made that expansion possible is fragmentary. In addition to the attraction of the gifts being offered, a series of Spanish successes against French intruders enhanced the Spaniards' image as allies worth cultivating. A personal embassy by a leading Christianized Indian from Nombre de Dios may have swayed Utina's most prestigious leader. Use of a mailed fist to punish the killing of Spaniards brought a reversal of hostility on the part of the Potano and Surruque. For some, such as Utina's head chief and Apalachee leaders who asked for friars, the change of heart may have been abetted by loss of faith in the native religious system as a bulwark for their power. Such chiefs may have viewed exotic goods provided by Spaniards and esoteric knowledge and skills Spaniards made available as enhancing the chiefs' prestige in the eyes of their people. That may explain the eagerness of many of the early converts to learn to read and write and the Utina chief's willingness to permit

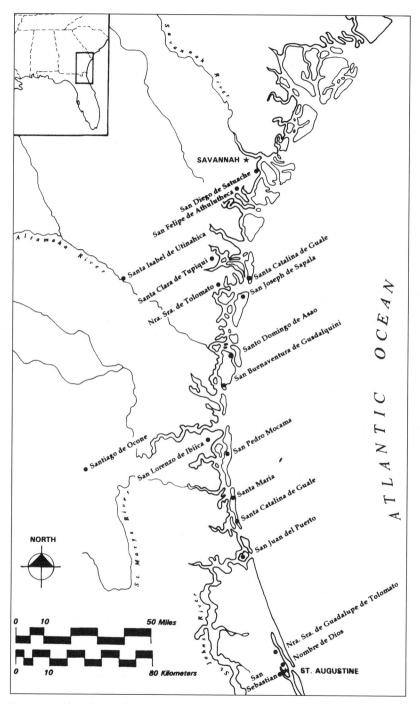

Names and locations of Franciscan missions at St. Augustine and north along the Atlantic coast in the seventeenth century.

destruction of the idols in five villages under his immediate jurisdiction. The Apalachee leaders' request for friars was motivated in part at least by belief that a Spanish alliance would enable leaders to regain control over their subjects that they had lost. For that and other reasons, Spanish authorities delayed the missionization of Apalachee for a generation.

Florida's missions contrast with those of California in that their friars generally did not alter the natives' settlement pattern, which consisted of a large central village under a head chief, smaller ones under subordinate chiefs, and still smaller chiefless hamlets. Friars established their doctrinas in the head villages, visiting subordinate villages and hamlets to give instructions and building churches in some of the subordinate villages. Some such subordinate villages eventually became missions, at least for a time. In 1602, however, a friar advocated consolidation of the many small hamlets surrounding the coastal missions. There is no indication that it was done, but as populations dwindled, consolidation may have occurred in some cases. In Apalachee, best known of the mission provinces, the settlement pattern persisted virtually intact until destruction of the missions in 1704. Guale is the one area where consolidation and extensive moving about of missions is known to have occurred. Between 1604 and the 1670s, many Christian Guale from former mainland doctrinas and their subordinate villages moved to the islands off Georgia's coast. Little is known of the timing and circumstances of those moves, except for the Tolomato, whose chief led the 1597 revolt. In the 1620s, the governor pressured its inhabitants to move to a site near St. Augustine to provide ferry service and assist in the unloading of ships at St. Augustine. In this earlier period, the desire for greater security from attacks by Westo and Yuchi probably motivated such moves. A later consolidation on Amelia Island resulted from British attacks.

Florida's inland missions in general were not missions of conquest as were those of the coast to a degree. This difference also sets those missions apart from those of New Mexico and California. Soldiers did not accompany the first friars who began work in the hinterland, following a policy laid down explicitly by the Crown in that era. This seemingly posed no problem for the friars in Utina, but the situation was different in Potano, Yustaga, and Apalachee. Even though Potano's head chief had been baptized in St. Augustine prior to the launching of the formal mission effort in his land, his authority did not suffice to assure the priests a friendly reception. Jeering, jostling, and even threats of bodily harm greeted the friars' first efforts there. The first friars venturing into Apalachee between 1608 and 1612 at the invitation of its most prestigious chief were twice forced to leave because of the

Names and locations of Franciscan missions in the interior of Florida in the seventeenth century.

unruliness of Indians who did not obey their chiefs well. In deferring the effort there, both governor and friars cited a need for soldiers among their reasons for doing so. Yustaga's head chief initially refused friars entry to work in his territory. Even after admitting two friars, for a time he forbade any of his subjects to be baptized. In the hinterland, Spaniards resorted to a degree of compulsion only among the Chacato of the Panhandle, a few months after the launching of missions there, when opposition to the friars' presence developed.

Steady and, at times, spectacular shrinking of the population accompanied spread of the missions, resulting largely from the Indians' exposure to new diseases brought by outsiders. The magnitude of the population loss is unknown because demographic information is scant and usually imprecise. There are no global estimates for any people in the sixteenth century and none for the first three-quarters of the seventeenth century, except for the Apalachee.

The size of Guale's population in the 1560s or later when they began to be Christianized is among the least known. The only data recorded are that more than 1,200 had been baptized by 1597, that Guale were more populous in 1602 than the coastal and Freshwater Timucua, and that 756 Guale were confirmed by Cuba's bishop in 1606. There are no indications of the size of individual villages until 1675.

For coastal and Freshwater Timucua in the 1560s, there are offhand statements about the numbers of warriors whom leaders assembled on several occasions. Based on those statements, demographer Henry Dobyns suggested a total Saltwater population of 7,500 to 10,000 for that era. In 1602, friars provided precise figures on the Christian population of each of the three Saltwater missions of that period (San Pedro 792, San Juan 500, Nombre de Dios 200) and, in the case of San Pedro, figures for its individual subordinate villages. The figures for San Pedro (500) represented the entire population of Cumberland Island at that time. Six Freshwater villages on the St. Johns and Mayaca held about 200 Christians in 1602, and Mayaca had about 100 people yet to be baptized. The other Freshwater villages on the St. Johns presumably were still heathen. Most of San Sebastian's people perished in a hurricane shortly before 1602. In 1606 a visiting bishop from Cuba confirmed 1,003 Saltwater Timucua and 315 Freshwater Timucua and Mayaca. On the south Georgia coastal mainland, the 1,100 people in Ycafui's eight villages had been catechized by 1602, but the 700 to 800 in Ibi's five settlements were still heathen. The scant data for the 1560s suggest that the

Saltwater and Freshwater Timucua populations had declined drastically by 1602.

Among the hinterland Timucua in this period, the data are best for Potano. Early in November 1607, two friars reported more than 1,000 adult baptisms among the Potano over the previous year. The friar who launched the work in four settlements in the vicinity of Gainesville baptized the 400 people of each of two of the settlements and 200 people in a third. Together with the children they were a major portion of the more than 4,000 baptized between mid-1606 and the end of 1607. By then another 1,000-plus were being catechized. Over the next nine years the number of Christianized natives rose to more than 16,000, but a series of epidemics beginning in 1614 halved that Christian population and undoubtedly took an equally heavy toll on the non-Christianized who were in contact with them.

We have the fewest data about the size of Utina's population in the mission era and earlier. Hernando de Soto found it to be more populous and better provisioned than lands such as Potano that he had passed through earlier. A remark in 1616 that after the first five years of a friar's work at Tarihica there were 712 living Christian Indians may provide an indicator of Utina mission size. If Tarihica's Christian population lost half its numbers in the 1614–16 epidemics, it would rank with the largest Apalachee mission centers of 1675, as did the head chief's jurisdiction of Ayaocuto with its 1,500 people distributed over five settlements.

Dobyns used a French remark that Yustaga's head chief of the 1560s could put 3,000 or 4,000 warriors in battle to estimate a total population of 15,000 or 20,000. The baptism of 13,000 people during the first twelve years of the friars' work in Yustaga suggests at least that large a population, as does the marked preponderance of Yustaga among western Timucua's surviving population in 1675.

Global estimates made from 1608 to the 1630s placed Apalachee's population during those years at 30,000 to 34,000. Other estimates from the 1630s placed it at 15,000 or 16,000. A friar gave a late 1640s figure of 20,000. The higher estimates are not inconceivable in view of Apalachee's surviving population of about 10,000 as late as 1675. At the start of missionization in the 1630s that population was distributed over more than forty settlements under the jurisdiction of ten principal chiefs who headed the missions in existence in 1657. Until the 1650s Apalachee was less affected by epidemics than were the other mission territories.

By the 1670s an eleventh Apalachee mission had been established, and

An artistic reconstruction of the Franciscan mission church of San Luis de Talimali at Tallahassee. Archaeological excavations reveal that the Apalachee churches were constructed of plank and thatch. The dimensions of this particular church in the Florida hinterland, 110 by 50 feet, make it as large as the seventeenth-century parish church in the capital city of St. Augustine. Artist: John LoCastro; original watercolor, 1993, *Afternoon at Mission San Luis.*

the province was host to six or more other peoples who migrated into the province. Three missions were established among the immigrant Chine, Amacano, Pacara, Chacato, and Tama-Yamasee. The sixth group, Tocobaga from the Tampa Bay region, apparently never showed interest in receiving a friar. The Chacato migrants were refugees from one of the last efforts to expand the scope of the missions. In mid-1674, two months after the establishment of the Chine-Amacano-Pacara mission, friars established two missions in the Chacato homeland near Marianna, which ended a year later with the revolt and flight of most of the Chacato. A contemporaneous short-lived third mission on the Apalachicola River served a small band of Sabacola who had migrated downriver from the vicinity of Columbus, Georgia.

Governor Pablo de Hita Salazar gave impetus to the last expansion of the Florida missions. It began with resurrection of missions at Anacape near Welatka and Mayaca to serve Yamasee who had moved to the upper St. Johns River. Friars then moved southward from Mayaca into the lakes district to establish five short-lived missions among the Mayaca-speaking

Jororo and the Aypaja by the 1690s. The effort collapsed essentially in 1696–97 when the Jororo of Atoyquime killed their friar and his Guale assistants. A renewed approach to the Calusa in September 1697 ended several months later when Indians stripped the friars of even their clothing and deposited them on Matecumbe Key, where a Spanish vessel eventually rescued them.

The following is a listing of the more enduring missions arranged by province or geographic area. Those marked with a pound sign probably had died out by 1655. Those marked with an asterisk had ceased to exist by 1675 or had merged with another mission. Population statistics are given for most of the missions that existed in 1675 and in 1689. The first figure is the one for 1675.

COASTAL TIMUCUA

Nombre de Dios	—	100
San Sebastian#		
San Juan del Puerto	30	125
San Pedro Mocama*		
San Buenaventura de Guadalquini	40	300
San Lorenzo de Ibiica#		
Santiago de Ocone*		

ST. JOHNS AND OCKLAWAHA VALLEYS

San Antonio de Anacape*	—	150
San Diego de Laca or Salamototo	40	200
San Salvador de Mayaca*		
Santa Lucia de Acuera*		
San Luis de Acuera or Avino*		

GUALE AND OTHER NORTH GEORGIA MISSIONS

Santa Catalina de Guale	140	150
Santo Domingo de Asao or Talaje	30	125
San Pedro or San Felipe de Athuluteca	36	200
Santa Clara de Tupiqui*		
San Diego de Satuache*		
San Joseph de Sapala	50	—
Nra. Sra. de Guadalupe de Tolomato	—	125

WESTERN TIMUCUA

San Francisco de Potano	60	125
Santa Fe	110	180
San Martin de Ayaocuto*		
Sta. Cruz de Tarihica	80	100
San Agustin or/and Sta. Catalina de Ahoica	60	200
Sta. Catalina	80	—
San Juan Guacara	80	150

Sta. Cruz de Cachipile*
San Agustin de Urihica*
San Francisco de Chuaquin*
San Ildefonso de Chamini*
Sta. Maria de los Angeles de Arapaha*
Sta. Isabel de Utinahica#
San Luis de Eloquale (Ocale)#

San Pedro y San Pablo de Potohiriba	300	750
Sta. Elena de Machaba	300	500
San Matheo de Tolapatafi	300	250
San Miguel de Asile	40	150

CHACATO

San Carlos de Yatcatani	400	150
San Nicolas de Tolentino	100	350

APALACHEE

San Lorenzo de Ivitachuco	1200	1000
San Luis de Talimali	1400	1500
Sta. Maria de Ayubale	800	1200
San Francisco de Oconi	200	400
San Joseph de Ocuia	900	1000
San Juan de Aspalaga	800	250
San Pedro y San Pablo de Patale	500	600
San Antonio de Bacuqua	120	250
San Cosme y San Damian de Cupaica or Escambe	900	2000
San Martin de Tomole	700	650
Sta. Cruz de Capoli or Ychutafun	60	150
Purificacion de Tama or Candelaria	300	400
San Pedro de los Chines	300	150

Intervillage migration and flight from Apalachee villages such as Tomole and Aspalaga probably account for some discrepancies in the data from 1675 and from 1689. Evidence for Apalachee in particular indicates that its people were undercounted in 1675. In that year a visiting bishop of Santiago de Cuba confirmed 13,152 Indians, a figure that probably did not include young children. It suggests a population of at least 10,000 in Apalachee, as does a remark by the bishop that he provided long dresses for 4,081 women in Apalachee who were wearing nothing but short skirts that covered them from knees to waist. The standard translation of his letter omitted the detail that identified the women as "from Apalachee."[1] Evidence from the 1680s shows that Guale and Mocama populations also were understated in 1675.

Many of the older missions and their peoples probably disappeared during the years 1649–56, when a series of epidemics devastated the remaining populations of the Guale and Timucua. Another epidemic in 1659 report-edly killed 10,000, many of them probably in Apalachee in view of a remark by the governor that the 1655 smallpox epidemic had left very few Indians in Guale and Timucua. A 1656 revolt among the Potano, Utina, and Yustaga, directed at the governor and his soldiers but not against the friars, also has-tened the demise of many missions. An imprudent governor's disrespect for privileges of rank enjoyed by Indian leaders provided a pretext for the re-volt, but those leaders' dismay over their steady loss of power and influence as the number of their subjects declined was a more fundamental cause. The governor's relocation of the people of a northern tier of the western Timucuan missions—most of whom had not participated in the revolt—to revive the depopulated rebel missions of southern Utina and Potano that were on the Spanish trail led many of the migrants to flee from mission territory. His policy caused the disappearance of all western Timucuan mis-sions with asterisks in the list.

The establishment of Charleston brought a new threat to the missions. Indians armed by the British of Virginia had attacked missions as early as the 1620s. But the threat intensified in the 1680s from pirates as well as new and closer Indian groups allied with the British, leading ultimately to complete destruction of the missions by 1704–5. The mission Indians' dis-satisfaction with Spanish rule intensified as the British threat moved Spain to begin building the stone castillo at St. Augustine in the mid-1670s, in-creasing the demand for Indian labor and foodstuffs to feed the laborers. British-inspired attacks eliminated all the Georgia coast's missions in the 1680s. Many of the Guale and Yamasee living there migrated to Creek coun-try or to South Carolina. The rest, consisting mainly of Guale, relocated to three mission villages on Amelia Island. The Mocama of Guadalquini moved from St. Simons Island to the north side of the St. Johns River just west of Fort George Island, changing the mission's name to Santa Cruz de Guadalquini. In 1685, Utina Province's Santa Catalina de Ahoica was the first of the remaining hinterland missions to be destroyed. The last perished in the first half of the 1690s, leaving only the four Yustaga missions and two Potano missions in western Timucua territory. Creek struck a Chacato mis-sion on the Apalachicola River in 1695.

South Carolina's governor, James Moore, destroyed the remaining coastal missions and St. Augustine itself in 1702 and put its castillo under siege for a time. That same year, hostile Indians attacked Potano's Santa Fé mis-sion and Apalachee's Ocuia. Just prior to Moore's attack on St. Augustine, a Spanish-led 800-man Apalachee force marching toward the Chattahoochee to retaliate against the Creek for the attacks on Santa Fé and Ocuia was routed at a Flint River crossing in an ambush set by a Creek force moving toward Apalachee. Most destructive of all were two attacks the Creek and the English launched in 1704 that destroyed all but three of Apalachee's twelve surviving missions. At the start of the first attack, at least fifty Apalachee warriors went over to the enemy in revolt. Additional Apalachee joined the attackers during ensuing battles. Thirteen hundred Apalachee surrendered, agreeing to leave for South Carolina with a promise that they would not be enslaved. A considerable number who were captured, probably about 1,000, were carried off to Carolina as slaves in what seems to have been the largest slave raid in the South, if not the nation. When the remnant of the Spanish garrison abandoned Apalachee at the end of July 1704, about 400 Apalachee from Ivitachuco under the province's most prestigious chief moved eastward with the soldiers, settling in southern Potano for a short time before continued harassment forced them to move on to the vicinity of St. Augustine. Most surviving inhabitants of the two largest Apalachee missions, San Luis de Talimali and Cupaica, together with the Chacato, migrated to Pensacola and Mobile.

Except for the few who remained at Pensacola, the only mission Indians left in Florida huddled in a few insecure villages under the protective guns of St. Augustine, where disease and continuing raids by Carolinians and their native cohorts steadily reduced their numbers. By 1711, their number had fallen to 401 who lived in seven camps that bore the names of former Guale, Timucua, and Apalachee missions. A native rebellion against the Carolinians in 1715, known as the Yamasee War, removed pressure on Florida's Indians for a time and increased the number of Indians living near St. Augustine. Yamasee, one of the major predator peoples who destroyed the missions, were prominent among the immigrants. The refugees also included Apalachees, who were one of the many native peoples in British territory who participated in the uprising that bears the Yamasee name. By then, the immigrants also included Indians from south Florida who sought to escape English-inspired Creek slave-raiding expeditions that swept as far south as the Keys. By 1717, Florida's governor had reorganized and relocated the 946 natives in ten settlements. Three contained about 366 Yamasee speakers. Three Timucua settlements held about 248 people, about 100 of whom were Mocama. Two missions contained 189 Guale. About 54 Apalachee lived in the one Apalachee-speaking village or scattered through a number of the other settlements. The tenth settlement held 33 Jororo, a Mayaca-speaking south central Florida people missionized in the 1690s.

The rest were natives of other tribes who had not been missionized earlier. Yamasee and Apalachee numbering well over 200 established two villages near the rebuilt Fort St. Mark in Apalachee.

Expansion continued briefly as additional villages were established before 1723. By 1726, sixteen settlements contained 1,011 Indians despite renewal of English-inspired attacks that probably were mainly responsible for reducing the number of Yamasee to 167. But the number of Apalachee grew to 87, probably from immigration from the Creek country. The Guale remained stable at 187, while the Timucua fell to 154. Over the next two years, however, disease and hostilities reduced the population sharply. Decline continued until the British assumed control in 1763. By then few, if any, of Florida's aboriginal peoples remained in their homeland. All of the fewer than 100 Indians living in two villages in the vicinity of St. Augustine chose to depart for Cuba with the Spaniards.

Aside from the introduction of the church at the main village's center and, beside it, the residence of the friar, referred to as a *convento,* and a few Christian symbols such as the cross and bell tower, the missions in Florida do not seem to have altered the appearance of Florida's aboriginal native villages substantially. In contrast to the round or oval native structures, the two European structures, church and convent, were rectangular and put together with spikes and nails. Church walls were constructed of either vertical planks or wattle and daub, and the latter seem to have been usual for the convent. But the roofs of both European structures followed the native thatch pattern.

The missions brought many changes to the lives of Florida's Indians beyond the obvious ones of religious beliefs and practices. Friars sought to "civilize" the natives in the sense of imposing many European mores on them as well as indoctrinating them in the Christian faith. Friars or other Spaniards introduced the Indians to new cultigens, animal husbandry, and new tools and skills. The process began at baptism, at least, with imposition of a Spanish first name and the friars' insistence that Indian males cut their long hair to conform to Spanish usage. In the economic sphere, friars sought to convert Indians from their subsistence economy in which, as a friar phrased it, "they are idle most of the time, the men and the women alike,"[2] to one geared to produce surpluses for export that would enable them to acquire clothing and other goods. Labor itself became an export with introduction of the repartimiento labor system. For most of Florida's missionized Indians, except the Apalachees, the governor imposed that obligation as soon as Indian leaders gave obedience to the king.

The friars banned Indian dances that they considered obscene or that had ties to the Indians' pre-Christian religious practices. Dances that had continued for entire days and nights became shorter. Ultimately, Spaniards banned the Indians' ball game because of its religious associations, violence, and the intervillage hostilities it generated. Christian burial practices supplanted most of those native to the Indians, but archaeologists have found that they continued to bury grave goods with some of the deceased. The Indians' ceremonial wailing for the dead continued for a time at least, possibly because it was practiced by some Europeans.

In many respects, however, Indian society in the mission provinces remained strongly traditional. Leadership positions remained hereditary under a matrilineal system in which rule passed to a deceased chief's nephew (or niece, where female leaders existed) by his eldest sister. Matrilocality, which required that a man live with his wife's family in their village, remained the rule for the ordinary Indian. The council house remained by far the village's most impressive structure. It continued to be built in the traditional way and to serve both as the focus of the community's life and as a place for meeting with Spanish authorities other than the friar. Indians continued to build their houses in their round form, using traditional materials and none of the new iron tools other than the axe. Only in the building of churches and convents did they follow European models and techniques. They continued to use their traditional ceramic vessels to cook, eat, and store food. One distinctive style, known as León-Jefferson Ware, found from Potano westward through Apalachee, reached full development during the mission era. Certain vessel forms, known as Colono-Ware, contain direct copies of European pottery features. It is believed they were made for European rather than for Indian use.

Acculturation, the adapting to or borrowing of traits from another culture, was most intense in religious belief and practice. Over time, a substantial segment of Apalachee and Timucua society appears to have embraced Catholicism sincerely. For Timucua, the best indication is that the friars remained at their posts unharmed during the 1656 revolt. There is strong evidence on the faith of the Apalachee from the French who received the exiles at Mobile. The French noted their demand for the sacraments and stated that, in matters religious, the Apalachee were scarcely distinguishable from Europeans who had been Christians for centuries. Only in the gray area of recourse to the shaman as healer are traditional practices with religious overtones known to have survived until the end of the seventeenth century. For all but some from the older generations in Apalachee, and for everyone

Title page of a dictionary and grammar to the language of the Timucua natives of Florida, compiled by Franciscan missionary Francisco Pareja in 1614.

in western Timucua, the ball game had lost most of its religious overtones by the 1670s.

The Spanish intrusion had its most decisive impact in the material sphere on agriculture in adding many new cultigens and introducing new activities such as raising chickens and hogs, dairy farming, and animal husbandry in general. In contrast to missions in California and elsewhere, chickens, hogs, and cattle belonged to individual Indians or to Indian communities. Disposition of the cattle was controlled by Indian leaders, not the friars, but friars controlled communal plantings of maize, wheat, and other crops in support of the church and feeding of the poor and incapacitated. In Apalachee by 1695, the two keys for the building in which produce was stored were entrusted to the chief and another leading man chosen by the governor's deputy. Export of produce to St. Augustine and Havana increased the area under cultivation and, consequently, the labor performed by ordinary Indians. The degree to which the laborers benefitted, if any, is not known.

For Florida's aboriginal peoples, the coming of the Europeans and adoption of the mission way of life under Spanish auspices were disastrous in the long run. Their population collapse was an inevitable consequence of their encounter with the pathogens of Old World peoples. But in many cases their extinction resulted from preventable human factors: a politically and economically motivated struggle for empire among English, Spanish, and French; the English determination to oust the Spaniards from Florida and eliminate native peoples who had allied with the Spaniards; and the English demand for Indian slaves. Without such human factors, some of the missionized peoples eventually would have acquired immunity to the new diseases and may have survived to the present, as did their Creek neighbors and many southwestern native groups.

Notes

1. Gabriel Díaz Vara Calderón, letter to the queen, 1675 Archivo General de Indias (Seville), Santo Domingo, 151; microfilm furnished by William H. Marquardt. Cf. Lucy L. Wenhold, ed. and trans., *A 17th-Century Letter of Gabriel Díaz Vara Calderón, Bishop of Cuba, Describing the Indians and Indian Missions of Florida* (Washington: Smithsonian Miscellaneous Collections, vol. 95, no. 16, 1936).

2. Fray Francisco Alonso de Jesus, "1630 Memorial of Fray Francisco Alonso de Jesus on Spanish Florida's Missions and Natives," edited and translated by John H. Hann, *The Americas* 50, no. 1 (July 1993):88.

Bibliography

Boyd, Mark F., Hale G. Smith, and John W. Griffin. *Here They Once Stood: The Tragic End of the Apalachee Missions.* Gainesville: University of Florida Press, 1951.

Gannon, Michael V. *The Cross in the Sand: The Early Catholic Church in Florida, 1513–1870.* Rev. ed. Gainesville: University Presses of Florida, 1983.

———. [pseud. Charles W. Spellman]. "The 'Golden Age' of the Florida Missions, 1632–1674." *Catholic Historical Review* 51, no. 3 (October 1965):354–72.

Geiger, Maynard, O.F.M. *The Franciscan Conquest of Florida (1573–1618).* Washington: Catholic University of America, 1937.

Hann, John H. *Apalachee: The Land Between the Rivers.* Gainesville: University Presses of Florida, 1988.

———. "Demographic Patterns and Changes in Mid-Seventeenth-Century Timucua and Apalachee." *Florida Historical Quarterly* 64, no. 4 (April 1986):371–92.

———. *A History of the Timucua Indians and Missions.* Gainesville: University Press of Florida, 1996.

———. "The Indian Village on Apalachee Bay's RíoChachave on the Solana Map of 1683." *Florida Anthropologist* 48, no. 1 (March 1995):61–66.

———. "The Mayaca and Jororo and Missions to Them." In *The Spanish Missions of La Florida,* edited by Bonnie G. McEwan, pp. 111–40. Gainesville: University Press of Florida, 1993.

———. *Missions to the Calusa.* Gainesville: University of Florida Press/Florida Museum of Natural History, 1991.

———. "St. Augustine's Fallout from the Yamasee War." *Florida Historical Quarterly* 68, no. 2 (October 1989):180–200.

———. *Summary Guide to Spanish Florida Missions and Visitas with Churches in the Sixteenth and Seventeenth Centuries.* Washington: Academy of American Franciscan History, 1990 (reprint from *The Americas* 56, no. 4 [April 1990]:417–513, with illustrations added).

———. "Twilight of the Mocamo and Guale Aborigines as Portrayed in the 1695 Spanish Visitation." *Florida Historical Quarterly* 66, no. 1 (July 1987):1–24.

———. "Visitations and Revolts in Florida, 1656–1695." *Florida Archaeology* 7 (1993).

Kessell, John L. *Kiva, Cross, and Crown: The Pecos Indians and New Mexico 1540–1840.* Albuquerque: University of New Mexico Press, 1987 (originally published Washington: National Park Service, U.S. Department of the Interior, 1979).

Lyon, Eugene. *Richer Than We Thought: The Material Culture of Sixteenth-Century St. Augustine.* St. Augustine: St. Augustine Historical Society, 1992.

Oré, Luis Jerónimo de. *The Martyrs of Florida (1513–1616).* Translated by Maynard Geiger. New York: Joseph F. Wagner, 1936.

Vargas Ugarte, Ruben. "The First Jesuit Mission in Florida." In *Historical Records and Studies,* edited by Thomas F. Meehan, 35:59–148. New York: United States Catholic Historical Society, 1935.

Worth, John E. "The Timucuan. Missions of Spanish Florida and the Rebellion of 1656." Ph.D. diss., University of Florida, 1992.

7

Raids, Sieges, and International Wars

DANIEL L. SCHAFER

In the middle years of the seventeenth century, Spain's La Florida colony entered a period of steep decline from which it never recovered. Epidemic diseases, including yellow fever, smallpox, and plague, swept away thousands of Native Americans at the coastal and inland Franciscan mission villages. By 1655, only 26,000 Christian Indians remained at the thirty-eight mission villages. Four years later, a measles epidemic claimed 10,000 more lives. La Florida had become what the historian Amy Bushnell has called a "hollow peninsula" with only two population centers: the provincial capital of St. Augustine situated on the Atlantic coast at the northeast of the peninsula, and the Apalachee province located approximately 180 miles to the west amidst the rich agricultural lands of today's Leon and Jefferson Counties. A vast and mostly deserted core lay between, with a small number of farms and cattle ranches controlled by floridanos (persons of Spanish descent born in Florida) situated near the road from St. Augustine to Apalachee. Corn and other provisions transported from Apalachee by Native Americans subject to the Spanish-imposed labor levy represented a vital food supply for residents of St. Augustine.

Also along the road from Apalachee were strategically located mission villages populated by the survivors of epidemics, hostile attacks by pirates, predatory Indian warriors from La Florida, and after 1670, warfare between English and Spaniards engaged in a contest for empire. By 1690, Guale villages along the Georgia coast and sea islands had been abandoned and the surviving residents relocated to three Mocama missions within fifty miles of St. Augustine. The once numerous Timucua from Potano and along the St. Johns River had also suffered drastic demographic decline and been relocated to mission centers along the road from St. Augustine to Apalachee.

As the demographic decline continued, the annual levy of laborers sent

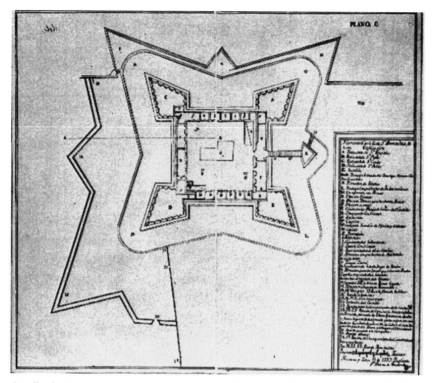

Castillo de San Marcos, St. Augustine, Florida. Courtesy of the National Archives, Kew, England.

to St. Augustine by the local chiefs bore more heavily on the surviving men in the villages. The burden intensified after Jamaica was conquered by English forces in 1655. Fearing an attack on La Florida, Governor Diego de Rebolledo demanded that 500 Apalachee and Timucua warriors be sent to St. Augustine, which led to a Timucua rebellion. By the time it was suppressed, many alienated mission Indians had migrated north of Spanish-controlled zones to join with the Apalachicola and Yamassee, who would later be known as the Lower Creek.

La Florida was victimized by hurricanes, drought, and severe food shortages, as well as raids by Native Americans and attacks by pirates. In 1668, Captain Robert Searles led a band of 100 murderous buccaneers on a midnight raid through the streets of St. Augustine. While Spanish soldiers fled to the woods or cowered in the fort, the raiders plundered houses and churches, killed sixty persons in the streets, and kidnapped women and children for ransom. Alarmed by the escalating violence, the viceroy of New Spain at Mexico City sent additional soldiers to the garrison and authorized funds for a stone fort to protect St. Augustine. Construction began in fall 1672, but the Castillo de San Marcos was not completed until 1695.

Even before construction began, a greater threat to the survival of La Florida occurred approximately 215 miles north of St. Augustine. In April 1670, acting under authorization of a charter granted by Charles II, the True and Absolute Lords and Proprietors of Carolina established a colony of 130 English men and women on the Ashley River, today at Charleston. English colonials from Barbados followed, bringing enslaved Africans with them. By 1690, they had accomplished what the Spanish at La Florida were unable to do in two centuries of colonial rule: establish a permanent and expanding base of settlers with a prospering economy based on cattle, naval stores, cultivation of rice, and exports of deerskins obtained in trade with Native Americans.

The Carolina colonists' interaction with Native Americans had a debilitating impact on Spanish Florida. Seeking to advance beyond their initial coastal settlements, the Carolina leaders took advantage of traditional hostilities between the natives of the region, providing trade goods and firearms to one group of Native Americans and encouraging them to attack another. The Westoes of Savannah River attacked and destroyed the coastal Indians and opened the way for inland expansion of English settlements. By 1680, however, it was the Westoes who were standing in the way. English traders therefore struck alliances with the Apalachicola and Yamassee and encouraged them to attack the Westoes. The enslaved Indians captured during these raids were purchased by the English and put to work on plantations or sold to planters in the Caribbean islands.

These tactics had direct impact on Spanish Florida. Apalachicola and Yamassee armed by English traders attacked the villages of Christian Indians at Franciscan missions among the Guale along the Georgia coast, enslaving captives and forcing survivors to relocate to sites farther south and closer to St. Augustine. Attacks next focused on the Timucua and the Apalachee. Within two decades of their arrival at the Ashley River, Carolina traders had moved west from Charleston and drawn into their trade network the Native Americans located north of Florida and to the west as far as today's central Alabama. They had also formed alliances with Native Americans that posed a serious threat to the continuation of Spanish Florida.

This threat to La Florida overlapped with a challenge from French explorers who were expanding from Quebec through the Great Lakes and down the Mississippi River to the Gulf of Mexico staking territorial claims for future settlements. In 1699, Pierre le Moyne, Sieur d'Iberville, led an expedition from France to establish a colony on the Gulf coast at Pensacola Bay. When he arrived, he discovered that Spaniards were already building a fort in a belated attempt to maintain control of the Gulf and protect Spanish settlements at Mexico. Iberville instead established Fort Maurepas at Biloxi Bay and Fort Mississippi, south of today's New Orleans. His goal was to control the Mississippi River delta and block access to ships from other European nations. From the French colony of Louisiana, traders established partnerships with Chickasaw, Choctaw, and other Native Americans in the vicinity, and proceeded upriver to strike similar partnerships along the numerous rivers feeding into the Mississippi.

With a dynamic French presence to the west at Louisiana and an aggressive and an expanding English colony to the north at Carolina, the residents of Spanish Florida were placed in a precarious position. To strengthen its controls, Spain authorized construction of a stone fort at St. Augustine, the Castillo de San Marcos, and to protect the Apalachee missions and their vital agricultural resources, the Castillo de San Marcos de Apalachee was built in 1680 on the St. Marks River, inland from Apalachee Bay (thirty miles south of Tallahassee in Wakulla County). In 1696, a two-story blockhouse with artillery and a palisade was built at Mission San Luis (in present-day Tallahassee).

A European conflict, the War of Spanish Succession (1701–14), known in the North American colonies as Queen Anne's War, brought devastation to Spanish Florida. Fear that the balance of power would be upset if the thrones of France and Spain merged following the death of Charles II of Spain and his succession by Philip V, the grandson of the king of France, led to a major European war. France and Spain faced off against England, Austria, the Netherlands, and Prussia. In North America, Governor James Moore of Carolina was determined to destroy Spain's Florida colony and follow that with an attack on the French in Louisiana. The first blow was struck in May 1702 by Creek warriors who burned Mission Santa Fe on the road from St. Augustine to Apalachee, and carried off Timucuan captives as slaves. In the failed Spanish counterattack that followed, the Creek killed or captured more than 400 Timucuan and Apalachee auxiliaries of the Spanish.

In November 1702, Governor Moore led a force of 1,200 men, primarily Creek warriors, against the Spanish at St. Augustine. Detachments under Colonel Robert Daniel debarked first at Amelia Island and destroyed the

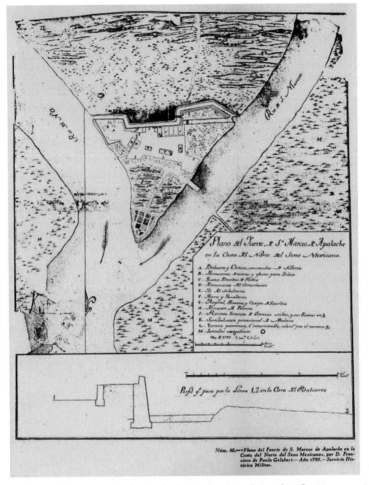

Castillo de San Marcos de Apalachee. The site of this fortification was inland from Apalachee Bay on the St. Marks River. The site can be visited at San Marcos State Park, off State Road 363 in Wakulla County, Florida, 30 miles south of Tallahassee. Courtesy of the National Archives, Kew, England.

missions and villages there. San Juan del Puerto at Fort George Island and Piritiriba, located south of the St. Johns on the west bank of the San Pablo, were destroyed next.

Governor Moore had proceeded by water to St. Augustine Inlet to block entrance to the harbor and join with Colonel Daniel's men, who arrived on November 10 and established headquarters at the south of town near the convent on St. Francis Street. Spanish Governor Joseph de Zúñiga y Zerda had already moved 1,500 town residents, soldiers, refugees, and stores of

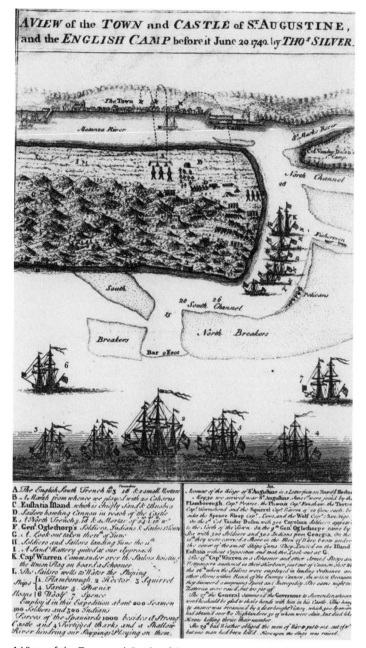

A View of the Town and Castle of St. Augustine, and the English Camp before it, June 20, 1740. General Oglethorpe and the British invaders from Georgia were unable to breach the walls of the Castillo de San Marcos and called off the siege of the Spanish town. By Thomas Silver. Courtesy of the University of Florida Digital Collections, http://ufdc.ufl.edu/UF90000078/00001.

corn inside the Castillo. He also arranged for soldiers to round up a herd of 160 cattle and drive the thundering beasts through the streets of the town. Startled English troops ran for cover as the cattle ran across the drawbridge over the moat. Behind the protective stone walls of the Castillo de San Marcos, the Spaniards waited anxiously, praying for the arrival of a relief force from Havana.

Unable to breach the walls of Castillo de San Marcos, Moore laid down a siege expecting to starve the inhabitants into submission. The Spanish relief force that arrived from Cuba on December 26 trapped the Carolina ships in the harbor and forced Moore to end the siege. His men torched their vessels and ignited a conflagration in the town that destroyed religious and governmental structures and left only twenty houses standing, along with Nuestra Señora de la Soledad, built in 1572, and the hospital attached in 1597, the first hospital in the continental United States. The English invaders marched northward, leaving more charred ruins in their path. At the entrance to the St. Johns they boarded English ships and returned to Charleston in disgrace.

In November 1703, former governor James Moore was offered a chance to redeem his reputation by leading fifty Carolina settlers and 1,000 Lower Creek and Yamassee in an invasion of Apalachee province. A census of thirteen Apalachee missions compiled in 1689 by the bishop of Cuba, Diego Ebelino de Compostela, listed nearly 10,000 residents. Between January and August 1704, the Apalachee, the Spanish friars and soldiers, and floridano ranchers and farmers were swept away in attacks by Moore's Carolina militia and allied Creek and Yamassee warriors. Between January and April 1704, Moore's army swept through Apalachee, destroying villages, killing or enslaving as many as 2,000 Apalachee converts to Christianity, and forcefully persuading between 1,300 and 2,000 Apalachee to follow his army to Charleston to avoid death or enslavement. Only the seven mission villages whose leaders paid ransoms to Moore remained after the invaders departed.

After Creek warriors raided Apalachee again in June and July, only the villages at San Luis, Ivitachuco, and Chacato remained. Spanish authorities in St. Augustine recognized it would be futile to resist further attacks and abandoned the Apalachee missions. A group of 800 Apalachee from San Luis decided to march westward to join the French at Mobile, while many more abandoned the Spaniards and migrated north and west to merge their families into Creek villages along the Apalachicola, Flint, and Chattahoochee Rivers. Patrice de Hinachuba, the leader of Ivitachuco, led his villagers eastward to Potano and established the new settlement of Abosaya near the La Chua cattle ranch. But the Creek raids continued, focused on

Yustaga, Potano, and the ranch at La Chua. The new town of Abosaya was attacked, forcing the survivors to seek safety in small settlements outside the town walls at St. Augustine.

Governor Zúñiga y Zerda ordered other mission villages and stockades rebuilt in the aftermath of the Carolina raids of 1702 and 1704, including at San Francisco Potano and at the La Chua cattle ranch. As a result of hostile Indian raids, all the new villages were destroyed or abandoned soon after they were completed. In *A History of the Timucua Indians and Missions*, John Hann describes an anonymous and undated map of Piritiriba dated circa 1704 that indicates a "four-bastioned fort" with "barracks, living quarters, and warehouses for supplies" was constructed—possibly as early as 1703—to protect two adjoining villages of refugee Guale and Mocama. Apparently, San Juan del Puerto was not rebuilt. Each village at Piritiriba had its own church, but prayers did not protect them from attacks that resulted in the death and capture of 500 Indians.

Governor Córcoles y Martínez estimated that, between 1702 and 1708, more than 10,000 Native Americans perished, yet the Creek and Yamassee attacks continued. Even the Indian villages outside the walls of St. Augustine were attacked. Without the corn and beef formerly supplied by the Guale, Timucua, and Apalachee, St. Augustine residents were dependent on imports by water. Severe shortages and hungry times lay ahead.

In 1715, it was the Carolina colonists who were attacked by Native Americans, this time by a confederation led by Yamassee warriors angered by English encroachment. More than 400 settlers were killed before the English regained control, which prompted several hundred Yamassee to take refuge with the Spanish at St. Augustine. Others who participated in the rebellion migrated to Creek villages along the Apalachicola and Chattahoochee Rivers.

It was to these villages that Lt. Diego Peña and a detachment of Spanish soldiers traveled in 1717 to promote trade opportunities and to encourage the residents to migrate to the abandoned fields formerly tilled by the Apalachee. In support of Lt. Peña's initiatives, the fort at St. Marks was rebuilt to facilitate trade with St. Augustine and Havana. Eventually, Creek migrants began moving into the rolling hills region near today's Tallahassee, but the more aggressive diplomatic and trade initiatives by the English minimized Spanish gains.

Between 1723 and 1728, the English waged persistent war on the Yamassee, relentlessly destroying their villages along the Apalachicola and Chattahoochee Rivers, as well as in Apalachee and near St. Augustine. An epidemic at St. Augustine in 1727 claimed the lives of approximately 500 Yamassee, and more lives were lost due to a raid on Mission Nombre de Dios led by Colonel John Palmer of Charleston in March 1728.

The next major threat to the continuation of Spanish Florida came in 1732 with the establishment of the English colony of Georgia in the disputed territory between Carolina and Florida. In the past, Carolina had claimed that their charter set the southern boundary at the thirty-first parallel, or just north of St. Augustine. Later, Carolina insisted that the border was even farther south, seventy miles beyond St. Augustine at Mosquito Inlet. The 1670 Treaty of Madrid, however, established the boundary much farther north, at the current line between South Carolina and Georgia, but the English colonists refused to comply with the treaty. The construction in 1721 of Fort King George on the Altamaha River was viewed as provocative by the Spaniards, who sent Native American auxiliaries to attack the fort in 1722. The attack was unsuccessful, but the unhealthiness of the site led to abandonment of the fort in 1727.

James Edward Oglethorpe, an original trustee and resident founder of Georgia, advocated aggressive military expansion to protect the British colonies from attacks by the Spanish. Oglethorpe ordered construction of a series of fortifications on the coastal islands, starting at Fort Frederica on St. Simons Island and extending as far south as the St. Johns River. In June 1736, Oglethorpe ordered Fort St. George constructed on Fort George Island, on the north bank of the St. Johns near its merger with the Atlantic. He left a small garrison in place overlooking a Spanish lookout on the opposite (south) bank of the river and returned to St. Simons Island.

Rather than go to war, Spain sought a diplomatic solution. In the meantime, a military engineer and cartographer, Antonio de Arredondo, assessed British strength and inspected Spanish defenses throughout Florida. He was appalled by the tiny palmetto hut that served as a lookout post at the entry to the St. Johns, and by the absence of defense posts farther upriver. Arredondo urged the Council of the Indies to authorize construction of additional forts and to send more ships and sailors and an additional 800 soldiers for the St. Augustine garrison. Under Arredondo's supervision, improvements were made to the earthwork defenses and town walls at St. Augustine, the forts at St. Augustine and St. Marks, and the small wooden blockhouses west of St. Augustine—Fort Picolata on the east and Fort San Francisco de Pupo on the west of the St. Johns River. With the exception of the Castillo de San Marcos, however, Spanish defenses were still woefully inadequate.

James Edward Oglethorpe, governor of Georgia, 1733–42. Oglethorpe led unsuccessful invasions of Spanish Florida in 1740 and 1743. Courtesy of the State Archives of Florida, *Florida Memory*, http://floridamemory.com/items/show/6278.

The weakness of Spain's defensive network in Florida became dramatically evident in 1739, when Britain declared war on Spain in what became known as the War of Jenkins' Ear. The war grew out of trade rivalries in the Americas and was in its early phases fought primarily in the Caribbean and South America. By 1742 it had evolved into a wider European conflict known as the War of Austrian Succession. In North America, the war was largely a conflict between the English at Georgia and the Spanish at Florida.

In January 1740, Oglethorpe sailed down the Inland Passage west of Amelia, Talbot, and Fort George Islands to post British ships at the entrance to the St. Johns and add men to his southern outpost at Fort St. George. He then proceeded upriver (south on the St. Johns) to capture Forts Picolata and Pupo, before returning to Frederica to form an army of Carolina and Georgia regiments and Native American allies. On May 20, the advance force of Oglethorpe's army encamped south of the entry to the St. Johns and marched south toward St. Augustine. The first impediment encountered was Fort San Diego, a wooden stronghold built by the Sanchez and

Plat map, 640 acres north of St. Augustine surveyed for David Yeats, 1770, showing paths that converge at the location of Fort Diego. British invaders from Georgia captured the fort in 1740. Image is from Treasury 77, Records of the Parliamentary Claims Commission, courtesy of the National Archives, Kew, England.

Espinosa families to protect their cattle herds from Creek raids. The two families, allied by marriage, had migrated to Florida from Spain and Cuba after 1670 and established ranches in the Diego Plains. Fort Diego delayed the British advance for less than a day.

Two miles north of St. Augustine, Oglethorpe called a halt outside the walls of Gracia Real de Santa Teresa de Mose, one of the most unique settlements in the North American colonies. Fort Mose was constructed in 1738 by free blacks who had, beginning in 1686, escaped from their owners in Carolina and found refuge and freedom in Spanish Florida. Instructed in the Catholic faith and employed in St. Augustine, the men had enrolled in the militia to serve as scouts and defenders of the northern frontier. The historian Jane Landers has carefully researched the history of Mose and its leader and commander, Francisco Menéndez, an African-born man who had fought alongside Native American warriors against the British during the Yamassee War. Forewarned of the powerful British force approaching St. Augustine, Governor Manuel de Montiano ordered the evacuation of Fort Mose and brought its 100 residents inside the protective walls of the

Castillo de San Marcos. Approximately 2,500 persons were crowded within those walls, short of provisions and hoping for resupply and reinforcement from Cuba.

After inexplicably marching his men back and forth between St. Augustine and the camp south of the St. Johns, Oglethorpe occupied Fort Diego and Fort Mose. His soldiers skirmished with Spanish militia while British ships patrolled offshore to block access to the Matanzas River. In late June, Oglethorpe sent artillery to a camp north of St. Augustine inlet and established a second artillery post on Anastasia Island across from the Castillo de San Marcos. On June 24th, daily bombardments of the fort and town commenced, but the shells fired by Oglethorpe's artillery batteries could not breach the sturdy walls of the Castillo. The walls were constructed of blocks of coquina, a soft and porous sedimentary rock composed of compacted shells and mineral calcite quarried in mines on Anastasia Island. The cannonballs fired by the Georgia artillerists that struck the walls of the Castillo either bounced off or were absorbed by the soft coquina blocks. Consequently, the siege settled into a lengthy stalemate.

On June 25, Governor Montiano ordered a nighttime attack on the Scot Highlanders garrisoned at Fort Mose. Free black militia men played a leading role in the daring recapture of their town, killing or capturing most of the defenders. Oglethorpe foolishly demanded a Spanish surrender, for which he received a curt and immediate refusal. Governor Montiano was encouraged by the victory at Mose and recognized the uplift in morale that it provided for the Spaniards inside the fort, yet he was deeply worried that unless he received a resupply of provisions, he would eventually be forced to either surrender or watch the Spanish defenders die of starvation.

He would not have to make that decision. On July 6, seven Spanish ships arrived at Mosquito Inlet with flour and other provisions that were offloaded to smaller vessels. In daring runs up the Matanzas Inlet through a gauntlet of British fire, the Spanish ships managed to deliver their valuable cargoes to the Castillo. Montiano also received a troop reinforcement that brought the number of soldiers under his command to 1,300. Oglethorpe, although he commanded 2,000 men, acknowledged the invincibility of the Castillo's walls and commanded his troops to begin an orderly withdrawal and return to Georgia. By July 20, the last of the British soldiers and artillery had been withdrawn. Oglethorpe, anticipating a retaliatory attack, began preparing defenses in Georgia.

That attack was delayed almost two years, until July 1742, when Spanish ships landed 400 men from Florida and 1,300 from Cuba at the south end of St. Simon's Island. Marching north toward Frederica through unfamiliar and swampy terrain, the Spanish soldiers suffered serious casualties in an ambush that became known as the Battle of Bloody Marsh. The survivors were reembarked on transports and withdrawn from the area, marking the end of Spanish incursions into the contested territory between Florida and Georgia.

Oglethorpe would make one more effort to drive the Spaniards from Florida. In 1743, he crossed the St. Johns with a force of Georgia rangers and Indian allies, and looted and burned Fort Diego and other Spanish settlements during the advance southward. The goal of the 1743 invasion was not to breach the walls of the Castillo or to capture St. Augustine, but to punish Spaniards and enhance the reputation of an inexperienced and minimally successful military leader.

After the withdrawal of Oglethorpe's army in 1743, Florida experienced two decades without invasions or Indian raids. These were not easy or prosperous times, but the era of Native American rebellions had ended along with the Franciscan missions. Small villages of Indians of several different ethnic identities surrounded the walls of St. Augustine. The few friars who remained in the province were assigned to Nombre de Dios, the free black town of Mose, and the portage village of Tolomato, where the residents still transported cargoes embarked at wharfs in St. Augustine over the land bridge separating the North and San Pablo Rivers, from where they were floated north to the St. Johns. Persistent shortages of provisions and the failure of subsidies from Spain often left Governor Montiano desperately searching for subsistence for the garrison and the town. To fill the need, Montiano implemented an admiralty court and licensed privateers to prey on ships of nations that, until 1848, were still at war with Spain.

Montiano and other pragmatic Florida governors, aware that they were violating Spanish mercantile trade restrictions, also negotiated trade agreements with a British merchant in Charleston, John Gordon, and another in New York, William W. Walton, to provide provisions for the garrison and town residents in times of great need. Charles Hicks, an employee of W. W. Walton and Company of New York, resided in St. Augustine as early as 1735. His apprentice clerk, Jesse Fish, arrived as a teenager and remained in St. Augustine for the next half century.

The Sanchez and Espinosa families survived Creek raids and the Oglethorpe invasions, and by the mid-1740s were reviving their cattle ranches and farm fields in the Diego Plains, twenty miles north of St. Augustine. West of the town, near the St. Johns, the Solana family was doing the same.

With the province at peace, a few Spaniards were able to export oranges to Charleston and to begin exploiting the forests for shipments of lumber and naval stores.

Small numbers of Creek began moving into vacant lands near today's Tallahassee that, prior to the 1704 invasion led by James Moore, had been inhabited for centuries by thousands of Apalachee. Chief Tonaby settled a village of approximately 300 Creek, and a larger village was located nearby at Lake Miccosukee. Farther south, on the west bank of the Suwannee River near the Gulf coast, a village of 300 to 400 Creek led by a chief known as the White King was established in the late 1750s. These newly settled Creek villages benefitted from proximity to trade opportunities at the fort on the St. Marks River, recently renovated and frequented by merchants who traveled to St. Augustine and Havana.

Other Creek migrants came to the Alachua Savanna near the former ranch of La Chua where cattle still grazed wild in the grasslands. Chief Cowkeeper and his brother Long Warrior had moved from the Chattahoochee River in central Georgia circa 1750 to settle Cuscowilla (near present-day Micanopy) with several hundred men, women, and children. The numbers of Creek migrants at Alachua and Apalachee were small at first, and their early settlements may have been seasonal camps where Creek hunters obtained skins to sell to European traders. By 1763, however, the seasonal habitations had become permanent towns. As Brent R. Weisman discusses later in this volume, the migrants were in the process of transforming their identity from Creek to Seminole.

After generations of failing to promote immigration to Florida, Spanish officials finally brought 363 settlers from the Canary Islands to St. Augustine in 1757. They settled on empty land north of the town between the Castillo and Fort Mose. According to the historian Paul E. Hoffman, three hundred more "Isleños" arrived the following year and settled outside the southern wall of the town. The population of Florida was slowly increasing during the years of peace following 1748, still concentrated on the east in the vicinity of St. Augustine, and on the west at Apalachee and near the fort at St. Marks. But the total number was miniscule in comparison to the thousands of indigenous Native Americans the Spaniards under Pedro Menéndez de Aviles had encountered in Florida in 1565.

These promising signs of progress were endangered in January 1762, when Spain once again declared war on England in the final year of the Seven Years' War (1756–63). It had been a massive international conflict fought in Europe and the Americas, even in India and the Philippines. In

North America, it was known as the French and Indian War. Fears of Indian raids originating in Georgia or Carolina were rekindled in St. Augustine, but the significant military operations took place to the north and west of Florida. However, the trade arrangements that Spanish governors had worked out with British colonial merchants in New York and Charleston were suspended. Once again, licenses were issued to captains of privateer vessels, and captured cargoes of vital provisions were unloaded at St. Augustine's wharfs.

The most important event of the Seven Years' War, as far as Spanish residents of Florida were concerned, was the capture of Havana by English troops in August 1762. The war ended only a few months after Havana fell. During peace negotiations, Spanish officials decided that restoration of the rich sugar island of Cuba was more important than retaining Florida. In the Treaty of Paris signed in February 1763, Florida was exchanged for Cuba. The residents of Florida were told that the Crown would provide transportation to new homes in Cuba for colonists who departed St. Augustine within thirteen months. With the exception of three families, all the Spanish residents of St. Augustine decided to say good-bye to Florida. Another eighty families, possibly the last remnants of the Calusa Indians from southwest Florida who had resettled near the fort at St. Marks, were transported to Veracruz. The Creek who had recently migrated to Apalachee and the lower Suwannee remained. Englishmen who began arriving in July 1763 were already calling them "cimmarones," for "runaways," or people who moved from their traditional villages to become Seminoles in Florida.

In *The Oldest City: St. Augustine, Saga of Survival*, St. Augustine native Jean Parker Waterbury described the "transfer of an entire population out of Florida to Cuba, some three thousand men, women and children, soldiers, slaves, Indians and priests, Germans and Catalans, floridanos, Canary Islanders, free blacks, the mix which made up St. Augustine for so many decades." Thirteen hundred Spaniards left in August 1763; the others followed four months later. Only the floridano families of Francisco Xavier Sanchez, Manuel Solana, and Luciano de Herrera remained, along with a transplant from New York named Jesse Fish whose roots in Florida reached back to the 1730s. He would find kindred spirits among the incoming English colonials from Georgia and South Carolina, and the Scots, English, and Irish that moved their families into the houses of the old Spanish city.

Bibliography

Arnade, Charles W. "Raids, Sieges, and International Wars." In *The New History of Florida*, edited by Michael Gannon. Gainesville: University Press of Florida, 1996.

Ashley, Keith H. "Straddling the Georgia-Florida State Line: Ceramic Chronology of the St. Marys Region AD 1400–1700)." In *From Santa Elena to St. Augustine: Indigenous Ceramic Variability (A.D. 1400–1700)*, edited by Kathleen Deagan and David Hurst, 125–99. New York: American Museum of Natural History, 2009.

Bushnell, Amy. *The King's Coffer: Proprietors of the Spanish Florida Treasury, 1565–1702*. Gainesville: University Presses of Florida, 1981.

———. "The Noble and Loyal City, 1565–1668." In *The Oldest City: St. Augustine, Saga of Survival*, edited by Jean Parker Waterbury. St. Augustine Historical Society, 1983.

———. "Patricio de Hinachuba: Defender of the Word of God, the Crown of the King, and the Little Children of Ivitachuco." *American Indian Culture and Research Journal* 3, no. 3 (1979).

———. "Republic of Spaniards, Republic of Indians." In *The New History of Florida*, edited by Michael Gannon. Gainesville: University Press of Florida, 1996.

Coker, William S. "Pensacola, 1686–1763." In *The New History of Florida*, edited by Michael Gannon. Gainesville: University Press of Florida, 1996.

Deagan, Kathleen, and Darcie MacMahon. *Fort Mose: Colonial America's Black Fortress of Freedom*. Gainesville: University Press of Florida, 1995.

Edgar, Walter B. *South Carolina: A History*. Columbia: University of South Carolina Press, 1998.

Hann, John H. *Apalachee: The Land between the Rivers*. Gainesville: University Presses of Florida, 1988.

———. *A History of the Timucua Indians and Missions*. Gainesville: University Press of Florida, 1996.

Hann, John H., and Bonnie G. McEwan. *The Apalachee Indians and Mission San Luis*. Gainesville: University Press of Florida, 1998.

Hoffman, Paul E. *Florida's Frontiers*. Bloomington: Indiana University Press, 2002.

Landers, Jane. *Atlantic Creoles in the Age of Revolutions*. Cambridge: Harvard University Press, 2010.

———. "Fort Mose. Gracia Real de Santa Teresa de Mose: A Free Black Town in Spanish Colonial Florida." *American Historical Review* 95, no. 1 (February 1990):9–30.

Mahon, John K., and Brent R. Weisman. "Florida's Seminole and Miccosukee Peoples." In *The New History of Florida*, edited by Michael Gannon, 183–206. Gainesville: University Press of Florida, 1996.

Waterbury, Jean Parker. "The Castillo Years, 1668–1763." In *The Oldest City: St. Augustine, Saga of Survival*, edited by Waterbury. St. Augustine Historical Society, 1983.

Worth, John E. *The Timucuan Chiefdoms of Spanish Florida*. 2 vols. Gainesville: University Press of Florida, 1998.

8

Pensacola, 1686–1763

WILLIAM S. COKER

The Sieur de La Salle's 1685 voyage to the Texas coast created near-panic among the Spanish officials in New Spain (México). It also prompted Spain to plant a colony on the northern Gulf coast, although some years passed before it was done.

Eleven expeditions by land and by sea searched for the La Salle colony. The first of the sea expeditions, that of Juan Enríquez Barroto and Antonio Romero in 1686, examined the Bahía Santa María Filipina, the site of the Luna colony of 1559–61. The pilot, Ensign Juan Jordán de Reina, called the bay "the best that I have ever seen in my life." He also noted that the Indians there referred to the bay as Panzacola, a Choctaw word that means "long haired people," because the men and women both wore their hair long.

This was not the earliest reference to Panzacola, also spelled Pansacola. A 1657 report listed Pansacola as a satellite village of San Juan de Aspalaga in the Apalachee area and the name of its cacique as Manuel. Pansacola was also a common surname there. Interestingly, the natives who occupied the Pansacola village in 1657 were Apalachee. It is believed that some Pansacola were in that area at a much earlier period. There were also some Panzacola in the Choctawhatchee and Mobile areas at a later date. But those met by Jordán de Reina in 1686 were a separate tribe. Seven years later, in 1693, Laureano de Torres y Ayala visited Pensacola Bay and found the Panzacola village abandoned. He reported that these natives had been exterminated by their mortal enemies, the Mobila. About 1725, some forty Panzacola and Biloxi were living on the Pearl River, but whether they were survivors from the Pensacola Bay village is unknown. Little is known about the Panzacola natives after 1725.

Jordán de Reina's glowing report of the Bahía de Panzacola prompted officials to recommend a settlement there to prevent the French from occupying the bay. The viceroy sent Captain Andrés de Pez, one of the advocates of the Panzacola site, to Spain to obtain permission and support for such a settlement. Because of Panzacola's superior harbor, Pez recommended abandoning San Agustin de la Florida (St. Augustine) and making Panzacola the capital of La Florida. For only half of the money spent on St. Augustine, 48,000 pesos annually, he stated, Spain could maintain a fort at Pensacola and have an excellent harbor to go with it. In addition, the Indians at Pensacola (the English spelling) were ready to be converted to Christianity.

The Council of War in Madrid disapproved Pez's plan, but Carlos II, king of Spain, ordered that Panzacola be settled without abandoning St. Augustine. The council acquiesced but directed that first a scientific survey be made of Pensacola Bay.

The viceroy sent two expeditions to Pensacola Bay in 1693. The first, by sea, was headed by Admiral Pez, accompanied by Dr. Carlos de Sigüenza y Góngora, a noted retired professor from the University of México, and Captain Jordán de Reina. They rechristened the bay Bahía de Santa María de Galve, for the Virgin Mary and the viceroy, the Conde de Galve. The only site still bearing a name given it in 1693 is Punta de Sigüenza (Point Sigüenza), the western end of Santa Rosa Island. After their survey of the bay, Sigüenza joined Pez as one of the staunchest supporters of a settlement there.

Laureano de Torres y Ayala, governor-to-be of St. Augustine, commanded a land expedition that arrived at Pensacola Bay on 2 July 1693. His report indicated that Pensacola was a good port that could easily be fortified but that it lacked building stone.

As a result of these expeditions, a royal order issued on 13 July 1694 directed that Pensacola Bay be occupied and fortified without delay. The initial force was to come from México, but because of a lack of troops and money in México, and the fact that Spain was involved in King William's War (1689–97), nothing was done. There matters rested until 1698.

In that year, two events pushed the Spaniards to occupy Pensacola Bay. Reports indicated that a French expedition led by the Sieur d'Iberville was preparing to sail for Pensacola Bay. The French had been spurred to action by the plans of Dr. Daniel Coxe of London, who hoped to establish a large settlement of exiled French Huguenots in his province of Carolana

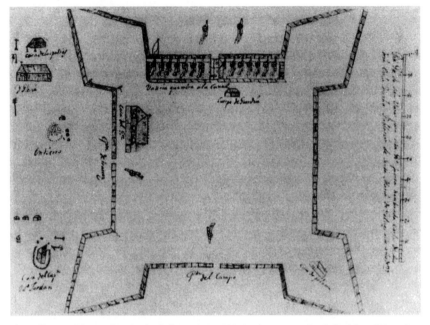

The village of Santa María de Galve, 1698–1722, is shown to the left side of Fort San Carlos de Austria. From top to bottom at left are the rectory, church, cemetery, seven cabins, and the residence of Captain Juan Jordán [de Reina]. The governor's residence was inside the fort. The first-known European settlement on the Barrancas coloradas, or Red Cliffs, the village and fort were captured by the French from Mobile and Dauphin Island in 1719 and then abandoned after the Spaniards returned to the site in 1722. Electing to move to Santa Rosa Island, the Spaniards would not occupy the cliffs again until the 1790s.

(Florida). The Gulf of Mexico was his objective. Spain ordered the viceroy in México to occupy Pensacola Bay without delay. Captain Jordán de Reina, who was in Spain at the time, left immediately for Havana to secure the necessary troops and supplies and sail for Pensacola Bay.

Jordán de Reina reached Pensacola Bay on 17 November 1698 with two ships and sixty soldiers. Four days later, Andrés de Arriola, the appointed governor, who had visited Pensacola Bay in 1695, arrived from Veracruz with three ships and 357 persons. Captain Jaime Franck, an Austrian, was the military engineer. Franck selected a site for the fort near the Barranca de Santo Tomé, which overlooked the entrance to the harbor, and began to build. He named the fort San Carlos de Austria, for thirteen-year-old Charles of Austria, later Charles VI of the Holy Roman Empire. Built of pine logs, each side of the planned fort measured 275 feet with a bastion on each corner. Immediate construction was restricted to building the front wall facing the harbor entrance, and there sixteen cannon were mounted to discourage any foreign ships from entering the bay. Neither Arriola nor Franck liked Pensacola, and both wanted to leave as soon as possible.

The situation at Pensacola was far from good. Many of the troops and workers had been released from jails in México and were not desirable settlers. Forty of the criminals deserted soon after their arrival, but most were recaptured. The camp split into factions, and stealing was common. On 4 January 1699, a fire caused by some careless gamblers destroyed a number of buildings, including the main storehouse for provisions, and the garrison there faced the possibility of starvation.

To add to the Spaniards' woes, the anticipated French squadron arrived on 26 January. The commander of the fleet, the marquis de Chasteaumorant, informed Arriola that they were only in search of some Canadian adventurers. But Arriola was not deceived; he was sure that it was d'Iberville's expedition and that it intended to establish a base on the Gulf coast. Arriola refused permission to enter the harbor, and the French sailed westward. Soon after they departed, Arriola left for México to warn the viceroy about the French and to secure supplies and reinforcements.

Upon arriving at Veracruz, Arriola learned that because the Scots were planning a colony at Darién (Panama) and the Spaniards were preparing

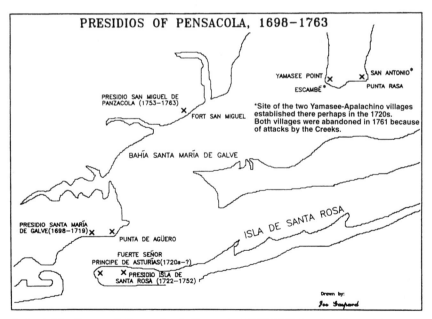

A plan of the Pensacola Bay region in the period 1698–1763 showing the various presidios. Drawn by Joe Gaspard.

an expedition to oust them, no help could be provided him. Reports also reached México that Englishmen were planning a settlement near Pensacola. Fortunately, the Scottish threat was soon over, and Arriola finally secured 100 men from Mexican slums and prisons whom he carried to Pensacola to assist him in driving both the French and English from the Gulf coast.

Arriola departed Pensacola on 4 March 1700 to accomplish his mission. The so-called Englishmen turned out to be Frenchmen whom Arriola captured and carried to the French at Fort Maurepas (Ocean Springs, Mississippi). The Spaniards were received with great hospitality. Arriola warned, however, that the French fort was in Spanish territory and must be abandoned. The French countered that they had been ordered by their king to establish the fort on the Gulf coast to prevent the English from doing so and that they could not leave without orders from France. Arriola decided to give up his plans to oust the French and sailed for Pensacola. A hurricane hit en route, and the Spaniards lost all their ships but one. After much suffering, the survivors returned to Fort Maurepas, where, again, they were well treated by the French, who returned them to Pensacola.

The Pensacola garrison suffered constantly from a lack of supplies. Efforts to grow foodstuffs failed in the sandy soil. The garrison engaged in raising sheep and, much later, cattle. An abundant supply of large pine trees enabled them to produce ships' masts for export, but that industry never made Pensacola self-sufficient and the settlement was forced to rely heavily upon outside sources for its survival.

France and Spain had a basic difference in their reasons for being on the northern Gulf coast. The Spaniards came to prevent the French from settling there. The French came to make money through trade with the Indians and Spaniards. They mistakenly thought they were near the silver mines of northern México, but they also hoped to discover rich mineral deposits in the Mississippi Valley. The one aim Spain and France had in common was to prevent the English from settling on the Gulf coast.

When the French sold goods at Pensacola, they usually received cash because the Spaniards were most often paid in specie when the situado, or annual subsidy, was received. Unfortunately, it did not always arrive on time, and even when it did, it usually contained only a fraction of the money due the presidio.

The relationship between Spain and France over their Gulf coast settlements during the early years reflected their differing goals. In 1701, France requested that Spain cede Pensacola to them. In turn, Spain wanted French

Louisiana to be placed under the jurisdiction of the viceroy of New Spain. Neither side succeeded in these diplomatic efforts, although the French continued to want Pensacola. Later, they argued over the boundary between Florida and Louisiana: The Spaniards claimed jurisdiction to the east bank of Mobile Bay, while the French held out for the Perdido River and Bay as the boundary. This dispute went on for years, but Spain finally, and not willingly, recognized the Perdido as the boundary.

The death of Carlos II on 1 November 1700 soon brought on the War of the Spanish Succession (Queen Anne's War in the colonies). Carlos II had no children. Before he died, and after much diplomatic maneuvering, he had designated Philip of Anjou, grandson of Louis XIV, as his heir. Other European countries including England, not wanting to see France and Spain united under one crown, formed the Grand Alliance, which declared war on 4 May 1702. These events were to have a direct bearing on Spanish Pensacola and on Mobile, where by 1702 the French had built Fort St. Louis de La Mobile at the mouth of the Dog River. The French at Mobile were much better supplied than were the Spaniards, and, fortunately for the Spaniards, they were generous with what they had. The Spanish garrison would have been forced to abandon Pensacola, or to surrender it to the English, if it had not been for supplies and military support furnished by the French.

After their military success in the Apalachee area in 1704, the English and their Indian allies tried several times—unsuccessfully—to capture the Pensacola presidio. They destroyed the fort in the winter of 1704–5, but the French came to the Spaniards' rescue. Between 1707 and 1713, the Anglo-allied Indians, usually led by a few Englishmen, laid siege to Pensacola on several occasions, but help from Mobile forced them to retire. Almost miraculously, the war ended with Pensacola still in Spanish hands.

Some but not much information is available on the priests who served the presidio during its early years. Three priests arrived with Arriola in 1698: Fathers Rodrigo de la Barreda, Alfonso Ximénez de Cisneros, and Miguel Gómez Alvarez. In 1702, Arriola purchased a house from one of the soldiers and converted it into a hospital, Nuestra Señora de las Angustias (Our Lady of Afflictions). Fray Joseph de Salazar, a friar-surgeon, served in this hospital as did several others of the Order of San Juan de Dios. About 1709, the hospital moved inside the fort; and Fray Juan de Chavarria and Fray Felipe de Orbalaes y Abreo served as medico-friars there, but they were gone by 1713. Some gossip about several of the presidio's priests, along with some information about Pensacola's population, was recorded by Father François Le Maire, a visiting priest from Mobile.

Le Maire arrived in Pensacola in 1712 and stayed as acting pastor for three years. He came, he wrote, because two priests had been murdered there in just punishment for the wicked life they led. Nothing more is known about this incident unless it is in some way related to the murder of one priest and the capture of another by enemy Indians in 1711. But Le Maire had more to say about Pensacola.

The fort there, he wrote, was a "land galley," garrisoned by 250 soldiers, who were well known by the Indians for their cowardice. He classified the civil population as "scum" who had escaped torture or execution in México by being sent to Pensacola. These residents, Le Maire observed, were his "fine parishioners." Despite his caustic comments about Pensacola's citizens, Le Maire was an outstanding cartographer, whose significance in North American mapmaking has only recently been recognized. His map of 1713 is of special interest because of the canal or channel shown on Santa Rosa Island.

The period of peace for Pensacola lasted only from the end of Queen Anne's War in 1713 to the outbreak of the War of the Quadruple Alliance in 1718. Cooperation between Pensacola and Mobile was not as good as it had been during the war years. The French wanted to sell merchandise in Pensacola, but Spain opposed the practice. The result was an extensive contraband trade which was estimated, by 1717, at 12,000 pesos a year. Even so, the French grumbled that they made little money from the Spaniards.

England, Holland, Austria, and France formed the Quadruple Alliance in 1718 to check the ambitions of Philip V of Spain. France declared war on Spain on 9 January 1719. Two days previously, the Company of the Indies had ordered the Sieur de Bienville, the governor of Louisiana, to take possession of Pensacola. On 14 May, the French captured the recently built battery on Point Sigüenza, then crossed the channel to Fort San Carlos de Austria and engaged in a brief cannonade with the fort. Governor Juan Pedro Matamoros de Isla, unaware that France and Spain were at war, quickly surrendered.

The French took their Spanish prisoners to Cuba, where they planned to leave them. But when they reached Havana, its commander, Captain General Gregorio Guazo Calderón, refused to recognize the French flag of truce on the grounds that the French had attacked Pensacola without proper warning. The Spaniards prepared to recapture Pensacola, and Admiral Alfonso Carrascosa de la Torre, commander of a Spanish fleet of twelve ships and 1,800 men, reached Pensacola on 6 August. When the Spaniards landed, about ninety French soldiers (the numbers vary) deserted to join them. The French officer in charge at the site, the Sieur de Châteaugué, Bien-ville's brother, still had about 200 soldiers under his command, but they put up such a feeble defense he had no choice but to surrender. The Frenchmen were sent to Cuba for imprisonment in Havana's notorious Moro Castle.

When word reached Mobile that the Spanish fleet was at Pensacola, French troops accompanied by several bands of Indians rushed there but arrived too late. The Chevalier de Noyan, who commanded one of the French-Indian forces, talked with Matamoros de Isla and learned that the next Spanish objective was Mobile and Dauphin Island. Noyan quickly re-turned to Mobile, and the French prepared to defend the area.

Part of the Spanish fleet led by Captain Antonio de Mendieta quickly set sail for Dauphin Island. After twelve days and nights of frustrating efforts to capture Dauphin Island, and without the arrival of expected assistance from México, the Spaniards finally gave up and departed Mobile Bay on 25 August.

In early September, the French made plans to recapture Pensacola. Bien-ville led a force of 400 Indians overland, while the recently arrived French fleet under the command of Admiral Desnos de Champeslin left Mobile and reached Pensacola on the sixteenth. Pensacola was well defended because the Spanish *flota* from Havana was still there, but the naval battle that en-sued lasted only an hour before the Spaniards gave up. The reinforced Span-ish battery at Point Sigüenza put up a stout defense but ran out of ammuni-tion and surrendered. Matamoros de Isla at Fort San Carlos de Austria had planned a strong defense, but fear of Bienville's Indian warriors persuaded him to give up without a fight.

The French sent 625 privateersmen and noncombatants back to Havana in exchange for the French soldiers under Châteaugué. The soldiers and the officers, including Matamoros de Isla, were taken as prisoners to Brest, in France. When the Spaniards departed, the French permitted the Indians to plunder the Spanish presidio. Forty-seven of the Frenchmen who had surrendered to the Spaniards in August were court-martialed. Twelve were hanged, the others were sentenced to forced labor. Twelve French soldiers and eight Indians were left at Pensacola under the command of the Sieur Delisle with orders to give token opposition if the Spaniards returned. He was then to destroy what was left of the fort and retreat to Mobile.

A long-awaited Spanish fleet from Veracruz, commanded by Admiral Francisco de Cornejo, finally sailed for Pensacola but went instead to St. Joseph's Bay. There Cornejo was warned that Champeslin and his ships were still at Pensacola. Fearful that he might not succeed in an attack upon the

French, Cornejo went to Havana to await reinforcements. Plans to recapture Pensacola continued, but nothing was actually done. By early 1720, peace overtures were under way in Europe.

France planned to keep Pensacola under any circumstances, while Spain demanded its return. For nearly a year they negotiated an end to the war. Finally, France recognized that it would be impossible to obtain Spanish cooperation unless Pensacola was restored to Spain, so, in the treaty of 27 March 1721, France gave up its claim.

Bienville received orders on 6 April 1722 to return Pensacola to Spain. Lieutenant Colonel Alejandro Wauchope, the Spanish governor-to-be of the Pensacola presidio, visited Mobile in June. He carried instructions for the French to return Pensacola and all of the armament and supplies that were there in 1719, but Bienville could not comply with the Spanish demands: The Indians had destroyed virtually everything in the presidio except some cannon, which were buried in the sand.

After some delay, Wauchope reached Pensacola with three ships and an infantry company. Wauchope (also written Wauchop) was a Scotsman who had served in Spain's Irish Brigade. He received possession of the site from Lieutenant Jean Baptiste Rebue (also Reboul) on 26 November. All that remained was one dilapidated cabin, a bake oven, and a lidless cistern.

Wauchope's orders called for a canal to be dug across Santa Rosa Island to lower the water level in Pensacola Bay to prevent large enemy ships of war from entering the harbor. An engineer, Don José de Berbegal, accompanied Wauchope to supervise the project. If it proved to be an impractical plan, they were to move the presidio to Santa Rosa Island. The projected fort to be built on Point Sigüenza was to be manned by 150 soldiers of infantry and artillery but supplemented by the garrison from St. Joseph. In February 1723, Captain Pedro Primo de Rivera and men from St. Joseph's Bay were brought to Pensacola. By that date considerable progress had been made in building the new Presidio Isla de Santa Rosa/Punta de Sigüenza about three-quarters of a mile east of Point Sigüenza. The canal across the island was not attempted.

The new presidio consisted of a church, warehouse, powder magazine, quarters for the officers, barracks for the soldiers, twenty-four small buildings for the workmen, convicts, and others, a bake oven, a house for the governor, and a look-out tower sixty feet high.

But for the Spaniards, troubles in Pensacola were far from over. Wauchope had the same basic problem that his predecessors confronted: Supplies for the garrison were uniformly inadequate and late in arriving. Once more, Pensacola turned to its French neighbors for help. Bienville complied with Wauchope's plea for assistance and sent supplies from New Orleans to Pensacola via Mobile. In spite of this help, Wauchope intended to observe royal orders that directed that all contraband French goods arriving for sale at Pensacola were to be burned and those involved punished.

In 1724, Wauchope complied strictly with these orders when a Madame Olivier and others from Mobile visited Pensacola. The madame, it seems, came to visit friends, while her companions brought some goods to sell. The Spaniards seized and burned the boats including the merchandise and put all the Frenchmen except Madame Olivier and her daughter in irons. This was only one of several similar incidents.

If contraband trade was not enough, hostile Indians presented the Spaniards with additional trouble. An attack upon Pensacola by the pro-English Talapoosa in 1727 may well have spelled disaster for the Spaniards had it not been for the Sieur de Perier, governor of Louisiana, who came to the rescue. He warned the Talapoosa that, if they did not cease their attack upon the Spanish presidio, he would turn loose a large force of Choctaw that would destroy them. As a result, the Talapoosa lifted the siege and retreated from Pensacola.

Illegal trade between the French and Spaniards could not be prevented, despite the best efforts of officers like Wauchope. In 1738, the Spanish secretary of state wrote the viceroy of New Spain that he should take action against the commandant and officers at Pensacola unless they stopped trading with the French. Such warnings had little effect, but one policy did affect this trade. In 1743, Louisiana officials forbade French merchants at Mobile and New Orleans to carry merchandise to Pensacola because the Spaniards had not paid their outstanding debts. The Spaniards were thus forced to go to New Orleans for their goods and to pay cash for them.

The year 1743 was important to Pensacola for reasons other than the trade imbroglio. An artist's sketch of the Santa Rosa Island presidio and orders for a report on the remote outpost would be significant in the history of Pensacola.

Dominic Serres, a Frenchman serving on a trading ship that visited Pensacola in 1743, made the sketch of the presidio. He later became a seascape painter in London. When the British learned that Florida was to be traded to Great Britain in 1763, Serres's drawing was published in William Roberts's *Natural History of Florida* (London, 1763). Several of the buildings are identified in the sketch, including the octagon-shaped church. This drawing is the only existing representation of the island presidio.

On 15 April, the viceroy in Mexico City directed Field Marshal Pedro de Rivera y Villalón to prepare a report on the Pensacola presidio. Rivera had made an extended inspection of the presidios west of Louisiana some years earlier, which had had a strong impact on those fortifications.

In the preparation of his Pensacola study he did not visit the site but relied for his observations on the letters and recommendations of men who had served there. In his report, dated 29 May 1744, Rivera briefly, and with some errors, traced the history of Pensacola's presidios and the ebb and flow of the three-way struggle for Florida among France, Great Britain, and Spain. He noted that the violent storms that had virtually destroyed the presidio on several occasions were an ever-present danger. He also recognized that, in the event of war, the presidio would easily fall prey to an attacking force but that it would cost thousands of pesos to build a more suitable fort, which would then require more manpower. In spite of its problems, Rivera recommended retaining Pensacola but with a reduction in the size of the garrison. He did not have a recommendation on whether the presidio should remain on the island or be moved back to the mainland.

The only part of Rivera's report that seems to have been implemented was the reduction in manpower. In 1750, two companies of infantry were stationed there, only sixty-two men with thirty-six fit for duty. The labor battalion had twenty-four men.

Sometime in the 1740s the Spaniards built a small blockhouse on the mainland which they named Fort San Miguel. Its purpose and that of the small detachment of soldiers stationed there was to help protect the Yamasee-Apalachino Indians living nearby from attacks by British-allied Indians. Located in present-day downtown Pensacola, the little fort was soon to be the site of Pensacola's third presidio.

On 3 November 1752, a hurricane struck Santa Rosa Island. It destroyed all of the buildings except a storehouse and the hospital. Nearly three years later, a fort built of stakes, a warehouse for supplies, and another for gunpowder were located on the site of the old presidio. Some distance to the west were the church, hospital, commandant's quarters, and a camp for the garrison. In August 1755, the buildings were reported to be deteriorating.

The following summer, the Marqués de las Amarillas, the viceroy of New Spain, ordered that the presidio be relocated to the site of Fort San Miguel on the mainland and that it be named the Presidio San Miguel de las Amarillas. A royal order of October 1757 changed the name to the Presidio San Miguel de Panzacola. Although the area had long been familiarly known as Panzacola, it was now officially so recognized. The new presidio was to be

In 1743, a Frenchman, Dominic Serres, serving as a seaman on a Spanish merchant ship, made a drawing of the presidio on Santa Rosa Island, the only illustration of the presidio that exists. The view is from the interior of the bay looking south. Notable among the buildings shown is an octagon-shaped church, the first such building in Pensacola's history. Serres later became famous as a seascape painter for King George III of England.

manned by 200 soldiers, although it would be some time before that many were in place.

A new commandant, Colonel Miguel Román de Castilla y Lugo, reached Pensacola in early 1757. En route from Veracruz, he had been shipwrecked on Massacre (Dauphin) Island and had lost most of the supplies and some of the troops he was bringing to Pensacola. The soldiers who survived increased the garrison to about 150 men. By August 1757, that number had grown to 180. Still, the new location was in no condition to defend itself in the event of Indian hostilities, which were expected any day. Román de Castilla quickly set about building a new stockade and establishing other defensive measures for the presidio.

The walls of the new stockade, built of vertical pointed stakes, were soon completed except for the one facing the water. The walls eventually measured 365 by 700 feet. Within the stockade were the government house, a church, warehouses, barracks, bake ovens, and a brick house for the governor. Outside the stockade, seven or eight paces distant, was a single line of dwellings for the civilians, officers, and married soldiers.

Except for periodic scares, Pensacola escaped attacks by hostile Indians for several years after Román de Castilla arrived, despite the fact that the French and Indian War swept the hinterland. During that time the number of soldiers increased to 224, including two infantry companies and one of light artillery. Even supplies and provisions arrived more frequently. By the summer of 1760, however, conditions began to deteriorate.

In June, fear of an attack by unfriendly Indians prompted the governor to clear the area around the stockade, destroying the houses and moving the occupants into the fort. If the Indian menace was not enough, in August a hurricane destroyed half of the stockade and blew the roofs off the houses. The Spaniards were unable to secure new cypress bark, so Pensacola's houses went through the winter of 1760–61 without roofs.

The year 1761 was more trying. In February, the Alibama Indians attacked the Spanish Indian village of Punta Rasa on Garçon Point, killing several soldiers and resident Indians. Such attacks continued periodically, and the situation became so alarming that, in May, Román de Castilla moved the friendly Yamasee-Apalachino Indians from the villages on Garçon Point into the stockade. In June, the captain-general of Cuba dispatched two infantry companies of *pardos* (mulattoes) commanded by Captain Vizente Manuel de Zéspedes to Pensacola. In turn, some of the women from Pensacola went to Havana, but about 200 women and children remained. For the most part, the residents were confined to the stockade, although cavalrymen did escort them to the nearby creek for water.

Again, the French came to the rescue. In September, the governor of Louisiana, Chevalier de Kerlerec, sent a representative, M. Baudin, to help establish peace between the Indians and the Spaniards. Baudin succeeded, and the peace accord was signed on 14 September 1761. The Indians agreed to cease their attacks, and arrangements were made for an exchange of prisoners.

The question of why the French were usually successful in such negotiations has a simple answer: They carried on an extensive trade with the Indians, while the Spaniards did not. The French traded guns and provisions for deerskins and other furs, and if they stopped this exchange, the Indians, heavily dependent upon such trade, would suffer. Thus the French exercised great influence among the natives of the area. But for Spanish Governor Román de Castilla, the French solution of the Indian problem came too late.

By the summer of 1761, officials in New Spain replaced the Pensacola governor with an officer who was an experienced Indian fighter, Colonel Diego Ortiz Parrilla. Although opposed to his new assignment, he assumed command on 21 October. The new governor was appalled at the terrible condition of the presidio. He accused Román de Castilla and some of the other officers of gross mismanagement. He also believed Román de Castilla to be involved in illicit trade, which seemed to be confirmed when a British ship belonging to William Walton & Co. arrived later that year. In addition, Román de Castilla and some of the officers owned and operated stores in the stockade which charged exorbitant prices for the goods sold. But the official residencia, the investigation into the former governor's conduct in office, was still not complete by May 1762, when Román de Castilla left Pensacola.

For his part, Ortiz Parrilla spent the next year and more rebuilding the presidio and preparing its defenses in the event that the French and Indian War should again reach Pensacola. Spain finally entered the war in 1762 as an ally of France. As a result, France ceded Louisiana west of the Mississippi River including the Isle of Orleans, to Spain. But Spain quickly lost Havana to the British. When the war ended in February 1763, Spain exchanged La Florida for Havana. Thus Pensacola became a British possession.

In June 1763, a British entrepreneur, James Noble, arrived at Pensacola. He quickly purchased a number of town lots from the departing Spaniards. He also bought all of the lands claimed by the Yamasee-Apalachinos, probably a million or more acres, for $100,000. Later, this purchase from the Indians was disallowed for a lack of proof of his claim.

Finally, on 6 August 1763, British Lieutenant Colonel Augustin Prevost and accompanying troops reached Pensacola. He officially accepted its transfer to Great Britain from Spanish Colonel Ortiz Parrilla. All of the Spaniards, with one exception, and all of the Yamasee-Apalachinos left for Havana and Veracruz in early September. The British were happy with the strategic location that they had acquired on the Gulf coast, but they were sorely disappointed with its ruinous condition.

What had it cost the Spaniards to maintain Pensacola's presidios from 1698 to 1763? Over 4.5 million pesos:

Presidio Santa Maria de Galve (1698–1719)	971,763 pesos
War of the Quadruple Alliance (1719–22)	1,070,284 pesos
Presidio Isla de Santa Rosa (1722–52)	572,505 pesos
Presidio San Miguel de Panzacola (1753–63)	435,826 pesos
Other expenses charged the presidios	1,515,442 pesos
Total	**4,565,820 pesos**

Excluding expenses for the war of 1719–22, the cost was divided into salaries, 45.9 percent; provisions, 38.9 percent; fortifications, 4.7 percent; materiél, 9.5 percent; other, 1.0 percent.

Spain had accomplished only half of its original objective in occupying Pensacola. With the assistance of the French, it had prevented the British

This British plan of the harbor and settlement of Pensacola was made in the year 1763, when Great Britain assumed rule over Florida. It contains a number of inaccuracies.

from establishing a base on the Gulf of Mexico for sixty-five years. But it had not accomplished its other major purpose, the ouster of France from Louisiana. The British victories accomplished that ouster, but they also cost Spain Pensacola and all of La Florida.

Bibliography

Coker, William S. "The Financial History of Pensacola's Spanish Presidios, 1698–1763." *Pensacola Historical Society Quarterly* 9, no. 4 (Spring 1979):1–20.

———. "The Village on the Red Cliffs." *Pensacola History Illustrated* 1, no. 2 (1984):22–26.

———. "West Florida (The Spanish Presidios of Pensacola), 1686–1763." In *A Guide to the History of Florida*, edited by Paul S. George, pp. 49–56. New York: Greenwood Press, 1989.

Coker, William S., et al. "Pedro de Rivera's Report on the Presidio of Punta de Sigüenza, Alias Panzacola, 1744." *Pensacola Historical Society Quarterly* 8, no. 4 (Winter 1975; rev. ed. 1980):1–22.

Cox, Daniel. *A Description of the English Province of CAROLANA, by the Spaniards call'd FLORIDA, And by the French La LOUISIANE*. Introduction by William S. Coker. Gainesville: University Presses of Florida, 1976.

Dunn, William Edward. *Spanish and French Rivalry in the Gulf Region of the United States, 1678–1702: The Beginnings of Texas and Pensacola.* Austin: University of Texas Bulletin, no. 1705, 1917.

Dunn transcripts, 1700–1703. "Autos Made upon the Measures taken for the Occupation and Fortification of Santa María de Galve." University of Texas, Austin.

Faye, Stanley. "The Spanish and British Fortifications of Pensacola, 1698–1821." *Pensacola Historical Society Quarterly* 6, no. 4 (April 1972):151–292. Reprinted from *Florida Historical Quarterly.*

Folmer, Henry. *Franco-Spanish Rivalry in North America.* Glendale, Calif.: Arthur H. Clark Co., 1953.

Ford, Lawrence C. *The Triangular Struggle for Spanish Pensacola, 1689–1739.* The Catholic University of America Studies in Hispanic-American History, vol. 2. Washington, 1939.

Griffen, William B. "Spanish Pensacola, 1700–1763." *Florida Historical Quarterly* 27, nos. 3, 4 (January–April 1959):242–62.

Griffith, Wendell Lamar. "The Royal Spanish Presidio of San Miguel de Panzacola, 1753–1763." Master's thesis, University of West Florida, 1988.

Hann, John H. "Florida's Terra Incognita: West Florida's Natives in the Sixteenth and Seventeenth Century." *Florida Anthropologist* 41, no. 1 (March 1988):61–107.

Holmes, Jack D. L. "Dauphin Island in the Franco-Spanish War, 1719–1722." In *Frenchmen and French Ways in the Mississippi Valley,* edited by John Francis McDermott, pp. 103–25. Urbana: University of Illinois Press, 1969.

Jackson, Jack, Robert S. Weddle, and Winston Deville. *Mapping Texas and the Gulf coast: The Contributions of Saint-Denis, Oliván, and Le Maire.* College Station: Texas A&M University Press, 1990.

Leónard, Irving A. "Don Andrés de Arriola and the Occupation of Pensacola Bay." In *New Spain and the Anglo-American West: Historical Contributions Presented to Herbert Eugene Bolton,* edited by George P. Hammond, pp. 81–106. Lancaster, Pa.: Lancaster Press, 1932.

———, ed. and trans. "The Spanish Re-Exploration of the Gulf coast in 1686." *Mississippi Valley Historical Review* 22, no. 1 (June 1935):547–57.

Manucy, Albert. "The Founding of Pensacola—Reasons and Reality." *Florida Historical Quarterly* 37, nos. 3, 4 (January–April 1959):223–41.

Rowland, Dunbar, and A. G. Sanders, eds. *Mississippi Provincial Archives: French Dominion, 1701–1743.* 3 vols. Jackson: Press of the Mississippi Department of Archives and History, 1927–29.

Spain. Archivo General de Indias. Testimony of Autos, no. 5, México 633, 1709.

Weddle, Robert S. *The French Thorn: Rival Explorers in the Spanish Sea, 1682–1762.* College Station: Texas A&M University Press, 1991.

9

British Rule in the Floridas

ROBIN F. A. FABEL AND DANIEL L. SCHAFER

In February 1763, representatives of Spain, France, and Great Britain signed a peace treaty to end the Seven Years' War (called the French and Indian War in North America). In the massive reshuffling of overseas territories that followed Britain's victories in the Caribbean, India, and North America, Florida was acquired from Spain in exchange for Cuba, captured by British troops in 1762. From France, Britain gained Canada, along with territory adjoining Florida to the west and extending to the Mississippi River, with the exception of the city of New Orleans and the Isle of Orleans, which went to Spain. French claims to land west of the Mississippi were also ceded to Spain.

Britain divided the newly acquired Florida and Gulf coast territories into two provinces separated by the Apalachicola River. The land east of the Apalachicola River and south of the St. Marys River became the province of East Florida, with St. Augustine as its capital. West Florida extended westward from the Apalachicola to the Mississippi River and incorporated the Panhandle region of today's state of Florida, much of Alabama and Mississippi, and a portion of Louisiana. After a northward border adjustment in 1764, West Florida stretched from the Gulf of Mexico to the juncture of the Mississippi and Yazoo Rivers, and from there eastward to the Apalachicola. This border extension incorporated the rich farmland on the east bank of the Mississippi in the Natchez region.

On July 20, 1763, Captain John Hedges and four companies of the British First Regiment, later known as the "Royal Scots," arrived at St. Augustine. After observing ceremonies in honor of the Spanish king and queen, Captain Hedges raised the flag of Great Britain—the Union Jack—over the Castillo de San Marcos, the imposing coquina stone fortification alongside the

Map of British West Florida, showing the 1763 and 1764 boundaries and the few towns that existed at the time. Courtesy of the Mississippi Department of Archives and History, http://mdah.state.ms.us/.

British East Florida, 1763, by Thomas Jefferys. London: W. Nicoll, 1769. Courtesy of University of South Florida Libraries, Special and Digital Collections, http://digital.lib.usf.edu/civ/?doi=U15-0025.

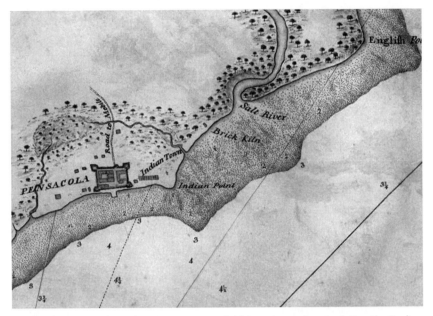

Pensacola ca. 1763, drawn by an anonymous British cartographer depicting the "Indian Town" adjacent to Spanish Fort San Miguel. Approximately 120 Yamasee and Apalachee inhabited the town in 1763; they were transported to Vera Cruz, Mexico, when the British took control of West Florida. Courtesy of Professor John Worth, University of West Florida, http://www.uwf.edu/jworth/colonialfrontiers.htm.

Matanzas River at the northeast corner of the city. For the next two decades, the Castillo would be known as Castle, or Fort, St. Mark.

Ten days after the British flag was raised, Major Francis Ogilvie of the Ninth Regiment assumed command. Soldiers who arrived with Hedges were given the choice of joining the Ninth Regiment or mustering out of the army to become civilian residents of St. Augustine. Major Ogilvie and Spanish governor Melchoir Feliú maintained peaceful relations until transports carried away the last of the 3,500 Spanish residents on January 21, 1764. Only three Spanish families remained under British rule.

At Pensacola, the designated seat of government for British West Florida, British troops under Lieutenant Colonel Augustine Prevost arrived on August 5, 1763. One month later, 800 Spanish subjects departed Pensacola for Havana and Veracruz, leaving behind approximately 350 French residents of Mobile and another ninety French families settled on farms nearby. Colonel Prevost complained about the miserable conditions of the fort and the absence of cultivated fields in the surrounding countryside.

Prevost and Ogilvie recognized the necessity of establishing peaceful relations with the Native Americans of their respective provinces. The combined populations of the Chickasaw, Choctaw, and Creek nations of West Florida totaled nearly 28,000, whereas the total European population of West Florida as late as 1765 was only 2,315. In East Florida, Major Ogilvie traveled to the Creek villages in the Alachua region west of St. Augustine with gifts for Chief Cowkeeper and his brother, the Long Warrior. Several years before, Chief Cowkeeper and 130 families had left Oconee in Georgia and settled in the rich farming and grazing lands near today's city of Gainesville. Land there had been vacant since the former inhabitants, the Timucua Indians, had been decimated to the point of extinction by epidemic diseases. The Creek under Cowkeeper were in the process of establishing a separate identity as the Seminole.

Mico-chlucco. Portrait by the famed naturalist William Bartram, who visited the Seminole villages in Alachua during his second exploration of East Florida in 1774. Elsewhere, Bartram mistakenly identified him as "King of the Muscogulges or Cricks called the Long Warrior." Long Warrior was not "King of the Muscogulges"; rather, he was the war leader for the Creek under Chief Cowkeeper who migrated from Oconee in Georgia to Alachua in north Florida. Image courtesy of the American Philosophical Society, Philadelphia.

Mico Chlucco the Long Warrior, or King of the Siminoles.

The former Spanish Governor's House on the plaza in St. Augustine served the British governors of East Florida from 1763 to 1784. This watercolor sketch, dated November 1764, is reproduced courtesy of th British Library, London.

The first governor of East Florida, Colonel James Grant, arrived at St. Augustine in August 1764. A native of Scotland, Grant was shocked by the miniscule size of the provincial capital. Passengers who debarked at a wharf on the Matanzas River and walked westward on the city's sand-filled streets crossed only four intersecting streets before reaching the barricade and redoubts at the edge of town. The distance from the town's barrier wall on the north to the southern barricade was less than one mile. The 300 dwellings within the walled town were less than fifty years old. Fires, wood rot, termites, and the English siege of 1702 had destroyed most traces of the sixteenth- and seventeenth-century city. The dwellings standing in 1763 were mostly one-story, made of quarried coquina stone, tabby, or wood.

In typical Spanish colonial fashion, St. Augustine centered on a plaza surrounded by important public buildings. Streets radiated north and south bounded by stores and residences. The dominant structures were the Governor's House at the west end of the plaza and Fort St. Mark. The governor distributed town lots and houses among British officials, merchants, and settlers.

When Captain George Johnstone of the Royal Navy, the first governor of British West Florida, arrived at Pensacola in October 1764, he found an impressive natural harbor but only 112 dilapidated and abandoned dwellings. Elias Durnford, the provincial surveyor, drew up a plan for a new Pensacola that allocated town lots to incoming settlers without charge, but it was 1768 before two hundred houses were standing. Members of the Royal Council for each province were appointed by King George III and were called into session soon after the arrival of their respective governors. Despite

Johnstone's reputation as a combative and ill-tempered man, he extended suffrage to leaseholders and landowners alike and authorized elections to a colonial assembly for West Florida in 1766. In striking contrast, a colonial assembly in East Florida was not seated until 1781.

The major challenge for both Grant and Johnstone was attracting settlers. Grant characterized East Florida as a "New World in a State of Nature when I landed in Augustine 1764. Not an acre of land planted in this country and nobody to work or at work." He was alarmed, however, when he discovered "straggling woodsmen" settling on rural lands without acquiring land titles. Farmers and laborers were desperately needed, but Grant was determined to prevent the American frontiersmen he contemptuously referred to as "crackers" from settling in his province. Like Grant, Governor Johnstone wanted a ban on the frontiersmen who wandered through the province without establishing permanent settlements and whom Johnstone called "the refuse of the Jails of great Citys, and the overflowing scum of the empire." Johnstone's goal was to recruit French, German, and Swiss immigrants, and to coax residents of New Orleans to cross the border and settle in West Florida.

Both governors were hindered by policies that awarded 10,000- and 20,000-acre tracts to men of wealth and influence in Britain who had no

Portrait of George Johnstone, the first governor of British West Florida. Courtesy of the State Archives of Florida, *Florida Memory*, http://floridamemory.com/items/show/19984.

James Grant, the first governor of British East Florida. Portrait courtesy of the National Galleries of Scotland, and Lady Clare and Sir Oliver Russell, Ballindalloch, Scotland.

intention of establishing settlements. Grant warned that absentee landlords would claim the best land and let it sit idle to speculate on rising prices rather than send settlers to develop their tracts. "No Lands ought to be granted, but to People who are actually to reside in the Colony," Grant reasoned, but his advice was not heeded. Recognizing the inevitable, Grant urged the "great grantees" to send settlers and to invest in the development of their tracts. He wrote repeatedly to the grantees in Britain urging them to employ enslaved black men and women rather than white Europeans, who became debilitated by the heat in Florida and abandoned the rural settlements for the colonial towns. Even the often praised German immigrants "won't do here. Upon their landing they are immediately seized with the pride which every man is possessed of who wears a white face in America and they say they won't be slaves and so they make their escape." He told one grantee: "no produce will answer the expense of white labor," and another: "Settlements in this warm climate must be formed by Negroes."

Governor Grant promised government support and free land to entice South Carolina and Georgia planters to migrate to East Florida and bring with them their experienced slave laborers. In addition, Grant attempted to "put a spur" to proprietors by developing one of his own rural tracts, called Grant's Villa, as a model indigo plantation. When the proceeds of four years of profits from indigo exports repaid all of Grant's startup expenses, including the cost of seventy-eight slaves, planters paid attention. Soon after, nearly all of the field laborers in East Florida were enslaved black men and women.

Numerous St. Augustine residents acquired farms west of the town toward the St. Johns River, and to the north alongside the North, Guana, and Pablo Rivers. George Grassell, a carpenter in the town, owned four farms. Englishman Spencer Mann ran a mercantile business in St. Augustine from 1764 to 1784, while his overseer and sixty slaves cultivated rice, indigo, and corn, and harvested lumber, shingles, and naval stores at nine rural properties. Francis Philip Fatio and Francis Levett had houses in St. Augustine plus estates of ten thousand acres west of St. Augustine on the St. Johns River. James Penman came to East Florida in 1767 as the agent for the planting fortunes of absentee owner Peter Taylor at a 10,000-acre estate at today's Daytona Beach. Penman became a leading St. Augustine merchant, and the owner of six rural estates and 188 black slaves. Several other large estates were developed south of St. Augustine by Lt. Governor John Moultrie, Captain Robert Bissett, London merchant William Elliot, and others, all worked by enslaved Africans. The wealthy London merchant Richard

Oswald shipped Africans from Bance Island, Sierra Leone, to Mount Oswald, a 20,000-acre plantation at today's Ormond Beach where 240 enslaved men and women were domiciled.

The major exception to Governor Grant's proviso that Florida settlements "must be formed by Negroes" was Dr. Andrew Turnbull's Smyrnea settlement located south of St. Augustine at Mosquito Inlet (present-day New Smyrna Beach and Edgewater). More than one hundred slaves were purchased for work at Smyrnea, but indentured Europeans became the mainstay of the labor force. Turnbull, a Scotland-born physician who resided for years at Smyrna, Turkey, while employed by the Levant Company, partnered with William Duncan, a baronet and physician to King George III, and Prime Minister George Grenville to develop three 20,000-acre tracts of land with the labor of indentured Europeans. Turnbull traveled to the Mediterranean to recruit 1,400 Greek, Italian, and Minorcan indentures. The scale of development envisioned for Smyrnea exceeded anything attempted elsewhere in the North American colonies, but the agonizingly high sickness and mortality rates, food and funding shortages, labor unrest, rebellion, and charges of brutal treatment led to the collapse of the settlement in 1777 and 1778. Those who survived the high disease and death rates and the sometimes oppressive labor conditions abandoned Smyrnea and settled in what became known as the "Minorcan Quarter" of St. Augustine. They rented vacant farmland near the town walls, became fishermen, laborers, and merchants, and distinguished themselves as enduring pioneer families whose descendants are still prominent Florida citizens.

At West Florida, migrants began arriving soon after accession, but infertile soil near Pensacola and high sickness and mortality rates slowed the inflow. Settlement of the Natchez region along the Mississippi River, where some of the finest agricultural land in North America could be found, was frustratingly slow. This was in part the result of the decision in 1768 by the War Office in London to withdraw the garrisons from the frontier outposts at Manchac and Natchez. The only significant products exported in the province's first decade were the deerskins, beaver pelts, and furs shipped out of Mobile.

By the early 1770s, however, news of the abundant fertile soil along the western rivers had spread to Britain's other North American colonies and prompted a rush of emigrants to set out for West Florida. The Company of Military Adventurers, led by General Phineas Lyman of Connecticut and joined by dozens of veterans of the Seven Years' War, had formulated plans to settle New Englanders on the Mississippi River as early as 1763. At a meeting of the Adventurers at Hartford in June of that year, dues were collected and General Lyman was elected to represent them in London to lobby for a massive land grant, possibly even a separate province. Lyman unwisely chose to transform his assignment into a nine-year sojourn while he sought a personal grant of 20,000 acres and chased after an aristocratic title. Lyman's personal ambitions delayed the project unnecessarily and diminished the actual number of settlers who eventually traveled to West Florida to claim land.

In addition to problems recruiting settlers, both governors faced challenges as they negotiated land concessions and trade agreements with Native Americans. It was Grant's conviction that migrants needed to know they could settle safely on rural Florida plantations, and that Native Americans should feel confident that British rule would be just and generous. Grant learned early that the Creek and the Seminole were "very tenacious of their lands" and unlikely to make concessions if doing so would diminish their annual harvests of deer- and bearskins. To avoid conflict, Grant imposed strict rules on British fur traders and informed British planters that Creek hunters had the right to pass through British farms in pursuit of game.

In November 1765, Grant convened a congress with fifty headmen of the Lower Creek and the Seminole at Fort Picolata, located twenty miles west of St. Augustine on the St. Johns River. With the crucial assistance of John Stuart, superintendent of Indian Affairs for the Southern Department, a treaty was arranged that resulted in a land concession that permitted the British to occupy the land lying between the St. Johns River and the Atlantic Ocean, and to the west and south as far as the tidal waters flowed. Grant entertained lavishly and distributed gifts generously on this occasion, and again in November 1767 when another congress was convened at Fort Picolata. After the congress, Grant informed the Board of Trade that he had countered suspicion with generosity by "load[ing] those Indians who attended the Congress with presents, I fed them plentifully, and gave them as much provisions as they could carry away with them." The congress had been expensive, but the governor believed "money could not be better applied, as it certainly prevented an Indian War." Similar meetings were held in the remaining years of Britain's brief tenure in Florida.

Governor Johnstone's problems were more severe because of a greater population imbalance, and also because of British policies that pitted one Native American nation against another. This policy was most evident in the continuing warfare between the Creek and the Choctaw. Johnstone possessed a stubborn and truculent nature and advocated a bellicose policy

Portrait of Patrick Tonyn, the second governor of British East Florida. An early absentee planter in East Florida, Tonyn was appointed governor in 1774 and efficiently organized the militia and the defense of the colony during the American War of Independence. Courtesy of the State Archives of Florida, *Florida Memory*, http://florida memory.com/items/ show/128483.

toward his Native American neighbors. In an effort to promote cordial relations, Superintendent Stuart encouraged Johnstone to join him in a meeting with tribal leaders to distribute gifts and negotiate differences. Johnstone's extreme demands for reinforcements of more than 3,000 British regulars, provincial militia and marines, and 1,000 Indian allies to conduct a war against the Creek led to his removal from office in January 1767. Political instability was a continuing problem in West Florida.

In East Florida, Governor Grant served well and energetically from 1764 until 1771, when he returned to Britain for health reasons and was replaced on an interim basis by a competent administrator, Lieutenant Governor John Moultrie, a native of South Carolina and a planter with a degree in medicine from Edinburgh University. Grant never returned to East Florida. He was elected to the House of Commons in 1773 and resigned his governorship in April of that year.

Colonel Patrick Tonyn, a naval officer who was appointed the second governor of East Florida, arrived at St. Augustine in March 1774. Prior to his appointment as governor, Tonyn had established a St. Johns River plantation, although as an absentee owner. Like his predecessor, Governor Tonyn worked in concert with John Stuart to maintain peaceful relations with the Indians. After the War of Rebellion began in 1775, Tonyn ordered a census of white inhabitants in the province fit to bear arms, and of the enslaved men who could be trusted with weapons. By August 1776 he had formed the East Florida Rangers, a provincial militia of seven companies of white volunteers and four companies of enslaved black men serving under white officers. Thomas Brown, a Loyalist refugee from Georgia, was given command.

Forming an alliance between his loyal colony and the Creek and Seminole was one of Tonyn's wartime achievements. He first sought their allegiance in December 1775 at a congress held at the Cowford under the branches of the "Treaty Oak," a giant live oak tree that still stands near the south bank of the St. Johns River opposite Jacksonville's downtown business district. Anticipating the need for well-armed Native American allies to repel invaders from Georgia, Tonyn supplied the Creek and Seminole with weapons and gunpowder and deployed them as scouts and soldiers.

The war in East Florida devolved into border warfare as Georgia militia crossed into Florida in August 1776 to destroy settlements and steal cattle and slaves. Within weeks, Florida's Rangers retaliated with raids into Georgia. The violent raids back and forth across the border continued for the remainder of the war and turned the area between the St. Marys and the St. Johns Rivers into a "no man's land" of debris and ashes where dwellings and farm buildings once stood, and scorched stubble where corn and indigo fields once thrived. Following Patriot raids in 1776, East Florida forces crossed into Georgia and captured Fort McIntosh on the Satilla River in February 1777, and returned to St. Augustine with two thousand head of cattle and sixty-eight prisoners. A Georgia invasion force struck back in May but was stopped short of the St. Johns River. John Moultrie remarked: "The common frontier quite abandoned on both sides, horses and crops destroyed, people and cattle moved away; numbers of refugees . . . fled to us, they almost eat up our provisions, but . . . we drive off as many cattle from the Georgians as have hitherto supplied our market."

In March 1778, the East Florida Rangers invaded Georgia to burn Fort Barrington on the Altamaha River. An American force of two thousand retaliated in June, driving the Rangers south to the Alligator Creek Bridge on Nassau River, where they were defeated by Florida troops. This would be the last major invasion of the war in East Florida. Reinforcements were rushed to St. Augustine in the summer of 1778. In November, British forces under General Augustine Prevost crossed the Florida/Georgia border and marched north toward Savannah. The besieged city was surrendered on December 29, 1778, and Prevost's army continued northward to assist in the capture of Charleston in May 1780.

For West Florida, the outbreak of war came as a significant migratory movement was under way. Increasing numbers of settlers had heard of the rich agricultural lands along the western rivers and were initiating settlements. General Phyneas Lyman had returned to Connecticut in 1772 and arranged another meeting of the Company of Military Adventurers at Hartford. Members of an exploratory committee traveled to West Florida to select land for settlements. Committee members arrived at Pensacola on February 28, 1773, and after exploring possible sites along the Mississippi as far as the Yazoo River, submitted claims for nineteen townships averaging 23,000 acres each. Thaddeus Lyman, son of the general, and the other committee members observed several groups of colonists from New England, North Carolina, and Virginia searching for land or already established on farms, and rightfully concluded that a major rush of settlement was under way. But it was not until March 1774 that two ships chartered by the Adventurers arrived at Pensacola, each carrying approximately 100 passengers. From Pensacola, they journeyed up the Mississippi to begin the arduous task of establishing settlements in the Natchez district. The total number of emigrants representing the Company of Military Adventurers was probably less than two hundred, and they were only beginning their settlements when the American Revolution broke out.

In 1774, Elias Durnford estimated that 3,100 persons (2,500 white and 600 black) resided at the east bank of the Mississippi between the Iberville and Yazoo Rivers. Migration was stagnated by the onset of the American Revolution, yet the settlements along the Mississippi, Amite, and Comite Rivers were temporarily unaffected by the violence that occurred to the east of the province. That tranquil state ended in February 1778, when a Patriot naval captain, James Willing, a former planter in the Natchez district, floated past a sentinel post at today's Vicksburg and, with fewer than one hundred men, gained control of Natchez before continuing downriver to New Orleans. His presumed goal was to gain support for the Revolutionary cause, but looting and unobstructed mayhem characterized his career on the lower Mississippi. After selling the plundered treasure at New Orleans, the threat from Willing and his bandits dissipated. Bernardo de Gálvez, the governor of Spanish Louisiana, was greatly embarrassed by the incident. Spain and Britain were not then at war, and the presence of British frigates on the Mississippi gave British forces a decided advantage in armament.

Britain responded to the Willing raid by sending regular troops to the abandoned forts at Natchez and Manchac and building a new fort at Baton Rouge, thus strengthening the defenses of West Florida. John Stuart, who had moved to Pensacola in 1776, organized a company of mounted rangers and an infantry regiment that provided settlers with a sense of security and stabilized the economy. With the war under way, New England's merchants were cut off from markets in the British West Indies, enabling entrepreneurs and planters in both West and East Florida to prosper from exports of lumber, naval stores, fish from the Atlantic Ocean and Gulf of Mexico, and rice and other foodstuffs to Jamaica and other British colonies.

The principal restraint on optimism was the prospect of war with Spain. When the Spanish monarch, Charles III, declared war on Britain on June 21, 1779, the thinly garrisoned forts in the western districts were placed in jeopardy. To sever the link between West Florida's capital and the settlements in the Natchez district, Bernardo de Gálvez focused his first military campaign against the tiny trade center of Manchac, at the junction of the Mississippi River and the Iberville Bayou. Galvez's army of 1,000 easily captured the twenty-three-man garrison at Manchac and followed that victory with the conquest of the British forts at Baton Rouge and Natchez by September 1779. Fort Charlotte at Mobile fell to the Spanish army in March 1780, and after a two-month siege of Fort George and Pensacola, Major General John Campbell and Governor Peter Chester surrendered to Gálvez on May 10, 1781. With the surrender of Pensacola, West Florida became again part of the Spanish colonial empire.

In East Florida, however, British strength increased during the Revolution's latter stages. As early as the latter months of 1775, supporters of King George III living in the Georgia and South Carolina backcountry began fleeing to woods and swamps to escape zealous revolutionaries. Hundreds made their way overland to loyal East Florida, where Governor Tonyn made unoccupied land available for settlement. Without land, it was feared the refugee Loyalists would drift toward the rebel cause.

In August 1776, John Moultrie described St. Augustine as "full of people who have fled for safety. Our planting thrives finely; good indigo, plenty of provisions . . . [and] the consumption of the town at present is great." Moultrie decided to "plant nothing but what is to go into the mouth." In the summer of 1778, troop reinforcements began pouring into St. Augustine

Portrait of Bernardo de Gálvez, colonial governor of Spanish Louisiana and Cuba, and the viceroy of New Spain. Gálvez commanded Spanish troops in victories over the British at Manchac, Baton Rouge, and Natchez in 1779, and at Mobile and Pensacola in 1780, effectively terminating British rule in West Florida. Courtesy of the State Archives of Florida, *Florida Memory*, http://floridamemory.com/items/show/128368.

accompanied by carpenters, dock workers, and hundreds of sailors on shore leave. For local farmers and businessmen, the influx meant unprecedented opportunity.

After the disturbing capitulations of Baton Rouge, Natchez, and Mobile to the Spanish in 1779 and 1780 and the capture of Pensacola in May 1781, Loyalists in East Florida were shocked to learn that Lord Charles Cornwallis had surrendered his 8,000-man British army to General George Washington at Yorktown, Virginia, on October 19, 1781. In the early months of 1782, Spain gained control of Minorca and the Bahamas from Britain, and France seized St. Eustasius, galvanizing the House of Commons vote at the end of February that terminated offensive actions against the Patriots in North America and forced Lord Frederick North to resign as prime minister. Peace negotiations began in earnest in Paris.

On May 20, 1782, General Sir Guy Carleton, commander of British forces in North America, ordered the withdrawal of British garrisons at St. Augustine, Charleston, and Savannah. East Florida Loyalists were disillusioned and devastated. In June, David Yeats, a medical doctor and the plantation agent for James Grant, confided in the former governor: "I am totally ruined and see nothing but want and misery before me."

One month later, however, Yeats was again optimistic. Admiral George Rodney's British fleet had achieved a victory over a French fleet in the West Indies, Jamaica was secure, and St. Lucia had been successfully defended by British forces under James Grant, by then a major general. Carleton rescinded his order for the evacuation of the St. Augustine garrison, and designated East Florida a haven for disheartened Loyalists from other British provinces. Between July and October, British transports carried thousands of Loyalists to East Florida, Jamaica, Nova Scotia, and other British colonies. Governor Tonyn reported that many of the refugees that debarked at St. Augustine had survived "truly deplorable" circumstances, while others succumbed to sickness. The historian Charles Mowat called the conditions experienced by many of the refugees "pitiful indeed . . . having already been forced to move two or three times from plantation to plantation, from country to town . . . herded together, prosperous and poor alike on the quays of Savannah and Charleston, surrounded by cases and bundles containing their few salvaged effects, and waiting to embark with their Negroes." By the end of December, more than 6,147 refugees had arrived in East Florida.

The refugees were provided emergency rations, tools, and seeds for planting provisions crops at unoccupied rural tracts marked out by order of the governor. New farms were created on vacant land along the rivers north and south of St. Augustine and the banks of creeks and rivers feeding into the St. Johns. The new planters focused on forest products for export to Britain's other Caribbean colonies, where demand was high for naval stores, lumber, and provisions. Seemingly overnight, a new town of between two and three hundred houses was created at St. Johns Bluff, six miles inland from the Atlantic Ocean on the south bank of the St. Johns River. Governor Tonyn was optimistic that the influx of refugees, which eventually increased the population to between 17,000 and 18,000, would result in "a happy Era [for] this Province," and that the new settlers would regard it a "safe asylum and permanent residence." Tonyn felt confident enough to authorize elections for delegates to a Lower House of Assembly.

These hopes were dashed in January 1783 when British, Spanish, French, and American negotiators meeting in Paris agreed to preliminary terms of another Treaty of Paris. The colonies in rebellion were granted independence, and East and West Florida were ceded to Spain. In June, John

Moultrie informed his friend James Grant he had decided to leave East Florida. After achieving a life of "real plenty, ease and elegance," he expected "to be turned adrift, and again seek a resting place. . . . England, I think, will bring me up. My feelings, principles, everything prevents me having any idea of remaining in America."

Moultrie grieved for the other British residents of the colony. "What shall become of these poor unfortunate but virtuous people I cannot divine. . . . Thousands . . . have settled here and were just made comfortable, and quite happy, astonished at the crops in the ground. . . . Had this province not been ceded in the course of this year every part would have been full of industrious people, the only thing wanted to make it great and flourishing."

David Yeats had also decided to depart. In May 1784 he lamented: "The idea of keeping possession of Estates in this Province under the Spanish government is now I suppose vanished, we being told that such as choose to remain must publicly profess the Catholic religion or absolutely quit their Estates." Yeats and the other British Loyalists were faced with a bitter choice: stay in Florida under the terms of Spanish rule, or sacrifice wealth and property and embark on a ship of the evacuation fleet.

On July 12, 1784, Spanish Governor Vizente Manuel de Zéspedes witnessed the formal change of flags at the Plaza in St. Augustine. For the next year, two governors—one Spanish, the other British—resided in the town. Eventually Patrick Tonyn moved to the St. Marys River to supervise the final departures, but it was not until November 10, 1785, that a troop transport carried him and the last of the Loyalists away. British rule in the Floridas had ended.

Bibliography

Manuscripts

British Library, London
> Egmont Papers, Additional Manuscripts: 46920-47213, 17720, 27980–90.
> Haldimand Collection, Additional MSS 21661-21892.
Colonial Williamsburg, Inc. Williamsburg, Va.
> Carleton Papers.
National Archives of Scotland, Edinburgh
> Amherst Papers, War Office 34.
> James Grant of Ballindalloch Papers. Governorship Series. Microfilm copies are at David Library of the American Revolution, Washington Crossing, Pennsylvania; Library of Congress, Washington, D.C.; Jay I. Kislak Foundation, Miami Lakes, Florida.

National Archives of the United Kingdom, Kew, England
  Colonial Office Papers 5 (vols. 540–73 for East Florida; vols. 574–635 for West Florida).
  Treasury 77, Papers of the East Florida Claims Commission.
William L. Clements Library, University of Michigan, Ann Arbor
  Gage Papers.

Published Sources

Alden, John Richard. *John Stuart and the Southern Colonial Frontier: A Study of Indian Relations, War, Trade, and Land Problems in the Southern Wilderness, 1754–1775*. New York: Gordian Press, 1966.

Bailyn, Bernard. *Voyagers to the West: A Passage in the Peopling of America on the Eve of the Revolution*. New York: Knopf, 1986, chaps. 12 and 13.

Braund, Kathryn E. Holland. *Deerskins and Duffels: Creek Indian Trade with Anglo-America, 1685–1815*. Lincoln and London: University of Nebraska Press, 1993.

Cashin, Edward J. *The King's Ranger: Thomas Brown and the American Revolution on the Southern Frontier*. Athens: University of Georgia Press, 1989.

Covington, James W. *The British Meet the Seminoles: Negotiations between British Authorities in East Florida and the Indians: 1763–68*. Gainesville: University of Florida Press, 1961.

Fabel, Robin F. A. *Bombast and Broadsides: The Lives of George Johnstone*. Tuscaloosa: University of Alabama Press, 1987.

———. *The Economy of British West Florida, 1763–1783*. Tuscaloosa: University of Alabama Press, 1988.

Gold, Robert L. *Borderland Empires in Transition: The Triple Nation Transfer of Florida*. Carbondale: Southern Illinois University Press, 1969.

Griffin, Patricia C. "Blue Gold: Andrew Turnbull's New Smyrna Plantation." In *Colonial Plantations and Economy in Florida*, edited by Jane Landers. Gainesville: University Press of Florida, 2000, chap. 2.

———. *Mullet on the Beach: The Minorcans of Florida, 1768–1788*. Jacksonville: University of North Florida Press, 1991.

Hancock, David. *Citizens of the World: London Merchants and the Integration of the British Atlantic Community, 1735–1785*. New York and Cambridge: Cambridge University Press, 1995.

Johnson, Cecil. *British West Florida, 1763–1783*. New York: Archon, 1971.

Lewis, James A. *The Final Campaign of the American Revolution: Rise and Fall of the Spanish Bahamas*. Columbia: University of South Carolina Press, 1991.

Mowat, Charles Loch. *East Florida as a British Province, 1763–1784*. 1943. Facsimile reprint, Gainesville: University of Florida Press, 1964.

Nelson, Paul David. *General James Grant: Scottish Soldier and Royal Governor of East Florida*. Gainesville: University Presses of Florida, 1993.

Panagopoulos, Epaminondas P. *New Smyrna: An Eighteenth-Century Greek Colony*. Gainesville: University of Florida Press, 1966.

Rea, Robert R. "'Graveyard for Britons,' West Florida, 1763–1781." *Florida Historical Quarterly* 47 (1969).

———. "Pensacola under the British (1763–1781)." In *Colonial Pensacola*, edited by James R. McGovern. Hattiesburg: University of Southern Mississippi Press, 1972.

Schafer, Daniel L. *Governor James Grant's Villa: A British East Florida Indigo Plantation*. St. Augustine: St. Augustine Historical Society, 2000.

———. "'Not So Gay a Town in America as This': St. Augustine, 1763–1784." In *The Oldest City: St. Augustine, Saga of Survival*, edited by Jean Parker Waterbury. St. Augustine: St. Augustine Historical Society, 1983, chap. 4.

———. "Plantation Development in British East Florida: A Case Study of the Earl of Egmont." *Florida Historical Quarterly* 43 (October 1984):172–83.

———. *St. Augustine's British Years, 1763–1784*. St. Augustine: St. Augustine Historical Society, 2001.

———. "'A Swamp of an Investment'? Richard Oswald's British East Florida Plantation Experiment." In *Colonial Plantations and Economy in Florida*, edited by Jane Landers. Gainesville: University Press of Florida, 2000, chap. 1.

———. *William Bartram and the Ghost Plantations of British East Florida*. Gainesville: University Press of Florida, 2010.

———. "'Yellow Silk Ferret Tied Round Their Wrists': African Americans in British East Florida, 1763–1784." In *The African American Heritage of Florida*, edited by David R. Colburn and Jane L. Landers, Gainesville: University Press of Florida, 1995, chap. 4.

Searcy, Martha Condray. *The Georgia-Florida Contest in the American Revolution, 1776–1778*. Tuscaloosa: University of Alabama Press, 1988.

Siebert, Wilbur Henry. *Loyalists in East Florida 1774 to 1785*. 2 vols. Deland: Florida State Historical Society, 1929.

Snapp, J. Russell. *John Stuart and the Struggle for Empire on the Southern Frontier*. New York: Cambridge University Press, 1995.

Starr, J. Barton. *Tories, Dons, and Rebels: The American Revolution in British West Florida*. Gainesville: University Presses of Florida, 1976.

TePaske, John Jay. *The Governorship of Spanish Florida, 1700–1763*. Durham: Duke University Press, 1964.

Troxler, Carole Watterson. "Loyalist Refugees and the British Evacuation of East Florida, 1783–1785." *Florida Historical Quarterly* 60, no. 1 (July 1981):1–28.

Weisman, Brent R. *Like Beads on a String: A Cultural History of the Seminole Indians in North Peninsular Florida*. Tuscaloosa: University of Alabama Press, 1989.

———. *Unconquered Peoples: Florida's Seminole and Miccosukee Indians*. Gainesville: University Press of Florida, 1999.

Williams, Linda K. "East Florida as a Loyalist Haven." *Florida Historical Quarterly* 54 (1976).

Wright, J. Leitch, Jr. *British St. Augustine*. St. Augustine: Historic St. Augustine Preservation Board, 1975.

———. *Florida in the American Revolution*. Gainesville: University Presses of Florida, 1975.

10

The Second Spanish Period in the Two Floridas

SUSAN RICHBOURG PARKER AND WILLIAM S. COKER

Spanish rule returned to East and West Florida in 1784. Spain regained its former colonies at the peace negotiations for the Treaty of Versailles; Spain had declared war on Great Britain in 1779 during the War of the American Revolution. The newly restored Spanish rule claimed sway over the same colonial boundaries in Florida as established by the British: two separate colonies, West and East, divided at the Apalachicola River, ranging west as far as the Mississippi and governed from two capitals, Pensacola and St. Augustine. The St Marys River formed the boundary between Spanish East Florida and the new U.S. state of Georgia. West Florida was the larger of the two Floridas. It extended from the Chattahoochee and Apalachicola Rivers on the east to the Mississippi River and the Isle of Orleans on the west. The Gulf of Mexico and the Louisiana Lakes Borgne, Ponchartrain, and Maurepas formed its southern boundary. There was disagreement over the northern boundary of West Florida. Initially, the northern border had been set at latitude 31° north, but in 1764 it was moved up to 32°28" in order to include more fertile lands and fur-trapping ranges. The United States and Great Britain accepted the thirty-first parallel as the boundary. Spain considered the international line to lie considerably northward, and the boundary dispute immediately embittered relations between the United States and Spain. As a result, Spanish West Florida became the first victim of what some historians would later call Manifest Destiny. The history of Spanish West Florida from 1783 to 1821 is really a history of defeats—some economic, some diplomatic, and a few military—that ultimately cost Spain her newly regained colony.

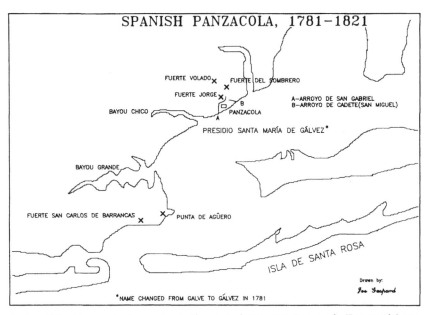

SPANISH PANZACOLA, 1781–1821

FUERTE VOLADO
FUERTE JORGE
FUERTE DEL SOMBRERO
BAYOU CHICO
PANZACOLA
A—ARROYO DE SAN GABRIEL
B—ARROYO DE CADETE(SAN MIGUEL)
PRESIDIO SANTA MARÍA DE GÁLVEZ*
BAYOU GRANDE
FUERTE SAN CARLOS DE BARRANCAS
PUNTA DE AGÜERO
ISLA DE SANTA ROSA
Drawn by:
Joe Gaspard
*NAME CHANGED FROM GALVE TO GÁLVEZ IN 1781

A plan of the Pensacola Bay region in the period 1781–1821. Pensacola (Panzacola) was the capital of Spanish West Florida. Other towns of consequence in the colony were Mobile, Baton Rouge, and Natchez. Drawn by Joe Gaspard.

For a long time, most histories of the Second Spanish Period of the Floridas reflected the Anglophile viewpoints of earlier historians. The era is generally portrayed as an interval of decline wedged between the British and American periods, merely awaiting an inevitable takeover by the United States and its institutions. That view arose largely from reliance upon English-language sources, which aggrandized conditions during the two periods when English was the official language while minimizing developments during the Spanish period. David J. Weber observed that Englishmen and Anglo-Americans writing at the time of the Second Spanish Period "uniformly condemned Spanish rule." They saw only Spanish misgovernment, which "seemed the inevitable result of the defective character of Spaniards themselves."[1] More recent attention to Spanish-language documents questions that negative assessment.

In 1784 there was widespread doubt that the republican government of the new United States could control even its large landmass awarded in treaty negotiations, much less take over additional territory in the Floridas. Only four towns of any consequence contained the urban populations of West Florida: Mobile, Baton Rouge, Natchez, and Pensacola, the capital. In addition to the military forts in each of those towns, there were two others in the interior, Fort Choiseul (York) and Fort Toulouse. Without counting the native peoples, the population of West Florida was approximately 3,660 in 1785 and 8,390 in 1795. Between 1795 and 1814, the population grew significantly, but substantial territorial losses to the United States reduced the area and population of West Florida by 50 percent or more.

In St. Augustine, troops sent from Cuba again walked the capital's streets gossiping in Spanish, former émigré residents moved in to reclaim old homes, and Mass was heard again in the parish church. In the countryside, English-speaking settlers debated what their fate might be under the new regime while they planted their crops and felled timber. Many British citizens remained in East Florida in the hope of taking advantage of a failure of the United States. These former British subjects joined Spanish soldiers and returning families, their slaves, free blacks, white and black immigrants from the United States, refugees of both races from the Caribbean, especially Saint-Domingue (Haiti), sailors and opportunists of many nationalities, and Seminole Indians in the interior of the peninsula to make East Florida's Second Spanish Period the most culturally and racially heterogeneous era of its history until the second half of the twentieth century. The population of the countryside was more homogeneous than that of the towns and ports. In the first years of the Second Spanish Period, rural residents beyond the immediate outskirts of St. Augustine were overwhelmingly Protestant; they were planters or farmers and natives of the southern British colonies, especially South Carolina, and about half owned slaves. The diversity among the province's populace contributed to the unsettledness of the era.

The role and power of the military and the Roman Catholic Church during the Second Spanish Period were diminished in comparison to the first two centuries, although both institutions remained strong presences. Spanish West Florida was under the jurisdiction of the civil and military commandant stationed at Pensacola. The title of his office was later changed to governor, but the duties remained essentially the same. All of West Florida's commandants/governors were military officers, normally appointed to serve a term of five years. In practice, they stayed until they were formally relieved of duty. Thirteen officers served as commandant/governor of the colony between 1781 and 1821. Colonel Vicente Folch y Juan held office the longest, 1796–1811; Colonel Arturo O'Neill y Tyrone was second in length of service, 1781–94.

The duties of these officers included supervision of the military, Indian affairs, foreign relations directly affecting the colony, financial matters and the economy, land grants, and the church. These officers were under the supervision of the governor-general and the intendant of Louisiana and West Florida until 1806. After that date, the captain-general of Cuba assumed direct command over West Florida's governors. Although within the boundaries of Spanish West Florida, the Natchez District, whose principal officer was changed from a commandant to a governor in 1787, was under the direct command of the governor-general of Louisiana. Colonel Manuel Gayoso de Lemos served there from 1789 to 1797, by which time the United States had acquired the area. Gayoso then became the governor-general of Louisiana and West Florida.

The Roman Catholic faith was the only religion officially permitted in the Spanish Floridas although persons of other religious denominations could worship in private. The church in West Florida followed the same pattern of jurisdiction as did the civil and military government: It was under the governor of West Florida except for strictly religious matters. For religious matters, after 1787, it was under the auxiliary bishop of Louisiana and West Florida. Father James Coleman served as the priest of the parish of San Miguel in Pensacola from 1794 until 1822. In 1806, he was appointed the vicar-general and ecclesiastical judge of West Florida. He became perhaps the best known of all the priests in colonial West Florida. After 1806, confusion reigns about who had official jurisdiction over the church in West Florida, but Father Coleman looked to the bishop of Havana.

By 1795, it is estimated, about 15 percent of the population of West Florida was Protestant. Father Coleman's religious censuses of Pensacola in 1796–1801 indicated that about 25 percent of its population was Protestant; this strong showing resulted from the presence of British residents who decided to remain in West Florida, as well as from Protestant immigration after 1783. Mobile, with its large French population, remained predominantly Catholic.

Spain continued to subsidize a military presence in East Florida financially disproportionate to the colony's productivity, for East Florida's raison d'être was still to protect the richer areas belonging to the Crown, particularly the mineral wealth of Mexico. But the military budget no longer overwhelmingly supplied the financial base of the province, as in the First Spanish Period, and over the years it became an ever-smaller part of the economy, reflecting the vicissitudes of the Spanish Crown and government. East Florida's governors complained about the irregular arrival of monies needed to maintain the troops and fortifications, but the accounting records reveal that the funds usually did arrive and were usually on time; the problem lay with the manner of distributing funds in an annual lump sum. Over the years, diminishing troop strength meant smaller budgets, which translated into the ever-decreasing financial and social influence of the military. Between 1790 and 1800, East Florida lost 30 percent of its soldiery, and units continued to diminish in strength although at a slower rate.

The weakened role of the church in East Florida reflected its position throughout the Spanish empire, as the monarchy and its bureaucracy gained power by taking over functions once performed by the church, such as approval of marriages. In East Florida, the financial well-being of the church was tied to that of the provincial government through its inclusion in the defense budget. Although the Franciscans had wished to return, there was no revival of the missions in Florida to parallel the prosperity of the order's missions in California during the late eighteenth century. Catholic priests visited East Florida's largely Protestant rural population soon after the Spaniards returned and baptized many young children, but there was no subsequent establishment of parishes or church-sponsored schools outside of St. Augustine. Thus, the opportunity to incorporate the residents of the countryside into the province's society was lost, and they remained English-speaking, unchurched, and omitted from most official festivals and celebrations—events that revolved around religious feast days and commemorative rituals. For example, in 1789, when the residents of St. Augustine staged a three-day festival for the coronation of King Carlos IV, featuring Masses, an enthroning reenactment, parades, and plays, no counterpart took place in the rural area to involve the settlers in that moment of national celebration.

West Florida had the potential of being an important colony economically. Early on, the area did reasonably well with tobacco, indigo, and lumber. Tobacco flourished but soon lost out from overproduction and competition from Mexico. Indigo also did well until pollution problems developed. Timber, especially ships' masts, yielded a good return, but the market was limited. And, unfortunately, a cotton boom came too late. Seafood and livestock production never reached their potential. The population was too small to support large-scale manufacturing and related industries. For Spain, West Florida was simply not a profit-making colony. Its importance lay in its strategic position on the Gulf coast. There was one way to make a profit—the Indian trade—but the profit went to the British, not to the Spanish.

The person who was to have an important economic impact on West Florida was the Scotsman William Panton, one of the partners in the Indian trading firm of Panton, Leslie and Company. The company had already achieved considerable success in East Florida. Panton and his assistant John

Thirteen years after their return, Spanish residents of St. Augustine enjoyed use of a new Roman Catholic church, larger than any that had stood in the city before. Designed by royal engineer-architect Mariano de la Rocque, the coquina stone structure was erected on the north side of the central plaza during the years 1793–97. Its neoclassic facade was typical of parish and mission churches built elsewhere in the Spanish Americas during the period. This photograph was taken one hundred years after its completion.

Forbes reached Pensacola in 1784, shortly after the Spaniards had reached an agreement with the Creeks to supply them with trade goods. Panton was a friend of Alexander McGillivray, an influential mixed-blood Upper Creek chief, and, with McGillivray's support, Panton, Leslie and Company eventually secured a large part of the Indian trade.

The company traded English-made goods, especially guns, powder, and shot, for deerskins and other furs. It extended credit to the Indians who were soon heavily in debt—$200,000 or more—to the firm. Panton and his partners spent years collecting these debts. One thing worked to their advantage: The Indians owned large tracts of land which they traded, not always willingly, to cancel their debts.

Since the United States eagerly wanted Indian lands, the company pressured the Indians in 1805 into trading 8 million acres to the United States. The land was actually in U.S. territory. With the cash that they received, the Indians paid off part of their debts to the company. Later, the Indians and the Spanish government gave the company 2.7 million acres in West Florida as recompense for losses sustained by the company during the War of 1812. Eventually, and because of a technicality, the United States confirmed only 1.4 million acres of this grant, known as Forbes Grant I. At its peak, Panton, Leslie and its successor firm, John Forbes & Co., exercised significant control over the Indians of the Floridas and played an important role in the history of both East and West Florida during the years 1783 to 1821.

Residents of East Florida participated in the Atlantic-wide economy that was fed by the mass production of the emerging Industrial Revolution. It was a period marked by the rise of the British navy and merchant marine and the lifting of Spanish trade restrictions. East Florida's reliance on imports probably was in line with the economic activity in surrounding areas of both the Caribbean and the United States. Foodstuffs from ports in the United States were the major imported item. Manufactured goods arrived in East Florida in vessels from England and the United States; wine, sugar, rum, coffee, and some tablewares were shipped via Cuba. In the early years of the Second Spanish Period, Florida planters saw planting rice as a way to riches. Others with fewer resources or less capital looked to timber and cattle raising for profit. As the nineteenth century arrived, cotton was replacing corn, rice, and other staples on East Florida's acreage. Planter Francis Fatio claimed that an acre of cotton would yield ten times the profit of an acre of corn. The departure of money from the province to the United States to purchase food for slaves in East Florida now engaged in raising inedible cotton so alarmed Spanish Governor Enrique White in 1800 that he officially prohibited the planting of cotton and ordered the immediate sowing of corn.

Even before it acquired the Indian lands in 1805, the United States had begun its acquisition of Spanish West Florida, a piece at a time. The area between the 31st parallel and 32° 28" north was in dispute between Spain and the United States from 1783 until 1795. Despite the differences between the first and second Spanish regimes in its Florida territories, the continuing role of the provinces as adjuncts of a European power meant a close connection with wars in Europe. Spain's enemies were the Floridas' enemies, whatever the reality within the provinces. By 1795, Spain's problems in Europe, and the French Revolution and its consequences, pushed it to resolve its dispute with the United States. The result was Pinckney's Treaty, or the Treaty of 1795, which gave the disputed area, including the Natchez District, to the United States. The United States had then sovereignty over all the lands north of 31° to the Great Lakes and from the Appalachian Mountains to the Mississippi River.

In 1803, the United States purchased Louisiana from France and although Spain protested, the sale stood. The United States claimed, without any justification, that the Louisiana Purchase included all lands from the Mississippi River east to the Perdido River, an area that had been part of French Louisiana prior to 1763. Officially, those lands had been included in British West Florida from 1763 to 1783 and in Spanish West Florida after that.

In order to confirm its claim to the disputed area, Spain commissioned a number of persons to write the history of that region. Among those who contributed was John Forbes, Panton's successor, who now headed the Forbes company, but his paper was more concerned with the economic improvement of West Florida than with its history. He believed that it could be developed into one of the best agricultural and commercial colonies in the Spanish empire, but his recommendations were lost in the international intrigue of the time.

Unfortunately, conditions did not improve for West Florida, and plots to acquire the area west of the Perdido River continued until 1810. In September of that year, insurgents took the fort at Baton Rouge, quickly declared their independence, and created the Republic of West Florida. They adopted a constitution modeled after that of the United States and elected as their governor Fulwar Skipwith. Their flag had a white star on a blue field, thus making West Florida the first lone star republic. By 1812, the United States had annexed all of the territory between the Perdido and Mississippi Rivers. The area between the Pearl and Perdido Rivers was made a part of the Mississippi Territory, while the area west of the Pearl was incorporated into the State of Louisiana. By 1814, the United States had occupied Mobile and had built Fort Bowyer on Mobile Point and a lookout post on the Perdido River. The Spaniards at Pensacola continually protested such blatant aggression, but because of the Peninsular War then raging in Europe, they could do little about it.

The National Assembly (Cortes) of Spain enacted a constitution in March 1812, which also became the law of the two Floridas. The Spanish constitution of 1812 applied to all of Spain's territories as well to as the mother country.

News of the constitution reached St. Augustine in August 1812, and in October an official promulgation took place with a military parade and religious service. Under the provisions of the Spanish constitution, St. Augustine's and Pensacola's voters elected their first city councils (*ayuntamientos*). Correspondence written by Gerónimo Alvarez, first mayor of St. Augustine, and the minutes book of the Council indicate that Spanish Floridians accepted their role of civic responsibility with enthusiasm. The St. Augustine City Council built a monument to commemorate the constitution of 1812 in the city's main plaza. The monument stands today. In Pensacola and St. Augustine, the respective city councils and military governors contended over the lines of authority. On 4 May 1814, Spain's King Fernando VII rescinded the constitution, and within a few months the city councils in both Florida capitals disbanded and authority over local affairs reverted to the military governors. In September 1820, St. Augustine celebrated the king's repromulgation of the constitution and reinstatement of the city council. The Spanish constitution continued in effect until the Floridas were transferred to the United States. Although short-lived in the Floridas, the Spanish constitution offered rights and privileges similar to those of the U.S. Constitution, and with more benefits for black citizens.

The War of 1812 reached the Gulf of Mexico in 1814. General Andrew Jackson, who had just led the U.S. forces to victory in the Creek War, commanded the military at Mobile. The British decided to use Pensacola as their base of operations in the planned attack upon Fort Bowyer, Mobile, and New Orleans. Their justification was that Great Britain and Spain were allies in the Peninsular War. More important, if the British succeeded in their Gulf coast campaign and captured Mobile and New Orleans, it was clear that they would return those places to Spain. Thus, a British victory would have serious consequences for the United States. Jackson learned of the British plans from James Innerarity, a Scottish merchant in Mobile. He had received the warning from his brother, John, in Pensacola and from a Havana merchant, Vincent Gray. John Innerarity had also sent a rider to warn the Americans at Fort Bowyer of the anticipated British attack. Thus, Americans were prepared when the attack began on 15 September 1814. But after the destruction of one of their warships, *Hermes,* by the fort's cannon, the British withdrew and returned to Pensacola. Two months later, Jackson commanded a U.S. force that attacked Pensacola to drive the British out.

Because the Spaniards were not at war with the United States, they refused to assist the British against the Americans. The British then abandoned Pensacola, but they took out their anger at the Spaniards by destroying their

This engraving of Andrew Jackson (1767–1845) was based on a painting for which Jackson sat in 1815. Leading Tennessee troops, Jackson made two invasions of the Spanish Floridas, first during the War of 1812 and again during the First Seminole War of 1818. In 1821, when Florida became a possession of the United States, he returned a third time to serve a brief stint as military governor. At Pensacola he clashed repeatedly with the outgoing Spanish governor, José Callava, over change-of-flag details, at one point clapping the Spaniard in jail. Jacksonville, a site he never visited, is named for him.

Fort San Carlos de Barrancas and the redoubt on Santa Rosa Island before leaving. The British actively recruited blacks and Indians to assist them in their efforts to capture New Orleans, which, by December 1814, had become their main objective. The results of that battle are well known: Once again, the Americans were victorious. After the Battle of New Orleans, the British occupied Dauphin Island near Mobile. Determined to win a victory over the Americans, the British attacked Fort Bowyer on Mobile Point on 9 February 1815. This time they succeeded, but two days after their victory they received word that the war was over. They quickly abandoned Fort Bowyer and left the Gulf coast. This was the last battle of the war of 1812. Fortunately for the United States, the Stars and Stripes still flew over Fort Bowyer, Mobile, and New Orleans.

In the years after the Creek War and the War of 1812, some of the Indians who had fled the Spanish Floridas, the so-called Red Sticks, and their black allies conducted raids into Alabama and Georgia. In retaliation, the United States in July 1816 attacked and destroyed Negro Fort, one of their strongholds, on the Apalachicola River. But this did not end the problem, and in March 1818, General Jackson again invaded Spanish West Florida.

Jackson marched to the Suwannee River, where he engaged in a limited skirmish with the Indians before they slipped away. Although frustrated by this failure, he captured a British soldier of fortune, Robert Chrystie Ambrister, and learned that the Red Sticks had been forewarned. Jackson then took the Spanish fort, San Marcos de Apalache, which he suspected of supplying the Red Sticks. He also took prisoner a British merchant, Alexander Arbuthnot, who was in the fort, and two Red Stick chiefs. Jackson summarily had the chiefs executed and court-martialed the two Englishmen for assisting the Red Sticks in their war against the United States. Both were found guilty. Ambrister was shot by a firing squad; Arbuthnot was hanged from the yardarm of his own ship, *The Last Chance*. Thus, two British subjects had been tried and executed in Spanish territory by U.S. troops.

After San Marcos, Jackson marched west to Pensacola. He believed the Spaniards there were still supplying the Indians and encouraging them to raid nearby Alabama territory. The Spaniards put up a brief defense, but the main body of troops, led by Colonel José Masot, abandoned the city and took refuge in the reconstructed Fort San Carlos de Barrancas. Jackson engaged them, and after a short fight, Masot surrendered. The Spanish officials and soldiers were put aboard ship and sent to Havana. Pensacola's Spanish archives went with them. En route, however, the ship was captured by corsairs and the records were thrown overboard, consigning much of Pensacola's written history to the depths.

For the next nine months, 26 May 1818 to 4 February 1819, Colonel William King, a Jackson appointee, served as the civil and military governor of Pensacola and West Florida. The Spanish minister in Washington, Luis de Onís, voiced Spain's disapproval of the invasion of Spanish territory but accomplished little. Finally, the Spaniards returned to Pensacola in February 1819, and Colonel José Callava became the last Spanish governor of West Florida.

East Florida's border with the United States offered constant problems as neither the United States nor East Florida's colonial government was able to control border violations, and raids and rustling persisted. U.S. citizens found the availability of land to be encouragement enough to immigrate, particularly when, in 1790, the king of Spain invited foreigners to settle in East Florida by offering homestead grants. Settlers from the southern states especially began to move in. The Crown granted each head of a household 100 acres, and each additional family member or slave qualified for an additional 50 acres. Title to the land passed to the homesteaders after ten years of occupancy, farming, erecting appropriate buildings, and maintaining livestock. Two events tied to the international conflicts, however, were devastating to the settlement and development of the province. Both were insurgent military activities fomented in the United States.

In 1793, some residents of Georgia, ostensibly acting on the precepts of the French Revolution, joined together to take over East Florida militarily in order to free the Spanish province of what they considered monarchical tyranny. According to their plan, an expeditionary force would provide support for Florida residents who might wish to establish an independent republic in East Florida and subsequently request annexation into the United States. Doubtful of the loyalty of residents in the northern part of his province in the presence of such a force, Governor Juan Nepomuceno de Quesada and his council of war ordered the evacuation of the area between the St. Marys and St. Johns Rivers during the first week of 1794. To deprive the invasion of the force of any assistance, the council also demanded that crops be harvested or destroyed, buildings in the area burned, and residents either removed to another part of the province or made to leave the colony. These decisions reflected East Florida's role as a military outpost, where strategic requirements superseded all other considerations in time of threat. Not until 9 July 1795, however, did the strike against Spanish sovereignty come, when Florida residents and compatriots from the United States seized the Spanish fortification of San Nicolás in present-day downtown Jacksonville. The rebels persisted in their affiliation with the French cause, identifying themselves as French forces and cheering for the Republic of France during the skirmish. But, by mid-October, Spanish troops had routed the insurgents from the province, and settlers had relocated in the northern region to take advantage of newly available lands, abandoned by those who had fled.

The "Patriot War" in East Florida was a conflict that reflected expansionist desires on the part of United States and the anger of slave owners in the southern United States over the less-controlled existence of blacks in Spanish East Florida. American slave owners wanted especially to eliminate the frightening example of African Americans in Florida possessing firearms. Complicating matters, Amelia Island, the northeasternmost settlement site in East Florida, had developed since 1807 into an important "neutral" transshipping port for U.S. merchants who wished to bypass their own government's embargo. In 1812, James Madison's administration supported actions against Spain's colony of East Florida in order to expand the jurisdiction of the U.S. Non-Importation Act, to assert U.S. hegemony in the region, and to preempt any self-serving British activity in Florida.

Crossing into Spanish Florida on 10 March 1812, the Georgian expeditionary force, led by General George Mathews, did not find the anticipated cooperation from East Florida residents. The invaders took the town and port of Fernandina on Amelia Island, and by mid-April they were encamped at the site of Fort Mose, two miles north of St. Augustine, when President Madison withdrew official support for the venture in the face of public disapproval. But the filibusters did not withdraw. That summer, the Seminole Indians and their African American allies entered the conflict. The Patriots turned toward the interior and then occupied lands claimed by the Seminoles.

Die-hard adherents of the Patriot cause held on in East Florida until May 1814, causing widespread devastation. Various factions burned plantations and farmsteads on the Florida side of the St. Marys River, both sides of the St. Johns River, and the estuaries of today's Intracoastal Waterway as far south as present-day New Smyrna Beach although they bypassed St. Augustine and left a two-mile swath around the capital unharmed. Livestock strayed or were consumed by invading troops. John Fraser of Greenfields Plantation at the mouth of the St. Johns River claimed that he lost $111,000 in property and potential profit from his unplanted cotton crop. Equally important to a smaller farmer was the destruction of his houses and barns, food crops, rifles and miscellany such as a coffee mill, a fiddle and sheet music, and a fishing net. One rancher never recovered the 800 head of cattle he owned before the disruptions. Judge Isaac Bronson would declare that by the time the invaders retired, "the whole inhabited part of the province was in a state of utter desolation and ruin."[2] The depredation discouraged a number of settlers who had opted to remain in East Florida after their losses in 1794, and they departed the province in disgust after the so-called Patriot War.

When Spaniards returned to occupy St. Augustine after the twenty-one-year British interregnum, they found the physical appearance of the city substantially unchanged. In 1808, the Spanish Crown built a new, more impressive gate for the north entry through the wall that protected the capital city. Inside the walled city, wood-plank balconies of the coquina houses still cast their shadows over the old streets.

East Florida continued to be prey to the designs of invaders. Citizens of the U.S. southern states favored acquiring Florida as an American possession in order to eliminate the province as a destination for runaway slaves and to remove the Seminole presence from the northern region of the colony. The good harbor at the mouth of the St. Marys River at Fernandina attracted smugglers and adventurers. East Florida's last colonial governor, José María Coppinger, endeavored to maintain Spain's presence with dignity despite minimal support from his superiors in Cuba and troops who were inadequate both in number and in character. Coppinger even endured the experience of smugglers kidnapping his son and holding him ransom for food and other supplies from St. Augustine.

To encourage the loyalty of the residents in the northern area, Coppinger wisely instituted a form of local government that allowed some degree of representative decision making through the election of militia officials and magistrates, although the practice violated Spanish law. The capture of

Amelia Island in July 1817 by English-born Gregor MacGregor, a notorious insurgent, again disrupted peace in the region as well as Coppinger's successes with the citizenry. In December, U.S. soldiers, not Spanish troops, expelled MacGregor and occupied Amelia Island. In the second half of the following year, Coppinger readied for another invasion by MacGregor while residents lived also in fear of troops from the United States.

The incursions of Andrew Jackson into West Florida and Gregor MacGregor into East Florida mirrored the rebellions, revolutions, and violations of sovereign territories in the Americas and as well as in Spain, where French troops held areas of Spain itself. Spain's financial state was terrible. The Peninsular War had drained the country of much of its resources. Spain's King Fernando VII played politics with his countrymen and with the French. On top of that, rebellion was rampant in the Americas and soldiers revolted in Spain itself. Meanwhile, to no one's surprise, U.S. Secretary of State John Quincy Adams and Luis de Onís were negotiating for the transfer of the Floridas to the United States.

On 22 February 1819, the often discussed treaty ceding the Floridas to the United States was finally negotiated and signed in Washington by Adams and Onís. The Spanish Crown vacillated on affirming the treaty, and the United States threatened instead to take East Florida forcibly in 1820. Among the items in dispute were new, large land grants to Spanish nobles, which would eliminate the acreage from the public domain under American rule and make the parcels either unavailable for settlement or unacceptably expensive.

On 22 February 1821, the treaty of cession was finally ratified by both countries. According to its terms, the United States assumed $5 million worth of Spanish debts to American citizens and surrendered any claims to Texas. Governor Coppinger urged East Florida residents to emigrate to Cuba, Texas, or México. He received instructions to encourage the relocation of the Seminoles to the U.S.-Texas border, where they could serve as a valuable and strategic buffer to America penetration of Texas. On 10 July 1821, at 5:00 a.m., the Spanish flag was raised at St. Augustine for the last time. By 6:00 p.m., the last remaining Spanish soldier had departed from the city to the vessels waiting to take Spanish subjects to new posts and homes. A formal transfer of flags took place at Pensacola on 17 July.

More than three centuries of sunrises and sunsets lay between the first and final appearances of the Spanish flag in Florida. It will be the twenty-second century before the same can be said about the flag of the United States.

Notes

1. Weber, *Spanish Frontier*, 336.
2. Patrick, *Florida Fiasco*, 302.

Bibliography

Bermúdez, Ligia. "The Situado: A Study in the Dynamics of East Florida's Economy during the Second Spanish Period, 1785–1820." Master's thesis, University of Florida, 1989.

Coker, William S. "Father James Coleman, Vicar and Ecclesiastical Judge, Parish of San Miguel de Panzacola, 1794–1822." In *The Spanish Missionary Heritage of the United States,* edited by Howard Benoist and Sr. María Carolina Flories, C.P., pp. 29–45. San Antonio: U.S. Department of the Interior/National Park Service and Los Compadres de San Antonio Missions, National Historical Park [1991].

———. "How General Andrew Jackson Learned of the British Plans before the Battle of New Orleans." *Gulf coast Historical Review* 3, no. 1 (1987):85–95.

———. "The Last Battle of the War of 1812: New Orleans. No Fort Bowyer!" *Alabama Historical Quarterly* 43, no. 1 (Spring 1981):42–63.

Coker, William S., and Douglas G. Inglis. *The Spanish Censuses of Pensacola, 1784–1820: A Genealogical Guide to Spanish Pensacola.* Pensacola: Perdido Bay Press, 1980.

Coker, William S., and Jerrell H. Shofner. *Florida: From the Beginning to 1992.* Houston, Tex.: Pioneer, 1992.

Coker, William S., and Thomas D. Watson. *Indian Traders of the Southeastern Spanish Borderlands: Panton, Leslie & Company and John Forbes & Company, 1783–1847.* Gainesville: University Presses of Florida, 1986.

Coker, William S., et al. *John Forbes' Description of the Spanish Floridas, 1804.* Pensacola: Perdido Bay Press, 1979.

Cusick, James Gregory. "Ethnic Groups and Class in an Emerging Market Economy: Spaniards and Minorcans in Late Colonial St. Augustine." Ph.D. diss., University of Florida, 1993.

East Florida Papers Manuscript Collection, Library of Congress. Microfilm.

Gannon, Michael V. *The Cross in the Sand: The Early Catholic Church in Florida, 1513–1870.* Gainesville: University of Florida Press, 1965.

Holmes, Jack D. L. "West Florida, 1779–1821." In *A Guide to the History of Florida,* edited by Paul S. George, pp. 63–76. New York: Greenwood Press, 1989.

Marchena, Fernández, Juan. "The Defense Structure of East Florida, 1700–1820." *El Escribano* 21 (1984):37–52.

McAlister, L. N. "Pensacola during the Second Spanish Period." *Florida Historical Quarterly* 37 (1959):281–327.

McGovern, James R., ed. *Colonial Pensacola.* Pensacola: Pensacola-Escambia Development Commission, 1974.

Murdoch, Richard K. *The Georgia-Florida Frontier, 1793–1796: Spanish Reaction to French Intrigue and American Designs.* Berkeley: University of California Press, 1951.

Norris, L. David. "The Squeeze: Spain Cedes Florida to the United States." In *Clash be-

tween Cultures: Spanish East Florida, 1784–1821, edited by Jacqueline K. Fretwell and Susan R. Parker. St. Augustine: St. Augustine Historical Society, 1988.

Parker, Susan R. "Men Without God or King: Rural Settlers of East Florida, 1784–1790." Master's thesis, University of Florida, 1990.

———. "The Spanish Constitution in St. Augustine." *El Escribano* 49 (2011).

Patrick, Rembert. *Florida Fiasco: Rampant Rebels on the Georgia Florida Border, 1810–1813.* Athens: University of Georgia Press, 1954.

Patriot War Claims. Manuscript Collection 31. St. Augustine Historical Society.

Spanish Land Grant Claims. State Archives of Florida, Tallahassee.

Tanner, Helen Hornbeck. *Zéspedes in East Florida, 1784–1790.* Gainesville: University Presses of Florida, 1989.

Ward, Christopher. "The Commerce of East Florida during the Embargo of 1806–1812: The Role of Amelia Island." *Florida Historical Quarterly* 68(1989):160–79.

Weaver, Paul L., III. "The Constitution Obelisk of St. Augustine, Florida: A Unique Historic Resource." *El Escribano* 49 (2011).

Weber, David J. *The Spanish Frontier in North America.* New Haven: Yale University Press, 1992.

Wright, J. Leitch, Jr. *Anglo-Spanish Rivalry in North America.* Athens: University of Georgia Press, 1971.

11

Free and Enslaved

JANE LANDERS

The African presence in the Americas and in Florida dates to the earliest days of Spanish exploration, yet persons of African descent remain largely "invisible" in the historical literature. This absence is due, in part, to the difficulty of the sources (their locations are scattered and their language is eighteenth-century Spanish) and in part to the lack of interest among earlier scholars. But the Spaniards were meticulous bureaucrats, and the exceptionally rich documentary evidence on Africans in Florida tells much about their long-neglected history.

Florida was part of the Spanish Caribbean world for more than 300 years before it became an American possession in 1821, and the influence of Spanish legal traditions and race relations had a lasting impact on the African experience in the region.

Like other areas in the Spanish Caribbean, Florida suffered from early and dramatic Indian depopulation and a shortage of European manpower, and this demographic imperative created a demand for the labor, artisanal, and military skills of blacks. Once Africans entered Florida they interacted closely with the remaining Indian populations and, in effect, became culture brokers on the frontier, moving between the Spanish and Indian worlds.

Florida's first slaves came from southern Spain, where a significant African population filled a variety of important functions—laboring in mines and agriculture and in less onerous tasks as artisans, petty merchants, and domestics. Although most Africans in Spain were slaves, not all were. Spanish law and custom granted slaves a moral and legal personality, as well as certain rights and protections not found in other slave systems. They had the right to personal security and legal mechanisms by which to escape a cruel master. Further, slaves were permitted to hold and transfer property and to initiate legal suits—a significant right that in the Americas evolved into the right of self-purchase. Social and religious values in Spanish society promoted honor, charity, and paternalism toward "miserable classes," which often ameliorated the hardships slaves suffered and sometimes led owners to manumit them. This is not to suggest that Spain or its New World colonies were free of racial prejudice. Nevertheless, the emphasis on a slave's humanity and rights, and the lenient attitude toward manumission embodied in Spanish slave codes and social practice, made it possible for a significant free black class to exist, first in Spain, later in the Spanish Americas.

Africans, both free and enslaved, crossed the Atlantic on the early voyages and participated in the conquest and settlement of the new territories claimed by Spain. With the Europeans they formed a specialized pool of human resources circulating throughout the circum-Caribbean in many different expeditions. One member of this tightly knit group, a free African named Juan Gárrido, sailed from Seville to Hispaniola, where he befriended other blacks such as Juan González [Ponce] de León, an interpreter of the Taíno language. The two adventurers took part in Juan Ponce de León's "pacification" campaigns against the native populations of Hispaniola, his expedition to explore and conquer Puerto Rico (San Juan de Boriquen) in 1508, and in slaving raids against the Carib Indians on surrounding islands.

When Juan Ponce de León made his "discovery" in 1513 and initiated European exploration of the American Southeast, the free Africans Juan Gárrido and Juan González [Ponce] de León accompanied him. Although Juan Ponce de León's first contact with the Florida natives was hostile, it enabled Spain to claim exclusive sovereignty over the continent and led to further attempts to explore its interior.

After a second trip to Florida proved fatal to Juan Ponce de León, another Spanish adventurer (and slave raider), Lucas Vázquez de Ayllón, attempted a settlement on the Atlantic coast in 1526. The site, called San Miguel de Gualdape, is believed to be near present-day Sapelo Sound in Georgia (see chapter 2). Ayllón's expedition included 600 Spanish men, women, and children as well as the first-known contingent of African slaves brought to the present-day United States. As historian Paul E. Hoffman has pointed out, these were probably skilled artisans and domestics from Spain rather than African-born field hands. Ayllón's ambitious enterprise was undermined by disease, starvation, and his own death. Mutiny ensued, African slaves set fires to the compound, and the Guale Indians rebelled. The surviving Europeans straggled back to the Caribbean, but ethnohistorians maintain that the Africans took up residence among the Guales, becoming maroons, as

The free African Juan Gárrido participated in the early Spanish exploration in the Caribbean, in Ponce de León's 1513 voyage to Florida and in the conquest of the Aztec empire of México by Hernán Cortés. He is shown here as a spear carrier behind Cortés in an illustration from Fray Diego Durán, *Historia de las Indias de Nueva España y islas de Tierra Firme.*

many of their counterparts were doing in Hispaniola, Puerto Rico, Jamaica, Cuba, and México.

Despite the slave arson at Gualdape, African slaves were included in the next expedition to La Florida—that of Pánfilo de Narváez, who landed somewhere near Tampa in 1528. Like Ayllón's, his was a major colonization effort involving approximately 600 persons and unknown numbers of Africans. This colony, too, proved a disastrous failure, undone by hurricanes, supply losses, and separation of the forces. Of the four survivors who "came back from the dead" after eight years of wandering along the Gulf coast and westward to the Pacific Ocean, the most famous was the expedition's treasurer, Alvar Núñez Cabeza de Vaca, who left a written account of his trials. A less noted survivor was Estevan, the African slave of Andrés Dorantes, who quickly learned the language and belief systems of indigenous groups and whose skills helped sustain his party.

Hernando de Soto next took up the challenge of exploring the Southeast. Many of the men who accompanied de Soto to Florida in 1539 took with them their African slaves. De Soto's secretary wrote of Gómez, the slave of André de Vasconcelos, who helped the chieftainess of Cofitachequi to escape from the Spaniards and later became her husband. Other slaves and Spaniards from the de Soto expedition also "went over" to the Indians, further blending the Indian, African, and European populations of the Southeast.

Other Africans remained with de Soto's force for the duration. Bernaldo, a free caulker from Vizcaya and formerly the slave of one of de Soto's captains, survived the many bloody Indian battles, severe hunger, killing marches, and finally a voyage down the Mississippi River in hastily constructed boats. After an epic voyage of more than four years, during which the expeditionaries traversed 3,700 miles and ten of the present-day United States, Bernaldo was among those who limped back to Mexico City dressed only in animal skins.

Several more attempts failed before Pedro Menéndez de Avilés finally established the first permanent settlement at St. Augustine in 1565. By that time persons of African descent had already taken up residence in the peninsula. When Menéndez first explored his claim, he found a shipwrecked mulatto named Luis living among the fiercely resistant Ais nation to the south. Luis's knowledge of the Ais language had saved other shipwreck victims whose freedom Menéndez negotiated, among them an unnamed black woman. Luis became a translator for Menéndez and returned to live among the Spaniards, but other "captives" chose to stay with the Indians. Menéndez complained later that slaves from St. Augustine ran to and intermarried with the Ais. The possibility of an alternative life among the Indians would temper race relations in Florida well into the nineteenth century.

Although a royal charter permitted Menéndez to import 500 African slaves to do the difficult labor required in settling a new colony, he never filled that contract, and probably fewer than fifty slaves may have accompanied the first settlers. The loss of those slaves who ran to the Ais was significant. White manpower was in short supply in Florida, as it was in other areas of the Caribbean, and Spaniards considered Indians to be too weak, lazy, and transient to be a dependable labor force. Moreover, the native populations were extremely vulnerable to European diseases which had already ravaged their counterparts in the Antilles. Thus, the slaves who remained performed many critical functions in Spanish Florida, first at St. Augustine and later at Santa Elena, Spain's northernmost settlement, in present-day South Carolina. Slaves logged and sawed the timber for fortifications and ships, built structures, and cleared and planted the fields, "with no other expense but their oil and salt."[1] The Crown considered black labor indispensable to the maintenance of Florida, noting that the entire government subsidy would not suffice if wages had to be paid for their labor. By the seventeenth century, the government was depending on royal slaves to quarry coquina from Anastasia Island, make lime, load and unload government ships, and row government galleys. Private owners of slaves employed them in domestic occupations, as cattlemen and overseers on Florida's vast cattle ranches, and in a myriad of plantation jobs.

In times of crisis slaves and free Africans were also expected to help defend the colony and provide military reserves for the badly understaffed military garrison. After the late sixteenth century, the "Spanish Lake" was infested with corsairs from England, France, and Holland who raided Spanish shipping and settlements with seeming impunity. Florida's long exposed coastline made it particularly vulnerable to attack. By 1683 free blacks in St. Augustine had formed themselves into a formal militia unit and were commanded by officers of their own election. Similar units served in Hispaniola, Cuba, México, Puerto Rico, Cartagena, and throughout Central America.

The men who formed the black militias were usually free black artisans or skilled workers. They were Catholics who lived as Spaniards and were integrated into their communities through powerful social institutions such as godparentage and patron/client networks. Leading useful and orderly lives, they mirrored the early free African communities of Spain and enjoyed the protections promised by Spanish law and custom. Military service was an important way for free blacks to prove themselves to their community and also to advance themselves through occasional opportunities for plunder. Moreover, through the militias, free blacks acquired titles and status and eventually full military privileges. It is possible that the militia units also functioned to reinforce relationships within the African community, as "natural" leaders rose to command and assumed responsibility for their men. Parish registers from St. Augustine show that militia families commonly intermarried and served as godparents and marriage sponsors for one another. Church records also suggest that the double connection of family and military corporatism may have worked to move some men out of slavery. Although their slave past was certainly not forgotten, it was in a sense excused by appropriate behavior, valuable services, and the sponsorship of Africans of whom the community already approved.

Michael Mullin's recent study of slavery in the contemporary British Caribbean demonstrates how geographic context and the organization of labor shaped the institution of slavery. In Florida slavery exhibited a number of the features that Mullin contends mitigated its oppressive nature: it was generally organized by the task system, and slaves had free time to engage in their own social and economic activities; slaves were able to utilize the resources of both frontier and coast to their advantage; the trade in slaves was never massive; and the paternal model of plantation management prevailed, even on Florida's largest ranches and plantations. Moreover, the geopolitical pressures exerted by Spain's circum-Caribbean rivals meant additional leverage for slaves and more Spanish dependence upon free people of color.

In 1670 English planters from Barbados challenged Spain's claim to exclusive control of the Atlantic seaboard by establishing Charles Town. St. Augustine lacked sufficient force to mount a major attack against the usurpers, but Spanish governors initiated a campaign of harassment against the English colony that included slave raids by the Spaniards and their black and Indian allies. These contacts may have pointed the way to St. Augustine and suggested to English-owned black slaves the possibility of a refuge among the enemy, for in 1687, after a dramatic escape by canoe, eight men, two women, and a nursing child appeared in Florida. The fugitive slaves requested religious sanctuary in St. Augustine, and, despite an early ambiguity about their legal condition, only in one known example were the runaways returned to their English masters. The rest were sheltered in St. Augustine, instructed and baptized in the Catholic faith, married, and employed, ostensibly for wages. Royal policy regarding the fugitives was finally set in 1693 when Charles II granted the newcomers to Florida freedom on the basis of religious conversion, "the men as well as the women . . . so that by their example and by my liberality others will do the same."[2] In gratitude the freedmen vowed to shed their "last drop of blood in defense of the Great Crown of Spain and the Holy Faith, and to be the most cruel enemies of the English."[3] The runaways had considered their options and made their choices.

During the next decades more fugitives from Carolina flowed into St. Augustine, and in 1738 the Spanish governor established the freedmen and -women in the town of Gracia Real de Santa Teresa de Mose, about two miles north of St. Augustine. Florida's governor recognized the group's spokesman and the captain of their newly formed militia, Francisco Menéndez, as the "chief" of Mose and referred to the others living at the village as his "subjects." The residents of Mose established complex family and fictive kin networks over several generations and successfully incorporated into the founding group incoming fugitives, Indians from nearby villages, and slaves from St. Augustine. Community and familial ties were further reinforced by a tradition of militia service at Mose.

MILICIAS de MORENOS LIBRES de VERACRUZ y de LA HABANA 1770-1776. Segun Reglamentos y Modelos de la Época, Archivo Gral. de las Indias, Sevilla.

Many former slaves and free African Americans served in Spanish militias in Florida and throughout the circum-Caribbean in the eighteenth century. The soldiers depicted here were posted at Havana, Cuba, and Veracruz, México.

However, despite the best efforts of Menéndez and his men, the first town of Mose was destroyed when General James Oglethorpe commanded a joint naval and land assault against St. Augustine in 1740. Mose's inhabitants took up residence in St. Augustine until Governor Fulgencio García de Solís attempted to relocate the freedmen to Mose in 1752. The former residents feared further attacks and did not want to move back, but after the governor promised to fortify the settlement better and to post soldiers at the site, the freedmen rebuilt Mose, constructing a church and a house for the Franciscan priest within an enclosed fort as well as twenty-two shelters outside the fort for their own households.

Kathleen Deagan of the Florida Museum of Natural History directed an interdisciplinary investigation of Mose that has added to the documentary record archaeological, or material, evidence about daily life at this unique site. In two seasons of excavations her team uncovered the foundations and earthen walls of the fort, parts of the palisade, sections of the moat, and several of the interior structures. They also recovered military artifacts such as bullets, gunflints, and buttons and domestic items such as bone buttons, pins and thimbles, clay pipe bowls, beads, and a variety of eighteenth-century ceramics and bottles. One valuable find was a handmade pewter St. Christopher's medal, which may be a reference to the Africans' travels over water or suggest links to Havana, for which St. Christopher was the patron.

While conditions at Mose were rugged, the homesteaders were at least free to farm their own lands, build their own homes, and live in them with their families. A house-by-house census of Mose from 1759 identified thirty-seven men, fifteen women, seven boys, and eight girls living at the site. Included were members of the Mandinga, Congo, and Carabalí nations, as well as many others, but over time the diverse ethnic-linguistic groups formed a cohesive community that survived until 1763. Then, through the fortunes of war, Spain lost Florida to the British, and the Spanish Crown evacuated St. Augustine and its black and Indian allies to Cuba.

Under British rule (1763–84), black freedom in Florida became only a remote possibility. Anglo planters established vast indigo, rice, sugar, and sea island cotton plantations modeled after those in South Carolina and Georgia. Historian Daniel L. Schafer has found that wealthy planters, such as Richard Oswald and John Fraser, imported large numbers of African slaves from Sierra Leóne for the back-breaking work involved in establishing new plantations. Soon Africans were the most numerous element of Florida's population. The American Revolution accelerated that trend, for after the Patriots took Charleston and Savannah, planters shifted whole workforces

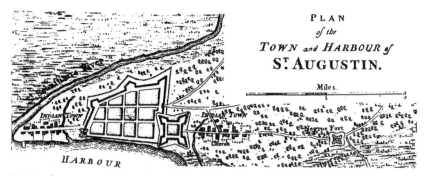

In 1738, slave runaways from Carolina and Georgia received civil and religious sanctuary in Spanish Florida. With support from Governor Manuel de Montiano, they established the legally sanctioned free community of Gracia Real de Santa Teresa de Mose. Two miles north of St. Augustine, Mose is shown as "Negroe Fort" (*right*) on this 1762 plan by English cartographer Thomas Jefferys (1699–1775).

into East Florida, the last Loyalist haven in North America. The colony's population grew by about 12,000 persons, over half of whom were black, making the black-white ratio approximately three to one. Although a small number of these blacks were free—for example, those who had performed military service for George III—most were not. British Floridians restricted the movement of free blacks, adopted a slave code based on that of South Carolina, and often subjected slaves to brutal punishments.

At the conclusion of the North American revolution, Florida was retroceded to Spain, and many slaves took advantage of the chaos of war and the subsequent colonial transfer to escape British control. Untold numbers found sanctuary among the Seminole nation, which had established flourishing villages in the central plains of north Florida. Others, however, claimed a refuge among the incoming Spaniards on the grounds of religious conversion; although the Spanish governor doubted their religious motivation, the 1693 sanctuary policy was still in effect, and he was forced to honor it. After appearing before notaries to be documented and to show proof of work, at least 251 individuals were manumitted under the sanctuary provisions.

Prince Witten, his wife, Judy, and their children, Polly and Glasgow, were among those presenting themselves to be manumitted, and their lives demonstrate how ambitious persons were able to maximize the benefits of free status in Spanish Florida. Prince and Judy were Guinea-born slaves who escaped from Georgia. Runaway notices reported that Prince had fled to Florida "to avoid a separation from his family to which he is much attached."[4]

Once Witten and his family were granted sanctuary in Florida, they adapted to the civil, religious, and military expectations of successive Spanish governments and prospered. The family's freedom was dependent upon religious conversion, and the children were baptized within a year of entering the province. Adult baptism required religious instruction and usually took somewhat longer to accomplish, but in 1792 Prince and Judy were also baptized. Later they had their marriage of twenty-one years legitimized by the Catholic Church and became favored godparents for the black community, free and slave. Prince served as godfather to twenty-three children, and Judy was godmother to thirty-one children, including the child of her own slave. When Polly and Glasgow grew older, they, too, were popular godparents.

Witten was a skilled carpenter and hired himself out to a variety of employers. He also earned money working on government construction projects, and by 1793 he and his family were living between prominent white neighbors in the city. By the following year, Judy, a laundress and cook,

Some escaped slaves found refuge among the Seminole villages of Florida and later joined in three wars against U.S. forces bent on removing the Seminole from their lands (see chapter 12).

owned a female slave. Prince joined the free black militia and defended St. Augustine on numerous occasions, including the French-inspired invasion of 1795, the State of Muskogee's war against Spain from 1800 to 1803, and the Patriot War of 1812, in which he earned heroic status and the rank of lieutenant.

While the free black population grew during the second Spanish rule of Florida (1784–1821), so did the enslaved African population. Englishmen who accepted Spanish dominion in Florida and Spaniards alike operated plantations and cattle ranches with sizable labor forces of 50 to 200 slaves. One large planter, Zephaniah Kingsley, credited his success to a moderate view of race relations, the task system, and the employment of highly skilled slaves in management positions on his diversified estates. Other successful operations such as the plantations of Francisco Xavier Sánchez were devoted to cattle, which required a mobile and fairly autonomous workforce, as did Sánchez's timbering operations. A black overseer, Edimboro, managed Sánchez's enterprises when Sánchez was in Cuba. The corporate establishments of the Panton, Leslie trading company, which included trading stores, agricultural plantations, and cattle ranches, employed African workforces of up to 250 laborers, as well as black linguists and black Indian traders.

On both corporate and privately owned plantations, it was common for several generations of slave families to live and work together. The paternal model of slave management was reinforced by religion, law, and community norms. Slave masters were often linked to their slaves as godparents, which further underscored paternal obligations. Slaves used these intangible but real assets to improve their conditions, petitioning the courts when they were ill treated, were not materially provided for in the required manner, or wished to change owners. They also went to court to effect self-purchase arrangements. Even slaves on remote plantations were linked to urban institutions and networks through economic activities, the mobility of free blacks, and visits of the parish priest and other city dwellers.

Treasury accounts, census returns, notarized instruments, and civil petitions provide insights into the lives of St. Augustine's black community. Although censuses are inconsistent and must be used with caution, they show that the black population of the Second Spanish Period in Florida ranged from 27 percent of the total recorded population in 1786 to 57 percent in 1814. Whatever the limitations of the counts, it is obvious that Spanish Florida had a sizable and growing population of African descent. A variety of economic opportunities existed in this Atlantic port city, and as they had in the First Spanish Period, many black males worked for the government, on fortifications projects, in the royal armory, unloading ships at the wharf, delivering the mails, cutting timber, and as pilots and oarsmen on government boats. Although in some major cities of Spanish America blacks were forbidden to compete with whites in the marketplace, no such restrictions operated in St. Augustine. Free blacks were cartwrights, jewelers, shoemakers, tanners, butchers, and innkeepers, to name a few of their varied occupations. Antonio Coleman was a skilled tailor who also supported himself by playing the fiddle at dances. Manuel Alzendorf fished for turtles when he was not barbering. One black entrepreneur, Juan Bautista Collins, had mercantile links to South Carolina, Havana, New Orleans, Pensacola, and the Seminole nation in the heart of Florida. He bought and sold everything from butter to large herds of cattle, acquired property, and, like other ambitious free men of color in St. Augustine, observed the Catholic faith and joined the black militia.

Although the lives of women are more difficult to document, records show that free black women in St. Augustine were laundresses or cooks or had small businesses, selling crafts or foodstuffs. Others, like Nancy Wiggins and Anna Madgigine Jai, advanced themselves through unions with, and sometimes marriages to, white men of property. They managed homesteads and even sizable plantations, bought and sold property, including slaves, and entered into business agreements with both black and white townspeople. Miscegenation was a common and accepted feature of life in St. Augustine, and although most white fathers did not marry black women, they routinely acknowledged their children at baptism and in their wills. Children of interracial unions in St. Augustine often received education, training, or property from their white fathers. Free black parents also left more modest properties to their children. They tried to arrange good marriages for their daughters and sought to advance their sons by enrolling them in St. Augustine's parochial school or by apprenticing them to tradesmen.

But while some of their former slaves went about creating new lives for themselves, Georgian slave owners complained bitterly about the provocation inherent in Florida's sanctuary policy. Finally, in 1790, Spain bowed to the pressures of the new U.S. government delivered through its forceful secretary of state, Thomas Jefferson, and abrogated Florida's religious sanctuary policy. But all escaped slaves who had already claimed freedom in Florida remained free.

Enslaved people could no longer utilize Florida's religious sanctuary provision to achieve freedom, but they still had the possibility of purchased or granted freedom. Military service to the Crown was another avenue out of bondage. During the slave revolt in Saint-Domingue, thousands of former slaves allied themselves to the Spanish Crown and were organized into a force known as the Black Auxiliaries of Carlos IV. Among its leaders was Jorge Biassou, who commanded an army of 40,000 men and outranked the famous Toussaint Louverture. When Spain concluded a peace treaty with the Directory of the French Republic, the Black Auxiliaries were disbanded and dispersed to various locations in the Caribbean and Spain. The decorated and well-pensioned Biassou, and his "family" of kin and dependent troops, chose relocation in St. Augustine, where they were absorbed into the polyglot black community.

Despite major language and cultural differences, Biassou's "family" quickly blended into the free black community. Within three months of their arrival in St. Augustine, Biassou's brother-in-law and heir apparent, Jorge Jacobo, married Prince Witten's daughter, María (Polly) Rafaela, effectively linking the leading families among the North American and Haitian refugee communities.

The Spanish governors were not pleased by the "proud and vain character" and "high temper" Biassou displayed and worried about the bad example he and his band might set. Still, they had no choice but to receive him. Biassou and his men were quick to remind Florida's governors and the captain general of Cuba of their service in various campaigns in Hispaniola, of the promises made them by the Spanish king, and of their status as his loyal and free vassals. Biassou retained the title of caudillo in St. Augustine, and Florida's governors employed him and his battle-hardened men in guerrilla operations against hostile Indians who terrorized Spanish Florida from 1800 to 1803.

The violence of the Saint-Domingue slave revolt and the establishment of Haiti's free black government had hemispheric implications, and Florida's dependence upon black military forces was a continuing and grave concern to Anglo planters on its borders. Governor David Mitchell of Georgia warned President James Monroe that the Spaniards "have armed every able-bodied negro within their power. . . . Our southern country will soon be in a state of insurrection." In 1812, with the covert support of the U.S. government, John McIntosh led the so-called Patriot rebels to try to overthrow Spanish rule in Florida. He echoed Mitchell's sentiments in his own letter to

Monroe, complaining that Florida was a refuge for fugitive slaves and that its emissaries "will be detached to bring about the revolt of the black population of the United States."[5]

Violations of Spain's territorial sovereignty in Florida were a regular feature of U.S. foreign policy for the remainder of the decade: the Patriot War of 1812, a naval attack on the black and Indian fort and settlement at Prospect Bluff on the Apalachicola River in 1815, and Andrew Jackson's devastating raids against Seminole villages along the Suwannee in 1818. The same U.S. hostility toward free blacks living among the Seminole, and the Seminole refusal to return their allies and family members to slavery, contributed to the three Seminole wars from 1818 to 1858.

Florida's black troops were able to slow but not stem the tide of U.S. expansionism. When Spain finally turned Florida over to the officials of the U.S. territorial government in 1821, it did not abandon its free black citizens. As in Louisiana, cession treaties required that the legal status and property rights of free blacks be respected by the incoming government. Some free blacks, like Prince Witten and Edimboro Sánchez, who had won his freedom despite the protests of his former owner, had acquired property and invested years of hard work in improving it. They decided to stay in Florida and risk trusting the newcomers to honor their treaty promises. But Prince's daughter, María, and Edimboro's daughter, Nicolasa, joined their husbands and most of the free black community in a second exodus to Cuba. Like their predecessors in 1763, these exiles received government assistance as they remade their lives in Cuba.

Meanwhile, African Americans who had made their free lives among the Seminole rather than among the Spanish were still at risk from the incoming Americans, who brought with them chattel slavery and a firm conviction of their racial superiority. These new homesteaders had long objected to the free blacks living in Florida, fearing their militancy, their alliance with Native Americans, and the dangerous example they set for plantation slaves. Finding the racial climate in Florida increasingly restrictive, more free blacks from St. Augustine left for Cuba in the American territorial years, and in 1857 another community of free blacks living in Pensacola departed for México.

These new migrations underscored the fact that Florida was an extension of the Caribbean, where Native Americans, Europeans, and Africans had interacted for centuries. Embroiled in the struggles of the European "superpowers" of their day, Africans in Florida and in the circum-Caribbean became adroit at reading the political tides. They were pragmatic diplomats, shifting allegiances when they saw the need. In some areas of the Southeast their strategic advantage lasted well into the eighteenth century, and in Florida it ended only when the region became part of the American South in the nineteenth century. Historians Daniel Schafer and Canter Brown Jr. have shown that even then Spanish legal traditions and customs left an imprint in northeastern Florida that blunted some of the more restrictive and punitive aspects of territorial race legislation.

Free and enslaved Africans helped shape international geopolitics in the Southeast for more than three centuries before slavery was finally abolished in Florida, yet their existence and their impact has been obscured by traditional historiography. As new historical and archaeological investigations are determining, African Americans exercised more important and varied roles in the colonial history of the Spanish frontiers of the United States than has previously been appreciated. These studies make it clear that no history of Florida, or the Southeast, is complete without considering this complex and multidimensional African experience.

Notes

1. Fernando Miranda to the King, 20 August 1583, cited in Verne E. Chatelain, *The Defenses of Spanish Florida, 1565–1763* (Washington: Carnegie Institution of Washington, 1941), p. 138.

2. Royal edict, 7 November 1693, Santo Domingo 58-1-26 in the John B. Stetson Collection, P. K. Yonge Library of Florida History, University of Florida, Gainesville (hereafter cited as PKY).

3. Fugitive Negroes of the English plantations to the King, 10 June 1738, SD 844, on microfilm reel 15, PKY.

4. Letter of Alexander Semple, 16 December 1786, "To and from the United States, 1784–1821," on microfilm reel 41, EFP, PKY. According to this letter, Prince had attempted twice before to escape.

5. J. H. Alexander, "The Ambush of Captain John Williams, U.S.M.C.: Failure of the East Florida Invasion," *Florida Historical Quarterly* 56, no. 3 (July 1977):286.

Bibliography

Colburn, David, and Jane Landers, eds. *The African American Heritage of Florida.* Gainesville: University Press of Florida, 1995.

Ferguson, Leland. *Uncommon Ground: Archaeology and Early African America, 1650–1800.* Washington: Smithsonian Press, 1992.

Hall, Gwendolyn Midlo. *Africans in Colonial Louisiana: The Development of Afro-Creole Culture in the Eighteenth Century.* Baton Rouge: Louisiana State University Press, 1992.

Landers, Jane. "Africans in the Land of Ayllón: The Exploration and Settlement of the Southeast." In *Columbus and the Land of Ayllón,* edited by Jeaninne Cook, pp. 105–230. Darien, Ga.: Lower Altamaha Historical Society, 1992.

——. "An Examination of Racial Conflict and Cooperation in Spanish St. Augustine: The Career of Jorge Biassou, Black Caudillo." *El Escribano* (December 1988):85–100.

——. "Gracia Real de Santa Teresa de Mose: A Free Black Town in Spanish Colonial Florida." *American Historical Review* 95, no. 1 (February 1990):9–30.

Mullin, Michael. *Africa in America: Slave Acculturation and Resistance in the American South and the British Caribbean, 1736–1831.* Urbana: University of Illinois Press, 1992.

Mulroy, Kevin. *Freedom on the Border: The Seminole Maroons in Florida, the Indian Territory, Coahuila, and Texas.* Lubbock: Texas Tech University Press, 1993.

Patrick, Rembert W. *Florida Fiasco: Rampant Rebels on the Georgia-Florida Border.* Athens: University of Georgia Press, 1954.

Porter, Kenneth Wiggins. *The Negro on the American Frontier.* New York: Arno Press, 1971.

Thornton, John. *Africa and Africans in the Making of the Atlantic World, 1400–1680.* Cambridge: Cambridge University Press, 1992.

Usner, Daniel H., Jr. *Indians, Settlers, and Slaves in a Frontier Exchange Economy: The Lower Mississippi Valley Before 1783.* Chapel Hill: University of North Carolina Press, 1992.

Wood, Peter W. *Black Majority: Negroes in Colonial South Carolina from 1670 through the Stono Rebellion.* New York: Norton Press, 1974.

12

Florida's Seminole and Miccosukee Peoples

BRENT R. WEISMAN

Origins

The Native Americans that today compose Florida's Seminole and Miccosukee tribes have roots deep in the cultural prehistory of southeastern North America. The modern political division between the two tribes, dating formally only to the 1950s, belies their fundamental cultural similarity and shared historical origin in the lower piedmont of present-day Georgia and Alabama. Here dwelled the Creeks, Yuchis, and other related groups, the immediate cultural ancestors of the Indians to be known in Florida as *cimmarones*. This word, of Spanish origin, meant in the usage of the time people separate from, or apart from, their major ancestral population center. In the native Muskogean tongue, the Spanish word became "Seminole," forms of which were in use in British Florida by 1765. The transformation of Creek into Seminole is the story of both cultural adaptation to the environmental, political, and economic conditions of a rapidly globalizing world and the cultural persistence of ancient customs and beliefs deeply seated in place and time.

The foundations of both Creek and Seminole culture lie in the aboriginal mound-building chiefdoms of the lower Southeast. By the tenth century A.D., or C.E., such societies were presided over by hereditary chiefs and a priestly elite who resided in formal towns consisting of temple and residential mounds arranged around a central plaza. Much of the populace lived in the surrounding countryside in small farming hamlets on the banks of streams or tributary creeks. Society was divided into matrilineal clans, that is, clan membership was determined through the mother's line. In this system, a man's sons were not members of his clan, nor could they inherit to him. Instead, he had a set of responsibilities and obligations to his sister's sons, and they to him. Thus we see in Creek and early Seminole leadership the succession of chiefly power from a man to his nephew. It is likely also that the women and their families living together in the farming hamlets shared clan membership. In the historic Creek period, these small maternal clan groups were known as *huti,* while in Seminole society of the recent past such groups were known as *istihapo,* or clan camps.

Creek religion stressed purity of mind and body, which was achieved through the ritual use of tobacco, scratching or blood-letting, and imbibing the "black drink," a tea brewed from Ilex (holly) leaves and other herbs, to induce vomiting. Annual or seasonal ceremonies held in the plaza or squareground emphasized community purity and solidarity. The most important and enduring of these ceremonies was the Green Corn Dance, or busk (from the Creek *poskita,* to fast), still practiced by the Creeks and Seminoles today. This event, typically lasting four days, consisted of scheduled social, political, and religious activities. Males and females, armed with webbed ball sticks, played vigorously at the ball game. Boys would step up to become young men through the naming ritual and puberty rites. Crimes were atoned for and grievances heard by the tribal council on Court day. The medicine man would publicly examine the medicine bundle, then secrete it away until next year. Then there were the dances, in which the dancers circled a ritually prepared low mound of earth or moved in patterned formation across the dance ground. Above all, the goal was to produce harmony and a sense of well-being for both the individual and the larger community.

The Creek cosmos, inherited from the Mississippian mound builders, was shaped by beliefs associated with the four cardinal directions. The east, for instance, associated with the rising sun, was thought to have beneficial power. Mythical serpents, horned monsters, and other creatures had their place in the Creek and Seminole cosmos. Colors also were given symbolic meaning, with red being the color of war, and white associated with peace.

In daily life, the principal occupation of men was to hunt and make war. Both activities usually required small groups of men to be absent from their households for extended periods of time, during which time the women would tend garden plots, fish and gather plant foods available closer to home, take care of the children, make pottery and clothing, and engage in numerous other domestic tasks. Warfare was not the mass frontal assault familiar to Europeans, but instead consisted of raids on the enemy. The rewards for personal bravery and stealth shown in such raids included increased prestige among the warrior's peers, the privilege to wear a tattoo, and the opportunity for a young man to earn an adult, or warrior's, name.

The coming of the Europeans to the interior Southeast, beginning with the Spanish *conquistadores* in the mid-sixteenth century, had drastic and far-reaching consequences for the aboriginal populations of the region. The Creeks, possibly owing to their interior, buffered location, were spared immediate extinction, although the effects of depopulation due both to introduced disease and direct conflict with the Europeans and the movement of towns did much to unsettle the traditional social structure. However, with the arrival of British colonists, first on the Carolina coast and, by 1670, in Georgia, the Creeks, by virtue of their location, assumed a pivotal position in the trade networks opening up on the emerging colonial frontier. Deerskins, in great demand in Europe for making clothing, saddles, and other items, passed from Indian hands to traders located at posts on the fall line or on the coasts, while the Indians reaped iron tools and utensils, beads, coarse "stroud" cloth, and guns and ammunition in the exchange. The Creeks were quickly and deeply enmeshed in an expanding commercial economy. Meanwhile, in Florida, things had not gone well with the native tribes. The more populous groups—the Calusa of the southwest coast, the Timucua-speaking peoples of the central interior, the Apalachee of the Panhandle—had borne the brunt of the first encounters with the Spanish conquistadores beginning early in the sixteenth century. Following the establishment of St. Augustine in 1565 by Pedro Menéndez de Avilés, the serious missionizing of the Florida Indians began. After a failed Jesuit effort, Franciscan priests concentrated on the conversion of the surviving Timucua and Apalachee Indians of north Florida. Besides the earnest desire on the part of the mission priests to bring Catholicism to the natives, the Spanish colonial government in St. Augustine looked upon the mission chain to provide a first line of defense should the British decide to expand southward. When the inevitable push did come, the small, isolated mission settlements, most of which were not garrisoned, could not hold. First in the 1680s, and then more seriously between 1702 and 1706, the Florida missions were assaulted by well-armed, British-backed Yamasees and Creeks, who swept some 1,000 Florida Indians into plantation slavery on the rice coast of Carolina.

Despite the apparent good feeling between the British and the Creeks, in 1715 "Emperor" Brim of the Coweta Creeks attempted to organize a unified strike against the British, French, and Spanish colonists in former Indian

Map showing locations mentioned in the text.

territory. When the first attack of the so-called Yamasee War failed, some of the Creek towns moved from their former locations to avoid retaliation, while these and other towns in the Lower Creek region of central Georgia began a cautious realignment toward the Spanish in Florida. Taking advantage of this turn in allegiance, in 1716, 1717, and 1718 the Spanish sent Diego Pena among the Lower Creeks in an attempt to entice them to move to the largely vacant Florida peninsula. A number of towns—Oconee, Yuchi, Sawokli, Apalachicola—responded favorably to Pena's offer, and the gradual native repopulation of Florida was begun. Slowly, in the middle decades of the eighteenth century, the old Apalachee area around present-day Tallahassee, the Apalachicola drainage, the central Florida region surrounding the great Alachua Savanna (Paynes Prairie), and, to a lesser extent, the rolling uplands northeast of Tampa Bay, witnessed the transformation of Creek into Seminole. With these peoples came languages new to the Florida peninsula. Hitchiti, ancestral to the Mikasuki language spoken by members of the contemporary Seminole and Miccosukee tribes, could be heard in the Alachua Savanna, Apalachicola, and Tallahassee areas. Muskogee, or Creek, today spoken on the Brighton Seminole reservation, was also to be heard in some of the Tallahassee towns and in the settlements above Tampa Bay.

Early Seminole history can be divided into two periods: Colonization (1716–1767), the initial migrations of the Creek towns into Florida; and Enterprise (1767–1821), the era of prosperity under British and Spanish rule of Florida prior to the American presence.

Colonization (1716–1767)

The exact dates for the settlement of Florida by the Creeks are not certain, nor are they likely to be, given the uneven documentation of the time. It does not appear, however, that these first Florida towns virtually replicated in architecture and social structure the Creek settlements to the north. Squareground towns, notably at Latchua or Latchaway (on the rim of today's Paynes Prairie) and on the west bank of the Suwannee River in the vicinity of Old Town (Dixie County) continued to be the hub of social and political life. A squareground typically consisted of four open pavilions at each side of the square, one of them specially designated for the chief like Cowkeeper of Latchaway and White King of the Suwannee town. In the central plaza of the square was the dance circle. Red towns still battled White towns in the ballgame, as they had in Creek country, the peace pipe or calumet ceremony still opened important proceedings, and the black drink (actually known to the Indians as the "white drink") still purified both mind and spirit.

Although there was a basic continuity of the Creek culture pattern, there was an increasing and purposeful separation by the Florida Indians from the political affairs of their Creek counterparts to the north. In 1765, when Governor James Grant of the British colonial government called the Creek leaders together for the Picolata Congress, at which he hoped to gain from them boundary concessions to land east of the St. Johns River, the shrewd Cowkeeper was not in attendance, preferring to pay the governor a personal visit a month later. By Cowkeeper's own testimony, he had little formal contact with the Creek leadership during the decade previous. Cowkeeper's case also illustrates how difficult it is to characterize any aspect of Seminole history with simple generality, for while he led his band of Oconees to settle in Spanish Florida, he boasted of killing eighty-six Spaniards and hoped to do away with more. Yet he seemed to have little use for the British in Florida (although he was regarded as friendly), and little direct interest in Anglo-Creek politics. Perhaps his strongest inclination was in maintaining a degree of autonomy for his people. At St. Marks in the former Apalachee territory, the Spanish established a trading post in 1745, hoping to lure neighboring Lower Creeks into permanent settlement. For a time this was successful, with the founding of Creek towns in the area under the overall leadership of Secoffee, the son of Brim. However, the Spanish had difficulty provisioning the store to meet demand as the quantity of deerskins brought in far surpassed their expectation. Indian restlessness grew in this part of Spanish Florida.

The archaeological remains, what few there are that can be confidently dated to the colonization period, show a strong continuity of Creek material culture. Pottery vessels, the best collection of which is from the Suwannee River, are of the same form and function as similarly dated Creek vessels, and bear the same "brushed" surface treatment and styles of rim decoration. Trade goods found, such as razors, knives, gun parts, glass beads, silver cones and earrings, buckles, and horse tack indicate full participation in the trade economy.

As the native involvement in trade intensified, and as tensions between Indian, Anglo, French, and Spanish on the colonial frontier continued to mount, the underpinnings of traditional Creek society began, slowly at first, to give way. The power of hereditary leadership began to diminish as traders plied the interior looking to make deals with whomever they could. As socially sanctioned warfare became an unacceptable means for young men to gain their manhood because of the turbulence and disruption it caused for the colonists, gangs of mounted warriors roamed the frontier looking for opportunities to test their bravery and courage. Such was the temper of Indian Florida when the British gained control in 1763 in accordance with the terms of the Treaty of Paris. By the end of British rule twenty-one years later, it could be said that there were no longer any Creeks in Florida, only Seminoles.

The Period of Enterprise (1767–1817)

Despite their overall administrative prowess, the British in Florida seemed ill-prepared to deal with the increasingly complex question of Indian trade and land rights. Through a series of conferences with the Creeks set to clarify these concerns, at Augusta in 1763, St. Marks in 1764, and Picolata in 1765, John Stuart, Indian agent for the Southern District, became aware of increasing Indian dissatisfaction and demands relating to trade and of the emerging separateness of the Seminole from Creek. Specific treaty negotiations also imply that there was separateness, perhaps even antagonism, between the Alachua and St. Marks settlements. Although the beginning date for the period of enterprise could be set at 1763, when Great Britain took possession of Florida, by 1767 Anglo-Indian relations were relatively stable and the term "Seminole" or some derivative thereof was coming into common use. In between the lines, to judge from Stuart's letters of 1767, this term was used to designate those natives of Creek origin living beyond the control and reach of the Creek Confederacy and was understood to mean "wild people" more than "runaway."

This was a time of tremendous radiation of the Seminoles across the Florida landscape and, of course, a great increase in their numbers. In addition to the Cowkeeper's Alachua Seminoles, now settled at Cuscowilla, major towns were found at Talahasochte on the Suwannee River, on the St. Johns River near present-day Palatka, and Chukochatty near present-day Brooksville. By 1774, nine substantial towns, most, if not all, with squaregrounds, were present in Florida; by 1821, this number had increased fourfold. In the old Apalachee area, major villages were located at Mickasuki (also called Newtown), and Tallahassee.

The impetus for this Seminole expansion was trade. Using fire drives and firearms obtained by trade or direct gift, Indian hunters took large numbers of deer for the skin trade, ranging far south to the Everglades. For 18 pounds of skins a hunter could obtain a new gun; for 60 pounds (a not unrealistic take in a good year) a new saddle could be had. The British "one trader–one town" policy, designed to prevent competitive traders from unduly promoting village factionalism, had the unintended effect of stimulating the formation of new towns. Not all the Seminoles supplied to the traders came from the forest. Particularly in the fertile uplands east and northeast of Tampa Bay, plantation agriculture developed. Corn, rice, watermelons, peaches, potatoes, and pumpkins grown in plantation fields were taken to St. Augustine to provision the perpetually needy citizens of that city.

Using large, seaworthy canoes, Seminoles from the Suwannee towns and from a town at the head of today's Charlotte Harbor traveled to Spanish Cuba to trade in the hope of getting better prices than those offered by the British. However, when Spain again took possession of Florida in 1783 following the American Revolution, trading houses established under British rule were encouraged to remain by Governor Zespedes to ensure continuity in trade relations. The leader of the Creek Confederacy, Alexander McGillivray, attempted to promote peaceful conditions among the Creeks and Seminoles and the Spanish by nurturing the Indian trading company of Panton and Leslie, while fending off increasing pressure from the encroaching Americans. But peace in Spanish Florida was not to be. Tensions mounted between the Florida Seminoles and the new American residents of Georgia, and armed conflict, to be detailed in the next section, erupted in the border regions. The tensions culminated in what amounted to the American invasion of Spanish Florida and the inevitable cession of Florida to the United States. For the Seminoles, as we will see, this event was to have cataclysmic results.

The prosperity of the Enterprise period has left an archaeological landscape strewn with an abundance of trade goods. Glass beads, glass bottle sherds, transfer-print and shell-edged pearlware ceramics, iron and brass kettles, kaolin smoking pipes, gun hardware, metal belt buckles, and silver earrings and brooches mark Seminole archaeological sites of this period. Brushed and decorated aboriginal pottery found at these sites illustrates a basic continuity with the Creek tradition. Yet prosperity also brought a break with Creek tradition. Inheritance may have passed less frequently along matrilineal lines than was customary, instead passing from father to son. By the first decades of the nineteenth century, major Seminole settlements may have resembled more the typical southern plantation than the traditional Creek squareground. Certainly elements of both were combined. This seems to have been the case at Paynestown, the settlement of Payne, successor to Cowkeeper, where the archaeological concentrations of artifacts are thought to represent numerous outbuildings associated with the main house. A harbinger of things to come, Payne was wounded in an 1812 campaign against his town led by Col. Daniel Newnan of the Georgia militia, and died shortly thereafter.

Coming into history at this time are the bands of Seminole blacks, referred to as Black Seminoles or maroons. These were the descendants of those who had fought for the Spanish at Fort Mose, above St. Augustine, established in 1738, or more recent runaways from plantation slavery in Carolina and Georgia. Locating themselves in separate villages near Seminole towns, the blacks entered into a peculiar type of vassalage with the Seminoles, supplying them with agricultural produce and expecting some degree of protection in return. Having the blacks in Spanish Florida became a major point of antagonism between the Seminoles and the Georgians, while attempts to separate the blacks from their Seminole owners (as the Indians felt themselves to be) by the Americans after 1821 became a contributing cause of the Second Seminole War.

Warfare and Revitalization

The next period of Seminole history is the time of the three Seminole wars, covering the years between 1817 and 1858. Without question, these were the years of great trauma and upheaval for the Seminole people. From death in combat or deportation to Indian Territory, the Seminole population decreased from about 5,000 persons in the late pre-American period to perhaps fewer than 200 by 1858. Yet this was the period that most strongly shaped the cultural identity of the modern Seminoles. Through the adversity, indeed perhaps because of it, a revival of traditional Creek religion and customs took place. Archaeological and documentary evidence suggests the presence of a nativistic pulse during the early years of the Second Seminole War, driven, perhaps, by influences from militant Red Stick Creeks who had unsuccessfully resisted the increasing American presence in Alabama. Because there was not any significant in-migration to swell Seminole ranks in the twentieth century, the cultural repertoire of Florida's contemporary Seminole Indians—including the Green Corn Dance—must have been passed down by those few Seminoles remaining in 1858. This is true also for the politically distinct Miccosukee Tribe, whose members share a cultural, historical, and linguistic past largely indistinguishable from that of the Seminoles.

The First Seminole War (1817–1818)

It is hard to isolate the so-called First Seminole War from the constant violence that characterized Florida during the opening decades of the nineteenth century. Incursions by the militia of Georgia and Tennessee at the start of the War of 1812, besides resulting in the death of Payne, scattered the Alachua Seminoles widely throughout the peninsula, some as far as present-day Miami. The weakness of Spain coupled with pressure by the United States to acquire Florida contributed to the turmoil. White men and non-Florida Indians raided into the peninsula to capture slaves, red and black. Slaves from Georgia and Alabama escaped to mingle with the Seminoles, as was mentioned, in a form of servitude less onerous than the chattel slavery from which they ran away. The institution of slavery determined much that went on in troubled Spanish Florida. It was clear, too, that Native Americans and Americans of European descent could not live in proximity without friction, often violent.

In 1816 the United States established Fort Scott in the southwestern corner of Georgia just a few miles from the Spanish boundary. The administration decided to supply the fort by boats sent up the Apalachicola River through Spanish territory. Spain protested but not militarily. The major military obstacle was the so-called Negro Fort sixty miles south of Fort Scott overlooking the river and garrisoned by 334 blacks armed with ample military supplies left by the British after the War of 1812. If these blacks opposed the advance, they would give the United States the chance it sought to eliminate them. They did attempt to block the passage upstream, but were blown sky-high on 27 July 1816 when a lucky hotshot exploded the open powder magazines. The blast killed 270 blacks and injured more, depriving the Seminoles of efficient black warriors and tons of military stores.

Across the Flint River from Fort Scott was the Mikasuki village of Fowltown. The spelling "Mikasuki" is used intentionally here to reflect the historically accurate usage in identifying a specific band of Seminoles and to avoid confusion with the modern Miccosukee Tribe. The chief of Fowltown, Neamathla, warned Colonel Edmund P. Gaines not to cross the river. Irritated by so blunt a threat, Gaines moved with 250 men to attack the town on 21 November 1817, killing five Indians and later burning the place. In retaliation, the Indians opened fire on a boat coming up the river and killed thirty-seven of the forty soldiers aboard, six women and four children. This, with other retaliatory acts, caused Secretary of War John C. Calhoun to order Major General Andrew Jackson to Fort Scott with power to wage war as he judged best. Jackson reached the fort on 9 March 1818. His force of 4,800, 1,500 of whom were Creek Indians, facing 1,000 Seminoles and 300 blacks, easily advanced southwestward, destroying Indian settlements and crops. Late in March he obliterated Kenache's (or Kinhajo) town (close to Lake Miccosukee), the largest in Florida. His next conquest was not Indian, but the Spanish town of St. Marks. Then he wiped out the town of Bowlegs, brother of Payne, on the Suwannee River in April 1818. Bowlegs's band, displaced from the Alachua area by the Georgians in 1813, this time moved far south to the vicinity of Lake Harris (Lake County). Jackson had eliminated the fighting power of the Indians west of the Suwannee River, and dispersed the bands there. He had cleared the Indians from the Georgia border and closed one route into Florida to escaping slaves.

Jackson wrote to the secretary of war, "Let it be signified to me through any channel that the possession of Florida would be desirable . . . and in sixty days it will be accomplished." Convinced that he had government approval, he turned back westward to capture Pensacola. Late in May 1818, he retook the city which he had occupied once before in 1814. Only St. Augustine remained under effective Spanish control. But the general looked beyond that. Given permission, some shipping, and a few more troops, he wrote, "I will assure you that Cuba will be ours in a few days."

President Monroe, in justifying the First Seminole War to Congress, said that the Seminoles had provoked the United States into punitive action. The latter had been purely defensive. According to Jackson, his campaign had been "to chastise a savage foe, combined with a lawless band of negro brigands" carrying on a "cruel and unprovoked war against the citizens of the United States." One result of the American invasions of Florida was the transfer in 1821 of the peninsula and Panhandle to the United States.

For a half century before this transfer, the Florida Seminoles had prospered and increased their numbers tenfold. They carried on a profitable trade with British suppliers even during the Second Spanish Period. The trading system in that fifty years had the effect of diminishing the power of chiefs and increasing the power of autonomous bands, as has been mentioned. When the United States acquired Florida, there was no longer any strong central leadership among the Seminoles.

The prosperity of the Seminoles, described in the discussion of the Enterprise period, was their undoing. Florida had become economically desirable. Therefore the policy of the United States was first to restrict the Seminoles within a limited area, then remove them altogether to the west. Removal would end their threat to the institution of slavery. In a series of treaties, the government undertook to carry out its policy but was hampered by the lack of central Indian command to deal with. It could always find Indians to sign treaties, but the signers were usually not acknowledged by the bands to have the authority to commit them to crowd into a reservation or to leave Florida.

Second Seminole War (1835–1842)

During the 1820s and early 1830s, white encroachments drove the Florida Indians toward war. Slave raiders harassed them and their black associates. The United States, by the Treaty of Moultrie Creek (1823), confined them to a reservation. They became dependent on the government for food, but were usually hungry, with some actually starving. In 1835 there were between 800 and 1,400 warriors fragmented into numerous bands. These warriors had 400 black men as allies, rated by whites as better fighters than the Indians. Each band had a hereditary chief, but there was still no principal chief over them all. Closest to a head chief was Micanopy, a descendant of Cowkeeper (possibly nephew to Payne and Bowlegs), but he did not take the initiative against white encroachment.

The man who did was Osceola, son of the Englishman William Powell and a Creek Indian woman named Polly Coppinger. White men often referred to him simply as Powell. He came to Florida with the Red Stick Creeks as a boy of ten. Lacking any claim to hereditary leadership, he nevertheless personified the determination of the Seminoles to keep their homeland. It was he who planned the destruction of Major Francis Dade's detachment of 108 soldiers and the murder of agent Wiley Thompson with four other men on 28 December 1835. Three days later he led the Indian force that prevented a small army under Brevet Brigadier General Duncan L. Clinch from penetrating the Seminole refuge, about 100 square miles, known as the Cove of the Withlacoochee (in present-day Citrus County). Simultaneously with Osceola's offensive, Phillip, a hereditary chief, perhaps in coordination with Osceola, ravaged plantations along the St. Johns River.

The United States force in Florida had one commander, but he was rotated until seven had served. Clinch gave way to Brevet Major General Winfield Scott. Like all of his successors, Scott had to mix disparate types—regular army, volunteers, militia, and Indians hostile to the Seminoles—to make a fighting force. This mixture was an uneasy one throughout the seven years of war. In March 1836, Scott conducted his campaign in the European tactical tradition. He, too, aimed at the Cove, but by the time his three heavy columns converged on it, the Indians had already split into their basic bands and left.

Brevet Major General Edmund Pendleton Gaines, in New Orleans, hearing of the fighting, assembled 1,000 men and landed them in Florida without orders. After some marching and countermarching, he was entrapped and besieged 26 February to 5 March 1836, until relieved by troops sent by

Osceola, Chief of the Seminole. Painting by George Catlin, 1838. Catlin painting A-499, American Museum of Natural History. Courtesy of the Department of Library Services, American Museum of Natural History (Neg. No. 327045).

General Clinch. Gaines departed from Florida to the border of Texas. Scott charged him with spoiling his campaign, necessitating a court of inquiry, late in November 1836. The two generals vilified each other, but the court found both blameless.

When President Jackson relieved Scott on 21 June 1836, he made a political rather than a military appointment. His selection to command in Florida was a civilian, Richard Keith Call, governor of Florida Territory. Call assembled 2,500 men, a mixture of Tennessee volunteers, Florida militiamen, regulars, and Creek Indians, once again to penetrate the Cove. On 13 November he found it abandoned. Desperate to make a creditable showing, he received evidence that a substantial body of warriors was in Wahoo Swamp at the southern tip of the Cove. He attacked on 21 November, but after several hours of fighting drew back without overcoming the foe. Jackson did not forgive him for this. He dispatched Brevet Major General Thomas S. Jesup, quartermaster general of the army, to take command in Florida.

A year of conflict had borne hard on the Indians. Several chiefs, including Micanopy, entered into an agreement on 6 March 1837 to migrate. They stalled, enjoying the provisions and liquor provided by the government. At length, though, 700 encamped near Fort Brooke, waiting to be shipped west. Jesup thought the war was over. Then, during the night of 2 June, the 700 slipped away. Although Osceola's power had diminished, he, with the medicine man of the Mikasukis, Arpeika (Sam Jones to the white men), by some means convinced or coerced the camped Indians to decamp. This exodus so disillusioned Jesup that he determined to subdue the Seminoles by any means. The latter, hungry and impoverished, were willing to come to the military camps to talk, eat well, and drink whiskey. At such a meeting on 9 September 1837, the general seized Coacoochee (Wildcat), who had arrived under a flag of truce. Wildcat's father was Philip, his mother a sister of Micanopy. He had a chief's lineage but was not yet a chief. Like Osceola, he lacked formal authority and had to lead by force of personality.

More notorious was Jesup's seizing of Osceola on 27 October under a white flag. These two vital leaders were imprisoned in the old Spanish coquina fortress Castillo de San Marcos at St. Augustine, known to the Americans as Fort Marion. Wildcat, with nineteen followers, made a miraculous escape on 29 November, then slipped southward to join the intransigents under Arpeika and Otulke Thlocco, the Prophet. Arpeika, after hearing Wildcat's story, would never again risk attending a white council. Osceola, now too unwell to influence the war, died at Fort Moultrie, South Carolina, on 31 January 1838.

General Jesup held to this strategy. On 14 December 1837 he seized Micanopy, three other chiefs, and 78 followers who had come in to his camp to talk. He had by that time seriously cut into Seminole leadership. Still there were frequent skirmishes and the major pitched battle of the war. Colonel Zachary Taylor attacked a prepared position near Lake Okeechobee on Christmas Day 1837. Halpatter Tustenuggee (known to the whites as

Alligator), a close associate of Micanopy, commanded the center of the Indian line; Wildcat held the left with about eighty men, while Sam Jones and the Prophet directed half the force on the right. Soldiers numbering 1,032, most of them regulars, assailed 480 Seminoles from diverse bands with no overall commander. Taylor's army drove the warriors out of their prepared position at a cost of 26 killed and 112 wounded. Because it was closer to a pitched battle than any other action during the conflict, it focused public attention on Zachary Taylor. He was commissioned a brigadier general for it, and in the end became the only white commander to emerge from the war with an enhanced reputation.

In May 1838 General Jesup requested relief from the Florida command. He had crippled Indian fighting power, shipping 1,978 persons west and killing perhaps 400. He created opportunities for captured blacks to serve as guides and interpreters and helped set them against each other. Although he vacillated on what to do with the Seminole blacks, finally he sent most of them west with their masters.

Thomas S. Jesup continued as quartermaster general until his death in 1860, but he never lived down the stigma attached to his seizing Indian leaders, particularly Osceola, under white flags.

Brigadier General Zachary Taylor assumed command on 15 May 1838. One thousand Indians remained in the territory; a cluster of bands in Middle Florida (the Panhandle region), another in central Florida, and a third in the southwest region of the Big Cypress. They had little contact with each other, but the leaders in the southwest, Holata Micco (known as Billy Bowlegs), Arpeika, and Otulke Thlocco sometimes met together. The Prophet was a refugee Creek who escaped out of Georgia after the Creek War of 1816. He became the messiah figure of the Second Seminole War. Because the other leaders feared his occult powers, he controlled much of the action in southwest Florida. In the end, though, he could not keep an army detachment from destroying his own camp.

Zachary Taylor initiated a new strategy. He divided the territory north of the Withlacoochee River into squares twenty miles on each side, with a fort in the middle garrisoned by soldiers who built roads and regularly patrolled their squares. He intended to enlarge the area covered by squares when the commanding general of the army, Major General Alexander Macomb, arrived in Florida. Macomb met with such chiefs as he could assemble and in mid-May 1839 arranged with them to end the conflict. His peace document permitted the Seminoles to remain in 6,700 square miles of southwestern Florida, about half of the Big Cypress Swamp. Floridians detested this settlement, but they were not the instruments terminating the peace. Certain Indian leaders who had not signed Macomb's pact struck at the new trading post on the Caloosahatchee River on 23 July 1839, totally destroying it and killing several soldiers. This ended the peace. Taylor's strategy of squares was not continued. During his command, 800 Indians and 400 blacks had been shipped west.

At his request, Taylor was relieved by Brigadier General Walker K. Armistead in May 1840. The new commander established detachments of 100 men and sent them to explore little-known parts of Florida and ferret out Indian hideaways. But when it seemed that all the Indians had been pushed into south Florida, destructive raids occurred in northeast and central Florida, where none had taken place for months. Armistead did what he could to suppress these, and to corral more Seminoles to ship west. At the end of the year in which he commanded, 700 Seminoles and blacks were deported to Indian Territory.

Under a policy to rely fully on regular troops, militia generals left the federal service. Once they were no longer present to outrank United States officers, it was possible for the first time to place a colonel, William Jenkins Worth, in command. At a council in April 1841, Bowlegs, Arpeika, and the Prophet reaffirmed their determination not to leave Florida, and pronounced death for any Indian who carried messages from the whites. Far north in the Long Swamp east of Fort King, two months later, one Mikasuki chief, two Seminole chiefs, and Octiarche, a Creek fugitive from Georgia, took the same intransigent stand. No peace terms involving removal were acceptable.

When Colonel Worth took command in June 1841, he began to change his strategy. First, in Worth's plan, rid north Florida of hostiles, because of their proximity to new white settlements. The Indians had returned to the Cove of the Withlacoochee, and he divided his force into detachments of twenty men to clean them out. Second, using partisan tactics, he kept his troops campaigning right on through the sickly season in the swamps of south Florida. White Floridians approved of his strategy, but howled when he sharply reduced the number of civilians and militiamen employed by the United States.

In June 1841 Major Childs seized Coacoochee when he came into Fort Pierce. An officer shipped him west, but Worth ordered him returned to be used to induce other bands to surrender. Not even Wildcat could persuade Arpeika to place himself in white hands. All in all, though, Worth's system was so successful that by April 1842 only 300 Indians remained in Florida, 112 of them warriors. They were hungry and miserable, especially the women and children. Worth, from his base of operations near Cedar Key, proposed to the War Department that this remnant be allowed to remain in Florida in the same 6,700-square-mile reservation proposed by General Macomb in 1839. White Floridians cried that it was shameful to tolerate any Indians in the peninsula, but in August 1842 the administration accepted the plan and the war ended.

Shipment of some of the 300 continued until, by the end of 1843, 3,824 were gone. It is not known how many died during the war, but the Seminoles had shown a rare ability to adapt to new circumstances and to survive as a culture. Their resilience would serve them well in the years ahead. Their fight to stay in their homeland is as gallant as any in history. That they held out for seven years is all the more remarkable because of the diversity of bands among them and their lack of continuous central leadership. It had been total war for them.

Not so for the United States where the war required a limited commitment from the people. It did require a full commitment from the army. Every regular army regiment served in Florida, straining the logistical and personnel staffs more than at any time since the War of 1812. There were 1,466 deaths in the regular army, 328 of them combat-related. Seventy-four of the dead were officers while the corps was reduced sharply due to resignations of officers who saw no glory or honor for their service in Florida. Fifty-five citizen soldiers were killed, while unknown hundreds died of disease. On the plus side, the war amounted to field training for officers who served later in the Mexican War and Civil War.

The army had to change its strategy and tactics more than once during the seven years of conflict. The Seminoles proved tactically adept at engaging the soldiers on terrain of their choosing, and used natural features of the landscape to their advantage. In response, the heavy columns, supported by logistical trains used by General Scott, gave way bit by bit to small units carrying their supplies on their backs. These detachments had to penetrate nearly inaccessible hideaways, live in part off the land, recruit Indians and blacks as guides and interpreters, destroy the Seminoles' food sources, endure extreme hardship, and throughout also protect white settlements. The partisan style was not carried into the Mexican or Civil Wars, but the Union did finally employ a strategy against a people, not just against the military portion of it.

Third Seminole War

Following the end of the Second Seminole War in August 1842, Billy Bowlegs became principal chief over the 300 to 400 Indians remaining in Florida. Twenty warriors refused to acknowledge his authority. He and Sam Jones, a trusted leader and head of one of the bands, strove to abide by the terms of the peace settlement. Thus, when in July 1849, after seven quiet years, five defiant young warriors killed and pillaged outside the reservation, Bowlegs and Jones undertook to deliver the miscreants to the whites for justice. They did deliver three, and the hand of one killed, but the fifth had escaped. The next year they handed over three other rovers who had killed young Daniel Hubbard of Marion County. Floridians were little affected by the conscientious effort that the chiefs had made. They simply wanted to be rid of the Seminoles altogether. An editorial in a St. Augustine newspaper on 10 August 1850 asked that the natives be outlawed and a bounty of $1,000 placed on every male delivered dead or alive and $500 for every woman or child delivered alive. Senator Stephen Mallory said that they must get out or be exterminated.

For a time the United States government sought to achieve removal without war. Powerful chiefs were brought from among the Seminoles in Indian Territory to persuade the Florida remnant to come west. In 1850, Major General David Twiggs, in command, offered Bowlegs $10,000 to remove the entire group with a fee to each migrating Indian. In 1852, the government put the matter in the private sector. It designated Luther Blake to achieve the removal peacefully. Blake took Bowlegs to Washington with three sub-chiefs to show them the power of the United States. When Jefferson Davis was secretary of war, he heeded the cries of the Floridians, and inaugurated a policy calculated either to make the Seminoles leave or fight. It included an embargo on trade with them and survey of land within the reservation, followed by some sales. Efforts were made to rebuild some of the abandoned roads made during the Second Seminole War and to patrol them. Boats, too, appeared for use in the swamps. These white invasions of the reserved land did indeed push the Seminoles into war. Some accounts say that it was the vandalizing of one of Bowlegs's camps "to see how Billy would cut up" that started the conflict. But it is more likely that the chiefs had decided earlier that they must fight. In any case, thirty warriors opened fire on Lt. George Hartsuff's detachment (the vandalizers) at 5:00 a.m. on 18 December 1855, wounding four of the ten and killing four. Thus began the Third Seminole War.

The United States commander, Colonel John Monroe, had at his disposal 800 regulars, 260 Florida militia in federal service, and 400 not in federal service. Since there were about 100 warriors left, the manpower odds were fourteen to one. White organization, however, was faulty, there being poor communication between federal and state commanders.

The Seminoles without a planned strategy isolated habitations and small detachments at random. For six months they held the initiative. During 1856, they made fifteen raids and killed 28 people. In September 1856, Brevet Brigadier General William S. Harney took command in Florida. He commenced a system of patrols that reduced the raiding, but never found the retreats of Billy Bowlegs and Sam Jones. Harney left Florida in April 1857, followed in the command by Colonel Gustavus Loomis.

Governor James Broome insisted that citizen soldiers would be required to defeat the Indians. He ordered militia companies into service, appealing in all cases to the federal government to muster them into United States service. In July 1857 he called for ten companies. Not all of the companies that he ordered into service were acceptable to the War Department, and some of them, never officially mustered by regular officers, waited decades before receiving any pay. Nevertheless, as the conflict lengthened, the number of citizen soldiers in the field increased, while the number of regulars declined. In the fall of 1857, only four companies of regulars remained in Florida.

Since the volunteers and militia from south Florida were in the main ranchers, they insisted on serving as horse troops. But horsemen could not penetrate the swamps and lakes where the last refuges of the Indians were. In the summer of 1857, the State of Florida organized three boat companies, equipped with shallow-draft vessels carrying 16 men each. Manned by a motley, unmilitary assortment, this flotilla forced its way through the swamps and sawgrass into Bowlegs's refuge on 19 November 1857. For two years the white forces had been unsuccessfully hunting this place. There the boat people burned down more than fifty dwellings, took large quantities of corn and rice, some oxen, and destroyed food growing in several hundred acres.

Captain John Casey worked before and during the conflict to limit the violence. Because of his influence, the chiefs knew that they were safe from seizure when they entered white camps for talks. Sam Jones never came in. He was by this time more than 100 years old, senile, and represented in meetings by Assinwah, Bowlegs's son-in-law. To induce migration, Congress in August 1856 created an area of 2 million acres in Indian Territory for Florida Indians, separating them from the Creeks, toward whom they were hostile. Congress also made substantial funds available to pay Seminoles who removed.

Bowlegs, beaten down by the destruction of his ultimate refuge, finally accepted money to go west: $6,500 for himself, $1,000 each for four sub-chiefs, $500 each for all other warriors, and $100 for women and children. Under these terms, 164 persons shipped out on 4 May 1858: all of Bowlegs's band, all of Assinwah's, and ten from Sam Jones's band. They received a total of $44,600. Sam Jones, with perhaps 17 warriors, remained hidden on an island deep in the Everglades. He died in Florida at an estimated age of 111.

Colonel Gustavus Loomis, who succeeded Harney in command, received permission officially to declare the war ended on 8 May 1858. In this third conflict, there had been no action classifiable as a battle. About 40 warriors had lost their lives in combat and the same number of white fighters. Whereas in the Second Seminole War the regular soldiers had done the final mopping up, in this one the citizen soldiers did it.

No more than 200 Indians remained in the state, but they preserved the Seminole culture, and were the basis for a slowly increasing number of inheritors.

Isolation (1858–1880)

Following the Third Seminole War, the remaining Seminoles understandably withdrew from any but the most fleeting contacts with the few non-Indian Floridians inhabiting the lower portion of the peninsula. Settlement for the most part was in small, remote, matrilocal camps located on tree islands in the Everglades and Big Cypress regions. The familiar open-air pole and thatch Seminole chickee (from the word in the Mikasuki language meaning "house") typified such settlements, which also had outdoor cooking and work areas and garden plots. Gradually a coalescence of settlements occurred, with locations on the north side of Lake Okeechobee, the northern edge of the Big Cypress, and the Pine Island Ridge area west of Fort Lauderdale regularly inhabited. The Okeechobee settlements would give rise to the Muskogee-speaking Cow Creek Seminole, ancestors of today's Brighton group occupying a reservation in the same area. The Mikasuki-speaking Big Cypress and Pine Island groups were generally ancestral to the present populations of the Big Cypress and Hollywood reservations, respectively, and contributed to the ancestry of the Miccosukee Indians living along the Tamiami Trail as well.

Seminole chickee in the Big Cypress Swamp drawn by Clay MacCauley in 1881. Courtesy of the National Anthropological Archives, National Museum of Natural History, Smithsonian Institution (Neg. No. 1178-N-8[1]).

Travel between islands was accomplished by dugout canoe. Trade contacts were established with stores on both coasts, with skins and pelts being exchanged for cloth, corn, beads, pots and pans, rifles, and ammunition. Ceremonial life centered on the Green Corn Dance, when scattered camps would come together to a shared dance or busk ground. Each busk group also shared in common a medicine bundle, a gathering of sacred objects bundled in a deerskin pouch under the exclusive care of the medicine man. Major busk grounds were located at Pine Island, although the Cow Creek and Big Cypress groups also possessed medicine bundles and held separate busks.

Development of Modern Tribalism

After 1880, Seminole contact with whites became more frequent and, inevitably with this increased interaction grew the making of more "Indian trouble." The government again developed a plan of removal to Indian Territory. A succession of federal agents from the Bureau of Indian Affairs and government-sponsored investigators were sent to assess the current Seminole situation and determine the feasibility of removal. During this time various plans were put forth by groups of Seminole sympathizers to purchase reservation lands in Florida for the Indians, and private funds were raised for this purpose. However, the problem of getting the Seminoles to move to such lands was more complex than had been thought, and these plans came to naught. By 1891, the State of Florida agreed to set aside a 5,000-acre tract for an Indian reservation, to include lands then currently inhabited by the Seminoles, but no allocation was made for proper boundary survey. By 1917, however, largely through the efforts of Minnie Moore-Willson, the state designed nearly 100,000 acres for reservation use in the swamps of Monroe County, although few if any Indians actually ever resided there. With the creation of Everglades National Park in 1935, the Monroe County lands were exchanged for acreage in Broward and Palm Beach Counties.

Through the diligence of Lucian Spencer, U.S. government special commissioner to the Seminoles, and a few others, the Seminoles gradually began moving to federal reservation lands during the 1920s, particularly to a small tract at Dania where the current Hollywood reservation is located. The opening of the Tamiami Trail highway (U.S. 41) across the Everglades in 1928 attracted far-flung northern and southern bands to establish tourist camps along the road. Here motorists could see colorful patchwork, palmetto dolls, split palmetto baskets, animal skins, live baby alligators, wooden spoons, and other items for sale. These groups and others still living in remote camps showed little interest in the reservation policy of the federal administration. Through the early 1930s, less than 10 percent of the Seminole population lived on reservation lands. Exhibition villages, primarily in and around Miami, also housed a number of Seminole families in the early to middle decades of the twentieth century.

A burst of success by Christian missionaries in the 1940s led by the Creek Baptist preacher Stanley Smith created a schism between the new converts and those adhering to traditional religion, with the result that Christian Seminoles began to move to reservations where they could establish churches. As the reservations at Dania, Big Cypress, and Brighton became true population centers, the Bureau of Indian Affairs had less difficulty in developing formal governing bodies through which new policies and programs could be introduced and administered. The Seminoles living along the Trail continued to be little interested in formal relationships with the federal government, and resented efforts to lump them with the reservation Seminoles for administrative purposes.

Antagonisms between the Trail Indians and the reservation Seminoles were accelerated in 1950, when a small group of reservation Seminole with legal representation filed a land claims lawsuit before the Indian Claims Commission. The suit, filed under terms specified in the Indian Claims Commission Act of 1946, sought financial compensation for land taken from the Seminoles in treaties before and during the Second Seminole War and for the land lost to Everglades National Park in 1935. The Trail Indians wanted nothing to do with the Seminole suit, fearing the government would accept no future claims once this case was settled. In fact, fully one-third of the adult reservation Seminoles did not back the case. Partly due to the impetus of the land claims case, a central tribal government was formed in which the Big Cypress, Brighton, and Dania reservations were politically linked. In 1957, the Seminole Tribe of Florida was officially recognized by the United States government.

The Trail Indians also found it necessary to organize, and in 1962 they were granted federal recognition as the Miccosukee Tribe of Florida.

In 1970, after years of expensive legal maneuvers by both sides and the entry and exit of numerous third parties, the commission determined that the Seminoles should be awarded a little more than $12 million for lands taken in the 1820s and 1830s at less than market value. Unfortunately, the commission failed to specify how the money was to be divided among the Seminole, Miccosukee, and Oklahoma Seminole Tribes. After an appeal by the Seminoles, the commission awarded the tribes $16 million in 1976 but did not resolve the distribution problem. In 1990, twenty years after the initial award, Congress mandated a 75/25 split of the $50 million settlement (the 1976 award plus interest) between the Oklahoma and Florida Seminoles. The Florida share, amounting to some $12.3 million, was divided between the Seminole tribe (77.2 percent), the Miccosukees (18.6 percent), and independent Seminoles, legally recognized full-blooded Indians who are not tribal members (4.6 percent).

The Seminole Tribe, based at the Hollywood Reservation, is governed by an elected tribal council representing each of the reservations and, through its corporate branch, engages in many sophisticated and complex business ventures. The smaller Miccosukee Tribe—organized similarly to the Seminole Tribe—conducts tribal business from its headquarters on the Tamiami Trail reservation. In recent years, both tribes have made bold forays into the world of high-stakes gaming.

Too frequently the Seminoles and Miccosukees have been defined in the public mind by popular media reports on legal battles with state or federal authorities over gaming, land- and water-use rights, and the civil rights of citizens of Indian nations. Federal law recognizes the sovereign status of designated Indian tribes and nations, but sovereignty as both a political and civil concept is not well understood at the state and local governmental levels. The Seminoles, Miccosukees, and many other Indian nations have used their sovereign status to build economic self-sufficiency through the sales of tax-free cigarettes and bingo revenues. The Seminole Tribe in particular parlayed these revenues into surprising political clout and bold financial investments. In 2006, the Seminole Tribe purchased the Hard Rock Corporation. The $965 million deal included 124 Hard Rock Cafes, four Hard Rock Hotels, two Hard Rock Casinos (already doing business on reservation property in Tampa and Hollywood), and a variety of subsidiary enterprises. Although most of the tribal revenue comes from gaming, more conventional pursuits such as cattle ranching, particularly on the Brighton reservation (where it has become a multimillion-dollar enterprise), and growing lemons, grapefruits, and oranges have added to the diversified economic portfolio. In 2009, the Seminole Tribe negotiated a compact with the State of Florida for initial payments of $150 million per year to state coffers in exchange for exclusive rights to offer blackjack and slot machines at tribal casinos. Negotiations such as these often polarize public opinion and encourage misconceptions about the integrity of Seminole culture. To the Seminoles, however, there are no misconceptions. The economic success of their gaming enterprise underwrites the survival of their cultural identity. They can continue to be Seminoles because they have found a viable way to maintain their independence. They take pride in their self-designation as the "Unconquered People," an homage to their survival through the era of the Seminole wars.

Although modern ranch-style houses with manicured lawns have largely replaced the standard reservation-style concrete block house, which largely replaced the traditional chickee, and Christianity has been long since accepted, much remains of traditional Seminole culture. In early summer, dance grounds are prepared for the annual Green Corn Dance, directed by a tribal medicine man, much as was done in the nineteenth century and before. Here families come and children learn the traditional ways. Cultural education takes place in the reservation schools and through programming offered through the tribal Ah-Tah-Thi-Ki museum. The simple wood-framed "Red Barn" on the Brighton Reservation, built to stable Seminole horses in the early years of the cattle industry, was listed on the National Register of Historic Places in 2008 and will become another educational point of pride for Seminole youth. Combined Seminole and Miccosukee population numbers now approximate their pre–Second Seminole War total. Despite unprecedented levels of wealth that would have been beyond the comprehension of earlier generations, much uncertainty remains and new generations must be prepared for the future. If history can serve as a guide, the Seminoles will find a way to endure.

Bibliography

Blackard, David M. *Patchwork and Palmettos: Seminole Miccosukee Folk Art since 1820.* Fort Lauderdale: Fort Lauderdale Historical Society, 1990.

Cattelino, Jessica R. *High Stakes: Florida Seminole Gaming and Sovereignty.* Durham: Duke University Press, 2008.

Covington, James W. *The Seminoles of Florida.* Gainesville: University Press of Florida, 1993.

Garbarino, Merwyn S. *Big Cypress: A Changing Seminole Community.* New York: Holt, Rinehart, and Winston, 1972.

Kersey, Harry A., Jr. *An Assumption of Sovereignty: Social and Political Transformation among the Florida Seminoles, 1953–1979.* Lincoln: University of Nebraska Press, 1996.

MacCauley, Clay. "The Seminole Indians of Florida." In *Fifth Annual Report of the Bureau of Ethnology*, pp. 469–531. Washington, 1887.

Mahon, John K. *History of the Second Seminole War, 1835–1842.* Gainesville: University of Florida Press, 1967.

Sprague, John T. *The Origin, Progress, and Conclusion of the Florida War.* 1848. Gainesville: University of Florida Press, 1964.

Sturtevant, William C., editor. *A Seminole Source Book.* New York: Garland, 1987.

Weisman, Brent R. *Unconquered People: Florida's Seminole and Miccosukee Indians.* Gainesville: University Press of Florida, 1999.

West, Patsy. *The Enduring Seminoles: From Alligator Wrestling to Ecotourism.* Gainesville: University Press of Florida, 1998.

Wickman, Patricia R. *Osceola's Legacy.* Tuscaloosa: University of Alabama Press, 1991.

Wright, J. Leitch, Jr. *Creeks and Seminoles: The Destruction and Regeneration of the Muscogulge People.* Lincoln: University of Nebraska Press, 1987.

13

U.S. Territory and State

DANIEL L. SCHAFER

On 17 July 1821, as the Stars and Stripes replaced the Spanish flag in the public square outside Government House in Pensacola, America's greatest living military hero, General Andrew Jackson, supervised the ceremony. Jackson, the man from Tennessee who in March 1814 led a coalition of Americans and Indian allies in the decisive defeat of the Upper Creek at the Battle of Horseshoe Bend that ended the Creek War, and nine months later led the American army in a historic victory over a British army at the Battle of New Orleans, had accepted President James Monroe's offer to become the first American governor of Florida. Jackson had led American armies on punishing invasions of the Spanish East and West Florida provinces in 1814 and 1818. The latter campaign, known as the First Seminole War, persuaded Spain to cede East and West Florida to the United States. Instead of praise from Washington, however, Jackson's political opponents impugned his Florida victory as an outrageous usurpation of military power. Presiding over the ceremonies in which Spain relinquished all claims to territories east of the Mississippi River was for Jackson a triumphal moment.

There had been frustrating delays and vexations in the months of negotiations that preceded the exchange of flags. The Adams-Onís Treaty was signed by the principal negotiators on 22 February 1819 and approved by the U.S. Senate within days, yet Spanish officials delayed approval until 24 October 1820. The U.S. Senate again ratified the treaty on 19 February 1821, and President James Monroe and Secretary of State John Quincy Adams appointed Jackson governor of the two provinces on 12 March and ordered him to proceed to Pensacola. Jackson appointed a subordinate, Lt. Robert Butler, to manage the transition in St. Augustine. After further delays, the exchange of flags finally took place on 10 July 1821 in St. Augustine and 17 July in Pensacola.

Portrait of Richard K. Call. Courtesy of the State Archives of Florida, *Florida Memory*, http://floridamemory.com/items/show/128615.

Jackson's tenure as governor was brief and tempestuous. He resigned his office in September and departed Pensacola in early October. Before leaving, however, the hot-tempered Jackson ordered Spanish governor José Callava jailed briefly for obstructing delivery of documents pertinent to a lawsuit. In an attempt to justify this serious diplomatic blunder, Jackson said he had acted to protect the rights of a free quadroon woman who had been cheated of her inheritance, an injustice that had been perpetuated for fifteen years. His motive, Jackson explained later, had been to prevent "men of high standing" from "trampl[ing] on the rights of the weak."[1]

The incident soon passed from public consciousness, but the new governor's prickly temperament continued to raise alarm bells in Washington. Jackson was greatly troubled when President Monroe refused to accept his nominees for the principal posts in the Florida administration. Jackson had expected wide powers of patronage to reward his loyal associates. Instead, Monroe appointed the higher-ranking secretaries, judges, and attorneys. Jackson chose officeholders for Escambia and St. Johns Counties, two vast administrative units that were reminiscent of the separate provinces of Spanish East and West Florida. He also chose the judges for the county courts and the mayors and aldermen of St. Augustine and Pensacola.

Richard Keith Call, who would serve with distinction in Florida for the next four decades, was the most important of Jackson's appointees. He had joined a volunteer unit under Jackson's command in 1813, and participated in the Battle of New Orleans and both Florida campaigns. Call handled the early negotiations with Governor Callava and was named to the Pensacola Town Council. He established a thriving law practice, served on the Florida Legislative Council in 1822 and 1823 and as territorial delegate to Congress in 1824. He also became a brigadier general in the Florida militia, and was twice named governor of the territory. Call became the leader of American Florida's first governing elite, known popularly as the "Nucleus." After Jackson's resignation, however, it was William P. Duval, a U.S. judge at Pensacola, who succeeded him. Duval was a supporter of Jackson and generally followed his policies.

In March 1822, Congress replaced the provisional structure with a single territorial government. Executive and legislative leadership for the territory would come from a governor, a secretary, and a legislative council—all to be appointed by the president. Federal courts were established at Pensacola and St. Augustine, with judges to be appointed by the president. Only the delegate to Congress would be elected.

Governor Duval called the first Legislative Council into session on 10 June 1822 at Pensacola, but the ship carrying the St. Johns delegates that departed St. Augustine on 30 May experienced storms and shipwreck and did not arrive until 22 July. Another shipwreck claimed the life of a council member. A yellow fever outbreak forced the council members to reconvene at temporary quarters north of Pensacola and claimed the life of the chairman, Dr. James C. Bronaugh. Despite these adversities, the first council created civil offices, courts, a militia, and revenue measures and carved two new counties, Duval and Jackson, from the unmanageably large counties of St. Johns and Escambia.

Congress ordered that annual sessions of the council should alternate between St. Augustine and Pensacola, but dangers and delays experienced by the delegates from Escambia to the 1823 session in St. Augustine convinced Governor Duval that the system was untenable. He commissioned Dr. William H. Simmons and John Lee Williams to select a compromise site for a permanent capital between the Ochlockonee and Suwannee Rivers, midway between St. Augustine and Pensacola. Simmons and Williams selected

Portrait of William P. Duval. Courtesy of the State Archives of Florida, *Florida Memory*, http://florida memory.com/items/show/128200.

Tallahassee, where the old fields and council houses of the Apalachee once stood.

Hernando de Soto had camped near the site of the new capital in the winter of 1539–40; Franciscans built missions there a century later; and in the eighteenth century, Creek migrants established Tallahassee Taloofa, and Mikasuki, towns that were burned by Andrew Jackson's army in 1818. The opposition of Seminole leaders Neamathla and Chefixico was disregarded, and Tallahassee became the permanent capital in March 1824.

Settlers began arriving at the site in the following month, living in tents while they acquired land and built houses. By the time the council met in November 1824, a hotel had been constructed for legislators. Governor Duval lived briefly in a log cabin adjacent to the site of the log-and-board structure that became the Capitol in 1824. A two-story brick building replaced the log building in 1826, and was in turn superseded by a more permanent structure in 1839.

Congress made the legislative council elective in 1826, and bicameral in 1838. Members of the House of Representatives were elected at the county level based roughly on population, and the initial eleven senators were chosen from four judicial districts, with three each from the east and west, four from the middle, and one from the sparsely populated south. The most important elected official in the territory was the delegate to Congress, although the first delegate was appointed by the legislative council. Joseph M. Hernández, an East Florida planter and lawyer of Minorcan ancestry, was selected for the 1823 term. Hernández was the first Hispanic to serve in Congress. Subsequent delegates were elected by the voters of the territory, with suffrage open to white males at least twenty-one years old who had resided in the Florida Territory for at least three months. In the 1824 elections, Richard K. Call became the first elected delegate.

Delegates from Florida were not eligible to vote in Congress, but they were able to lobby for the interests of residents of the Territory. Hernández and Call, as well as subsequent delegates advocated for naval projects, road construction, bridges, and other internal improvements. Joseph M. White served as delegate from 1825 to 1838. By the time his successor was elected, candidates were pledged to political parties. Charles Downing was elected as a representative of the Whig Party.

Until Florida became a state in 1845, its governors were presidential appointees. William Duval served until 1834, when President Andrew Jackson appointed John H. Eaton to succeed him. Richard Call, still a Jackson favorite despite his opposition to Democratic Party policies in Florida, was appointed governor in 1836. President Martin Van Buren replaced Call with a Democrat, Robert R. Reid, in 1839. Call supported Whig Party candidate William Henry Harrison's successful presidential campaign in 1840 and was rewarded with a return to the governor's office from 1841 to 1844. Democrat John Branch served as governor for the last year that Florida was a territory.

During the early territorial years, Florida residents were more concerned with acquiring and cultivating land than with political affairs in Tallahassee. Some had migrated to Florida even before it became an American territory. More than 450 settlers from the United States were living near Pensacola prior to final approval of the Adams-Onís Treaty. Two thousand Americans had marched with Jackson from the Suwannee River to Pensacola in 1818. Some remained, and others returned home to tell family and friends of the fertile and unclaimed land they had seen, prompting land-hungry pioneers on the southern frontier to move to Florida.

The journalist and historian Clifton Paisley identified 300 persons living in log cabins and planting crops at the Spring Creek settlement in northwestern Jackson County in the months before the Stars and Stripes were raised at Pensacola. By 1825, Jackson County had 2,156 residents, a group that included cotton planters and approximately 720 enslaved black men and women. In 1819, Henry Yonge was living in today's Gadsden County on the Apalachicola River after migrating from Georgia with twenty slaves. He was already clearing land and erecting buildings, waiting for the American flag to catch up.

Middle Florida, between the Apalachicola and the Suwannee Rivers, attracted the majority of settlers in the territorial years. Tallahassee grew to 1,500 residents by 1835, a combination government town and merchant center. Men from aristocratic families in Virginia and Maryland brought large numbers of slaves to cultivate sugar and cotton in the fertile Red Hills of Florida. Thomas E. Randolph and his son-in-law, Francis Eppes, a grandson of Thomas Jefferson, settled in today's Leon County. John G. and Robert Gamble migrated from Richmond, Virginia. Thomas Randall, William B. Nuttall, and Hector Braden also came from Virginia.

Thomas Brown arrived in Middle Florida during the winter of 1826–27 with an advance party of slaves that immediately built shelters, cleared land, and planted crops. In 1828, Brown led a wagon caravan of twenty-one planters, their families and slaves, from Virginia to Middle Florida. Brown himself brought 140 slaves to Florida. Following statehood, Brown was elected governor, serving from 1849 to 1853.

Dr. John A. Craig migrated from Maryland. Benjamin Chaires, the wealthiest of the Middle Florida planters, moved from North Carolina. James Gadsden came from South Carolina, Richard K. Call from Virginia via Kentucky, and Joseph White from Kentucky. Prince Achille Murat, son of the exiled king of Naples and married to the sister of Napoleon Bonaparte, created Lipona, an estate in Jefferson County known for elegant entertainment. With such personages, Middle Florida became the center of an aristocratic social life and the dominant political and economic region of Florida from 1821 to 1861.

Census takers counted fewer than 2,400 persons living in Middle Florida in 1825 and 11,000 in the rest of the territory. By 1830, Middle Florida had grown to nearly 16,000, approximately 45 percent of the territory's total population. Ten years later it had 34,000 residents, West Florida only 5,500, and East Florida 15,000. The Middle Florida counties, where the majority of the population consisted of enslaved blacks, harvested 80 percent of the cotton produced in Florida in 1840.

Migrants came to East Florida as well, many fording the St. Marys River and following the King's Road to homesteads in today's Nassau and Duval

Counties. Others continued southward, crossing the St. Johns River at a narrow bend known as Cowford. They found the best land already under cultivation by families who had been living in the area for decades. The family of Francisco Xavier Sánchez witnessed three changes of flags at St. Augustine, and acquired cattle ranches and plantations as early as the 1670s. Francis P. Fatio's family lived on St. Johns River properties acquired from the British government in the 1770s. Francis Richard arrived in 1791, in flight from the violence associated with the slave rebellion in Saint-Domingue. By 1821, the Richard family had acquired a sawmill and thousands of acres of prime woodlands and plantation fields. There were also Browards, Williamses, Christophers, Houstons, Flemings, McIntoshes, Clarks, Perpalls, Solanas, Ugartes, Bethunes, and Hartleys among the families with long tenure in northeast Florida.

Zephaniah Kingsley, an African slave trader, maritime merchant, shipbuilder, and planter, arrived in northeast Florida in 1803. The African woman he acknowledged as his wife and emancipated, Anna Madgigine Jai Kingsley, a woman from a royal family in Jolof, Senegal, became a planter and slave owner herself. In 1821, Kingsley lived with his free African American family at Fort George Island, where the St. Johns River meets the Atlantic Ocean. He acquired title to numerous plantations located in what became six northeast Florida counties, cultivated by more than 300 slaves.

Slave Quarters at Kingsley Plantation, Fort George Island. Stereographic image, ca. 1870. Courtesy of Kevin Hooper, Middleburg, Fla.

For Isaiah David Hart, another longtime resident of northeast Florida, the exchange of flags and the onrush of migrants was an opportunity to profit. One of the Patriot rebels in 1812–14, Hart was living on the St. Marys River at the time the treaty of cession was signed, one of the *banditti* raiding for cattle and slaves. In 1820, he traded cattle for acreage near the ferry crossing at Cowford on the St. Johns and built a boardinghouse and store. The acreage became the heart of the town of Jacksonville when it was founded in 1822, and Hart became a wealthy merchant, planter, and influential officeholder.

In 1821, St. Augustine was the only town of significant size in East Florida. Greek and Minorcan descendants of the failed Smyrnea settlement established by Dr. Andrew Turnbull (today at New Smyrna Beach and Edgewater), occupied one-quarter of the town; Anglo-Americans, Europeans, free blacks, and slaves resided in the remainder of the town. Seminoles from the Alachua Prairie often came to St. Augustine to sell cattle and horses. After 1842, Jacksonville, Fernandina, and other new towns eclipsed the old Spanish capital's commercial importance. In the decade before 1861, tourism became a staple of St. Augustine's economy. To the south, along the Matanzas, Tomoka, Halifax, and other coastal rivers, large plantations had been carved from the Florida wilderness by British absentee owners between 1763 and 1783. Initially indigo, rice, and naval stores plantations, many were converted to sugar cultivation after the change of flags. These continued to be large estates, some worked by more than one hundred slaves.

West of the St. Johns River, travelers heading toward Tallahassee encountered Seminole villages whose established inhabitants resisted Anglo-American intrusion. General Duncan Clinch, John H. McIntosh, and Moses Elias Levy had plantations in the interior district of Alachua. Levy, a Sephardic Jew who had lived in Morocco, Spain, the Danish Island of St. Thomas, and Cuba before arriving in East Florida in 1818, had purchased 60,000 acres from Fernando de la Maza Arredondo, a Spanish Florida merchant. Levy planned to establish a colony of Jewish settlers from Europe. When recruiting efforts failed, he purchased African slaves. His son, David Levy Yulee, an attorney in St. Augustine and a sugar planter in Alachua County, became one of Florida's leading politicians.

Throughout the territory, two issues were of fundamental importance: access to land (or validation of existing deeds) and removal of the Seminole Indians. Spain ceded nearly 40 million acres of land to the United States, much of it uninhabited and a potential bonanza to speculators and settlers.

The absence of land records for West Florida complicated transmittal of deeds. For East Florida, where the bulk of Spanish and British land grants had been made, records were acquired by U.S. marshal James Grant Forbes (born in St. Augustine in 1769, the son of the Reverend Johns Forbes, an Anglican minister) during a mission to Havana in 1821. Forbes became the first mayor of American St. Augustine. Land claims dragged through the court for decades. Particularly vexing were legal problems associated with the Arredondo Grant of 300,000 acres in Alachua, and the Forbes Purchase, a grant to John Forbes and Company by the Spanish Crown of 1 million acres on both sides of the Apalachicola River.

Under terms of the Adams-Onís Treaty, the United States agreed to honor valid Spanish titles, and Congress created a board of commissioners for Pensacola and St. Augustine to adjudicate the claims. In 1826, unsettled Spanish land grant claims were assigned to the receiver of the Land Office, and later to the federal courts. Congress also passed a Donation Act in 1824 to permit squatters to acquire valid titles to a maximum of 640 acres. In 1828, it became legal to "pre-empt" previously settled land from public sale for a fee of $1.25 an acre. Land offices for sale of surveyed public land were established in Tallahassee and St. Augustine in 1825 and 1826 and in New-nansville after 1842. During the territorial years, most of the public land that sold was located in Middle Florida, for prices that averaged $1.25 an acre. Over time, as the population increased and the demand for land led to increased prices, speculators made fortunes.

The appointment of Andrew Jackson as the first governor of the Territory of Florida sent a warning to the Seminole that their days in Florida were limited. Removal of Native Americans of the Southeast to reservations west of the Mississippi River became national policy, and no one would administer it more efficiently than the man the Creek called "Sharp Knife." After defeating the Creek at Horseshoe Bend in 1814, Jackson forced the vanquished Creek to cede nearly 20 million acres of land. Few among the Creek and Seminole in Florida doubted that Jackson would attempt to remove them. Jackson's elections to the presidency in 1828 and 1832 and passage of the Indian Removal Law of 1830 only hastened the inevitable.

Governor Duval insisted that the 5,000 Seminole living in villages along the Apalachicola and Suwannee Rivers, in Alachua, and near Tallahassee evacuate the territory, but their leaders refused to leave. Violent conflicts with encroaching settlers prompted volumes of angry letters and petitions to the governor and the president. Plantation owners accused the Seminole of killing their cattle and enticing slaves to escape; newspaper editors called for speedy removal of the "murderous savages." Seminole leaders also solicited the governor's protection, accusing the settlers of stealing cattle and capturing free blacks and slaves from Native American villages.

In September 1823, a commission headed by James Gadsden met with seventy Seminole leaders at Moultrie Creek, five miles south of St. Augustine. After two weeks of intense negotiations, thirty-two of the chiefs reluctantly agreed to terminate their rights of occupancy in north Florida in exchange for a reserve of 4 million acres located between the Peace and Withlacoochee Rivers. Gadsden promised that the U.S. government would provide financial subsidies to the Seminole for twenty years. The government thus added 24 million acres in north Florida to the public domain, much of it prime planting land, in exchange for what even Governor Duval thought to be worthless land. Duval and Gadsden agreed, however, that it was of paramount importance to move the Seminole to the reserve and concentrate them to facilitate removal to west of the Mississippi.

Further pressure was required to prompt reluctant Seminoles to begin trekking south, and once on the reserve they discovered the land was infertile. After suffering drought and crop failure, an army officer who observed their plight predicted they would either starve or be forced to leave the reserve and steal from nearby settlers. Colonel George F. Brooke distributed rations rather than watch them die of starvation.

The Seminole soon began returning to their former homes in north Florida, renewing conflicts with settlers and intensifying pressures for removal. In 1832, President Jackson sent Gadsden to renegotiate. The resulting Treaty of Payne's Landing has been embroiled in controversy since it was marked, in lieu of signatures, by fifteen Seminole leaders on 9 May. Gadsden insisted the Seminole agreed to a mass evacuation within three years. The Seminole vehemently disagreed, claiming their intention had been to send a delegation to inspect the lands in the west and report back. Departure was contingent on a favorable vote of their people.

The delegation of seven Seminoles that visited the western lands signed another pact on 28 March 1833, often referred to as the Treaty of Fort Gibson. John Phagan, the Indian agent representing the government, interpreted it as an agreement that the land was acceptable even though it was controlled by Creek factions whom Seminole leaders considered hostile. Seminole leaders adamantly insisted they would never agree to merge with their bitter enemies despite having common cultural origins. Furthermore, they charged that Phagan refused to transport them back to Florida unless they signed the pact.

James Gadsden. Born at Charleston, South Carolina in 1788, Gadsden served as an aide to General Andrew Jackson in 1818 during the First Seminole War. He is best known in Florida for heading the U.S. delegations in negotiations with the Seminole that resulted in the Treaty of Moultrie Creek in 1823 and the Treaty of Payne's Landing in 1832. Courtesy of the State Archives of Florida, *Florida Memory*, http://floridamemory.com/items/show/26225.

Historian John K. Mahon, the leading authority on the subject, concluded that coercion, bribery, and deceit produced the signatures at Payne's Landing and Fort Gibson. Andrew Jackson, however, gave orders to expedite removal. The outraged Seminole refused to cooperate and began planning to attack the Americans. These attacks escalated to become the Second Seminole War, 1835–42, and the Third Seminole War, 1855–58. Battle casualties and the forced removal of the Seminole to the trans-Mississippi West reduced their numbers to approximately 200 persons living in small, scattered bands in the remote regions of south Florida.

At the conclusion of the Second Seminole War, Congress passed the Armed Occupation Act of 1842 (AOA) to encourage white population growth in south Florida and to further pressure any remaining Seminole to leave. The act permitted a head of family or a single man capable of armed defense to claim 160 acres of land south of Gainesville and north of the Peace River. Nearly 1,200 individuals received title to 200,000 acres of land, and 6,000 persons moved to south Florida as a result of this legislation. Claimants rushed to lands on the Indian River on the Atlantic coast, and Hillsborough County in southwest Florida, which previously had been inhabited by Seminole.

Near the deactivated military outpost at Fort Pierce on Indian River, a colony of migrants from Augusta, Georgia, created a thriving settlement. Caleb Lyndon Brayton, one of the Augusta migrants, had moved from Massachusetts to Augusta in the 1830s and prospered as a merchant. Passage

Major Robert Gamble. After the Second Seminole War and the forced migration of the Seminole to reservations west of the Mississippi River, Major Robert Gamble moved seventy slaves from Middle Florida to establish a 3,500-acre sugarcane plantation along the Manatee River in Hillsborough County. Gamble's massive sugar mill was destroyed during the Civil War, but the Gamble Mansion still stands at Gamble Plantation Historic State Park at Ellenton, Florida. Courtesy of the State Archives of Florida, *Florida Memory*, http://floridamemory.com/items/show/29750.

of the AOA prompted him to move to the south Florida frontier. Despite periodic bouts with tuberculosis, Brayton threw himself into pioneer life with remarkable energy, clearing land and building a cabin on high ground overlooking the Indian River. By 1845, he had planted more than 140 acres of arrowroot, pumpkins, and other produce and had begun to market poultry, dried fish, and green turtles in Key West. He acquired a schooner to facilitate his trade and dreamed of the wealth he would gain from pineapples and other fruits and vegetables planted on an additional 160-acre tract he purchased. Filled with unbridled enthusiasm, Brayton's letters to his wife in Augusta are an enduring testimonial to the rigors as well as to the exhilarations of pioneer life. The letters also document the profound loneliness of life on the south Florida frontier.

Across the peninsula from Fort Pierce, the AOA stimulated development of Hillsborough County, where only ninety-six permanent residents had been counted in 1840. Families that had moved from Virginia and Maryland to Middle Florida in the 1820s and had prospered there until the national depression of 1837 moved to their second Florida frontier after passage of the AOA. Sons of the Braden, Gamble, and Craig families moved their slave communities to tracts along the Manatee River, where a longer growing season protected sugarcane from the early frosts that hindered sugar production in north Florida. Men like Jacob Summerlin drove herds of cattle from northeast Florida to graze free on the vast open range of Hillsborough County. By 1860, more than 30,000 head of cattle roamed the inland grasslands and more than 900 people lived among the prosperous Manatee River plantations. Historian Janet Snyder Mathews has characterized the Hillsborough settlements as "the edge of wilderness" and an important part of "a new American frontier."[2]

The Gambles and Bradens were frontier aristocrats, not the "plain folk" who pioneered in Florida from adjacent southern states after 1842. Historian James M. Denham has written with understanding of the culture of the Florida "crackers" who brought their families and farm animals to Florida seeking affordable and fertile land. Highly individualistic and mobile, fiercely dedicated to popular democracy, generally possessing antipathy toward Native Americans and African Americans, and quick to anger, the crackers would become the majority of the population in farming regions of the state.

Seminole removal also contributed to the growth and development of northeast Florida. The rural plantations had been periodically disrupted by Indian attacks between 1835 and 1842, but the stimulus of a military garrison

Jacob Summerlin, known as the King of the Crackers. Summerlin was born in Alachua County in 1820. As a young man, he moved to central Florida and started a career as a cattle rancher by rounding up wild cattle that roamed the Florida grasslands. Cracking long whips, Summerlin and his men drove the cattle to ports on the Gulf for shipment to Cuba. Prior to the Civil War, Summerlin grazed more than 15,000 cattle in the Peace and Kissimmee River valleys. Courtesy of the State Archives of Florida, *Florida Memory*, http://floridamemory.com/items/show/26245.

and supply post at Jacksonville led to the doubling of Duval County's population between 1830 and 1840. After 1842, wagon caravans of settlers and their slaves rolled through Jacksonville with the tools and supplies needed to build homes in the backcountry that became Clay County and beyond to the Alachua Prairie. The wagons soon rolled farther south and west, carrying Georgians and South Carolinians to cotton plantations in Marion and Columbia Counties. A record 530 vessels carried exports from Jacksonville in 1855. Reports of streets jammed with wagons and carts prompted the editor of the *Jacksonville News* to boast on 18 December 1856 that Florida's "crop is greater in quantity of cotton, and aggregate value, than any State in proportion to its population."

By 1842, three steam-powered sawmills were cutting lumber on the St. Johns River, supported by commerce with the military. On October 11, 1851, a newsman reported in the *Florida Republican* that Jacksonville was "the largest lumber market in the South." Three years later, twenty sawmills were producing boards for export. Mills on the Nassau and St. Marys Rivers and Black Creek also cut yellow pine and shipped Florida lumber to ports throughout the world. Late in the 1850s, railroads tapped new timberlands, sustaining an economic enterprise of major significance and encouraging an influx of additional small farmers.

As the loggers cut the pine, new homesteads were cleared for settlement. In 1860, Clay County was a land of white yeoman farmers; 73 percent of its population was white, 93 percent of whom had been born in slave states. Only 19 percent of the heads of Clay County households owned slaves, and more than half of all bondsmen were held at only six estates.

Whites were 57 percent of Duval County's 5,074 residents in 1860. Slaves in Duval numbered 2,046 (40 percent), and free black persons totaled 164 (3 percent). Approximately 41 percent of all Duval residents lived in the City of Jacksonville in 1860, working at diverse occupations that reflected the expansion of the region's economy. There were slightly more whites than blacks among the 2,128 residents of the town, and 44 percent of the heads of household had been born in the North or in foreign countries. Outside the town, however, four of every five white household heads were from slave-holding states. Just north of Jacksonville, the growing town of Fernandina, with a population of 1,360 residents in 1860, showed similar patterns.

By the 1840s and 1850s, governmental affairs in Florida were dominated by a coalition of elites known as the "Nucleus," led by Richard K. Call. This combination of early Monroe and Jackson appointees and wealthy migrants from Virginia who had settled in Middle Florida had gained control of the Florida Land Office as well as executive and judicial posts throughout the territory. Often land speculators, slave owners, and cotton planters, as members of the Whig Party they advocated government-assisted internal improvements and liberal bank charters. Their banking policies evolved into the most controversial political issue of the territorial years.

Between 1831 and 1835, the Legislative Council approved bank charters for groups in Pensacola, Tallahassee, and St. Augustine. Directors of the banks, their stockholders, and the individuals who received loans were all members of the ruling elite. With inflated evaluations of their property from bank officers who were friends and relatives, planters traded mortgages for stock in the Union Bank of Tallahassee and then received generous loans to finance additional purchases of land and slaves. Additional capital came from bond sales to investors in New York City, Boston, Amsterdam, and London, sales made possible by the "good faith" promise of the Legislative Council to back the bonds. Call and his associates had been followers of Old Hickory in earlier years, but in Florida they evolved into a conservative ruling class opposed to the policies advocated in the 1830s by the Jacksonian Democrats.

In less troubled times, the banks may have prospered, but the bitterly cold winter of 1835 that destroyed the citrus industry in East Florida, coupled with the economic dislocations caused by the Second Seminole War and the repercussions of the Panic of 1837, led to bank failures throughout the nation. In Florida, the legislative council passed laws to tax Florida residents as a means to pay interest on the "faith bonds" as the council had promised to bond holders. Outraged Florida residents condemned the laws and taxes as evidence that politicians were corrupt and protecting only the interests of the "Nucleus."

Men outside of this circle of influence were also eager to acquire properties and business, and became resentful of the antidemocratic politics of the Florida elite. They denounced inherited privileges and monopolies that denied opportunities to the common man. In response, leaders like Robert R. Reid, David Levy, and James D. Westcott formed the Jacksonian Democratic Party as a vehicle to unseat the entrenched aristocracy.

The Florida "Bank War" opened on an unlikely front: as the feature issue in the drive for statehood that Richard Call and his Whig Party colleagues spearheaded in the mid-1830s. Call pointed to the millions of acres of land in the territory, controlled by Congress, that could be granted to Florida and used by state officials as inducements for internal improvements, and claimed that wealth, population growth, and economic development were certain to come to Florida with statehood. When a referendum in May 1838 produced a majority of voters in favor of statehood, Governor Call authorized elections of delegates to a constitutional convention to be held in December at St. Joseph, the new Gulf coast port near Apalachicola. During the elections of delegates to the convention, candidates pledged to antibank positions denounced speculators and aristocrats who profited from the banks and excluded the laboring classes. The antibank delegates won the majority of the seats.

The leading men of the territory assembled at St. Joseph on 3 December. Future governors Robert R. Reid, Thomas Brown, and William Marvin were in attendance, as were future U.S. senators from Florida James D. Westcott, Jackson Morton, and David Levy Yulee (who had adopted his family's honorary Moorish title). Delegates debated until 11 January 1839, when a constitution was approved containing provisions that severely restricted banking policies. It was a clear repudiation of the conservative elite. In a referendum conducted in May, voters of the territory approved the constitution, but the ratification campaign was again controversial and closely contested.

It was the leadership of congressional delegate Yulee that most directly led to admission of Florida to the Union. He wrote numerous letters, gave countless speeches, and published an influential pamphlet in support of statehood. A convincing theme in the speeches was Yulee's claim that once statehood was approved, Congress would make federal lands available to support railroad construction and other internal improvement projects that would result in national prominence for Florida and additional population growth.

In Washington, Yulee worked through southern congressmen, reminding them that admitting Florida would correct the imbalance of free and slave states expected to occur in 1846 with the admission of Iowa as a free state. In January 1845, the House of Representatives reported out a bill calling for admission of Iowa and Florida that was approved and signed by President John Tyler. On 3 March 1845, Florida became the twenty-seventh state of the United States of America.

Governor John Branch declared 26 May 1845 as the date for election of officers for the new State of Florida. Voters chose Democrats William D. Moseley, a planter from Jefferson County for governor, and David Yulee for congressman. Democrats also won majorities in both houses of the General Assembly, and at the initial meeting in June 1845 chose Yulee and David Westcott as Florida's first United States senators. By adjournment on 26 July, the assembly had created the executive and judicial structure of the new state and passed tax and revenue bills to support it.

Democrats remained in control of Florida politics until after the Civil War. The party became adamantly insistent on states' rights and made increasingly radical demands for secession from the Union. While some twentieth-century Floridians have argued that secession and the Civil War were not related to defense of the institution of slavery, political leaders in Florida during the late antebellum years would have unapologetically and strenuously disagreed. "Southern rights" to Florida's Democrats meant the

David Levy Yulee, U.S. senator from Florida, born at Charlotte Amalie on the Island of St. Thomas, the son of Moses Levy, a Jewish merchant from Morocco who acquired a huge estate in Florida. David Levy Yulee became an attorney at St. Augustine and the Territory of Florida's leading advocate for statehood. He was twice elected to the U.S. Senate, the first Jew to serve in that body, and a radical supporter of secession from the Union. Yulee was the founder and president of the Florida Railroad. Courtesy of the State Archives of Florida, *Florida Memory*, http://floridamemory.com/items/show/174.

implicit and unrestricted right to own slave property and to move slaves into the western territories. Defense of property rights came to mean protection of slave property from abolitionists.

From Florida's inception as a territory, slave labor was considered essential to economic development. During Florida's British years, and during the Spanish period that followed, large-scale importation of enslaved Africans was considered essential for development and economic prosperity. In 1830, slaves comprised 47 percent and free blacks 5 percent of the total population of three northeast Florida counties: St. Johns, Duval, and Nassau. Nearly every owner of six or more slaves had been a Spanish colonial. By 1860, the Spanish holdovers were deceased and the ratio of slaves to total population had dropped to 30 percent, but slaves were still considered vital to the economy.

In Alachua, in Middle Florida, along the Gulf coast south of Tallahassee, and in south Florida there were no holdover planters. Native American populations concentrated in several locations inhibited expansion of American plantations until 1842, yet as early as 1830 enslaved persons comprised 41 percent of Gadsden County's 4,894 residents. By 1860, the total population had nearly doubled and the slave population had increased to 58 percent. Jefferson County's slave ratios increased from 48 to 65 percent in the same period. By 1860, Leon County's population of 12,243 was 74 percent enslaved. Free blacks were rarely seen in the Middle Florida counties. Migrant planters brought with them the slave codes and the two-caste racial system, with strong biases against emancipation and the presence of free blacks in the general population that had prevailed in their states of origin.

Slaves in the populous Middle Florida counties produced and transported cotton crops, ran sawmills, made brick, and were masons, carpenters, blacksmiths, and even overseers. The Jefferson County cotton crop of 11,000 bales ranked second in Florida in 1860, its value estimated at $1.3 million. As historian Larry Rivers has shown, slaves were the most valuable property in Florida, and slave owning was the preferred route to status and power. Middle Florida's slave owners included judges, legislators, attorneys, merchants, medical doctors, single and married women, and even preachers.

In East Florida, the Spanish three-caste system of race relations (white owners, free blacks, and black slaves) was operative when the United States took possession in 1821. The territorial government quickly implemented a two-caste system. Blaming free blacks for creating discontent among slaves, the Legislative Council passed restrictive laws aimed at eliminating emancipation and free black status. Discriminatory laws against free blacks, and harsh punishments for those found guilty of minor infractions, prompted more than 150 free blacks from Pensacola to flee to Mexico in the 1850s. Free blacks from St. Augustine and Pensacola emigrated to Cuba and the free black Republic of Haiti. In 1837, Zephaniah Kingsley moved his mixed-race family from Duval County to a 36,000-acre settlement in Haiti that he established for free persons of color. He liberated fifty slaves from his Florida plantations and moved them to Haiti under indentured labor contracts for his son's estate near Puerto Plata in today's Dominican Republic.

Cotton cultivation, U.S. South, 1875. Black men and women covering cotton seed while a noise-maker contraption is installed to prevent birds from picking out the seed. Although the image depicts a postwar event, it is reminiscent of the labor of thousands of black men and women in Florida's cotton fields prior to 1865. Source: *Harper's Weekly*, April 24, 1875. Courtesy of www.slaveryimages.org, compiled by Jerome Handler and Michael Tuite, and sponsored by the Virginia Foundation for the Humanities and the University of Virginia Library.

On 12 July 1851, the editor of St. Augustine's *Ancient City* castigated free blacks as "useless" troublemakers and "hopeless, degraded, wretched, and forbidden outcasts." This was not the last deliberate misreading of the historical record. St. Augustine had long been home to educated free blacks who owned property, held responsible jobs, and led productive lives. With a single exception during the Second Seminole War, free blacks had not acted to overthrow slavery. In fact, some were slave owners. The newspaper editor was reacting to the racial hysteria and heightened attachment to white supremacy that escalated in the 1850s.

Cotton prices were at record highs in the 1850s. Slave prices doubled, leading some politicians to suggest that the African slave trade should be reopened. Lumber mills boomed from Pensacola to Jacksonville, and subsidiary industries were being established. At the end of the decade, the Florida Railroad, under direction of David Yulee and spurred on by generous grants of land by the federal and state governments, was under construction between Fernandina on the Atlantic and Cedar Keys on the Gulf. South Florida cattlemen were furious that the western terminus would not be at nearby Tampa Bay, but Yulee proceeded to link the two towns where he had acquired title to a majority of the property. The Florida, Atlantic and Gulf Central Railroad ran from Jacksonville to Lake City; from there the Pensacola and Georgia Railroad extended to Tallahassee. It was an era of unparalleled expansion, with the population increasing from 87,000 to 140,000 during the 1850s. White workingmen from northern and southern states were migrating to Florida's growing towns, and yet there were labor shortages that prompted employers to advertise for black or white laborers. By mid-decade, Irish immigrants could be found on local work crews.

Fear of slave rebellions became common after the Nat Turner rebellion in Virginia in 1831, and was intensified in Florida by the black warriors who fought alongside the Seminole from 1835 to 1842. The *Jacksonville News* printed accounts of runaway attempts in May 1852 that led angry citizens of Jacksonville to meet and denounce "abolitionists and their tools" who were allegedly attempting to entice our slave population to abscond." Citizens demanded new laws to impose more rigid restrictions on the town's free blacks and slaves. White workingmen supported hefty license fees for free blacks and prohibitions on slaves arranging their own employment and living apart from their owners. Despite a rapid influx of northern and foreign-born workers, the flourishing urban labor force was still mostly black, prompting white fears of insurrection unless blacks were restrained.

National political passions of the 1850s added to racial tensions in Florida. At town meetings in 1850, speakers angry about debates in Congress over the admission of California to the Union and the resultant Compromise of 1850 denounced northern-born residents of Florida as abolitionists. They called on fellow citizens to defend southern rights and secede from the Union rather than compromise away the rights of slaveholders to carry human property into the western territories. Firebrand speakers warned that further compromises would encourage northern abolitionists to place chains of slavery around the necks of white Floridians. Democrats in Florida overwhelmingly opposed the Compromise of 1850, calling it abolitionist inspired.

In early 1860, Florida's Democrats joined with Democrats in other southern states to block Stephen Douglas as the party's nominee for president. Events in Kansas had convinced them that the Douglas policy of popular sovereignty jeopardized the cause of extending slavery into the western territories. When northern delegates insisted on a Douglas candidacy at the

Charleston convention in April, southern delegates withdrew and backed John C. Breckenridge of Kentucky as the candidate for the southern branch of the Democratic Party. The Republican Party chose Abraham Lincoln, and the remnants of the southern Whigs hoped for a miracle behind John Bell of Tennessee, the candidate for the Constitutional Union Party.

Lincoln was not on the ballot in the 7 November elections in Florida, and Douglas received only 367 votes. John Bell polled 5,437 votes, running strong in east coast cities, while the southern Democrats and Breckenridge tallied 8,543 votes to lead the field. Breckenridge had been supported by eighteen of the state's twenty-four newspapers.

In the race for governor, Democrat John Milton tallied 6,994 votes to Constitutional Union candidate Edward Hopkins's 5,248 votes. Although Democrats swept the statewide races and controlled both legislative and congressional delegations, it was clear from the votes for Bell and the Constitutional Union Party that many Floridians were still hoping to find a compromise and remain in the Union.

Lincoln's victory triggered mob rallies, newspaper denunciations, and calls for immediate secession. On 10 November, a story in the *Tallahassee Floridian and Journal* read: "Lincoln is elected. There is a beginning of the end. Sectionalism has triumphed. What is to be done? We say resist." Regulators and other vigilantes increased their activities, and the ranks of militia companies swelled.

Newspapers throughout the state demanded that the General Assembly authorize a convention to consider secession. On 26 November, Governor Perry told the General Assembly to either consider secession or to prepare for slave insurrection. He announced that an election would be held on 22 December to elect delegates to attend a 3 January 1861 convention.

While candidates campaigned, a South Carolina convention voted to sever ties with the Union, inciting extremists in Florida to make increasingly shrill demands for secession. In some counties, Duval and Clay, for example, delegates elected to the convention had campaigned on platforms embracing moderation and Union. Others planned to delay secession and insist that the final document be submitted to the voters for approval.

The Florida convention opened in an atmosphere of secessionist euphoria. John C. McGehee of Madison County was elected president. With leading secessionists from South Carolina and Alabama in the galleries, the delegates prepared an ordinance of secession by 9 January. Efforts by Jackson Morton and George T. Ward to submit the ordinance to the voters in a referendum were defeated. Secession fever had spread too rapidly.

On 10 January 1861 the delegates voted sixty-two to seven in favor of secession. By 4 February, Florida representatives were in Montgomery for the formation of the Confederate States of America. It was time to change the flags again, write another constitution, and hold new elections, all under the shadow of a looming war.

The parades, speeches and toasts, and the jubilation that greeted the news of secession occurred in every hamlet in Florida. Crowds filled the hotels in Pensacola, Tallahassee, and Jacksonville, and revelers danced in the streets amidst torchlight parades and fireworks. Bonfires and the sounds of church bells and cannon firings were common. Militia units paraded, while Unionists became cautious and silent.

John Darling of Tampa would later claim that his advocacy of secession had not been motivated by thoughts of war but rather by the "conviction that it was a rightful and proper remedy to break down the policy of Negro emancipation believed to be intended by the Republican Administration then about to come into office." Confederate Congressman John Sanderson, a Vermont-born attorney and planter in Duval County, said that he had not voted for secession with the expectation that war would follow. Rather, Sanderson said, he had acted on behalf of those "states interested in the institution of slavery" expecting to "secure permanent guarantees for the interests and institutions of the South."

Whig Unionist Richard Call had no such illusions as the galleries erupted in applause when the secession vote was counted on 10 January. He rose to condemn the delegates and shout loudly: "You have opened the gates of Hell, from which shall flow the curses of the damned which shall sink you to perdition."[3] Strong words, but, by late 1863, many Florida secessionists would come to agree with him.

Notes

1. Remini, *The Life of Andrew Jackson*, 134.
2. Mathews, *Edge of Wilderness*, 137.
3. Doherty, *Richard Keith Call: Southern Unionist*, 158.

Bibliography

Brown, Canter, Jr. *Florida's Peace River Frontier*. Gainesville: University Presses of Florida, 1991.

———. *Ossian Bingley Hart, Florida's Loyalist Reconstruction Governor*. Baton Rouge: Louisiana State University Press, 1997.

Buker, George E. "The Americanization of St. Augustine, 1821–1865." In *The Oldest City: St. Augustine, Saga of Survival*, edited by Jean Parker Waterbury, 151–80. St. Augustine: St. Augustine Historical Society, 1983.

Coker, Edward Caleb, and Daniel L. Schafer. "A New Englander on the Indian River Frontier: Caleb Lyndon Brayton and the View from Brayton's Bluff." *Florida Historical Quarterly* 70, no. 3 (January 1992):305–32.

Covington, James W. *The Seminoles of Florida*. Gainesville: University Press of Florida, 1993.

Dodd, Dorothy. *Florida Becomes a State*. Tallahassee: Florida Centennial Commission, 1945.

Doherty, Herbert J. *Richard Keith Call, Southern Unionist*. Gainesville: University of Florida Press, 1961.

———. *The Whigs of Florida, 1845–1854*. Gainesville: University of Florida Press, 1959.

Dovell, Junius E. *Florida: Historic, Dramatic, Contemporary*. Vol. 1. New York: Lewis Historical Publishing, 1952.

Ellsworth, Linda, and Lucius Ellsworth. *Pensacola: The Deep Water City*. Tulsa: Continental Heritage Press, 1982.

Hoffman, Paul E. *Florida's Frontiers*. Bloomington: Indiana University Press, 2002.

Mahon, John K. *History of the Second Seminole War, 1835–1842*. Gainesville: University of Florida Press, 1967.

Mahon, John K., and Brent R. Weisman. "Florida's Seminole and Miccosukee Peoples." In *The New History of Florida*, edited by Michael Gannon, 183–206. Gainesville: University Press of Florida, 1996.

Mathews, Janet Snyder. *Edge of Wilderness: A Settlement History of Manatee River and Sarasota Bay, 1528–1885*. Tulsa: Caprine Press, 1983.

Monaco, C. S. *Moses Levy of Florida: Jewish Utopian and Antebellum Reformer*. Baton Rouge: Louisiana State University Press, 2005.

Paisley, Clifton. *The Red Hills of Florida, 1528–1865*. Tuscaloosa: University of Alabama Press, 1989.

Reiger, John F. "Secession of Florida from the Union—A Minority Decision?" *Florida Historical Quarterly* 46, no. 4 (April 1968):358–68.

Remini, Robert V. *The Life of Andrew Jackson*. New York: Harper and Row, 1988.

Rivers, Larry. *Slavery in Florida: Territorial Days to Emancipation*. Gainesville: University Press of Florida, 2000.

Schafer, Daniel L. "'A class of people neither free men nor slaves': From Spanish to American Relations in Florida, 1821–1861." *Journal of Social History* 26, no. 3 (Spring 1993):587–609.

———. *Thunder on the River: The Civil War in Northeast Florida*. Gainesville: University Press of Florida, 2010.

Thompson, Arthur W. *Jacksonian Democracy on the Florida Frontier*. Gainesville: University of Florida Press, 1961.

14

The Civil War, 1861–1865

ROBERT A. TAYLOR

Florida's road to civil war began with a disputed presidential election. The year 1860 saw a dividing nation select a new chief executive from four possible candidates of whom one, the new Republican Party's Abraham Lincoln, did not appear on state ballots. Florida voters were very unlikely to support a "black Republican" in any case that year. John C. Breckinridge, the sitting vice president of the United States, gained Florida's electoral votes by a comfortable margin. But when the final tally was made, Lincoln won the White House without the vote of a single southern state. The stage was now set for the ultimate national crisis.

The vast majority of Floridians along with their neighbors to the north refused to accept the idea of a Republican president who they believed would move against the South's "peculiar institution" of slavery with all his constitutional powers. Seemingly the only option was secession from the Union and perhaps joining some sort of new slave-state-based republic. Those calling for immediate secession, even before Lincoln took office, dominated the political climate in Tallahassee. Governor Madison S. Perry completely agreed with such sentiments. Despite this very vocal bloc, there were other Florida leaders who took a more cautious approach, as they feared the consequences of being the first state to secede and test the resolve of the federal government.

All eyes were on the capital in Tallahassee in January 1861 as a convention of Floridians met to debate the question of Florida remaining a part of the United States. Hard-core "fire-eating" secessionists failed to gain control of the meeting. Most of the delegates tended toward cooperation with other slave states or waiting for some overt act from the Lincoln administration. The secession convention also sat members who did not support what they considered drastic and unnecessary action. Pockets of such Union sympathy existed around the state and would later loom large in Florida's war experience. Argument raged between the factions, with some calling for secession even before it was clear that Georgia and Alabama would act in the same fashion. In the end, the radicals won the day, and an ordinance of secession was approved on January 10, 1861, by a sixty-two to seven vote. Joyous crowds filled the streets of Tallahassee and other Florida towns to celebrate the birth of an independent Florida republic. Unionist ex-governor Richard Keith Call dared to publicly speak out against what he considered the madness of this course of action, but he was ignored.[1]

Why did leaders like Call fail to stop Florida from seceding? There is no simple answer to such a complicated question, but some points do stand out. First, large numbers of Floridians had moved to the peninsula from South Carolina to make their futures with fresh, new lands. Political and emotional ties to the Palmetto State, and its radicalism, remained strong. Second, many feared that an isolated Florida, cut off from the Lower South's economy, might not be able to survive. Third, Floridians in large numbers were convinced that Lincoln and his abolitionist supporters would unleash a reign of terror with assaults on the slave system that would result in racial warfare. As Florida had only been a state since 1845, being apart from the United States seemed something less than terrifying.

Events moved even while the secessionist solons debated in Tallahassee. Local militia forces promptly moved to seize important federal installations around the state. Eager troops took control of the arsenal at Chattahoochee, Fernandina's Fort Clinch, and even the formidable old Spanish fortress, then called Fort Marion, in Saint Augustine. Other bases in the state seemed ripe for the taking in the face of little to no Union resistance. This failure to react confirmed in many minds that the North, as predicted, would acquiesce to southern independence without an armed conflict. Floridians worked to convince themselves that should war break out, it would be short, easy, and glorious for southern arms.

Florida would exist as an independent country for only a matter of weeks in 1861. By February delegates from the peninsula journeyed to Montgomery, Alabama, to meet with other seceded states to form a new nation, the Confederate States of America. In short order this convention produced a new constitution, selected Jefferson Davis to be its provisional president, and laid plans to create an army and navy. Former U.S. senator Stephen R. Mallory, of Key West, joined the Davis administration as the Confederacy's first (and only) secretary of the navy. He would prove to be an able leader for the Confederate Navy Department, though his tenure did not lack for controversy as the naval arm failed in the end to defeat the more powerful Union fleets.[2]

America's bloodiest war could have easily started in Florida. In January 1861, a small force under Union Lieutenant Adam J. Slemmer abandoned fortifications he could not hold around Pensacola and concentrated his men in Fort Pickens at the entrance to Pensacola Bay. This lonely fort on Santa Rosa Island effectively blocked the new Confederacy's largest harbor, and rebel forces flocked there in hopes of taking it by force of arms. A very uneasy truce held as the Lincoln administration groped in its early days to formulate a strategy and get reinforcements to Slemmer. Before the inevitable clash occurred, South Carolinians opened fire on Fort Sumter on April 12, thus unleashing civil war.[3]

The attack on Sumter resulted in President Lincoln calling for 75,000 volunteers to put down what he considered to be a rebellion in the southern states, as well as a naval blockade of the new Confederacy including Florida. Under the laws of nations, a blockade is an act of war against another country. The result of all this was the secession of four more slave states and the threat of others opting for the Confederate States of America. Peaceful separation would not be a possibility, as Floridians were soon to find out.

Male Floridians of military age, and many who were not, flocked to join local companies quickly growing into regiments. These moved out of Florida to join the growing rebel armies soon to be committed to battle. Amazingly, between 14,000 and 15,000 men from Florida served in the ranks for the Confederate army and navy out of the state's roughly 140,000 inhabitants. This proved to be the highest percentage of fighting men in any of the Confederate states. The troops exhibited their valor on the many battlefields seen by the Army of Northern Virginia and the Army of Tennessee. Their numbers thinned as the war progressed from combat deaths, wounds, and illnesses, but they truly made their mark from Gettysburg to Chickamauga.[4]

Florida provided leaders as well as private soldiers to the Confederate cause. General officers like Edmund Kirby Smith, William W. Loring, and Joseph Finegan represented Florida well as general officers in the Confederate army and shared its victories as well as its setbacks and final defeat. They joined many brave lower-ranking Floridians as the fighting grew in intensity and cost from Tennessee to the fields of Virginia.

Organizing and equipping all these new Florida troops fell on the shoulders of newly elected Governor John Milton. A Jackson County planter and strong Confederate, Milton proved to be a hardworking and competent war governor for Florida. He believed that the only realistic path to southern independence was cooperation with the government now located in Richmond. Tragically, his efforts ended with the failure of the rebel cause, and depression drove him to take his own life in April 1865.

Governor Milton had a myriad of problems from the start of his administration. One looming large was how to defend a state the size and shape of Florida with limited or no military resources. Things grew even worse when, in the spring of 1862, the Confederate high command made the strategic decision to withdraw troops from areas they deemed of secondary importance, like Florida. Most of the new Florida troops found themselves serving in Virginia and Tennessee and not defending their home state. Confederate officials like General Robert E. Lee told Floridians at home that they would have to look after their own defenses. Such words rang hollow as time passed and the Yankee threat to Florida loomed larger each day.[5]

Even if Milton could somehow scare up enough manpower for state defense, a tall order, deploying them would be crippled by a shortage of weapons and military equipment. He grew frustrated and angry with Richmond bureaucrats who seemed clueless about conditions outside Virginia. Suggestions that weapons could be had if he simply filled out the right forms and sent them through proper military channels drove him to distraction. The governor knew the Federals would sooner or later move on a weak, exposed Florida, and wondered what was taking them so long to attack. In the troubled days ahead, Florida would receive precious little help from Richmond or any other part of the Confederate States.

Milton also had to keep in mind another problem with the potential to sap Florida's war effort. The people of Florida had never been completely united behind secession and a war for independence. Defeats, shortages, and sacrifices would only increase Unionist influence as the struggle went on. A serious social fault line ran through Florida, and could potentially bring the horrors of real civil war to the home front. And Milton could never forget that Florida's slave population might not stay complacent as freedom beckoned in the form of the Union military.

Such pressures on Florida society began with the establishment of the Union naval blockade. Apalachicola became Florida's first port crippled when the USS *Montgomery* appeared offshore on June 11, 1861. Pensacola and Key West were already under Federal control, and by mid-1862 they were joined by Fernandina, Saint Augustine, and Jacksonville (one of several Union occupations of that city). These gains supported the U.S. Navy's presence in Florida waters, and created ready bases for strikes into the interior of the peninsula. In time, blockaders sealed off Tampa Bay, leaving only small ports like Punta Rassa and Saint Marks on the Gulf open. Smugglers soon began using what was then called Mosquito Inlet near New Smyrna to unload cargoes. Even with such advantages, the Union navy still had to patrol some 1,300 miles of coastline without the aid of modern devices like radar and aircraft.[6]

Soon blockade-runners used Florida waters as a destination for goods needed by the South. Items like shoes, blankets, medical supplies, and rifles came through, along with increasingly difficult-to-find civilian consumer goods. The volume of smuggled supplies coming into the state did, however, pale in comparison with that entering ports like Charleston or Mobile. The primary reason for this was the fact that Florida's primitive transportation system made moving bulky shipments out almost impossible. There were no good roads, and the major river, the Saint Johns, was soon filled with Yankee gunboats. What little railroad mileage that did exist in Florida in the early 1860s offered little help as rail operations quickly ground to a halt. No direct link to Georgia's railroads existed until the spring of 1865. It simply did not pay to try Florida as a major conduit for such supplies.

If that was the case, why did illicit traffic continue from the Bahamas and Cuba toward Florida? By continuing even at low levels, blockade-runners forced the Union navy to tie down dozens of warships on patrol off Florida, ships that could have been used against major rebel ports sooner and strangled needed imports. Also, the limited amount of goods moved into Florida did contribute something to the Confederate war effort and helped civilian morale. Despite the nagging problems of transportation, material run into Florida did make its way northward and was available in markets as far north as Atlanta.[7]

While the naval blockade was originally quite leaky, over time it tightened up and helped to dry up sources of certain critical supplies. Combined with the loss of productive areas due to advancing Federal armies, the Confederate South increasingly was forced to rely on its own resources to provide for both its armies and the home-front population. Florida quickly grew into a major source for the Confederate government east of the Mississippi River. Despite herculean efforts, time would show that Florida would never be able to meet all the demands placed upon it. Rebel expectations of what the state could provide proved overly optimistic.

Florida's most important contribution to the Confederate war effort was ordinary salt, which was absolutely essential for preserving meat and for tanning leather. Before the war, southern salt came from salt mines in the Upper South and from the Caribbean islands. The coming of civil war choked off both sources just as demand for salted meat for army rations soared. By the spring of 1862, the South faced a salt famine with the potential to cripple military operations. The only real solution was to turn to domestic resources behind Confederate lines. Boiling water from the Atlantic and Gulf of Mexico for its saline had to be done, and many eyes looked to the Florida peninsula as an inviting place to begin.

Saltworks soon sprang up on both Florida coasts and ranged from large-scale factories to single families using old sugar kettles. Eventually everything was pressed into service from used steam boilers to adapted metal channel buoys to manufacture the precious mineral. Plentiful firewood for the boiler fires was needed, as well as labor to tend those flames and harvest the salt at the end of the process. Slaves often toiled at Florida coast saltworks, and whites flocked to them as well. Such men enjoyed an exemption from the 1862 Confederate conscription law as well as a share in the considerable profits saltworks generated.[8]

The heaviest concentration of Florida saltworks was on the Gulf coast in an area ranging from Saint Marks to Saint Andrews Bay (the site of modern-day Panama City). Salty marshes along Saint Andrews Bay offered protection from sudden attacks from Federal warships in the Gulf, and boasted a number of trails into Georgia and Alabama that made transporting wagonloads of salt fairly easy. The hot, smelly, but lucrative work kept men on the bay, and investors from other states hoped for tidy profits from their ventures. Newspapers like the *Macon (Ga.) Daily Telegraph* warned that far too many people on the Florida coast were making salt for the monetary gain and not a sense of Confederate patriotism.[9]

The Union military quickly learned how important Florida salt making was to the rebels, and attacked it at every opportunity. Landing parties of Yankee sailors and marines rowed ashore and wrecked salt plants from Tampa Bay all the way to Saint Andrews Bay with a vengeance. But despite countless raids from the blockading vessels, most saltworks rose phoenix-like from the ashes and debris to resume production. In fact, some were repaired and boiling before the blue-clad enemy could return to their waiting warships. Only a physical permanent occupation of the major salt locations by Federal ground troops could stop its production. And as the Union high command considered Florida a secondary theater of war at best, soldiers would never be assigned in sufficient number to carry out this mission.

Florida would make salt for the Confederacy well into 1865. It is estimated that millions of dollars were invested in what was indeed a war industry, and the salt produced had an impact on meeting the desperate need for salt during the conflict. Thousands of workers, free and unfree, toiled at the works and manufactured enough to at least partially ease shortages in lower Alabama and Georgia. Without Florida's contributions in this area, it is difficult to see the Confederacy solving the salt problem.

Florida's agricultural bounty would also be tapped more and more as the Civil War dragged on. Its farms and plantations provided food for rebel soldiers, civilians, and the animals they depended on to move their armies. Such forces were literally horse-powered, and needed mountains of fodder to feed their cavalry and artillery horses daily. Such demand for all types of food leaped upward with the 1863 fall of Vicksburg and the isolation of the Confederate trans-Mississippi region. Southern newspapers glowingly referred to Florida as the "granary of the Confederacy" and the South's garden farm. Unfortunately, Florida was never able to live up to such unrealistic expectations and often failed to meet demands placed on it.[10]

The peninsula state did manage in the face of poor transportation and enemy disruptions to send agricultural products northward. Corn (sometimes distilled into whisky for the Confederate Medical Department), citrus, sugar, pork, and fish made its way to Georgia and South Carolina. Though Florida never provided enough to ward off hunger in the ranks, Florida food did free up local produce in those states for needy rebel regiments in other areas. In the spring of 1865, the government supply depot in Lake City bulged with considerable stores of corn, sugar, and horse feed for the rebel government, but, as the Confederacy collapsed, there was no one to whom to ship it.[11]

Florida's primary food contribution to the Confederacy ironically walked itself to supply depots. A large number of Florida beef cattle made the long journey from the piney prairies of the southern half of the peninsula to rebel forces north of Atlanta and to the besieged garrison of Charleston. As with the rest of Florida agriculture, there were high hopes that its herds could fill all food needs in short order. And the less than expected results turned out to be the same for beef as all the other foodstuffs despite considerable efforts.

Early in 1861 the new Confederate government began buying Florida bovines for army rations. A contract was let to Jacob Summerlin, a legendary cattleman, to deliver 25,000 head for eight to ten Confederate dollars per head. "Uncle Jake," however, soon tired of running cattle all the way to Charleston for rebel currency of dubious value. Soon he and Tampa's James McKay entered the far more profitable business of shipping cows to Cuba in exchange for Spanish gold. This cattle "leakage" only made supplying beef more difficult as ranchers had to choose between supporting a distant government in Richmond or protecting their economic futures in the form of their herds.[12]

By mid-1863 it had become clear to even Confederate Commissary Department bureaucrats at the Virginia capital that the war for their independence would not be a quick or easy one, and that measures needed to be taken at once to maximize supply sources east of the Mississippi. Without drastic changes, the rebel armies might disband for lack of food. Richmond announced a new program in April 1863 that divided the remaining Confederate states into districts commanded by a state chief commissary officer. Such an arrangement, it was hoped, would make the collection of all supplies more efficient and get food to the mouths of hungry soldiers. Florida was cast as a leading player in this new effort.

Major Pleasant W. White, a Quincy lawyer, took the position of chief commissary of Florida, and began the thankless job of convincing Floridians to contribute their cattle and other products to the Confederate government. White drew five commissary district lines to ensure the widest possible coverage. The fifth district encompassed the major cattle areas of south Florida and contained Hernando, Hillsborough, Manatee, Polk, Brevard, Dade, and Monroe Counties. Veteran businessman James McKay took command of this vital area.[13]

Numerous problems faced White and his men as orders for Florida beef flooded in from the fighting fronts and other segments of the Confederate government. Cows soon became harder to find as herds shrank and cattlemen grew less likely to sell their animals for low prices and payment in Confederate script. The Confederate Impressment Act of 1863, which gave officials the power to seize needed supplies from farmers, did little to foster cooperation with supply officers and wounded civilian morale. When cattle were collected, they somehow had to be driven northward to at least the Georgia rail network for further shipment. That took experienced "cracker" cowboys able to move the nearly wild cattle and to protect them from Union attacks that became all the more frequent on the trail. One solution was to form a special unit of cattle herders, known as Munnerlyn's Battalion or the Cow Cavalry, to ensure the cows got through. Their efforts made the difference between success and failure in these operations.[14]

By war's end, rebel forces had received at least 50,000 head of Florida beef, and the stringy meat filled many a Johnny Reb's stomach. The Confederate Army of Tennessee and troops around Charleston depended heavily on it as a part of their daily meals. Others subsisted, albeit poorly, on Florida cattle, and these included the starving Union prisoners of war languishing at Andersonville. But in the final analysis, the peninsula state was never able to keep up with the demands forced on it by rebel officials who lacked a clear sense of what Florida could realistically provide.

By 1863 the Civil War was having a definite impact on Florida's frontier society as the strains on the home front increased. People now knew full well that this struggle would not be quick or cheap, and that toil and sacrifice was required from all Floridians. How the segments of Florida's population responded to these challenges reveals much about what Florida was like in the early 1860s. The fiery trial of war tore at the state's social fabric and impacted all from plantations in Leon County to Seminoles living on the fringes of the Everglades. No Floridian could escape from it.

Florida women watched as their men marched off to fight in 1861, and only a few truly realized what their absences would mean in their lives. Shortages of once common consumer items became the new norm for them, and demanded that they seek them out or manufacture substitutes themselves. Farms and plantations still had to be managed and worked without a large segment of the male population. Florida women took up the slack, and found the strength and self-confidence to step in and run family businesses and raise children often alone. They made the clothes their families needed, taught their children when no schools were operating, and dealt with the fear and the loneliness of separation.

Upper-class women could at least often count on relatives and the labor of their slaves to keep things going. But the wives of common soldiers had to somehow get by without the support of their husbands and sons, and by 1863 were joining their sisters in other Confederate states in demanding some sort of relief from the government. While Florida women did not riot in the street as happened in Richmond, they clearly could understand the desperation that caused such unrest. Florida women had even more to fear from Union troops, lawless deserter bands, Unionist raiders, and perhaps even the Seminoles.[15]

Florida's African American slave population soon felt wartime changes like tremors from an earthquake. Slaves were often rented, or impressed, into service for the Confederate government for tasks like building fortification or collecting food supplies. Whether there or on the farm, slaves provided labor desperately needed to make up for the absence of so many white males in the army. When Union forces made their presence known around the state, they offered freedom for those with the courage to grasp for it. Soon, crossing the Saint Johns River into Union-controlled territory meant emancipation for many black Floridians. Those working at the salt-works could escape bondage when Yankee sailors came on raids from the sea.[16]

Even in the face of such disruptions, the bulk of Florida's slave population stayed at work producing what was needed for survival. Without them the state's war effort would have withered at a much faster rate than it did. In hindsight, the Federal forces should have targeted those areas of Florida with the highest concentration of slaves, like the greater Tallahassee area, for military operations. Perhaps the Confederacy would have collapsed a bit sooner through disruption of Florida's economic support of the South.

The Seminoles also lived through the Florida Civil War experience in their homes deep in the interior. After three devastating conflicts with whites, news that their former foes were now waging war on each other must have seemed strange to them. Florida officials began to worry about whether the Seminoles would be emboldened to take the war path yet again and seek vengeance from scattered Florida settlements? Would they be forced to raid to secure the trade goods they needed to live? Government leaders worked to maintain good relations by providing them with supplies in the hope of at least keeping them neutral. Tribal leaders made certain Tallahassee knew about Union contacts Seminoles were having as a means to ensure trade items would keep arriving.[17]

Such native interaction with Federals was real, as in the case of a small group of Mikasukis who visited Union troops based at Fort Myers in May 1864. They complained of poor treatment by Confederates and gladly accepted presents from the Yankees. The Indians looked with awe at African Americans clad in blue uniforms serving with the garrison. In the end the chances of a fourth Seminole war during the larger Civil War were slim, but Florida's native population was involved in the struggle and played a significant role.[18]

Seminoles were not the only nonwhite Florida ethnic group living through the Civil War. At least eighty citizens of Hispanic descent donned gray uniforms out of the 15,000 or so male Floridians to do so. A significant number of Florida Hispanics served in the Eight Florida Infantry Regiment, which saw action from Fredericksburg to the end at Appomattox Court House. One such soldier, William Baya of Saint Augustine, rose from sergeant to lieutenant colonel by 1865. Others, like Captain Celestine Gonzales, were killed in action or died from wounds or disease. The war experiences of this important part of the Florida community deserve to be acknowledged in any account of the war.[19]

As the war raged on, cracks in Florida's social order widened. Many people grew increasingly skeptical of Confederate victory, and of a national government in Richmond that wanted much and seemingly gave little back. Many soldier families lacked food or other essentials and begged for state help. Unionist sentiment, existing in the state since 1861, grew as time and home-front suffering went on. Confederate government policies like impressment and the unpopular 1862 Conscription Act pushed many Floridians into outright opposition to the Confederacy. By 1863 many sections of the state hosted armed bands of Unionists as well as gangs of draft evaders and army deserters. The true terrors of civil war came home to the state as these groups clashed violently with pro-rebel forces like those led by cavalryman J. J. Dickison.

Northerners soon looked at Florida as a section ripe for reclamation for the Union, and schemes to colonize Yankees there were in the works. The Union army looked to Florida for recruits and managed to raise enough volunteers to field two cavalry regiments for field service. Florida blacks took the oath and joined units of the new United States Colored Troops or the Union navy. Such forces were helped by Florida Unionists across the state who served as an effective fifth column and aid to Federal troops operating in Florida.[20]

Those Union soldiers stationed in Florida found themselves having a very unique Civil War experience. They occupied many Florida cities and towns and were in little danger from direct Confederate assaults. Most offensive operations were "expeditions" or raids into the interior seeking cattle and other supplies to make their garrison life more comfortable. Of course any slaves or cotton encountered would be promptly liberated for the Union cause. The war in Florida for the most part was a low-intensity conflict that stood in stark contrast to the titanic battles going on to the north.

Union troops serving in the Florida theater often found it delightful duty. Limited combat and relatively low casualties made it attractive, as did the balmy climate. Soldiers from Connecticut or New York looked on in wonder at palm trees and picked fresh citrus fruit from nearby groves. The warm winters stood in stark contrast to those at home, and many of these armed tourists vowed they would return after the war. Those who did played a vital role in Florida's post-1865 growth and development.[21]

The state did not totally escape the fury of Civil War combat, however. By early 1864, plans were under way for a campaign that would end in bloody battle. The Olustee campaign had its roots in the Union high command's frustration with its failure to capture the city of Charleston, South Carolina.

Union Major General Quincy A. Gilmore, whose command included much of Florida, wanted to exert more pressure on besieged Charleston by cutting its supplies coming up from the peninsula. Capturing Jacksonville once again would open a ready port to export cotton and other supplies for the North. Slaves could be freed and enlisted into the Union ranks, and with luck Florida could be politically reconstructed just in time to help President Lincoln win reelection later that year. An assault on northern Florida seemed to make perfect sense to Gilmore.[22]

The attack began with an amphibious strike at war-weary Jacksonville, which once again brought it under Federal control. Gunboats and troops continued up the St. Johns River to capture Palatka and Picolata. Soldiers under the immediate command of Brigadier General Truman A. Seymour pushed westward from Jacksonville for the railroad junction at Baldwin. Abandoned rebel supplies were seized there without resistance, and Seymour bragged to his superiors in a message that if they "want to see what Florida is good for come out to Baldwin."[23] Seymour's confidence would soon be shaken as Confederate officers reacted to his incursion by sending reinforcements to the area at the fastest possible speed.

Confederate forces marched to meet Seymour's 5,500 men at Olustee (or Ocean Pond) just outside Lake City. Led by General Joseph Finegan, rebel forces stood their ground and mauled Seymour's force in a day of bitter fighting on February 20. Poorly trained and badly led Yankee soldiers beat a retreat back toward the safety of Jacksonville. Only the rearguard effort of the famous Fifty-Fourth Massachusetts Infantry and the First North Carolina, both African American regiments, saved the day from being a total disaster. Finegan's victorious men followed to the gates of Jacksonville, but chose not to take on its fortifications. Olustee would turn out to be a Confederate victory and Florida's largest Civil War battle. Union casualties ran to 1,861, while Finegan reported losses of roughly 946 men.[24]

The Confederate victory at Olustee was a bit of bright news for a South hungry for it in early 1864. Newspapers crowed about Confederate success and Yankee ineptness. One Georgia editor summed it up by stating the Federals "marched forty miles in the most barren part of the South, fighting the salamanders and gophers, and getting a terrible thrashing."[25] Northern newspapers, not surprisingly, attacked General Seymour and President Lincoln for yet another bloody military blunder by northern forces. One blue-clad veteran of Olustee summed up his feeling by exclaiming that "the whole of Florida is not worth half the suffering and anguish this battle has caused."[26]

The first months of 1865 brought one last Union effort to take control of a large section of Florida. On March 4 a Federal force of about 1,000 splashed ashore at Saint Marks with Tallahassee as their ultimate objective. Local forces scrambled to stop them south of the capital. Frightened Tallahassee citizens began digging defensive trenches (still visible today) in case they failed. On March 6, the Unionists stalled at Natural Bridge and then fell back to the Gulf coast. The battle at Natural Bridge ironically turned out to be one of the last Confederate victories of the war. Union losses were almost 140 men, and certainly no Yankee soldier wanted to add his name to such a casualty list when the war seemed almost won. Confederates claimed only twenty-five casualties.[27]

There would be no more triumphs for the South in the spring of 1865. Lee surrendered to Grant in Virginia on April 9, and only a very few rebel supporters in Florida thought the war could go on after that. Governor Milton's death by his own hand deprived the state of executive leadership at a crucial moment in its history. Floridians still in the Confederate forces began making their way home after taking an oath of allegiance to the United States. Federal troops finally rode into Tallahassee on May 20 and raised the Stars and Stripes over the capital city once more. Florida's Civil War was over.

Confederate veterans returned and pondered how they would make a living in a state with a barely functioning economy. Ardent ex-rebels now had to learn how to live in peace with equally strident Unionists and re-build a Florida community. And what of Florida's slave population, now free but very uncertain of its future without political or economic rights? These questions hung over Florida as the postwar era began.

Physically, Florida emerged from the war in far better shape than many of its neighbors. Some towns like Jacksonville suffered major damage, while others like Apalachicola were destined to never regain their prewar prosperity. The peninsula's abundant natural resources and pleasing climate still beckoned, and before long the state would commence economic reconstruction. In the end, Floridians old and new prepared to enter a radically new time.

Notes

1. Dorothy Dodd, "The Secession Movement in Florida, 1850–1861." *Florida Historical Quarterly* 12 (1933–34):45–66.

2. Emory M. Thomas, *The Confederate Nation: 1861–1865* (New York: Harper, 1970), pp. 76–77; James M. McPherson, *Ordeal by Fire: The Civil War and Reconstruction* (New York: Knopf, 1982), p. 129.

3. J. H. Gilman. "With Slemmer in Pensacola Harbor." In *Battles and Leaders of the Civil War*, edited by Robert U. Johnson and Clarence C. Buell (New York: Century, 1885–87), 1:26–32.

4. Zack C. Waters and James C. Edmonds, *A Small but Spartan Band: The Florida Brigade in Lee's Army of Northern Virginia* (Tuscaloosa: University of Alabama Press, 2010), pp. 1–3.

5. Milton to Jefferson Davis, 18 October, 19 November 1861, John Milton Papers, Collection of the Florida Historical Society, Cocoa; Robert E. Lee to John Milton, 24 February 1862, Lee to James M. Trapier, 19 February 1862, in *The Wartime Papers of R. E. Lee*, edited by Clifford Dowdey and Louis H. Manarian (New York: Bramble House, 1961), pp. 116–17, 130.

6. U.S. War Department, *Official Records of the Union and Confederate Navies in the War of the Rebellion* (Washington, D.C.: 1901): ser. 1, vol. 17, pp. 240, 381.

7. *Atlanta Southern Confederate*, 27 May 1862.

8. William B. Braswell to Daniel C. Barrow, 3, 11 December 1863, 15 January 1864, box 3, folders 27, 29, Daniel C. Barrow Papers, Special Collections Division, University of Georgia Libraries.

9. *Macon Daily Telegraph*, 6 December 1862.

10. *Southern Cultivator* 22 (February 1864):39; Macon *Daily Telegraph*, 23 May 1863.

11. Major William B. Teasdale Account Book, in J. R. Adams Papers, Florida Collection, Florida State Archives, Tallahassee.

12. George H. Dacy, *Four Centuries of Florida Ranching* (Saint Louis: Britt Printing, 1940), p. 52.

13. U.S. War Department, *War of the Rebellion: A Compilation of the Official Records of the Union and Confederate Armies*, 128 vols. (Washington, D.C.: 1880–1901), ser. 4, vol. 2, pp. 18–19 (hereafter *ORA)*; White to A. G. Summer, 13 August 1863, box 2, Pleasant W. White Papers, Collection of the Florida Historical Society, Cocoa.

14. James McKay to White, 25 March 1864, White to L. B. Northrop, 25 February 1864, box 1, 2, White Papers.

15. Octavia Stephens to Winston Stephens, 10, 12 March 1862, in *Rose Cottage Chronicles: Civil War Letters of the Bryant-Stephens Families of North Florida*, edited by Arch F. Blakey, Ann S. Lainhart, and Winston Bryant Stephens Jr. (Gainesville: University Press of Florida, 1998), pp. 106–9.

16. *ORA*, ser. 1, vol. 53, p. 260; "List of Commissary Department Employees," February 1864, box 1, White Papers.

17. Milton to John Griffin, 25 March 1862, Milton to George W. Randolph, 16 October 1862, Milton Papers.

18. Henry A. Crane to James D. Green, 2 April 1864, Crane to H. W. Bowers, 15 April 1864, U.S. War Department Letters Received, Department and District of Key West, 1861–1865, record group 393, National Archives, Washington, D.C.

19. Compiled Service Records of Confederate Soldiers Who Served in Organizations from the State of Florida, Rolls, 81, 27, *ORA*, ser. 1, vol. 49, part II, pp. 428–29.

20. "Memoirs," p. 56, Calvin L. Robinson Papers, Florida Collection, Florida State Archives, Tallahassee; George E. Buker, *Blockaders, Refugees, and Contrabands: Civil War on Florida's Gulf coast, 1861–1865* (Tuscaloosa: University of Alabama Press, 1993), pp. 116–31.

21. *ORA*, ser. 1, vol. 35, part I, p. 376, "Reminiscences," Albert W. Peck Papers, Florida Collection, Florida State Archives, Tallahassee, pp. 43–44; Alfred S. Roe, *Twenty-Fourth Regiment, Massachusetts Volunteers 1861–186* (Worcester, Mass.: Twenty-Fourth Veteran Association, 1907), p. 237.

22. *ORA*, ser. 1, vol. 35, part I, pp. 276, 279.

23. *ORA*, ser. 1, vol. 35, part I, p. 293.

24. *ORA*, ser. 1, vol. 35, part I, pp. 302, 337, 298.

25. *Macon Daily Telegraph,* 25 February 1864.

26. *New York Tribune,* 29 February 1864.

27. *ORA*, ser. 1, vol. 49, part I, p. 63.

Bibliography

Ash, Stephen V. *Firebrand of Liberty: The Story of Two Black Regiments That Changed the Course of the Civil War*. New York: Norton, 2008.

Brown, Canter. *Tampa in the Civil War and Reconstruction*. Tampa: University of Tampa Press, 2000.

Buker, George E. *Blockaders, Refugees, and Contrabands*. Tuscaloosa: University of Alabama Press, 1993.

Coles, David J. "'A Fight, A Licking, and a Footrace': The 1864 Florida Campaign and the Battle of Olustee." Master's thesis, Florida State University, 1985.

Curenton, Mark. *Tories and Deserters: The First Florida Federal Cavalry*. Laurel Hill: privately published, 1988.

Davis, William Watson. *The Civil War and Reconstruction in Florida*. 1913. Reprint, Gainesville: University of Florida Press, 1964.

Dickison, John J. "Military History of Florida." In *Confederate Military History*, edited by Clement A. Evans, 12 vols., vol. 11, pt. 2, pp. 1–198. Atlanta: Confederate Publishing Company, 1898.

Dickison, Mary Elizabeth. *Dickison and His Men: Reminiscences of the War in Florida, 1890*. Edited by Samuel Proctor. Gainesville: University of Florida Press, 1962.

Dillon, Rodney E., Jr. "The Civil War in South Florida." Master's thesis, University of Florida, 1980.

Gannon, Michael V. *Rebel Bishop: The Life and Era of Augustin Verot*. Milwaukee: Bruce Publishing, 1964.

Johns, John E. *Florida during the Civil War*. Gainesville: University of Florida Press, 1963. Reprint, Macclenny: Richard J. Ferry, 1989.

Loderhouse, Gary. *Far, Far from Home: The Ninth Florida Regiment in the Confederate Army*. Carmel, Ind.: Guild Press, 1999.

Nulty, William H. *Confederate Florida: The Road to Olustee*. Tuscaloosa: University of Alabama Press, 1990.

Pearce, George F. *Pensacola during the Civil War: A Thorn in the Side of the Confederacy*. Gainesville: University Press of Florida, 2000.

Reiger, John F. "Anti-War and Pro-Union Sentiment in Confederate Florida." Master's thesis, University of Florida, 1966.

Revels, Tracy J. *Grander in Her Daughters: Florida's Women during the Civil War*. Columbia: University of South Carolina Press, 2004.

Schafer, Daniel L. *Thunder on the River: The Civil War in Northeast Florida*. Gainesville: University Press of Florida, 2010.

Taylor, Robert A. *Rebel Storehouse: Florida in the Confederate Economy*. Tuscaloosa: University of Alabama Press, 1995.

Waters, Zack C., and James C. Edmonds. *A Small but Spartan Band: The Florida Brigade in Lee's Army of Northern Virginia*. Tuscaloosa: University of Alabama Press, 2010.

15

Reconstruction and Renewal, 1865–1877

JERRELL H. SHOFNER

The fighting was over in the spring of 1865, but there was much to be done. Everything was at a standstill. There was no government. After Governor John Milton killed himself, Union General Edward McCook had suppressed efforts to reorganize a civil government. There was no inkling of how or when Florida would resume relations with the United States. Abraham Lincoln's assassination had removed the only person who had plans to bring the seceded states back into the Union. Newly inaugurated President Andrew Johnson was still formulating his ideas. There was no economy. Money and credit had disappeared with the fall of the Confederacy. The means of production had ended with the abolition of slavery. There were no markets and little transportation. It was planting time, and while the new president pondered the situation, something had to be done if crops were to be put in so that people could eat the following winter.

In the existing political vacuum, military officials took the initiative. General John Newton instructed Florida planters to assemble their former slaves, explain that they were now free, and ask them to remain on the plantations and work for wages. Compensation was to be paid in shares of the harvest. When the Freedmen's Bureau agents reached the field, the freedmen were already at work. The agents subsequently supervised the contracts between freedmen and their former owners, but they did so in accordance with the system implemented by the U.S. Army as an emergency measure. The Florida Legislature legitimized the system with appropriate legislation. There would be years of controversy over the legal status of freedmen, but the labor system that replaced the institution of slavery came by military order.

Sharecropping, crop liens, and tenant farming extended across the old plantation belt and affected both black and white farmers for decades after the Civil War. Cotton was produced by this inefficient system at a time when demand for it was constantly declining. The result was that the economy of old Middle Florida languished at the same time that East Florida and the peninsula began to grow.

Florida's readmission to the Union and the status of freedmen as citizens were matters that consumed much time and left a bitter legacy. Lincoln had anticipated the anger and bitterness that eventually engulfed the nation over these matters. Wishing to avoid as much conflict as possible, he had tried to rebuild loyal governments in Union-occupied territories such as northeastern Florida while the war was still being fought. Eager Florida Unionists such as Lyman Stickney, Calvin Robinson, and John Sammis seized upon the president's "ten-percent plan," but their efforts were thwarted by the Union military defeat at Olustee in early 1864. Little more was heard of Lincoln's plan, but the Direct Tax Commission, of which Stickney and Sammis were original members, carried out its duties to foreclose upon and sell Confederate property within Union lines. The ensuing "direct tax sales" transferred hundreds of pieces of property from Confederate owners to Unionists, many of whom were freedmen, and caused tremendous difficulties when President Andrew Johnson subsequently restored ownership to the former Confederates. The problem that arose is illustrated by the case of Confederate General Joseph Finegan's home in Fernandina. It was auctioned to Chloe Merrick of Syracuse, New York, for twenty-five dollars. Miss Merrick, who later married Republican governor Harrison Reed, made the house into an orphanage for black children. When General Finegan marched home with President Johnson's amnesty proclamation in hand and found little black children playing on his veranda and the U.S. Army guarding them, the tenuous peace of Fernandina was sorely tested. Much of the tax-sale land was eventually returned to its former Confederate owners, but the matter exacerbated the struggle over Reconstruction in Florida and remained an issue until the 1890s.

With Freedmen's Bureau agents encountering increasing resistance from planters unaccustomed to limits on their autonomy, and confrontations between contesting owners of tax-sale property, President Johnson's Reconstruction plan was implemented. Following Lincoln's nonpunitive ideas,

Johnson permitted most former Confederates to participate in forming a new government. He appointed William Marvin, a former federal judge from Key West, as provisional governor. Working closely with Major General John Foster, the military commander, Marvin registered those adult white males who took the requisite oath and called an election for delegates to a constitutional convention. The convention wrote a new constitution to conform with recent developments. Slavery was repudiated, as was the right of a state to secede from the Union. All debts incurred in support of the Confederacy were also repudiated. Laws enacted by Congress since 1861 were recognized, and a committee was appointed to review the state statutes and make recommendations for necessary changes when the first legislature met. In the ensuing election, David Walker became the new governor, and Ferdinand McLeod was elected to the national House of Representatives.

The legislature was composed of many prominent former Confederates. There were, of course, no black members, and James Dopson Green of Manatee County was the only former Unionist named to the body. Former governor William Marvin and former Confederate Wilkinson Call were elected by the legislature to the U.S. Senate. There was some grumbling among congressmen in Washington about the predominance of Confederates in Florida's restored government, but the major portent of future difficulties came with the report of the three-member committee on statutory changes. Speaking for the committee, Anderson J. Peeler recommended that the legislature preserve, insofar as possible, the beneficial features of the "benign, but much abused and greatly misunderstood institution of slavery."[1] The legislature complied. Freedmen were given customary civil rights except that they were not permitted to give testimony in cases involving white people. Since most of their difficulties were with their employers, this was a major shortcoming. Beyond that, a lengthy series of laws clearly discriminated between white and black citizens, even to the extent of substituting corporal punishment for fines and imprisonment for blacks convicted of crimes.

Already angered by President Johnson's decision to proceed with "presidential Reconstruction" without calling them into session, some congressmen watched with growing alarm as Florida and most other southern states enacted legislation denying equal citizenship to the freedmen. When it convened in December 1865, Congress refused to recognize Johnson's efforts. Marvin, Call, and McLeod were denied seats in their respective Houses along with everyone elected from the other former Confederate states. A joint committee was named to investigate the conditions in the South and recommend an alternative course of action.

An acrimonious deadlock developed between President Johnson and Congress. It became increasingly clear that Johnson's program would not be approved without significant modifications. It was equally clear that the president was unwilling to compromise. The standoff became ugly. Congress enacted a civil rights law in April which expanded the rights of national citizens and gave enforcement authority to the U.S. Army. President Johnson vetoed the legislation and proclaimed an end to the "insurrection" in the South, with the apparent intention of removing martial law. Floridians applauded the president, but their elation was premature. Angered by the president's arbitrary actions and unwilling to readmit the seceded states without some guarantees of fair treatment of the freedmen, Congress voted to override the president's veto of the Civil Rights Act and another measure extending the life of the Freedmen's Bureau.

The continuing controversy between president and Congress gradually eroded the effectiveness of both the army and the bureau in protecting freedmen and Unionists in Florida. As chief of staff of the U.S. Army, General Ulysses S. Grant had at first instructed his field commanders to protect all freedmen and Unionists from abuses of their civil and property rights. But he was acting under the laws of Congress while his commander-in-chief was at odds with those laws.

In Florida, General John Foster tried to follow General Grant's instructions. Governor David Walker understandably agreed with the proclamations of the president. Both were reasonable men, and they tried to keep order in a situation that was becoming increasingly unclear. When the U.S. Army and a Nassau County sheriff's posse faced each other in the street in front of General Finegan's house, the two men went on the same train to Fernandina and prevented a violent confrontation. But they could not give personal attention to the hundreds of incidents arising throughout the northern Florida counties. Freedmen were treated atrociously by the county criminal courts. When Freedmen's Bureau agents attempted to intercede, they often confronted county sheriffs with large armed posses. General Foster felt compelled to declare martial law in nine counties in the summer of 1866. His action angered Governor Walker and did little to improve the plight of the freedmen.

The deteriorating situation in Florida was accompanied by increasing acrimony between President Johnson and Congress in Washington. In August 1866, Johnson issued an even stronger proclamation restoring civil law in Florida. Still sympathetic with congressional efforts to protect freedmen in their civil rights, General Grant was, after all, accountable to the president, who was commander-in-chief of all armed forces. The general accordingly issued new instructions to the field commanders which left their authority unclear. Increasingly frustrated at his inability to protect freedman from mistreatment, General Foster resigned in November 1866. He told his superiors that he would happily return to Florida but only if the laws were made adequate for him to execute his duties to protect all citizens in their civil rights.

The failure of President Johnson's Reconstruction plan in Florida coincided with the eclipse of his authority in Washington. Congress wrested control from him and implemented its own plan. Under congressional Reconstruction, martial law was reinstated with Major General John Pope in command. He appointed Ossian B. Hart of Jacksonville as supervisor of registration for a new electorate, which this time included all adult black males. New elections were held for delegates to yet another constitutional convention. The new document was to include a guarantee of black suffrage. When a suitable constitution was ratified by Florida voters and the legislature ratified the Fourteenth Amendment to the U.S. Constitution, military occupation would be ended and the state would be able to resume its normal place in the Union.

At the end of the war many native white Floridians had time only "to worship the Confederate dead and hate the Yankee living," but they had "gradually learned to manage" under the Johnson plan of Reconstruction.[2] Now, nearly two years after the war, Congress was forcing black suffrage upon them. There was talk of white immigration to Latin America or the unsettled American West, and a few Floridians did resettle in Brazil. A larger number simply abandoned Middle Florida and moved southward to Brevard, Orange, Hillsborough, and other sparsely populated central Florida counties. Most of them remained where they were, but they were badly divided over what course to follow. Some chose not to participate in elections involving blacks, but Hart's registration teams administered the oath of loyalty to several thousand who decided to make the best of the situation.

The demoralization and division of the white population left an open field for the evolving Republican Party, but it was also badly divided. At a convention called by Hart in the summer of 1867, vigorous disagreements emerged. A group led by Daniel Richards, a former tax commissioner; Liberty Billings, a former commander of a black regiment; and William U. Saunders, a representative of the Union League, joined by Charles H. Pearce, a Canadian minister of the African Methodist Episcopal Church, wanted to emphasize rights for blacks at the expense of native whites. Another faction

A Florida family photographed in the 1870s. Despite the fact that a few African Americans won election to government offices, Reconstruction did not result in securing for blacks an equal part in Florida society. In his book on Florida during that period, *Nor Is It Over Yet,* Jerrell Shofner writes: "The moderate Republicans who implemented the 1867 Reconstruction acts in Florida had never given Negro rights more than secondary consideration. Black voters contributed more to the Republican Party than they received from it. Even their basic right to vote was diluted by provisions for disproportionate legislative representation. Yet their situation between 1868 and 1877 was infinitely better than it was to be for the next seventy-five years."

headed by Harrison Reed, William H. Gleason, and Thomas W. Osborn, among others, took a more moderate position. They realized that congressional requirements would have to be met, but they were more interested in developing the vast vacant lands of the state. They were willing to include blacks in the new electorate, but they also wanted the native whites to participate in the new government.

The Republicans elected nearly all of the forty-three delegates to the convention, which met in January 1868, but they were varying kinds of

Republicans. The Radical Republican Billings-Richards faction was able to control the organization of the convention and seemingly would be able to write a constitution suitable to them. White delegates sympathetic to Reed and Gleason bolted the convention and wrote a contesting document with the cooperation of Charles E. Dyke and McQueen McIntosh, both of whom represented the native white leadership of the state. They then returned to Tallahassee in the middle of the night, took possession of the assembly hall, and reorganized the convention while the Billings-Richards delegates slept. The Radical delegates were dumbfounded that following morning to find themselves locked out of the assembly hall by a cordon of U.S. soldiers. After several stormy days and some amazing decisions by Congress, the moderate version of the constitution—despite its unorthodox origin—was sent to the polls and approved by Florida voters. Harrison Reed was elected governor and William H. Gleason lieutenant governor. At a Fourth of July ceremony, Colonel John T. Sprague, commander of the occupation force, relinquished authority to Governor Reed. Radical Reconstruction had led to a constitution which, according to the new governor, would "prevent a Negro legislature."[3]

Reed's was a stormy administration. In his continuing effort to retain the support of native whites for the new government, he appointed Robert Gamble and James Westcott to cabinet positions, but that move backfired when Gamble openly opposed Reed's deficit financing plans. Having supported him against the Billings-Richard faction, Charles E. Dyke now leveled the powerful guns of his *Tallahassee Floridian* against the governor in particular and all Republicans in general. A sizable minority of native white legislators calling themselves Conservatives used their votes in the legislature to thwart Reed and embarrass the new Republican Party. Attempting to tread the narrow path between Conservatives on one hand and black legislators on the other, the governor angered both. His ambitious lieutenant governor was not much help either: Gleason supported a move to impeach Reed and remove him from office. The wily governor bested him, retained his office, and strengthened his position by appointing Jonathan C. Gibbs, a capable and influential black, as secretary of state. Gleason subsequently turned his considerable abilities to developing vacant lands in peninsular Florida and founding the town of Eau Gallie on the Indian River.

While Conservative editors and legislators fought Reed in Tallahassee, others took more direct action in the outlying areas. Controlling most of the land and credit, Conservative planters and merchants denied credit and land rentals to freedmen who continued to vote the Republican ticket.

Born a slave in Virginia, Josiah T. Walls served in the Union army and settled in Florida after Appomattox. Aided by Republican Reconstruction politics, he entered public life as a state representative and senator. Then, in 1870, he became Florida's first African American member of the U.S. House of Representatives, to which he was elected twice more. Following politics he turned to truck farming. Other black politicians in Florida during the 1870s were John Wallace, Henry Harmon, Charles Pearce, Robert Meacham, and the Dartmouth-educated Jonathan Gibbs, who became secretary of state under Governor Harrison Reed (1868–73).

Vigilantes such as the Ku Klux Klan and the Young Men's Democratic Clubs used violence and intimidation to discourage or prevent newly enfranchised blacks from exercising their voting privileges. Leaders were threatened, beaten, and killed. Polling places were disrupted by gunfire and threats. Former Confederate cavalry commander J. J. Dickison even led bands of mounted men in cavalry charges through crowds of potential voters. Without financial and personnel resources, Reed was obliged to rely on the U.S. Army garrison to maintain order. But its numbers were small, it was far removed from the many scenes of violence, human life was lightly regarded, the stakes were high, and the violence continued.

Congress ultimately responded with legislation empowering the president to restore martial law, but violence and disorder remained serious problems during most of Reed's four and a half years in office. Intraparty factionalism and repeated impeachments of the governor, some of which were inspired and encouraged by U.S. Senator Thomas W. Osborn, kept the state in turmoil and discredited both the Reed administration and the Republican Party.

While Reconstruction brought unwelcome changes and political and racial strife to the Middle Florida plantation belt, it concomitantly helped to open up peninsular Florida to settlement. Until the 1860s the Florida peninsula had been a sparsely populated cattle range where drovers grazed their herds over miles and miles of open range. When William Gleason accompanied Freedmen's Bureau agent George F. Thompson on a tour of southern Florida in 1865–66, they reported vast open lands and a balmy climate—only the first of many touting the Florida peninsula to receptive audiences across the nation. Northerners were attracted by available open land where the winters were mild. Southerners liked the idea of an unsettled region where they could escape the conditions of Reconstruction.

Soon magazines, newspapers, and railroad companies were sending reporters to observe and report on this paradise. By 1870 Floridians were publishing the *Florida New Yorker* to attract settlers and investors. Jacksonville, which had been almost destroyed by the frequent invasions of the war years, bounced back to become the center of winter tourism, the gateway to southern Florida via the St. Johns River, and a budding financial center where northern capital was increasingly available for investment. Hubbard Hart's line of steamers was one of several which carried passengers and freight up the St. Johns. He and others made a tourist attraction of Harriet Beecher Stowe's winter home at Mandarin, easily visible to passengers eager to catch a glimpse of the lady who Abraham Lincoln had once credited with starting

President and former Union general Ulysses S. Grant (*seated, left front*) and a party of northern friends journey down Florida's most picturesque river, the Ocklawaha, on the paddle steamer *Osceola*. Similar steamboats plied the St. Johns, Suwannee, and Apalachicola Rivers. One nervous passenger on the Ocklawaha recorded: "The hull of the steamer went bumping against one cypress-butt, then another, suggesting to the tyro in this kind of aquatic adventure that possibly he might be wrecked, and sub-jected, even if he escaped a watery grave, to a miserable death, through the agency of mosquitoes, buzzards, and huge alligators."

the Civil War. But Hart also added a popular tourist attraction by opening up the Ocklawaha River to Silver Springs, which by 1873 was being visited by 50,000 tourists annually.

Frederick DeBary, a Belgian wine merchant, also transported visitors up the St. Johns as far as Lake Monroe, where he built a hotel at the new community named for him. The Brock Line operated between Jacksonville and Enterprise on the northern shore of Lake Monroe. Small shallow-draft steamers plied the tortuous channels of the upper St. Johns with passengers and cargo bound for the Indian River settlements of Titusville, Rockledge, and Eau Gallie. With three large hotels, Rockledge soon became known as the southernmost winter resort in the nation.

One of the Yankees who invested largely in peninsular Florida was Henry S. Sanford, a former Union general and powerful member of the national Republican Party. He founded the town of Sanford about 1870 on Lake Monroe's south shore. Using both Swedish immigrant and native black labor, he developed two large orange groves. He also sold numerous tracts to other northerners, among whom were William Tecumseh Sherman, Senator Henry Anthony of Rhode Island, and Orville Babcock, personal secretary to President Grant. With Sanford's vigorous support, several Boston investors started the South Florida Railroad to run southward through Orlando to Kissimmee, thus opening more of the peninsula to settlers. President Grant was induced to turn the first shovel of earth in 1879.

In the absence of suitable transportation, settlement of the western part of the peninsula lagged behind the St. Johns River valley, but Tampa boasted a few hundred inhabitants near the old Fort Brooke army reservation in the early 1870s. A colony of "Downeasters" settled at Sarasota in 1868, and tourists were able to find lodging at several locations in Manatee County by the early 1870s. Jacob Summerlin, Zibe King, Francis A. Hendry, the Curry family, and others continued grazing their herds uninterrupted on the south Florida range, but the citrus and tourist industries were already on their way during the Reconstruction years.

The missing link was suitable railroad transportation, but the state's Internal Improvement Fund was unable to use its millions of acres of public lands as incentive to potential builders because of a complicated lawsuit that prevented it from conveying clear titles. Efforts in 1866 to revive the war-damaged Florida Railroad from Fernandina to Cedar Keys had resulted in a federal court injunction prohibiting sale of state lands except for cash. Unable to effect such a sale, the state could not clear the so-called Vose injunction until 1881. The Reed administration assisted Milton Littlefield and

George W. Swepson with their Jacksonville, Pensacola, and Mobile Railroad venture, but that firm also became embroiled in litigation which was not settled until 1879. Railroad construction in Florida had to wait until the 1880s.

Events surrounding the Jacksonville, Pensacola, and Mobile Company were catalysts for one of the four attempts to remove Governor Reed from office by impeachment. These internecine squabbles added to the confusion that brought Reed's administration to an end in 1873. A fractious Republican convention bypassed him in 1872 and nominated for governor Ossian B. Hart, the native Florida Unionist who had good relations with black leaders. His running mate was Marcellus L. Stearns, a former bureau agent and prominent legislator who was aligned with white party leaders.

The Hart-Stearns ticket defeated a straight-out Conservative-Democratic slate headed by former Confederate William D. Bloxham. Hart guided several progressive measures through the 1873 legislature, the most important of which was a funding law that helped improve the state's financial condition. It seemed for a time that some political harmony had been achieved by the bickering Republican Party, but Hart became ill and remained hospitalized for months before he died. In the meantime, Stearns first acted in Hart's absence and then became governor in fact. His elevation to the governorship did little to nurture harmony in the party. Blacks felt increasingly alienated as Stearns tried to build his strength with the white, officeholding faction of the party. His actions led to new feuds. Congressman William J. Purman and Senator Simon B. Conover both broke with him, and the newspapers were filled with their acrimonious assaults on each other.

The Conservative-Democrats had not been idle. Despite Bloxham's poor showing in 1872, they were steadily gaining seats in both legislative branches. After the 1874 election, they claimed a small majority in the assembly and a 12–12 tie in the senate. The assassination of Republican senator Elisha Johnson broke the tie, but reminded everyone of the fragility of relations between native white Conservatives and their Republican opponents. Although they denied involvement in the murder, many Conservatives noted the political result. One of them wrote privately that "in losing Johnson we gain a county. Who could not afford to make this sacrifice?"[4] The 1876 election was approaching, and "bloody shirt politics" was back in the headlines.

Lingering memories of the war and Confederate defeat, abolition of slavery and enfranchisement of the freedmen, military occupation, and a disorderly and fractious government allegedly controlled by "carpetbaggers" and "scalawags" had left a heavy burden on native white Floridians by the mid-1870s. Ellen Call Long was reminded of this when she sought assistance from her friends to place a Florida exhibit at the Philadelphia centennial celebration to be held in 1876. Old acquaintances from all over the state found myriad reasons why they could not help, but the problem was summed up when a friend wrote, "I'm sorry your effort in behalf of our oppressed state has been abortive . . . fifteen years bitter struggle has crushed nearly every spark of patriotism from the Southern breast . . . and it will be hard to bury the past."[5]

Despite such sentiments, which were widely held, Conservative-Democratic leaders were much more pragmatic in 1876 than they had been four years earlier. They had noticed that many newcomers to peninsular Florida, while still favoring the national Republican Party, were tired of the disruptiveness in the state capital for which they blamed Florida Republicans. Henry Sanford, for example, expressed willingness to support a Conservative-Democrat for governor while voting for a Republican presidential candidate. Determined to take advantage of such a split ticket opportunity, the Conservative-Democrats named George F. Drew, a prominent lumberman and former Unionist, for governor.

Still fighting among themselves, the Republicans renominated Marcellus Stearns for the position he held. In an election that was overshadowed by the national presidential contest between Democrat Samuel Tilden and Republican Rutherford Hayes, about 48,000 Floridians voted in an election that was so close that fewer than a hundred votes would decide the outcome. With the presidential election depending on the outcome of the elections in Florida, Louisiana, and South Carolina, "visiting statesmen" from both parties rushed to the three state capitals to do what they could for their respective candidates. They joined numerous curious observers and several companies of U.S. soldiers and literally overran Florida's small capital city.

The newcomers in the peninsular counties who had split their tickets had created a dilemma for the state canvassing board, composed of two Republicans and one Democrat. Since the presidential election depended on fewer than 100 votes, it appeared that Republican Hayes deserved Florida's four electoral votes, but split tickets had left Stearns and the Florida Republicans several hundred votes behind Hayes. Governor Stearns told some of the "visiting statesmen" that he would not be pleased with a Hayes victory in which he did not share. The majority of the canvassing board voted to throw out several hundred votes on the grounds that they were improper. Those excluded votes tended to come from counties which returned Conservative-Democratic majorities. The result was majorities for Republicans at both presidential and state levels. The "visiting statesmen" left Tallahassee believing that Florida would be counted in the Republican column.

Local Conservative-Democrats had said nothing until the visitors were gone. They then induced the state supreme court to order a recount of the votes as they had been received from the counties, that is, to restore those votes which had been thrown out for various reasons. The recount showed that Hayes still had a small majority, but that Democrat George F. Drew had defeated Stearns for governor. Drew was inaugurated without incident on 2 January 1877.

The dispute over the presidency caused a near deadlock in Washington. After nearly three months, an electoral commission declared Hayes victorious, and he was sworn in as president in March 1877. In April, he removed the remaining U.S. troops from Louisiana and South Carolina. There were none in Florida after 23 January 1877. This disputed election and the so-called Compromise of 1877, which involved the withdrawal of the troops, came to symbolize the end of Reconstruction.

An immediate result of the events of late 1876 and early 1877 was consolidation of their control of the state by the newly empowered Conservative-Democrats. Drew used the extensive powers of his office in the same way that his Republican predecessors had. Soon his party controlled most state and county offices, including the all-important election machinery. Blacks continued to hold some local offices but in diminished numbers. Many of the defeated Republican officials left the state, but a number made Florida their home. Harrison Reed, for example, remained in Jacksonville and died in his adopted state in 1899. Senator Simon Conover and Secretary of State Samuel B. McLin joined several others who lived out their lives in the developing citrus country of peninsular Florida. Horatio Bisbee was elected to Congress from east Florida in 1882. But the Republicans' political strength was waning. In 1884 they attempted to fuse with a dissident wing of the Democratic Party, but the fusion ticket was easily defeated by the regular Democratic candidate, former Confederate General Edward A. Perry.

By 1884, Democrats, who had by then dropped the "Conservative" from their party name, were confident that they had solidified their majority status in Florida. In an attempt to rid themselves of one more reminder of Reconstruction days, a majority of them voted in 1884 for a constitutional convention to write still another fundamental law for the state. It would replace the onerous 1868 document which they still regarded as an imposition on the state from outsiders. Dominated by Democrats, the convention wrote a new constitution that weakened the powers of the governor, made

Florida's Capitol at Tallahassee as it appeared in the 1870s. A cupola would be added in 1891, and the building would serve until a new Capitol was built nearby in 1978.

most offices at state and local levels elective, and strengthened the powers of local officials. It also provided for a poll tax, which was enacted by the 1889 legislature. That law effectively kept most black voters away from the polls. The Republican Party ceased to be a serious challenge to Democratic control of the state, and Florida would be a one-party state for many decades.

The years of Reconstruction had been turbulent and traumatic for many Floridians, and the Democrats successfully used recollections of those years to cement political control, but there were other important results. There was a definite shift of the population southward and a corresponding diminution of the hegemony of Middle Florida planters. The plantation belt remained comparatively static until well into the twentieth century, while the peninsula, all the way from Jacksonville southward, was settled by both permanent inhabitants and winter residents. Many of both groups engaged in citrus culture and tourism. Others turned to railroad construction to bind the new section to the rest of the nation. These changes were set in motion during the Reconstruction era, but their development is a matter for later chapters.

Notes

1. Florida, *House Journal,* 1865–66.
2. Helen Moore Edwards, *Memoirs* (privately printed, n.d.).
3. H. Reed to D. L. Yulee, 16 February 1868, David L. Yulee Papers, P. K. Yonge Library of Florida History, University of Florida, Gainesville.
4. Henry L'Engle to E. M. L'Engle, 23 July 1875, Edward M. L'Engle Papers, Southern Historical Collection, University of North Carolina, Chapel Hill.
5. Ida Wood to Mrs. Long, 8 April 1872, Richard Keith Call Papers, Southern Historical Collection, University of North Carolina, Chapel Hill.

Bibliography

Brown, Canter, Jr. "'Where Are Now the Hopes I Cherished?' The Life and Times of Robert Meacham." *Florida Historical Quarterly* 69, no. 1 (July 1990):1–36.

Clark, James C. "John Wallace and the Writing of Reconstruction History." *Florida Historical Quarterly* 67, no. 4 (April 1989):409–27.

Cox, Merlin G. "Military Reconstruction in Florida." *Florida Historical Quarterly* 46, no. 3 (January 1968):219–33.

Cresse, Lewis H., Jr. "A Study of William Henry Gleason: Carpetbagger, Politician, Land Developer." Ph.D. dissertation, University of South Carolina, 1977.

Davis, William Watson. *The Civil War and Reconstruction in Florida.* New York: Columbia University, 1913.

Reid, Whitelaw. *After the War: A Southern Tour.* Cincinnati and New York: Moore, Wilstach & Baldwin, 1866.

Richardson, Joe M. "The Florida Black Codes." *Florida Historical Quarterly* 47 (1969).

———. *The Negro in the Reconstruction of Florida, 1865–1877.* Tallahassee: Florida State University, 1965.

Shofner, Jerrell H. "Andrew Johnson and the Fernandina Unionists." *Prologue: The Journal of the National Archives* (Winter 1978):211–24.

———. "The Constitution of 1868." *Florida Historical Quarterly* 41, no. 2 (April 1963): 356–74.

———. "A Merchant Planter in the Reconstruction South." *Agricultural History* 46, no. 2 (April 1972):291–96.

———. "Militant Negro Laborers in Reconstruction Florida." *Journal of Southern History* 39 (1973).

———. *Nor Is It Over Yet: Florida in the Era of Reconstruction 1865–1877.* Gainesville: University of Florida Press, 1974.

———. "Political Reconstruction in Florida." *Florida Historical Quarterly* 45, no. 2 (October 1966):145–70.

Wallace, John. *Carpetbag Rule in Florida: The Inside Workings of the Reconstruction of Civil Government in Florida after the Close of the Civil War.* 1888. Gainesville: University of Florida Press, 1964.

16

The First Developers

THOMAS GRAHAM

In 1877, Florida ranked as the least populous and most thinly settled state east of the Mississippi River, with only about 250,000 residents. However, over the following forty years Florida would grow at a rate approaching twice the pace of the United States. Floridians could sense that change was on the way. Both large developers and individual pioneers saw Florida as a raw wilderness ripe for improvement.

Florida's political leaders understood that the state needed to attract both immigrants from the North and investment capital to build its economy. To encourage rich outsiders to invest in the state, they pursued policies of low taxes and minimal government interference with businesses. The most important field of investment was railroad building. While steamboats could serve in areas with navigable rivers, most regions of the state would remain undeveloped until railroads could be built to connect them with the outside world.

Before the Civil War, the state had been a Deep South cotton and slave state much like its neighbors Georgia and Alabama. Most of Florida's population clustered along its northern border. As railroads extended down the peninsula, the center of population moved southward. New enterprises such as citrus growing, phosphate mining, and tourism moved Florida society away from the cotton culture. In 1872 Henry Sanford, a former U.S. diplomat, established a plantation on Lake Monroe in central Florida to grow winter vegetables, and in 1876 Henry DeLand founded a town that he hoped would prosper with the cultivation of oranges. Many people continued to eke out a living as tenant farmers or sharecroppers, growing corn, cotton, and tobacco or catching open-range cattle just as their fathers had, but the future clearly lay along the path of the steel rails into the peninsula in what was emerging as the Sunshine State.

The governor who took office in January 1877, George F. Drew, had been selected by the Democrats to raise as little controversy as possible at a time when Reconstruction was coming to an end. Drew had been born in New Hampshire but had lived in Florida before the war. He operated a large sawmill at Ellaville on the Suwannee River and was a businessman, not a politician. Since he had been a Whig before the war and supported the Union during the war, he could appeal to moderate white men and still be acceptable to conservative Democrats. Black Floridians hoped that he would not reverse the gains made by black citizens during Reconstruction.

Drew and the legislature focused their attention on putting the state's economic house in order. They embarked on a program of reducing government spending that severely impacted support for public schools. A proposal to establish a state college at Eau Gallie was dropped. The legislature passed a law that provided for the leasing of state penitentiary inmates to private businesses. The measure served to cut state expenses but raised serious questions about the exploitation and abuse of prisoners by private contractors. Often convict laborers were employed in arduous work that free men could not be induced to undertake.

By 1880, the Democrats felt they no longer needed the compromise candidate Drew and nominated their champion, William D. Bloxham, a native-born Florida plantation owner and lawyer from Tallahassee and a veteran of the Confederate military. Though he had fought for the Old South, he now envisioned a New South of modern businesses and industries. He stressed the need for sound finances in state government. The previous legislature's enthusiasm for cutting taxes, combined with the nationwide economic recession of the 1870s, had left the state with a large public debt.

The only major financial asset of the state, its public lands, had been used as collateral for bonds issued by various railroad ventures that subsequently went bankrupt, leaving the state responsible for a $1 million debt, which constantly grew because of the accumulation of unpaid interest. When the state continued to make deals to give away land in exchange for promises to build railroads and drain swamps, one of the major bondholders, Francis Vose, a New York investor, filed suit in federal court, which placed the state's custodian of lands, the Internal Improvement Commission, into receivership and refused to allow any further alienation of state lands except for hard cash or until the bonded debt was paid. This effectively blocked the most promising way of encouraging investment in the state. Since the governor served as head of the Internal Improvement Commission, responsibility for resolving this impasse fell to him.

Hamilton Disston's dredges floated on barges that cut a pathway through wetlands to excavate drainage canals. This photo was taken on the St. Cloud Canal south of Orlando. Courtesy of the State Archives of Florida, *Florida Memory*, http://floridamemory. com/items/show/138343.

Bloxham traveled north and personally negotiated an agreement with Philadelphia industrialist Hamilton Disston to eliminate the Internal Improvement Commission's debt. The deal had two parts: for $1 million in cash, Disston purchased 4 million acres of land outright, and he also gained the option to drain an additional 9 million acres of swampland at his own expense, dividing the drained land equally between himself and the state. The land to be drained encompassed the Kissimmee River and Lake Okeechobee water basins. Disston established real estate companies in the North and in Europe to sell land to immigrants, making him one of the largest promoters of Florida.

His dredges began digging south from the town of Kissimmee to straighten the Kissimmee River so that it would carry water rapidly into Lake Okeechobee. At the same time, another crew excavated a canal from the mouth of the Caloosahatchee into Lake Okeechobee at Moore Haven so that water from the lake would flow into the Gulf of Mexico. Disston established a sugar plantation at St. Cloud south of Orlando on drained land. After a few years it became clear that lowering the water table of Lake Okeechobee would require dredging many more canals.

The Disston land deals became a major issue in state politics. Critics argued that Governor Bloxham had been too hasty in making a deal that sold land for twenty-five cents per acre when the usual price for undeveloped government land was $1.25 per acre. Opponents also said that Disston claimed land that he had not drained and that he had pushed pioneer squatters off the land they had been living on. Moreover, many felt that it was simply wrong for a handful of wealthy men to own so much of the state.

Another of Florida's important developers, Henry Bradley Plant, helped to connect the remote frontier state of Florida with the rest of the country by modernizing the South's railroads. Born in Connecticut, Plant rose in the ranks of the Adams Express Company before the war to become superintendent of its shipping operations in the South. When war came, Plant organized his own firm to serve the Confederacy. After the war, Plant purchased a railroad he renamed the Savannah, Florida and Western, and in 1881 he extended its line directly to Jacksonville. Plant established his home in New York City on Fifth Avenue to be near the financial markets and to attract northern investors in his growing railroad system.

Reaching out from his foothold in Jacksonville, Plant purchased controlling interest in the South Florida Railroad in 1883 and extended its southernmost terminus from Kissimmee to Tampa, a town of 700 souls. He began to turn Tampa into a major metropolis by building a deepwater port on Tampa Bay from which his steamships could trade with Cuba and the Caribbean. In 1891 he opened the fantastic Tampa Bay Hotel as an attraction for wealthy northern visitors during the winter months. Eventually Plant would own eight hotels in central Florida and along the Gulf coast. All the while he continued either to purchase or to build additional railroad lines until most of the western half of the peninsula as far south as Punta Gorda seemed to be Plant's domain.

One of Plant's neighbors in New York City, living a block away on Fifth Avenue, was Henry M. Flagler, a partner with John D. Rockefeller in Standard Oil Company. Flagler invested in Plant's Southern railway ventures. He came to Florida in 1878 with his first wife, Mary, and traveled to St. Augustine in the hope that warm air and sunlight might improve her health. However, Flagler found the surroundings in America's oldest city depressing. He quickly returned north, where Mary soon died. Six years later, following Flagler's remarriage to his second wife, Alice, he returned to St. Augustine and was surprised to discover that the town was filled with healthy, prosperous northerners who had come simply to enjoy themselves.[1]

Flagler saw that improvements in the South's railroad connections made

Henry Plant opened his Tampa Bay Hotel in 1891. Legend has it that when Henry Flagler asked how to find Tampa, Plant replied, "Just follow the crowds." Actually, the hotel was not a commercial success, but it briefly became famous as headquarters for U.S. Army officers during the Spanish-American War. Courtesy of the State Archives of Florida, *Florida Memory*, http://floridamemory.com/items/show/31956.

it practical for the growing class of affluent people in northern states to travel to Florida. Flagler realized he could profit from this significant development in American transportation by opening fine winter resort hotels in Florida and building a railroad to connect them with customers coming down in search of sunshine and pleasure.

In 1885 he began construction of the elegant Hotel Ponce de Leon and its companion, the Hotel Alcazar in St. Augustine. When they opened in 1888, they were the first large buildings in America to be constructed of concrete. Designed by architects Thomas Hastings and John Carrère, the hotels introduced Spanish-style architecture to modern Florida.

To ensure convenient, reliable transportation to his hotels, Flagler purchased the Jacksonville, St. Augustine & Halifax River Railroad in 1885. The acquisition of this railroad, with charter rights to build all the way to Daytona, gave Flagler an incentive to extend his range down the east coast. In 1890, Flagler built a steel railroad bridge across the St. Johns River in downtown Jacksonville, making it possible for travelers to reach St. Augustine from New York in just thirty-one hours without changing trains. They rode in plush Pullman cars on trains with names such as the "Florida Special." The way had been opened for development of one of Florida's now primary industries: Tourism.

Flagler extended his empire southward, reaching Palm Beach in 1894 where he built, first, the Hotel Royal Poinciana overlooking Lake Worth and then the Breakers on the shore of the Atlantic. Flagler's St. Augustine hotels had attracted the elite of northern high society (and some noted politicians, including President Grover Cleveland), and now Palm Beach became known as a premier winter resort for the country's millionaires.[2]

Julia Tuttle had been imploring both Plant and Flagler to build their railroads to her pioneer settlement of Miami when, in December 1894 and February 1895, two killer freezes struck, devastating Florida's citrus industry. Tuttle may have (as a story has it) sent Flagler a sprig of orange blossoms to show him that the frost had not reached Miami, but, in any case, Tuttle and Biscayne Bay's other pioneer, William Brickell, made an agreement to donate half of their large land holdings to Flagler if he would build his railroad to Miami. Flagler's railroad, now named the Florida East Coast Railway, reached Miami in April 1896. There he built the Hotel Royal Palm and

Henry Flagler's Hotel Ponce de Leon opened in January 1888 as the most luxurious winter resort in the country. Today Flagler College coeds live in rooms once occupied by millionaires. Courtesy of the State Archives of Florida, *Florida Memory*, http://florida memory.com/items/show/24086.

dredged a channel across shallow Biscayne Bay so that his steamships could carry passengers to his Hotel Colonial in Nassau.

Unfortunately, Flagler's private life was struck by tragedy when his second wife, Alice, became incurably insane. In 1901, Flagler lobbied the state legislature to change state law to include insanity as grounds for divorce, and, shortly after passage of the law, he married his third wife, Mary Lily Kenan, and built a palatial home for her, Whitehall, in Palm Beach. Afterward, what came to be called the "Flagler divorce law" emerged as a political issue since it was charged that Flagler had bribed the legislature to secure passage of a bill tailor-made to fit his personal needs. It seemed to be a blatant example of how rich special interests controlled the state government. Flagler's railroad building would terminate with his overseas extension to Key West in 1912.

The Panhandle region of the state benefitted from its own foremost developer, William D. Chipley. Born in Georgia but raised in Kentucky, Chipley had fought for the Confederate army. After the war he became involved in constructing railroads in Georgia, and then settled in Pensacola, from which he expanded his road-building efforts. Plant merged his railroads with the Louisville and Nashville Railroad. Then he obtained a charter from the State of Florida in 1881 for the Pensacola and Atlantic Railroad to build a railroad linking Pensacola with the rest of the state. To encourage this effort, the state granted the P & A more than 2 million acres of land. By 1883, Chipley's road had bridged the Apalachicola River and linked with lines in Georgia and the rest of Florida. Plant also built docks and warehouses in Pensacola to make it an important seaport.

Unlike Plant and Flagler, Chipley inserted himself personally into Florida politics. He was elected mayor of Pensacola and later became a state senator. In 1891, he failed to unseat U.S. senator Wilkinson Call in a contest that pitted a railroad man against an anticorporation politician. Six years later, while serving in the Florida Senate, Chipley again contested Call for his U.S. Senate seat. He was able to block Call's reelection, and Stephen R. Mallory II won as a compromise candidate. Shortly thereafter Chipley died unexpectedly.

The Civil War and Reconstruction had forced all white Floridians to unite within the Democratic Party in common cause against the Republicans. However, forced unity in the Democratic Party pushed politicians of widely varying philosophies and interests into an artificial alliance. As the Republican Party's influence in Florida began to wane, fractures appeared among the Democrats, leading in the early 1880s to an "Independent" movement.

The Independents claimed to speak for the common people and voiced their opposition to railroads, banks, corporations, and the politicians who supported these "special interests." The Disston land deals became an additional issue highlighting supposed favoritism for the rich. Another question was the constitution of 1868, which gave the governor power to appoint county officials. Independents declared that this led to domination of the whole state by a "Tallahassee Ring."

In June, a convention of disaffected Democrats met in Live Oak and nominated Frank Pope, a young former mayor of Madison, for governor. The Independents' only hope for victory in the election lay in an alliance with the Republicans, but this raised the race issue because most Republican voters were black. The Republicans realized they were in a predicament. If they nominated their own slate of candidates, they would split the anti-Democratic vote. If they nominated the same ticket as the Independents, they would brand Pope as the "black man's candidate." Thus the Republicans fielded no separate ticket and only "endorsed" the Independent nominee.

The Democrats held their convention in Pensacola just days after the Independents. Realizing that the Independent-Republican alliance posed a serious threat, they passed over controversial Governor Bloxham and nominated General Edward A. Perry of Pensacola, who had commanded the Florida Brigade during the Civil War. He ran as a war hero rather than as a politician.

The election was hard fought, but the Democrats prevailed. The black vote diminished from previous contests and did not go completely to the Independents, probably because of intimidation by Democrats at the polls. Also, the Democrats partly defused the question of a new constitution by vowing that, if elected, they too would call a constitutional convention. After their defeat, the Independent politicians moved back into the ranks of the Democrats, but the issues that put the "common folk" and the special interests at odds did not go away.

In June 1885, delegates elected from the various counties met in Tallahassee to draft a new constitution. Only 20 of the 108 delegates were Republicans, and only 7 were black. Conservative Democrats dominated the proceedings. Considering the controversial atmosphere in the state at the time, the delegates did their work well and the constitution they drafted and that the voters ratified stayed in effect until 1968.

In an overreaction to the control the governor had wielded under the 1868 constitution, the powers of the executive office were curtailed in several ways. The governor was limited to a single term in office. An elected cabinet would share decision making with the governor, making cabinet officers, who could be reelected indefinitely, very powerful. The office of lieutenant governor was abolished. On the legislative side, the practice of the state legislature meeting only every other year was written into the constitution.

The most controversial measures dealt with restoring home rule. The power to appoint county officers had been given to the governor in 1868 to prevent "Negro rule" in the old plantation-belt counties that had large populations of black residents. Restoring the right to elect county officers would mean the election of some black officeholders unless some way could be devised to minimize the black vote. The solution was a poll tax. Although the tax would not be high, it would discourage black men from registering to vote, especially if they knew that other pressures would be brought upon them to keep them away from the polls. In the ratification election, black voters strongly opposed the new constitution. After the poll tax was implemented by law, black voting dropped off precipitously. In some areas, such as the city of Jacksonville, black citizens continued to vote, but over the next decade white Floridians made a concerted effort to eliminate black voting once and for all. By the turn of the twentieth century, black voting had been reduced to just a few citizens, and black officeholding on both the state and local level ended.

When the poll tax was proposed, some lower-income white men protested that the tax would also discourage white voting. While black voter turnout dropped between the elections of 1888 and 1892 from 62 percent to 11 percent, white voting also fell from 86 percent to 59 percent.[3] Segregation of the races had always been the norm, but the color line was drawn more severely in the late nineteenth century. In 1887, the legislature passed an ordinance requiring separate cars for white and black passengers in railroad trains.

Florida's economy received a stimulus in the mid-1880s when deposits of phosphate were found along the Peace River in the central part of the state. Phosphate comes from the bones and shells of ancient animals so that the prospectors who rushed into the area found the bones of ancient beasts such as mastodons along with the phosphate. They dubbed the area "Bone Valley." Phosphate could be used in fertilizers and as an ingredient in a wide variety of products. Soon large companies using huge steam shovels to scoop out the mineral-rich earth replaced the early independent prospectors. Towns such as Arcadia and Dunnellon boomed, and the port of Tampa enjoyed profits from exporting phosphate to the world.

Some traditional enterprises continued to flourish. The cattle population thrived in the pine barrens and prairies west of Lake Okeechobee. Florida remained "open range," meaning cattle owners did not have to fence in their stock. Most of Florida's beef was exported on the hoof to the Cuban market.

Lumbering entered a period of extensive activity.[4] The advent of railroads made it easier to ship lumber out of Florida to more northerly states, and timber companies sent many temporary spur railroads snaking into remote areas to haul out logs. Some of the most valuable trees cut were cypress, but most of the lumber was yellow pine, often called heart pine. The destruction of Jacksonville by fire in 1901, to cite just one of many examples, resulted from the prevalence of buildings constructed with pine lumber. By the twentieth century, the cutting of the old-growth forests had become so rampant that concerns were raised about destruction of the environment. The first national forest east of the Mississippi River, the Ocala Forest, was created by President Theodore Roosevelt in 1908.

Naval stores had a long history in Florida. For centuries pine trees had been tapped for their resin to be turned into tar for use on wooden ships. With the advent of the Industrial Revolution, many more applications were found for the pine sap. Workers would be sent into the woods with sharp blades to hack "cat faces" into the trunks of pine. The sap would run down the scarred face of the trunk into clay cups and then would be taken back to a camp to be distilled into turpentine. Turpentine camps became notorious for their abysmal living conditions.

The making of tobacco products, especially cigars, ranked as the largest manufacturing industry in Florida.[5] With the outbreak of the first war of Cuban independence in 1868, some Cuban cigar manufacturers had moved their workshops to nearby Key West. In 1885, the City of Tampa offered to give one of Key West's cigar makers, Vicente Ybor, a tract of land east of town if he would build a factory there. Ybor took up the offer, and soon Ybor City grew into a cosmopolitan community of Cubans, Italians, and Spaniards with a vibrant culture all its own. Other Florida towns also had cigar factories operated by immigrants from Cuba.

Commercial fishing off both the Atlantic and Gulf coasts grew in importance as railroads and refrigerator cars made it possible to market catch in the North. Before the Civil War, beds of sponges had been discovered growing off Key West, but it would not be until the 1880s that demand for sponges soared. New sponge grounds were found off Florida's west coast, and Tarpon Springs became home port for a fleet of boats that sent out Greek divers in metal helmets attached to air hoses to go down and bring up the sponges.

Workers hacked "faces" into the bark of pine trees to create a flow of sap into cups. Since the work had to be done in remote forested areas, leased convict labor was often employed since free men would not have tolerated the harsh living conditions. Courtesy of the State Archives of Florida, *Florida Memory*, http://floridamemory.com/items/show/11021.

Oranges had long been an iconic symbol of Florida, but the industry suffered periodic setbacks. Freezing-cold snaps in 1886, 1894, and 1895 wiped out many of the groves and forced replanting to take place farther down the peninsula. Along the southeast coast, pineapple cultivation enjoyed a short-lived bonanza in the 1890s. Winter vegetables actually produced more income for Florida farmers than oranges, partly because it took seven years for an orange grove to mature while vegetables could yield profits within a few weeks. Cold Yankees in wintertime had an insatiable appetite for Florida carrots, cabbages, tomatoes, and beans. St. Johns County discovered that Irish potatoes grew very well in Florida soil. The profitability of these perishable crops depended upon rapid railroad transportation to northern markets.

At this time fashionable women wore large, elaborate hats often decorated with the delicate snow-white feathers of "plume birds." The highest-quality feathers came from birds shot at nesting season. Florida was home to millions of plume birds, and frontier hunters would make difficult treks into wetlands seeking out the rookeries where great flocks of birds nested in colonies. Killing the birds was comparatively easy since the parent birds would hover over their nests trying to protect their chicks.

This wanton slaughter of birds aroused the indignation of early conservationists, many of them women. Florida passed a law in 1879 that forbade noncitizens from killing plume birds and in 1891 outlawed their commercial hunting. In 1900, the Florida Audubon Society was organized to disseminate information about the destruction of the state's bird life and to encourage women to boycott feathers used as decorations. In 1901, the Florida legislature passed another law to prohibit hunting of plume birds, but made the penalty for violation a small fine, with no provision to hire game wardens to enforce the law. The Audubon Society employed and paid its own wardens, but when two of them were murdered, the society gave up the battle. At least some parks were created as sanctuaries. President Roosevelt established Pelican Island Wildlife Refuge on Indian River in 1903, and the state set aside Royal Palm Park in the Everglades in 1916 as Florida's first state park.[6]

The presence of tropical fevers had long been a deterrent to the settlement of Florida. In June 1887, people in Key West began dying of yellow fever. Outbreaks followed in Tampa and along the rail lines leading away from Tampa. Towns in Florida not touched by the epidemic imposed quarantines against outsiders entering their borders. With the arrival of winter frosts, the fever usually disappeared, but in the dead of winter stories began to circulate again of yellow fever in Tampa. Those reports were denounced as false and malicious, but proved to be all too true. Once more cities across the state raised quarantines against their neighbors. Jacksonville suffered by far the worst, with 430 people there succumbing to the disease. As a result, the incoming governor, Francis P. Fleming of Jacksonville, called a special session of the state legislature in 1889 to establish a State Board of Health.

Although the Independents had been defeated in 1884, their spirit lived on. In 1887, anticorporation feelings found expression in the creation of a three-man railroad commission appointed by the governor to investigate, set rates, and prohibit railroads from discriminating among shippers. The railroads opposed the commission, saying it violated sound economic principles and discouraged investment in the state. In 1891, the state legislature abolished the commission.

Farmers made an effort to organize so they could promote their own welfare. The Grange, a national organization, established branches in the state in the 1870s. Their appeal was mainly to traditional small farmers growing crops such as cotton that were suffering from declining market prices. The Grange urged farmers to stick together and cooperate in buying and selling.

The Grange maintained a policy of staying out of politics, but the Farmers Alliance, which entered the state in 1887, did not. Rather than form a political party, the Alliance drew up a list of principles and endorsed politicians who agreed to support the Alliance platform. By 1890, most Democrats had pledged their support to the Alliance.

In December 1890, the national convention of the Farmers Alliance met at Ocala. They adopted the "Ocala Demands" that asked for stronger regulation of the railroads, free coinage of silver, a graduated income tax, election of U.S. senators directly by the voters, and other reforms. The Alliance soon disappeared as an organized movement, but the nationwide economic depression of the 1890s increased the discontent of farmers.

Conservative leader William Bloxham returned as governor in 1897. Progressives, however, scored some victories. In 1897, the legislature established a new, more powerful railroad commission. By this time the frantic rate of railroad building was mostly over. The state's rail system was reaching a state of maturity, and even many business interests saw the desirability of government supervision.

In another victory, the reformers enacted a primary election method of nominating party candidates. This took the nominating power out of the hands of the party elite and meant that men from all parts of the state stood a chance of winning nomination for governor. Since by this time the Republican Party had become powerless due to the decline in black voting, the Democratic primary election virtually decided who would hold office.

Cuban rebellion against Spanish colonial rule resumed in the early 1890s. Many Cubans lived in Florida, working in cigar factories, and Florida had other connections to Cuba through investments, cattle sales, and tourism. José Martí and other exiled rebel leaders traveled frequently in Florida enlisting support and smuggling arms to Cuba. Napoleon Bonaparte Broward of Jacksonville gained fame by running guns to Cuba with his tugboat, the *Three Friends*.

When the United States declared war against Spain following the sinking of the battleship *Maine* in Havana harbor on February 15, 1898, Florida played a large part in the conflict. Tampa was selected as the primary point of assembly for a U.S. invasion force. Plant's Tampa Bay Hotel served as headquarters for the officers. (Teddy Roosevelt would later brag that he had camped in tents with his Rough Riders, but he also spent some time in the hotel with his wife.) The government dredged the harbor channel deeper, an improvement that would benefit the port after the war. Army camps became a bonanza for local businessmen and laborers, not only in Tampa but also in

Jacksonville, Fernandina, and Miami, where troops were also stationed. Key West served as the navy's closest base to the scene of the conflict in Cuba.

Twelve units of local Florida militia were organized into the First Florida Regiment, but were never sent to Cuba. Most of the casualties in the war came from typhoid contracted in camp, not Spanish rifles. United States authorities feared an outbreak of yellow fever, but none occurred.

Florida gained publicity from newspaper coverage of the war and from soldiers returning North with stories of their time in Florida. A second benefit from the war came with the discovery of the cause of yellow fever. While stationed in Cuba, Major Walter Reed performed experiments that proved yellow fever microbes were transmitted by mosquito bites. With Reed's discovery, Floridians launched a war on mosquitoes. Finally, northerners could settle in Florida rather than just visiting during the winters. Florida's rate of population growth increased after the turn of the century.

With the return of economic prosperity, America entered a period of progressive reform. William S. Jennings, cousin of the populist Democratic presidential contender William Jennings Bryan, was elected governor in 1900 on his promise to fight special interests. He attempted to prevent the railroads from taking possession of state lands that had been promised to them. The railroads sued, but ultimately failed to acquire much of the land they thought they deserved.

As the end of his term as governor approached in 1904, Jennings threw his support to another progressive, Napoleon B. Broward, who won with a promise to drain the Everglades, sell the reclaimed land for settlement by Floridians, and use the profits to fund the government. "The railroads are draining the people instead of the swamps," was his battle cry.[7]

Once in office, Broward found little support for his proposal to drain the Everglades because the legislature was reluctant to appropriate funds. Instead, it voted for a constitutional amendment to create a drainage tax district to fund the plan. Without waiting for the public's action on the amendment, Broward, on July 4, 1906, sent a dredge off from the north branch of New River in Ft. Lauderdale to excavate west and north toward Lake Okeechobee.

In November, the voters overwhelmingly rejected the amendment authorizing a drainage tax. Shortly thereafter, Broward began working out compromises with the railroads and other corporations to settle lawsuits and clear the way for new land deals. It also became clear that the two dredges Broward had in operation were not making substantial progress in lowering water levels, so Broward constructed two more dredges to join the work.

Prohibited by the constitution from running for governor again, Broward turned the drainage of the Everglades over to his successor, Albert Gilchrist. During the latter's administration, the state continued to make settlements with claimants in the lawsuits over land grants and actually began to collect a drainage tax at a lower rate. By this time, it had become clear to everyone that lowering water levels in the Everglades was a much more complex problem than it had first appeared.

Yet a great endeavor had been set in motion that would not stop for generations. Very little concern was shown at the time for the questions raised by modern-day conservationists. Both progressives and conservatives agreed that draining the big swamp was a good idea.

During his time in office, Broward realized that the citizens in modern times needed more education than they had been receiving in their backward, agrarian state. He spoke out for greater spending on public schools and oversaw a more orderly organization of the state's public school system, although his proposal to provide free textbooks failed to pass the legislature.

Before the turn of the century, private schools played a large role in providing college-level education. Stetson University had been established in DeLand in 1883, and Rollins College, in Winter Park, was founded in 1885. In 1904, Mary McLeod Bethune established the Daytona Training School for Negro Girls that would later develop into Bethune-Cookman College. The leading state-sponsored college was the Florida Agricultural College in Lake City, established in 1870, but the state also gave meager support to a handful of other institutions, including the State Normal School for Negroes in Tallahassee that had been organized in 1887. Funding for all of these institutions fell far short of the requirements of true colleges, and enrollments were meager.

Broward's most notable achievement in education came with passage of the Buckman Act in 1905, which established the basis for orderly support of higher education in the state. The Buckman Act provided for the creation of a state board to oversee all state-sponsored colleges, with the intention that over time the state would develop a system of higher education. The Normal School for black students in Tallahassee became Florida Agricultural and Mechanical College, and, also in Tallahassee, the Florida Female College became Florida State College for Women, and, after World War II, with the admission of male students, Florida State University. The location of the other school, Florida Agricultural College, which enrolled only white men, became a major controversy. Gainesville managed to lure the college away from Lake City, partly because the city offered to furnish the college with free water from the municipal system. It was renamed the University of Florida.

In step with the ideas current among progressives nationwide, Broward saw to the passage of a law prohibiting child labor in factories, mines, and saloons, as well as a pure food law to create state inspection of meat and vegetables. Broward also advocated the building of modern, hard-surface roads around the state for the use of automobiles and trucks. A "good roads" movement had started back in the 1890s before automobiles entered the picture, but once cars began to appear in Florida, the demand for better roads increased dramatically. Every major county had its organization to promote road improvement. The state passed its first laws regulating automobiles and required that autos be registered at a cost of two dollars, with the money going to build roads. In 1908, 733 cars were recorded.

The movement to prohibit alcoholic drinks had been gaining momentum across the country during the final decades of the nineteenth century. Religious leaders and progressive reformers who saw alcoholism as a serious social problem joined hands to support local and state laws limiting the consumption of alcoholic beverages. By 1908, Gainesville, Tallahassee, and Live Oak had adopted "local option" laws prohibiting alcoholic beverages within their boundaries.

In the 1916 Democratic primary election, state comptroller William V. Knott, a mainstream party leader, faced four other opponents, including outsider Sidney J. Catts, who had recently moved to DeFuniak Springs in the Panhandle from Alabama. An impressive man with red hair who had lost one eye in a childhood accident, Catts had been a Baptist minister, but went into the business of selling life insurance. His career had given him a strong sense of how the common people in backwoods areas viewed life. Catts realized that he needed an issue that would separate him from the other candidates, and he found it in anti-Catholicism.

Religion had never played a major role in state politics since the population was overwhelmingly Protestant Christian. The two Stephen R. Mallorys, father and son, had been elected to the U.S. Senate, in widely separate eras, without their Catholic religion being a hindrance. However, Catts found that it did not seem to matter that the Catholic population of Florida was small; in rural areas, fears of an unseen threat lurking just over the horizon could be amplified and exploited. The Democratic Party's executive committee inadvertently added fuel to this fear by passing a provision known as the Sturkie Resolution declaring that voters should not be influenced by religion in their choice of candidates and should not belong to any secret society advocating religious discrimination. The motion was prompted by the rise of an organization called the Guardians of Liberty, dedicated to protecting native-born Americans against immigrant Catholics. Catts seized upon the Sturkie Resolution as evidence that the leaders of the state's Democratic Party sympathized with Catholics and opposed anyone who stood up for the rights of Protestants.

Lacking campaign money and newspaper support, Catts toured the state's rural areas declaring that he was the only candidate who cared about the welfare of small-town people and farm families. When the primary ballots were counted, Catts seemed to have won. However, the second-place finisher, Knott, appealed to the state Supreme Court, which recounted the ballots and declared Knott the victor by 270 votes. Claiming that the Democratic Party had stolen the nomination from him, Catts ran in the fall general election as the candidate of the Prohibition Party. Adding a modern touch to his campaign, Catts purchased a Model T Ford that allowed him to reach even remote areas where the railroads did not go. Catts often brandished two six-shooters, saying that he carried them for protection. He won the general election by a good margin.

Catts rode to his inauguration in a procession of automobiles, including his Model T, rather than the traditional carriages. Once in office, Catts adopted a moderate course. In most respects, the legislature continued to enact laws that contributed to making Florida a modern state. Catts did push for ratification of the Eighteenth Amendment outlawing alcoholic drinks, and it was passed in December 1918. However, even in this case, Catts did not act outside the mainstream of public opinion since most of the state's counties had already passed laws prohibiting alcoholic drinks, and the whole United States went dry following ratification of the Eighteenth Amendment in 1919.

In other ways, Catts advanced the progressive agenda. He supported a law that required youngsters between the ages of seven and fourteen to attend school. He advocated two acts passed by the legislature in 1917 and 1919 that ended the leasing of state prisoners, although convict leasing continued on the county level. Henceforth the state would use prisoners to maintain the state's developing road system.

In 1915, the legislature created a state road department. In October of that year, the "Dixie Highway Motorcade" arrived in Jacksonville, having driven in cars down from Chicago. Communities along the east coast of Florida joined the movement and built roads that would be designated part of the Dixie Highway. Florida's future love affair with tourists in their automobiles was already blossoming.

The United States went to war against Germany just four months after Catts took office. In December 1917, at the start of the tourist season, President Wilson took possession of all the railroads in the United States. This, and the general disruptions of the war, caused the number of Florida tourists to decrease during the 1918 season. In addition, overseas exports of phosphate and lumber declined since European markets were closed during the fighting.

However, the Florida economy boomed during the war. Railroad traffic actually increased as the movement of soldiers and building supplies for military bases were added to the usual civilian traffic in lumber, winter vegetables, citrus, and tourists. Shipyards in Jacksonville and Tampa increased production of ships for civilian owners. Lumber went to neighboring states to build army camps. A labor shortage developed during the fighting. One factor that added to the shortage was the increased migration of black Floridians to the North in search of better employment opportunities and greater freedom.

Florida's most significant contribution to the military came from aviation training bases established in the state. With year-round good weather, Florida made an ideal place to train aviators. The U.S. Navy had already established Pensacola Naval Air Station 1914 as its primary base for training pilots. Miami received two fields: Curtiss and Chapman, while Arcadia was home to Carlstrom and Dorr Fields.

Key West became noted as a base for submarines and as the U.S. Navy's home port for the Caribbean basin. A south Jacksonville location served as the U.S. Army's Camp Joseph E. Johnston (today's Jacksonville Naval Air Station).

The war imposed few hardships on civilians. Floridians voluntarily rationed their consumption of meat and planted more land in corn and potatoes to increase the available food supply. Some farmers earned enough money to replace their mules with tractors. However, prices for food, clothing, and rent went up rapidly due to increased demand. During the war, 42,000 Floridians served in the military. Approximately 1,100 died in combat.

Just as the war was being won in Europe in the fall of 1918, an influenza pandemic engulfed the world. The flu first appeared in Florida in the port cities of Key West and Pensacola. Across the state, people wore squares of gauze over their mouths and noses. Schools, movie theaters, churches, and other places of public gatherings closed. Jacksonville recorded 234 deaths, by far the most, and statewide probably more than 1,000 died.

On November 5, 1915, Lieutenant Commander Henry C. Mustin flew the first aircraft launched from a ship by catapult. He flew a Curtiss AB-2 flying boat off the stern of the USS *North Carolina* anchored in Pensacola Bay. Before he began designing aircraft, Glenn Curtiss had set a world speed record for motorcycles on Daytona Beach. Courtesy of the State Archives of Florida, *Florida Memory*, http://floridamemory.com/items/show/6943.

Following the war, the United States was engulfed in labor disputes. Wages had not kept up with inflation in the prices of consumer goods. Strikes broke out in Florida cities with large numbers of unionized workers. Tampa and Jacksonville had the largest strikes, but strikes also occurred in other cities. Even some policemen and firemen went on strike. Racial tensions rose as employers brought in black men to replace striking white workers. Black men, who had been forced out of many skilled trades in previous decades, saw this as a chance to improve their employment status. Fortunately, the strikes were settled without the kind of major violence that happened in some northern cities.

Soon good times returned, and Sunny Florida stood poised to lead America into the Roaring Twenties.

Notes

1. Akin, *Flagler*, 117.
2. Braden, *Architecture of Leisure*, 221.
3. Colburn, *Government in the Sunshine*, 12.
4. Stronge, *Sunshine Economy*, 13.
5. Ibid., 34–35.
6. Davis, *Paradise Lost*, 243–51.
7. Proctor, *Broward*, 190.

Bibliography

Akin, Edward N. *Flagler: Rockefeller Partner and Florida Baron*. Kent, Ohio: Kent State University Press, 1988.

Blake, Nelson M. *Land into Water—Water into Land: A History of Water Management in Florida*. Gainesville: University Presses of Florida, 1980.

Braden, Susan R. *The Architecture of Leisure: The Florida Resort Hotels of Henry Flagler and Henry Plant*. Gainesville: University Press of Florida, 2002.

Colburn, David R., and Lance deHaven-Smith. *Government in the Sunshine State: Florida since Statehood*. Gainesville: University Press of Florida, 1999.

Davis, Jack E., and Raymond Arsenault, eds. *Paradise Lost? The Environmental History of Florida*. Gainesville: University Press of Florida, 2005.

Flynt, Wayne. *Cracker Messiah: Governor Sidney J. Catts of Florida*. Baton Rouge: Louisiana State University Press, 1977.

Knetsch, Joe, and Nick Wynne. *Florida in the Spanish-American War*. Charleston: History Press, 2011.

Proctor, Samuel. *Napoleon Bonaparte Broward: Florida's Fighting Democrat*. Gainesville: University of Florida Press, 1950.

Stronge, William B. *The Sunshine Economy: An Economic History of Florida since the Civil War*. Gainesville: University Press of Florida, 2008.

Turner, Gregg M. *A Journey into Florida Railroad History*. Gainesville: University Press of Florida, 2008.

Turner, Gregg M., and Seth H. Bramson. *The Plant System of Railroads, Steamships and Hotels: The South's First Great Industrial Enterprise*. Laurys Station, Pa.: Garrigues House, 2004.

Williamson, Edward C. *Florida Politics in the Gilded Age, 1877–1893*. Gainesville: University Presses of Florida, 1976.

17

Fortune and Misfortune

The Paradoxical 1920s

WILLIAM W. ROGERS

Florida's social matrix in the 1920s combined reality and fantasy. Its parts included people, land, automobiles and highways, banks, hurricanes, insects (Mediterranean fruit flies and mosquitoes), ticks, and the intangible—but no less real—emotions of greed, optimism, faith, and despair. Politics was less prominent than usual, but there was no lack of strong candidates and hard-fought campaigns. The biggest race of 1920, a year in which women gained the right to vote with the adoption of the Nineteenth Amendment, was for the U.S. Senate. It was decided by the Democratic primary victory of incumbent conservative-progressive Duncan U. Fletcher over the populist and flamboyant governor Sydney J. Catts. In the general election, Fletcher easily defeated his Socialist and Republican opponents.

The state's one-party system had been dominated since the end of Reconstruction by the Democrats, whose shibboleths were honesty, frugality, efficiency in government, and white supremacy. Tainted by the alleged and real corruption of Reconstruction, the Republicans offered only token opposition. Nomination in the Democratic primary guaranteed victory in the general election. Black voters had been disfranchised, first by extralegal means and since the 1890s by legal means, especially by laws that permitted Democratic officials to exclude them from participating in the primaries. Beyond that, the poll tax eliminated many black voters (and poor whites as well). By the 1920s, black citizens were no longer a viable part of the political process.

In the 1920 gubernatorial primary, Cary A. Hardee, a Live Oak banker and lawyer, won over two rivals before vanquishing his Republican and

Socialist adversaries in the general election. In the primary for that office in 1924, John W. Martin, a lawyer and longtime mayor of Jacksonville, ran as the businessman's candidate. Emphasizing a road-building program, he was nominated over three opponents. Two years later, Senator Fletcher won another term with his primary victory over Florida's colorful hotel commissioner, Jerry W. Carter, a Catts appointee. In 1920 and 1924, Republicans won the White House, but Florida routinely awarded its electoral votes to Democrats James M. Cox and John W. Davis.

Vote tallies in 1928 produced no surprises at the state level, but Florida joined four other states in deviating from the South's solid Democratic norm in the national presidential contest, which pitted Republican Herbert Hoover against New York's Democratic governor Alfred E. Smith. Wauchula's Doyle E. Carlton, descendant of a pioneer family, defeated four primary opponents, including perennial candidate Catts, in the gubernatorial race. Catts supported the victorious Hoover, but Carlton went on to win the general election. U.S. Senator Park Trammell defeated former governor John Martin in the primary and easily bested Republican Barclay H. Warburton.

Al Smith had won the Democratic presidential nomination without any delegate support from Florida. Senator Joseph T. Robinson of Arkansas had received the vice-presidential nomination to placate southern voters, most of them Protestants who opposed electing a Catholic president. Smith's liabilities in Florida and the South included his "shanty Irish" immigrant background, ties with Tammany Hall and eastern big-city politics, and opposition to Prohibition. His East Side accent and wardrobe of spats, bowler derby, and striped suits further repelled southern voters. Many Florida politicians gave only tepid support to the national ticket. Local and statewide church groups, antiliquor organizations, and civic leaders endorsed Hoover. Many women voters also approved of the Republican candidate's support of Prohibition. Besides, Hoover promised to continue Republican prosperity begun under Calvin Coolidge, and by 1928, still reeling from a real estate bust, Floridians had good cause to want prosperity.

Hoover received 144,168 votes to Al Smith's 101,764, and carried Florida with 56.8 percent of the popular vote. Socialist Norman Thomas got 4,036 votes and Communist William Z. Foster 3,704. Large victory margins by other Democratic candidates in the state suggested no massive shift by white voters to the Republican Party. Their voting patterns in the 1930s would remain solidly Democratic. Hoover owed his victory to special circumstances: Democratic overconfidence, the Prohibition issue, and strong religious feelings of Florida's voters.

Too much was going on in Florida during the 1920s for citizens to concentrate solely on politics. Prohibition, for example, went into effect in 1919. Subsequently, enforcement became a major problem. With 3,800 miles of tidal shoreline containing an extensive system of bays and inlets, Florida became a major port of entry for alcoholic beverages. Airplanes, speedboats, and other vessels came in under cover of darkness from the Bahamas and Caribbean islands. While smugglers operated with near impunity, native Floridians set up moonshine stills and put their imaginations to full use devising innovative marketing techniques. One Duval County bootlegger was caught dispensing "white lightning" from the back of a truck, where he kept it hidden beneath sacks of pecans and sweet potatoes.

As one British traveler put it, "Florida, from my personal experience in it, was the wettest country I have ever known."[1] Noted gangster Al Capone, no novice to liquor trafficking, came to Miami in the 1920s, presumably to escape the stress of Chicago and Cicero, Illinois. However law-abiding he may have tried to be, the mobster's presence set off official but unsuccessful efforts to bar him from the state.

Religion, especially the modernist-fundamentalist controversy over teaching evolution in the public schools, also diverted attention from politics. Florida remained a Protestant stronghold, although it had substantial numbers of Catholics and Jews. Many whites and blacks were devout church members, and ministers, especially black ministers, exercised great influence in their communities. An eclectic theological domain, Florida sheltered groups ranging from evangelical preachers thundering hellfire and damnation to tent audiences to Episcopalian ministers intoning scriptures to upper-class congregations.

The Great Commoner, William Jennings Bryan, a three-time Democratic presidential candidate who had made Florida his residence, was a devout fundamentalist, as were many educational, civic, and political leaders. Despite pressure from such persons, and numerous heated debates on the subject, the state—unlike Tennessee, Arkansas, and Mississippi—did not statutorily forbid the teaching of evolution in the public schools. Such acts were known popularly as Monkey Laws. Even so, in 1923 the legislature did pass a joint resolution opposing the teaching of Darwinian thought. There was ongoing controversy over bills banning textbooks that denied spontaneous creation as described in the Book of Genesis, and certain scientific books were placed on restricted use or were taken from university and college library shelves, but no anti-evolution law passed as such. The controversy did not end until well after the Scopes trial in 1925 at Dayton, Tennessee.

Fundamentalists also frowned on gambling. They and a majority of citizens did not approve of efforts to establish thoroughbred racing in Florida. Despite antibetting laws, sporadic meets were held in the 1920s at sportsman Frank A. Kenney's track between Jacksonville and St. Augustine. In 1925, Joseph M. Smoot's Miami Jockey Club (renamed Hialeah in 1931) opened. But public outcry curtailed racing until the 1931 legislature, desperate to raise revenue, legalized pari-mutuel wagering.

Politics and popular distractions aside, the state's spectacular land boom became the main object of attention. It remained so until supplanted by an equally spectacular bust. In economic decline at the turn of the decade, Florida was on the road to prosperity by 1923. The rapid recovery was based largely on a dramatic rise in real estate transactions and land development. The phenomenon began at Miami Beach, spread through Dade County, moved up the east and west coasts, and infused central Florida before finding its way north to Tallahassee and west to the Panhandle. To many, Florida seemed a lotus land, and there was no shortage of individuals anxious to exploit its potential.

Near-legendary figures of Florida's development included John Collins, who created Miami Beach from mangrove swamps and salt marshes in the 1910s. His efforts were furthered by Carl G. Fisher, an Indiana native. Nearby to the south, George E. Merrick promoted Coral Gables, a planned community featuring Mediterranean architecture and distinguished by an artful blending of exotic landscaping and canals. Northward lay Hollywood, another designed community founded in 1921 by Joseph W. Young and his California associates. Even farther north, Addison Mizner, an extraordinary promoter-architect, designed homes for the wealthy at Palm Beach. His Mediterranean style was enhanced by the use of pastel colors—utilitarian in combatting the sun's rays and aesthetic in their soft-hued variety. Backed by eastern millionaires, Mizner's most ambitious project was Boca Raton. Unfortunately, he fell victim to the collapse of the land boom, and his corporation failed in 1926.

Elsewhere, other projects transformed the state. The distance between Tampa and St. Petersburg was more than halved by George S. Gandy's toll bridge, erected with financial assistance from St. Petersburg promoter Eugene M. Elliott. In Tampa, D. P. "Doc" Davis converted three land spits into the lucrative Davis Islands network, but another Davis effort failed at St. Augustine with the end of the land boom. Orlando's growth resulted from the early work of H. Carl Dann. William Lee Popham of Kentucky, a Baptist minister who combined oyster production with real estate deals, raised hopes in the Apalachicola area. His ventures on St. George Island ultimately failed, but not before his fame spread far and wide. Pensacola, Panama City, and Jacksonville also expanded, and supposedly staid Tallahassee opened numerous subdivisions.

Chambers of Commerce advertised their cities and initiated beautification projects, as the state touted its advantages and strengthened its transportation network. Public auctions of lots attracted large crowds and combined economics with entertainment. Private business groups trumpeted the message that one did not have to be rich to own a winter home in Florida. No less an authority than the Bible was utilized to lure settlers. One promoter quoted chapter and verse: "Arise, and go toward the south" (Acts 8:26); "I have bought a piece of ground and I must needs go and see it" (Luke 14:18); and "Search you out a place to pitch your tents in" (Deuteronomy 1:33).

Railroad construction increased, and trains traveling on the rival Seaboard Air Line and Atlantic Coast Line roads were packed with passengers. Thousands of Americans still had savings accumulated from wartime prosperity. Florida was easily accessible to most states east of the Mississippi River, and countless northerners longed to exchange cold winters for the semitropical paradise. So much of the state was still undeveloped that land was supposedly inexpensive. Urged on by controversial state comptroller Ernest Amos, state senator John P. Stokes of Pensacola, and others with eyes toward improving the money crop, the legislature amended the state constitution to prohibit income taxes and inheritance taxes. One newspaper commented perceptively that the move was "a very unique way of encouraging capitalists and investors to bring their money to this state."[2]

Real estate promoters and developers swarmed into Florida, and an estimated 300,000 people settled there between 1923 and 1925. Thirteen new counties were created, nine of them in south Florida. One result of the boom was a permanent population increase. Florida started the 1920s with 968,470 people, and by 1930 had 1,468,211. The white population rose from 638,153 to 1,035,205, blacks from 329,487 to 431,828. The number of men and women in both races was almost equally divided. Jacksonville remained the largest city (129,549), but Miami had moved from fourth place to second by 1930. Florida's urban population in 1930 was 72.3 percent white and 27.7 percent black.

An awed northern journalist asked, "Was there ever anything like the migration to Florida? From the time the Hebrews went into Egypt, or since the hegira of Mohammed the prophet, what can compare to this evacuation?

Land auctions were conducted everywhere in Florida during the 1920s land boom. Often what was offered was just-filled mangrove swamps or just-cleared pinelands, with rough-scraped dirt roads to outline subdivisions. But in the land delirium of mid-decade, even that sold quickly to northern "snowbirds" who wanted a piece of paradise. Bused to these rude sites by spellbinding promoters, their phantasmagoria was such that, having alighted, the visitors beheld not a barren landscape but a mirage of finished pleasure domes waiting for occupancy.

The Forty-Niners did not go out in such great numbers, nor can the gold rush to the Klondike be put in the same class with this flight to Florida. Entire populations are moving away bodily. The personal columns of our local press are unable to chronicle the daily departures."[3]

In 1925 alone, 2.5 million tourists visited Florida. The majority arrived by automobile on an expanding road system. Jacksonville and Lake City were the main entry points. Floridians, like other Americans, loved automobiles and by 1916 owned ninety different models. Besides those familiar today, they favored such cars as the Aurora, Metz, Kritt, Regal, Peerless, and Empire. By the 1920s, assembly-line production and installment buying had made Model T Fords and similar cars inexpensive and available to the masses so that less affluent citizens could afford transportation to Florida. Cars arrived packed with people and supplies. Their occupants camped out, thus creating tourist camps. In 1919, at Tampa's DeSoto Park, a number of them happily adopted an egalitarian nickname, the "Tin Can Tourists of the World." Annual meetings were held among parked vehicles and pitched tents, as visitors engaged in socializing, dancing, eating, and sports.

Privately owned tourist courts opened, and Florida was on the threshold of achieving what became its mammoth motel industry.

The creation of a state road department in 1915 enabled Florida to take advantage of the Federal Road Aid Act of 1916 and the Federal Highway Act of 1921. The section of U.S. 90 between Jacksonville and Lake City opened in 1923 as the state's first concrete highway. Later, it was extended to Pensacola. Not far behind were north-south connectors U.S. 1, 41, and 27. Earlier plans for the Tamiami Trail connecting Fort Myers and Miami were resurrected, and the highway across the Everglades was officially opened on 25 April 1928. Florida entered the decade with fewer than 1,000 miles of roadway, but by 1930 had 3,800 miles surfaced with everything from clay to grouted brick, Macadam, concrete, and asphalt.

Airplanes, as well as automobiles, revolutionized transportation, and by the end of the 1920s, commercial airlines were carrying passengers to and within Florida. The first airplane flight in Florida was at Orlando in 1910, and the state's first airport opened at Miami Beach in 1912. By 1926, nine Florida cities had airports, and early mail flights had added passengers. Eastern Air Transport (later Eastern Airlines) and Pan American were among the burgeoning and increasingly important corporations offering passenger service.

To accommodate newcomers eager to invest in Miami real estate, a large freelance sales force emerged. Called "Binder Boys," these fast-talking hucksters, in golf knickers and two-toned shoes, purchased lots for 10 percent down (a binder that held a property for thirty days), then sold the binders for a profit to other speculators. A binder could be sold and resold many times before payment became due. Paper profits rose to dizzying heights. At one time, Miami had 25,000 such street brokers, many of them men who had quit jobs in the North as butchers, taxi drivers, or railroad conductors, to take advantage of the Florida bonanza. Promoting real estate, not necessarily selling it, became another industry, with such luminaries as William Jennings Bryan, who informed outlanders about the attractions of Merrick's Coral Gables.

By 1925, the *Miami Herald* was the world's largest newspaper in terms of advertising linage. One issue of the *Miami News* set a record by publishing twenty-two sections containing a total of 504 pages. Clearly ignored, one critic observed, were certain biblical admonitions: "If riches increase, set not your heart upon them" (Psalms 62:10) and "Thou shall neither vex a stranger nor oppress him" (Exodus 22:21).

Property prices soared with inflated land values and affected the entire economy: transportation, construction, and banking. Some worried that if all of Florida basked in the sunshine of prosperity, a collapse would be equally widespread, but it seemed folly to engage in such gloomy musings when there was so much profit to be made. One movie of 1923 that attracted Floridians to theaters (also growing in number) was appropriately titled *Money, Money, Money*.

The expansion of banking was a concrete indication of economic growth. State and national bank deposits peaked in 1925 at $900 million. The number of national banks increased but lagged behind new state banks that benefitted from lower capital requirements and less strict regulations for loans and investments. When 1923 ended, Florida had 194 banks. The state comptroller and his increased staff moved into more commodious quarters. The legislature failed to enact any major banking laws, and the comptroller boasted that in the typical Florida bank, "deposits exceed loans by a very material and substantial margin."[4] No national banks failed from 1920 until 1925, but, ominously, in the same period eighty state banks failed.

The years 1925 and 1926 were pivotal for Florida. Problems began in 1925 with a national backlash of hostility against the excesses of the real estate boom. Promoters and "Binder Boys" were lacerated by the northern press. Governor Martin and a group of leading Floridians met with editors and publishers at the Waldorf Astoria Hotel in New York City. Their mollifying efforts to "tell the truth about Florida" were not completely successful.

The problems were compounded when, in October 1925, a strike on the Atlantic Coast Line Railroad swamped competing lines with freight. The Interstate Commerce Commission called an embargo so that railyards and freight houses could be cleared of the backlog. In the meantime, Florida builders were left without materials, retailers could not obtain merchandise, and travelers—frustrated by cancellations and long delays—raised an angry chorus. In January 1926, a ship sank in Miami harbor and further disrupted the flow of supplies. The embargo was short-lived, but trains ran irregularly as late as February and thousands of vacationers spurned Florida. Their boycott dealt the economy a stinging jolt.

The most dramatic blow was just that: a violent hurricane that ripped across south Florida in September 1926, killing 400 people, injuring 6,300, and leaving 50,000 homeless. Many newcomers abruptly left the state but not before withdrawing their money from banks. Realtors and developers began leaving also, and, adding to the problems, the cost of living soared.

A languorous day, 7 May 1926, at Boca Grande Beach near Charlotte Harbor. The Florida real estate boom had collapsed, but the sun still shone and the water was fine.

The boom was over, and worse conditions lay ahead. Few Floridians who had basked in prosperity just one year before would have predicted such an abrupt reversal.

The banking situation remained volatile. Sheer volume of activity forced an increase in the number of state bank examiners to eight. A new law required state banks to be examined annually and "more often if necessary."[5] Comptroller Amos, who had easily been reelected in 1924, was full of confidence and exhibited impressive statistics about 1925. As illustrated by his example, there was an absence of prudence and cautious skepticism in Florida. H. R. Doughy, sales manager and lecturer for Daytona Shores, said, "The sunshine state is now entering upon the most extraordinary era of substantial growth and business activity ever known in the history of the world." The January 1926 issue of a national financial journal featured several articles on Florida's economic stability. Governor Martin and the mayor of Miami were among its contributors. Speculating on the future, the publication's editor declared, "The bubble will not burst for the very good reason that there is no bubble."[6]

The truth was that in 1925 and 1926 numerous Floridians went from riches to rags, and sometimes not even rags were left. As 1925 ended, even Comptroller Amos grew glum and admonished state banks to maintain strong cash positions. He wanted "plenty of leeway" between deposits and loans.[7] The directive was academic. It was already too late. Inflation was at its peak. Although the average state bank had a comfortable cash reserve in 1925, the new year was a different story. Money flowed out and deposits dropped as previously stable banks had difficulty obtaining call money. Emergency meetings produced some funds but not enough to meet needs, and banks saw their cash reserves melt away.

Bank heads and state officials met to discuss a crisis they could not solve. Unable to maintain cash reserves, more banks failed in the last months of 1926. A stoical Amos appealed for calm. One newspaper warned against rumors and innuendoes: "The whisperer who talks about banks is a good deal like the purveyor of backstairs gossip about a good woman. They are

On the night of 18 September 1926, a hurricane packing winds of 130 to 150 miles per hour caught the boomtime population of Dade County unaware. Ninety-two coastal residents were killed by the storm, the first in the region since 1910; another 300 were drowned at Moore Haven in the interior. More than 600 persons were injured and 18,000 made homeless. From Miami (see downtown damage, *above*) to Fort Lauderdale, 5,000 homes were destroyed and 9,000 were damaged. Boomtime tent cities and tourist camps were leveled. Two years later, almost to the day (16 September), a hurricane of equal strength hit the Florida shoreline at Palm Beach and caused Lake Okeechobee to overflow, deluging surrounding communities. Nearly 2,000 persons drowned, three-quarters of them black farmworkers.

equally dangerous members of society."[8] An additional serious problem resulted from various Florida cities floating large bond issues, which caused a slump in the bond market.

Despite a reeling economy, Floridians partly regained their optimism in 1927 and 1928 as tourism rebounded and real estate made a comeback. The two years proved only a prelude, though, to the stock market crash of 1929. During this period, even national banks were hard pressed to hold their own. It was probably just as well that Florida's citizens could not foresee coming afflictions.

With some exceptions, state banks suffered crippling declines in deposits, loans, and cash reserves. In 1927, many were unable to meet depositors' demands, and failures became daily headlines. Amos was indicted in 1927 on charges of permitting two insolvent banks to remain open, but the state supreme court ruled in his favor. Unchastened and undaunted, he was reelected in 1928, carrying every county and receiving more votes than any candidate for state office. Other questionable activities earned the comptroller additional charges in 1930, but again the court dismissed the case. One cynical observer was prompted to declare that Florida needed "more bankers in Raiford [prison], and more leadership in Tallahassee."[9]

The state's malaise would soon be repeated nationally. A restoration of public confidence in Florida's banking institutions was needed, but conferences of state leaders failed to restore morale. Few doubted that the boom was over. Walter Fuller, a candid land developer in St. Petersburg, wrote: "We just ran out of suckers. That's all. We got all their money, then started trading with ourselves. . . . That isn't quite correct. We became the suckers."[10] A requiem from the *Nation* declared, "Like a mad, bad dream the real-estate delirium passed." The phenomenon "vanished like a soap bubble."[11]

If hope sprang eternal, it was blown away by a series of tropical disturbances followed by a devastating hurricane in the fall of 1928. Floridians had learned something from their 1926 experience, but they could do nothing about a storm that contained wind gusts of 130 miles per hour. Striking first at Palm Beach, the hurricane caused Lake Okeechobee to flood nearby communities. An estimated 2,000 lives were lost. Even that figure may have been low because emergency burials in mass graves proved necessary to avoid the possibility of epidemics. Most of the casualties were black seasonal workers, some of them from the Bahamas.

For some Floridians, Doyle Carlton's election as governor in 1928 signaled better times, but no one realistically expected a return to the halcyon days of the first half of the 1920s. Others expected national leadership to revive the state, but President Hoover's administration was crippled by the beginning of the Great Depression. An accumulation of events and circumstances caused the nation's economic collapse: high tariff walls and an insistence on debt repayment in gold effected a drastic decline in the export market; a worldwide glut of raw materials and agricultural products sent prices plummeting; the cost of consumer goods exceeded the range of most Americans' buying power, causing overproduction and rising inventories; and there was a serious maldistribution of the nation's wealth—a few people had too much money, and too many people had too little.

Historians and economists usually date the Great Depression from the panic that hit the Wall Street stock market in late October 1929. Frenzied liquidation ended an unprecedented bull market that had lasted for six years. The collapse in values halted the optimistic and speculative enthusiasm that had permeated American society. Making money had seemed simple and automatic. Now, in October 1929, the country had a bear market, and things were dismally different.

Hoover moved to offset the panic by obtaining promises from management to sustain production and wages and from organized labor not to strike or seek pay increases. Even so, matters grew increasingly worse, while distress of Old Testament proportions continued in much of Florida. In April 1929, the Mediterranean fruit fly was found at a grapefruit grove in Orlando. From there it spread across the state, requiring quarantines and embargoes on the shipment of fruit and agricultural products. The destruction wrought by the insect (the "Medfly" resembled an ordinary house fly but was slightly smaller and had yellow and black wings) forced the destruction of citrus groves and temporarily devastated the industry.

Economic and fruit fly problems notwithstanding, agriculture remained Florida's predominant source of wealth. The number of farms had increased from 54,005 in 1920 to 58,906 in 1930; 5,244 farmers had traded in their mules and horses for tractors; 3,525 farm families had telephones, and 7,559 had water piped into their homes. In 1930, the state's 300,000 acres of fruit and truck products represented 10 percent of the total value of such crops in the country. By contrast, Florida's traditional field crops, such as corn and cotton, had declined in value from well over $27 million to about $10.2 million.

The number and worth of livestock increased during the decade. The costly presence of ticks had hampered the cattle industry, but in 1923 a compulsory statewide eradication plan was enacted. The difficulty of rounding up free-ranging livestock caused opposition from some cattlemen, but a tick quarantine was put in place. Some ranchers sold their herds rather than comply, but corrals and dipping vats became commonplace, and the program succeeded. Significant and permanent upgrading occurred but was hampered by the lack of a fence law—an acrimonious economic and political issue involving public safety that was not resolved until 1949.

As the 1920s came to a close, the large number of bank failures was attributed to an excess of localities dependent on a single industry or crop, too few restrictions on banks, and "too many unknown rascals and bad management."[12] Banking scholar Raymond B. Vickers contends that many banks failed through the machinations of grasping men who were outright crooks. In 1929, the wily Amos told a state bankers' convention that Florida had "new blood and new money" and was "on the road to a safe and sound banking system."[13] With strong public backing, Governor Carlton demanded banking legislation. The legislature responded with a major statute that changed capitalization requirements, tightened loan limitations, limited dividends, raised requirements, and increased bank directors' and stockholders' obligations. Failure continued, but in the fall of 1929 some banks reopened and a few new ones were established.

Many prominent officials, including Senator Fletcher and Governor Carlton, attempted to quiet fears by treating the Depression as if it could be talked away or written off with positive thinking. In January 1930, one paper noted: "The state is enjoying its best tourist season. . . . Almost every city and county has pledged itself to its greatest effort this year in construction work. The outlook is indeed bright."[14] Those were hollow words to the person whose property had been lost or whose savings had disappeared. In 1930, Florida's bank failures were still as ubiquitous as mosquitoes.

Looking back over the era, objective Floridians saw a mixed record of accomplishments. Women began entering the workforce in greater numbers, but their entrance and acceptance in the professions was slow. In the field of penal reform, Florida abolished the inhumane convict lease system with its lash and sweatbox that had been in place since 1877. Convict leasing by the state was prohibited in 1919 and at the county level in 1923. The latter action resulted from a scandal involving the beating death at a lumber camp of Martin Tabert, a young white man from South Dakota who had been arrested for vagrancy.

Although public education remained rigidly segregated, the state could claim "progress." In 1920, Florida's school-age population (six to twenty-one years) was 292,199; there were 193,302 whites and 98,898 blacks. Of those, 64 percent of the eligible whites attended school and 47 percent of the blacks. Teaching was one of the few professions in which women were dominant: 5,077 white female teachers as opposed to 902 white males and 1,444 black women teachers contrasted to 196 black men. The doctrine of "separate but equal" as enunciated by the U.S. Supreme Court in 1896 was only half-fulfilled in Florida: separate, yes; equal, no. The average monthly wage in 1920 for a white male teacher was $143.06; his black male counterpart received $71.51. The monthly salaries for white and black women teachers were $99.96 and $51.08, respectively. Total school expenditure for white schools was $8,262,903; for black schools, $643,701. Whites were more numerous than blacks, but the lopsided funding indicates a pronounced bias for whites.

Yet there were persons of good faith, such as State Superintendent of Public Instruction W. S. Cawthon, who reported, "While our progress has been slow [in funding education for blacks], still we are getting more definite and tangible results accomplished and under way."[15] No major educational changes were implemented by 1930, although improvements had been made. The number of white and black teachers, their salaries, and the physical plants where they taught reflected the existing Jim Crow society. The average length of the school year for blacks was 132 days; for whites, it was 160 days. In higher education, the state provided three public institutions: Florida Agricultural and Mechanical College for Negroes and Florida State College for Women, both at Tallahassee, and the University of Florida, for white males, at Gainesville. A number of private institutions existed, including the University of Miami, which opened its doors in 1926.

In race relations, Florida's record was bad, although lynchings declined from eight in 1920 to one in 1930. The revived Ku Klux Klan had a large membership, influenced politics, and used extralegal violence to perpetuate white superiority and black inferiority. The Klan declined toward the decade's end but kept its organization into the 1930s. The 1920s had witnessed some frightful racial episodes. On election day in 1920, a pitched battle at Ocoee in Orange County resulted in the deaths of whites and blacks. A combination lynching and race riot occurred at the small Levy County community of Rosewood during the first week of January 1923. Before it ended, at least eight people, two of them whites, were killed, and the homes and churches owned by blacks were burned.

In many ways, black and white cultures, though separate, ran parallel and often overlapped. The mass of Florida's blacks remained second-class citizens and victims of prejudice throughout the 1920s. Still, there was more progress than retrogression, as some blacks—in the professions and in business—gained economic independence and became a part of the middle class.

Several black Floridians were beginning or continuing distinguished careers. Zora Neale Hurston, born at Eatonville in 1907, would soon establish an enduring literary reputation. Crescent City was the birthplace of A. Philip Randolph, who organized the Brotherhood of Sleeping Car Porters in 1925 and became one of the nation's leaders in both the trade union movement and the civil rights crusade. James Weldon Johnson, born in Jacksonville, achieved national prominence as a poet, editor, teacher, and leader in the National Association for the Advancement of Colored People (NAACP).

The 1920s were a significant period in Florida's modern history. The state gained an international reputation as a vacation spot for tourists and as a desirable place in which to live. Increasingly, retirees selected the peninsula and Panhandle as the domicile of their senior years. Although southern in many ways, Florida had moved into the mainstream of American life. Florida's rate of urbanization was greater than that experienced by its neighboring states. Its image became one of vitality and excitement, of shining cities, of "skyscraper" hotels and banks, of business opportunity, and of the good life. Floridians knew that, despite the prevailing economic crisis, the sun would still shine brightly, the Atlantic and the Gulf would continue to bathe paradise with their warm waters, the fish would bite, and the soil would provide.

Notes

1. See James A. Carter III, "Florida and Rumrunning during National Prohibition." Patricia Buchanan, in "Miami's Bootleg Boom" (1960), quotes Congressman (later mayor of New York City) Fiorello LaGuardia, from the notoriously wet state of New York, as saying, "There are more prohibition lawbreakers in Florida than in my state."

2. *Tallahassee Democrat*, 8 June 1923.

3. Ibid., 16 October 1925, quoting an unnamed northern publication.

4. *Annual Report Banking Department [Florida]*, 1924, 9, hereafter cited as *ARBD*.

5. *Florida Laws 1925*, 1:64–66, 58.

6. *Annual Report Florida Comptroller 1925 and First Six Months 1926*, pp. xiii–xxiv.

7. *ARBD*, 20 June 1926, n.p.

8. *Tallahassee Democrat*, 29 July 1926.

9. Quoted ibid., 14 July 1930.

10. Walter P. Fuller, *This Was Florida's Boom* (St. Petersburg: n.p., n.d.), p. 8.

11. Henry S. Villard, "Florida Aftermath," *Nation*, 6 June 1928, p. 635.

12. H. E. Bierly, in "Open Forum," a column in the *Tallahassee Democrat*, 24 April 1929.

13. The remarks were made at the Florida Bankers Association meeting at Pensacola (see *Tallahassee Democrat,* 22 April 1929).

14. *Tallahassee Democrat,* 16 February 1930.

15. For Cawthon's quote, see *Biennial Report of the Superintendent of Public Instruction of the State of Florida, 1920–1922,* p. 131. For other educational statistics, see ibid., pp. 36, 38–39, 44–45, 76–77.

Bibliography

Buchanan, Patricia. "Miami's Bootleg Boom." *Tequesta* 30 (1970):13–31.

Carper, N. Gordon. "Martin Tabert, Martyr of an Era." *Florida Historical Quarterly* 52, no. 2 (October 1973):115–31.

Carter, James A., III. "Florida Rumrunning during National Prohibition." *Florida Historical Quarterly* 48, no. 1 (July 1969):47–56.

Chalmers, David. "The Ku Klux Klan in the Sunshine State: The 1920s." *Florida Historical Quarterly* 42, no. 3 (January 1964):209–15.

Colburn, David R., and Richard K. Scher. *Florida's Gubernatorial Politics in the Twentieth Century.* Tallahassee: University Presses of Florida, 1980.

Doherty, Herbert J., Jr. "Florida and the Presidential Election of 1928." *Florida Historical Quarterly* 26, no. 2 (October 1947):174–86.

Dovell, Junius E. *History of Banking in Florida,* 1828–1954. Orlando, 1955.

Flynt, Wayne. *Cracker Messiah: Governor Sidney J. Catts of Florida.* Baton Rouge: Louisiana State University Press, 1977.

———. *Duncan Upshaw Fletcher: Dixie's Reluctant Progressive.* Tallahassee: Florida State University Press, 1971.

France, Mary Duncan. "'A Year of Monkey War': The Anti-Evolution Campaign and the Florida Legislature." *Florida Historical Quarterly* 44, no. 2 (October 1975):156–77.

Fuller, Walter P. *This Was Florida's Boom.* St. Petersburg, n.d.

George, Paul S. "Passage to the New Eden: Tourism in Miami from Flagler through Everest G. Sewell." *Florida Historical Quarterly* 59, no. 4 (April 1981):440–63.

Gross, Eric L. "'Somebody Got Drowned, Lord': The Great Okeechobee Hurricane Disaster of 1928." Master's thesis, Florida State University, 1991.

Hughes, M. Edward. "Florida Preachers and the Election of 1928." *Florida Historical Quarterly* 67, no. 2 (October 1988):131–46.

McDonnell, Victoria H. "The Businessman's Politician: A Study of the Administration of John Wellborn Martin, 1925–1929." Master's thesis, University of Florida, 1968.

Nolan, David. *Fifty Feet in Paradise: The Booming of Florida.* New York: Harcourt Brace Jovanovich, 1984.

Rogers, William Warren. *Outposts on the Gulf: Saint George Island and Apalachicola from Early Exploration to World War II.* Gainesville: University Presses of Florida, 1986.

Sessa, Frank B. "Anti-Florida Propaganda and Counter Measures during the 1920s." *Tequesta* 21 (1961):41–51.

———. "Miami in 1926." *Tequesta* 16 (1956):15–36.

———. "Miami on the Eve of the Boom, 1923." *Tequesta* 21 (1961):41–51.

————. "The Real Estate Boom in Miami and Its Environs [1923–1926]." Ph.D. dissertation, University of Pittsburgh, 1950.

Shofner, Jerrell H. "Florida and Black Migration." *Florida Historical Quarterly* 57, no. 3 (January 1979):267–88.

Vickers, Raymond B. *Panic in Paradise: Florida's Banking Crash of 1926*. Tuscaloosa: University of Alabama Press, 1994.

18

The Great Depression

WILLIAM W. ROGERS

Governor Doyle Carlton and state legislators faced hard times in 1931. Old problems had persisted, and new ones demanded attention. Economic news was dismal—both the Florida East Coast and the Seaboard Air Line railroads sank into receivership that year—and the state's financial structure appeared ready to collapse. As Carlton told the legislature, "In the minds of many banking presents the major issue."[1] No one challenged his analysis. The legislature responded with the Banking Act of 1931, which limited depositor withdrawals and directed some banks to call loans in to meet existing obligations. Comptroller Ernest Amos anticipated New Deal legislation to protect deposits. "I know the mere mention of 'guaranteeing deposits' is 'arsenic to banks' but some effective plan could be designed," he asserted.[2]

Florida banks, like those in other states, continued to fail in 1931. Whether large (the Central National Bank of St. Petersburg) or small (the Bank of Chipley), failures did not respect age or prestige. The situation prompted a bit of doggerel: Lawyers are red / Business is blue / If you were a banker / You'd be white-headed too.[3]

The governor and the legislature also grappled with the overall economic crisis. The presidential election would determine the state's and the nation's direction but not until November 1932. Florida's constitution, which forbade bonded indebtedness, prevented bankruptcy, but it also prohibited emergency borrowing. Cities, counties, political subdivisions, and special tax districts were not so limited. Here Florida's debt liability led the nation and was largely in default. The state's lack of funds effectively barred borrowing money on a matching basis from the federal government. Even so, governors Dave Sholtz (1932–36) and Fred P. Cone (1936–40) adroitly obtained money from Washington that did not require matching.

Carlton trimmed services, recommended governmental streamlining, suggested paving roads on a pay-as-you-go basis, and argued for restricting local government bonding. He backed a sales tax to increase revenue while insisting that an income tax would cause the affluent to avoid Florida. His veto of an inheritance tax bill was sustained. The governor opposed another potential revenue source, legalized gambling, on moral grounds, but in 1931 the legislature created a State Racing Commission, legalized pari-mutuel betting, and taxed the proceeds. Joseph E. Widener of Miami's Hialeah race-track lobbied the measure to enactment. When Carlton vetoed it, the solons overrode him and thus began the state's important involvement with horse and dog tracks and jai alai frontons. In 1934, income from admission taxes, commissions on pari-mutuel sales, occupational licenses, and other related receipts totaled $1,072,364; six years later it was $2,348,348.

Cities cut budgets and reduced tax millages. Chambers of commerce urged merchants to offer bargains for citizen home-improvement projects. "Buy Now" campaigns were launched. Typically, in Jacksonville, the Community Chest opened a soup kitchen for the hungry, and the city hired the unemployed on public works. Millionaire Alfred DuPont donated money to employ workers for its public parks. A Lee County commissioner remarked, "We've spent a pile of money but we haven't spent a cent that shouldn't have been spent."[4] Other cities and counties had similar programs, but none could cope with escalating unemployment problems. The state Board of Public Welfare, created in 1927, lacked resources to undertake large-scale relief. Accordingly, municipal and county relief efforts, however inadequate, were much more important before 1935 than was state aid. Pride and insufficient knowledge prompted one state committee on the unemployed to oppose federal assistance and strongly reject the dole system of relief.

Floridians who believed a depression could not occur in their vacation-land deluded themselves. They fantasized that at worst—and always excluding affluent Palm Beach—a few thousand tourists would cancel or abbreviate their annual visits. Lacking smokestack urban centers, Florida presented no stark image of closed factories with padlocked gates. A balmy climate made it difficult to conjure long lines of out-of-work men wearing threadbare overcoats. Yet the Great Depression engulfed Florida and left many of its citizens in misery and out of work, just as elsewhere in the nation.

Of necessity, Florida soon abandoned its philosophy of self-sufficiency; fewer than twenty counties operated public welfare programs. Turning to Washington, Floridians suffered disappointment. President Herbert Hoover, while sympathetic, declined to order direct governmental economic intervention. By 1930 a political stalemate had developed between the White House and the Democratic Congress. Hoover's private relief policy had foundered. A discontented "Bonus Army" of veterans marched on Washington; their hovels and tents at Anacostia Flats were burned and the marchers were dispelled by force; a food strike was threatened by midwestern farmers; violence flared intermittently; and communist agitators stirred discontent. Across America the homeless huddled in their "Hoovervilles"— hastily constructed clusters of shacks. Many young men and women joined adult transients to ride the rails and camp in hobo jungles. Florida drew them like a magnet, and relief rolls swelled. Immigration was discouraged, and for three winter seasons state policemen blocked roads and refused to let indigent transients cross into Florida. Indecision, resentment, despair, and fear were evident everywhere—the United States had lost its confidence.

The impasse was broken partially in July 1932, when Hoover approved a law that extended Reconstruction Finance Corporation powers, but it was too little, too late. Governor Carlton asked for $500,000, and Florida got its first relief funds in September. The number of families that went on relief represented 36 percent of the black and 22 percent of the white population. Per capita income had reached a low of $289. The presidential elections of 1932 promised new directions in the government's attack on the depression. Hoover became the scapegoat for what had gone wrong, and, as the election approached, the nation demanded change. Florida Democrats, who controlled state politics, supported New York's governor Franklin D. Roosevelt against Hoover. Promising relief, recovery, and reform through a New Deal for the American people, Roosevelt won the White House and easily carried Florida, where he received 74.9 percent of the popular vote.

Significant contests in state elections, including the race for state comptroller, also occurred in 1932. Besides running against two strong candidates, John M. Lee and Van C. Swearinger, Ernest Amos had an extra burden. J. Tom Watson, his nemesis from a previous impeachment attempt, based a gubernatorial campaign on removing the comptroller from office. Prosperity would never return, Watson declared, until the political power of Amos and the state banking interests was broken. Lee won the runoff primary comfortably and ended the career of Florida's most controversial comptroller. In the general election Lee had no difficulty defeating Republican Armonis F. Knotts.

The gubernatorial primary bulged with eight candidates, among them former governors Cary A. Hardee and John W. Martin. Brooklyn-born David Sholtz, a Jewish lawyer from Daytona Beach, placed second to Martin in the first primary. Known for his state Chamber of Commerce work, Sholtz advocated improved education. Despite traces of anti-Semitism, he carried the runoff to win by more than 71,000 votes. Sholtz then defeated Republican William J. Howey, winning as a strong Roosevelt supporter. The Prohibition issue prompted some cynics to say that Sholtz won because people confused him with Schlitz and thought they were voting to bring back beer. Repeal came with ratification of the Twenty-First Amendment on 5 December 1933.

Unlike the hotly contested governor's race, U.S. Senator Duncan U. Fletcher faced no opposition in 1932. Two years later, the Senate election pitted incumbent Park Trammell against former Alabamian Claude Pepper and three other candidates, one of them Hortense E. Wells, a World War I ambulance driver and Democratic National Committeewoman. Trammell won easily.

Politics remained important to Floridians throughout the decade. In 1936 they reaffirmed their support of Roosevelt by giving him 76.1 percent of the vote over Republican Alfred M. Landon. The deaths of Senators Trammell and Fletcher in 1936 forced the calling of a special primary to fill their seats. Pepper was elected to one seat without opposition. Charles O. Andrews beat former governor Carlton in a close primary, then defeated Republican H. C. Babcock. After serving an uncompleted two-year Senate term, Pepper ran for reelection in 1938 and did so as a strong New Dealer. Facing four opponents, including former governor Sholtz, he won the primary without a runoff. Pepper's 82.4 percent of the vote in the general election was a stinging defeat for Republican Thomas E. Swanson.

Even by Florida standards, the fourteen opponents who sought the Democratic nomination for governor in 1936 were a large number. The field included former governor Martin, as well as Raleigh W. Petteway, who finished first, and Fred P. Cone, who trailed by 5,000 votes. Although voters gave Roosevelt a landslide, Cone's performance demonstrated their independence. The Lake City banker's conservative campaign called for "lowering the budget to balance taxes instead of raising taxes to balance the budget." The voters agreed, and Cone handily defeated Petteway in the runoff primary. He then swamped Elvey E. Callaway, his Republican adversary.

The 1940 contests likewise commanded state attention. Roosevelt won an unprecedented third term over Republican Wendell L. Willkie, taking Florida by 359,334 to 126,158 votes. Seeking reelection to his Senate seat, Charles O. Andrews faced five opponents, among them Jerry W. Carter, former governor Cone, and Bernarr McFadden, a political novice better known as a physical culturalist and publisher of true romance magazines. Andrews led runner-up Carter by 100,000 votes and increased his margin in the runoff primary. Republican Miles H. Draper withdrew, leaving the incumbent unopposed. The Democratic gubernatorial nomination was sought by eleven candidates. Future governor Fuller Warren was one of them, but the leading aspirants were Polk County's Spessard L. Holland and Volusia County's Francis P. Whitehair. Holland finished first, but Whitehair forced a runoff in which Holland repeated his primary victory. Republicans declined to oppose him in the general election.

Florida's politics were highly partisan and individualistic during the Great Depression, which resulted in a string of one-term governors and the absence of political machines. Within the framework of a one-party system, the politics were deceptively complex. Roosevelt's personality and federal government activities overshadowed state politicians and their accomplishments. No sweeping political changes occurred, although in 1937 the poll tax, a means of disfranchising blacks, was repealed. Repeal meant the addition of more poor white voters but had no significant impact on blacks. Women did not vote as a bloc, but they became important in the overall political process. Increasingly they sought political office, especially at the local level. At the decade's end the state was still solidly Democratic, and, with few exceptions, Roosevelt was a folk hero. Many named their children after him.

Early in the decade, though, Floridians had been too caught up in the present to worry about future politics. Even before the new president took office in March 1933, the national experience became an action movie with the film speeded up. Sometimes in the frantic whir of the reels, images blurred. An air of unreality loomed, for instance, around an event in Florida that occurred on 15 February. President-elect Roosevelt had begun to speak at Miami's Bayfront Park when pistol shots rang out. An assassin's bullets missed him but wounded five others. Unemployed bricklayer Guiseppe Zangara was arrested as the assailant. After wounded Chicago mayor Anton Cermak died, Zangara was retried for murder, convicted, and electrocuted.

Roosevelt's election as such accomplished little toward calming fears. Before he took office, the banking crisis became so serious that numerous governors began calling "banking holidays," and the index of industrial production continued to drop. Runs on banks and hoarding of currency were rampant. On 4 March, Governor Sholtz, in Washington for the inauguration, declared a five-day banking holiday for Florida (later extended to 15 March). Roosevelt then decreed a four-day national banking holiday effective 6 March. The use of scrip was briefly allowed, and an embargo was put on the export of gold, silver, and currency. The public responded well, and within two weeks stock prices rose, some hoarded currency was reinvested, and gold and gold certificates were returned to the treasury and reserve banks. With the prompt passage of a banking act and a reassuring fireside chat from Roosevelt, confidence rose and the banking crisis was checked.

Sholtz soon permitted state banks to resume business under certain conditions. He promised "banking laws with teeth," and the legislature responded by increasing the powers of liquidators and receivers, regulating how banks issued preferred stock, and toughening penalties. Floridians took the crisis calmly. Instead of hoarding money, they used their cash for local purchases. Many stores took personal checks even though they could not be deposited, and credit was extended. Businesses advertised that they would accept checks and held "New Deal Sales." In a statewide radio address, Sholtz proclaimed that he wanted each citizen to "keep your chin where you have it now—up. If you have confidence in God and man, maintain that confidence."[5] Many state banks and a number of national banks were operating by 14 March, and Comptroller Lee remarked in June, "I believe that we are soon to be on the threshold of a new era in banking."[6] He was correct. The decade's remaining legislative sessions did not have to deal with either the deflation of the 1920s or the severe depression of the early 1930s.

During the special congressional session of 1933, known as the "Hundred Days," a record number of acts permanently changed Florida and the nation. They spawned a bewildering array of bureaus and agencies. A bemused public called the mixture "alphabet soup." Confusion and conflict inevitably arose. Some of the programs succeeded; others did not. Even so, the American people got the action Roosevelt had promised: the Emergency Banking Act; the Glass-Stegall Act, which divorced investment banking from deposit banking and created the Federal Deposit Insurance Corporation (FDIC); the Securities and Exchange Act; and many others. Rural and urban citizens were helped by the Emergency Farm Mortgage Act and the Home Owners Loan Corporation Act (HOLC). To aid in distributing relief funds, the Federal Emergency Relief Administration (FERA) was created. Interior Secretary Harold L. Ickes directed a massive building program known as the Public Works Administration (PWA). To offer relief even faster and more directly, the short-lived Civil Works Administration (CWA) was established. It gave the word "boondoggle" to the country and was criticized in Florida by some turpentine operators and citrus growers who objected to "high" CWA payment levels.

Southern states such as Florida benefitted from a myriad of other programs. The most popular New Deal agency was the Civilian Conservation Corps (CCC). Known as the "tree army," the CCC engaged in various reforestation and conservation projects. Nationally it provided work for more than 2 million young men between the ages of eighteen and twenty-five. Most were from economically impoverished families, and no state benefitted more than did Florida. Agricultural problems were addressed through allotment and crop-reduction programs established under the Agricultural Adjustment Act. The AAA affected all of Florida's farmers. Because industry and organized labor were no less devastated than agriculture, Congress created the National Recovery Administration (NRA). With its symbolic Blue Eagle, the NRA attempted to put into effect industrial codes of fair competition and prices among the nation's industries. Its other aim was to secure collective bargaining for organized labor.

The popular New Deal measures resulted in a great Democratic victory in the 1934 off-year elections, and set in motion the Second New Deal. What followed was a policy of deficit financing—the idea that direct government intervention or "pump priming" was sometimes necessary in a capitalist economy. While continuing some relief and recovery programs, the administration concentrated on long-range reform. One many-faceted program was the Works Progress Administration (WPA), which aimed to provide work for the employable in positions they were able to handle. Between 1935 and 1941, the WPA completed almost 1.5 million projects, although critics claimed that the initials meant "We Poke Along." Many WPA projects benefitted Florida, including the work of its subdivisions such as the National Youth Administration (NYA), Federal Theatre Project, Federal Writers' Project, and Federal Art Project. By 1935 the WPA was primarily responsible for most of the able-bodied workers on Florida's relief rolls. Opposition to the National Social Security Act of 1935 yielded eventually to acceptance, and Social Security became a permanent part of American life. Also in 1935, the National Labor Relations Act (NLRA) reflected the New Deal's sympathy toward organized labor, and its provisions spurred the growth of the AFL (American Federation of Labor) and especially the CIO (Congress of Industrial Organizations).

In the late 1930s, leftist radicals attacked the New Deal for not going far enough, while extreme conservatives believed that it had gone too far. After 1938, conservative southern politicians often allied with Republicans to defeat or emasculate New Deal measures, and popular support also declined. Roosevelt had cause to be grateful to Florida's Senator Pepper, whose campaign included support of a stalled wages and hours bill. Pepper's reelection assured congressional passage. Roosevelt's attempted "purge" of conservative Democratic senators and representatives in 1938 failed. As New Deal support waned, gathering threats to world peace by Germany, Italy, and Japan resulted in war in Asia and Europe. Roosevelt, by shifting his emphasis to a program of domestic preparedness and support for the Allied powers, held the Democratic coalition of liberals, southerners, blacks, ethnic groups, and organized labor together and won a third term.

The experiences of Apalachicola and Franklin County were a microcosm of the New Deal. People there were reassured on seeing evidence of FDIC membership posted in the local bank's window and the Blue Eagle posters in various stores. The WPA took over local public works projects and employed hundreds of people. FERA funds financed a Carrabelle mattress factory and an airport at Apalachicola. Other WPA and PWA allocations further stimulated the economy. A new courthouse was built and opened with federal monies. In 1937, forty-six county men were enrolled in the CCC. By 1938, the county had 125 citizens working on federal projects and another 281 engaged in part-time work. The most visible achievement was the opening of the John Gorrie Bridge. Contact with east Florida had been restricted for more than 100 years by Apalachicola Bay; the townspeople now had a convenient modern bridge and causeway, which stood as a symbol of hope.

State and local politics and programs also had their influence. The state's most valuable possession was its people. The state grew more slowly than during the 1920s, but it did not stagnate. Total population increased between 1930 and 1940 by 409,203. There were 1,897,414 Floridians in 1940; blacks numbered 433,714 and whites 1,037,198. Black and white women slightly outnumbered their male counterparts.

Few jobs in urban centers, reduced living expenses, and greater availability of food caused many people to remain in rural areas. Between 1930 and 1940, Florida's urban white population increased only slightly, from 72.3 to 72.5 percent. Its black urban population actually declined from 27.7 to 27.4 percent. The number of farms grew by 3,500, and the average acreage rose from 85.2 to 133.0. With 173,065 residents, Jacksonville was only marginally larger than Miami, which had 171,172. Tampa was the state's third-most-populous city, with more than 100,000 residents. Florida was urban, but St. Petersburg was the only other city with more than 50,000. Otherwise, only Orlando and West Palm Beach had more than 30,000 people.

Changes during the Depression also affected the state's Native Americans. In 1930 Florida had approximately 500 Indians. Known collectively as Seminoles, they were dispersed through much of south Florida. Poverty, lack of organization, and the presence of at least two distinct groups threatened their tribal integrity. In 1934, the federal government offered a program that encouraged tribal government, land purchases to permit concentration of population, and education. This Indian New Deal fostered a sense of viability. Aid was channeled through CCC–Indian Division work programs to help fight persistent social problems.

Since its people were Florida's greatest asset, their overall health was fundamentally important. In the 1930s significant progress was made in this area. The Florida constitution of 1885 had mandated a State Board of Public Health, but the agency remained underfunded and neglected until 1931, when the legislature provided for county health departments. Counties were allowed to levy special taxes to support them, and Taylor County was the first to establish a health unit. Ultimately the activities of these units included communicable disease control, hygienic programs, protection of food and milk, and extensive laboratory work. After the Social Security Act of 1935, more health funds became available. By 1940 the state board operated a mobile X-ray unit and had many clinics (segregated by race). Because Florida led the nation in deaths from syphilis, sixty-seven clinics were set up, and they proved effective. Important work was accomplished in combatting hookworm, malaria, and pneumonia. In 1939, state officials drafted a school health plan and coordinated it with community health programs. WPA funds also were expended for sanitation and various medical projects.

For Floridians to achieve their potential, the state had to have an efficient public school system. The Depression dealt a crippling blow to that ambition. Funding for public education dropped, and in 1931 Florida ranked forty-third in average teacher pay and thirty-ninth in money spent annually per student. A wrenching austerity program eliminated small high schools, enlarged elementary classes, retained old textbooks, pooled library books countrywide, and reduced purchases of equipment. Tallahassee and Leon County were among Florida's more stable areas, yet in 1933 many schools, most of them black, were closed, and the academic year was reduced to six months. In 1934 Florida had 446 school buses with factory-made bodies and 752 with homemade ones. Salary reductions meant that by 1934 the state owed teachers $312,408 in back pay. The average salary in 1936 was $1,039 for a white and $495 for a black teacher. In the mid-1930s the state department of education estimated that only 10 to 15 percent of schoolchildren

Seminole family members gather outside Miami in 1929.

would attend college. Based on that projection, the department opposed making the achievement of college entrance requirements a goal of a high school education.

With returning prosperity in the late 1930s, the public school system improved. The educational budget was increased under Governor Cone, although teachers' salaries remained low and tied to race, with blacks always at a disadvantage. On the plus side, the average length of school terms in grades one through twelve achieved near equality: for blacks 165 and for whites 175 days. State laws required compulsory school attendance. By the end of the 1930s, while much remained to be done, progress had been made, especially by blacks. Of the 663,547 young white people of school age, 54.7 percent attended in 1940. There were 195,274 blacks eligible to attend school, and 49.2 percent of them did so.

Federal funds greatly helped Florida education. More than 500 schools, in addition to playgrounds and athletic fields, were built or refurbished by the WPA. Its funds were also used to provide school lunches. The state's colleges received WPA appropriations for capital improvements programs, and the WPA's education division employed more than 1,600 teachers. Vocational courses were encouraged, including home economics, agriculture, trade and industrial education, distributive education, and rehabilitation.

Beginning in 1935, the National Youth Administration (NYA) administered a work-relief and employment program for school-age persons and provided part-time employment for needy secondary, college, and graduate students.

The state's school program, including higher education, remained segregated by race. Florida Agricultural and Mechanical College for Negroes at Tallahassee continued as one of two land grant institutions. It offered a variety of courses other than engineering and agriculture. A much larger choice of fields was possible at Gainesville's all-white, all-male University of Florida. It boasted a College of Law and a broad liberal arts program, while no state law school was available for blacks. The Florida State College for Women at Tallahassee had programs in teacher education but built its strongest reputation in the liberal arts.

Private colleges and universities, such as the University of Miami, begun in 1926, struggled to survive. Despite the times, the University of Tampa opened as Tampa Junior College in 1931 and in 1933 became a four-year institution. Palm Beach Junior College was established in 1933, and the next year Jacksonville Junior College began classes (it became Jacksonville University in 1956). St. Petersburg Junior College, Stetson University, Florida Southern College, and Rollins College all weathered the storm. Black private institutions such as Edward Waters College and Bethune-Cookman College continued to serve their students.

Because of Florida's climate, geographical location, and soil, agriculture was of paramount importance. In 1940 Florida had 4,500 more white farm owners or operators than in 1930; black owners and operators decreased by 2,700. Only slight increases in farm mechanization were registered. The greatest change came in the number of farm dwellings lighted by electricity. Federal programs helped reduce regional utility rates of private corporations, and Floridians benefitted directly from the Rural Electrification Administration, which, after its creation in 1935, generated and distributed electricity in isolated rural areas. The 11 percent of Florida farm homes lighted by electricity in 1930 increased to 26.5 percent in 1940.

From the decade's beginning to its end, the state's production of beef cattle and chickens increased. Income from milk ($15,859,946) grew fivefold. Florida established itself as a permanent major producer of winter vegetables. Plant pathologist Herman Hamilton Wedgworth developed viable fertilizers for the rich muck soil of the Everglades and grew disease-resistant vegetables, and by 1934 his Belle Glade plant was shipping vegetables in refrigerated railroad cars to northern markets. The Duda family and

Picking and crating celery in April 1930 at Sanford, where one-third of the nation's celery supply was grown.

others soon transferred the new techniques to the muckland north of Lake Apopka. By 1940 tomatoes, watermelons, string beans, lima beans, green peas, cucumbers, peppers, and celery offered significant sources of income. The Everglades' persistent flooding problems were eliminated when FERA and WPA funds were used to build a dike around Lake Okeechobee and improve the adjacent drainage canals. This work, plus the establishment of a federal sugarcane experiment station at Canal, made possible the development of a lucrative private sugar industry. Corn brought in $4 million in 1940; it remained an important money crop, as did Irish potatoes, peanuts, velvet beans, and tobacco. The cotton crop of 1940 generated less cash ($1,225,000) than did cabbage ($2,620,533).

Timber was considered a crop, and from it emerged a large pulp paper industry. The Florida Forest Service (created in 1935), the CCC, and private individuals launched reforestation programs. At the same time, Charles H. Henry developed an inexpensive way to manufacture paper from southern slash pine. Cutover land was replanted, and existing forests offered the possibility of cheap paper products. The decision of the nation's newspaper owners to convert to pulp paper newsprint was especially important to Florida. In 1931 the International Paper Company's operation at Panama City became Florida's first mill. Other companies followed, and by the late

1930s pulp mills also were operating at Pensacola, Port St. Joe, Jacksonville, Fernandina, and Palatka. Alfred I. DuPont purchased 70,000 acres of land in the Gulf counties of Walton, Bay, and Franklin. His Port St. Joe mill, opened in 1938 at a cost of $7 million, was the largest in Florida.

The citrus industry expanded. Dating from the establishment in 1909 of the Florida Citrus Exchange, growers had attempted to formulate industry-wide policy. The advantages of volume buying and selling were advocated by local exchanges, but many growers preferred independent marketing. Such practices prevented uniformity of product, and grove owners who shipped green fruit injured the industry. Improvements came in 1935 when the state legislature created the Florida Citrus Commission. The agency, which was financed by a tax on citrus, encouraged growers to ship quality fruit and engaged in an effective advertising campaign. The state's share of the 1940 citrus market was impressive: tangerines brought in $1,671,656, grapefruit $7,637,836, and oranges $25,342,079.

Federal land banks aided Florida's farmers by providing long-term loans, and federal involvement in the broad area of agrarian life was profound: government subsidy payments in 1935 amounted to $1,129,878. AAA agents, county agents, and various agricultural specialists were funded in part from Washington. Nathan Mayo, Florida's commissioner of agriculture, established farmers' markets with New Deal financing. The WPA attempted to aid Florida's commercial fishing industry, which rewarded its participants mostly with hard work and meager incomes. The agency worked out a cooperative program of replanting and renewing the geographically limited industry. The main profits came from oyster beds located along the upper Florida coast from Cedar Key in Levy County to Panama City in Bay County. The shrimp industry soon became an additional means of income.

Changes in farming operations that had long-run benefits were sometimes painful in the short run. As large-scale agriculture became necessary for economic survival, increased use of machinery diminished the number of tenant farmers. Although the transition for tenants was difficult, the curse of sharecropping was ending. Unskilled fruit and vegetable pickers received low pay for their seasonal work. The migrant laborers followed the harvest seasons, working the Florida vegetable farms and fruit groves in the fall and winter and moving north for the spring and summer berries and vegetables. No labor was more difficult than the relentless leaning over required of cutters in Florida's sugarcane fields, where charges of peonage occasionally were raised.

New Deal legislation favored union activity, resulting in tense confrontation between some owners and workers. A Polk County citrus workers' union, for instance, met physical opposition. In 1938 the United Cannery, Agriculture, Packing and Allied Workers of America, a CIO union, struck over wage reductions. Governor Cone helped to mediate the dispute, which ended in compromise.

The natural environment, as well as the work environment, was fostered by governmental action. The national government bought land in north Florida for the St. Marks Wildlife Refuge and elsewhere added many acres to the Ocala, Apalachicola, Osceola, and other national forests. The CCC's work also had environmental and aesthetic consequences. By the 1930s naval stores and logging firms had practically depleted longleaf yellow pine forests, and the timber industry had declined. Profits were low, and operators kept their black workers in virtual peonage, especially in the turpentine camps. The turnaround came through reseeding programs led by the CCC. Many of the twenty-six agency camps were in national forests. In its nine years in Florida, the agency enrolled more than 50,000 young men in segregated camps and about $30 million was expended. The CCC planted 13,605,000 trees, cut 14,554 miles of firebreaks, and improved thousands of acres of forest land. It cooperated with the Florida Parks Service and the National Park Service to build Torreya State Park and similar projects that became models for the nation.

In these and other ways the New Deal left an indelible mark on Florida. The WPA's public works projects continued into the early 1940s. Florida led the nation in WPA airport construction. Tampa benefitted, for example, by expansion of its airport and construction of a large dry dock. Statewide, the WPA built 800 public buildings and constructed bridges, roads (more than 6,000 miles), culverts, parks, playgrounds, athletic fields, public housing, and hospitals. It conserved beaches against erosion, built seawalls, and helped complete the intracoastal waterway. Artists, writers, sculptors, musicians, and teachers were funded in their work. The Federal Writers' Project employed historians and others to collect public records, and an excellent guide to Florida was compiled. The Federal Theatre's productions at Miami, Jacksonville, and Tampa, plus its statewide touring company, employed out-of-work actors, playwrights, and stage personnel.

In 1935, Key West became a monument to federal-state-local cooperation. Bankrupt, and with 80 percent of their citizens on relief, local officials asked the governor to declare a state of emergency. His decree authorized the FERA to take over the city. By those means Key West was revitalized,

The Civilian Conservation Corps (CCC), the first New Deal agency to operate in Florida, began at Eastport in Duval County in 1933. Before its termination in 1942, the CCC gave work to more than 50,000 Floridians between the ages of eighteen and twenty-five. Though best known for planting millions of trees and clearing thousands of miles of firebreaks, the agency also helped to establish wildlife preserves and numerous state parks, including Hillsborough near Tampa and O'Leno near High Springs. In the photograph, a CCC official is shown in September 1936 inspecting a bridge and road fill constructed at O'Leno State Park.

as citizens contributed long hours to cleaning streets, developing beaches, renovating houses and hotels, and improving sanitation facilities. New Deal funds enabled the town to become a bustling resort city, aided by construction of a highway to the mainland, 100 miles away. The project was threatened when disaster struck on Labor Day, 2 September 1935. A hurricane slashed the Keys, where about 400 lives were lost. Henry Flagler's Overseas Railroad, completed in 1912, was so badly damaged that it was sold to the state. With federal and state assistance, the Monroe County Toll Bridge Commission took it over, and U.S. Highway 1 was completed to Key West in 1938.

At the state level, the State Board of Public Welfare, backed by Governor Sholtz, concerned itself with a broad range of social problems, including child welfare. After 1935, when state participation in relief programs increased, the board enlarged its operations and in 1937 became the Department of Social Welfare. Sholtz pushed the state toward a greater role but was restrained when the state supreme court declared unconstitutional his attempt to pledge Florida's credit on a loan. Sholtz persisted, and in 1935 the state allocated $2 million toward its responsibility for the welfare program. Tax revenues were to be applied to relief payments (this required the successful passage of a constitutional amendment), for schools, for the State Welfare Board, and for a State Planning Board.

After 1935, Florida evolved past its traditional status as a small-government state. The forces of change were inexorable, and the result was inevitable: complex, complicated government on a scale necessary to meet the needs of a growing state. The trend took on momentum as the economic situation improved toward the end of the Sholtz administration and throughout that of Governor Cone. Setbacks occurred, but the line on the prosperity graph was upward. Floridians welcomed a constitutional change that authorized a homestead tax exemption. State government action and recovery were further aided by the Murphy Act. The collapse of the 1920s land boom had left much real estate abandoned and subject to delinquent taxes. Cone wanted taxes collected and homesteads settled on the lands. In 1937, the Murphy Act allowed the sale of tax-delinquent land for tax certificates, whereby shrewd buyers obtained deeds at a fraction of land value. The public gained by having the land restored to the tax rolls.

Tourism and its economic benefits experienced renewed vigor. The number of tourists had dropped to a half million in 1932, but a comeback was evident by 1934. The 2 million who came in 1935 created the largest tourist season in state history, and Floridians welcomed the $625 million they left behind. In 1936, the *Tampa Tribune* boasted that tourism "is our richest crop. . . . It rides in and rides out, leaving its money as it goes."[7] Building permits for hotel and residential construction had dropped to less than $400,000 in 1932—one real estate developer was reduced to advertising five-acre farms for $60 each—but in 1936 building permits exceeded $9 million, and on Miami Beach's Collins Avenue a line of Art Deco hotels rose from the sand.

Commercial aviation, begun in the 1920s, expanded. By 1939 Florida had three scheduled airlines: Pan American, Eastern, and National. Adding to the growing private freight and passenger service was the decision of the Army Air Corps to train many of its pilots in Florida. By 1940 Army and Navy airfields were established at Miami, Tampa, Orlando, Jacksonville, Pensacola, Valparaiso, and Arcadia. Others followed as military aviation became a major industry.

Marjorie Kinnan Rawlings came to Florida from Rochester, New York, in 1928. Living in the sparsely settled scrub at Cross Creek south of Gainesville, she divided her time between growing oranges and writing fiction. In several notable books, which included *South Moon Under* (1933); *The Yearling* (1938), which won a Pulitzer Prize; and the autobiographical *Cross Creek* (1942), she took as her subjects the proud taciturn Crackers who eked out a bare subsistence from the fields, woods, and lakes of Florida's half-wild interior. In a fitting tribute, her friend and attorney Philip S. May, of Jacksonville, wrote her in 1947: "Ponce de León discovered Florida in 1513, but he had found only the physical and material Florida. Then, more than 400 years later, you came to discover the heart and spirit of Florida and revealed them to the world in writings of rare beauty and sensitiveness."

New Deal programs did not solve unemployment in Florida, nor did they end the Great Depression. World War II did that. Yet they galvanized Floridians and reversed the slide of economic decline. Without question the New Deal supplied desperately needed funds, and Roosevelt's leadership gave Florida citizens a powerful psychological boost. The 1930s were a massive lesson in overcoming adversity. During the decade the state's physical contours, urban and rural, changed. A new concept of state government responsibilities emerged, and the necessary agencies to fulfill the obligations became fact.

The Miami Beach Lions Club exhibits its optimism in the midst of the Great Depression.

Floridians sought ways to lift themselves out of their misery (hence the popularity of Margaret Mitchell's novel *Gone with the Wind* and the movie that followed). Unable to afford membership in a country club, they seized on miniature golf as a leisure-time substitute. In numerous inspiring ways they discovered that they possessed reservoirs of fortitude, strength, and good humor. As one writer noted, the title song of Walt Disney's cartoon "Who's Afraid of the Big Bad Wolf" became a metaphor for their struggle against the Great Depression.

Notes

1. *Tallahassee Daily Democrat,* 18 April 1931.

2. *Annual Report Banking Department [Florida],* 30 June 1931, p. 5, hereafter cited as *ARBD.*

3. *Tallahassee Daily Democrat,* 2 February 1933.

4. Lyn Rainard, "Ready Cash on Easy Terms: Local Responses to the Depression in Lee County," p. 297.

5. *Jacksonville Florida Times Union,* 10 March 1933.

6. *ARBD,* 30 June 1933, p. 6.

7. *Tampa Tribune,* 6 April 1936.

Bibliography

Buchanan, Patricia. "Miami's Bootleg Boom." *Tequesta* 30 (1970):13–31.

Cox, Merlin G. "David Sholtz: New Deal Governor of Florida." *Florida Historical Quarterly* 43, no. 2 (October 1964):142–52.

Dunn, James William. "The New Deal and Florida Politics." Ph.D. dissertation, Florida State University, 1971.

Ginzl, David J. "The Politics of Patronage Florida Republicans during the Hoover Administration." *Florida Historical Quarterly* 61, no. 1 (July 1982):1–19.

Hughes, Melvin Edward, Jr. "William J. Howey and His Florida Dreams." *Florida Historical Quarterly* 66, no. 3 (January 1988):243–64.

Kersey, Harry A., Jr. *The Florida Seminoles and the New Deal, 1933–1942.* Boca Raton: Florida Atlantic University Press, 1989.

La Godna, Martin M. "Greens, Grist and Guernseys: Development of the Florida State Agricultural Marketing System." *Florida Historical Quarterly* 53, no. 2 (October 1974): 146–63.

Loftin, Bernadette K. "A Woman Liberated: Lillian C. West, Editor." *Florida Historical Quarterly* 52, no. 4 (April 1974):396–403.

Long, Durward. "Key West and the New Deal, 1934–1936." *Florida Historical Quarterly* 46, no. 3 (January 1968):209–18.

Lowry, Charles B. "The PWA in Tampa: A Case Study." *Florida Historical Quarterly* 52, no. 4 (April 1974):363–80.

Mardis, John. "Federal Theatre in Florida." Ph.D. dissertation, University of Florida, 1972.

Rainard, R. Lyn. "Ready Cash on Easy Terms: Local Responses to the Depression in Lee County." *Florida Historical Quarterly* 64, no. 3 (January 1986):284–300.

Sewell, J. Richard. "Cross-Florida Barge Canal, 1927–1968." *Florida Historical Quarterly* 46, no. 4 (April 1968):369–83.

Shofner, Jerrell H. "Roosevelt's 'Tree Army': The Civilian Conservation Corps in Florida." *Florida Historical Quarterly* 65, no. 4 (April 1987):433–56.

Snyder, Robert E. "Marion Post and the Farm Security Administration in Florida." *Florida Historical Quarterly* 65, no. 4 (April 1987):457–79.

Stoesen, Alexander R. "The Senatorial Career of Claude D. Pepper." Ph.D. dissertation, University of North Carolina, 1965.

19

World War II

GARY R. MORMINO

For a state that trafficked in hyperbole, Florida had ample reasons to welcome the first Sunday in December 1941. Not since the giddy days of the mid-1920s had residents of the Sunshine State expressed such optimism. Symbolically, the first Sunday of December marked the official beginning of Florida's tourism season, but by the Sunday afternoon of December 7, news of Pearl Harbor shattered the expectations of beaches filled with free-spending tourists.

On the eve of Pearl Harbor, Floridians, like most Americans, were deeply divided over the questions of isolationism, neutrality, and intervention. But as the *Tallahassee Democrat* editorialized: "Japan has done one thing for us. The cowardly attack . . . has united the nation as nothing else could have done."[1] A surge of patriotism swept the state. In Pensacola and Quincy, civic clubs pledged cash prizes to the first aviator to drop a bomb on Tokyo or the first Florida boy to kill a Japanese soldier.

The realities of war quickly hit home. In the weeks after Pearl Harbor, at a time when Allied hopes were dimmed by Japanese and German successes, two Floridians offered hope. Alexander Ramsey "Sandy" Nininger Jr., a Fort Lauderdale resident and graduate of West Point, was killed on 12 January 1942 in the Philippines. For his gallantry, he was awarded the first Medal of Honor of the war.[2] Arguably the war's first American hero was a twenty-six-year-old north Florida farm boy. For the duration, editorial writers and war bond promoters summoned Americans to cherish the name and deeds of Colin Purdie Kelly Jr. A West Point graduate, Kelly stirred American spirits when newspaper reports recorded that, after the Japanese attacked the Philippines, Kelly saved his air crew and then sank an enemy battleship by ramming it with his crippled B-17 bomber. Later reports revised the narrative. Today, Four Freedoms Park in Madison honors Kelly.

The explosive growth of military establishments represented the most tangible evidence of war. Florida, once the Campground State, had become a citadel. Home to a handful of military installations before 1939, Florida soon bristled with 172 military installations, ranging from megacomplexes at the U.S. Army's Camp Blanding and Eglin Army Air Field to fledgling facilities such as the Sopchoppy Bombing Range and the Naples Army Air Field.

Year-round sunshine, sandy beaches, and a jungle-like terrain made Florida especially attractive for military training. Pork-barrel politics, masterfully practiced by U.S. Senator Claude Pepper and Congressman Robert "He-Coon" Sikes, also contributed to Florida's makeover. The evolution of northwest Florida graphically illustrates the success of Sikes. Elected to Congress in 1940, he procured nine military bases before his retirement in the 1970s.

Camp Blanding also represented the transforming wand of federal largess. Conceived in 1939 as a summer camp for the Florida National Guard, Blanding was carved from a 27,000-acre preserve in rural Clay County. With the coming of war, construction companies employed 21,000 carpenters and laborers to expand the base. So many migrants flocked to the site that the Florida Welfare Board distributed food to the needy. To relieve the congested roads, a special train carried more than one thousand workers between Jacksonville and Starke. In a February 16, 1942, article in the *New York Sun,* reporter Ward Morehouse captured the frantic mood:

> Starke is gauche. In its present incarnation it is a town created and spoiled by defense dollars. With its over-lighted facades, its blazing interiors, its fluorescent tubing, its while-u-wait photo studios, its hell-red neons, its cheap jewelry displays and its gaudy movie palaces . . . Starke had gone from a population of 1,500 (Home of the Sweetest Strawberries This Side of Heaven) to a population of nobody knows what. Starke, an overnight gold-rush town as a result of the national emergency, is as fantastic a spot as America now presents.

The urgency of mobilization imposed limits on future Camp Blandings. An expedient solution was found in an unlikely setting: Florida's resort beach hotels. Humorists initially spoofed the notion of raw recruits sleeping in the splendorous Don CeSar or Ponce de Leon Hotels, but Undersecretary of War Robert Patterson disarmed critics by insisting that "the best hotel room is none too good for the American soldier." Florida's hoteliers, expecting a banner 1942 season, initially balked at the proposal, but traveling

Army Air Forces trainees march to their classroom in Miami Beach. The Air Forces occupied 70,000 hotel rooms on the beach, where one-fourth of all air officers and one-fifth of all air enlisted men received basic training. The largest ground army basic training center in the state was Camp Blanding, near Starke. At its peak during World War II, Blanding was Florida's fourth-largest city (after Jacksonville, Miami, and Tampa).

restrictions, the presence of German U-boats, and appeals to patriotism and pocketbook persuaded the industry to turn over the keys to the military. Every major hotel but the Suwannee in St. Petersburg was transformed into a training facility. By February 1942, the first wave of ninety-day wonders arrived in Miami. By fall, almost 300 hotels in Miami and Miami Beach hosted 78,000 military "guests." The government purchased some of the elegant hotels, including the Biltmore in Coral Gables. The Hollywood Beach Hotel became a naval training school, the Breakers in Palm Beach saw service as an army hospital, and the rustic Everglades Rod and Gun Club hosted the Coast Guard during the war. Dan Moody's experience must have been repeated many times. The young Virginian arrived at Miami Beach on 29 January 1944, and dutifully wrote his parents on Hotel Blackstone stationary: "Mother, this is the most beautiful place that I have ever seen. . . . I really think when the war is over, I'll move down here."[3]

The Sunshine State became the Garrison State. In Fort Pierce, 150,000 men passed through the Naval Amphibious Training Base, home of future frogmen and underwater demolition experts. Along the Big Bend, at Camp Gordon Johnston in Carrabelle, thousands of soldiers perfected future invasion tactics that would be employed on beaches in North Africa, Normandy, and Tarawa. Daytona Beach hosted a WAC (Women's Army Corps) base as a result of Mary McLeod Bethune's lobbying of Eleanor Roosevelt.

Wings over Florida became a familiar sight. In 1939, Florida boasted six aviation schools; by the end of the war, the state claimed forty aviation installations. Residents became accustomed to the distinctive sounds and silhouettes of Navy Hellcats, B-17 Flying Fortresses, and TBM Avengers. Airfields offered specialized training. Pilots at the Lake City and Sanford naval air stations perfected dive bombing.

Although the count is imprecise, as many as 2 million military recruits spent some time in Florida from 1941 to 1945. George Herbert Walker Bush learned to fly torpedo bombers at the Fort Lauderdale Naval Air Station. Ted Williams served as a flight instructor at the Pensacola Naval Air Station. George C. Wallace trained as a flight engineer in Miami while Paul Newman completed radio school and gunnery training in Jacksonville and Miami. Andy Rooney spent time at Camp Blanding, where he wrote for *Stars and Stripes*. Already an accomplished artist, Jacob Lawrence was stationed in St. Augustine, where he served in the Coast Guard. His lodging consisted of a room formerly assigned to kitchen help in the Ponce de Leon Hotel. Clark Gable endured basic training at Miami Beach and excelled at the Flexible Gunnery School at Tyndall Field in Panama City.

Floridians escaped to the Dixie Theatre in Apalachicola or the Athens in DeLand to watch war movies filmed in Florida: *Air Force, A Guy Named Joe*, and *They Were Expendable*. But Floridians living along the east coast watched the real war come to them. German submarines seized a strategic opportunity in January 1942, launching Operation Drumbeat. German U-boats sank twenty-four ships off Florida's coasts. Residents and tourists at Jacksonville Beach and Cocoa Beach, among others, watched in horror as tankers burned and thick oil coated the white sand. Hundreds of lives were lost, along with critical cargo and resources, until the Allies developed an effective convoy system and perfected the use of sonar. Volunteers softened the human tragedy. *Miami Herald* columnist Helen Muir wrote a story of a young nurse wiping tar off a bedraggled merchant mariner, asking him, "Is this your first visit to Florida?"[4]

Floridians welcomed the sight of men and women in uniform. But German prisoners of war evoked suspicion and fear. Of the 372,000 German POWs incarcerated in the United States, almost 12,000 spent time in Florida. They picked oranges in Dade City, Leesburg, and Winter Haven, cut sugarcane in Clewiston, and swept the streets of Miami Beach. The largest group was stationed at Camp Blanding. In one of the war's more ironic moments, German POWs picked cotton at El Destino, one of Jefferson County's great antebellum plantations.[5]

World War II, not the New Deal, ended the Great Depression and unleashed one of the greatest economic booms in American history. From 1940 to 1945, federal expenditures soared from $9 billion to $98.4 billion. Nationally, per capita income doubled during the war, while personal savings increased tenfold and the labor force expanded by 9 million workers—all during a two-front war that absorbed 16 American million soldiers. The war wrought extraordinary changes to two neglected regions—the American West and South. The South, often a subject of derision and pity, and once identified by President Roosevelt as the "Nation's No. 1 economic problem," was swept into the vortex of prosperity and change. *Fortune* magazine translated the heady events into understandable terms: "For the first time since the War Between the States, almost any native of the Deep South who wants a job can get one."[6] The war funneled huge sums of money into Florida's underdeveloped economy that had rested for decades upon an uneasy tripod of tourism, extractive industries, and agriculture. Statistics reveal the dramatic impact. War contracts revived the state's slumbering agricultural and manufacturing sectors. The war also rejuvenated Florida's moribund shipbuilding industry.

In 1940, Bay County languished in poverty, an isolated wedge supporting 20,000 residents along the state's Big Bend. The county boomed as the result of Tyndall Field and government contracts. The population trebled by 1945. The Wainwright Company constructed 108 vessels during the war, including 102 Liberty ships. At its peak, the Panama City shipyards employed 15,000 workers, earning premium wages. The general contractor, J. A. Jones, assumed the role of urban planner and city boss, building homes for workers and delivering milk and ice to families.

Defense buoyed Tampa, a city reeling since the Great Depression had devastated the once-vaunted cigar industry. The construction of MacDill and Drew Air Fields and the reconstruction of a shipbuilding industry spelled a new prosperity. The Tampa Shipbuilding Company employed 9,000 workers by 1942 and desperately searched for new laborers, a problem exacerbated with the establishment of a second major shipyard at Hooker's Point. The shipyards paid union wages; skilled workers averaged $1.03 an hour, with unlimited overtime. The companies sponsored athletic teams, published newspapers, and even provided alarm clocks for workers.[7]

Twenty-four U.S. and Allied freighters and tankers were sunk in Florida coastal waters by German submarines (U-boats) during World War II, particularly during the period February–July 1942. Many torpedoed merchant vessels could be seen burning from the front porches of beach houses and from the balconies of tourist hotels. Here a stricken tanker burns off Hobe Sound.

The war's cornucopia also enriched the economies of Pensacola, Jacksonville, and Miami. The Pensacola Shipyard and Engineering Company employed 7,000 workers; in addition, the government spent $55 million expanding the Pensacola Naval Air Station and constructing auxiliary fields. Jacksonville's docks bustled. Local firms built 82 Liberty ships and scores of minesweepers and PT (patrol torpedo) boats. The city also served as headquarters for the Naval Overhaul and Repair facility. In Miami, vessels from the Caribbean and South America thronged the Miami River docks. Miami's economy surged from streams of military recruits, defense contracts, and, improbably, tourist spending. The home of Eastern Airlines and Pan American Airlines, Miami solidified its hold as the most important hub for South American flights.

The parade of industrial statistics might lead one to believe that the Sunshine State had transformed its economy into an arsenal. For all the new and revived industries, the state's economic standing changed little during the war; indeed, one can argue that Florida actually slipped in sectors critical to postwar growth. And once the war ended, the bustling shipyards largely disappeared. Moreover, in industries critical to sustained growth—chemicals, oil refining, iron and steel foundries, aircraft manufacturing, electronics, automobiles—Florida cities fared poorly, even when compared to southern rivals Atlanta, Mobile, Norfolk, Galveston, and Houston.

Agriculture achieved dramatic gains during the war, realizing new profits and incorporating new technologies. Southern farmers in general, and Florida in particular, had endured two lean decades since the flush times of World War I. But World War II brought good times back. North Florida cotton planters prospered with the rise of cotton prices from 10 cents to 22 cents per pound between 1939 and 1945.

Grove owners harvested orange gold during the war. Notable milestones in the marketing and processing of citrus occurred. Florida's citrus harvest surpassed California's for the first time in 1942–43, producing 80 million boxes of oranges and grapefruit. That year's yield also marked Florida's first $100 million crop. Scientists helped solve a problem long vexing the industry: waste and spoilage. Chemists at the Florida Citrus Commission patented a process to make frozen concentrated orange juice. Few realized the significance of the development, because in 1944, few American homes or stores had freezers. But frozen concentrate revolutionized the citrus industry and the consumption of juice after the war.

The war also wrought a green revolution. While researchers at the Bureau of Entomology in Orlando advanced the frontiers of jungle warfare, they discovered an insecticide with revolutionary implications. By 1945, DDT was available for commercial use, promising an end to a tropical Florida teeming with palmetto bugs, cattle ticks, and voracious mosquitoes. *Time* magazine, however, cautioned against careless optimism: "Not much is known as yet about the full effect of DDT on large areas."[8] Undeterred, Floridians rushed to saturate the new witch's brew on swamps and backlots. Not until 1962 with the publication of Rachel Carson's seminal book *Silent Spring* would they learn how damaging pesticides were, particularly DDT, to the environment.

The war's new technologies augured a bright future for grove owners and planters, but scientists had yet to invent machines to pick oranges and cut sugarcane. A drastic labor shortage confronted farmers. Historically, African Americans had performed low-paid agricultural work. But the once reliable and pliable workforce disintegrated, as blacks enlisted in the service or accepted better-paying positions in northern industries or Florida cities.

Florida confronted a labor crisis as experts predicted a shortage of 10,000 pickers for the 1943–44 citrus season. Across Florida, cities and officials passed new vagrancy laws or enforced old ones, determined to punish slackers and obtain seasonal laborers. Governor Spessard Holland and many municipalities promulgated "Work or Fight" laws. In Clearwater, charged the *Tampa Morning Tribune,* "The city has put more than fifty chronic loafers, including some gigolos, to work. . . . Many were Negroes who borrowed money from their girlfriends to aid their loafing."[9] In Apopka, officials citing vagrancy laws arrested scores of African Americans, assigning them to labor in the celery fields. In 1945, Governor Millard Caldwell ordered Florida sheriffs to eliminate indolence. The sheriff of Martin County openly admitted that his office would cooperate with farmers, sawmill operators, and others doing essential work in seeing they received all the help they needed.

Nowhere was the line between freedom and bondage more blurred than on the vast sugar plantations of south Florida. Historically, the cane fields attracted the most desperate workers. When the war began, the United States Sugar Corporation controlled 86 percent of the state market, although the massive expansion of sugar production that created Big Sugar did not occur until the postwar years. With the fall of the Philippines in 1942, U.S. Sugar successfully lobbied the government to lift the domestic quotas on sugar production.

The short- and long-term solution to Florida's shortage of agricultural laborers came from afar. The U.S. Department of Agriculture (USDA) signed agreements with the governments of the Bahamas and Jamaica to allow the temporary emigration of 75,000 workers, and to pay for their transportation. To planters and corporations, the policy was a godsend. L. L. Chandler, chair of the Dade County USDA War Board, observed candidly: "The vast difference between the Bahama Islands labor and the domestic . . . is that the labor transported from the Bahama Islands can be deported and sent home if it does not work."[10] The face—and faces—of Florida agricultural work were changing.

What happened in Florida may have been a harvest of shame, but it was also a harvest of plenty. The bittersweet truth remains: For all of the war's horrors, the conflict enriched the American home front. The war provided Floridians, accustomed to decades of depression and scarcity, a taste of prosperity and abundance.

City dwellers were forced to come to terms with the dizzying changes wrought by war. In September 1940, the *National Municipal Review* prophesied that American cities were threatened less by Stuka dive bombers than by mounting crises in public health. Had the editor visited wartime Jacksonville, Miami, or Pensacola, he might have added alarming crises in public education, urban services, and affordable housing.

World War II accelerated Americans' mobile tendencies. Fifteen million Americans, in search of new opportunities, moved their residences and workplaces between 1940 and 1945. Another 16 million men and women served in the armed forces, moving still greater distances. For most Americans, the war was more *Odyssey* than *Iliad*. Florida cities functioned as dynamic hives of activity. Never static, the cities shuffled constant streams of defense workers, rural migrants, tourists, and military personnel, who all competed for scarce housing and transportation.

Jacksonville and Pensacola shared a symbiotic relationship with the Georgia and Alabama hinterlands. Jacksonville drew large numbers of rural migrants from south Georgia. "Jacksonville came up in conversations like the weather," reminisced novelist Harry Crews, whose family left Bacon County for opportunities in Florida.[11] Pensacola's "official" population increased modestly, from 37,000 in 1940 to 43,000 in 1945. But these statistics ignore at least 100,000 temporary residents who spent some time in the city. Trailers and tents became commonplace as Pensacola groaned under the burden of accommodating newcomers, many of whom spilled into unincorporated areas.

In 1940, Key West slumbered as a colorful community of 13,000 residents. Five years later, 45,000 persons crammed the "Gibraltar of the Gulf."

It became, once again, a navy town, a home for PT boats, submarines, and pleasure craft drafted into service. "War has brought about many changes in Key West," lamented the *Miami Herald* in 1943. "One of the last of the picturesque island's customs to disappear was the closing of doors to stores while a funeral procession passed. All business along the line of a funeral procession must be suspended as a final tribute to the dead. But the war ended that."[12] In what must have been the strangest conflict ever fought on Florida soil or water, on 13 July 1943, a navy blimp and a German U-boat engaged in battle forty miles south of Key West. Perhaps the most palatable change was the completion of the long-awaited pipeline and aqueduct that brought freshwater from an Everglades well field to Key West.

Miami hummed with the surging currents of war, as "the Magic City" became a crossroads of travelers, workers, and soldiers. Tourists returned to the city in 1943 when the county's hotels returned to the business of pleasure. Officially, Miami's population increased from 173,065 residents in 1940 to 192,122 in 1945. Unofficially, the city's population fluctuated wildly. In January 1944, the *Miami Herald* estimated the city was "home" to 325,000 persons, including winter visitors, soldiers, and visitors. "Except for the land boom of 1925," wrote journalist Nixon Smiley, "no other event in Miami's history had done so much to change the city as World War II. At the war's beginnings Miami still had many of the qualities of a small town. As you walked down Miami Avenue or Flagler Street you met person after person you called by their first name. . . . The war changed all that."[13]

Small-town Florida was not immune to wartime tumult. The *New York Times'* Dora Byron toured Panama City, Ocala, and Homestead in the fall of 1942. "Dime stores are thronged on Saturday night and churches filled on Sundays," Byron wrote. Pointing out the inevitable loss of community that came with rapid growth, she stated: "Everywhere there is noise and hurry and crowds. All three quickly are strangers to small Florida towns."[14] In Stuart, older residents criticized improper wearing apparel, especially "the very short shorts and halter tops" of the new female residents shopping downtown.[15]

Tallahassee, a small community of 16,000 residents in 1940, felt the war's tremors. Over one-third of the city's lawyers enlisted in the service. By 1944, the Florida State College for Women reached its largest enrollment ever, registering 2,227 students. On weekends, male students and soldiers from Dale Mabry Field, Camp Gordon Johnston, and the University of Florida, desperate for female companionship, descended upon the capital, many of them forced to sleep in hotel lobbies and on park benches.

President Doak Campbell (*foreground*) and student members of the Victory Club at Florida State College for Women form a *V* for victory on the Tallahassee campus. The students tilled "victory gardens" as part of the war effort.

In big cities and rural hamlets, residents expressed in words and deeds an outpouring of patriotic gestures and voluntary activities. Home-front Florida recycled scrap metal, planted victory gardens, and rolled bandages at the Red Cross. In Lakeland, the Florida Citrus Bomber Fleet Committee raised funds to purchase fifteen Flying Fortresses. During one rally, Pine Island residents rescued ten tons of metal. In Zellwood, local children collected tons of paper and scrap metal during assorted drives. Victory gardens flourished. Floridians everywhere endured dimouts, gasless Sundays, and ration coupons. In every community, a window flag bearing a blue star meant a son in the military. A gold star signaled the somber news of a family's supreme sacrifice.

The collective struggle to vanquish totalitarianism, leaders argued, bound society together. While that proved true in part, the war's dynamism also created new fears and widened old fissures. War revealed how fragile unity and patriotism were and how crises challenged democratic institutions. The wartime struggle for racial justice, in particular, is illuminating. Inspired by President Roosevelt's call for "Four Freedoms," and committed to defeating the evil empires of Japan and Germany, African Americans enthusiastically joined in the fighting. The war instilled new hopes for change. African American leaders championed a "Double V" campaign, supporting the war against totalitarianism abroad while continuing the fight against racism at home.

On the eve of Pearl Harbor, 515,000 African Americans resided in Florida. While Deep South states had hemorrhaged black migrants since 1915, the Great Migration had affected Florida less severely. Many southern black migrants had moved to places such as Jacksonville, Miami, and Tampa. The "Second Great Migration," begun during the war, only intensified that pattern.

World War II represented the last American conflict fought with segregated units. Daniel "Chappie" James, born in Pensacola in 1920, entered the Air Corps and in 1975 became a four-star general. The famed Ninety-Ninth Fighter Squadron, comprised of black fighter pilots, trained at Tallahassee's Dale Mabry Field.

Nostalgia and distant memories depict the home-front war as a time when all Americans came together. But competing visions of the American dream collided in Florida and the South. In the maelstrom of war, as soldiers and civilians competed for services and respect, Floridians saw no reason to adjust the color line. A series of racial incidents stained Florida's wartime image, including melees involving black troops (especially northern-born servicemen) and white military police.[16] In August 1942, the Fort Myers City Council unanimously enacted an "emergency ordinance to define the customs which promote and preserve the inter-racial disorders." The ordinance made it unlawful for whites and blacks to "loiter upon the streets" or to "patronize establishments serving food and intoxicating beverages . . . [without respect to] the divisional areas set apart by long established customs for colored and white occupancy and patronage."[17]

Florida officials expected the worst. The State Defense Council and Army Service Forces prepared a secret plan in the event of serious race riots at Tallahassee, Jacksonville, Orlando, St. Petersburg, Tampa, or Miami. "In the City of Orlando," the press release explained, "there is an undercurrent of tension, activated by union organizers and the presence of Northern Negro soldiers in the community."[18] Officials made plans to impose martial law in the afflicted cities. Detailed maps indicated key neighborhoods and institutions such as radio stations and newspaper offices.

The war forced some Floridians to confront racial boundaries. In 1943, Herbert Krensky was traveling by train from Miami to Jacksonville. At a

USO clubs throughout the state entertained the 2,122,100 servicemen and -women who trained at Florida bases and camps. These GIs enjoyed a USO banquet at Tampa in April 1943.

stop in Ocala, a platoon of German POWs, dressed in their Afrika Corps uniforms, boarded the train. "When our train stopped at Waldo," remembered Krensky, "we stopped for a moment. . . . On the platform were these colored servicemen, one of them wounded and hobbling on crutches. They tried to board with their tickets in hand. The conductor refused to let them board. . . . He told them that since there were no colored coaches, that they would have to ride in the baggage car."[19]

The most sensational and horrifying racial episode occurred in Madison County. Jesse Payne, a black sharecropper, was lynched following a dispute with a white farmer. The spectacle brought ignominious attention to Florida since it was America's only lynching in 1945. A black army corporal wrote Governor Millard Caldwell: "I had no idea that I would hear of similar acts of Fascism upon return to our great arsenal of democracy, America."[20]

But the war also offered real hope and the promise of change. On the eve of World War II, the NAACP had launched an attack upon the pillars of segregation and inequality. Counsel Thurgood Marshall, representing the NAACP and black teachers, won several court cases in Florida, awarding

African American teachers salaries equal to those of their white counterparts. By war's end, black men served on juries in Escambia and Pinellas Counties, while cities such as Miami and Tampa hired black policemen. On 3 April 1944, the U.S. Supreme Court struck down the white primary in *Smith v. Allwright*. By 1946, African Americans in Florida—or at least those who lived in urban counties—broke the political color line in Florida, registered as Democrats, and voted in primaries.

African Americans, long denied the right to enjoy white beaches, envisioned a new day in the sun. In May 1945, Miami's Colored Ministerial Alliance orchestrated a "swim-in." The target was Baker's Haulover Beach, a county white beach. Chagrined city and county leaders responded by offering blacks a separate beach at Virginia Key. The seeds of the modern civil rights movement had been sown.

World War II served as a great watershed for American women. The most visible and powerful symbol of the war's impact on the home front was the presence of women in the workplace. The *Daytona Beach Evening News* wrote: "Womanpower is available everywhere. Women are eager to give it whenever and wherever they can. Why does not the government take steps to organize, recognize, and use this valuable asset?"[21]

The *Tampa Morning Tribune* saw the war as a harbinger. "It may hurt the masculine pride a little to think that a woman can handle a man's job, but pretty soon a lot of Tampa women may be working at the benches and docks where men used to be." The *Tribune* might have expanded the list to include groves, welding shops, shipyards, and aircraft hangars.

Across America, the number of working women rose from 14.6 million in 1941 to 20 million in 1944. By war's end, married women outnumbered single women in the workplace, a landmark event. Florida newspapers expressed wonderment over the novelty and substance of change. And change could be seen everywhere. One official estimated that at least one-quarter of the state's farmworkers were women. "Women are doing virtually all of the cultivating and harvesting," observed the *Tampa Morning Tribune*, noting that 700 of Hillsborough County's farmworkers were females.[22] In Miami, milkmaids replaced milkmen at Southern Dairy, while women took jobs as pole painters at Florida Power & Light and as clerks and elevator operators at area hotels. Tallahassee hired Elizabeth McLean as the city's first policewoman. Women replaced men as transit workers in St. Petersburg. "Lumberjills [have] invaded Florida," announced the *Miami Herald*. "They are doing practically every job in the saw mill today, and they are even felling trees in the woods with a soprano "Timber!"[23]

The war effort relied heavily upon civic volunteerism, a field historically dominated by women. The day after Pearl Harbor, the *Tampa Morning Tribune* pleaded for "Tampa girls . . . to attend dances for soldiers." In Miami Beach, 18,000 volunteers refurbished and staffed the Minskie Pier, a favorite recreational destination for soldiers. In St. Petersburg, hundreds of young women volunteered as "Bomb-a-Dears," while the more matronly Grey Ladies distributed cigars and postcards at the Bay Pines Veterans Hospital.

In the 1943 Florida Legislature, a single woman took her place among the solons. State Representative Mary Lou Baker introduced a measure popularly known as the "Women's Emancipation Bill." Passed after a spirited debate, the law strengthened the rights of married women to manage their separate estates and to sue and be sued independently of their husbands. A bill to ensure the rights of women to serve on juries failed. The measure would be passed in 1949.

Historians continue to debate the sheer impact of World War II upon American women. One school of thought argues that, for all their individual efforts outside the home, and for all of the wartime service within and outside the military, American women returned to the "traditional" home roles of mother and housewife when the war ended. Other scholars contend that one can directly trace the beginnings of a feminist revolution and the modern women's movement to the war, that the conflict profoundly changed the participants *and* the home front, and that, while many women did return to their homes, their expectations and experiences were incorporated into a changing American culture.

Headlines depict Florida as consumed with alarming questions about morality and the sins (and afflictions) of the flesh. The war, with its supercharged atmosphere of patriotism and sacrifice, strained the swirling world of gender and sexual relationships. Newspapers conveniently blamed the problem on "Victory Girls," "VD Girls," and "Khaki Wackies." Certainly it is difficult to stereotype wartime conduct or assign labels of "victim" and "villain."

The reality is that prostitution posed a serious problem around military bases and in large cities. In 1944, Pensacola's "VD Control Officer" estimated that Escambia County's population included 11,000 syphilitics. In Miami and Tampa, the military pressured city officials to eliminate red-light districts. The urges and demands for illicit sex spawned new opportunities in new places. Helen Muir remarked that "Miami teenagers turned prostitute in Bayfront Park. . . . Early park closings and extra police failed to stop this mass prostitution until all shrubbery was ordered trimmed."[24] Some military commanders, such as Col. Edmund Gaines at Tallahassee's Dale Mabry Field, threatened to declare infected cities "off limits" to soldiers. The 1943 Florida Legislature passed a State Quarantine Bill, converting four CCC camps at Miami, Ocala, Wakulla, and Jacksonville into VD hospitals.

Thousands of wives, sweethearts, and children followed servicemen to Florida, hoping to reconstitute war-torn families or simply to be closer to loved ones. Florida, they learned, could be a cold place. Finding a home or apartment in crowded cities proved to be frustrating and often heartbreaking. Many called it a disgrace that servicemen and small children were turned away from homes and apartments. An "irate Navy wife" complained to a newspaper in 1944 that housing seemed to be for tourists only.

A mood of Spartan sacrifice overtook Florida. The military imposed a ban on deep-sea fishing. Armed guards patrolled the beaches, imposing a ban on bonfires. St. Petersburg canceled its Festival of States Parade "for the duration." Minor-league baseball leagues canceled their schedules. The crosshairs of a home-front war soon found new targets. Total war, with its obligatory strictures against waste and folly, demanded old-fashioned virtues of patriotism, community, and deferred gratification. Florida's tropical casinos and tourist centers appealed to a new taste of leisure, individualism, and conspicuous consumption.

Florida tourism, like American baseball, proved resilient even in wartime. Appeals to help revive the state's flagging tourist industry began. *Florida Highways* reminded readers in New Jersey and Illinois that "sunshine was *not* being rationed." The Daytona Beach Chamber of Commerce ran a brochure in New York newspapers with the tempting message, "Like a soldier, YOU need a civilian furlough." Florida press agents unleashed a "blitzkrieg of joy" campaign on civilian morale. The owners of Tallahassee's Cherokee Hotel offered soap bars in red, white, and blue wrappers. In St. Petersburg, the Lakewood Country Club provided an electric shuttle service between downtown hotels and the golf course. Horse and dog racing tracks encouraged winning bettors to purchase war bonds.

The image of Florida at Play clashed sharply with the image of America at War. So many tourists arrived in January 1944 (the first winter season Gold Coast hotels had been reconverted to civilian use) that passengers simply overwhelmed the transportation system. In Fort Lauderdale, a journalist noted, every day resembled a "Christmas weekend." Governor Holland appealed to the Office of Defense to add more railcars. The FBI's sensational arrests of sixteen Miami hotel operators and ticket agents only reinforced J. Edgar Hoover's opinion of Miami as "a lodestar for criminals, gangsters, racketeers and federal fugitives from justice during the winter season." Helen Muir wrote, "Miami Beach never had it so gay as titled European refugees, wartime manufacturers, and government bigwigs crowded the nightspots, attended the horse races, and brunched at cabanas."[25]

Philip Wylie, a trenchant critic and keen observer, expressed outrage over the juxtaposition of the idle rich and the deserving poor in Miami. "Women and children walk the street," he complained in the *New Republic*. "The men who have sacrificed most meet in Miami those who have sacrificed the least."[26] But Wylie desperately wanted Miami to soar to new heights after the war and bristled when sunshine patriots attacked his hometown. In an extraordinary 1943 essay in the *Miami Herald*, he defended the charge that "Greater Miami is a third-rate city, garish, vulgar and trivial." He wrote at war's end, Miami "can seize the gigantic opportunities at hand and develop this unique region into a new heart of the new world—or we can go on being a tropical Coney Island."[27]

News of the Japanese surrender ending the war swept across the peninsula and panhandle on 14 August 1945. Collectively and spontaneously, V-J Day was the most deliriously happy day in Florida history. Floridians were tired of war and sacrifice, ready for peace and homecoming. In Key West, ten long blasts alerted the Conchs; in Clewiston, locomotive whistles at the U.S. Sugar Company heralded the message; while in Quincy, "Big Jim," the giant whistle at the Fuller's Earth plant, thundered the news. No city escaped V-J Day's pandemonium. Gainesville's *Daily Sun* described the scene at University Avenue and First Street: "Automobiles, motorcycles, trucks and anything else with wheels jammed the streets for a mile or so, while occupants of the vehicles sounded horns, screamed, rang cow bells, and hysterically expressed joy." On Biscayne Bay, one observer thought Miami "looked like Rio at Carnival." In Tampa, the *Tribune* reported gingerly, "Young and old joined in the kissing contests. Acquaintance was not necessary although some girls insisted on kissing only sailors and some servicemen preferred blondes."

V-J Day was especially poignant for the inhabitants of 1716 SW Twelfth Avenue in Miami. The parents of pilot Lt. Col. Paul Tibbets Jr. resided there, and after August 14, Enola Gay Tibbets (after whom Paul's atomic bomber was named) was the most famous woman in America. At the dawn of the nuclear age, technology seemed both terrifying and liberating. Just hours after Hiroshima's destruction, Lee County commissioners offered the government a 7,500-acre tract of land "as a base for the atomic bombing of hurricanes."[28] Understandably, Floridians had understood the war as a triumph of technology, and there was little reason to believe America could not harness atomic power. The war had also introduced the wonder drug penicillin. Daily C-46 flights were saturating Florida cities with DDT spray. Year-round living on Gulf beaches would soon be possible. By 1947, Floridians were all too eager to read new stories of technology's leap. "Now's the time for comfort lovers to order one-room air conditioners," announced the *Miami Herald*.[29]

At the end of the war, Floridians still relied upon radio and newspapers for their news. Daily, newsboys still delivered a morning and afternoon paper. Evening rituals included chatting with neighbors and reading the day's papers on the front porch. Still another revolution began on the evening of 21 March 1949. Inside the venerable Capitol Theatre in downtown Miami, technicians broadcast the first television signals from Florida.

Before the war, few Floridians had ever flown in an airplane. The war ushered in an era of flight, and Florida benefitted handsomely from the aviation boom. Scores of New Deal and World War II–era airfields became municipal airports. By 1947, the commentator John Gunther proclaimed Miami "one of the great international airports of the world."[30] The conversion of airfields to international airports illustrated the conversion of hundreds of World War II installations to civilian use. Civic leaders scrambled to hold on to their economic lifelines. "Crestview," philosophized the editor of the *Okaloosa News Journal*, "like all other small towns of around 2,500, will have to sink or swim after the war is finished. What will we do after the war?" Crestview need not have worried. Congressman Bob Sikes vowed to take care of his hometown like a He-Coon protects the defenseless coons.[31] Many small towns—Arcadia, Lake City, and Naples—did lose their beloved military bases. Other communities found creative ways to utilize abandoned barracks and aircraft runways. Sebring's Hendricks Field had welcomed crews learning to fly B-17 bombers. In 1950, the Sebring Grand Prix was born. Marianna Air Field became a tuberculosis hospital. Dale Mabry Field housed the first males to attend the Florida State College for Women, which would soon become Florida State University. The Richmond Naval Air Station exchanged blimps and seaplanes for tigers, lions, and the Miami Metro Zoo. Lakeland's Lodwick School of Aeronautics became the new spring training home for the Detroit Tigers baseball team. The Vero Beach Naval Air Station became the legendary "Dodgertown," spring home for the Brooklyn Dodgers.

Perhaps most dramatically, the romantic-sounding Banana River Naval Air Station was closed and then reappeared as Patrick Air Field. Its new mission was to protect Cape Canaveral. For centuries, Cape Canaveral stood as a lighthouse and geographic destination, and one of the most isolated places in Florida. In 1946, a reporter had described the place: "Canaveral, a small community on the sparsely populated cape of a scrub-covered key . . . has no port, and no commerce, nothing but a battered pier."[32] The following year, the Joint Chiefs of Staff identified 15,000 acres of Brevard County as a site for the Joint Long Range Proving Ground. A vanguard of scientists arrived in 1947.

America's space race began there in 1949.

Notes

1. *Tallahassee Democrat,* 9 December 1941.

2. "How Tough Is a Hero?" *Time,* 9 February 1942.

3. Hemphill, *Aerial Gunner from Virginia,* 9.

4. Helen Muir, *Miami U.S.A.* (Gainesville: University Press of Florida, 2000), 205. For an overview of the U-boat Atlantic campaign, see Michael Gannon, *Operation Drumbeat* (New York: Harper and Row, 1990).

5. Robert Billinger, *Hitler's Soldiers in the Sunshine Stat: German POWs in Florida* (Gainesville: University Press of Florida, 2000).

6. "The South Looks Up," *Fortune,* July 1943, 95.

7. Gary R. Mormino, *Hillsborough County Goes to War: The Home Front, 1940–1945* (Tampa: Tampa Bay History Center, 2001), 51–58.

8. "Careful with DDT," *Time,* 22 October 1945.

9. *Tampa Morning Tribune,* 27 November 1942.

10. Chandler quoted in *Miami Herald,* 26 July 1943.

11. Harry Crews, *A Childhood* (New York: Harper and Row, 1978), 128.

12. *Miami Herald,* 26 July 1943.

13. Nixon Smiley, *Knights of the Fourth Estate: The Story of the Miami Herald* (Miami: E. A. Seamann Publishing, 1974), 209; Gary R. Mormino, "Midas Returns: Miami Goes to War," *Tequesta* 57 (1997):5–53.

14. "'Welcome' and 'Keep Out' Signs to Dot Florida Winter Scene," *New York Times,* 27 July 1941.

15. "Around Florida," *Miami Herald,* 26 July 1943.

16. Gary R. Mormino, "GI Joe Meets Jim Crow: Racial Violence and Reform in World War II Florida," *Florida Historical Quarterly* 73 (July 1994):23–42.

17. *Fort Myers News-Press,* 18 August 1942.

18. State Defense Council, Record Group 191, Series 419, Box 5, p. 7, Florida State Archives, Tallahassee.

19. Krensky memoir in *Miami Herald,* 7 May 1985.

20. Millard F. Caldwell Papers, Florida State Archives, Tallahassee.

21. *Daytona Beach Evening News,* 5 October 1942.

22. "700 Women Work On County Farms," *Tampa Morning Tribune,* 14 March 1943.

23. "Lady Lumberjacks Work in Forests," *Miami Herald*, 22 August 1943.

24. Muir, *Miami U.S.A.*, 211.

25. Ibid., 201.

26. *New Republic*, 21 February 1944.

27. Philip Wylie, "True Greatness," *Miami Herald*, 5 December 1943.

28. "Lee Offers Base to Bomb Storms," *Tampa Daily Times,* 9 August 1945.

29. *Miami Herald*, 1 June 1947.

30. John Gunther, *Inside U.S.A.* (New York: Harper and Bros., 1947), p. 655.

31. *Okaloosa News Journal,* 5 May 1944.

32. "Canaveral," *Tampa Morning Tribune*, 17 February 1946.

Bibliography

Primary Sources

Newspapers constitute an invaluable source for studying the war on the home front. Almost any town of significance published a newspaper during the industry's golden age of the 1940s. Two out-of-state newspapers, the *Pittsburgh Courier* (Florida edition) and the *Atlanta Daily World*, offer valuable insights into race relations.

The P. K. Yonge Library of Florida History at the University of Florida and the State Historical Library and the State Archives in Tallahassee provide the best holdings of primary materials related to the home front. The Archives' Millard Caldwell and Spessard Holland Papers are especially interesting. The Claude Pepper Library houses the papers of a powerful and influential Floridian and can be accessed at Florida State University.

Secondary Sources

Billinger, Robert D., Jr. *Hitler's Soldiers in the Sunshine State: German POWs in Florida.* Gainesville: University Press of Florida, 2000.

Craft, Stephen G. *Embry-Riddle at War: Aviation Training during World War II.* Gainesville: University Press of Florida, 2009.

Davis, Jack. "'Whitewash' in Florida: The Lynching of Jesse James Payne and Its Aftermath." *Florida Historical Quarterly* 68 (January 1990):277–90.

Freitus, Joseph, and Anne Freitus. *Florida: The War Years.* Niceville, Fla.: Wind Canyon Publishing, 1998.

Gannon, Michael. *Operation Drumbeat: The Dramatic True Story of Germany's First U-Boat Attacks along the Atlantic Coast in World War II.* New York: Harper and Row, 1990.

George, Paul S. "Submarines and Soldiers: Fort Lauderdale and World War II." *Broward Legacy* 14 (Winter-Spring 1991):2–14.

McGovern, James R. *The Emergence of a City in the Modern South: Pensacola, 1900–1945.* DeLeon Springs, Fla.: E. O. Painter, 1976.

Mormino, Gary R. "GI Joe Meets Jim Crow: Racial Violence and Reform in World War II Florida. *Florida Historical Quarterly* 73 (July 1994):23–42.

Patterson, Gordon. "Hurston Goes to War: The Army Signal Corps in Saint Augustine." *Florida Historical Quarterly* 74 (Fall 1995):166–83.

Rogers, Ben F. "Florida in World War II: Tourists and Citrus." *Florida Historical Quarterly* 39 (July 1960):34–41.

Shofner, Jerrell H. "Forced Labor in the Florida Forests." *Journal of Forest History* 25 (January 1981):14–25.

Sikes, Bob. *He-Coon: The Bob Sikes Story.* Pensacola: Perdido Bay Press, 1984.

Taylor, Robert A. "The Frogmen in Florida: U.S. Navy Combat Demolition Training in Fort Pierce, 1943–1946." *Florida Historical Quarterly* 75 (Winter 1997):289–302.

Waldek, Jacqueline Ashton. "How Boca Won the War." *Boca Raton* 37 (Winter 1988): 140–47.

"War! How World War II Changed the Face of Florida." *Forum: The Magazine of the Florida Humanities Council* (Fall 1999):1–42.

Wynne, Lewis N., ed., *Florida at War.* Saint Leo, Fla.: Saint Leo College Press, 1993.

20

Florida by Nature

A Survey of Extrahuman Historical Agency

JACK E. DAVIS

The abolitionist author Harriet Beecher Stowe is best known for her abiding interest in the human condition. The foremost example of this sentiment is *Uncle Tom's Cabin*, her searing indictment of the American tolerance of slavery. Two decades later, her *Palmetto Leaves* followed familiar formula by attending to the abject conditions of the formerly enslaved. Yet the state of the nonhuman world moved Stowe, too. *Palmetto Leaves* was inspired by winters she spent on Florida's picturesque St. Johns River. A best seller in its day, the book devotes considerable attention to the wildlife, wilderness, water, and climate of her adopted state. "Nature," Stowe wrote, "has raptures and frenzies of growth, and conducts herself like a crazy, drunken, but beautiful *bacchante*."[1]

Implicit in her statement is the idea of nature as an independent force. That idea put her one conceptual step ahead of historians of more recent times. It is hard to write about Florida without including a line or clause about its natural aura. Any researcher experiencing the state firsthand encounters its visual, aural, and aromatic assertions. This is to say nothing of his or her source material. A diary, letter, or postcard of the past would be from another place if it failed to give due to colors at sunset, a flight of shorebirds, a rush of fish, or the bellow of alligators. That said, historians may paint the natural backdrop behind their human subjects or mention civilization's impact on the environment, but typically they show little curiosity in nature's imposition in the human journey. They seldom reflect on its historical agency.

Yet consider this: the geological character and the ecology of twenty-first-century Florida is only around 2,500 years old. In the preceding age,

Florida was the flip side of the sunshine state. It was cold, dry, and wind-swept. Ten thousand years ago, the peninsula was twice as wide, expanding as much as 100 miles into the Gulf of Mexico from the present-day coastline. Imagine if Florida were still the same. Imagine if it had winters as cold as Minnesota, a rocky shoreline similar to Maine's, or a terra firma as parched as the Arizona desert. The narrative of Florida's past would be very different from the one we read and write today. Marjory Stoneman Douglas put it this way: Florida constitutes a "region in the greatest possible contrast to the others of this continent. It has shaped uniquely the history of man within it."[2]

Florida has a history all its own in part because it has wild flora and fauna and a climate found nowhere else in the country. It is the only continental state that reaches below the temperate climate zone and supports the growth of tropical plants, which have attracted tropical animals and tropical people. It has white-sand beaches and warmth, and quantities of insistent sunshine that compare with its quantities of water—wetlands, lakes, bays, ocean, and gulf. Floridians have always organized their societies around natural distinctions. At the daybreak of modern Florida, to cite one example, the infirm and the retired elderly began flocking to the southernmost state. Credit for this migration typically goes to the railroad, automobile, Social Security, World War II, cheap living, and the state's boosters. In truth, the newcomers were pursuing soothing ocean breezes and healing sunshine. A consumptive Ralph Waldo Emerson went to Florida in the 1830s seeking restoration, and he found it. "Yet much is here," he wrote of the St. Augustine region in 1830s, "That can beguile the months of banishment / To the pale travelers whom Disease hath sent / Hither for genial air from Northern homes."[3]

Awareness of Florida's genial offerings has typically been a matter of proximity. Those who dwelled intimately with the land or water, or lived more distantly in the past, seem to have been the most attentive to, and more humble about, their place in nature.

The Calusa of pre-Spanish Florida were such a people. Although mighty among indigenous groups, they were deferential toward the nonhuman world. In studying the Calusa, anthropologists have had to learn much about the ecology of their day and place. It was in fact ecology, specifically tarpon striking in the Gulf, that brought their lost civilization to the attention of researchers. Still a frontier, south Florida in the late nineteenth century was particularly attractive to rod-and-reel tourists spoiling for a good fight with a big fish, an activity the *Washington Post* called the "titanic sport." Typically wealthy and well-connected men, they learned from locals about aboriginal artifacts buried in sandy hummocks and swamplands. News of these ante-diluvian finds eventually reached Frank Hamilton Cushing of the Bureau of American Ethnology in Washington, D.C. Not yet forty, the slight-of-build, heavily mustached Cushing was a leading authority on aboriginal cultures when he organized a Florida expedition in 1895. His time on the Gulf coast produced one of the most fruitful excavations in the history of U.S. archaeology. He uncovered thousands of artifacts, mostly carved wooden animals, amazingly well preserved in the anaerobic muck of a coastal pond on a small shell key, then called Key Marco (which in the 1960s became a point connected, courtesy of a dredge-and-fill project, to the north side of Marco Island). What he learned from the artifacts, and from Spanish documents, is that the Calusa were a sedentary people who flourished without agriculture.

This was remarkable. Rare was the hunter-gatherer society that settled permanently. Cushing, who was foremost an ethnographer, looked at physical objects of a culture much as a historian looks at the archived documents of a republic. In them he read the story of his subjects. He concluded that the people whom he called the Key Dwellers had established a well-ordered polity structured around numerous tribal chiefs and a superchief. Long after his time, other researchers confirmed his findings, determining that the Calusa chiefdom—which included a paramount chief, religious chief, and military chief—ran the sandy coast from Charlotte Harbor to Cape Sable. Its control reached to other primary Indian groups across the peninsula's southern quarter—the Ais, Tequesta, Myaimi, and Jeaga—who paid tribute to the Calusa.

The Calusa demonstrated their power upon their first contact with the Spanish. Recognizing the Europeans as hostile invaders of their sovereignty, they attacked Juan Ponce de León's exploratory party during its first sweep of the southern coast in 1513. Eight years later, Florida's original conquistador died following a second encounter with the Calusa, succumbing to a wound from an arrow poisoned with sap of the native manchineel tree. Bearing a physical stature to match their defensive might, the Calusa commanded a height that impressed their European visitors. The "stout old soldier" Bernal Diaz, who was involved in a brief skirmish with Calusa in 1517, described them as having "large powerful bodies." Others recorded the Calusa men to stand between five feet six and five feet ten inches. Their eventual conquerors, an agrarian people, averaged around five feet four inches or less.[4]

What bound the Calusa to a single place was water. That flowing through and around south Florida brimmed with a natural bounty. Hunter-gatherer societies on other parts of the continent suffered food shortages and starvation in winter months, an uncertain time for the weak and elderly. Not the Calusa. The coastal estuaries—now called Charlotte Harbor, Pine Island Sound, and Estero Bay—and the inner waterways—the modern Peace, Myakka, and Caloosahatchee Rivers—were a constant source of protein. It was self-generating, perpetual, no cultivation required. Although they supported the densest population in south Florida, the Calusa had no need for agriculture. Big fish, little fish, shrimp, sea turtles, crabs, lobsters, manatees, and even sharks, whales, and the West Indian seal were easily gathered with spear, net, or quick hand. Bird meat, venison, and wild plant food (saw palmetto berries, cocoplums, seagrapes, coontie roots) contributed slightly to the local diet; marine habitats supplied more than 90 percent. When adelantado Pedro Menéndez de Avilés dined with the Calusa six months after founding St. Augustine, his hosts presented a feast of fish and oysters, the latter served boiled, roasted, and raw. The honorary spread included no plant foods.

Food sources were more than nourishment. Nearly all in some way had a utilitarian purpose. As stone defined the age and culture of peoples elsewhere, shell and bone were the stock of Calusa civilization. Shells were used as dippers, spoons, bowls, clubs, hammers, awls, and digging and hacking tools. Few things were as important as nets. Individual fish were harvested with spears or harpoons made from alligator and fish bones and stingray spines, which were also fashioned into cutting edges and gaffs. Nets—seine, cast, and gill—were the more efficient means for catching fish. At the Key Marco site, Cushing found several intact examples, which in their way were objects of refined beauty. Busy hands had meticulously woven them from cord equally meticulously fabricated out of palm-fiber (cabbage palm or saw palmetto) and Spanish moss. The net makers attached gourds—domesticated papaya or *cucurbita pepo*—to the upper course of cording (today known as the cork line). To the lower course, they carefully wove in pierced mollusk shells for bottom weights, to stand the nets in the water vertically.

Symbolic of the cultural importance of shells were conspicuous mounds, which had raised the curiosity of frontier dwellers, who had told the fishing tourists about them, who got the word out to scientists, who came to study them. Cushing eventually recognized the shell heaps as more than midden, or refuse piles. They were constructed sites that had supported houses and temples. Many indigenous groups built mounds to elevate a place of worship or political honor. The Calusa did that, but they were also sensitive to the weather. They responded to hurricanes and tidal surges by building on higher ground, where they could also catch sea breezes to keep at bay mosquitoes and biting midges, the latter of which frontier settlers of another century called "no-see-ums." Shell was an accessible substrate for high-and-dry houses, and those not raised on a shell or natural mound usually were on pilings. Palm and grass thatch was another important material in the construction of dwellings, suitable for roofs and woven to make lattice walls and floor mats. The cacique who hosted Menéndez with a feast of fish did so in a thatched council house that held 2,000 people.

The Spanish ultimately conquered the Calusa. Armed conflict and en-slavement took their toll, but rampaging pathogens conveyed across the Atlantic were the real scourge in the demise of indigenous populations. Be-fore European contact, the worlds on either side of the ocean lived more or less in ecological isolation. Compared with its hemispheric counterpart, the New World had few domesticated animals, and outside the llama and canine, none ideally suitable as beasts of burden or as draft animals. Europe-ans consequently had been exposed to animal-borne diseases, such as cow-pox, utterly foreign to Western Hemisphere natives, whose immune system was ill-prepared for the viral assault, primarily in the form of smallpox and measles. By the time the Spanish surrendered Florida to the British in 1763, the Calusa were a people of the past.

The traditional narrative of Florida and the Americas attributes European conquest to the actions of men. In no small measure the strength of empire relied on the ambitions and resolution, not to mention arrogance and brutal ways, of conquistadors like Juan Ponce de León and Pedro Menéndez de Avilés. But empire building also relied on nature—the ocean currents and the wind that propelled and the stars that guided flotillas of sailing vessels, the natural resources from which those vessels were constructed, and those that paid dividends in exchange for risk taking in exploration. No conquis-tadors were more closely in touch with nature than the pilots who navigated ships, and one of the most knowledgeable was Antón Alaminos. He sailed with Christopher Columbus on his fourth Indies voyage and piloted the first recorded Spanish expedition to the Yucatán Peninsula (in 1517). Four years earlier, he had guided Juan Ponce to La Florida, up the east coast (probably no farther than Melbourne) and then back and around the curving end of the peninsula, through the shipwrecking Florida Straits without mishap (at least none recorded), and into the Gulf of Mexico, a nameless sea at the time. The southbound journey coasting the eastern shore against the current took twice as long as the northbound, with some days yielding no headway. Alaminos took note, saw abetment rather than hindrance, and in 1519 used this novel and great ocean current for the first time to propel ships of the Spanish treasure fleet back to Europe. Flowing up to seventy miles per day, carrying a volume of water greater than all the rivers that pour into the Atlantic Ocean, the Gulf Stream revolutionized cross-Atlantic travel. The Spanish, wrote geographer Carl Ortwin Sauer, converted this new expeditious route into the "lifeline" of "empire." No other Spanish discovery in Florida was as important, aside from that of Florida itself. It in turn gave urgency to Spanish settlement on the peninsula. Sailing along a coast controlled by others would risk exposing the treasure fleet to freebooters.[5]

Sailing the Gulf Stream posed dangers beyond the human kind, too. Ships had to navigate through the Florida Straits and the Bahama Channel, gingerly around the coral reefs of the Florida Keys and the shoals of the east coast. Given the obstacles, the Straits were a shipwreck alley. The word Bahama derives from *baja mar*, meaning shallow sea; Juan Ponce referred to the Keys as Los Martires, The Martyred; the Spanish name for Key West was Cayo Hueso, Bone Island; and the name for the two Matecumbe keys apparently derives from *mata hombre*, kill man. Poorly charted, swirled by swift currents and countercurrents, becalmed and windless on hot summer days, routinely pummeled by storms, the area demanded an alert helmsman and pilot, especially those of gold- and silver-laden cargo ships that responded sluggishly to commands at the helm.

The hazards off the coast spurred an indigenous salvaging industry that is older than European settlement in Florida. Locally known as shipwrecking, the industry began with native coast dwellers, who by virtue of their diet were expert free divers. As it turned out, the little precious metal that conquistadors found in Florida was in the possession of natives. It came from no natural deposits but from trade with other Indians and, quite often, from wrecked cargo ships carrying the New World plunder of the Spanish empire. By the nineteenth century, long after the treasure-ship era, salvaging lost cargo routed from Apalachicola, Pensacola, Mobile, New Orleans, the Yucatan, Jamaica, and Cuba made Key West one of the country's wealthiest cities. Captains of salvage schooners, wrote Douglas, "built ample two-storied white houses with balconies and shutters against the heat, shaded by mangoes, coconuts, sapodillas, limes and other tropical trees. . . . The streets filled with a babble of Spanish and French, slave accents from West Africa, and American voices from everywhere." Recovered furniture, silver, china, women's finery, and men's garments went to auction houses in New Orleans, Savannah, and elsewhere. The federal court licensed some fifty Key West salvage operations in the 1850s, when ships were "piling up on the

[Florida] reef at the rate of nearly one a week." The decade averaged nearly five Atlantic hurricanes per year.[6]

Hurricanes are conveyors of history. They have always been a part of the Florida experience, but they are not simply a Florida phenomenon. They come from somewhere distant, do their damage, and move on to some-place else. Although they blow things away, they also bring things with them. Many of Florida's tropical plants and some of its fauna were carried on strong winds or heavy seas to the peninsula from across the Caribbean. Tropical storms washed in the spoil of shipwrecks, too, of course. While salvage crews welcomed big blows, most Floridians generally feared them. They represented God's wrath or nature's fury, depending on one's perspective. They were not the sort of phenomenon that endeared one to nature's power. "Florida," writes Neil Frank, former director of the National Hurricane Center, "has had a long and brutal hurricane history." This is not surprising for a landmass such as the 450-mile-plus Florida peninsula, which exposes itself to the vagaries of Atlantic Ocean weather on the east and the Gulf of Mexico on the west. Most Atlantic hurricanes form north of the equator and move east to west, a good many of them drawn to the shallow, warm waters of the Gulf. Nearly 40 percent of all U.S. hurricanes hit Florida. Sixty-two did so in the twentieth century.[7]

The Spanish dealt with a perplexing number during the conquest period. What may in part account for Florida's strong aboriginal defense against initial Spanish encounters were early warnings. More than likely, the Indians who resisted Juan Ponce in 1513 had previously encountered bearded, strangely clad men, dead and alive, in the storm wash onshore. Shipwrecked at the age of thirteen in 1549 or 1550, Hernando d'Escalante Fontaneda lived with Florida Indians for seventeen years, learning their languages and teaching them his. Pedro Menéndez de Avilés found him in 1566 living with the Calusa and used him as an interpreter. Historians would know less about Florida's indigenous people if not for the memoir of his captivity and, foremost, for the storm that wrecked his ship.

The French, not the Spanish, might have found him if not for an Atlantic gale the year before. Florida was contested territory by the time Menéndez landed at present-day St. Augustine in September 1565. The French had already begun building a fort north of the St. Johns River and were determined to subvert Spanish claims to Florida. Under the leadership of Jean Ribault, the French attempted the first strike from sea before a nor'easter drove the ships down the coast. Menéndez knew the fate such weather could deliver. He had previously lost a son somewhere off Florida to a storm, and of the nineteen ships that had left Spain under his command, only five made it to Florida. Fortune turned for him when the nor'easter thwarted Ribault's assault, giving the Spanish the advantage over their superior rival. Menéndez hunted down the shipwrecked French. Upon their slaughter, he secured Spanish sovereignty in Florida and, with it, east coast harbors of safe refuge for ships of the treasure fleet.

One place where the Spanish failed initially to find security from nature was the Florida panhandle. In 1559, Pensacola was poised to become the first successfully settled European city north of Mexico when conquistador Tristán de Luna y Arellano set sail in June from Vera Cruz with thirteen ships carrying a ready-made colony of 1,500 soldiers and settlers, the requisite missionaries, and necessary provisions. They raised the flag of empire and planted the cross of Christianity on a red bluff along the eastern shores of Pensacola's deep and well-protected bay, seemingly ideal for safe harborage. The "best port in the Indies," de Luna called it in a letter to the king. Proving that claim wrong, a hurricane came up the Gulf of Mexico that September and scattered the colony, which was fully abandoned two years later. The viceroy in Mexico declared the region off-limits to settlement, and the Spanish kept their distance for 137 years. They finally secured a colonized footing in Pensacola in 1698. Once again, they were responding to their French rivals, who were searching for the mouth of the Mississippi River to establish a natural waterway between the Gulf of Mexico and their North American claims.[8]

Bad weather 163 years later deprived Pensacola of another first, the opening shots of the Civil War. After Florida seceded from the Union, Federal forces retained control of Pensacola's four brick forts. President Lincoln dispatched supply ships and reinforcements to Fort Sumter, South Carolina, and to Pensacola to prevent Confederate takeovers. An Atlantic gale delayed the convoy, and the same foul weather foiled Confederate plans to attack Pensacola's Fort Pickens. By the time reinforcements arrived, violating a truce between the two sides, Federal forces, on April 13, 1861, had already surrendered Fort Sumter to the Confederates.

Forts withstood hurricanes better than private dwellings, compelling Floridians to contemplate their location. The Apostle Matthew maintained, "A foolish man built his house upon the sand, and the rain fell, and the floods came, and the winds blew and beat against that house, and it fell." For a while, Floridians heeded Matthew's admonition. Charles Pierce, who grew up in south Florida in the 1870s, said, "No one thought of building much near the ocean, because it would eventually sweep any structure away." Fort Myers was founded under those circumstances. When an 1841 hurricane wiped out the Second Seminole War outpost Fort Dulany at Punta Rassa, the military retreated from the Gulf shores and built a new installation at present-day Fort Myers. Ultimately, Floridians threw caution to the wind and lined the seacoast with homes and hotels, only to see a big blow pummel them time and again. After the 1926 Miami hurricane, John J. Farrey, chief building inspector for Miami Beach, which had been flattened in the storm, drew up the first building codes instituted in Florida. (Farrey has been honored by the state as a Great Floridian for his initiative.) Persistent dwelling damage from a long string of storms in the 1950s (including Baker, Easy, King, Love, How, Able, Florence, Hazel, Brenda, Flossy, Greta, Debbie, Ella, and Judith) forced a widespread restructuring of poorly conceived municipal and county building codes. Some had been imported from the North, addressing irrelevant issues such as snow loading and soil frost lines but not wind loading. Requiring more rigid construction, however, mitigated apprehensions about inhabiting danger's alley. Beginning in 1970, the state took modest initiatives, though still bold in real-estate-crazed Florida, to move the population to safer ground. It instituted a mean-high-tide setback of fifteen meters for new construction. That rule was followed a few years later by the Coastal Construction Control Line, which is based on a 100-year storm surge.[9] Houses had to be built on deep-set pilings with living space limited to levels above floodwaters. Insurance companies and the Federal Emergency Management Agency also required these regulations.[10]

Architectural design that bent away from nature was inconsistent with earlier inclinations. A regional wood-frame vernacular emerged in the early nineteenth century built to the elements. Today, the form is called Cracker architecture. It had two principal requirements: limiting direct sun exposure and maintaining natural ventilation. Situating a house on a lot to minimize the hottest rays of late afternoon and to take advantage of shade trees was a first consideration. Using local materials, in particular pine and cedar, both of which are resistant to indigenous termites, homesteaders constructed the foundation a foot or two above the ground on piers of brick (later of concrete block or poured cement). Elevating the house not only enhanced air flow; it kept occupants above flooding water. Windows in every wall and a dog trot—an open space running from the front to the back—between two halves of the house brought flowing air inside. Tall ceilings and steeply angled roofs gathered the warmest air above living areas. On the Gulf shores, the vernacular changed slightly; roofs were usually drawn to a shallow pitch to withstand storm winds. Porches were designed to provide outside shade but also to keep the sun from penetrating the interior. When they could afford to do so, Floridians built front and back porches and even side porches.

New architectural styles were coming into vogue by the next century. A leading figure who introduced a Mediterranean style was architect and Boca Raton visionary Addison Mizner. The arches, colonnades, French doorways, barrel-tile roofs, and pastel colors all seemed to fit with the palm trees, flowering frangipanis, waterscape, and general warmth and sunshine of the American Mediterranean. When architects like Mizner incorporated new designs, they usually borrowed the passive technologies of the Cracker house. Even brick and block homes were raised on suspended foundations with a ventilated crawl space below. The dog trot was enclosed and turned into a hallway between left and right rooms but remained front-to-rear breezeways with an exterior door at each end. Windows were plentiful and ceilings high. Mizner typically kept the footprint one-room deep to facilitate cross-ventilation. Home designs changed sharply with the advent of residential air-conditioning, which by 2000 had become as common in Florida homes as a kitchen or bathroom. Houses were built on slab foundations, ceilings were lowered, windows grew smaller and fewer, and the dog trot and porch disappeared. Florida was turning into an indoor culture. Its residents were losing touch with the natural conditions that had attracted so many to the Sunshine State.

Environmental historian Alfred Crosby argues that in the era of global conquests, parts of the world with natural conditions most familiar to Europeans pulled strongest. The English tended to regions with a temperate climate, and the Spanish concentrated in subtropical and tropical places. Settlement was facilitated when Europeans were able to reproduce plants and animals that had sustained them in the Old World. Florida may have lacked the craggy countryside of Spain, but it suggested other ecological possibilities. The new settlers brought citrus from southern Spain to plant in Florida's sandy soil and beef cattle to graze on its prairies. Florida had the first European horses and cattle introduced north of Mexico. The line of the latter never died out. They were left to forage on indigenous vegetation until needed for market or table, and after the Spanish left Florida, the hardy animals went feral. Seminoles and yeomen farmers plucked them from the wild, bred them, consumed them, and sold them. Modern-day ranchers learned the Spanish breed required no winter feed as did imported western cattle; they quietly fended for themselves. Although the Spanish never succeeded in developing a profitable beef industry, Floridians of subsequent generations stuck with the Spanish vision. In 2007, the oldest cattle-raising state ranked eleventh among U.S. states in the number of beef cattle.

Cattle are not a species that comes to mind at the thought of Florida. What does evoke familiarity is lemon, lime, grapefruit, and orange trees. Pastoral Florida was not the conventional farmhouse on a hillside surrounded by verdant or amber fields carved out of the wooded wilderness. It was instead the perfect green of citrus accented with white blossoms and ripening fruit planted in neat rows opening to the flat interior horizon. A citrus grove is what environmental historians call second nature, a human-modified environment that resembles an indigenous one. But Florida has been associated with the round, dimple-skinned fruit that ripens into sunshine colors for so long that it seems organic. Much like the Fountain of Youth, its juicy savoriness and persistence stand with the idea of vitality and youthful endeavor that defines the Sunshine State. Stowe observed long ago, "The orange-tree is, in our view, the best worthy to represent the tree of life of any that grows on our earth." Citrus evolved into Florida's chief export at the same time it transformed into a cultural icon.[11] With appropriate irony, the state with so many non-native residents chose a non-native species, the orange, as the state fruit and its blossom as the state flower. Backyard citrus trees became as common as shrubbery. Streets, subdivisions, buildings, counties, festivals, and a championship college-football bowl adopted names from the fruit. In 1998, the legislature selected the orange as the background graphic of standard automobile license plates.[12]

Popular literature credits Juan Ponce de Léon, who brought the first cattle to Florida, with planting the first orange trees in Florida. No one really knows which Spaniard introduced the fruit. From nearly the first European contact, Florida elicited comparisons with the Mediterranean. Indeed, the province lay closer to the equator than Valencia, the great citrus-growing region of Spain, and it seemed an ideal place in which to expand New World production. Writer John McPhee says that Spain mandated that ships going to the New World take citrus for planting. But the Spanish never managed to make much of a citriculture in Florida. For one, the Spanish variety was sour in taste. The fruit escaped settled areas, like Columbus's swine in the Caribbean, and began growing in the wild. Indians harvested oranges from feral groves, roasted them, and sweetened them with honey. After the British took possession of Florida, citrus production turned into a genuine export, with varieties harvested in north Florida, Georgia, and South

Carolina. Growers continued to ship oranges, lemons, and limes during the second Spanish occupation of Florida, and by the time the territory went to the Americans, nurseries were falling behind grower demand for saplings. Within two decades, citrus took over as the leading agricultural product on Florida's east coast. The year before the cataclysmic freeze of 1894–95, the state's growers packed 5 million ninety-pound crates of oranges.

The first central growing area encompassed the lower St. Johns River in northeast Florida. A slow-moving mass with more than a dozen tributaries, the St. Johns begins in the south from a series of watershed marshes in Indian River County. It flows north 310 miles to its mouth on the Atlantic Ocean at Jacksonville. The St. Johns is Florida's longest river. Up to three miles wide, it is also the most navigable. The Timucuan Indians thrived alongside it, and Jean Ribault and the French saw logic in settling its mouth (despite underestimating the ruthlessness of Menéndez). In the heyday of river commerce, no other Florida river produced the same bustle. Some of the state's most important cities resided on its banks. Much of the land around it lay above flood levels, and, as does any large body of water, it curbed temperature extremes. The Spanish, British, and Americans grew cotton, indigo, and citrus in the region. Harriet Beecher Stowe tended a small grove at her riverside Mandarin home. From the basin of the St. Johns, citrus growing spread down the Ridge, a highland region running through the upper center of the peninsula. The scent of the orange blossom was strong in Palatka and Gainesville, where groves were planted along city streets and next to municipal buildings. But occasional hard freezes, beginning with one in 1835, which Floridians blamed on a renegade iceberg floating off the coast, gradually forced the center of the industry southward toward Orlando and the Tampa Bay area and down to the Indian River on the east.

Citrus was the product of Spanish initiative, but climate allowed it to endure—or not. Following the most memorable freeze of the century, that of 1894–95, the event some argue is responsible for the founding of Miami, land speculators began promoting south Florida to northerners as the frost-free American Mediterranean. South Florida was not frost free, but the temperatures along the east coast were moderated by the Gulf Stream. The region owes its "tropical exuberance" to the ocean current, observes historian Mark Derr, a climate that not only attracted citrus but generated a phenomenal tourist industry and real estate market. By the late twentieth century, south Florida had become the new home to the citrus industry. As historian Christopher Warren writes, the "geographic and climatic history of citrus may be interpreted as growers' lessons from nature's catechism, a rigorous tutorial in respecting the limits of climate, season, and geography." Truth be told, growers unwittingly contributed to the conditions that forced their continual southern migration, never quite mastering the catechism. Scientists concluded that Florida's facility in destroying wetlands to make way for cultivatable cropland and the layered concrete and asphalt of cities and suburbs pushed the freeze line southward and altered local climate. The state logged an estimated 12-percent-lower annual rainfall average at the end of the twentieth century than at the beginning and endured greater temperature extremes in winter and summer. "Ironically," notes journalist Cynthia Barnett, "when farmers drain wetlands for crops, they increase the likelihood that freezes will harm those very crops."[13]

Freezes were not the lone impetus for the southward drift of citrus. The rush of people moving to Florida after World War II put growers in the unwanted position of competing with real estate agents. The latter kept a hawk's gaze on land that citrus growers had made high and dry and, unintentionally, exquisitely suitable for housing developments. When they succeeded in flipping groveland to real estate, developers often left a few citrus trees on a new-home lot to entice buyers. As the price of land increased, retiring growers often sold their grove rather than pass it on to the next generation. This was particularly true in the center of the state, escape grounds for growers after the devastating 1890s. Ninety years later, history repeated itself with a little prompting from the land boom ignited by the opening of Walt Disney World in 1971. After two hard freezes in the 1980s, tract homes quickly replaced miles and miles of ruined citrus trees on the rolling groveland that encircled Orlando. Once the producer of 40 percent of the state's orange crop, central Florida acquired a new ranking as one of the nation's leading sprawl areas. In 2000, a mere 6 percent of the state's oranges shipped from the area.

The industry again had moved deeper into the peninsula to survive outside popular growth areas. By 2000, 61 percent of the crop was grown in the southwestern interior. Overall, citrus occupied 830,000 acres, down from 1 million in 1992. Still, with more than $1.6 billion in cash receipts, "Big Citrus" survived. Hybridization, breeding, fertilizer, and pesticides allowed late-twentieth-century growers to produce ten to fifteen times the amount of product per acre, with trees holding two to three times more fruit, than their predecessors did a century earlier. The innovation of frozen concentrate to aid the Allied effort during World War II and the skyrocketing demand toward the end of the century for refrigerated single-strength juice revolutionized citriculture. Growers harvested 244 million crates of oranges in 1998, with only 5 percent of that fruit consumed fresh. Big Citrus had gone liquid.

Florida could support citrus and cattle because it had a lot of land, nearly 40 million acres of it. Although the state boasts the oldest European-established city in the United States, nearly three hundred years passed before whites settled the lower peninsula with conviction. As Douglas pointed out, Florida had a "long frontier." Her measure was both geographic and chronological. The shrinking availability of land in northern states and worn-out soil in traditional agricultural regions such as the Piedmont and the Carolinas were sending Americans west and south. Beginning with the second Spanish occupation, an expanding number were putting down stakes in Florida. The U.S. territorial government set up land sales offices and hired land surveyors, and Congress passed the Donation Act in 1824 and the Armed Occupation Act in 1842 to advance the frontier line southward. The progression of homesteading whites was a foreboding development for Florida Indians—Seminoles, Miccosukees, Creeks, Yuchi, and Choctaws—many of them agrarian people engaged in local trade and the territorial economy. The Florida militia and U.S. military waged war to force the Indians onto a reserve. Compared with the "rich prairies of Alachua," where many had lived, the agricultural potential of the first reserve, in central Florida, was poor enough to compel the Indians to war. Even territorial Governor William Duval conceded that the "lands are wretchedly poor and cannot support them." Following seven years of conflict, the few hundred Indians who had avoided relocation to the West were restricted to a second reserve, located roughly between the Peace River and the Gulf of Mexico. This time, authorities tolerated no complaint, believing the reserve was blessed by nature's providence. Captain John T. Sprague, the federal officer in charge of Florida Indian affairs, wrote military authorities in Washington, "The game of the country, climate and natural productions places them [the Indians] above sympathy or charity, every necessary want is supplied." Another war, nevertheless, broke out.[14]

During both, Indians used water and wetland as a defensive bulwark. It was an effective strategy. George A. McCall, aide-de-camp to General Edmund P. Gaines during the Second Seminole War, noted in a letter to his father, "it is much to be apprehended that the Seminole will retreat to the lower part of the peninsula, and cause the troops much fatigue to bring them to bay." Indeed, the Seminoles led the military into the "almost inaccessible" Big Cypress Swamp and Everglades. "Today officers as well as men have been compelled to wade in the mud, sawgrass, and water, and assist the sailors in dragging the canoes," wrote midshipman George Henry Preble in his diary. "On the sick-list," he noted a month later, "foot badly inflamed and legs ulcerated; poisoned by the sawgrass of the Everglades and exposure to the mud." For fifty-eight days, the expedition of eighty marines and sailors trudged through the nation's largest wetland, locating numerous enemy encampments but arriving after the Indians had departed. Many soldiers were, nevertheless, taken with the hospitable parts of Florida. "Florida as far as my own experience extends is as healthy as any other parts of the United States," wrote James B. Dallam of Baltimore to his brother. "I shall undoubtedly permanently establish here." Paradise eluded him, though. He was killed during an Indian raid on his encampment near Charlotte Harbor. After the final war, perhaps 200 Indians remained behind in Florida. They lived in the Big Cypress, Everglades, and the Ten Thousand Islands, which one soldier called a "most hideous region." "It seems," said another, "expressly intended as a retreat for the rascally Indian." The Everglades was a savage land to many soldiers, suitable for only a savage people.[15]

Despite the removal and seclusion of Indians, the migration stream of white settlers slowed. At the start of the Civil War, the U.S. census counted only 140,000 free and slave people living in Florida, fewer than any other southern state. At the turn of the century, the population density, 9.8 people per square mile, was less than half the national average. Open range remained plentiful (for the time being). Cattle roamed freely. They "wandered the swamp edges and the big pine and palmetto flats" of the interior, writes storyteller Leo Lovel. They "had to be hunted, gathered, branded, treated for screwworms, counted, eventually herded up and sold." This was the job of cracker cowboys, who communicated with each other and their cows using frayed- or braided-leather bullwhips to crack the air, "louder than a rifle shot," a sound that some say gave the Florida herdsmen their name. "Those 'Crackers,'" says Lovel, "had to be woodsmen," making do "with what the land provided like swamp cabbage, wild onion, fish and game, gator meat, the much prized gopher turtle." They drove cattle across the prairies much as would the more familiar cowboys of the American West. There were panthers plenty to take a steer. Equal threats on the drive to Punta Rassa and Tampa, where ships conducted cattle to Cuba and other locations, materialized in deadly lightning strikes, more common in Florida than any other state, and in storm floods. Average annual rainfall reached between fifty and sixty inches, with south Florida's portion usually slightly higher. In wetter years, some parts of the state could endure up to 100 inches. Florida was well known for pregnant clouds pulling a gray wall of rain across blue afternoons, leaving behind several inches in a matter of hours. Where the ground had been dry the day before, a river, wetland, or lake would soon appear.[16]

Water was another obstacle to the advance of white settlement. Florida had plenty of it, fresh and salt. The state is surrounded by so much of the latter that the Spanish for many years mistook the peninsula for an island. Only Alaska's 6,640 miles of coastline beats Florida's 1,350 (Florida's tidal shoreline is 8,426 miles). Yet there was a time when saltwater and sandy beaches were not yet the marvel that bewitched visitors. Interior Florida stirred imaginations, as it did that of the early American naturalist William Bartram. It was, as he put it in the published journal of his explorations, *The Travels* (1791), an enchanting living natural museum of the most amazing specimens of plants and animals. Contemporary readers of *The Travels* accused him of engaging in fiction writing because he recorded such incredible things in Florida: 25- to 30-pound large-mouth bass; water thick with alligators, a primordial beast unknown to most fellow colonists; and 125 species of flora not known to whites. Historian Tom Berson argues that as much as prairies, mountains, and deserts formed the aesthetic of the continent's interior, springs, rivers, and wetlands did the same for Florida's. In his famous 1907 travelogue, *The American Scene*, the prickly Henry James expressed misgivings about Florida's principal city, Jacksonville, and its beaches; they "in especial were to acquire a trick of getting on one's nerves!" Yet a trip up the St. Johns left him "Byronically foolish" about the interior river.[17]

Before major drainage projects and development booms in the twentieth century, half of Florida's surface area was covered with freshwater, too much from the point of view of settlers. To deal with it, the state lobbied aggressively for the passage of the 1850 Swamp Land Act, congressional legislation that allowed states to annex and drain federally owned wetlands. In the end, the act nearly doubled the landmass belonging to the state of Florida. But the actual historical agent here is water. Indians and European settlers alike tended to settle near freshwater sources. There was the obvious need of sustenance, and there was utility in waterways as avenues of transportation for people and trade. As the population grew, water got in the way. The state wanted to open more land and to expand railroad service, which was pathetically insufficient. The Swamp Land Act was the answer. But false starts hampered successful drainage operations until the early twentieth century. In the meantime, the long coastline and 11,000-mile infrastructure of rivers lessened the urgency of railroad development.

Somewhere along the winding course of many of those rivers is a freshwater spring. The Spanish called them fountains. They were the sparkling, animated centerpieces of Florida's vast water endowment. The Suwannee River alone has 200 springs. Geologists have counted more than 900 in the state, giving Florida the highest concentration of springs in existence. Thirty-three are first-magnitude springs, meaning each discharges 100 cubic feet or more per second. The daily output of all springs combined reaches 7 billion gallons. That is a lot of water boiling, gushing, and bubbling from down below and feeding rivers and streams above. The source of much of this effusiveness is the Floridan Aquifer, one of the world's most productive artesian systems. All of Florida and parts of Georgia, Alabama, South Carolina, and Mississippi sit atop the Floridan, where more than a quadrillion gallons of water winnow unseen through cracks, crevices, and corridors of this fossilized limestone underbelly, and through time itself. Some of the water has been around since the Middle Ages. In the twentieth century, municipal utilities—including those in Jacksonville, Tallahassee, Gainesville, Daytona, Tampa, and St. Petersburg—and the fields and groves of agriculture came to depend on that ancient source.

Suffused with wetness, Florida's natural richness captivated the nation. Ornithologist Mark Catesby and artist Titian Ramsay Peale were among the earliest to affirm in their work the exotic, the paradise, the Eden Bartram had discovered. They were followed by John James Audubon, who early in the nineteenth century was lured by Florida's most remarkable bird population, profuse and colorful and unique in North America. It was the artists and writers—the famous and the not-so famous, the newsprint and book illustrator, the journalist, the literary writer, and the travelogue writer— who crafted the lyrical imagery of Florida. It leaped into the imagination of not only Stowe and James but Sidney Lanier, Stephen Crane, Edward King, and the former slave turned poet Albery Allson Whitman. Winslow Homer, James Wells Champney, John Singer Sargent, Thomas Moran, Laura Woodward, and Martin Johnson Heade, artists generally associated with other places and themes, traveled south to capture Florida's living aesthetic—panthers and birds, palm and hardwood hammocks, river ox-bows and wet prairies, orange light and dark silhouettes at sunset. Descriptions of these sorts, illustrated and literary, appeared in countless magazine and newspaper articles beginning in the nineteenth century, and Florida's tourism industry was born.

The first tourists harbored the hope of catching a glimpse of the wildlife and wilderness they had read about or seen in artwork. They did encounter it, most often from the deck of sternwheel riverboats steaming up the St. Johns River, into the Ocklawaha and Silver Rivers. Lanier called the Ocklawaha the "sweetest water-lane in the world"; King said it coursed through "sylvan peace and perfect beauty." The tourists' final destination was Silver Springs, Florida's first major commercial attraction. Fifty thousand visitors a year made the river voyage to peer into the spring's glassy depth, unwittingly down into the Floridan Aquifer, that fountain of life if not youth. The same mystique that enraptured Bartram endured two centuries later when the late Florida writer Al Burt put down these thoughts.[18]

> Those old Spanish conquistadors who came here in the 16th century looking for the fountain of youth found one but they were looking for the wrong thing. Though they never understood it, this really was a place of rejuvenation, but it was not located in a single magical spring as they had hoped. Instead, it was in the nature of this place. Rather than one spring that restored youth there was a dazzling array of natural gifts—*many* springs, rivers, and lakes and an extraordinary range of geography, climate, plant and animal life.[19]

Floridians who had to contend with water frequently checked their enthusiasm. There often seemed too much where it was not wanted and too little where it was wanted. In the early days of statehood, leadership in Tallahassee was intent on removing excess water to open up fresh land to prospective farmers, ranchers, and growers. No place in Florida was more inundated than the Everglades, and beneath their shallow, limpid waters, boosters claimed, lay the most fecund soil in the world. In the 1880s, Philadelphia saw manufacturer and Florida land speculator Hamilton Disston launched a private venture to reclaim the Everglades. The drainage canals his dredges dug redirected millions of gallons a day to the Gulf of Mexico, but in terms of agricultural expansion and capital return, the Disston project was a failure. The state followed with its own initiative two decades later, only to meet with its own limited success. It sent even more water into the Gulf and into the Atlantic. But when the inevitable heavy rains came, thousands of drained acres reflooded. The people who had been lured by the idea of a prosperous life on Everglades farmland found themselves living and working in a dangerous place.

Hurricanes struck with this harsh reality. One of the worst in history did so on September 16, 1928. It pushed up a fifteen-foot storm surge and breached the state's flood-control dike along parts of the 750-square-mile Lake Okeechobee, the headwater of the Everglades. More than 2,000 people, most of them black farmworkers, drowned. The federal government afterward helped the state build a bigger and better dike. But that was not enough. When hurricanes careened across the peninsula in September and October 1947—accompanied by a rainfall of 100 inches for the year—it was clear that the new dike had given false security to the continued settlement of the Everglades. The human toll reached only twenty-three deaths, yet the storms washed away 178 homes and drowned 4,298 domestic animals. The public outcry was loud enough to prompt the Army Corps of Engineers to move quickly to devise a comprehensive flood-control and drainage project that was unprecedented in size and scope. By the time the Corps completed the last phase of the flood-control project in 1971, it had destroyed nearly half of the Everglades and wrested the remaining ecosystem under the control of a fossil-fuel-powered system consisting of pumps, dams, locks, levees, and canals.

By then, the Corps had realized that much that had been done needed to be undone. The control of nature had gone too far; the Everglades were on the verge of extinction. Unyielding activism, protective legislation, and consistent bureaucratic wheel spinning at the state level culminated in the congressional authorization of the Comprehensive Everglades Restoration Plan (CERP) of 2000. Although controversial for its $8 billion price tag (with escalating costs estimated to reach $30 billion), CERP represented a renewed environmental commitment similar to the enthusiasm of the 1970s. It was then that the American people launched Earth Day, Congress adopted rigorous clean water and air legislation, and a worthless swamp and abject wasteland—the Everglades—gained new credibility as a vital and valued natural endowment. Yet restoring the ecosystem, environmentalists revealed, was not the top priority in Everglades restoration. The huge investment in CERP was for the benefit of the ever-expanding human population along the coast of south Florida. Water management and ecological destruction had spoiled the very natural system on which the big, morphing cities relied for freshwater.

Long before, recreational interest in Florida's interior had flagged. Tourists had begun heading to the coast, and joining them there was an intense interest in developing seaside areas. Like citrus, beaches soon became part of Florida's identity.

Their popularity is relatively recent in the long course of history. In the days of sailing ships, the sea was the perilous sea, and beaches were its outer edge. They suggested cold isolation and danger, not rest and relaxation. When the Spanish came to Florida, the beach was the threshold to new land, and not always an inviting one. Beaches were typically lined with tall sand dunes, behind which were long walls of jungle-like vegetation. Behind this natural bulkhead, still, were natives with spears and poison arrows capable of piercing chain mail. For their part, the Spanish may have claimed to have come in peace, but they came ashore in full armor, often with war dogs, and bearing the weapons and disease of conquest. The beach was battleground. Even upon securing their position against natives, international rivals tested Spanish claims. A "succession of dons and governors regarded the coast dispassionately," writes Gary Mormino, "nervously watching for marauding Protestants." Remember Menéndez, who butchered French Protestants on the beach. The place where it happened is still called Matanzas, a Spanish word for massacres. Centuries were required for playground to replace battleground. When vacationing was becoming vogue in the nineteenth century, Americans initially flocked to lakeshore but not seashore. Northern Michigan was a far more popular vacation spot than beachfront Florida. Middle- and upper-class easterners joined the Grand Tour, a vacation excursion that took them to natural attractions in the continental interior—to odd spectacles of nature, such as a geyser, or to natural monuments, such as a waterfall or mountain. Spring bathing, not beach bathing, was the rage, although preferences were changing.

After railroad builders Henry Flagler and Henry Plant located their first resorts to give easy access to inland fishing and hunting, they realized profit making was moving beachside. They subsequently built resorts to take advantage of the new interest in what the *Halifax Journal* in 1886 called "surf bathing, a perfectly safe gigantic bathing trough provided by nature." The activity had been in full swing for years in the Northeast—Coney Island, Newport, and the Jersey Shore, in particular—providing a reprieve from the stale confines of the city. By the 1880s, beaches on the Florida panhandle's

Santa Rosa and St. George Islands and at Jacksonville had begun accommodating leisure seekers (with restrictions to whites only). In 1898, a *New York
Times* travel correspondent recommended the Italian Riviera as a wintering
spot for Americans, though with one qualification: Its beaches could not be
"mentioned in the same breath with our Florida beaches." For a time, when
the automobile was still a novelty, the national media was more interested in
the beach at Ormond and Daytona as a place to set land speed records (produced on the hard-packed interbedded sands and coquina from the Anastasia Formation) than as one for surf bathers. Ormond nicknamed itself the
Birthplace of Speed, although by the 1910s, the sport had migrated to Utah's
Bonneville Salt Flats. Heightened interest in Florida's beaches followed the
democratization of vacationing. New roads were directed to coastal retreats.
Bridges were built across the water from mainland to barrier islands, most
of which before had been left to the wildlife, the odd beach hermit, or a
handful of fishing families.

Early beachgoing was a return to nature. Recreators went into the surf, a
tidal lagoon, or an inlet to hunt and gather. They built a beach fire to cook
their spoil—frying fish, smoking mullet, boiling crabs, roasting oysters—
mimicking the indigenous peoples of forgotten times. Sunset hues, salt air,
drumming surf, and refreshing breezes enlivened their senses. Swimwear
covered less and less through the years until beachgoers were wearing little
more than what the Calusa had worn, doing so to duplicate the complex-
ion of aboriginal peoples. No place was more suitable than Florida for the
modern-day sun worshipper. St. Petersburg captured a spot in *The Guinness
Book of World Records* with a run of 768 sun-filled days, from February
9, 1967, to March 17, 1969. Before concerns of atmospheric ozone deple-
tion and ultraviolet-light radiation, white Americans associated bronze skin
with health and natural beauty. Sun lotions appeared on the consumer market in the 1940s, not to block damaging sun rays but to deepen skin color.[20]
In 1967, a Volusia County high-school chemistry teacher named Ron Rice
mixed a batch of oils in a twenty-gallon garbage can, and two years later
founded Hawaiian Tropic tanning products. Unlike his chief competitor,
Coppertone, Rice used only natural oils in his product. When Platex Products, Inc. bought him out in 2007, his Daytona Beach company was posting
$200 million in annual sales. By that time, the sun had turned into a menace
in the minds of many, the source of deadly skin cancer, and suntan-lotion
manufacturers started calling their products sunscreens. Beaches nevertheless preserved their luster. Even after Walt Disney World opened in 1971,

they remained the state's primary draw. In the middle of the twentieth century, 2.6 more Floridians lived in coastal counties than landlocked ones. By 2000, the coast absorbed 12 million residents and 20 million annual tourists. Fewer than 4 million Floridians lived in the counties of the mostly ignored interior.

Not surprisingly, Florida officials worried incessantly about the condition of the sandy coast. In the 1990s, scientists concluded that six to ten feet of beachfront annually were washing away, and that most areas depended on routine replenishments of sand. Beaches naturally shift and change, expand and recede, and it seemed as if nature was taking away one of Florida's most prized assets. But after looking closely, researchers discovered that dredging operations, jetty building, and, most significantly, inlet construction contributed to as much as 85 percent of the erosion. (This is to say nothing of what sea-level rise, induced by climate change, holds for the future of Florida's beaches.) Florida adopted aggressive measures to preserve the tourist economy. In four decades following the 1970s, the state and local governments relocated 1.8 billion cubic feet of sand, at a cost of $10 per cubic foot, to restore beaches. By the 1990s, Florida was spending $30 to $50 million a year on beach renourishment.

Florida's coast has not been about leisure alone. The score or more fishing villages that formed in the nineteenth and twentieth centuries represented a work-ethic inverse to fun-in-the-sun Florida. Historically, the Gulf of Mexico has been home to Florida's most productive working waterfronts. "You can do a lot of things in the Gulf that you can't do in the Atlantic," said Mike Davis, whose family had fished in Cedar Key for more than a century. "The East Coast you got beaches. Over here we got marsh and estuarine areas, and there's a living to be made in those areas." "It was all there," author Ben Green writes of the Gulf's bounty, "within easy reach of young men and women with strong backs and determination to work hard." By the second half of the twentieth century, the Gulf's marine reserves were yielding more than the combined fisheries of the U.S. East Coast. In 2009, the Gulf accommodated four of the seven most productive fishing ports in the United States. Eighty-three percent of the nation's commercial shrimp and 56 percent of its oysters were culled from its waters. Both were major contributors to the state's $6-billion commercial- and sportfishing industry, which employed 60,000 people.

Fish are the oldest-known commodity of inter-mainland trade in Florida. Using dugout canoes that held up to thirty people, pre-Spanish coastal

Indians maintained a fish-trade network that reached to Cuba. The earliest European explorers had no interest in this particular commodity exchange. For them, the consumption of seafood was more often than not a desperate act in time of crisis and starvation. Once whites settled the Gulf, marine life became an important article in local commerce. During the second Spanish occupation, the bays from Tampa to Port Charlotte supported fish ranchos. As with coastal Indians, seafood filled the diet of fishing villagers. Ben Green's mother, who grew up in the Gulf town of Cortez, remembered, "We'd eat fish during the week and then try to have chicken or roast for Sunday dinner, except during the Depression, and then we ate it every night." The people of Cortez may have been "money-poor," said Green, but they were "food rich." Locals called their bay "the kitchen." "There was no way to starve to death," said Davis of the people of Cedar Key. "And they found it was pretty easy to make a living." As the fruits of the sea put food on the table, they put money in pockets.[21]

Mullet was the main commercial and food fish of Gulf coasters, as meaningful to their culture as hogs were to southern rural life. Like the southern barbecue, the mullet fry became west coast Florida's ubiquitous fund-raiser. "You know how many churches and band uniforms [were paid for] with mullet?" asked Mike Davis. In the mid-nineteenth century, seasonal, palm-thatched shanties cropped up on barrier islands, at the end of bights, and along inlets close to fish runs. A vegetarian that habituated sea grass beds, mullet were easily taken with a cast net thrown from the stern of a flat-bottomed skiff or a gill net struck from the same. Once known as the poor man's dinner, mullet became a popular restaurant and fish-store selection in the last quarter of the twentieth century, and the roe of the red mullet a high-end commodity worldwide, particularly in Japan. Leo Lovel, a long-time Big Bend commercial fisherman and restaurateur, calls mullet "Mother Nature's finest," the "basis of the food chain in the sea."

> Poor ole mullet. Everybody and everything in the sea, air and on land love 'em. . . .
> By far the porpoise's food. . . .
> Pelicans dive on 'em when the mullet are trying to run up the river.
> Eagles and osprey snatch at every one that gets close to the surface.
> All your fish in the ocean eat mullet. From trout feeding on the finger mullet in the estuaries to the marlin eating three-pound mullet offshore.

Cormorants chase 'em underwater.
Seagulls pick up the small fry in the grass.
Gators eat 'em.[22]

Mullet leaping in the Anclote River, not far up the Gulf coast from Tampa Bay, gave the town of Tarpon Springs its name. Newcomers to the area mistook the near-shore fish for the bigger, broad-mouthed tarpon. As it happened, neither fish had much to do with the town's importance. Its identity became wrapped up with a sedentary aquatic animal, the sponge. For decades, Gulf coast dwellers pulled sponges from the shallows for personal use before realizing, in the 1840s, their commercial value. Key West initially dominated the sponge trade and did so until the end of the century. By then, the industry had begun a permanent migration up the coast, where yellow, grass, wire, glove, and sheepswool sponges grew. Hospitals used the grass species as surgical sponges, and everyday consumers used sheepswool sponges for bathing and washing carriages and, later, automobiles. Before the turn of the century, Apalachicola emerged as an important port for these sponges. This was before the panhandle town cornered the market with its own brand of oysters. They were harvested from its bay where Gulf saltwater mingled with the freshwater of the town's namesake river, producing plump, sweet-tasting oysters.

Ultimately, Tarpon Springs was better situated to the Gulf's 9,000-square-mile sponge habitat. In 1890, Gulf sponge beds delivered to one local firm $1 million in sales. Such success encouraged Tarpon residents John E. Cheney and John Cocoris, a Greek immigrant, to recruit skilled sponge divers from the Dodecanese Islands. Tarpon Springs evolved into a true Greek American city. In the 1940s, the Anclote River harbored 150 sponge boats, each designed from an original thirty-foot imported Mediterranean model with high-curving bow and stern. They rode the water, said a writer for the Work Progress Administration, "like a crescent moon." Before the fleet got under way for two- to four-week trips, the priest of St. Nicholas Greek Orthodox Cathedral blessed each boat. Tarpon Springs was the world's most productive sponge port. Its natural product washed America. But not even the sacraments of the priest could prevent the first red tide from striking the Gulf coast. The result of nutrient overloading from human activity, the 1947 algae bloom obliterated the industry. Sponging never returned to the same level.[23]

Cedar Key was another Gulf coast community that owed its existence to nature. "The Gulf is what made this place what it is," said Mike Davis. That place is a cluster of barrier islands in a region once called the lonesome leg, later renamed the Nature Coast in the wake of development and artificiality rampaging across Florida. Like the state's other barrier islands—more than 4,500 of ten or more acres—Cedar Key's fourteen date to the retreat of glaciers thousands of years ago when ocean levels rose. They may have been attached to the mainland or to each other at one time, or they may have materialized on their own from the buildup of sediment washing down rivers that emptied into the Gulf. John Muir, who traveled to the area in 1867, described the islands as "looking like a clump of palms, arranged like a tasteful bouquet, and placed in the sea to be kept fresh." The surrounding water is shallow above a continental shelf that rises gently up to grassy—cordgrass and needlerush—intertidal salt marshes from Tarpon Springs north and around west to Ochlockonee Bay, a 200-mile coastal region known as the Big Bend. There is no breaking surf or sand-dune beaches to lure the surfers and beachgoers who frequent the panhandle from Panama City to Pensacola. The Big Bend has historically accommodated quiet recreational and commercial fishing and crabbing. Scientists call it a low-energy coastline. The current is too mild to carry much sediment and sand, and in fair weather the water laps against the shore. These conditions were right for the expanse of tidal marsh, and the gentle surf combined with the sunlight-penetrated shallows encouraged the growth of sea grasses, primarily turtle and manatee grass. They sprawled into a 1,200-square-mile underwater prairie. Seventy percent of Florida's Gulf recreational fish spend part of their lives there, and scallops, shrimp, crabs, seahorses, and sea stars hide out there from predators. In the warmer months, manatees, nicknamed sea cows, migrate north to graze on the grass.

Cedar Key's past is a triangular relationship between water, land, and place. The estuarine environment set the rhythm of human life. This prime marine habitat, which includes grouper, red fish, mullet, green turtles, stone and blue crabs, oysters, and much more, has fed people back to the indigenous inhabitants. Like the Calusa, they built mounds to elevate their settlement above surging water and to capture cooling, mosquito-blowing breezes. They also hunted terrestrial game. In the loblolly and longleaf pine forests reaching deep into the mainland, deer, bear, and gopher tortoise were abundant. But then, in the narrative common to all of North America, European weapons, enslavement, and diseases wiped out nearly all of the aborigines of Florida by the early eighteenth century. The next occupants of the Cedar Keys were once again Indians, this time Seminoles. The U.S. military detained captives at Seahorse Key during the Second Seminole War in preparation for removal to a trans-Mississippi reservation.

After the war, whites began settling the keys and the reedy coast, where mullet jumped in profusion. The fish and forests were the main draw to settlers and businessmen. David Levy Yulee completed his cross-Florida railroad in 1861, connecting the port of Fernandina with Way Key, the main island in the Cedar Key cluster. The Gulf port handled naval stores, lumber, cotton, salt, and more. The Civil War disrupted rail service but peace restored the commercial momentum, enough to make Cedar Key the busiest port on the peninsula's Gulf coast. Sea turtles, its meat a sweet delicacy around the world, were part of that revival. The hundreds that came out of Cedar Key each year—600 to 800 pounds each—were among the 15,000 green turtles Florida and the Caribbean were exporting annually to England by 1878. Fishing, sponging, and salt manufacturing were integral to the local economy, too, and for many years, a cottage industry formed around the horseshoe crab, which on every full moon stormed the beach like Eisenhower's Normandy invaders. They were caught and ground up for animal feed and fertilizer, and the medical industry later extracted their blood to test for bacterial contamination in medical equipment and commercial drugs. When Daniel Andrews retired to Cedar Key from the Midwest around 1909, he patented a whisk broom (trademarked Donax-whisk) and began manufacturing it and brushes from palm fiber, consuming up to 3,000 sabal palm saplings a month. The factory employed roughly 100 people and operated until competition from synthetic fibers and a hurricane, one of those agents of history, shut it down in 1950.

A glance northward from Cedar Key, millions of board feet of cypress and pine once spilled from the Suwannee River, floated down by timber crews from interior forests to be milled at Cedar Key or shipped to ports elsewhere. The most important wood for the people of Cedar Key came from their namesake tree. There were a number of lumber mills in the area, employing more than 100 people, including John Muir for a few days during his three-month stay. The mill of perhaps greatest importance was that of Eberhard Faber on Atsena Otie (Muskogee Creek words for cedar island). A Bavarian immigrant, Faber bought large tracts of wooded land in Levy County for 50 cents an acre to supply the raw material for his New York pencil factory, the first mass-production pencil manufacturing in the United States. On Atsena Otie, he milled red cedar into pencil blanks and penholders shipped to New York and European pencil factories. In 1890, the

Florida Times-Union estimated that Cedar Key's three pencil factories were consuming 100,000 cedar logs a year and producing enough pencil blanks to circle the globe nearly five times.

Muir saw all of this and more. In 1867, twenty-nine years old and auburn bearded, he had months before left Indiana on a pivotal 1,000-mile walk to the Gulf. He entered Florida at Fernandina and walked Yulee's railroad tracks across the peninsula to Cedar Key. En route, in the vine-tangled, water-soaked wilderness landscape he was struck by the wisdom that secured his future as the father of American conservation. It happened with a mosquito bite that infected him with malaria, which to fellow humans reflected the dark side of Florida paradise. Muir developed a different view, however. While convalescing at Cedar Key, he took the opportunity to get to know the area's natural characteristics and began to reassess the human place on earth, that is, the stratification of culture over nature. His encounter with "venomous beasts" and "thorny plants," most especially Florida's Spanish bayonet, combined with his fever convinced him that "certain parts of the earth prove that the whole world was not made for" humans. Nature is the "one great unit of creation," he concluded. It makes human existence possible, yet nature's purpose is not solely for humans. Its purpose is for all.[24]

Nature's richness had its limits. Few in young Muir's day understood this. Lessons often came the hard way. The pencil factories shut down in the 1890s. Locals liked to attribute the demise of the mill economy to an 1896 hurricane that leveled houses and manufacturing on Atsena Otie. It is true that the hurricane marked a shift in the local economy to a near complete dependence on commercial fishing. But it made little sense for the mills to rebuild, even if they had so chosen. Prior to the hurricane, they had logged out the area's cedar stands.

Their activities were a growing trend. Along the coastline south of Cedar Key and on the other side of the state in the Mosquito Lagoon area north of Merritt Island, loggers cut out miles upon miles of red mangroves for tannin, used in the treatment of leather, and for fine-grained wood, coveted by furniture makers. The result was the widespread elimination of avian and marine habitat, key to the Gulf's natural bounty. Pine and cypress were the fish of inland Florida, exploited for a living and profit but to a near end. Pines, like mullet, were ubiquitous and easily harvested. Extracting cypress from its wetland habitat was more complicated but the payoff was usually higher for the owner of the timber rights.

Cypresses were Florida's sequoias of the swamp, ancient and beautiful and inspiring. Captain George McCall, writing a letter from the Withlacoochee

River in 1828 in the vein of the naturalist rather than military officer, noted that he had found "enough to excite his wonder, if not his admiration" in the "enormous shafts of the cypress trees, which support their broad, flat umbrella-shaped tops at the distance of a hundred and twenty feet above the earth." Yet the forest pantheon stirred different sensibilities in different people. The romanticist and the businessman might be equally awed by the trees and note the handiwork of God, but as one would contemplate spiritual enrichment the other would calculate monetary enrichment. "The cypress timber to-day was magnificent," McCall wrote in another passage, "the largest I have ever seen, towering to a height I am afraid to estimate." *Timber* is the key word here, one the utilitarian, not the spiritualist, used when referencing a product rather than the living aesthetic, when estimating dollars in board feet rather than pondering peaceful solitude. Cypress was insect- and rot-resistant, making it an excellent marketable wood for shingles and fencing. Once soldiers like McCall reduced the Seminoles to harmless numbers, timber concerns swarmed to Florida's trees. On the land side of the Big Bend, two of nature's commercial attractions were the Tide Swamp, ranging inland from the coast, and the Mallory Swamp–San Pedro Bay wetland area, the watershed for the Econfina, Fenholloway, and Steinhatchee Rivers. Both were home to mature cypress trees. A sawmill worker recalled the sylvan landscape in 1919, not long after the harvesting had begun: "There were miles and miles of trees never touched by an ax. . . . I can still remember the wind in the trees, with sunlight filtering through the branches. . . . And the woods were full of game." Nearby in Perry, the Burton-Swartz Cypress Company operated the largest cypress mill in the country, which served a nationwide demand the local stock could not satiate.[25]

The mills turned to the Big Cypress Swamp. Trains traveled 318 miles from the Big Cypress to the Big Bend to deliver forty carloads each of cut timber. Some of the toppled giants were more than a thousand years old; some were twelve feet in diameter.[26] The timber trains repeated the journey 915 times between 1943 and 1957, until loggers finished clearing 150,000 acres of old-growth forest. At the same time, more than 400,000 acres of cypress, cedar, and pine fell in the Big Bend region. Burton-Swartz shut down in 1942. There were no more trees to cut. Wildlife of the cypress ecology also disappeared, including another titan of the forest, the now possibly extinct ivory-billed woodpecker. The cypress industry, too, ecologist Howard Odum pointed out, "effectively went extinct"—but only temporarily. Odum was writing in the 1980s, when a second growth of cypress was "coming back" and the industry was "reforming," this time to turn the young trees into landscaping mulch. The "cycle," Odum wrote, "continues."[27]

Nature's attraction as commodity had few sylvan rivals to the pine tree. In the commonwealth of the species, the longleaf was the monarch. It ranged across 92 million acres from southern Virginia down to Lake Okeechobee and across to Texas. A traveler in the old Southeast could not avoid the statuesque tree, straight and spare of branches to its crown. Bartram talked of the solemn symphony of the steady Western breezes . . . playing incessantly, rising and falling through the thick and wavy foliage." Muir liked the spare density of the longleaf forest, the "sunny spaces between full of beautiful abounding grasses," where he "sauntered in delightful freedom." When the protagonist in Zora Neale Hurston's "The Gilded Six-bits" wishes for the well-fed physique of rich white men, to pretend the look of wealth for himself, his wife assures him, "God took pattern after a pine tree and built you noble." The milled wood of the longleaf, dense and clear and tight-grained, ideal for sturdy ship- and home building, prized for its natural resistance to termites, created real wealth for a relative few. The market and fire (exacerbated by timbering) had taken 17 million acres of Florida pine by 1918. By the end of the twentieth century, barely 3 percent of the great longleaf ecosystem of the Southeast had survived. The loss exceeds that of hardwood in the Amazon rain forest, the old-growth Douglas firs of the Pacific Northwest, and the tallgrass prairies of the North American interior. Florida made over allowed no room for the woodland homes of cypresses and pines.[28]

Some longleafs escaped the saw, though not from exploitation and eventual extraction. The highly resinous trees were tapped for gum (oleoresin) to be distilled into spirits of turpentine, which had multiple purposes—from paint and varnish thinners to disinfectant to medicinal ointment—and into rosin, which had seemingly infinite uses—as a compound in soap, electrical insulation, leather dressing, fly paper, lipstick, hair spray, and more. The Spanish were the first to take advantage of this resource, and during their time in the Floridas the British developed a robust industry in naval stores traded across the Atlantic world. As many New South historians have pointed out, cotton was not the only king in the ante- and postbellum eras; so too were timber and turpentine, which on the eve of the Civil War were the South's number two and three export commodities. By the early twentieth century, 70 percent of the world supply of naval stores was drawn from the sap of the longleaf region, with Florida at the center.

Like cotton, timber exploited labor as it exploited the environment. Most of the industry's workers were black. Florida nature in yet another way bespoke economic potential, and the drudgery of subduing it fell ill-fatedly to the dispossessed. Remarkably, the cotton field as workplace was preferable to the industrialized pine forest. Researchers have found that southern blacks who spent peaceful lives in coniferous woods developed a special attachment to the forest and an acute lay knowledge of its ecology—the wildlife and wiregrass and the lightning that struck the columnar trees and ignited fires integral to healthy regeneration. But timber and turpentine camps cast a different glow on the woods. Too few men sought employment in the camps, where the work was toilsome and dangerous, and where one was perpetually at risk of involuntary internment. The industry relied on state and county penal institutions for labor, meaning their woodsy workplaces were veritable convict camps, nearly all black and corporeally brutal. The infamy of Florida's camps earned them the collective branding, the "American Siberia."

The state's convict-lease system lay at the intersection of environmental justice, where culture, economy, and nature formed the crossroads. When the ground was moist and the trees quenched, the gum ran strong. Unshackled after a short night's rest, turpentine crewmembers labored from sunup to sundown, exposed to heat, poisonous snakes, wild boars, and mosquitoes—vectors of malaria and yellow fever—day after life-threatening day. Workers went from tree to tree, hacking chevron-shaped streaks in the trunks for draining the gum. Hurston called the telltale hack marks the "10,000 faces of the piney woods," the trees' equivalent to the tormented countenances of the oppressed workers. Tapping did not bring the trees instant death. They lived ten years on average; a relative few survived into the twenty-first century. The mortality rate of the workers was little better, several times that of the state's already high rate for black males and perhaps twice that of the general prison population. "The onliest way out is to die out," a turpentine worker told Florida folklorist Stetson Kennedy in the late 1930s. Those who managed to survive were, like the turpentine tree, scarred for life. Whippings, maiming, and torture were routine. Researchers have accessed an incriminating paper trail of abuse, and in a state and of an industry that apparently felt no compulsion to cover the trail. Those who executed the brutality did so with a sense of security that their behavior was countenanced by the law and moral code of white society. Eventually, the nation awakened to the realities of the system. A spate of bad publicity exposed the inhumanity at a time when Florida was promoting itself as a natural paradise and tourist destination and hawking its real-estate as a good investment. Local and state officials were forced to reconsider their convict-for-hire practices. In 1919, Florida ended convict-leasing in the state penal system. It continued at the county level until the legislature ended it altogether in 1924 (too many county sheriffs were accepting kickbacks from the turpentine industry).[29]

For those who tapped the trees, the rural life was not the good life. Cassandra Y. Johnson and Josh McDaniel, students of the "turpentine Negro," argue that a long history of economic, political, and social disfranchisement segregated the black experience from a quality life on the land. "It is difficult," observes Florida nature lover Doug Alderson, "to contrast the lives of turpentiners with the peace of the piney woods." At the thought of wilderness, many blacks called up memories or stories of mistreatment and oppressed labor, a "context of exploitation" and horror, rather than tranquility and solitude. Memories could be potent and dark: fugitives escaping through the woods from the slave quarters, baying hounds chasing the wrongly accused through the swamp or pine barren, the stout bough of an oak tree employed for the noose strung by the lynch mob. Oppression in the wilderness reinforced the draw to the city, confounded by its own tragic history of racism. The social memory of the camps and the history of woodland abuse, according to researchers, contributed to a general aversion to outdoor recreation and conservation. For their part, champions of the predominantly white middle-class environmental movement failed to account for the wild outdoors filtering through the differing lenses of cultural experience. Nature that was acceptable to one group was unacceptable to another.[30]

As with the social consequences, the environmental consequences of the turpentine industry were lasting. When a tree could no longer produce, the sawyer came in to cut it. Relieved of its gum, the tree more surely floated downriver to sawmill. Once the longleafs were gone, the slash and loblolly pines that grew in their place, naturally and through planned propagation, were a poor substitute in stoutness but useful nevertheless. The substitutes were faster growing, bearing a softer wood that was the key element of the pulp and paper industry, which by the 1930s had begun spoiling the sky and water with noxious, foul-smelling toxins—sulfuric acid, ammonia, hydrochloric acid, methanol, and dioxins. It was a blight that persisted, along with massive consumptions of water drawn from the aquifer, into the twenty-first century.

Witness to this fate, Leo Lovel wrote at the beginning of that century,

"Mother Nature is the ultimate provider for all of our lives." For thousands of years, nature provided for the multiple cultures that occupied Florida. It gave food for the table, tranquility for the spirit, scenery for the artist and writer, health for the sickly, timber and thatch for shelter, transportation for goods and people, a way of life for a countless many, and recreation for all. Representatives of Western societies arrived in the sixteenth century with an appreciation for Florida's natural endowments. But they also carried a strong belief in their supremacy over all other cultures and things. One of the weaknesses of indigenous cultures, from the Western point of view, was their deep affiliation with other living systems. Westerners, by turn, expressed little or no humility toward nature. As they sought to possess and control other peoples, they sought to possess and control the nonhuman world. Rather than reconciling the natural world as beneficent ecosystem, Floridians continually summoned new genius to exploit its endowments, sometimes to their end, and to impose upon nature an unnatural regime. Like beauty that attracts the villain determined to destroy beauty, nature's allure in Florida was in the end nature's undoing. Long ago, Florida naturalist Charles Torrey Simpson lamented, "The only attraction belonging to the state that we do not ruin is the climate, and if it were possible to can and export it we would do so until Florida would be as bleak and desolate as Labrador." He was wrong in the first instance, of course. Floridians had already begun to change the climate.[31]

Humankind's damage to Florida's environment is a story historians of Florida have begun to tell with insight, detail, and objective passion.[32] As they continue in their service, they might avoid the oversight of those about whom they write. They might pay closer attention to nature's powerful narrative.

Notes

1. Harriet Beecher Stowe, *Palmetto Leaves* (Boston: James R. Osgood, 1873), 138.

2. Marjory Stoneman Douglas, *Florida: The Long Frontier* (New York: Harper and Row, 1967), 21.

3. Ralph Waldo Emerson, *Journals of Ralph Waldo Emerson: With Annotations* (Boston: Houghton Mifflin, 1909), 1:23.

4. Bernal Diaz del Castillo, John Ingram Lockhart trans., *The Memoirs of Bernal Diaz del Castillo* (London: J. Hatchard Lockhart, 1844), 1:14.

5. Carl Ortwin Sauer, *Sixteenth Century North America: The Land and the People as Seen by the Europeans* (Berkeley: University of California Press, 1975), 29.

6. Douglas, *Florida*, 142–43; John Viele, *The Florida Keys: The Wreckers* (Sarasota, Fla.: Pineapple Press, 2001), vi, 54–55; Sauer, *Sixteenth Century North America*, 191.

7. Jay Barnes, *Florida's Hurricane History* (Chapel Hill: University of North Carolina Press, 1998), 1–4.

8. Charles Arnade, "Tristan de Luna and Ochuse, 1559," *Florida Historical Quarterly* 37 (January–April 1959):208–20.

9. The 100-year storm surge refers to the magnitude of a storm surge expected to be equaled or exceeded every 100 years, or that has a 1 percent chance of being exceeded in a given year.

10. Gary R. Mormino, *Land of Sunshine, State of Dreams: The Social History of Modern Florida* (Gainesville: University Press of Florida, 2005), 301, 303.

11. In 2002, the production of sod grass and horticultural products, nonfood commodities officially defined as agriculture, surpassed oranges as the state's top agricultural commodity.

12. Stowe, 18.

13. Mark Derr, *Some Kind of Paradise: A Chronicle of Man and the Land in Florida* (New York: William Morrow, 1989), 40; Christopher Warren, "'Nature's Navel': An Overview of the Many Environmental Histories of Florida Citrus," in *Paradise Lost? The Environmental History of Florida*, ed. Jack E. Davis and Raymond Arsenault (Gainesville: University Press of Florida, 2005), 185; Cynthia Barnett, "Does Big Citrus Have a Future in Florida?" *Florida Trend* 46 (March 2003):46–51.

14. Douglas, *Florida*, 135; James W. Covington, ed., "The Florida Seminoles in 1847," *Tequesta* 24 (1964):49–57.

15. George A. McCall, *Letters from the Frontiers* (Bedford, Mass.: Applewood, 1868), 295; William D. Hoyt Jr. and James B. Dallam, "A Soldier's View of the Seminole War, 1838–39," *Florida Historical Quarterly* 25 (April 1947):359; Fort Myers *News Press*, April 18, 2011.

16. Leo Lovel, *Spring Creek Chronicles II: More Stories of Commercial Fishin', Huntin', Workin', and People along the Gulf coast* (Tallahassee: privately published by Leo Lovel, 2004), 88–89.

17. Henry James, *The American Scene* (New York: Harper and Bros., 1907), 417, 419.

18. Lanier, *Florida*, 20; Edward King, *The Great South: A Record of Journeys in Louisiana, Texas, Missouri, Arkansas, Mississippi, Alabama, Georgia, Florida, South Carolina, North Carolina, Kentucky, Tennessee, Virginia, West Virginia, and Maryland* (American Publishing Company, 1875), 408.

19. *Tallahassee Democrat*, April 27, 2003.

20. Coppertone, developed by a pharmacist in 1944, was originally intended as a sunscreen to protect servicemen, but it marketed its commercial product primarily as a tanning enhancer.

21. Ben Green, *Finest Kind: A Celebration of a Florida Fishing Village* (Cocoa: Florida Historical Society, 2007), 33, 47; Mike Davis, interview by the author, October 28, 2011.

22. Leo Lovel, *Spring Creek Chronicles: Stories of Commercial Fishin', Huntin', Workin', and People along the North Florida Gulf coast* (Tallahassee: privately published by Leo Lovel, 2000), 17, 18.

23. "Ten Fathoms Down in the Gulf," *Florida Highways* 10 (March 1942):14.

24. John Muir, *A Thousand-Mile Walk to the Gulf* (Boston: Houghton Mifflin, 1916), 138–39.

25. McCall, *Letters from the Frontiers*, 193–94; Jeffrey A. Drobney, *Lumbermen and Log*

Sawyers: Life, Labor, and Culture in the North Florida Timber Industry, 1830–1930 (Macon, Ga.: Mercer University Press, 1997), 52–54, 77.

26. The oldest recorded bald cypress in the world was located in Big Tree Park, a county park in Longwood, Florida. Nicknamed the Senator, it was 3,400 to 3,500 years old, 125 feet tall (a 1925 hurricane removed 40 feet from the top), and 17.5 feet in diameter. An arsonist destroyed it in 2012.

27. Howard T. Odum, "Cypress Swamps," in *Cypress Swamps*, ed. Katherine Ewel and Howard T. Odum (Gainesville: University of Florida Press, 1984), 421.

28. Lawrence S. Earley, *Looking for Longleaf: The Fall and Rise of an American Forest* (Chapel Hill: University of North Carolina Press, 2004), 7, 13; Zora Neale Hurston, "The Gilded Six-Bits," in *Black American Short Stories: One Hundred Years of the Best*, edited by John Henrik Clarke (New York: Hill and Wang, 1993), 67.

29. The account of the turpentine worker talking to Kennedy came from a visit to a Louisville, Georgia, camp and is found in Stetson Kennedy, *Southern Exposure: Making the South for Democracy* (Tuscaloosa: University of Alabama Press, 2011), 61.

30. Doug Alderson, *Waters Less Traveled: Exploring Florida's Big Bend Coast* (Gainesville: University Press of Florida, 2005), 75; Cassandra Y. Johnson and Josh McDaniel, "Turpentine Negro," *"To Love the Wind and the Rain": African Americans and Environmental History* (Pittsburgh: University of Pittsburgh Press, 2006), 51.

31. Lovel, *Spring Creek Chronicles*, 84. On Simpson, see Cynthia Barnett, *Mirage: Florida and the Vanishing Waters of the Eastern U.S.* (Ann Arbor: University of Michigan Press, 2007), 21, who responds to the Simpson quote with very similar words. Charles Torrey Simpson, *Out of Doors in Florida: The Adventures of a Naturalist, Together with Essays of the Wild Life and Geology of the State* (Miami: E. B. Douglas, 1923), 137.

32. Many of those sources have been cited in the notes. A selected few others include: David McCally, *The Everglades: An Environmental History* (Gainesville: University Press of Florida, 1999); Kathryn Ziewitz and June Wiaz, *Green Empire: The St. Joe Company and the Remaking of Florida's Panhandle* (Gainesville: University Press of Florida, 2004); Jack E. Davis, *An Everglades Providence: Marjory Stoneman Douglas and the American Environmental Century* (Athens: University of Georgia Press, 2009); Craig Pittman and Matthew Waite, *Paving Paradise: Florida's Vanishing Wetlands and the Failure of No Net Loss* (Gainesville: University Press of Florida, 2009); Craig Pittman, *Manatee Insanity: Inside the War over Florida's Most Famous Endangered Species* (Gainesville: University Press of Florida, 2010); Michael Grunwald, *The Swamp: The Everglades, Florida, and the Politics of Paradise* (New York: Simon and Schuster, 2006); Luther J. Carter, *The Florida Experience: Land and Water Policy in a Growth State* (Baltimore: Johns Hopkins University Press, 1974); Susan Cerulean et al., eds. *Unspoiled: Writers Speak for Florida's Coast* (Tallahassee, Fla.: Heart of the Earth, 2010).

Bibliography

Alderson, Doug. *Waters Less Traveled: Exploring Florida's Big Bend Coast.* Gainesville: University Press of Florida, 2005.

Arnade, Charles W. "Cattle Raising in Spanish Florida." *Agricultural History* 35 (July 1961):116–24.

Barnes, Jay. *Florida's Hurricane History.* Chapel Hill: University of North Carolina Press, 1998.

Barnett, Cynthia. "Does Big Citrus Have a Future in Florida?" *Florida Trend* 46 (March 2003):46–51.

———. *Mirage: Florida and the Vanishing Water of the Eastern U.S.* Ann Arbor: University of Michigan Press, 2007.

Berson, Thomas. "Silver Springs: The Florida Interior and the American Imagination." Ph.D. diss., University of Florida, 2011.

Clarke, John Henrik, ed. *Black American Short Stories: One Hundred Years of the Best.* New York: Hill and Wang, 1993.

Covington, James W., ed. "The Florida Seminoles in 1847." *Tequesta* 24 (1964):49–57.

Davis, Jack E., and Raymond Arsenault, eds. *Paradise Lost? The Environmental History of Florida.* Gainesville: University Press of Florida, 2005.

Davis, Mike. Interview by Jack E. Davis. October 28, 2011.

Derr, Mark. *Some Kind of Paradise: A Chronicle of Man and the Land in Florida.* New York: William Morrow, 1989.

Diaz del Castillo, Bernal. *The Memoirs of Bernal Diaz de Castillo volume 1.* Translated by John Ingram Lockhart. London: J. Hatchard Lockhart, 1844.

Douglas, Marjory Stoneman. *Florida: The Long Frontier.* New York: Harper and Row, 1967.

Drobney, Jeffrey A. *Lumbermen and Log Sawyers: Life, Labor, and Culture in the North Florida Timber Industry, 1830–1930.* Macon, Ga: Mercer University Press, 1997.

Earley, Laurence S. *Looking for Longleaf: The Fall and Rise of an American Forest.* Chapel Hill: University of North Carolina Press, 2004.

Emerson, Ralph Waldo. *Journals of Ralph Waldo Emerson: With Annotations.* Vol. 1. Boston: Houghton Mifflin, 1909.

Ewel, Katherine Carter, and Howard T. Odum, eds. *Cypress Swamps.* Gainesville: University Press of Florida, 1984.

Glave, Dianne D., and Mark Stoll, eds. *"To Love the Wind and the Rain": African Americans and Environmental History.* Pittsburgh: University of Pittsburgh Press, 2006.

Green, Ben. *Finest Kind: A Celebration of a Florida Fishing Village.* Cocoa: Florida Historical Society, 2007.

Hoyt, William D., Jr., and James B. Dallam. "A Soldier's View of the Seminole War, 1838–39." *Florida Historical Quarterly* 25 (April 1947):356–62.

James, Henry. *The American Scene.* New York: Harper and Bros., 1907.

Kennedy, Stetson. *Southern Exposure: Making the South for Democracy.* Tuscaloosa: University of Alabama Press, 2011.

King, Edward. *The Great South: A Record of Journeys in Louisiana, Texas, Missouri, Arkansas, Mississippi, Alabama, Georgia, Florida, South Carolina, North Carolina, Kentucky, Tennessee, Virginia, West Virginia, and Maryland.* American Publishing Company, 1875.

Lanier, Sidney. *Florida: Its Scenery, Climate, and History of Accounts of Charleston, Savannah, Augusta, and Aiken; A Chapter for Consumptives; Various Papers on Fruit-Culture; and Complete Handbook and Guide.* Philadelphia: Lippincott, 1876.

Lovel, Leo. *Spring Creek Chronicles: Stories of Commercial Fishin', Huntin', Workin', and People along the North Florida Gulf coast.* Tallahassee: privately published by Leo Lovel, 2000.

————. *Spring Creek Chronicles II: More Stories of Commercial Fishin', Huntin', Workin', and People along the Gulf coast.* Tallahassee: privately published by Leo Lovel, 2004.

McCall, George A. *Letters from the Frontiers.* Bedford, Mass.: Applewood, 1868.

Mormino, Gary R. *Land of Sunshine, State of Dreams: A Social History of Modern Florida.* Gainesville: University Press of Florida, 2005.

Muir, John. *A Thousand-Mile Walk to the Gulf.* Boston: Houghton Mifflin, 1916.

Sauer, Carl Ortwin. *Sixteenth Century North America: The Land and the People as Seen by the Europeans.* Berkeley: University of California Press, 1975.

Simpson, Charles Torrey. *Out of Doors in Florida: The Adventures of a Naturalist, Together with Essays of the Wild Life and Geology of the State.* Miami: E. B. Douglas, 1923.

Stowe, Harriet Beecher. *Palmetto Leaves.* Boston: James R. Osgood, 1873.

"Ten Fathoms Down in the Gulf." *Florida Highways* 10 (March 1942):10–14.

21

The Maritime Heritage of Florida

DELLA A. SCOTT-IRETON AND AMY M. MITCHELL-COOK

Prehistoric Florida

Florida is a maritime state, and its history has always been tied to the oceans surrounding the long peninsula and to the freshwater rivers meandering through the interior. Florida's maritime history began long before Europeans dreamed of a New World across the Atlantic. Approximately 12,000 years ago, the first people arrived in what is today the state of Florida. Nomadic groups who sustained themselves through hunting and gathering, these people, called Paleoindians, are known today only through their elegant stone tools. In Florida, they utilized the area's many springs and sinkholes to obtain water and to hunt game drawn to these oases in what was at that time an arid, savannah-like landscape. As described in chapter 1, the geography of Florida was much different 12,000 to 14,000 years ago, when much of the planet's water was caught up in massive ice sheets during the last great Ice Age. The resulting lower sea level made Florida much larger in land area, with vast parts of the continental shelf, which today are underwater, high and dry. Paleoindians lived in these now-submerged regions, and archaeologists find evidence of their habitation and hunting sites along relic river channels that once ran to the ancient coastline.

As sea levels rose over thousands of years, Florida's landmass changed, becoming the shape we are familiar with today. The first Floridians utilized the coasts to obtain maritime resources, such as fish and shellfish, for food and tools. Inland freshwater springs continued to be of major importance, and evidence of native use can still be found in many spring basins and sinkholes. For example, at Little Salt Spring hundreds of objects made of wood, shell, bone, and stone have been recovered and provide information about

Prehistoric canoes, such as this one recovered near Weedon Island, often are found along Florida's waterways. Courtesy of the Pinellas County Communications Department.

the people who lived around the spring in the late Paleoindian and early Archaic Periods (11,400–10,200 YBP [Years Before Present]). One especially amazing artifact appears to be an early calendar with incised markings representing the days of the month, one of the earliest date-keeping tools ever discovered in North America.

Watercraft appeared in Florida as early as the middle to early Archaic Period (at least 7,000 to 6,000 YBP); although earlier watercraft probably existed, archaeological evidence has not yet been found. Some Archaic vessels have been discovered, however, and currently more than 300 wooden dugout canoes have been identified in the state. Primarily discovered during droughts when lakes dry up and river levels are low, canoes offer a rare glimpse of the first maritime activity in Florida. For example, in the summer of 2000, a severe drought exposed dozens of prehistoric canoes in Newnan's Lake near Gainesville. With assistance from volunteers and students, archaeologists recorded canoes in a two-mile stretch of the exposed lake bed—the largest group of prehistoric canoes found to date in North America. About 75 percent of the watercraft dated to the late Archaic or early Woodland Periods in Florida's history, or approximately 2,300 to 5,000 years ago. The location of the finds was named the Lake Pithlachocco Canoe Site after an early Creek or Seminole name for Newnan's Lake, appropriately meaning "boat house." Ranging in length from about 15 feet to a little over 30 feet, all of the canoes were manufactured from solid logs using fire to char the wood and shell or stone tools to scrape the burned portions away. Probably associated with a village site on the lake shore, the canoes likely were abandoned when they became worn out, and in fact many showed evidence of wear and damage.

Early European explorers noted the indigenous watercraft they saw, describing them as seaworthy, agile, and expertly handled. Used for fishing and transport, the canoes carried native Florida peoples around the coast and throughout the interior. Wooden watercraft continued to be made and used by native Floridians into the contact, exploration, and colonization eras. Today, the native Floridian tradition of paddle-propelled watercraft survives. Seminoles still living in the Everglades preserve their ancestors' maritime skills in canoe construction and handling. Additionally, the clear, shallow, slow-flowing creeks of Florida's interior draw tens of thousands of visitors and residents to spend relaxing summer days in modern canoes.

European Contact and Colonization

On 7 June 1494, the Kingdom of Spain claimed Florida and all of the newly discovered and as-yet-undiscovered lands of the Americas as part of the Treaty of Tordesillas. The treaty, proposed by the pope, split the world down a line drawn about halfway between the Cape Verde Islands and the Caribbean islands. The Portuguese claimed lands east of the line, which included India and the rich spice islands of Malaysia, while the Spanish looked forward to sole control of the New World on the western side of the line. The treaty was, however, ignored by other European nations such as England, France, and the Netherlands, setting the stage for centuries of dispute, warfare, and colonial competition.

Spanish explorers soon expanded from the islands of the Caribbean into the heart of the New World. This expansion was, of course, enabled by waterborne transport. Within a few years, the Spanish developed a regular route between Spain and its New World colonies, called the Carrera de Indias, or the "Indies run." This round-trip voyage began in Spain with a convoy of ships carrying manufactured materials, clothing, horse tack, foods, books, and other goods that were in great demand in the colonies. After delivering the cargo to New Spain (Mexico), the ships took on spices, dyestuffs, precious metals, and exotic and expensive products of the colonies for the return voyage. Ideally, the fleet made the round-trip each year, avoiding the

New World fleets of the sixteenth century included vessels of different types and sizes, as shown in this 1594 engraving. Courtesy of the University Press of Florida.

late summer and fall season in the Caribbean that often brought hurricanes and tropical storms.

The large landform bounding the Gulf of Mexico to the east was largely unknown to the Spanish through the first decade of the sixteenth century. As explained in chapter 2, conquistador Juan Ponce de León generally is credited with European discovery of La Florida, named in part to honor the Easter season. Although Juan Ponce's first colonizing mission to La Florida proved unsuccessful, the Spanish Crown realized the need for establishing a permanent settlement in the newfound land. Other nations, including France and England, made uncontested forays into Spanish New World territory because no Spanish settlements or troops were there to prevent them. Further, a permanent settlement on the coast would provide aid to shipwrecked sailors. During the first half of the sixteenth century, exploratory voyages along the Gulf coast, including Pánfilo de Narváez in 1528 and Hernando de Soto in 1539, identified spacious harbors and sheltered bays. One bay in particular seemed especially well suited for a settlement, with deep water close to shore to facilitate loading cargo, good holding ground for anchored ships, and sheltering land to provide calm mooring. Called Ochuse or Polonza on early maps, the Spanish renamed it Bahía Filipina del Puerto de Santa María; today the harbor is called Pensacola Bay.

Don Tristán de Luna y Arellano led a colonizing mission to Bahía Filipina, which included families, slaves, Aztec mercenaries, livestock, and all the tools, equipment, and supplies to found a Spanish city on the edge of the empire. Leaving New Spain, Luna's fleet of eleven ships arrived in Pensacola in August 1559 with plans to clear land and construct houses for the settlers. Only a month later, however, a powerful hurricane struck the fledgling colony and sank most of the ships in the fleet and, with those losses, any chance for a successful colony. The survivors salvaged what they could from the wrecked ships, but, suffering from food shortages and privation, most marched north into the interior to try to obtain food from the native peoples. Failing to find adequate supplies, the survivors eventually returned to Pensacola and were evacuated back to New Spain. The Spanish did not return to Pensacola for more than a hundred years; in the meantime, the Spanish founded a permanent settlement in 1565 at St. Augustine on the east coast.

After Luna's failure on the Gulf coast of Florida, Don Pedro Menéndez de Avilés came to the Atlantic coast to accomplish the same goals of consolidating Spanish control, protecting the route of the treasure fleets, and aiding shipwrecked sailors. Menéndez also had an ambitious plan to establish mines and profitable agriculture, and, like other conquistadores, convert the native peoples to Christianity; he also hoped to find his son, lost in an earlier shipwreck on Florida's coast. Establishing Spanish control was especially crucial in east Florida because, in 1562, a French Protestant (Huguenot) expedition under Jean Ribault explored the area around St. Augustine before founding the settlement of Charlesfort in present-day South Carolina. A second French incursion in 1564 landed a small garrison at Fort Caroline on the St. Johns River, which the Spanish destroyed. Menéndez's flagship *San Pelayo*, along with four additional vessels, arrived off the coast on 8 September 1556 carrying colonists to found the first successful European town in what is now the United States. Despite hurricanes, disease, and attacks by English privateers, St. Augustine remains the nation's oldest continually inhabited city and port. Situated on a strategic harbor and relying on ships to bring supplies and additional settlers, St Augustine's maritime focus was reinforced by the construction of the Castillo de San Marcos in 1672–95.

Among the most exciting recent discoveries connected to these early Spanish maritime ventures in Florida was the finding of two ships from Luna's lost fleet. The only remains known to be associated with a Spanish colonization effort, these ships reveal information about seafaring in the Age of Discovery and Exploration and about the process of transporting an entire culture into a wilderness. State of Florida archaeologists discovered the first ship, called the Emanuel Point Ship (EPI) in 1992. Excavations revealed clues to colonial plans including ceramic containers for food and water, evidence of the Aztec mercenaries, butchered bones from cattle and swine, leather shoe soles, and hundreds of olive pits. The University of West Florida's maritime archaeology program in 2006 discovered the second vessel, Emanuel Point II (EPII), only 400 yards away from the first vessel. A smaller ship than EPI, EPII contained an array of ceramic items, as well as shafts for crossbow bolts and even bones from the ship's cat that likely perished in the wrecking.

Although Spain staked its claim to La Florida with a permanent settlement at St. Augustine, its hold was tenuous at best. To strengthen the claim, in 1698 a second colony was founded at Pensacola, located directly to the north of the pass leading into the bay from the Gulf, on today's Naval Air Station Pensacola, and called Presidio Santa María de Galve. Although Santa María had little to recommend it, the area boasted dense pine and live oak forests that provided ideal materials for ship construction and naval stores such as pitch and resin. From the early sixteenth century, shipyards in the New World took advantage of virgin forests and a profusion of natural resources to produce merchant vessels, warships, and a host of smaller watercraft. Although none of these ships survive, a few shipwrecks from this era have been discovered and archaeologically investigated. In Pensacola Bay, the Santa Rosa Island Wreck is an excellent example of an early-eighteenth-century Spanish warship. University of West Florida archaeologists identified the wreck, first recorded in 1992, as likely being *Nuestra Señora del Rosario y Santiago Apostol*. Built in Mexico in 1695, the vessel was approximately 130 feet long and was constructed of New World mahogany and other tropical hardwoods. In 1705, *Rosario* sailed to Pensacola to supply the garrison and then returned to Veracruz with a cargo of pine and cypress logs to be used for ship masts. *Rosario* was anchored in Pensacola Bay when a hurricane caused it to ground in shallow water on the north side of Santa Rosa Island. Stripped of everything useful, the damaged ship was abandoned and eventually broke apart, leaving the lower hull buried under sand and ballast stones. Archaeological investigations revealed personal possessions of the crew, stacks of brooms, and boxes of nails and replacement pulley sheaves probably meant for the shipyards of New Spain.

Many of the same ships that supplied Spain's colonies with basic necessities became annual treasure fleets when they returned with vast quantities of New World products, especially gold and silver. Due to the success of armed galleons in protecting those bullion shipments, only three fleets were captured by enemies, in 1628, 1657, and 1702. More ships, however, were destroyed by storms along Florida's shores: the 1622 fleet off the Marquesas and in the Dry Tortugas, the 1715 fleet off the east coast of Florida, and the 1733 fleet in the Keys. The loss of those fleets inspired pirates for hundreds of years. Historically, freebooters swarmed to wrecksites in an attempt to capture shipwrecked cargo, and the Spanish responded by developing sophisticated salvage techniques. Spanish salvage was so successful, in fact, that on the 1733 wrecks more precious metal was recovered than was listed on the ships' manifests—evidence of inevitable contraband and smuggling. Despite the damage caused by treasure hunters, especially since the 1960s, archaeological investigations have revealed a range of New World materials intended for the markets of Europe, including fine porcelain from China, religious figurines, weaponry, and jewelry from the workshops of native artisans. Today, the shipwrecks of the treasure fleets are among the oldest artificial reefs off Florida's shores.

British Florida and Return of the Spanish

When the Spanish left their colony of Florida in 1763 as part of the Treaty of Paris, they took with them everything of use, including tools, cannons, millstones, and household implements. As a result, British settlers had to import all of these mundane, yet necessary, items. At least one cargo ship carrying replacement goods wrecked while entering the port at St. Augustine, and historical documents indicate that other ships were lost as well. The transport sloop *Industry* ran aground in 1764 on the shallow bar at the entrance of St. Augustine harbor. Loaded with a varied cargo including cannons for the Castillo de San Marcos, millstones, chests of nails and tools, and ammunition, *Industry*'s cargo was vital to the establishment of the new British colony. The ship was discovered in 1997 during a survey of the historic port by archaeologists with Southern Oceans Archaeological Research, Inc., who found cannons still in position as they were loaded in *Industry*'s hold. Artifacts from *Industry* are on display at the St. Augustine Lighthouse & Museum. A second vessel, currently called the Storm Wreck, was discovered off St. Augustine in 2010 by archaeologists with the Lighthouse Museum's Lighthouse Archaeological Maritime Program, or LAMP. It, too, appears to have been a cargo vessel loaded with necessary goods such as cooking pots, cannons, ammunition, and tools. This shipwreck further illustrates the treacherous navigation often required to enter harbors and ports before the days of dredging and channel marking.

Wooden hulls in tropical waters needed frequent repairs to replace planks eaten by shipworm and fouled by barnacles and weed growth. Special places called careening grounds were used for these repairs and generally had sandy bottoms gently sloping to shallow water on wide beaches, which allowed the ships to be carefully leaned on their sides so repair crews could access the lower hull. A long-used careening ground in Pensacola Bay was located at Old Navy Cove on the modern Gulf Breeze Peninsula. The remains of several historic watercraft have been documented in the Cove, and the area also was used for quarantining ships suspected of carrying disease. In 1988, archaeologists with the University of West Florida conducted a survey of the land surrounding the Cove, called Deadman's Island. Investigations in the Cove's shallow water revealed a partially intact ship's hull, and State of Florida archaeologists conducted a maritime archaeology field school for UWF students. The field school, held in the summer of 1989, uncovered the port side of a British warship, identified by artifacts and historical documents as likely either HMS *Stork* or HMS *Florida*, both of which were careened in the Cove but, found to be unseaworthy, were abandoned. A second British vessel was also discovered at Deadman's Island, so likely both *Stork* and *Florida* have been found, although archaeologists are not certain which wreck is which ship.

The start of the American Revolution in 1775 caused British authorities to strengthen the defenses of their loyal colonies, East and West Florida. Armed warships and supplies were sent to St. Augustine and Pensacola. A British warship lost as a result of the war has long been a maritime mystery in Pensacola. HMS *Mentor* was built as the privateer *Who's Afraid* in Maryland in 1778. Captured by the British, the vessel was armed as a sloop-of-war and commissioned into the British navy in 1780. *Mentor* was sent to Pensacola to help defend the town during the Revolution. When a large Spanish fleet under command of Don Bernardo de Gálvez sailed into Pensacola Bay in 1781, *Mentor* was taken up the Blackwater River to prevent its falling into enemy hands. While in the river, a squall caused *Mentor* to capsize; her crew, unable to right the ship, set fire to the hull. To date, the wreck has not been found. The Battle of Pensacola resulted in Spanish forces taking the town, a major blow for British war efforts. The Treaty of Paris ending the American War of Independence gave Florida back to Spain.

The Second Spanish Period in Florida began with Spain resuming control of the colonies in 1784, after only twenty-one years of British occupation. Once again, ships brought settlers and supplies into the major ports of St. Augustine and Pensacola. The Spanish tended to remain along coasts and rivers for ease of trade and travel, leaving the interior of Florida unsettled and unprotected. Firms specializing in trade with Native American tribes flourished in the Spanish Floridas. For example, Panton, Leslie, and Company, founded in 1782–83, furnished Indians with trade goods such as guns, blankets, clothes, cooking ware, and rum in exchange for primarily deer hides but also exotic products such as furs, honey, and bear oil. Pensacola became the main port for the southern Indian trade, causing Panton, Leslie, and Company to locate their principal establishment in the town. Other company offices and trading posts were located at St. Augustine and at St. Marks. Import and export of Indian trading goods caused these ports to prosper, spurring further trade and settlement in Florida.

U.S. Territory and Statehood

As Florida entered the U.S. Territorial Period in 1821, the land was only sparsely settled. Pensacola and northeast Florida had reasonable centers of population but not until the end of the Second Seminole War, in 1842, did American settlements expand farther down the coasts and move slowly inland to take advantage of fertile soil and forest resources. Although some internal improvements occurred in Florida at this time, natural waterways, both inland and coastal, remained the primary means of transportation. Ships of all nations sailed Florida waters to take advantage of natural resources as well as a lack of official administration. Maritime activities along southern Florida waters came primarily from Bahamians who fished and smuggled goods to British Caribbean territory where they received better trade conditions. The numerous vessels sailing, and sometimes grounding, along the Keys contributed to the development of "wrecking," the profitable salvage of wrecked ships, by Keys inhabitants. Key West also became a major port for fishing and sponging.

As the territory grew in population, the paying of duties, or taxes, became an issue, and the U.S. government looked for ways to organize and consolidate shipping in and around Florida. During the Second Seminole War, the United States Revenue Cutter Service, a forerunner of the U.S. Coast Guard, had helped move troops and supplies through difficult-to-navigate waters. Despite U.S. control of Florida, commercial fishing was conducted primarily in Spanish or Native vessels. Fishermen typically salted and dried their catches at small villages, or "ranchos," and then traded their goods with Cuba, avoiding U.S. taxes. With an eye to broadening markets, U.S. fishermen moved into Florida to take advantage of the Havana trade. With the end of the Second Seminole War, many ranchos and indigenous communities disappeared or were destroyed, thus leaving the resource open to American nets and lines.

Like the Spanish and British before them, American colonists exploited the immense virgin forests in Florida's interior. Throughout the Territorial Period, ports like Jacksonville grew to accommodate a growing timber industry. Inland river transport increased due to improved steam technology, and logging became more efficient with the use of sawmills. After the wars, the interior opened up to cotton and agriculture that also relied on water transportation. As the Territorial Period ended, inland areas of Florida enjoyed some growth. However, problems of shallow-river navigation, inclement weather, the economic panic of 1839, and slowly spreading railroad tracks kept much of the area from developing further.

Some of Florida's best natural harbors, like Pensacola Bay, lacked navigable water routes to connect the coast to interior areas and industries, thus limiting their growth as viable ports. Apalachicola, with its convenient and relatively deep river, grew through trade while Pensacola remained primarily a military port. Overall, Florida's rivers and bays proved inadequate for shipping goods inland. Improved steamship construction did provide for regular communication and travel along the Gulf and Atlantic coastlines and helped tie Florida ports to larger markets, but internal travel remained limited with few ships able to steam up Florida's shallow rivers. In response to the growth of coastal shipping, several lighthouses were constructed to improve navigation.

Florida's agricultural and natural resources were not the only reasons why the region became essential to the U.S. economy. Florida provided safe anchorages and supplies for American ships, especially those carrying goods from the interior of the United States down the Mississippi River and into the Gulf and Atlantic. Some Americans feared that foreign vessels could block the Straits of Florida, the crucial passage between Florida and Cuba and the Bahamas, and hamper international trade coming from the United States. In addition, large bays such as Pensacola could harbor and supply enemy fleets if not patrolled carefully. After statehood in 1845, efforts were initiated to improve and protect the larger bays and waterways.

By 1822, the U.S. Navy's West Indies Squadron was based at the Pensacola Navy Yard (today's Naval Air Station Pensacola). The yard was the primary support facility for ships operating in the Gulf, Caribbean, and South Atlantic. Throughout the 1820s and 1830s, the United States constructed coastal forts to protect Pensacola Bay, including Fort Pickens, Fort McRee, and Fort Barrancas. The yard served as the main supply base for ships operating off Mexico and, as the closest naval base, it supported amphibious landings during the Mexican War (1846–48). By 1859, the yard had constructed USS *Pensacola* and USS *Seminole*; however, limited facilities prevented large-scale construction of steam-driven vessels, and shipbuilding fell into decline. The yard and nearby forts soon had different roles to play as the Civil War split control of the installations. Fort Pickens remained in Union hands and the others became Confederate strongholds.

Civil War

At the outbreak of the Civil War, the Union implemented a three-pronged offensive known as the Anaconda Plan. It called for taking the Confederate capital at Richmond, blockading southern coasts, and controlling the Mississippi River. While Florida played no part in the taking of Richmond, the state became a vital component in the Union's blockade and inland river campaigns. For the South, Florida remained an area ripe for blockade-runners, and it was a necessary buffer to maintain inland supplies. Blockade-runners operated out of several ports, especially those with interior railroad access such as Pensacola, Jacksonville, Apalachicola, and St. Marks. To maintain the blockade, the Union captured ports such as Jacksonville, Fernandina, and St. Augustine in the early months of the war, while Fort Taylor in Key West and Fort Pickens in Pensacola never fell to the Confederacy.

The blockade consisted of four squadrons, with three of those squadrons relying on Florida ports and coastlines for fuel and supplies. Key West was headquarters for the East Gulf Blockading Squadron, whose territory stretched from St. Andrews Bay, about 100 miles east of Pensacola, down the peninsula and halfway up the Atlantic coast to approximately Cape Canaveral. Due to the region's isolation from the rest of Confederacy, the East Coast Squadron dealt mainly with stopping blockade-runners and with destroying the coastal saltworks necessary for preserving the South's meat. The East Gulf Squadron also patrolled farther south to Spanish-controlled Cuba and east to the Bahamas. Although the East Gulf Squadron captured several blockade runners and seized Confederate property, it did not play a major role in the overall Union strategy to "strangle" the South. The squadron had too few vessels to block major ports and remained a forgotten post for most of the war.

Rather, Union efforts in Florida turned to areas closest to other southern states. The Atlantic and the West Gulf coast Squadrons picked up where the East Coast Squadron left off. The West Coast Squadron, under command of Admiral David Farragut, focused its efforts on taking the Mississippi River and on preventing blockade-runners from supplying New Orleans. Although emphasis had shifted farther west, Commander David Porter used his mortar flotilla to bombard Mobile. While he failed to accomplish much within Mobile Bay, his actions propelled Confederates to abandon Pensacola. With Union efforts concentrated on the Mississippi River, the blockade along ports such as Mobile remained porous and numerous southern vessels made it through unscathed. Once the West Gulf Squadron took New Orleans, Union efforts shifted back to the Gulf and closed Mobile in August 1863. With Mobile and New Orleans out of the war, fighting shifted west to Texas, which removed Florida even farther from hostilities.

On the east coast, Union attempts to take Jacksonville met with resistance. Although the North was unable to hold the town, several ships were left at the entrance of the St. Johns River to stop blockade-runners. Despite the Union's best efforts, traffic persisted along the river, and northeast

Florida remained in Confederate hands. Union strategy focused on important ports in South Carolina and Georgia, leaving few resources to maintain a permanent presence along the St. Johns. Throughout the war, and despite several battles, northeast Florida remained a contested theater, but always secondary to events farther north.

Meanwhile, the South strived to defy the blockade. Quiet sailing ships and fast steamships burning smokeless coal waited for moonless nights to "run the blockade," bringing material for war, medicines, foodstuffs, and scarce luxuries into southern ports. Shallow waters and small inlets prevented larger ships from gaining access and created perfect hiding places for shallow-draft vessels trying to avoid the blockade. Captains and crews risked their lives to evade Union ships, but could earn fabulous profits if successful. The Union pursued blockade-runners relentlessly, capturing, burning, and sinking the ships they caught. Two such ships, *Scottish Chief* and *Kate Dale*, are located in the Hillsborough River that flows into Tampa Bay. The stern-wheel steamship *Chief* and sailing vessel *Dale* were loaded with cotton when a Union raiding party burned them in 1863. Although in shallow water near a historic shipyard on the river, the remains were hidden by murky water until an archaeological survey sponsored by the Florida Aquarium discovered them in 2008–9.

Among the blockade-runners attacked was the two-masted schooner *William H. Judah,* in Pensacola Bay. The vessel was moored at the Pensacola Navy Yard, which was under Confederate control, while being readied for further service when, early in the morning of 14 September 1861, a Union party from the warship USS *Colorado* pounced, setting fire to the ship. The *Judah* broke free of the wharf and drifted west with the tide until sinking opposite Fort Barrancas.

More than twenty known Union vessels met their demise in and off Florida, as well as a score of British and international vessels. Only a few have been discovered and documented archaeologically. One of these vessels was *Maple Leaf.* The 173-foot-long vessel was built as a luxury passenger steamer, but the Union converted it to a troop transport. In 1864, *Maple Leaf* was traveling on the St. Johns River carrying 400 tons of gear, including personal possessions and supplies, when it hit a Confederate mine (called a torpedo at the time) and sank. The ship ultimately settled to the bottom of the river, where it was covered by more than seven feet of mud. The mines were effective; within six weeks, two other vessels met the same fate, and a third followed soon thereafter. *Maple Leaf* was rediscovered in the 1980s, and the State of Florida and the maritime archaeology program at East Carolina

University partnered to excavate a portion of the shipwreck. Artifacts recovered enabled historians to understand what possessions Civil War–era soldiers kept with them, such as photographs of loved ones, personal plates and eating utensils, sewing kits to repair shoes and clothes, and a variety of items that helped them to endure warfare, discomfort, loneliness, and long absences from home. Today, *Maple Leaf* artifacts are displayed in museums in Tallahassee and Jacksonville.

Just after the Civil War, the Navy's worst nonwartime disaster occurred off Tampa Bay. The tug USS *Narcissus* was traveling south from Pensacola to round the Florida peninsula and continue to New York when, along with USS *Althea*, she was caught in a storm off Tampa's Egmont Key. *Althea* managed to ride out the storm, but high waves breached *Narcissus's* hull and caused the ship's steam boiler to explode. *Narcissus* sank and all hands were lost; only a few pieces of the ship and the body of a fireman washed ashore. The shipwreck site was partially salvaged by treasure hunters in the 1980s, though the artifacts they recovered were never conserved and the salvors eventually threw away the rusty and corroded lumps of metal. Luckily, *Narcissus* was investigated archaeologically as part of the Florida Aquarium's Tampa Bay Shipwreck Project and, at this writing, has been nominated to join Florida's Underwater Archaeological Preserve system.

Reconstruction and Maritime Industry

After the war, steamboat traffic contributed to reconstruction of Florida's economy and also to the creation of a new industry that came to be called "tourism." Clear, spring-fed rivers, graceful overhanging trees festooned with Spanish moss, and an array of unusual wildlife drew visitors by the thousands to the peninsula and Panhandle. Steamboats travelling along slow-moving and easily navigable waters hosted some of the first tourists to Florida's natural attractions and helped promote the state as an exotic destination. Tourists helped to encourage maritime interests in general and boating trips of all types increased in these decades, providing a variety of excursions in and around Florida's waterways. Regular steam packets to various towns increased in number, as did vessels which serviced northern cities such as New York. By the late nineteenth century, Florida's waterways hosted ships from Charleston and Savannah on their ways to Fernandina and Jacksonville. Off the St. Johns River, Harriet Beecher Stowe wrote her famous letters "Back Home," and she became a tourist attraction in her own right. Side-wheelers and stern-wheelers moved agricultural goods, merchandise, mail, construction materials, groceries, and passengers throughout the state. Steamboats also carried cotton from interior agricultural regions to coastal ports for shipment to foreign manufacturing centers. Not until the advent of cross-Florida railroads in 1861 and afterwards, which moved people and goods faster and cheaper, did steamboating on Florida's rivers decline.

A few remnants of the state's steamboating heritage exist as ghostly wrecks in tannin-stained river water. *City of Hawkinsville* was the largest and last steamboat on the Suwannee River. Built in 1896, the stern-wheeler was 141 feet long with two decks. She moved along the river between Cedar Key, Branford, and Old Town until abandoned in 1922. Tied up on the west side of the river near Old Town, *Hawkinsville* was left to slowly sink into the Suwannee's dark depths. Now a state Underwater Archaeological Preserve, *Hawkinsville* provides an exciting diving opportunity and a tangible link to the steamboating era in Florida.

Into the last decades of the nineteenth century, industries such as tourism, lumber, and agriculture helped to boost shipping and increased the number of vessels along Florida's coastlines. Northern entrepreneurs took notice of postwar Florida's prospects and invested money in a variety of mills that fed ports like Jacksonville and Pensacola. The call for lumber continued. And there was new demand for naval stores and phosphates, the latter an important component of fertilizer. Tampa, especially, benefitted from a phosphate boom in the late nineteenth century. Smaller ports like Apalachicola, St. Marks, and Cedar Key also grew, but they lacked the infrastructure and convenience of major harbors. Southern portions of the state experienced increased production in fishing, cattle, and citrus.

By the end of the nineteenth century, Florida's lumber industry was engaged in heavy trans-Atlantic trade. It was the Florida ports that made possible shipments of lumber to foreign markets. Those sales led to harbor improvements and facilitated the growth of several port cities. Pensacola became the third-largest seaport on the Gulf coast. International demand for tar and turpentine increased as well and Florida became a major supplier of naval stores throughout the world.

While most ships loaded with pine, oak, and tropical hardwoods from Florida forests made their voyages successfully, some were lost on the state's shores. *Lofthus* was a Norwegian-owned, barque-rigged, iron-hulled sailing ship when she wrecked in 1898. Loaded with lumber, the ship left Pensacola bound for Buenos Aires, Argentina, when she was caught in a storm and grounded off the east coast of Florida near Boynton Beach. Now lying in

Florida's Shipwreck PRESERVES

USS MASSACHUSETTS
1 The Spanish-American War-era battleship USS *Massachusetts* was scuttled for target practice in the emerald-green waters off Pensacola in 1921.

Vamar
3 Admiral Richard Byrd used this steamer in his Antarctic expedition of 1928–30 and named her *Eleanor Bolling* in honor of his mother; later sold and renamed *Vamar*, she sank off Port St. Joe in 1942 under mysterious circumstances.

Regina
5 The Cuban tanker-barge *Regina*, loaded with 350,000 gallons of molasses, wrecked in a gale off Bradenton Beach in 1940.

SS Tarpon
2 The merchant steamer *SS Tarpon* plied the Gulf Coast for over 30 years before she was lost in a gale off Panama City in 1937.

CITY OF HAWKINSVILLE
4 The turn-of-the-century paddlewheel steamboat *City of Hawkinsville* lies submerged in the Suwannee River, a storybook ghost ship inhabited by catfish and sturgeon.

San Pedro
6 Victim of the 1733 Spanish Plate Fleet disaster, the galleon *San Pedro* was lost in a hurricane near Islamorada in the Florida Keys.

Urca De Lima
11 Part of the ill-fated 1715 Spanish Plate Fleet wrecked off Florida's east coast, *Urca de Lima* became the state's first Underwater Archaeological Preserve in 1987.

Georges Valentine
10 The Italian lumber bark *Georges Valentine* wrecked in 1904 offshore of the House of Refuge near Stuart, scattering her cargo of mahogany lumber on the beach.

Lofthus
9 The wreck of the Norwegian bark *Lofthus*, sunk during a storm in 1898 near Boynton Beach, was dynamited to salvage the valuable cargo of lumber.

SS Copenhagen
8 The steamship *SS Copenhagen*, wrecked in 1900, rests in clear blue water off Pompano Beach and is home to a variety of marine life.

Half Moon
7 *Half Moon*, originally christened *Germania*, was a famous racing yacht before being used as a floating cabaret in Miami and later wrecking on a shoal near Key Biscayne.

The steamboat City of *Hawkinsville* is one of Florida's Underwater Archaeological Preserves. Reprinted with permission of the Florida Department of State, Division of Historical Resources, http://www.flheritage.com/index.cfm.

twisted, jumbled pieces on the ocean bottom, *Lofthus* became an Underwater Archaeological Preserve in 2003. Similarly, the merchant ship *Catharine* wrecked in 1894 while attempting to enter Pensacola harbor to take on a load of lumber.

Other lumber vessels were abandoned when they reached the end of their useful life. In the Blackwater River, Shield's Cove is a historic ship graveyard. This maritime "junkyard" contains the sunken remains of ships and boats that were no longer useful or profitable for their owners. Four wooden-hulled lumber ships lie side by side where they were abandoned in the 1930s. *Palafox, George T. Locke, Dinty Moore,* and *Guanacastle* were all part of the northwest Florida lumber boom in the early twentieth century, hauling cargoes of timber from the river towns of Milton and Bagdad to the dockyards of Pensacola. Although not glamorous or famous, these working craft serve as reminders of the industry that helped to build northern Florida.

Another key maritime industry, fishing, has long been associated with Florida, from prehistoric peoples to the early modern era. The red snapper industry increased in the nineteenth century, as did the mullet and pompano markets. Oysters also became a new market for Gulf coast towns, which often relied on railroads to get shipments out quickly. By the 1890s, Florida was one of the top states engaged in commercial fisheries. Huge fleets of fishing boats were based in the major harbors of Tampa, St. Augustine, Apalachicola, Key West, and Pensacola. Many ports focused on pursuing a particular species, and port towns became famous for their signature catches, such as Apalachicola oysters, St. Augustine deep-water shrimp, Tarpon Springs and Key West sponges, and Pensacola red snapper. The ships and boats used in the industry were specialized for their tasks and reflected the particular needs of the crews. For example, a vessel type called a "smack" was used in the snapper fishing industry centered in the Gulf of Mexico. Smacks developed from fishing boats native to New England that were brought south to fish the offshore waters of the Gulf. These boats soon were modified with a live well that circulated ocean water to keep the fish alive during long voyages. The sound of the fish smacking against the hull is credited with inspiring the unusual name.

Despite the large numbers of smacks built and used around the Florida Gulf coast, no examples of the type remain afloat. A couple of wrecks, however, have been archaeologically investigated. A wooden-hulled wreck in the Blackwater River, appropriately called the Snapper Wreck, is an example of a locally used smack. Although the vessel's name is not known, it appears to have been abandoned in the 1930s, when motor-driven fishing boats proved more efficient than sailing craft. Another boat, called Hamilton's Wreck for its discoverer, lies in shallow water on the west side of Pensacola Bay. Probably wrecked during one of the hurricanes that struck Pensacola in the early twentieth century, this vessel's artifacts, along with construction features, suggest the vessel was used in the local fishing industry.

The expansion of maritime industries in Florida, like lumbering and fishing, relied on shipping and the necessary infrastructure to keep goods flowing. Through the 1870s and 1890s, small sums of money went to river and harbor improvement. For example, the Apalachicola River was opened to Columbus, Georgia, as a means to promote traffic; however, the harbor itself remained an issue. Dredging efforts at Cedar Key on the west coast and the St. Johns River in the east, especially around Jacksonville, helped with waterborne commerce and statewide transportation. By the 1880s, Jacksonville alone had seventy-four vessels operating from its port. Despite this improvement, however, Jacksonville, like other Florida ports, continued to face problems of shallow water, winding rivers, and shifting channels that limited the size and capabilities of watercraft. In response to these problems, throughout the latter part of the nineteenth century, Jacksonville implemented river and harbor improvements to make it a viable seaport; these improvements required continual maintenance well into the twentieth century.

Along with maritime improvements came advancements in other forms of moving goods. Railroads, a major means of transportation by the last decades of the nineteenth century, experienced a dramatic advance when in 1888 Standard Oil tycoon Henry Morrison Flagler began the railroad Florida East Coast System that descended the Atlantic coast from Jacksonville to Miami in 1896, and to Key West in 1912. As a result of increased traffic of people and goods, the port of Miami began much-needed harbor enhancements. Various other internal rail lines connected Jacksonville, Pensacola, and Tampa Bay to the rest of the United States. By 1900, the state had been transformed from a few minor ports and rail heads servicing a small and scattered population to a burgeoning network of modern harbors, steam lines, and railroad systems that mirrored developments in New York and New England.

While Florida focused on harbor and internal improvements, the United States recognized an increased need for coastal defense and improved marine safety. By the 1870s, the shoreline of Florida had several houses of refuge, including those located at Malabar, Gilbert's Bar, Indian River, and

The Gilbert's Bar house of refuge near Stuart in 1934. Courtesy of the U.S. Coast Guard.

Orange Grove. Often manned by a single keeper, the houses existed on sparsely settled beaches and gave shelter to stranded or shipwrecked sailors. A dramatic example of the need for such refuges occurred in 1904, when the Italian barque *Georges Valentine* wrecked on the east coast of Florida near the town of Stuart. Loaded with a cargo of milled mahogany, the ship was en route from Pensacola to Buenos Aires, Argentina, when she was caught in a powerful storm. Driven northward through the Straits of Florida, the vessel ran aground on a shoal, causing her three iron masts to fall and the hull to break apart; five of the crew were lost. Fortunately for the remainder, the ship had wrecked near the Gilbert's Bar house of refuge. Tired, cold, and injured, the men struggled to the house to alert the keeper, Captain William Rea, who provided aid, shelter, and food until the survivors could be sent home to Italy. Seven of the twelve-man crew were saved, proving the worth of the system of houses of refuge along Florida's coasts. Today, *Georges Valentine* is a Florida Underwater Archaeological Preserve and is listed on the National Register of Historic Places.

Modern Maritime Florida: Great Depression, World Wars, and Beyond

Into the twentieth century, Florida shipping solidified its place within worldwide commerce. The First World War disrupted some of this international trade, but the war itself did not come to Florida waters. Instead, the beginning of World War I brought about the birth of naval aviation at

Pensacola and, by 1919, seaplane, dirigible, and balloon pilots trained at the base. After the war, Florida's economy shifted to tourism and land sales. In the 1920s, southern Florida became a major tourist destination. Big-game fishing for marlin, tuna, and sailfish lured anglers to coastal towns including Key West, Miami, Ft. Lauderdale, and Destin. Projects such as the Overseas Highway boosted travel and tourism, and were a means to bring tourists to the Florida Keys. During winter months, the population of southern Florida expanded by 300 percent. Another project, first conceived in the late nineteenth century, the East Coast Canal (later renamed the Florida Intracoastal Waterway) provided a protected inland waterway for trade and shipping, but when opened, it proved to be more of a service to pleasure craft than a route for merchant ships. However, such improvements did not go without reverses. Collapsing land sales in 1926 and devastating hurricanes in 1926, 1928, and 1935 diminished growth, as did the Great Depression in 1929–40.

In 1920, Prohibition brought about a new emphasis on border security. At this time, the Revenue Cutter Service and the Life-Saving Service merged into the United States Coast Guard (USCG), and one of its major tasks was to enforce Prohibition and interrupt rumrunners bringing illegal alcohol into the United States. Large numbers of smugglers took advantage of Florida's sparsely settled coastlines and numerous inlets. Their boats and airplanes moved between the Bahamas and Florida, and Homestead became a main distribution center for alcohol imported from Cuba, while Key West served as an important stopover. Fast, quiet, sail-powered vessels often ran alcohol into Florida's hidden harbors. One relic of the rum-running days is *Governor Stone,* one of the last examples of the coastal schooners that once operated along the Gulf coast.

Built in 1877, *Governor Stone* was used as a cargo transport, an oyster buy-boat, and a merchant marine training vessel, as well as a rumrunner. Now restored as a sailing museum, *Stone* travels the Gulf coast offering educational activities, sailing excursions, and tours. Another Prohibition-era vessel lies on the sea floor near Miami. *Half Moon* was a German-built racing yacht originally called *Germania* when she was launched in 1908. After capture by the British at the start of World War I, *Half Moon* eventually was taken to Miami, where she was anchored offshore as a floating cabaret. *Half Moon* broke her moorings during a storm and ran aground off Key Biscayne, where she is located today. Now a popular snorkeling and diving site, the yacht also is a State Underwater Archaeological Preserve.

The rumrunners' problem came to a head when, in 1927, a smuggler shot and killed a Coastguardsman in Florida waters. The smuggler subsequently

The historic coastal schooner *Governor Stone* is now a floating museum and school. Courtesy of the Friends of the Governor Stone, Inc.

was tried and hanged at the USCG base in Ft. Lauderdale. The war against smuggling took a new direction soon afterwards as the need to locate smugglers farther out at sea led to an emphasis on air reconnaissance. The first Coast Guard Air Station was commissioned in Miami in 1926, followed by another at St. Petersburg in 1934. Thereafter, the USCG took a more active role along Florida's waters and beaches.

Shipping continued to provide some economic stability to Florida. With the state's long distances and limited roadways, coastal shipping remained the most convenient and viable method of moving people and goods around Florida. One of Florida's most famous coastal steamers, *Tarpon*, ran along the Panhandle from St. Andrews Bay (Panama City) to Pensacola and Mobile, Alabama, for more than thirty years. In 1937, *Tarpon*, heavily loaded, rounded the sea buoy at Pensacola bound for St. Andrews. Caught in a fierce gale, the ship began taking on water. Cargo was jettisoned and the vessel was turned toward shore to try to ground her, but *Tarpon* was still 11 miles offshore when she sank, taking eighteen people down with her. Today, the remains of *Tarpon* lie in 90 feet of water off Panama City and are designated a State Underwater Archaeological Preserve.

Shipping took on renewed importance with the outbreak of the Second World War. German submarines, or U-boats, operated in the Gulf of Mexico and in the Atlantic off Florida, prompting dim-out policies in coastal communities to help prevent ship silhouettes becoming visible against the

Half Moon, formerly *Germania*
UNDERWATER ARCHAEOLOGICAL PRESERVE
Miami, Florida

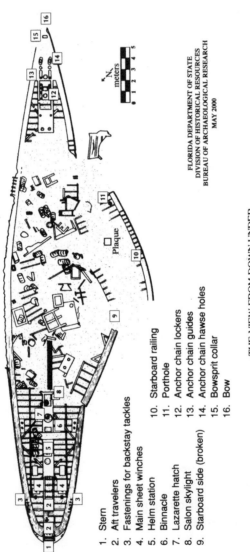

1. Stern
2. Aft travelers
3. Fastenings for backstay tackles
4. Main sheet winches
5. Helm station
6. Binnacle
7. Lazarette hatch
8. Salon skylight
9. Starboard side (broken)
10. Starboard railing
11. Porthole
12. Anchor chain lockers
13. Anchor chain guides
14. Anchor chain hawse holes
15. Bowsprit collar
16. Bow

Plaque

N
meters
0 1 2 3 4 5

FLORIDA DEPARTMENT OF STATE
DIVISION OF HISTORICAL RESOURCES
BUREAU OF ARCHAEOLOGICAL RESEARCH
MAY 2000

THE VIEW FROM DOWN UNDER

Half Moon lies imbedded in white sand on a shallow shoal off Key Biscayne, listing slightly to port, bow pointing southward. No traces of her masts are left and the starboard side has been broken outward, probably the result of a larger vessel colliding with the wreck. The yacht's internal framing is readily apparent, as are the forward anchor chain fittings and the bowsprit collar. The shipwreck is home to many species of tropical marine life, including fish, invertebrates, sponges, and corals. Please visit this preserve with care and respect.

The wreck of the yacht *Half Moon* is an Underwater Archaeological Preserve and is featured on the Florida Maritime Heritage Trail Shipwrecks poster. Reprinted with permission of the Florida Department of State, Division of Historical Resources, http://www.flheritage.com/index.cfm.

lighted backgrounds of cities. Nevertheless, U-boats succeeded in sinking twenty-four U.S. and Allied freighters and tankers off Florida's shores, most in the first six months of 1942. In April 1942, *Gulfamerica*, carrying 90,000 barrels of fuel oil, was hit by U-*123* and exploded in sight of horrified spectators at Jacksonville Beach.

Some of those casualties are now popular diving attractions. *Empire Mica*, a British steam tanker carrying a load of oil, was torpedoed by U-*67* in June 1942 south of St. George Island in the Gulf of Mexico. Today the shipwreck, located in 100 feet of water 45 miles offshore, is a top diving destination and is especially popular for spearfishing. Other, more mysterious, casualties of the maritime war include the tramp steamer *Vamar*, built as the British gunboat *Kilmarnock*, which sank under questionable circumstances off Port St. Joe in March 1942. Loaded with a cargo of lumber and bound for Cuba, *Vamar* sank in calm conditions and flat water, nearly blocking the shipping channel; local people suspected foreign sabotage although no conclusive evidence was found. Today the shipwreck is a state Underwater Archaeological Preserve and is listed on the National Register of Historic Places.

Naval bases at Key West, Tampa, and Valparaiso came back into action as World War II ramped up, and naval air stations trained Navy pilots in Pensacola, Jacksonville, Key West, Miami, Ft. Lauderdale, Vero Beach, Melbourne, Banana River, Daytona Beach, and DeLand. The Civil Air Patrol and the "Mosquito Fleet" were established to protect and patrol Florida's coasts. Military construction and the influx of military personnel helped to enlarge the economy and place Florida in a strong economic situation as the state entered the postwar era.

Into the Twenty-First Century

Florida has been, and will always be, a maritime state tied to the sea. Its unique geography and location make ocean commerce and recreation inevitable components of Florida's economy. As early as the 1960s, Floridians began to react to the negative effects of shipping, fishing, tourism, and other maritime-related activities. Pollution and destruction of natural resources led Florida's citizens to reevaluate the uses of precious rivers, bays, and coastal waters. Today, Florida's prosperity and destiny still lie with the sea as millions of tons of cargo and billions of dollars in revenue annually pass through the major ports of Miami, Tampa, and Jacksonville. Offshore exploration, both in the Gulf and the Atlantic, for petroleum resources such as oil and natural gas is becoming more prevalent. In the future, sites may be needed for wind farms and solar panel arrays, likely also impacting Florida's offshore and coastal areas.

The vacation and tourism industry also plays a part in Florida's maritime-focused economy. In addition to commercial cargo, Florida's ports support pleasure-cruising ships that host millions of vacationers each year. The Port of Miami and nearby Port Everglades are the two top cruise ship ports in the world. Commercial and recreational fishing supplies seafood for local tables and for distant markets and restaurants, while sportfishing draws anglers from around the world. Florida also is the nation's top scuba diving destination, with warm, clear water, colorful fish, historic shipwrecks, and the United States' only tropical coral reef. John Pennekamp Coral Reef State Park in Key Largo is the nation's first park dedicated to undersea marine life and includes shipwrecks as well as natural resources. National parks and preserves, such as Biscayne National Park near Miami, NOAA's Florida Keys National Marine Sanctuary, and Gulf Islands National Seashore in the Panhandle, preserve the natural beauty and cultural heritage of Florida's coasts and oceans, ensuring the state's historical maritime heritage is preserved for future generations. Even today, refugees seeking a better life build rafts and small boats to make the ocean journey to Florida.

Maritime Archaeology and the Underwater Cultural Heritage

With the exception of rare vessels like *Governor Stone* still afloat, information about Florida's maritime heritage can only be found in historical documents and in the archaeological record. When documents are missing or lost, archaeology is the only way we have of learning about the ships and boats that helped build the state. Florida's submerged heritage sites, including shipwrecks and prehistoric remains, are protected under federal and state law, just as historical and archaeological sites on land are protected. Federal laws including the National Historic Preservation Act of 1966 and the Archaeological Resources Protection Act of 1979 protect heritage sites on federal lands. The Abandoned Shipwreck Act of 1987 specifically extended protection to shipwrecks and mandated states in whose waters the wrecks are located to manage them for the public good. More recently, the Sunken Military Craft Act of 2005 established U.S. rights to any U.S. military craft sunk anywhere in the world and recognizes the rights of other sovereign nations to their sunken ships and planes in U.S. waters. Internationally, the

UNESCO Convention on the Protection of the Underwater Cultural Heritage has been ratified. Although the United States is not a signatory to the Convention, the United States does recognize the benefits of the Convention's Best Practices for shipwrecks and other underwater cultural heritage sites.

At the state level, Chapter 267 of the Florida Statutes, the Florida Historical Resources Act, proclaims that "all treasure trove, artifacts, and objects having historical or archaeological value which have been abandoned on state-owned submerged bottom lands belong to the people of Florida." The management of these heritage resources is the responsibility of the Florida Department of State's Division of Historical Resources. Within the Division, the Bureau of Archaeological Research's (BAR) Underwater Archaeology Program is responsible for managing submerged heritage sites on state lands. Two of its more successful programs are the Underwater Archaeological Preserves and the Florida Maritime Heritage Trail. The Preserves are historic shipwrecks around the state that are interpreted for the public while the Trail consists of informational literature on six coastal heritage themes including shipwrecks, lighthouses, coastal communities, coastal forts, environments, and ports.

Despite, or perhaps because of, Florida's uncommon wealth of maritime heritage sites, many of our state's underwater sites are under threat of damage or destruction. Rampant construction and development threaten coastal prehistoric and colonial sites. Florida's draw as a scuba diving destination leads tens of thousands of visitors a year to the state's historic shipwrecks and delicate coral reefs. Unfortunately, many divers, either ignorant or uncaring of state law, take "souvenirs," and in the process both damage archaeological context and destroy the marine ecosystem. So-called "treasure hunters" cause untold destruction of Florida's underwater cultural and ecological resources in the greedy, and usually futile, quest for riches. Florida historians and archaeologists urge everyone to be aware and to act as stewards to ensure that all of Florida's maritime heritage sites are protected and preserved for future generations to enjoy.

Bibliography

Bense, Judith. *Presidio Santa María de Galve: A Struggle for Survival in Colonial Spanish Pensacola.* Ripley P. Bullen Series. Gainesville: University Press of Florida, 2003.

Buker, George E. *Jacksonville: Riverport-Seaport.* Columbia: University of South Carolina Press, 1992.

Coker, William S., and Thomas D. Watson. *Indian Traders of the Southeastern Spanish Borderlands: Panton, Leslie & Company and John Forbes & Company, 1783–1847.* Gainesville: University Press of Florida, 1986.

Colburn, David R., and Lance DeHaven-Smith. *Florida's Megatrends: Critical Issues in Florida.* 2nd ed. Gainesville: University Press of Florida, 2010.

Dibble, Ernest. *Ante-Bellum Pensacola and the Military Presence,* Volume III. Pensacola, Fla.: Pensacola Bicentennial Series, 1974.

Gannon, Michael. *Operation Drumbeat: The Dramatic True Story of Germany's First U-boat Attacks along the American Coast in World War II.* New York: Harper and Row, 1990.

Hoffman, Paul E. *Florida's Frontiers.* Bloomington: Indiana University Press, 2001.

Holland, Keith V., and Lee B. Manley. *The Maple Leaf: An Extraordinary American Civil War Shipwreck.* Jacksonville, Fla.: St. Johns Archaeological Society, 2002.

Johnson, Brian. *Fly Navy: The History of Naval Aviation.* New York: William Morrow, 1981.

Konstam, Angus. *Confederate Blockade Runner 1861–65.* Westminster, Md.: Osprey, 2004.

Martin, S. Walter. *Florida during the Territorial Days.* Athens: University of Georgia Press, 1944.

McCarthy, Kevin M. *Thirty Florida Shipwrecks.* Sarasota, Fla.: Pineapple Press, 1992.

Milanich, Jerald T., and Susan Milbrath, eds. *First Encounters: Spanish Explorations in the Caribbean and the United States, 1492–1570.* Gainesville: University Press of Florida, 1989.

Molloy, Johnny. *From the Swamp to the Keys: A Paddle through Florida History.* Gainesville: University Press of Florida, 2003.

Mueller, Edward A. *Perilous Journeys: A History of Steamboating on the Chattahoochee, Apalachicola, and Flint Rivers, 1828–1928.* Chattahoochee, Fla.: Historic Chattahoochee, 1990.

Murphy, Leo F. *Flying Machines over Pensacola: An Early Aviation History from 1909 to 1929.* Gulf Breeze, Fla.: Pensacola Bay Flying Machines, 2003.

Schafer, Daniel L. *Thunder on the River: The Civil War in Northeast Florida.* Gainesville: University Press of Florida, 2010.

Smith, Roger C. "Treasure Ships of the Spanish Main: The Iberian-American Maritime Empires." In *Ships and Shipwrecks of the Americas: A History Based on Underwater Archaeology,* edited by George F. Bass, 85–106. New York: Thames and Hudson, 1988.

———. *Vanguard of Empire: Ships of Exploration in the Age of Columbus.* New York: Oxford University Press, 1993.

Stuart, John, and John Stack, eds. *The New Deal in the South.* Gainesville: University Press of Florida, 2008.

Weddle, Robert S. *Spanish Sea: The Gulf of Mexico in North American Discovery, 1500–1685.* College Station: Texas A&M University Press, 1995.

Wheeler, Ryan J., James J. Miller, Ray M. McGee, Donna Ruhl, Brenda Swann, and Melissa Memory. "Archaic Period Canoes from Newnan's Lake, Florida." *American Antiquity* 68, no. 3 (2003):533–51.

22

Florida Politics

The State Evolves into One of the Nation's Premier Political Battlegrounds

SUSAN A. MACMANUS AND DAVID R. COLBURN

(WITH THE ASSISTANCE OF TIFINI HILL)

Florida became a state in 1845. One hundred years later, the state was still being described as a sparsely populated, humid, swampy collection of country towns, fishing villages, migrant labor camps, Indian settlements, sugarcane fields, and orange groves, with a few plush coastal resorts catering to wealthy winter guests.[1] There were fewer than 2 million residents and the state ranked twenty-seventh in population. Political power rested in the northern tier of counties with the "pork choppers," who dominated the state legislature, the state's multiple executive offices, and the state's courts. *Florida politics was white, conservative, segregationist, and one-party Democratic.*

The state's politics began to change with the end of World War II. It was the beginning of a decades-long population boom that continued into the 2000s. The influx of newcomers from the Northeast, Midwest, and Latin and South America markedly transformed Florida economically and politically. The state changed "from one of the least appealing, most racially polarized, and poorest states to one of the most desired, most diverse, and most prosperous; from a state that had been anything but a bellwether of the nation to one that . . . is 'the whole deal, the real deal, a big deal.'"[2]

By the beginning of the twenty-first century, Florida had truly become one of the most politically competitive states in the United States. Nothing proved that more definitively than the 2000 presidential election when Republican George W. Bush bested Al Gore in Florida by a mere 537 votes—the closest vote in American presidential history and one of the most controversial. Other statewide contests (U.S. Senate, governor, cabinet) were being won by both Democrats and Republicans and were often close, with independents usually being the real swing voters. Diversity (racial/ethnic, gender, age, sexual preference, religion) among elected officials became more commonplace, especially in the state's large metropolitan areas. Political power shifted first from the north to the south, then to the center of the state. The now famous I-4 corridor that stretches from Daytona Beach east to the Tampa Bay area became "the swing part of the swing state."

The political transformation of the Sunshine State did not come without social and economic strife. Markedly different value systems stemming from diverse cultural backgrounds and experiences were often at the heart of the tug-of-war between newcomers demanding change and old-timers wedded to keeping the status quo. But eventually, a small, rural, one-party-dominated Deep South state of the Confederacy evolved into one of the nation's premier political battlegrounds. In the new Florida, the faces of its elected officials reflected the nation's racial and ethnic diversity, and its pressing issues often mirrored those facing the country at large. In some places, however, one can still observe the vestiges of the major fault lines, particularly racial, that characterized the state for so long, although they have faded considerably over the years. The new dividing lines are more partisan in nature.

Deep South, Confederate Florida: Agriculture, Whites, and Democrats Dominate in the 1800s

Florida seceded from the Union in 1861. Along with other southern states, it participated in the bloody war for independence in order to secure its southern economic, social, and cultural values. By joining the Confederacy, Florida was forced to share the costs of the conflict and the burden of military Reconstruction. It was a painful period for Floridians, and they remained isolated from the national mainstream and mired in rural poverty for much of the late nineteenth and early twentieth centuries as a result of this decision.

Florida's leaders did not accept the results of the Civil War gracefully. At every stage in the Reconstruction process, they took steps to preserve many of the traditions of the past. And in the aftermath of Reconstruction, they established a caste system, at first informally and then through law, that permeated the entire society, denying African Americans the rights promised them during Reconstruction. This Jim Crow system imposed a subservient status on African Americans until well into the second half of the twentieth century. The ramifications of this racial system had a profound impact on state politics during this era. The costs of civil war and the commitment to segregation hobbled Florida and the entire region for decades.

Florida's Unique Attributes: Land Area, Distance between Cities, Economic Diversity

While Florida was part of the Confederate Deep South, its frontier-like environment shaped its social and economic character and its politics in a manner different from the rest of the region during the first forty years of the twentieth century.

In 1900, Florida had the smallest population of any southern state, less than half that of the next smallest, and most of the state was undeveloped and often inaccessible wilderness. Political leaders recognized the critical importance of a development program if Florida was to prosper, but the state lacked the capital to spur development and population growth. The only resource political leaders had to barter was land, and they did just that by granting large sections of land indiscriminately in order to encourage ambitious and wealthy men to develop the state and to make it accessible to others.

The state's geography was a second aspect of its uniqueness. Its population was isolated and fragmented by enormous distances that stretched from as far as Key West to Pensacola—approximately the same road distance as that from Pensacola to Chicago. Tampa was as far from Miami as New York from Boston, and travel was so difficult that few passed from one city to the other. Even in the early twentieth century, Florida's southern region was closely linked to the Caribbean, and people from the islands moved freely to south Florida. Cubans settled in the Tampa Bay area around the turn of the century, where they established a substantial cigar industry. Other immigrants, including Italians and Greeks, also settled in the southern part of the state. Few residents of north Florida would have recognized the Tampa Bay area as part of their state.

A third unique attribute of Florida was its economic diversity. The state escaped the "curse" of cotton, a dependence on a one-crop economy and the oppression of tenant farming. Although Florida remained a poor state up to World War II, its economy varied significantly from cotton, tobacco, timber, and turpentine in the north to citrus, phosphate mining, cattle ranching, and tourism in the south. Florida thus never had the same commitment to the "southern way of life" that so influenced its southern neighbors.[3]

A One-Party (Democratic) State Controlled by North Florida Politicos

In examining southern politics prior to World War II, political scientist V. O. Key Jr. was the first to recognize Florida's differences and predict that Florida would be the first southern state to develop a viable two-party system. His projection was based on Florida's sharp geographical differences and the immigration of newcomers, each of which factionalized its politics and discouraged political cohesion. He also pointed to Florida's relatively small black population compared to other southern states as allowing for the reemergence of the Republican Party as it became less effective for white Democrats to portray blacks as a threat to white domination.[4]

Little did Key realize at the time that the Florida Democratic Party would dominate state politics every bit as thoroughly and for nearly as long as it did in those southern states with large black populations. *For approximately ninety years, from the post-Reconstruction period to the late 1960s, all state-wide elections were effectively decided within the Democratic Party.* The general election, during which Democrats seldom bothered to campaign, only confirmed the decisions of the party primary, better known as the "white primary." These same Democrats adopted a series of segregation ordinances in the late nineteenth and early twentieth centuries that prevented whites and blacks from being educated or socializing together, so that racial understanding and cooperation could not continue or develop further.[5]

North Florida's longer-than-anticipated political dominance was aided, ironically, by the massive flow of newcomers into the state beginning in the 1940s. The majority of them settled in the region south of Ocala. They often remained more attached to their native states and rarely got involved in Florida politics except at the local level to vote against any new taxes, having moved to the Sunshine State to get away from high taxes.

Meanwhile, north Florida politicos, most of whom lived within fifty miles of the Georgia border, dominated the state legislature and established an apportionment system that ensured the region's control until the late 1960s, when the courts ruled that both houses of a state legislature had to be apportioned based on population size—the "one person, one vote" principle.

The Early Twentieth Century: Segregation Clashes with Development Demands

Throughout the period from 1900 to 1940, state politics were dominated by a few central issues. National developments, especially those that occurred within the Democratic Party, occasionally impacted state politics in significant ways throughout this era from the age of progressivism to the New Deal. Race was never far from the forefront of state politics and played a particularly prominent role throughout the era from 1900 to 1924.

Development and who would determine its course in the state were other dominant concerns in the first decade of the twentieth century. Progressive Democrats like William Jennings (1901–5), Napoleon Bonaparte Broward (1905–9), and Broward's successor, Albert Gilchrist (1909–13), controlled the governor's office, but because of their limited ability to carry out their economic reforms and sharp divisions within the legislature, they gradually yielded power to more entrenched, conservative forces in the state.

The opponents of progressivism and even some of its allies believed that a cheap land policy and private development, even in areas as environmentally sensitive as the Everglades, were essential to the state's emergence from poverty. At this stage in Florida's development, environmental concerns took a distant second place to concerns about economic growth and expansion of the population. Florida's flirtation with progressivism was thus a short-lived affair, and by 1912 political power had fallen into the hands of pro-business spokesmen.

By the end of World War I, land developers had descended upon Florida. With the rise in popularity of the automobile, it became commonplace for people to vacation in Florida. Many tourists stayed on, and developers even sold land sight unseen to northerners persuaded by bogus advertisements.[6]

The gradual involvement in the war effort and the social dislocation that resulted from mobilization caused considerable consternation in the South over race relations. Having recently imposed segregation, white southerners by 1914 were in no mood to have this system altered. By contrast, black southerners viewed the war as an opportunity to cast off the oppressive blanket of segregation by demonstrating their patriotism.

Racial patterns in the South were additionally complicated by the massive migration of African Americans to the Midwest and Northeast beginning around 1910 to escape the oppression of segregation and the economic havoc created by the boll weevil's devastation of the cotton crop. They were also drawn to the North by the promise of economic opportunity and

Governor Sidney J. Catts (1917–21) is shown here (*seated, left front*) with his family on the Governor's Mansion steps. A resident of Florida only five years when he announced for governor, Catts campaigned in the rural counties as an anti-Catholic demagogue. Yet his administration was characterized by numerous progressive programs, including penal reform, support for organized labor, and improved status for women. And his official stance toward Catholicism was conciliatory (his executive secretary was Catholic, and his son Rozier, with his father's blessing, married a Catholic).

greater freedom. Labor agents from northern industries and railroads descended on the South in search of black workers.

As the massive exodus of African Americans continued from the northern counties of Florida during the war years, Governor Park Trammell (1913–17) and his successor, Sidney J. Catts (1917–21), essentially ignored it. Trammell, no friend of black Floridians, had disregarded the lynching of blacks when he was the state's attorney general and during his governorship.

When the NAACP complained about these lynchings, Catts denounced the organization and blacks generally.

Catts changed his tune when white business leaders, especially in the lumber and turpentine industries, began to complain that the continued outmigration of blacks was having a devastating effect on labor availability and labor costs in Florida. Suddenly, Catts urged blacks to stay in Florida and called for unity and harmony among the races. Few black citizens listened to him or were intimidated by threats of violence. The migration continued to escalate as a quiet protest against racial conditions in the South.

During the early 1920s, white Florida gradually suppressed the aspirations of its remaining black population. Its governors played a willing hand in this process. They defended their actions by asserting the inferiority and dependence of the black race and received ample encouragement from the writings of anthropologists and popular authors who claimed that scientific evidence documented black inferiority. Black citizens, however, resisted efforts to reimpose segregation by whatever means were at their disposal. In Ocoee, black residents marched to the polls in an effort to vote, only to be physically assaulted and to have their homes and property seriously damaged.[7]

The white commitment to maintaining segregation knew few bounds. In Perry and Rosewood, blacks were killed and their property destroyed following alleged assaults upon white women. When blacks in Rosewood tried to defend themselves against a white mob, their public buildings, churches, and homes were burned to the ground, six were reported murdered, and all were chased from the community in January 1923, never to return.[8] The promise of the war years and the great migration had been completely snuffed out in Florida by 1924, and state leaders were willing accessories in this process.

Although Catts and his allies remained political factors throughout the 1920s, the Democratic Party returned to the hands of party stalwarts in 1920 with the election of Cary Hardee (1921–25), who took office just in time to bask in the prosperity of the economic boom in south Florida. The economic development and population expansion that Florida had long sought began to stir, and Florida's leaders turned their backs on Catts and his allies and eagerly embraced the new investors. Unfortunately, like all roller coasters, Florida's economy suddenly lurched downward in late 1925 when the land bubble burst, money and credit ran out, and banks and investors abruptly ceased trusting developers. State leaders had done little to regulate speculators or to restrain the massive expansion.

The Depression: Fiscal Battles, Taxes Dominate State Politics

Florida became a metaphor for the boom and bust years of the 1920s, and no state experienced the highs and lows any more thoroughly. By the time the stock market collapsed in the fall of 1929, Florida was already mired in four years of depression.[9] The financial collapse paralyzed political leaders and left the state unprepared to meet the crisis. During this period, conservative campaign slogans, such as "no new taxes" and "make government run more efficiently," emerged. They became powerful political rallying cries for decades to come.

Governor Doyle Carlton (1929–33) attempted to counter the political ineptitude by urging the legislature to raise taxes to reduce a state deficit of $2.5 million and to assist counties in paying off their bonds. He also sought a gasoline tax to pay for roads and to keep schools open. But the governor's tax plan encountered stiff opposition from representatives whose counties

Senator Claude D. Pepper greets some of his Florida constituents in the 1940s. A vigorous advocate of President Roosevelt's New Deal, Pepper brought many millions of federal dollars to Florida during the Depression and war years. In his last years, as a member of the U.S. House of Representatives, he became the nation's staunchest advocate for senior citizens.

had small debts and who felt they were being forced to pay for the sins of those with large debts. At one point Carlton, totally exasperated, pleaded with legislators, "If the program that has been offered does not meet with your liking, then for God's sake provide one that does."[10]

Carlton's successors, David Sholtz (1933–37) and Fred Cone (1937–41), refused to follow Carlton's controversial lead. Both blamed Florida's problems on irresponsible leadership and called for a return to fiscal restraint, balanced budgets, and sound business principles. Decimated by the state and national depression, Florida looked to the federal government more than most states did for assistance.

Roosevelt's election and his New Deal programs provided the lifeline that kept Florida afloat during the 1930s. The Agricultural Adjustment Act, in particular, provided crucial assistance for financially desperate farmers and grove owners. For many, it was not enough. Florida continued to suffer greatly during the Depression, and as late as 1939 no end seemed in sight.[11]

World War II: Growth Begins, Tourism Takes Off, Fights for Political Power Intensify

World War II reinvigorated Florida. The state became a training center for troops, sailors, and airmen of the United States and its allies. Highway and airport construction was accelerated so that, by the war's end, Florida had an up-to-date transportation network ready for use by its citizens and by the visitors who seemed to arrive in an endless caravan.[12]

Led by Governor Spessard Holland (1941–45), Florida worked closely with the Roosevelt administration and the War Department to secure federal funds for Florida. Holland's successor, Governor Millard Caldwell (1945–49), dramatically expanded activities of the Florida Department of Commerce to attract new business and visitors into the state. Commerce Department employees seemed to take particular pleasure in sending photographs of beautiful young women, scantily clad and lounging round a pool or at the ocean, to northern newspapers in the dead of winter.

Caldwell and his successors also began a series of trips to the North and Midwest in an effort to recruit more business. Florida's sales pitch to prospective business interests and residents emphasized low taxes, a healthy environment, cheap land, and a pro-business political climate. These trips expanded in subsequent administrations to include foreign countries as Florida sought to internationalize its economy and its tourism. The state modernized its roads to accommodate increasing automobile traffic, and

Caldwell's successor, Governor Fuller Warren (1949–53), pushed through a fence law to keep the cattle from crossing the roads, killing the tourists, and damaging their cars.

World War II also created new opportunities for 500,000 black residents of Florida. The length of World War II in contrast to the twenty months of U.S. participation in World War I, and the resulting social and geographic dislocation, had mobilized the black community behind racial reform in ways the country (and state) had not seen. The war propaganda had given many hope that racial change would be forthcoming in the wake of the conflict. Change would not come quickly, however.

The state's white political leaders did what they could to keep race relations as they had been in the prewar era. Governor Caldwell and his successors, Fuller Warren (1949–53) and Dan McCarty (1953), did what the federal courts required of the state, but they stonewalled implementation at every turn.

In the postwar era, local leaders and law enforcement officials, often in cooperation with white militants, also took steps to make sure that segregation barriers remained intact. They systematically repressed black desires for equality and greater freedom. As an example to others in Florida, Klan leaders and allies in Orange County murdered Harry T. Moore, state leader of the NAACP, and his wife in their home on Christmas night 1950 for conducting a statewide campaign to register blacks to vote in Florida during 1949 and 1950. The FBI led the inquiry into Moore's death and found that there was a widespread network of local officials, police, and militant whites operating throughout central Florida to suppress the rights of blacks.[13]

By the late 1940s and throughout the 1950s, battle lines were drawn between proponents of traditional southern values and those who sought to build a "new" Florida. Racial and social traditions were steadily eroded by development policies embraced by political leaders. Business leaders and residents who had come predominantly from the Northeast and Midwest had no intention of having their interests jeopardized by a commitment to a long-dead southern past. A series of federal court rulings and congressional acts in the 1960s and 1970s reconfigured the state's political power structure racially and geographically, which sped up the state's transformation into a two-party political system.

Federal Actions on Civil Rights (Education, Voting, Reapportionment) Open up the State's Political System

With the infusion of newcomers into the state's urban areas, pressures to increase urban representation in the state legislature intensified. By 1950, the legislature remained unreapportioned; 13.6 percent of the state's population elected more than one-half of the state senators, and 18 percent of the population elected more than half the members of the House of Representatives. It was an all-white male legislature, with no women or minorities.

Governor LeRoy Collins (1955–61), who was elected with substantial backing from the urban regions of the state and with especially strong support from south Florida, made legislative reapportionment one of his top priorities. Collins introduced reapportionment in each legislative session, only to see it blocked by rural legislators, who dominated the senate leadership and held nearly a majority of the seats in the house.[14]

If Collins, south Florida legislators, and residents of that region had any hope of winning this fight, their plans were set back by the emergence of the civil rights movement. When the Supreme Court issued its *Brown v. Board of Education of Topeka* edict on 17 May 1954, few in Florida were prepared for such a decision. Pork Chop elements in the state legislature quickly seized the lead, denouncing the decisions and drafting proposals of resistance. Representatives from south Florida also criticized the Court's

Governor LeRoy Collins, whose administration (1955–61) was perhaps the most enlightened and successful in modern Florida history, promoted New South values of business pragmatism, social harmony, and governmental reform. During his first years in office, which directly followed the U.S. Supreme Court decision of 1954 ending racial segregation in the nation's schools, he adopted a moderate stance that prevented defiance of the court. On his death in 1991, the state House of Representatives unanimously named him "Floridian of the Century."

pronouncement, but they found themselves and their state being led by north Florida politicians who militantly rejected any compromise.

Locked in a struggle to win the governorship in a special election at the time of the Court's pronouncement, Collins announced his commitment to segregation. As a business progressive, however, Collins was not an extremist. Collins pursued a variety of measures that were designed to preserve school segregation but also sought to avoid racial extremism. The governor was able to keep the racial militants at bay so that he and Florida gained a reputation for racial moderation, and tourists, new residents, and new businesses continued to stream into the state. Only the veto of Governor LeRoy Collins prevented Florida from creating a private school system to avoid desegregation and jailing teachers who taught desegregated classes.[15]

The efforts by north Floridians to continue to hold on to the reins of power in the state took on a note of desperation in the 1960s. Without the political skill of a LeRoy Collins in the governor's chair and with Florida continuing to be a seedbed of change as a result of massive population growth, a burgeoning tourist economy, and an expanding civil rights movement, Governors Farris Bryant (1961–65) and Haydon Burns (1965–67), both of Jacksonville, together with rural, north Florida legislators, desperately sought to maintain the status quo. Attempts to stymie desegregation took on a harder edge. Florida's reputation for racial moderation slipped badly during the first half of the 1960s.[16]

Ironically, as Burns fought to block school desegregation, he led a statewide effort in 1965 to bring the Walt Disney Corporation to Florida. Disney and the other tourist operations that opted to follow Disney's new theme park in Orlando would further undermine racial extremism and the social instability that accompanied it. Above all, these businesses insisted on a secure environment in which to conduct their business operations.

Although the state's economic development program steadily eroded its commitment to a segregated past, there was no clear sign that political leaders were prepared to abandon Florida's racial heritage until the federal government intervened. Washington removed the civil rights issue from state control by adopting the Civil Rights Act of 1964 and the Voting Rights Act of 1965.

In 1967, in *Swann v. Adams*, the U.S. Supreme Court ordered the reapportionment of Florida to reflect "one man, one vote." Within months a new legislature was formed that oversaw the modernization of state government, the abandonment of segregation, and the rise of the Republican Party.[17] The world of the Pork Choppers had collapsed, and with it the southern cause they had so vigorously championed. In contrast to what happened in the Reconstruction era of nearly a century earlier, this time the federal government did not renege on its promises to black Americans. Although few white leaders would have acknowledged it in the 1960s, federal officials had done Florida an enormous favor by removing racial extremism and rural domination from its politics.

A New State Constitution and a Legislative Shake-Up

Without race-based politics and without a legislature dominated by rural north Florida, the state began to address important issues that had been ignored for years in the battle over segregation and, in the process, to revisit political loyalties that had gone unchallenged during the twentieth century. The most immediate impact of these developments was the adoption of a new constitution in 1968 which recognized the Court-ordered reapportionment in 1967, effectively gave legislative control to south Florida, and completely overhauled the old constitution of 1885.

The new constitution strengthened the hands of the governor by allowing him to serve two consecutive terms, consolidating the number of executive departments, and granting budgetary responsibilities to the chief executive. At the same time, however, it formally recognized the cabinet as a constitutional body and granted certain cabinet officers authority over the consolidated executive agencies. These changes, together with the Legislative Reorganization Act of 1969, which led to annual meetings of the legislature (as opposed to the biennial meetings) and the creation of permanent legislative staffs, effectively counterbalanced the new powers of the governor's office. Structural changes were one giant step taken to modernize Florida's government. Their importance became even more evident as the state's population continued to explode.

"Imported Politics": A Two-Party State Begins to Take Shape

In 1960, Florida was the nation's tenth-most-populous state; by 1980, it ranked seventh; and by 1990, it was fourth.[18] Projections are that it will become the nation's third-largest state by 2020. By the beginning of the twenty-first century, Florida had become a microcosm of the United States at large—a state whose politics was "imported" from other parts of the U.S. and from Latin and South America (see table 22.1).

As the state's population exploded, Florida's economy became increasingly

Table 22.1. Florida's Racial and Ethnic Composition: A Comparison with the United States

Race	Percentage of population Florida 2010 (%)	U.S. 2010 (%)
White	75.0	72.4
Non-Hispanic White	57.9	63.7
Hispanic/Latino	22.5	16.3
African American	16.0	12.6
Asian	2.4	4.8
Native American	0.4	0.9
Pacific Islander	0.1	0.2
Some other race	3.6	6.2
Two or more races	2.5	2.9

Source: U.S. Bureau of the Census, 2010 Census.

dependent on housing construction, high-technology manufacturing, and tourism, although agriculture and, to a lesser extent, the phosphate industry and cattle ranching still played prominent roles. The state's urban and sub-urban areas boomed. By the 2010 Census, more than 94 percent of Florida residents lived in one of the state's metropolitan statistical areas—one of the highest metropolitanization rates in the nation.[19]

The state's population center shifted from the Panhandle to central and south Florida. The state's centroid (exact population center) was in Jefferson County in 1830, but by 2005, it was in southwestern Polk County.[20] Political power in Florida shifted from the less-populated, rural north Florida counties to the urban centers in central Florida (Orlando, Daytona, Titusville, and the Space Center), Southwest Florida (from the Tampa–St. Petersburg–Clearwater area to Sarasota, Fort Myers, and Naples), and southeast Florida's "Gold Coast" (Palm Beach, Fort Lauderdale, and Miami).[21]

The infusion of new residents transformed Florida into a true "melting pot," prompting a change in the state's party, racial/ethnic, and gender makeup of its executive, legislative, and judicial officeholders. Redistricting, term limits enacted in 2000, and party recruitment of women and minority candidates helped change the faces of the state's elected officials to reflect a more representative picture of Florida's increasingly diverse population.

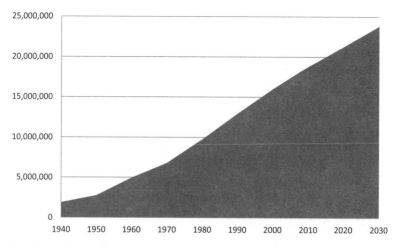

Florida's Explosive Population Growth. Source: Bureau of Economic and Business Research, "Florida Population: Census Summary 2010," April 2011. Bureau of Economic and Business Research, "Projections of Florida Population by County, 2009–2035," March 2010.

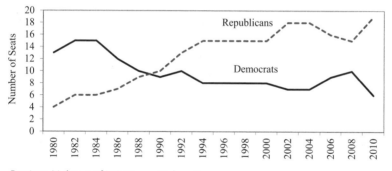

Partisan Makeup of U.S. House Delegation.

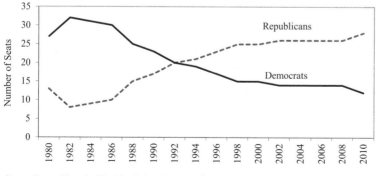

Party Seats Won in Florida State Senate Elections.

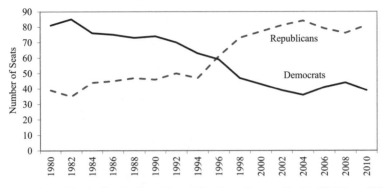

Party Seats Won in Florida State House Elections. Source: Florida Division of Elections.

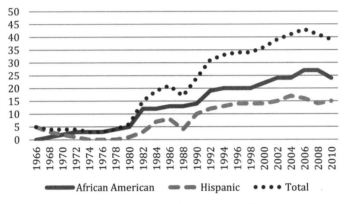

African American   Hispanic   Total

Minority Members of the Florida Legislature 1966–Present. Source: Compiled from Florida House and Senate records.

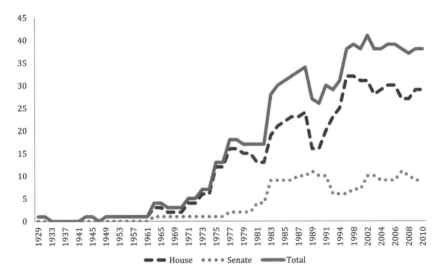

House   Senate   Total

Number of Women in the Florida Legislature. Source: Compiled from Florida House and Senate records.

Minority Pathbreakers

The first African American since Reconstruction (Joe Lang Kershaw) was elected to the state legislature in 1968. He was followed in 1970 by the first black female legislator, Gwen Cherry, a Miami attorney and FAMU graduate. The first black state senators since Reconstruction were elected in 1982: Arnett E. Girardeau from Jacksonville and Carrie Meek from Miami. The keys to more black political power in the state were the adoption of single-member legislative districts in 1982 and federal court-ordered redistricting in 1992. In that year, three districts (two in South Florida and one in Jacksonville) were crafted specifically with the intent to maximize the opportunity for black representation in the congressional delegation to comply with the federal Voting Rights Act. Joseph Hatchett was the first black appointed to the Florida Supreme Court by Governor Reubin Askew (D) in 1975. Hatchett became the first African American to win a statewide office in the entire South, when he won a contentious, racially charged election to keep the seat in 1976. In 2010, Jennifer Carroll, a native of Trinidad and a Republican, became the first black executive elected statewide when she became Florida's lieutenant governor.[22]

Most of the Hispanics serving in the Florida Legislature have been Cuban Americans, although some of the earliest Hispanic legislators were *Puerto Rican* Democrats Maurice Ferre from Miami and Elvin Martinez of Tampa. Both were first elected in 1966. Republican Roberto Casas became the first *Cuban American* legislator in the Florida House in fifty-seven years when he won a special election in 1982. Republican Ileana Ros-Lehtinen, who emigrated from Havana to Miami in 1960 at the age of eight, was the first female Cuban American legislator. She, too, was elected to the House in 1982. Both Ros-Lehtinen and Casas moved up to the state Senate in 1986. In 1988, Bob Martinez (R) made history by being the first Hispanic to be elected governor of Florida. Once the Democratic mayor of Tampa, Martinez had switched to the Republican Party before running for governor. Raoul G. Cantero III became the state's first Hispanic Supreme Court justice when Governor Jeb Bush (R) appointed him to the bench in 2002. Cantero is the grandson of Fulgencio Batista, the former Cuban dictator who was overthrown by Fidel Castro. At the congressional level, then State Senator Ileana Ros-Lehtinen won the special election for a vacant seat in the U.S. House of Representatives in 1989, becoming the first Hispanic in Congress from Florida in 166 years. (Joseph Marion Hernandez, who served from 1822 to 1823, was the first.) It was not until 2004 that Cuban-born Mel Martinez (R) beat Betty

Reubin O'Donovan Askew (*right*) served two terms as governor, 1971–79. The sedate, judicious former state senator from Pensacola was the first to be elected to two full terms. His administration was characterized by many progressive initiatives, including a Sunshine Law that required financial disclosure by all state officials and a state income tax on corporations. He is shown here at the Capitol on 14 April 1976 honoring Pensacola-born Air Force General Daniel "Chappie" James, the highest-ranking African American in the armed forces.

Castor (D) in a tight race to become the first Cuban American elected to the U.S. Senate.[23]

The Growing Strength of Republicans

The Republican Party gradually emerged as a viable second party in the 1960s. In 1966, the party captured the governorship in a stunning development, after having failed to challenge seriously for the office since 1900. The party's growth was principally the result of the influx of Republican-leaning retirees from the Midwest, immigrants from Cuba, conservatives from other southern states, and north Florida conservative Democrats who began voting Republican in the Reagan years as Democrats running nationally were perceived as too liberal.

Middle-class, suburban Republican retirees from midwestern states streamed via I-75 into central and southwest Florida, while senior Democrats from northeastern states poured into Florida via I-95 and settled in Miami-Dade, Broward (Fort Lauderdale), and Palm Beach Counties. Republican retirees are still more heavily concentrated on the southwest side of the state.[24]

Cuban Americans, who fled Communist Cuba in 1959 and settled in Dade County, made a rapid and remarkably successful adjustment to American life. Their middle-class status and the size of the Cuban community in south Florida facilitated their economic advancement and also made them a political force in Dade County and in Florida generally. Because of their opposition to Fidel Castro and communism, they focused their attention primarily on foreign affairs, but they were also strong advocates of an unfettered American capitalism. Beyond these concerns, they have been generally conservative on social programs and issues of race. The size of this community and its particular agenda have combined to add a further ethnic dynamic to Florida's politics. In some of the state's largest metropolitan areas, Hispanics and African Americans have become more competitive with each other than with Anglos for elective political posts, whether local, state, or congressional.

The Republican Party also gained support from some conservative Democrats who were drawn to Ronald Reagan's emphasis on smaller government and lower taxes. During the Reagan years (1981–89), Republican identification in Florida leaped from 20 to 40 percent of the electorate. For some Democrats, the national party and its presidential nominees were just too liberal, with the exception of southern Democrats (Lyndon Johnson from Texas, Jimmy Carter from Georgia, and Bill Clinton from Arkansas). As the GOP began winning races, they began attracting even more party identifiers once there was a viable option to the Democratic Party. However, as late as 1979, no statewide political office was held by a Republican, and only 26 percent of the seats in the legislature and three of fifteen congressional seats were held by Republicans.[25]

By 1990, the party had become so influential that it even constituted a powerful force in north Florida, a region where residents would have turned over in their graves before voting Republican in the period before 1960. In 1994, for the first time in the twentieth century, Republicans seized power in the state Senate. Republicans also held one of the two U.S. Senate seats and more than half of the Florida seats in the U.S. House of Representatives and barely lost the governor's race.

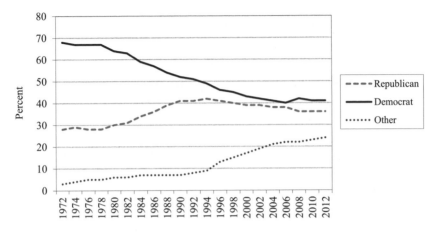

Florida Voter Party Registration Percentages: 1972–2012. Source: Compiled from data from the Florida Division of Elections.

It was the highly contentious 2000 presidential election, when Democrat Al Gore from Tennessee came within 537 votes of winning Florida, that sealed Florida's position as one of the nation's perennial premier battleground states. Presidential and gubernatorial races now routinely go down to the wire, with virtually each successive poll showing a lead change. Independents have become the fastest-growing portion of the electorate and the most volatile and unpredictable. In 2008, independents helped turn Florida blue for Democrat Barack Obama, then red in 2010, helping to elect Republican Governor Rick Scott and Republican U.S. Senator Marco Rubio. Florida's independents are, on average, younger than the state's Democrats and Republicans and the "swing voters in the swing state."

Geographically, north Florida remains a Democratic region of the state if measured by party identification and registration. But it looks Republican if measured by votes in presidential and gubernatorial elections. (The region often votes Republican in those contests, especially when Democratic candidates are too liberal.) The southeastern part of Florida, particularly Broward and Palm Beach Counties, is strongly Democratic while the southwest region is the most heavily Republican area. Central Florida, specifically the I-4 corridor (the Tampa Bay and Orlando media markets), has evolved into the most competitive part of the state.[26] The I-4 corridor is home to nearly half (44 percent) of all the state's registered voters and is almost equally divided between Democrats and Republicans, with a sizable and growing number of independents. The area is considered to be a microcosm of Florida at large in both its registration and voting patterns.[27]

The strength of the Republican Party in Florida lies with white voters, Cuban Hispanics, men, and more affluent, Protestant, college-educated, and conservative voters. Democrats draw greater support from blacks, some non-Cuban Hispanic groups, women, Jewish and nonreligious persons, lower-income, less-educated, and liberal voters. Support levels for each party's candidates may differ within these groups, depending on who is running, their platform, and their leadership skills during stressful times.[28]

Fifty Years of Population Growth (1960s to 2010s): An Increasingly Divided Electorate, Difficult Issues

Population growth created big challenges in a number of policy areas, including education, crime and law enforcement, transportation, taxation (equity), the environment, immigration, and health care. Depending on the specific policy debate, the state's historical divides became quite evident: regional—north vs. south; nativity—old-timer vs. newcomer; racial—black vs. white, or multiracial with the burgeoning Latino population; ideological—conservative vs. liberal; generational—young vs. old; and partisan—Democrats vs. Republicans.

Even the term "economic development" generated divisive politics, depending on whether it was a high-growth or stagnant economy. During high-growth periods, Florida's elected officials faced intense cross-pressures from citizens. Some pressured them to restrict growth or at least be smarter about it, while others favored continuing pro-growth policies. During economic downturns, there were disagreements about how to jump-start the economy. Some citizens pushed officials to offer tax breaks to bring new businesses (jobs) into the community, while others preferred higher taxes to create jobs, prevent more business closures, and stem further population out-migration.

Each governor who served from the 1960s to the 2010s had to deal with some type of crisis during his administration.[29] Claude Kirk dealt with a teacher strike, Bob Graham with the Mariel boatlift from Cuba to South Florida, Bob Martinez with a revolt against a proposed services tax, Lawton Chiles with Hurricane Andrew and widespread wildfires in central Florida during a drought, Jeb Bush with four Category 3 or higher hurricanes in six weeks, Charlie Crist with the BP oil spill in the Gulf of Mexico, and Rick

Scott with a budget crisis (a shortfall of almost $4 billion), a jobs crisis (one of the highest state unemployment rates in the country), and an ongoing housing crisis (with one of the highest home foreclosure rates in the country). In many ways, their successes and failures reflected the social, economic, and political landscape of the day. For some, it was their leadership style and skills that better explained their tenure in office.

Claude Roy Kirk Jr.-R (1967–1971)

Kirk won the last gubernatorial election in the 1960s before the new constitution and the new court-ordered redistricting took hold. He broke the Democratic monopoly on the governor's office by splitting the Democratic vote (conservative north Florida Democrats vs. the more liberal south Florida Democrats). He defeated Miami mayor Robert King High, who was perceived by many central and north Florida Democrats as too liberal on civil rights. Kirk's administration was both colorful and controversial, marked by confrontations with the Democratic legislature, an unprecedented statewide teachers' strike, and crises over forced school busing. On a more positive note, he did take some pro-environmental stances, helping to stop the Cross Florida Barge Canal from cutting across the state. His personal flamboyant leadership style came under attack from media around the state and turned off many former supporters. He was defeated in his bid for reelection in 1970 by a young Pensacola Democratic state senator, Reubin Askew.

Reubin O'Donovan Askew-D (1971–1979)

With a new constitution in place allowing governors to serve two terms, reformulated legislative districts based on population rather than county, and a fast-growing population, Askew successfully pushed comprehensive tax reform through the state legislature during his first term. Askew's corporate tax referendum won with over 70 percent of the vote. When the legislature failed to pass his "government in the sunshine" amendment, he lent his support to a citizen's initiative that won nearly 80 percent of vote. He failed in subsequent efforts to reform the cabinet system and strengthen the governorship, suffering voter rejection in 1978 of constitutional revisions that he supported. As a progressive Democrat from north Florida, Askew was able to reunite the Democratic base. He easily won reelection in 1974 to become the first Florida governor to serve two four-year terms. Askew named the first African American to the Florida Supreme Court and appointed the first woman to the Florida cabinet.

Daniel Robert "Bob" Graham-D (1979–1987)

Although from south Florida, Graham was a moderate Democrat who captured much of the same constituency that had voted for Askew. He maintained a moderate-to-conservative image—tough on crime and willing to sign death warrants to implement capital punishment. Education was his passion. He was a forceful advocate for public education, particularly higher education. He was easily reelected in 1982, as voters perceived that he was an effective leader who worked well with the Democratically controlled legislature. Graham pushed the far-reaching 1985 Florida Growth Management Act through the legislature. Among the more controversial provisions of this act was a "concurrency requirement" that barred private development, unless supporting public facilities (roads, schools, sewers, etc.) were either already in place or were built concurrently with new development. (The Growth Management Act was significantly altered in 2011 during an economic downturn when it was regarded by the Republican-controlled legislature as halting job growth.) Graham's flair for populism was evident in his famous "Workdays" that had begun during his first campaign and continued after his governorship.

Robert "Bob" Martinez-R (1987–1991)

A former Democratic mayor of Tampa took advantage of the state's conservative leanings in 1986 and used extensive television advertising to successfully label his Democratic opponent, Steve Pajcic from Jacksonville, as an unrepentant liberal. Martinez ran on a platform of low taxes and social conservatism. He lost support by first supporting—and later disavowing and repealing—a sales tax on services that would have enlarged the state's tax base. He also called an unsuccessful special session on abortion and generally had a difficult time with the Democratically controlled legislature. The tax issue doomed him politically, and he lost his 1990 bid for reelection to Democratic U.S. senator Lawton Chiles. The issue overshadowed some of Martinez's most significant accomplishments. He initiated and expanded a number of environmental initiatives, creating for the first time uniform policies for the management and protection of Florida's surface waters.

Martinez also played a major role in pushing Florida's Republican Party toward a more pro-environment position that ended up helping the party well beyond his tenure as governor.

Lawton Mainor Chiles Jr.-D (1991–1999)

In the first two years of his term, the moderate Democrat from Polk County faced tough budget times due to the national recession. He, like his predecessors, sought to revamp the state's tax system to make it more productive and fairer. He had little success. *Chiles was the first Democratic governor to face a legislature controlled by the opposition party.* In the 1992 midterm elections, the Republicans won a 20 to 20 tie in the state Senate and in 1994, a majority of the seats in both houses. Chiles barely won reelection in 1994 over Republican Jeb Bush by touting his more conservative policy positions on prison building, the death penalty, and opposition to unchecked immigration. Chiles joined with some other border state governors in suing the U.S. government to recover the costs of providing services to illegal immigrants. They lost the suit, but the governor's position resonated with Floridians. In his second term, Chiles's most notable success was a lawsuit against the tobacco industry demanding compensation and punitive damages for the ill effects of cigarette smoking on state-supported Medicaid patients. With the settlement funds he was able to expand health care opportunities for Florida children who lacked health care. Tragically, Chiles died of a heart attack in the gym of the Governor's Mansion with just twenty-four days remaining in his term. Lieutenant Governor Buddy MacKay filled out the last days of Chiles's term, having already lost his bid for governor to Republican Jeb Bush.

John Ellis "Jeb" Bush-R (1999–2007)

Bush won the governorship in 1998 by defeating Buddy MacKay using a catchy TV ad with the tag line, "Hey Buddy, you're a liberal." After his loss in 1994, Bush had repositioned himself as a "compassionate conservative" who reached out to minorities and sought to help the poor through innovative programs, while still keeping taxes low. Bush's finest moments were in crisis situations—first, the economic crisis that struck Florida's tourism industry after 9/11 when his creative fiscal policies helped jump-start the industry. Second, when powerful hurricanes ripped apart the lives of many Floridians. Bush also made his mark in several key policy areas—education (the A+ Plan), law enforcement (10-20-Life), and fiscal policy (tax cuts)—all controversial reforms he successfully pushed through the Republican-controlled legislature. Supporters credited the state's impressive economic growth and job creation during his tenure to the tax cuts, while critics saw them as delaying attention to major unmet growth-related needs of the state including education, welfare, and the environment. Bush had his share of other negative moments—the controversial 2000 election and a large protest march on Tallahassee by minority groups opposed to his "One Florida" program eliminating racial preferences in college admissions and government contracting. Yet he handily defeated Democrat Bill McBride in 2002 and became the first Republican Florida governor to be reelected. For *the first time in Florida's history, Republicans controlled the governorship, all three cabinet posts, 18 of 25 congressional seats, 26 of 40 state Senate seats, and 81 of 120 state House seats.* Jeb's success in garnering votes from both Cuban and *non-Cuban* Hispanics was aided by his fluency in Spanish, demonstrating the necessity of Spanish language-based political appeals in Latino-rich Florida.

Charles "Charlie" Joseph Crist Jr.-R, then NPA (2007–2011)

Crist became Florida's forty-fourth governor when he defeated Democrat Jim Davis. With no incumbent in the race, both major parties had a highly contested primary. Each nominee was from the Tampa Bay area—the state's largest media market. Crist ran as a populist, promising to be "the people's governor" and to govern by adhering to the core principles of fewer taxes, less government, and more freedom. The race was a classic "pocketbook" election driven by the high costs of growth in the form of rising homeowners' insurance rates and escalating property taxes. While a fiscal conservative, Crist was a social moderate, having expressed support for civil unions and embryonic stem cell research during his campaign. His governance style was more bipartisan than his predecessor's. But in reaching out more to Democrats, he often alienated the more conservative Republicans with such actions as restoring the voting rights of nonviolent felons, providing a paper trail for voting machines, hosting a major conference on global warming, vetoing a Republican-passed law that would have tied teacher pay raises to student performance as measured by test scores, and unapologetically taking federal stimulus dollars to stave off deep cuts to the state budget. His popularity was sky-high while he was dealing with the BP oil spill in the Gulf of Mexico and its cleanup, putting pressure on BP to provide more financial help to Florida families and businesses hurt by the spill. Eventually, his popularity among Republicans plummeted. Crist decided not to run for reelection as governor, but rather for the U.S. Senate—and as an independent. Although he lost, his switch reflected the state's growing rank of No Party Affiliation (NPA) voters.

Richard "Rick" Lynn Scott-R (2011–)

Rick Scott took office in the midst of a serious economic downturn. Florida's unemployment and foreclosure rates were among the highest in the country. The BP oil spill in the Gulf of Mexico (April) had wreaked havoc on the state's coastal counties' economies, particularly those in the Panhandle. It was a nationalized election, largely decided by voters, including Tea Party activists, who were angry at Washington and took it out on Democrats running for office at all levels. For those voters, Scott, the outsider, had more appeal with his "Let's Get to Work" anti-Washington message than his Democratic opponent Alex Sink, the insider (chief financial officer), with her honesty, integrity, and accountability message. The centerpiece of Scott's campaign was his 7-7-7 Plan that promised to create 700,000 new jobs over seven years using seven steps. Once elected, Scott faced a state legislature (Republican-controlled) that was *less* conservative than he and more interested in redistricting than focusing on the governor's pledge to put Florida back to work. The business community was Scott's strongest ally as he proposed regulatory relief, along with tax breaks, and spending cuts. He was highly unpopular with Democrats, local government officials, and other advocacy groups upset with his anti–public sector actions—preemployment and random drug testing for state employees, increased state employee contributions to their pensions, and rejection of $2.4 billion in federal grant money to build a $2.7 billion high-speed rail line from Orlando to Tampa. While Scott and his supporters thought that the project was wasteful, inefficient, and would be underutilized, thus putting the State of Florida on the hook for major building and operating expenses in the future, supporters saw the federal money going to other states, not saving taxpayers any money, and costing Florida thousands of construction and service jobs to build and operate the system. Whether because of the budget cuts, conservative social policy, or the bad economy, Florida citizens gave Governor Scott the lowest approval rating, 29 percent, of any governor in the country just four months after he was sworn into office. Scott's initial response was that he was not seeking to be the most popular, but rather to do what he said he would do—make hard choices that can no longer be avoided. The early Scott years affirmed what happens in periods of economic distress in a politically divided state—serious disagreements about the best way to reinvigorate the economy.

More Change to Come

Florida's political landscape will continue to change, especially its racial, ethnic, and age composition. The U.S. Census projects Florida will continue to grow over the next several decades, with growth rates among Hispanic and Asian populations exceeding those of blacks and whites. The age composition will change as well, along with the political party affiliations of the young and the old. The young will become the most solidly Democratic cohort, while the old will lean more Republican, mostly a consequence of the Baby Boomers replacing the solidly Democratic FDR generation of seniors.[30] The younger generations are more racially and ethnically diverse than the older generation—and more socially liberal—but they are increasingly more fiscally conservative.

Politics in the Sunshine State will always be different in boom times than during economic downturns. Governors will still do battle with the state legislature, urban area representatives with those from rural areas, liberals with conservatives, and Republicans with Democrats. Independents, the swing voters, will continue to be the "king"- or "queen"-makers, but the most difficult to sway. And Florida will become an even more important battleground state in national politics, while most likely retaining its "fiscally conservative, socially moderate" flavor.

Notes

1. See Gary R. Mormino, *Land of Sunshine, State of Dreams: A Social History of Modern Florida* (Gainesville: University Press of Florida, 2005).

2. David R. Colburn, *From Yellow Dog Democrats to Red State Republicans: Florida and Its Politics since 1940* (Gainesville: University Press of Florida, 2007), p. 4. The quote about Florida being the "real deal" was made by Dan Rather, former CBS Evening News anchor, during the 2000 election.

3. V. O. Key Jr., *Southern Politics in State and Nation* (New York: Knopf, 1949), pp. 86–87.

4. Ibid., pp. 82–105.

5. Jerrell H. Shofner, "Florida and Black Migration," *Florida Historical Quarterly* 57, no. 3 (January 1979):267–88.

6. Susan A. MacManus, Aubrey Jewett, Thomas R. Dye, and David J. Bonanza, *Politics in Florida*, 3rd ed. (Tallahassee: John Scott Dailey Florida Institute of Government, 2011): pp. 3–5.

7. John Higham, *Strangers in the Land: Patterns of American Nativism, 1860–1925* (New York: Athenaeum, 1965), pp. 149–57; Papers of the NAACP, pt. 7, Anti-Lynching Campaign, 1912–55, Lynching Ocoee, Florida (Series A: Anti-Lynching Investigative Files, 1912–53, reel 9, group 1, ser. C, Administrative Files, Box C-353, Microfilm, 1987, University Publications of America). See also Lester Dabbs Jr., "A Report of the Circumstances and Events of the Race Riot on 2 November 1920 in Ocoee, Florida" (master's thesis, Stetson University, 1969).

8. "A Documented History of the Incident Which Occurred at Rosewood, Florida, in January 1923," by Maxine D. Jones, Larry E. Rivers, David R. Colburn, R. Thomas Dye, and William W. Rogers (submitted to the Florida Board of Regents, 22 December 1993), 93 pages.

9. David R. Colburn and Richard K. Scher, *Florida's Gubernatorial Politics in the Twentieth Century* (Gainesville: University Presses of Florida, 1980), p. 190.

10. Ibid., pp. 191–92.

11. Ibid., p. 193

12. MacManus, Jewett, Dye, and Bonanza, *Politics in Florida*, 3rd ed., pp. 3–5.

13. James Clark, "Death Found Suspects before Justice," *Orlando Sentinel*, 17 October 1992.

14. William C. Harvard and Loren P. Beth, *The Politics of Mis-representation: Rural-Urban Conflict in the Florida Legislature* (Baton Rouge: Louisiana State University Press, 1962), pp. 50, 62; see also Colburn and Scher, *Florida's Gubernatorial Politics*, pp. 173–77.

15. David R. Colburn, "Florida's Legacy of Misdirected Reapportionment," *Ocala Star-Banner*, 13 May 2012.

16. David R. Colburn, *Racial Change and Community Crisis: St. Augustine, Florida, 1977–1980* (New York: Columbia University Press, 1985), pp. 104–9, 178, 187–88.

17. David R. Colburn, "Florida's Legacy of Misdirected Reapportionment," *Ocala Star-Banner*, 13 May 2012.

18. Bureau of Economic and Business Research, Florida Population: Census Summary 2010. Gainesville: University of Florida, April 2011.

19. Bureau of Economic and Business Research, Florida Population: Census Summary 2010, p. 5.

20. Scott K. Cody, "Florida's Population Center Migrates Through History," *Florida Focus 2* (April 2006).

21. MacManus, Jewett, Dye, and Bonanza, *Politics in Florida*, 3rd ed., pp. 6–9.

22. Ibid., pp. 20–24.

23. Ibid., pp. 26–31.

24. Ibid., p. 106.

25. See Edward Kallina, *Claude Kirk and the Politics of Confrontation* (Gainesville: University Press of Florida, 1993); and Mark Stern, "Florida's Elections," in *Florida's Politics and Government*, ed. Manning J. Dauer (Gainesville: University Presses of Florida, 1980), pp. 73–91.

26. Susan A. MacManus, "Florida Overview: Ten Media Markets—One Powerful State," in *Florida's Politics: Ten Media Markets, One Powerful State*, ed. Kevin A. Hill, Susan A. MacManus, and Dario Mareno (Tallahassee: John Scott Dailey Florida Institute of Government, 2004), pp. 1–64.

27. MacManus, Jewett, Dye, and Bonanza, *Politics in Florida*, 3rd ed., p. 111.

28. Ibid.

29. Ibid., chaps. 4, 7.

30. Susan A. MacManus, "V. O. Key Jr.'s Southern Politics: Demographic Changes Will Transform the Region: In-migration and Generational Shifts Speed up the Process," in *Unlocking V. O. Key Jr.: Southern Politics for the Twenty-First Century*, ed. Angie Maxwell and Todd G. Shields (Fayetteville: University of Arkansas Press, 2011), pp. 198–200.

23

Florida's African American Experience

The Twentieth Century and Beyond

LARRY EUGENE RIVERS

A mere forty years after slavery's demise, the president of the United States came to Florida to celebrate the progress made by a race. "The event is one that appeals to the loftiest patriotism of every colored man in Florida," a Jacksonville man recorded. "It matters not whether the President will speak one minute or not," he continued. "It is all sufficient to know he will be there." With encouragement from city councilman Judson Douglas Wetmore, Theodore Roosevelt had chosen Florida Baptist College as the site for his October 1905 remarks. A parade through Jacksonville led by fraternal, sororal, veterans, and civic organizations preceded Wetmore's introduction of the president to Florida Baptist's distinguished president Nathan W. Collier and other educators, dignitaries, and community leaders. "What a pleasure it has been, in driving through the streets to have the Governor and mayor point out to me house after house owned by colored citizens, who, by their own energy, industry and thrift, have accumulated a small fortune honestly and are spending it wisely," Roosevelt commented in remarks that, while pointed, lasted more than the acceptable one minute. "I say, all honor to teachers, all honor to preachers, but it is almost impossible that the whole of any people can be teachers or preachers," the president ultimately observed in conclusion. "The bulk have got to be men who follow trades and mechanical pursuits, who are first-class farmers, first-class tradesmen and carpenters, and who excel in any of these respects, and every man who makes that kind of good farmer or thrifty, progressive, saving mechanic, who gets to own his own house, to be free from debt, to be able to keep his wife as she should be kept. Every such man is not only a first-class citizen of this country, but is doing a mighty work in helping uplift the race."[1]

A family portrait by Vansickel Studios in Gainesville, 1900.

Given the tenor and direction of his remarks, President Roosevelt would have been hard-pressed to find a more apt setting than Jacksonville and Florida. In four short decades, the Sunshine State's African American residents had transitioned from conditions of abject servitude to a level of economic gain and merited respect almost unparalleled elsewhere in the South. In the process, their numbers, institutions, and possessions had swelled in magnitude to truly impressive figures. From a total of only about 92,000 black persons resident in 1870, for instance, African Americans would boast in 1900 a figure that topped 265,000. That amounted to over 43 percent of the total population at a time when the overwhelming majority of Floridians still lived within 50 miles of the Georgia state line. Twelve of forty-eight counties contained black majorities in 1900. These included Alachua, Columbia, Duval, Gadsden, Jackson, Jefferson, Leon, Liberty, Madison, Marion, Nassau, and Wakulla. This predominance found its echo in many of the state's principal towns and cities. As late as 1915, eleven of the incorporated places having populations of 1,000 or more held greater numbers of African Americans than whites. Numbered among them were Jacksonville, Tallahassee, Apalachicola, Daytona, Fernandina, Palatka, Quincy, Sanford, Green Cove Springs, Marianna, and Monticello.

In many respects, Jacksonville and Duval County stood at the summit of Florida's African American world. By far the state's most populous city and county, they contained within their limits achievements, circumstances, and conditions that many African Americans earnestly hoped would represent the future of the race. "Jacksonville in the Lead" a feature article in a nationally circulated race newspaper proclaimed in 1901.[2] Its correspondent waxed eloquent describing a thriving middle class based in part upon successful businessmen and proud professionals. Not forgotten were tradesmen and artisans, particularly carpenters, timber industry workers, and longshoremen. Service workers who catered to the burgeoning tourism industry belonged as well. James Johnson, the father of the writer, poet, lawyer, and race leader James Weldon Johnson, proudly served as a Baptist preacher, but he, with wife, Helen, raised their sons with his earnings as headwaiter at Jacksonville's posh St. James Hotel.

In a state of towns and cities pulsing with growth, opportunity abounded and rewards attended determined efforts. In the circumstances it did not appear all that unusual in 1901 when Jacksonville carpenter M. A. B. Brooks, with the gains of his Jacksonville labors, dispatched his son Charlie Brooks to the Meharry Medical School at Nashville or that banker Sylvanus H. Hart the next year would enroll Sylvanus H. Hart Jr. at New England's Phillips Exeter Academy. Meanwhile, black lawyers such as one-time state senator and Florida Reconstruction historian John Wallace might represent white clients just as black physicians, medical-school educated at a time when many white physicians lacked such formal training, treated white patients. It cannot be denied that poverty existed or that some individuals either lacked initiative or were inclined to crime to earn their living. The same state of affairs, though, existed among whites.

The very existence of Jacksonville's good schools—institutions that created educational legacies visible in the present day—offered an eloquent defense to a mounting chorus of racist voices that proclaimed without

Dr. Mary McLeod Bethune, president of Bethune-Cookman College in Daytona Beach, is shown at her desk in this photograph by Gordon Parks in February 1943. Daughter of former slaves in South Carolina, Dr. Bethune founded the Daytona Literary and Industrial Training School for Negro Girls in 1904, which merged with the Cookman Institute of Jacksonville in 1923. Until her death in 1955, she was Florida's best-known African American educator.

foundation the inferiority of the black man. Florida Baptist College (or Academy), where President Roosevelt spoke, ultimately would serve along with the Florida Institute of Live Oak and Florida Normal Collegiate Institute of Saint Augustine, as parent institutions of Florida Memorial College, now of Miami. The venerable Cookman Institute, a northern Methodist school founded in the 1870s, continued its traditions of service at Jacksonville into the twentieth century. In 1922, it merged with Mary McLeod Bethune's Daytona Literary and Industrial Training School for Negro Girls to create Bethune-Cookman College of Daytona Beach. Moreover, the African Methodist Episcopal Church late in the nineteenth century had sparked the creation of Edward Waters College. That institution also has pursued its mission on behalf of young people for well over a century.

These certainly were not the only schools of consequence in Florida or even Jacksonville. The State Normal and Industrial College for Negro Students at Tallahassee held premier status. Tracing its beginnings to 1887, the institution would emerge in 1909 as the Florida Agricultural and Mechanical College for Negroes, reflecting its special status as the state's only 1890 land grant institution. The name changed again in 1953 to become Florida Agricultural and Mechanical University. It remains the only publicly funded institution of higher learning for African Americans in Florida, as well as the nation's largest historically black college or university. This is not to say that, at the twentieth century's dawn, the State Normal School had no competition. In that category could be listed the Jacksonville institutions already mentioned, as well as Eatonville's Robert Hungerford Normal and Industrial School, founded in 1889 and modeled after Alabama's Tuskegee Institute. The Hungerford School today is operated as a public school by the Orange County School District.

At the twentieth century's beginning, black Floridians thus continued to embrace an appreciation for the power of education and illustrated that commitment through the institutions they supported. At a time when high schools could not be found in many white communities, African American schools at or approaching that caliber existed in many of the larger cities and towns. Typically, white-dominated school boards underfunded these institutions, leaving responsibility to black residents for making up the difference. The Stanton High School (once the Stanton Institute) at Jacksonville provides a good example. Founded with assistance from the Freedmen's Bureau and the American Missionary Association, it soon became a public institution that drew generations of students from the city and state. Similarly, children from throughout Florida sought out the Fessenden Academy at Martin near Ocala, an institution that dispatched its graduates to colleges and universities throughout the United States. In many places, the names and legacies of such schools live on. Representative of them were Lincoln Academy at Tallahassee; Union Academy, Gainesville and Bartow; Harlem Academy, Tampa; Howard Academy, Ocala; Central Academy, Palatka; Hopper Academy, Sanford; Douglass School, Key West; and Washington High School, Pensacola.

As Florida evolved into the most urban of southern states in the late nineteenth and early twentieth centuries, African Americans contributed to the dynamic in a variety of ways that might surprise residents today. Historian Canter Brown has pointed out that town and city governments run or heavily influenced by Republicans and sometimes dominated by black officeholders evidenced the foresight to plan for an urban future by bonding for water, sewerage, and electric power systems and otherwise to facilitate modern improvements such as paved streets and street railways. Democrats castigated the visionaries as spendthrift, at best; yet, with the future beckoning, the conservatives were forced to adopt the models pioneered by others.

Local whites often acknowledged the leadership debt. "When partisan and racial generalizations were set aside," Brown noted, "communities often retained sentiments of respect for individual black officeholders."[3] This did not deter efforts either to exclude blacks from the voting booth or to eliminate office holding by race representatives. Under the constitution of 1885, legislators imposed a variety of restrictions that included, among others, payment of a poll tax as a prerequisite for voter registration. Meanwhile, the state literally seized control for several years of cities such as Pensacola, Key West, and Jacksonville. Introduction of the partisan primary system followed beginning in 1897, leading to the notorious "white primary" system within the Democratic Party that excluded black voters entirely.

Thus, the principal dynamics that led to the ouster of African Americans from political power in the Sunshine State were not incompetence, corruption, or criminality as sometimes has been argued. Even in the face of economic pressures and physical violence, many black Floridians strove to maintain a voice at the government table. The white primary system guaranteed that they would do so as Republicans, and, within that limitation, leaders such as Jacksonville's Joseph E. Lee fostered persistence of black political influence within the national Republican Party into the 1920s. This helps to account for black postmaster Thomas S. Harris's presence at Live Oak in 1901 and the fact that Tallahassee's G. C. McPherson would be serving on a United States jury the same year. Meanwhile, African Americans at the century's turn continued to sit on city councils at Jacksonville, Key West, Fernandina, St. Augustine, Cedar Key, and other places. Two black councilmen, Albert Louis Browning and Joseph A. Nottage, in fact served Palatka as late as 1924. No wonder that, when woman's suffrage became the law of the land in 1920, African American women—technically exempt from payment of poll taxes—streamed to urban polling places at the urging of leaders such as Jacksonville's Eartha White and Daytona's Mary McLeod Bethune. They did so in direct defiance of Ku Klux Klan intimidation.

Contributions to Florida's urban-state orientation obviously did not stop with political influence and office holding. Credit also should be given to black truck farmers who, more so than did whites in many places, fed the growing populations of the towns and cities. The production of vegetables at F. W. Rutherford's 20-acre farm near Orlando provides an excellent illustration, as does the nutritious output of D. J. Williams's operations close to St. Augustine. Robert Aiken furnished Tallahasseans with cabbage and peas, while B. L. Brown offered up peas, beans, turnips, and mustard greens at Jacksonville. Examples of the same sort abound in virtually every locale and for almost every staple crop. Sometimes a particular community might even earn a reputation for specialization in a distinctive crop. Sanford's African American farmers, to cite one such instance, helped to perfect celery production and techniques that permitted shipment of the crop not only into town but also to northern markets.

Meat and poultry also came, in many places, from black stockmen and producers. William H. Ford specialized in turkeys at Tallahassee. J. D. McDuffie took pride in pork production at his Marion County properties, while his Alachua County compatriot James Hale offered quality beef. The premier Florida cowman, though, was Lawrence Silas of Kissimmee. In a career that spanned nearly three-quarters of the twentieth century, Silas contributed substantially to the growth and improvement of the state's cattle industry. "He is important," Zora Neale Hurston proclaimed in the *Saturday Evening Post*, "because his story is a sign and a symbol of the strength of the nation." She continued, "It helps to explain our history, and makes a promise for the future."[4]

Hurston was correct. Silas's accomplishments reflected broader and now largely forgotten contributions of black men and women to Florida agriculture. Take the citrus industry, for example. From the 1890s, the state's population progressively shifted southward with the extension of Florida's railroad networks. Especially after the disastrous Great Freeze of 1895, the development of citrus groves increasingly fueled new local economies and attracted settlers deeper into the peninsula. Already, black homesteaders of the Reconstruction era had undertaken citrus cultivation in Tampa and Hillsborough, Hernando, Polk, and Manatee Counties, providing vivid proof to potential northern émigrés at the terminus of Henry Plant's rail empire that the industry promised lucrative prospects.

Similar models greeted east coast arrivals. One such grower, Andrew Jackson, in 1870 had planted 500 orange trees near Titusville and within three years was earning the considerable sum of $1,000 per season. Jackson's operations by 1890 had grown to the point that his profits and the quality of his "first-class" fruit helped to establish industry standards in the region. In the same vein, at the peninsula's heart near Leesburg, black growers also provided a backbone for citrus production as "orange gold" lured investors. "This little chapel is completely surrounded by orange groves," African Methodist Episcopal Zion Church clergyman Joseph N. Clinton recorded in 1894 at Orange Bend, "and nearly every member of our church owns his grove, of, from three to five acres." Even where whites owned the land, black laborers' contributions were of critical importance. They typically provided the muscle and, not unusually, the expertise that kept newly settled white owners in business and profiting from their investments.[5]

Early-twentieth-century agricultural successes bespoke both an interest in further advancements and in building durable and effective ties across the state. State Normal and Industrial School president Nathan B. Young aided both goals by holding farmer's institutes as early as 1901 to stress crop diversification and truck farming techniques. These institutes led to more formal Educational and Farmers' Conferences held on the Tallahassee campus, as well as to the publication, beginning in 1909, of the helpful *Bulletin of the Agriculture Department*. The Hungerford Institute in the meantime also endeavored to improve the lot of African American agriculturalists. In 1903, it initiated the first annual Farmers' Conference at Eatonville. Ten years further into the century, Frank Robinson of Leon County aided the cause of agriculture as the state's first county demonstration agent. Soon thereafter, A. A. Turner covered much of the state as district agent.

Ties established through such efforts brought black Floridians closer together as the years passed, but they comprised only one element in a complex picture. Residents, if they enjoyed the means, delighted in traveling in order to relax, take cures, see friends and relations, manage business, or join with like-minded individuals in common causes and interests. Rail excursions from city to city brought collective delight, and trips to seaside locales developed by black entrepreneurs—including, for instance, Jacksonville's Manhattan Beach—allowed families the joy of Florida's coastal reaches. Probably the most famous beach destination was one of the latest to be opened as such. Amelia Island's American Beach near Fernandina long had welcomed black visitors, but not until 1935 did Afro-American Life Insurance Company president Abraham Lincoln Lewis purchase the site and undertake its formal development.

Institutional and organizational affiliations furnished near-constant justification for travel. Florida's churches paved the way, encompassing within their reach a significant portion of the African American population. "The church provided refuge from a cold, racist, and indifferent world," historian Maxine D. Jones has explained. "It was probably the only institution where blacks could seek solace, occupy leadership roles, make decisions, and maintain organizational control without interference from whites."[6] Tracing denominational origins in Florida to the Civil War and Reconstruction periods if not before, the AME Church, the AMEZ Church, the Colored (now

Christian) Methodist Episcopal Church, and the various Missionary and Primitive Baptist Churches competed with the Episcopalians, Presbyterians, Northern Methodists, and Roman Catholics for membership and attention. Church-sponsored conferences kept men and women on the move, as did related charitable and social undertakings.

In terms of bringing people together, church functions served only as the beginning. Clubs, associations, and social diversions proliferated, addressing a broad range of interests and social needs. West Palm Beach's Ever Ready Workers Civic Club afforded a good example, as did Jacksonville's Criterion Matrons Club. Eventually, the Florida Federation of Colored Women's Clubs brought many such groups under its nurturing wings. Masonic and other fraternal and sororal organizations likewise commanded time and interest. Masonry had entered the state's African American community in the late 1860s, with the Most Worshipful Grand Lodge organizing at Jacksonville the following year. As its reach extended, Masonic Benefit Associations began to appear as well. The 1890s saw the erection of a magnificent Masonic headquarters temple in Jacksonville. It burned in the 1901 fire, but a five-story structure built in 1942 and valued at $500,000 outshone earlier grandeur. The Eastern Star for women naturally accompanied Masonic expansion. From there, the list of groups lengthened with many organizations aimed at addressing benevolent causes including health coverage and burial benefits. Standouts included the Household of Ruth, the Daughters of Calanthe, the Lily White, and the Protective and Benevolent Order of Elks. Of special importance were the Independent Order of Odd Fellows and the Knights of Pythias. Each of them strove, as black political strength waned, to provide organizational support and statewide linkage for protection and resistance. In many places, the Odd Fellows Hall stood out as an unofficial black city hall.

Of additional importance, linkage among Florida's college-educated population—a vital leadership corps—flowed from college-based fraternities and sororities. From the early 1900s, these organizations have provided strong social ties and networks for information flow across the state, region, and nation. Alpha Phi Alpha, founded in 1906, came first. Alpha Kappa Alpha then debuted in 1908. Following were: Omega Psi Phi and Kappa Alpha Psi (1911); Delta Sigma Theta Sorority and Phi Beta Sigma (1913); Zeta Phi Beta Sorority (1920); and Sigma Gamma Rho Sorority (1922). These original eight were joined in 1966 by Iota Phi Theta. Especially at Bethune-Cookman and Florida A&M Colleges, these fraternities and sororities comprised an instrumental part of the institutional social scene.

The timing of the rise of the college fraternities and sororities coincided with increasing need for linkages within the state's African American community. As mentioned, the early 1900s saw intensification of racist rhetoric and heated demands for legally enforced racial segregation measures that often are remembered as Jim Crow discrimination. Not every white Floridian accepted the hate-filled verbiage, and in the century's opening years several attempts to enforce racial segregation in cities were beaten back. In 1905, however, former Duval County sheriff Napoleon Bonaparte Broward took the governor's chair and immediately requested Congress to segregate all black Americans in a separate territory, "either domestic or foreign." As biographer Samuel Proctor explained, "His attitude toward the Negro followed generally the definition given by Supreme Court Justice [Roger B.] Taney in 1857 when he said that the 'Negro had no rights or privileges but such as those who held the power and the government might choose to grant them.'"[7] Reinvigorated by such leadership, Jim Crow supporters renewed their fight for discriminatory laws. Central to these initiatives were efforts to mandate racial segregation on municipal streetcars. In places such as Jacksonville, Pensacola, and Tampa community members protested as black lawyers J. D. Wetmore, Isaac Lawrence Purcell, Charles H. Alston, and others fought in the courts. In 1905 they achieved a signal victory in the Supreme Court of Florida only to see the ruling negated within a matter of months.

The march of Jim Crow took place within the context of sometimes-violent subjugation of Florida's African American population, especially, but not always, in places remote from the larger cities. During the half century that began in 1880, Florida led in the nation in lynchings when computed on a per capita basis. The span of years from 1900 to 1917 alone saw about ninety black men put to death, often horribly, by extralegal violence. The supposed wrong might be as simple as an inadvertent insult to a white woman. Fifty more lynchings from 1918 to 1930 inflated the total. In fact, from 1900 to 1930 Florida's lynching rate ran nearly twice as high as that of Mississippi, Georgia, or Louisiana; more than three times that of Alabama; and six times that of South Carolina. The carnage did not end there. The nation watched aghast in 1934 at the travesty of justice involved in the cruel Jackson County murder of Claude Neal. One year later, Ku Klux Klansmen had dragged Reuben Stacy from a Fort Lauderdale jail before putting him to death by hanging and gunfire, while Tallahassee lawmen acting as Klansmen lynched Richard Hawkins and Ernest Ponder in 1937 virtually at Supreme Court Justice Glenn Terrell's front door. As late as 1945 Governor Millard Caldwell simply refused to investigate the lynching of Jesse James Payne in Madison County, creating another national scandal. In justification of his failure to act, the governor merely denied there had been a lynching.

The early 1910s brought dramatic change and not for the best. Florida's progressively evolving urban-oriented black culture and society collided with a rising tide of Jim Crow discrimination, racial violence, and economic intimidation. Adding to the problems were increasingly depressed conditions in rural areas produced by the cotton boll weevil and low cotton prices, a situation from which those who "sharecropped" and did not own their land suffered the most. Booker T. Washington's 1912 tour of the Sunshine State exemplified the transitory nature of the times. At Lake City, the famed educator credibly could assert, "In every community in the South where colored people live in large numbers there are white friends who stand by us." Then, days later at Jacksonville, Washington recoiled as a white mob unsuccessfully attempted to seize him from his automobile. Historian David H. Jackson Jr. described events occurring thereafter. "In the midst of his speech, Washington heard the howls of a mob in the distance on its way to lynch the accused murderers of [white grocer Simon] Silverstein at the jail," the historian wrote. To his credit, according to Jackson, Washington "launched into a fervid denunciation of lynching and ended with an earnest and eloquent appeal for better feeling between the races."[8]

In the years surrounding Booker T. Washington's close escape at Jacksonville, a tide shifted within Florida's African American population and, with the shift, large numbers of men, women, and children opted to abandon their Sunshine State homes for an uncertain future in the North. The "Great Migration" touched all of the Deep South states of the former Confederacy, but in Florida the impact evidenced itself unmistakably. A report detailed the net loss as of 1916. Live Oak had had seen "a large proportion of its colored population" depart, as had Dunnellon. One-third of black Lakelanders had left. "Not less than one-fourth of the black population of Orlando was swept into this movement," the report continued. "Probably half of the negroes of Palatka, Miami and DeLand, migrated as indicated by schools and churches, the membership of which decreased one-half." It added: "From 3,000 to 5,000 negroes migrated from Tampa and Hillsboro County. Jacksonville, the largest city in Florida, with a population of about 35,000 negroes, lost about 6,000 or 8,000 of its own black population and served as an assembling point for 14,000 or 15,000 others who went to the North."[9]

The emigration tide continued its urgent flow as another racist governor, Sidney J. Catts, took office in 1917. Known as "the Cracker Messiah," Catts's views ran to such extremes that he opposed, as his biographer Wayne Flynt put it, "both vocational and classical education for Negroes." The governor at first seemed pleased as black traveling parties crossed the state line headed north, but America's entry into World War I placed demands upon the state that a weakened labor pool could not begin to meet. Now, Catts delved into his experience as a Baptist preacher to urge African Americans, as Flynt noted, "to stay in a warm climate where 'the Creator had put them.'" When that overture proved of no avail, the state's chief executive launched a roundup of northern labor recruiters while prompting local governments to issue "work or fight" orders designed to compel black men to seek employment or be drafted into the military. In the end, laborers from the Bahamas filled the gap that Catts's misguided leadership could not.[10]

Long-term consequences, it hardly need be said, resulted from the flight of so many. To begin with, a significant percentage of the most talented and promising black Floridians departed, some for good, some fortunately only temporarily. James Weldon Johnson—who at Jacksonville in 1900 had authored the words to "Lift Every Voice and Sing," often called the Negro national anthem—already had gone, as had his composer brother Rosamond, a graduate of the New England Conservatory and the artist who added the music to "Lift Every Voice and Sing." Large enough numbers followed that Florida's contributions to what history has called the Harlem Renaissance of the 1920s and 1930s stood extraordinarily high. To name only a few individuals, James Weldon Johnson earned respect as a writer and poet while Zora Neale Hurston of Eatonville penned evocative fiction and insightful sociological studies focused back on her home state. Poet Alpheus Butler, son of Miami's first black medical doctor, James A. Butler, launched a creative career that flourished for four decades. Sculptor Augusta Savage of Green Cove Springs meanwhile developed talent of immense proportions. It is easily understandable why, in 1934, she would become the first African American selected to the National Association of Women Painters and Sculptors.

Along with the writers, poets, artists, sculptors, and intellectuals unfortunately went some of the greatest leadership potential. Florida's loss happily proved the nation's gain. If any one person embodied this fact, that person was Crescent City's A. Philip Randolph. Organizer of the Brotherhood of Sleeping Car Porters, he had emerged by the 1940s as one of the nation's most powerful labor leaders. Still active decades later, Randolph can be credited with organizing the 1963 March on Washington, the largest civil rights demonstration ever held in the United States.

Zora Neale Hurston left the all-black town of Eatonville, near Orlando, where she was born, to pursue an education and a writing career in New York City. With books such as *Mules and Men* (1935), *Their Eyes Were Watching God* (1937), and *Dust Tracks on a Road* (1942), she became a luminary of the Harlem Renaissance group of writers and drama- tists in 1930s. Though her last years were spent in poverty as a domestic servant in Fort Pierce, where she was buried in an unmarked grave in 1960, her name and books have since achieved international fame.

The Great Migration, when combined with growth in central and south Florida during the 1920s and afterward, additionally accelerated key de- mographic and economic trends. Black residents of rural areas, especially young people, increasingly sought lives in towns and cities, whether north- ern or in Florida. Unprepared by education or experience for the new en- vironment, the arrivals often found it difficult, if not impossible, to secure rewarding or even dependable employment. Florida's economic "bust" of

1926, which ushered in Depression-era conditions that, in places, would endure until World War II, made matters even worse. Urban poverty and associated problems grew as black contributions to Florida agriculture declined. Low commodity prices pressed African American owners and devastated sharecroppers. White-dominated state and local governments meanwhile permitted white owners to pay extraordinarily low wages while allowing importation of competing foreign workers. A 1963 report detailed the results. "The living and working conditions of the Negro farm worker in the State of Florida have already deteriorated far beyond the minimal standards of decency that are normally accepted in American society."[11]

The most urban of southern states in the process became even more urban as each year and decade of the twentieth century passed by. The state's population, including its African American population, grew by leaps and bounds after 1920. Always, though, whites arrived in far higher numbers

A. Philip Randolph was born in Crescent City in 1889. Educated in Jacksonville and New York in the 1920s, he organized the Brotherhood of Sleeping Car Porters, an all-black AFL union. As a result of his leadership, Pullman porters' working hours were cut, pay was increased, and working conditions were improved. During World War II and afterward, Randolph worked to end racial discrimination in defense factories and in the military. In 1963 he organized and directed a march on Washington that became the largest civil rights demonstration in the nation's history. He died in 1979.

than did blacks. Having constituted almost 44 percent of Florida's population in 1900, by World War II's end in 1945 the African American total stood at less than 25 percent. The slide continued to the point that blacks of non-Hispanic origin comprised by 2010 a slim 16 percent of 18.8 million persons. That low figure interestingly represented an uptick from 2000's 14.6 percent. Where a dozen counties had shown African American majorities in 1900, only two—Gadsden and Jefferson—did so in 1945. Gadsden alone claimed a black majority in 2010. Black majorities in high-population cities, too, had disappeared well before World War II's conclusion. Florida's demographic face had been altered irrevocably.

Back during the World War I era, when these trends were beginning to build, black residents remaining in Florida faced a serious and immediate challenge of protecting themselves against prevailing threats. Accordingly, protective leagues of various sorts were organized locally and groups such as the Odd Fellows and the Knights of Pythias attempted as best they could to afford statewide connections. Black lawyers—among them I. H. Purcell, Simuel D. McGill, Daniel Webster Perkins, and others—all the while continued to press the race's causes in court, a fact that threatened white leaders seriously enough to generate a sustained, although unsuccessful, effort in the mid-1910s to prohibit blacks from practicing law. Meanwhile, in 1909 the National Association for the Advancement of Colored People (NAACP) had coalesced.

The organization eschewed southern involvements at first, but this did not forestall inquiries from Florida. By November 1915, an NAACP branch had opened at Key West with former Monroe County sheriff Charles H. Dupont as its president. The next year Florida-born James Weldon Johnson took over national NAACP executive duties with the aim of southern expansion. In 1917 he opened branches at Jacksonville and Tampa—with others coming in the next several years—that, at first, promised to become centers for effective outreach. World War I ensued, however, and key leaders such as Tampa's D. W. Perkins entered the service. NAACP adherents continued valiant efforts, but, by the late 1920s, the organization essentially had become moribund within the state.

Into the gap stepped courageous individuals and, in particular, black journalists. Florida had spawned scores of race newspapers since the 1870s, even a daily at Jacksonville in the mid-1890s run during its brief life by James Weldon Johnson and businessman/Republican leader Milton J. Christopher. Into the late 1910s, Pensacola's *Florida Sentinel*, founded at Gainesville in 1887 and published by Matthew M. Lewey, ranked particularly high in terms of influence and reach. The opening in 1914 of the *Tampa Bulletin* by AME clergyman Marcellus D. Potter and his wife, Mary Ellen Davis Potter, nonetheless marked a turning point. In building a newspaper recognized nationally for its quality, the Potters strove to represent and defend the race vigorously and, often, courageously. Future civil rights leader Edward D. Davis lauded Potter as "Florida's foremost and most distinguished Negro journalist and publisher" and called the *Bulletin* "a brilliant tribute to his genius, ability, integrity, and worth." Davis added: "The road that he traveled was by no means strewn with roses. Buffered by hostility on the one hand, indifference and disloyalty on the other; confronted many times with threats, intimidation, and attempted bribery, he steered a straight course; he never wavered."[12]

If Potter and other men and women like him had not been of extraordinary character and capacity, conditions would have broken them. Despite the honorable and even heroic service of thousands of black Floridians during World War I, the Ku Klux Klan quickly entered the state with the peace and set an agenda of race hatred under their banner of "100% Americanism." Thus, when July Perry and friend Mose Norman, both property owners, attempted to vote at Ocoee near Orlando in November 1920, Klansmen occupied the town, lynched Perry, likely killed Norman, burned a good part of the black community, and drove out black residents so effectively that, according to report, no African American lived at Ocoee for the next sixty-one years. Added one correspondent from the scene, "The white men who killed [Perry] are well known, but have not been arrested."[13] All told, the Ocoee Riot claimed the lives of two whites and at least six blacks, and it signaled worse trouble to come. At Perry in 1922 and at Rosewood the following year, mob violence tragically produced needless deaths, painful dislocations, and wanton destruction of property. Many city and county governments all the while pursued stringent measures of racial discrimination including efforts to ban African Americans from residence. In one illustration, Miami as early as 1917 had barred blacks from driving automobiles within the city limits. When a white man's chauffeur broke the law, locals dynamited the Odd Fellows Hall in retribution. By 1925 the *Chicago Defender* had labeled fast-growing Miami as the "Hell-Hole of America." The city was, the *Defender* insisted, "Where to Be Right One Must Be White."[14]

In the 1920s and following decades, Klan influence extended deeply into law enforcement and judicial circles. Consequently, as a Polk County historian explained, "Increasingly, black fugitives refused to surrender and, instead, chose to fight it out with policemen and deputies."[15] Even in police custody, black suspects might be subjected to torture of various kinds. An incident of considerable significance arose at Pompano in 1933 where Isiah Chambers and three other men endured three days of extremely rough treatment at the hands of law enforcement authorities. Chambers, who maintained his innocence but was found guilty based upon confessions beaten from his fellow suspects, was sentenced to death. Attorneys S. D. McGill and Robert Crawford pressed to save Chambers's life, only to face rebuke from the Supreme Court of Florida. Justice Armstead Brown alone protested that the confessions were not "freely and voluntarily made." Eventually, NCAAP attorneys Leon Ransom and Thurgood Marshall aided McGill in taking Chambers's cause to the U.S. Supreme Court. That tribunal's landmark 1940 ruling in *Chambers, et al.* v. *Florida* reversed the conviction and barred the use in court of confessions derived from police torture. "We are not impressed by the argument that law enforcement methods such as those under review are necessary to uphold our laws," Justice Hugo Black wrote. "The Constitution proscribes such lawless means irrespective of the end."[16]

By the time Justice Black delivered his stinging rebuke of Florida law enforcement practices, the Sunshine State's atmosphere had begun to change insofar as the willingness of some black Floridians to risk everything by standing up and fighting for their cause was concerned. In 1929, at a low point, S. D. McGill had found it essential to inspirit Florida A&M graduates confronted by desperate times. "The world which will confront you is not an ideal world by any means," he acknowledged. "There is much to be done." Still, McGill insisted to the young men and women that they prepare for bringing a better day. "Education has furnished the beacon light of reason which is essential," he instructed them, "to the progress of any race."[17] Four months later, Black Thursday commenced the economic and social slide of the Great Depression. On the other hand, for many Floridians tough conditions had been the fact of life since 1926 if not before so they did not feel as hard a new blow as did much of the rest of the nation. Some segments of Florida's economy, such as citrus, phosphate mining, and even tourism, actually thrived over much of the decade that came after the crash. The novel problem confronting resident African Americans, as also was true of state and local leaders, involved men and women, black and white, flooding to the state for warmth and a taste of relative prosperity. Then, with the coming in 1933 of President Franklin D. Roosevelt's administration, circumstances for most slowly began to improve. The president's New Deal programs, though they might have been segregated by race, extended their benefits to the black man as well as to the white. Plus, the programs brought to black Floridians essential facilities on a scale previously unknown. The opening at Tampa in 1938 of its new $117,000 Clara Frye Hospital, for instance, launched a new era as far as improvements in black community health standards were concerned.

Within the more optimistic atmosphere of the New Deal era, certain black leaders endeavored once more to bring into being a statewide network to afford a united front against racism and discrimination. The Odd Fellows and the Knights of Pythias continued playing significant roles, but the Florida State Teachers Association emerged—particularly after Edward D. Davis of Tampa and Ocala became its president in 1935—as the most dynamic central organizational point. Aided by teachers Harry T. Moore and John Gilbert of Brevard County and Noah Griffin of St. Petersburg, Davis and his allies moved to confront laws and practices that denied equal opportunity to education for black children including equal pay for teachers. Their most effective weapon proved the lawsuit, with Griffin filing the first "equalization" suit in Pinellas County during 1937. Rejected by Florida's courts, the plaintiff found himself fired by the Pinellas school system.

The disappointing result of the Griffin suit led to other disappointments, but it also furthered a separate but not unrelated effort then ongoing that would aid the cause immensely. In 1934, inspired by the sordid horror of the *Chambers* case, Harry T. Moore and John Gilbert had breathed life into a Brevard County NAACP branch with Moore as president. Through their efforts, S. D. McGill was employed to represent Chambers. Now, in 1938, the NAACP contacts led to a second equalization suit, this one filed on Gilbert's behalf as principal of Cocoa Junior High School. This was the first such suit filed in the Deep South by the NAACP and served as a model for future action. Gilbert lost as had Griffin, but a subsequent 1940 action on behalf of Washington High School principal Vernon McDaniel of Pensacola forced a compromise settlement. Other school boards began to recognize the inevitable, and district after district over the next decade found itself compelled, voluntarily or otherwise, to address equalization.

The Escambia County victory in turn propelled Florida's civil rights advocates to take a second unique step as far as the NAACP was concerned. Nine branches then served the state's residents, and it occurred to most backers that coordinated, if not united, action was necessary. Through an informal agreement at first, the Florida State Conference of Branches came into being. The conference was the first of its kind in the nation. Formal organization came in October 1941 at St. Petersburg's Bethel Metropolitan

Baptist Church. With national executive secretary Walter White having blessed the conference's aims, delegates selected Harry T. Moore as their state president.

Meanwhile, actions were occurring on the local level that were breaking ground for future advances. Peninsular towns and cities had continued to grow, with Miami emerging as the state's largest city. There, the Ku Klux Klan openly strove to exercise its imposing strength. From within the Republican Party, local businessmen Samuel B. Solomon and Otis Mundy, with the Reverend John E. Culmer, in 1939 organized a black voter movement that brought nearly 1,000 individuals to the polls. As Miami chronicler Marvin Dunn explained, "[This marked] the first time in Miami's history that blacks had made a concerted effort to register and vote."[18] Four years later, as many thousands of Florida's African American residents served their country in World War II, Solomon again broke new ground. This time, as publisher of the *Miami Whip*, he ran for the Miami city commission as a Republican. He lost the election but gained two-thirds of his votes from whites. Meanwhile, attorney L. E. Thomas had put himself forward with a bid for justice of the peace, as had Stanley Sweeting for coroner.

Others soon would follow the examples set by Solomon, Thomas, and Sweeting, but mostly they did so as Democrats. The reason was a 1944 decision by the U. S. Supreme Court in the case of *Smith* v. *Allwright* that found the Democratic white primary to be unconstitutional. Wasting no time, Harry T. Moore and other NCAAP officials quickly organized the Progressive Voters' League and launched registration drives. After state officials had blustered and fumed for a while, Attorney General J. Tom Watson declared in November 1945 that the Florida party must comply. Arthesa D. Griffin and S. H. Bragg thereupon entered electoral politics as candidates, ultimately unsuccessful ones, for the Dade County school board.

Each year thereafter into the early 1950s, black voter access grew, at least in most major towns and cities. This could be credited in part to the actions of Dade County senator Ernest Graham, father of future governor Bob Graham, and Senator Spessard Holland of Polk County, who in 1937 performed what many thought of as a political miracle and achieved repeal of the poll tax. But, as the frequency of African Americans exercising political and other rights grew, so, too, did opposition and racial tensions. In some places, such as at Groveland in 1949, violence prevailed. As a testament to his character, Governor Fuller Warren sent the Florida National Guard to Groveland at the NCAAP's request, and, from the incident, Lake County sheriff Willis McCall entered the realm of infamy. Four suspects in an alleged rape of a white woman were beaten badly in his custody, while two of the men were shot by McCall under circumstances suggesting a personal execution attempt. County voters subsequently endorsed their sheriff by reelecting him to office every four years until 1972.

One important initiative especially stirred racial passions. This occurred beginning in 1949 when five black students, basing their actions on recent and expected U.S. Supreme Court decisions, sued for admission to various schools and colleges at the University of Florida. Virgil Hawkins, who desired to study law, persisted hardest and longest despite the adamant refusal of the Supreme Court of Florida to recognize his cause. Attempting to derail Hawkins's case, the state even created a law school at Florida A&M College (raised to university status in 1953). Hawkins refused to be sidetracked by all such diversions and for nine years fought to gain admission at Gainesville. In 1958 federal district judge Dozier De Vane ordered all University of Florida graduate programs opened to qualified black applicants, but the law school refused Hawkins as being, in its judgment, unqualified. George H. Starke, however, was admitted for the fall semester, and the home of the Gators began to come to grips with the U.S. Constitution and the civil rights era.

Unfortunately, the price in blood to be paid for the free exercise in Florida of constitutional rights by African Americans by no means had been satisfied by tragedies such as had occurred at Groveland. Tragically, activist Harry T. Moore and his wife, Harriette V. Moore, discovered this fact on Christmas night 1951. Ku Klux Klansmen planted dynamite under the bedroom floor at their home in the Brevard County community of Mims, and with its explosion their lives abruptly were forfeited. The brutal murders understandably shocked black and some white Floridians; yet, in doing so, the heinous act created obstacles of abject fear on the part of many when it came to participation in further civil rights activities.

Fear notwithstanding, the NAACP endeavored to reinvigorate the state's civil rights movement following the Moore murders, doing so in furtherance of a plan to utilize Florida and Mississippi as forums for trying out and perfecting civil rights initiatives. To head operations, the organization tapped Tampa native Robert W. Saunders as its Florida executive director. Saunders and his allies thereafter encountered repeated and steep hurdles that obstructed their movement forward, even after the famous 1954 and 1955 U.S. Supreme Court school desegregation decisions in the case of *Brown* v. *Board of Education of Topeka, Kansas.* The most notorious of the hurdles, except perhaps the Ku Klux Klan itself, involved the infamous Johns

Committee, named after Senator and Acting Governor Charlie Johns of Starke. A witch-hunting legislative panel that aimed to destroy the NAACP by seizing its records and membership lists, the committee in 1957 smeared civil rights activists as Communists and Communist dupes. Saunders and others stonewalled the committee's probes at the risk of their freedom but sent all Florida records to New York for safekeeping.

Meanwhile, rights crusaders elsewhere were gaining surer footing and pioneering new organizational structures, especially Dr. Martin Luther King Jr., and the Southern Christian Leadership Conference. One SCLC founder was Tallahassee's Rev. Charles Kenzie Steele, who also associated closely with the Florida NAACP. When in 1956 Florida A&M University students Wilhelmina Jakes and Carrie Patterson refused to give their seats on a city bus to white patrons, they were arrested and Steele found himself in a position to help organize and sustain community protest. The Tallahassee Bus Boycott followed, setting a model for action and achieving, over the next year, a signal victory for civil rights activists in need of a win.

In the years that followed, Floridians witnessed sit-ins and public beach wade-ins, among a myriad of other activities aimed at pushing back discriminatory barriers. Highlighting the struggle, in 1960 protesters at Jacksonville's downtown's Hemming Park endured baseball-bat attacks at the hands of Klansmen. Mayor and later governor Haydon Burns had absented himself from the city, and white policemen stood by as the violence flared. Four years afterward, at St. Augustine, the battles resumed, but this time they were featured throughout the nation on the televised nightly news. The city's quadricentennial celebration turned into a vividly panoramic presentation of protests demanding constitutional rights being countered by the immense power of prejudiced state and local government officials, hate-filled Klansmen, and their sympathizers. Most commentators accept that the experience contributed to passage in 1964 of the Civil Rights Act and, the next year, of the Voting Rights Act. Those measures and the federal authority they brought to bear finally and truly began to turn the corner forever on Jim Crow discrimination and racial segregation.

Although the Voting Rights Act effectively nurtured registration and voter turnout efforts, it did not assure the election of black men and women to public office. By the time of its passage in 1965, only a very few victories had been achieved. Worthy of remembrance, in 1962 Frank Malcolm Cunningham, a Riviera Beach attorney, became the first black candidate elected to a previously white city office (city commissioner in his case) since the city council election at Palatka four decades earlier. Safety Harbor voters followed two years later by placing William Blackshear on their commission. Although not in an elected office, James W. Matthews meanwhile received appointment as assistant United States attorney for South Florida. Four more years would elapse before Joe Lang Kershaw, the grandson of a Reconstruction-era AME minister and community leader, became in 1968 the first black legislator since 1889. Gwendolyn Cherry took honors as the first African American woman to sit in the Florida House in 1970. A dozen years then passed before Carrie P. Meek entered the Florida Senate. A decade more saw Meek, Corrine Brown, and Alcee Hastings elected to the U.S. Congress, following in the path last trod for Florida by Josiah Walls in 1876.

African Americans also began to serve in statewide offices, although they initially did so by appointment rather than election. Joseph W. Hatchett thus claimed a seat on the Supreme Court of Florida in 1975 thanks to Governor Bob Graham; one year later he kept the seat, however, becoming the first black candidate to win election to that tribunal. In 1979, Justice Hatchett achieved yet another distinction, becoming the first black judge to sit on a federal court of appeals in the South. Jesse J. McCrary the previous year had accepted the position of secretary of state, while former FAMU law professor Leander Shaw joined the Florida Supreme Court in 1983. He served as chief justice from 1990 to 1992. Governor Lawton Chiles, in the latter year, additionally designated Doug Jamerson as state commissioner of education. Jonathan C. Gibbs, his immediate African American predecessor, had served during 1873–74 in the administrations of Governors Ossian Bingley Hart and Marcellus Stearns.

The gains scored by Florida's African Americans during the civil rights era, as mentioned previously, came at a cost. The destruction of segregation barriers took a heavy toll on black businessmen and destroyed thriving black business districts in cities of consequential size. The deterioration of federally financed housing projects, urban renewal, and the construction of the interstate highway system contributed to breaking up historic urban centers of African American life and culture. The changing dynamics of the agriculture industry had purged most black owners and workers, leaving migrant workers—often of foreign origins—to capitalize on the need for seasonal manual labor required on the farm. Attempts to secure true integration of public education in the late 1960s and early 1970s brought resistance and, in more than a few places, violence onto their campuses and into school corridors. Governor Claude Kirk boldly manipulated such conditions for his political advantage, actually seizing control of the Manatee County school system until a federal judge convinced him to rethink his

Florida's first African American Supreme Court justice, Joseph W. Hatchett, of Pinellas County, poses with his family prior to taking the bench for the first time, 2 September 1975. Hatchett resigned from the court four years later in order to accept an appointment to the Federal Court of Appeals.

ill-advised action. Passions and frustrations simmered within much of the African American community, and they boiled over from time to time in the cities. Most notoriously, Overtown and Liberty City in Miami exploded in 1980 into what has been called one of the worse race riots in United States history.

At the twentieth century's turn and into the twenty-first century, the picture for Florida's African Americans remained a complicated one. Black entrepreneurs possessed the opportunity to enjoy the generous fruits of free enterprise, and a solid middle class lived a version of the American dream in every part of the state. Gone were the shackles of Jim Crow discrimination and the influence of the Ku Klux Klan. The law no longer limited advancement. Still, the picture evidenced less desirable aspects. To a community struggling to find rewarding employment opportunities, the first decade of the new century brought two recessions, the second of which approached conditions of the Great Depression and devastated the Sunshine State's economy. Thousands lost their homes through defaulted mortgages; others through killer hurricanes. Meanwhile, within the state a political revolution had occurred in the late 1990s that ushered in a Republican Party ascendency in state government and the subsequent marginalization of black political strength on the statewide level. Local, state, and national budget cuts raised the costs of education and training by considerable and, for many, prohibitive amounts. The election of a black president, Barack Obama, in 2008 brought joy, as did the fact that Florida added its electoral votes to his total. However, the reaction to President Obama by some whites in Florida and other southern states brought to the surface what many saw as renewed racism.

Looking forward, the community yearned for better understanding of its heritage, its successes, the price that had to be paid for what should have been guaranteed by law and constitution, and its enormous potential. In a sense, the gist of the thinking of many in 2010 reflected that of a Jacksonville man in 1901. Writing of the upcoming state fair, he had this to say about achievement, understanding, and ambition: "A large number of creditable exhibits in the colored department of the Florida State Fair will prove to the public that the large population of this people in Florida are more than dependents, void of a knowledge of the means of honorable livelihood, without industrial ambition, simply a mass from which numerous public evils emanate." He added hopefully, "The fairest dealing will be given every exhibitor, and the prizes offered will be open to all."[19]

Notes

1. *Jacksonville Evening Metropolis*, October 18, 23, 1905.

2. *Indianapolis Freeman*, December 21, 1901.

3. Canter Brown Jr., *Florida's Black Public Officials, 1867–1924* (Tuscaloosa: University of Alabama Press, 1998), 51.

4. Zora Neale Hurston, "Lawrence of the River," *Saturday Evening Post*, September 5, 1942, 18.

5. *New York Age*, January 21, 1888; *Salisbury (N.C.) Star of Zion*, August 23, 1894. See also Canter Brown Jr., "'Money was growing on trees . . . and here I come!': African American Pioneers of Florida's Citrus Industry," *Florida Frontier Gazette* 5 (Winter 2006):5–7.

6. Maxine D. Jones, "The African-American Experience in Twentieth-Century Florida," in *The New History of Florida*, ed. Michael Gannon (Gainesville: University Press of Florida, 1996), 386.

7. Samuel Proctor, *Napoleon Bonaparte Broward: Florida's Fighting Democrat* (Gainesville: University of Florida Press, 1950), 252, 296.

8. David H. Jackson Jr., *Booker T. Washington and the Struggle Against White Supremacy: The Southern Educational Tours, 1908–1912* (New York: Palgrave MacMillan, 2008), 162, 172–73.

9. Emmet J. Scott, *Negro Migration during the War* (New York: Oxford University Press, 1920), 63.

10. Wayne Flynt, *Cracker Messiah: Governor Sidney J. Catts of Florida* (Baton Rouge: Louisiana State University Press, 1977), 46, 190–91.

11. Herbert Hill, "The Tragedy of the Florida Farm Worker," *Crisis* 79 (December 1963):601.

12. Edward D. Davis, *A Half Century of Struggle for Freedom in Florida* (Orlando: Drake's, 1981), 70–71.

13. *Chicago Defender*, November 6, 1920.

14. Ibid., March 28, 1925.

15. Canter Brown Jr., *In the Midst of All That Makes Life Worth Living: Polk County, Florida, to 1940* (Tallahassee: Sentry Press, 2001), 295.

16. Walter W. Manley II and Canter Brown Jr., *The Supreme Court of Florida, 1917–1972* (Gainesville: University Press of Florida, 2006), 139–40.

17. *Chicago Defender*, June 8, 1929.

18. Marvin Dunn, *Black Miami in the Twentieth Century* (Gainesville: University Press of Florida, 1997), 195.

19. *Jacksonville Evening Metropolis*, October 25, 1901.

Bibliography

Bartley, Abel A. *Keeping the Faith: Race, Politics, and Social Development in Jacksonville, Florida, 1940–1970*. Westport, Conn.: Greenwood Press, 2000.

Brady, Rowena Ferrell. *Things Remembered: An Album of African Americans in Tampa*. Tampa: University of Tampa Press, 1997.

Brown, Canter, Jr. *Florida's Black Public Officials, 1867–1924*. Tuscaloosa: University of Alabama Press, 1998.

Colburn, David R., and Jane L. Landers, eds. *The African American Heritage of Florida*. Gainesville: University Press of Florida, 1995.

Davis, Edward D. *A Half Century of Struggle for Freedom in Florida*. Orlando: Drake's, 1981.

Dunn, Marvin. *Black Miami in the Twentieth Century*. Gainesville: University Press of Florida, 1997.

Green, Ben. *Before His Time: The Untold Story of Harry T. Moore, America's First Civil Rights Martyr*. New York: Free Press, 1999.

Jones, Maxine D., and Kevin McCarthy. *African Americans in Florida*. Sarasota, Fla.: Pineapple Press, 1993.

Manley, Walter W., II, and Canter Brown Jr. *The Supreme Court of Florida, 1917–1972*. Gainesville: University Press of Florida, 2006.

McCarthy, Kevin M. *African American Sites in Florida*. Sarasota, Fla.: Pineapple Press, 2007.

McDonogh, Gary W. *The Florida Negro: A Federal Writers' Project Legacy*. Jackson: University Press of Mississippi, 1993.

Newton, Michael. *The Invisible Empire: The Ku Klux Klan in Florida*. Gainesville: University Press of Florida, 2001.

Neyland, Leedell W. *Twelve Black Floridians*. Tallahassee: Florida Agricultural and Mechanical University Foundation, Inc., 1970.

Ortiz, Paul. *Emancipation Betrayed: The Hidden History of Black Organizing and White Violence in Florida from Reconstruction to the Bloody Election of 1920*. Berkeley: University of California Press, 2005.

Porter, Gilbert, and Leedell W. Neyland. *History of the Florida State Teachers Association*. Washington: National Education Association, 1977.

Saunders, Robert W., Sr. *Bridging the Gap: Continuing the Florida NAACP Legacy of Harry T. Moore*. Tampa: University of Tampa Press, 2000.

Scott, J. Irving. *The Education of Black People in Florida*. Philadelphia: Dorrance, 1974.

Smith, Walter Lee. *The Magnificent Twelve: Florida's Black Junior Colleges*. Winter Park, Fla.: Four-G, 1994.

24

Immigration and Ethnicity in Florida History

RAYMOND A. MOHL AND GEORGE E. POZZETTA

Powerful forces of transforming change buffeted the state of Florida throughout the twentieth century, none more important than rapid demographic growth. The fourth-largest state as early as the 1980s, and with a population surpassing 18.8 million in 2010, the year of the most recent U.S. census, Florida has been shaped in innumerable ways by internal migration and foreign immigration. Immigrant streams from Cuba and the Bahamas in the late nineteenth century provided a hint of things to come. By the late twentieth century, major concentrations of Caribbean, Latin American, and Asian immigrants had settled in all of the state's major metropolitan areas, as well as in some primarily rural central Florida agricultural counties. The census of 2010 reported almost 20 percent of Florida's population as foreign-born, more than three-fourths of whom came from Latin America. Perhaps surprisingly, in 2010 almost half (48.5 percent) of Florida's 3.7 million immigrants had become naturalized U.S. citizens. Florida remained the "Sunshine State" in the popular mind, but increasingly the state became identified as a significant center of new immigration.

It was not always so. Although blessed with abundant natural resources and available land, Florida struggled through its early history to attract people to its borders. As late as 1860, Florida had a population of only 140,423 (including 77,746 whites, 61,745 slaves, and 932 free blacks). These residents were clustered heavily in a thin band of settlement along the northern tier of the state. Until late in the nineteenth century, in fact, most of Florida existed in a frontier-like condition of virgin wilderness. The development of the state's lands, industries, and urban centers accordingly lagged far behind other sections of the nation, a fact that many residents linked to a lack of immigration.

Contemporary Florida responds to very different sets of population problems. Present-day residents of the state now debate proposals to limit population growth and discuss various strategies to curtail resource consumption. Increasingly burdened by the costs associated with refugee and immigrant influxes from the Caribbean and Latin America, and concerned about the social tensions engendered by multiculturalism and undocumented immigration, the state no longer worries about attracting newcomers. Rather, policymakers anxiously question whether Florida should continue to welcome new arrivals at all.

To understand how Florida has fluctuated to such curious extremes, it is necessary to comprehend the state's multifaceted encounter with migration, immigration, and settlement. A scrutiny of this history reveals that the many efforts to stimulate population movement to the state—and occasionally to repel it—varied over time and represented vastly different interests. Large landowners, for example, frequently devised schemes to populate unused land with settlers. Employers sought through various means to ensure an adequate and appropriate labor supply. Civic boosters similarly produced lavish plans to procure productive citizens for their communities. Superimposed over all of these initiatives were the strategies of ordinary migrants themselves, who often ignored the grand schemes of others and followed their own paths to a better future.

Vast acreages of undeveloped land and the need for resourceful settlers provided the two great motivating forces behind early human migration to Florida. The celebrated, if ill-fated, New Smyrna colonization experiment begun in 1768 represented an early such effort to settle productive immigrants on the land. Bolstered by a 20,000-acre land grant, a visionary London physician named Dr. Andrew Turnbull boldly transported 1,500 Greek, Italian, and Minorcan indentured servants to a site along the Atlantic coast of Florida to clear virgin forest for an indigo plantation. Within several years, mismanagement and disease undermined this colonization endeavor; the settlers drifted away, and Turnbull moved to Charleston to practice medicine. Both the Spanish and British governments made generous land grants to other individuals during their colonial administrations, hoping to stimulate substantial migration. These schemes generally produced results no better than the New Smyrna venture.

During the early years of statehood, Floridians became absorbed with the problems of the emerging sectional controversy and slavery, pushing aside concerns over immigration and new settlement. As the Civil War unfolded, Florida devoted its energies to the urgent demands of the conflict, leaving little opportunity for other initiatives. However, the immense human and economic dislocations that followed in the wake of war forced Florida's political and business leaders to focus on population growth. As one agricultural publication put it in 1881, "Unquestionably Florida's greatest need is immigration; next to immigration we need capital."[1] In fact, Florida had by far the fewest residents of any of the former Confederate states. In 1900, for example, Florida counted slightly more than a half million inhabitants, while Georgia and Alabama totaled 2,216,000 and 1,829,000, respectively. Such a small population in relationship to the state's vast land area meant a pronounced lack of development as defined by urbanization, industry, transportation facilities, and cultural amenities. Many Floridians believed that the state's deficiencies could most easily be erased by acquiring a class of industrious immigrants to populate unused lands, provide a stable labor force, and infuse the state with new ideas, enterprise, and energy.

Adding urgency to the desire for immigrants during this period was a pervasive white discontent with the black labor available in the state. In the years after the Civil War, many employers worried about the frequency with which former slaves exercised their new rights to mobility and deserted white-owned plantations and farms. Other Floridians reflected the racist attitudes of the time by claiming that without the coercive powers of the slave system, even those blacks willing to remain on the job would be unreliable and unproductive. The *Tallahassee Semi-Weekly Floridian*, for example, concluded in 1865 that a majority of citizens believed "negroes will not work on the plantations in a manner that will pay for the necessary investment of capital."[2] Thus, to solve the state's labor problem, anxious Floridians sought to divert to their state a portion of the rising tide of European immigration then flowing into the United States. For a few decades after 1868, Florida's official Bureau of Immigration promoted the state and its favorable prospects to prospective immigrants, but it was notably ineffective.

More energetic and effective immigration activities emanated from private interests. During the late nineteenth century, railroads, farm groups, real estate companies, wealthy landowners, mine operators, and industrialists directed an impressive volume of literature about Florida to distant parts of the globe. Italian immigrants received special attention in these campaigns. The prevalent perception of Florida as the "Italy of the South" and the common view that Italians excelled in citrus horticulture combined to make them appear particularly desirable. In 1873, citrus developer

Henry S. Sanford explained that Italians were "a most valuable class of im- migrants . . . intelligent and industrious, accustomed to orange and vine culture, and to a warm climate."[3] A similar enthusiasm for Chinese workers swept the state in these years, based on reports of their industriousness and skill in gardening. Nevertheless, promotional efforts attracted only insignifi- cant numbers of Italians and Chinese. When Florida turned away from sup- porting immigration by the first decades of the twentieth century, these two groups ironically came to be regarded as the least acceptable newcomers.

The drive to acquire foreign immigrants collapsed for several reasons. Since many Floridians supported foreign immigration as a means of re- placing black workers, they assumed that new arrivals would be content merely to change positions with the former slaves. Unsatisfactory crop lien and sharecropping arrangements characterized the fate of many early immi- grants who worked in Florida agriculture. Even worse, peonage exploitation was a common circumstance in turpentine camps, lumbering operations, and railroad construction projects. News of these conditions quickly spread outward and considerably dampened enthusiasm for Florida among poten- tial immigrants.

The attitudes of Floridians themselves similarly underwent a transfor- mation. Slowly in the 1890s and then with increasing speed after 1900, the state's earlier policy of open welcome turned to hostility toward foreign settlement. Florida had become engulfed in the rising tide of nativist senti- ment sweeping the nation. Concerns over the effects of introducing foreign religions, alien political ideologies, and potentially disturbing new racial strains rose to the surface. By 1910, most Floridians believed that if the state were to retain its racial integrity, preserve its unique "American" charac- ter, and protect its cherished institutions, it now had no room for foreign immigrants.

Even during the turn against immigration, however, a variety of promot- ers pursued colonizing plans. Immigrant colonies appealed to some land- owners and financiers on several grounds. This mode of settlement disposed of large tracts of land in one transaction and enhanced the value of adjacent property substantially. Moreover, this tactic seemed to offer the best pros- pects of permanent residence, since newcomers settled as a group could more easily perpetuate familiar customs and ease the difficult transition to life in the new land.

Florida's record of modern colony settlement included both success and abject failure. One effort to bring fifty Scottish settlers to Sarasota in 1885 foundered when the new arrivals found not the thriving community

In 1913, three members of the Japanese colony of Yamato near present-day Boca Raton posed for the camera outside what had once been their prosperous pineapple plantation. A blight destroyed the crop in 1908, and, owing to cheaper, earlier-maturing rail-transported pineapple exports from Cuba, the plantation never recovered. Courtesy of the State Archives of Florida, *Florida Memory*, http://floridamemory.com/items/show/12149.

promised to them but rather a "swampy wilderness" and a few scattered buildings. They soon abandoned their plans for a new life on Florida's tropical frontier. Similarly, in 1893 approximately 500 Danes purchased land at White City in St. Lucie County, only to learn shortly after arriving that their on-site manager had died and the group's financial agent had both sold them land he did not own and absconded with their money. This venture, however, was rescued at the last moment by the Florida East Coast Railway (FECR), which provided emergency supplies and financial backing.

It was no accident that the railroad was on hand to assist. The company owned vast tracts of land and supported a very active immigration bureau for many years. The settlement of Dania by Danish immigrants in 1898 grew out FECR operations, as did a 1904 venture to establish a Japanese colony called Yamato near the present-day location of Boca Raton. In the case of the Japanese, several years of successful pineapple farming raised expectations of a large-scale movement of people. By 1907 the FECR had established a rail station at Yamato, and several hundred industrious immigrants worked the land. A devastating attack of pineapple blight in 1908 ruined the colony's hopes, however, and most settlers eventually returned to Japan disillusioned with Florida's prospects.

As promoters and state officials vacillated over the wisdom of attempting to attract foreigners, immigrants themselves were often pursuing strategies of their own and independently creating centers of foreign settlement. The movement of Greeks to Tarpon Springs, for example, was guided by the business enterprise and vision of John Cocoris, a Greek immigrant who saw rich possibilities in the Florida sponge industry. Some Greek spong-ers had worked in Key West during the 1890s, using the "hook" method of harvesting from boats. But when huge sponge beds were found in the Gulf of Mexico off the coast of Tarpon Springs, Cocoris recognized that the tradi-tional Greek method of collecting, involving deep-water diving with special suits, would yield much better results. After initial harvesting successes in 1905, a steady flow of Greek immigrants came directly to Tarpon Springs, eventually dominating by force of numbers the small community's institu-tions and culture.

Two instances of large-scale migration during this period resulted in the creation of dense urban settlements capable of sustaining a full range of viable ethnic institutions and an enduring immigrant culture. The first of these emerged in Key West during and after Cuba's so-called Ten Years War of the 1860s. Expatriate Cuban and Spanish cigar workers and manufactur-ers flowed into Key West and established a major cigar-making center, while also turning the small island community for a time into Florida's largest city. By the 1870s, some 5,000 exiles labored in Key West's cigar factories, orga-nizing effective labor unions and community institutions. Key West was quickly eclipsed, however, by a cigar-making rival located to the north in Tampa.

During the years 1885–1924, thousands of Cubans, Italians, and Span-iards came to the small coastal village of Tampa and transformed it into a thriving industrial center. Drawn primarily to the cigar industry established in Tampa by Spanish industrialist V. M. Martinez Ybor, the immigrants—many moving from Key West—quickly made the city into the nation's lead-ing center for the production of high-quality, hand-rolled cigars. Settling in what was initially the separate community of Ybor City, the "Latins" of Tampa created a rich associational life that included immigrant labor unions, foreign-language newspapers, ethnic fraternal clubs, radical politi-cal organizations, and a thriving immigrant theater.

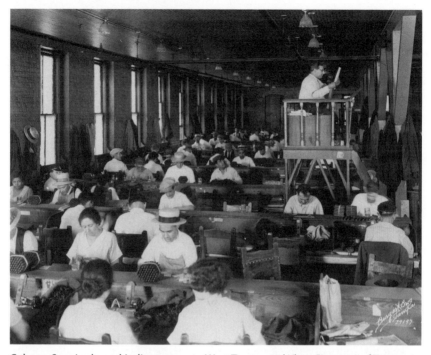

Cubans, Spaniards, and Italians came to West Tampa and Ybor City, east of Tampa, to work in the hand-rolled cigar industry. At the Cuesta Rey factory in West Tampa in 1929, these men and women silently rolled coronas, perfectos, and panatelas while *el lector* (the reader) on a raised platform (*right*) read to them in Spanish from newspapers, novels, and political tracts. Photo by Burgert Brothers. Courtesy of the State Archives of Florida, *Florida Memory*, http://floridamemory.com/items/show/27163.

No inquiry into the impact of immigrants on Florida during these years would be complete without recognition of the role played by transient foreign workers. Isolated work gangs of Italians, Greeks, Chinese, Portuguese, Spaniards, and many others crisscrossed the state laboring in plantation fields, drainage operations, and construction sites. The FECR, for example, regularly recruited work crews from far afield in its construction projects, hiring immigrant workers through labor agents located in major northeastern cities. In other economic sectors, such as sugarcane, citrus, and winter vegetables, the seasonal influx of migrant workers from the Bahamas and other locations became a long-term economic strategy that annually brought foreigners into Florida well into the twentieth century.

Black immigrants from the Bahamas added to the ethnic and racial diversity of nineteenth-century Florida. Black and white Bahamians had already established a distinctive presence in Key West by the mid-nineteenth century. Bahamian fishermen, shipwreck salvagers, and Indian traders, according to one Bahamian newspaper, regarded Florida "much as another island of the Bahamas."[4] Facing meager economic prospects at home, Bahamian blacks especially found better employment opportunities in the Florida island city. By the 1890s, Bahamians made up about a third of the population in Key West, where they worked primarily in sponging, turtling, and fishing. A large majority of today's Key West blacks trace their ancestry to Bahamian origins.

The black Bahamian migration to Florida intensified after the establishment of Miami in 1896. Like most other Caribbean islanders, Bahamians pursued a "livelihood migration" involving temporary labor elsewhere and regular return to the home island. The building up of Miami at the turn of the century created new opportunities for Bahamian migrant workers, who were attracted to the city by the prospect of better jobs and higher wages. As one Bahamian migrant remembered it, perhaps overstating the situation, "Miami was a young Magic City where money could be 'shaken from trees.'"[5] Bahamians who returned to the islands enticed others to follow with exaggerated tales of economic success in the "promised land"—a familiar theme in immigrant literature. The introduction of regular steamship service between Miami and Nassau by the early twentieth century made the trip to Florida cheap and convenient. According to Bahamian population studies, ten to twelve thousand Bahamians left the islands for Florida between 1900 and 1920—about one-fifth of the entire population of the Bahamas.

In early-twentieth-century Florida, Bahamian newcomers found work as railroad laborers, as construction workers and stevedores in early Miami, and in clearing land for agriculture and residential development. The emergence of Miami as a tourist center provided job opportunities for Bahamian women as maids, cooks, and laundry and service workers in the city's tourist hotels and restaurants. Large numbers of Bahamians also worked in the citrus industry and as field hands in south Florida agriculture. Many Bahamians came as migrant laborers during the harvest season, returning to the islands each summer. In the years before effective federal regulation of immigration, Bahamian blacks moved easily and often between the islands and south Florida.

The Bahamian presence in Miami and south Florida was proportionately large. By 1920, when Miami's population stood at 29,571, the foreign-born made up one-quarter of that total. More than 65 percent of Miami's immigrants—some 4,815 individuals—were blacks from the West Indies, mostly Bahamians. They comprised 52 percent of all Miami's blacks and 16.3

Agricultural, construction, and service workers from the Bahamas provided an important labor force over several decades during Miami's early history. This scene from a papaya plantation in the early twentieth century typified the Bahamian labor migration to Florida. R. E. Simpson postcard photograph from the personal collection of Raymond A. Mohl.

percent of the city's entire population. In 1920, Miami had a larger population of black immigrants than any other city in the United States except New York. As agriculture expanded along south Florida's Atlantic coastal region, Bahamians responded to new work opportunities. Consequently, the 1945 Florida state census reported more foreign-born blacks living in Palm Beach County (5,597) than in Dade County (4,609).

For thousands of Bahamians from the 1890s to the 1940s, the widespread perception of economic opportunity in Florida was too strong to resist.

Work was plentiful, but Bahamians routinely encountered racial segregation and discrimination in Florida. Racial confrontations involving Bahamian blacks and white policemen in Key West, Miami, and Jacksonville were not uncommon. Unaccustomed to harassment and racial barriers, Miami, Key West, and West Palm Beach Bahamians in large numbers joined the Universal Negro Improvement Association, the black nationalist movement led by Marcus Garvey.

As was true of Latins in Tampa, Bahamians built flourishing ethnic communities in Florida, especially in Key West and in Coconut Grove and Overtown, two black neighborhoods in early-twentieth-century Miami where they established businesses and laid the foundations for churches and a vibrant organizational life. The permanence and stability of these neighborhoods, along with strong links to the islands, contributed to cultural maintenance and an enduring ethnic identity. Unfettered Bahamian migration ended with World War II, when the agricultural labor supply in Florida came under governmental regulation. But enough Bahamians had already settled permanently in south Florida to sustain the growth of cohesive communities held together by a strong sense of identity and cultural distinctiveness.

Bahamian migration to Florida was paralleled by the early Cuban migration to Key West and Tampa. Florida's human connection to the Caribbean intensified as the twentieth century progressed. In retrospect, it is somewhat prophetic that the achievement of Cuban independence (1898) and the founding of Miami (1896) coincided at the end of the nineteenth century. The era of the Spanish-American War represented the first phase of that magnetic pull that has linked Miami and Havana as the twin cities of the Caribbean for much of the twentieth century. Key West, Tampa, and New York continued to be centers of Cuban exile life in the United States through the 1920s, but Miami was already beginning to emerge as a convenient place of political exile for Latin American revolutionaries, dissidents, and dictators. By the late 1920s, as many as 1,000 Cuban exiles, mostly young and radical university students opposed to the dictatorial regime of Gerardo Machado, had set up an exile headquarters in Miami. With the success of the 1933 Cuban Revolution, anti-Machado exiles in Florida returned home, with the blessing of the *Miami Herald*, which editorialized prophetically in 1933 that "Miami's gates will always be open to Cubans, should the time ever come again when they need a refuge."[6] Actually, that time came rather quickly, since ousted Machado supporters immediately took up new places in Miami exile.

Bahamian labor migrants continued to work in Florida agriculture well into the twentieth century. These farmworkers arriving in Miami by plane in April 1943 were part of a special temporary labor program during World War II. Courtesy of the State Archives of Florida, *Florida Memory*, http://floridamemory.com/items/show/29468.

It had become a natural pattern. As Harry Guggenheim, U.S. ambassador to Cuba in the early 1930s, noted at the time, Cuban exile leaders went to New York and Washington to solicit financial and political support, but the chief point of exile had already become Miami, where, Guggenheim said, "the rank and file of emigres and followers of the junta concentrate, since they can live more easily in Florida's sunshine."[7] Older communities of earlier Cuban immigrants were still thriving in Tampa and Key West, numbering about 7,400 and 1,600 respectively in 1930. But a new Cuban exile community began to emerge in Miami during the 1930s; by 1940, Miami had more than 1,100 Cuban-born residents, a colony that gradually grew even larger during the next two decades. Cuban-born workers, especially women, made up a large portion of the garment workers in Miami's needle trades in the early 1950s. Even before the success of Castro's revolution in 1959, a concentrated area of Cuban settlement had begun to take shape in Miami's central city, and the neighborhood was already being called "Little Havana." So the exiles who flowed out of Cuba in such astonishing numbers during the 1960s and after were only the latest in a long line of Cubans who historically sought refuge in Florida.

Despite the concentration of Latins in Tampa and of Bahamians and Cubans in Key West and Miami in the early twentieth century, Florida had not yet become a major destination for immigrants to the United States. In 1930, for instance, the foreign-born made up about 12 percent of the national population; by contrast, Florida had just under 70,000 white and black immigrants at the time, or about 4.7 percent of the state's total population. According to the 1930 U.S. census, more than half of those immigrants lived in the Tampa, Miami, and Jacksonville metropolitan districts. In addition to English, the most popular "mother tongues" of Florida's urban immigrants in 1930 were Spanish and Italian in Tampa; German, Yiddish, and Arabic in Jacksonville; and German, Yiddish, and Spanish in Miami. Despite small numbers of foreign-born, urban Florida was already displaying some ethnic and cultural diversity by the 1930s.

Over the next thirty years, immigration statistics for Florida converged with national patterns. By 1960, for example, the proportion of immigrants in Florida's population had increased marginally to 5.5 percent. For the nation as a whole, the immigrant proportion had declined to 5.4 percent of total population, reflecting the demographic consequences of the federal immigration restriction legislation of the 1920s. The foreign-born proportion for most of Florida's cities and counties hovered at or below the state average. But some dramatic exceptions appeared, such as in Miami Beach, where 33 percent of the city's population was foreign-born in 1960—mostly East European Jewish immigrants who had retired to Florida from northeastern states. Demographically speaking, Miami-Dade County appeared as an oddity in the 1960 U.S. census, with 113,000 foreign-born—over 40 percent of the state's total—whose mother tongues included German, Polish, Hungarian, Russian, and Yiddish, as well as English and Spanish. Pockets of immigrants clustered in other parts of Florida, too. Tarpon Springs, with many Greek immigrants, was almost one-quarter foreign-born. The foreign-born made up 14 percent of the population of Lake Worth, a small city in Palm Beach County where Finnish immigrants began settling in the 1930s. Jacksonville had a miniscule foreign-born population in 1960, but the city had long been home to several thousand Syrian-Lebanese people, a multigenerational ethnic community that grew to over 25,000 by the 1990s. Surprisingly, Canadian immigrants, largely a post–World War II phenomenon, comprised the largest foreign-born group in the Orlando, Jacksonville, Tampa–St. Petersburg, and Fort Lauderdale–Hollywood metropolitan areas. Finally, Miami-Dade County already had more than 50,000 Hispanics in 1960, reflecting both a growing Puerto Rican community and the early surge of Cubans just before and just after the fall of Batista in 1959.

The success of Fidel Castro's Cuban Revolution in 1959 permanently altered the trajectory of Florida's demography. The migration of Cuban exiles to the United States forms one of the most compelling and fascinating chapters in the history of American immigration. Over the course of a half century, more than 1.1 million Cuban exiles arrived in the United States, a large majority of whom settled in Florida, especially the Miami area. They came to the United States in several waves over five decades, an erratic migration flow dictated by the state of U.S.-Cuban relations at any particular time. This relationship also dictated the form of the exile movement. At various times, the Cubans arrived in Florida by airlift, boatlift, travel through third countries, or as escapees on small boats and rafts. American policymakers, beginning with the Eisenhower administration, encouraged the exile migration to destabilize and discredit Castro's communist regime. To a large degree, however, Castro controlled the timing and methods of exile migration, periodically opening and closing the doors, thus permitting the exodus of dissidents to defuse political opposition or internal economic problems. Humanitarian considerations had little to do with the Cuban migration on either side. Rather, as one recent Cuban American scholar has suggested, "the refugees became a prime weapon in the political war between the United States and Cuba," and Miami became a "front line in the Cold War."[8]

The great exodus of Cuban exiles to Florida reflected disenchantment with the outcome of the Cuban Revolution. The earliest exiles were ideological opponents of Castro, primarily the business and professional elite unhappy about the expropriation of property and the redistribution of wealth in socialist Cuba. Later exiles mostly had initially supported the Cuban Revolution, but pragmatic experience in the new Cuba had eroded their revolutionary zeal. Federal policy opened the gates to the early anticommunist Cuban exiles, who entered the United States unhindered by immigration quotas or other restrictions. Most of these Cuban newcomers entered the United States through Miami, which became one of the nation's chief immigration ports after 1959.

In 1960, the federal government established a Cuban Refugee Program and a Refugee Emergency Center in Miami to handle the processing and resettlement of exile Cubans. These agencies provided exiles with an unprecedented variety of social services, educational programs, medical assistance, and job training. By the mid-1970s, more than $1.3 billion had been spent by the federal government to assist Cuban resettlement in the United States. The refugee center also coordinated private aid from numerous religious and voluntary agencies, such as the Catholic Diocese of Miami, which played an important role in Cuban refugee assistance and resettlement. Tens of thousands of Cuban exiles were resettled throughout the United States, but a large number eventually returned to the Miami area. By the 1980s, more than 60 percent of all the Cubans in the United States resided in south Florida.

The arrival of the Cuban exiles in the 1960s initiated several decades of remarkable economic, political, and social change in south Florida. Given the professional and business backgrounds of first-wave exiles, the enormous amount of resettlement assistance they received, and their concentration in a single urban region, it is not really surprising that the Cubans adjusted well and prospered in their new home. They created a thriving ethnic community and carved out concentrated residential space in Miami's Little Havana, in Hialeah, and in other sections of metro Miami. After an initial period of adjustment, the initial wave of Florida Cubans generally became successful economically, creating an enclave economy that encouraged Spanish-language maintenance and provided jobs for a steady succession of Cuban newcomers. Later Cuban arrivals may not have been as successful, but statistical evidence gathered by the U.S. Census Bureau demonstrated that Cubans as a group have more education, better jobs, and higher incomes than the U.S. Hispanic population generally. The Cuban exiles and their Latin American connections sustained the emergence of Miami in the 1980s as a global city heavily reliant on international banking, trade, and tourism. On the downside, black Miamians consistently blamed Cuban exiles for displacing blacks in the local labor market and "taking over" the Miami-Dade County economy.

Florida's Cuban exiles adjusted to life in the United States, but they also held tenaciously to old-country language, culture, customs, religion, and foodways, even across several generations. Periodic political controversies in south Florida over immigration, bilingualism, and ethnic political power heightened the Cubans' sense of identity and the determination that language, culture, and community should be nurtured and defended. Second- and third-generation Cuban-Americans seemed to assimilate more quickly, but the constant infusion over time of new waves of Cuban exiles (such as with the 1980 Mariel boatlift that brought 125,000 newcomers to south Florida, as well as later waves of rafters) strengthened Cuban cultural maintenance. In Miami-Dade County, where the 2010 census reported the population to be 51.1 percent foreign-born, 65 percent Hispanic, and 71.9 percent non-English-speaking at home, the Cuban exile migration had an enormous cumulative impact over five decades.

Cuban exiles began arriving in Miami in 1959. They quickly carved out residential space just west of the city's central business district, while also establishing new cultural institutions and new businesses such as this "Little Havana" grocery store in a 1961 photo. Courtesy of the State Archives of Florida, *Florida Memory*, http://floridamemory.com/items/show/34744.

Since the 1970s, immigrant Cubans increasingly shared exile space in Florida with a growing refugee community of Haitians. Political repression, violence, and poverty in Haiti over several decades triggered a huge exile migration to Florida from that beleaguered Caribbean island. The rise of Francois "Papa Doc" Duvalier to power in Haiti in 1957 stimulated an early exodus of the country's professional and business elites, mostly to New York City, Montreal, and a few other northeastern cities. Metro Miami's Haitian community was initially quite small; the 1960 census reported only a few hundred Haitians living in Miami-Dade County. However, Haitian exile patterns changed dramatically by the mid-1970s, as Haiti's urban workers and rural peasantry began an exodus of their own to the United States, mostly in clandestine fashion by small boat, either directly to Florida or by way of the Bahamas, where tens of thousands of Haitians temporarily settled. The magnitude of this Haitian exile migration first was brought home to Floridians in 1980, when more than 25,000 Haitian boat people washed up on south Florida beaches, a desperate migration that occurred simultaneously with the Mariel boatlift. The parallel nature of the Haitian and Cuban exile migrations focused attention on the important place of Florida in the political economy of the Caribbean.

Federal policy on Haitian exiles has been controversial. Haitian newcomers received a less than enthusiastic welcome, especially when compared to the treatment accorded Cuban exiles. U.S. policy generally rejected Haitian appeals for political asylum. The U.S. Immigration and Naturalization Service (INS) sought to return the exiles to Haiti, interdict them at sea, or discourage their departure from Haiti. During the 1980s, the INS officially confined thousands of Haitian exiles at the Krome Refugee Center west of Miami; after awaiting deportation hearings, most were returned to Haiti. A new crisis emerged in the 1990s, when the United States detained tens of thousands of interdicted Haitians at the U.S. naval base in Guantanamo Bay, Cuba, before sending them back to Haiti, where they faced punishment or retribution. By contrast, Cuban exiles who arrived in the United States went free immediately under provisions of the Cuban Adjustment Act (1966),

In 1980, the Mariel boatlift brought 125,000 new Cuban exiles to south Florida. They crowded onto hundreds of vessels such as the *El Dorado* in their quest for a new life in the United States. Courtesy of the State Archives of Florida, *Florida Memory*, http://floridamemory.com/items/show/98693.

which granted them permanent resident alien status. To this day, Congress and federal immigration authorities have failed to resolve the double standard in American immigration policy—one that welcomed mostly white exiles from Cuba but rejected black refugees from Haiti.

The ongoing immigration of Haitian exiles reshaped once again the residential and ethnic structure of south Florida. Initially, Haitians settled heavily in the Edison–Little River section of Miami, an older, inner-city residential area soon labeled "Little Haiti." By the 1990s, Haitians also began moving into North Miami and then into Broward and Palm Beach Counties, mostly into a corridor of older, low-income residential neighborhoods stretching along Interstate 95. Thus, substantial Haitian communities emerged in Fort Lauderdale, Pompano Beach, Delray Beach, Boynton Beach, Lake Worth, West Palm Beach, and Riviera Beach, as well as in agricultural communities such as Pahokee, Belle Glade, and South Bay on Lake Okeechobee. According the U.S. Census Bureau, in 2009 some 376,000 Haitians and Haitian Americans resided in Florida, most in south Florida's three large urban counties.

In Florida, Haitian newcomers confronted the traditional immigrant task of adjustment and accommodation. Lacking the self-sufficient enclave economy of Cuban exiles, many Haitians entered the low end of the labor market, mainly in marginal service jobs and unskilled work in construction and landscaping; others participated in a local underground economy of car repair and handyman home-maintenance work. Florida's Haitians also built new ethnic communities with important institutional and cultural attributes. Pre-migration Haitian culture remained a powerful ingredient of community life. Haitian dress, food, music, and art prevailed in Miami's Little Haiti and in other Haitian communities. Frequent festivals and celebrations perpetuated the homeland flavor. The extended family structure served important functions, ranging from facilitating the chain migration process to providing job recruitment for new arrivals. Haitian Catholic parishes, with French- and Creole-speaking priests, provided a form of religious continuity. Haitians mixed organized religion with folk religion of African origins called voodoo—a mélange of music, magic, ceremony, ritual, natural medicine, and animal sacrifice that became an indelible part of Haitian immigrant culture. A powerful brand of exile politics testified to intense interest in the fate of their homeland, even as growing numbers of Haitians became U.S. citizens and voters.

Another large Florida exile community emerged after Nicaragua's Sandinista revolutionaries overthrew dictator Anastasio Somoza in 1979. By the

Haitian immigrants began arriving in south Florida during the 1970s. By 1985, when this photo of a Little Haiti botanica, or voodoo shop, was taken, Florida's Haitian community surpassed 100,000 people. Courtesy of the State Archives of Florida, *Florida Memory*, http://floridamemory.com/items/show/106159.

mid-1980s, some 75,000 opponents of the leftist Sandinistas had established an exile base in Miami-Dade County. The Nicaraguans found Miami, with its large population of anti-communist Cubans, a hospitable and convenient place of refuge. Much like the Cubans in the early days of their exile in Florida, the Nicaraguans initially hoped to return home. A peaceful transfer of power took place in Nicaragua in 1990, when the contras put down their arms and a pro-U.S. government was elected, thus short-circuiting the newest Latino migration stream to Florida.

What began as a temporary exile migration eventually resulted in a new and seemingly permanent immigrant community in Florida. It was a re-run of the Cuban exile migration. The earliest Nicaraguan exiles adjusted quickly, as Spanish-language use was beneficial rather than detrimental in Miami. Many Nicaraguans had business and professional backgrounds, which in the 1980s stimulated a new surge of immigrant entrepreneurialism.

The Cuban enclave economy absorbed many other newcomers from Central America. The Nicaraguans (or Nicas, as they are called in Miami) settled heavily in Sweetwater and Fontainebleau Park, communities on the western fringes of the Miami metropolitan area. In keeping with a well-established Miami tradition, this section of Miami-Dade County quickly earned the appellation "Little Managua." Miami's Nicaraguans possessed a strong sense of national identity that was sustained by transplanted communal institutions and Catholic parishes in Sweetwater and Little Havana. By 1990, the Nicaraguans had become the second-largest Hispanic group in Miami-Dade County, and Nicaraguan children supplanted Cubans as the largest-single group of foreign-born students in Miami-Dade County schools. The 2010 census reported some 135,000 Nicaraguans in Florida, most residing in metro Miami.

The heavy attention devoted to the Cuban, Haitian, and Nicaraguan migrations to south Florida has tended to obscure a wider pattern of recent immigration, especially Hispanic and Asian immigration, to Florida as a whole. The foreign-born and the Hispanic populations of Florida have been rising rapidly for the past half century. Between 1960 and 1990, Florida's foreign-born population increased from 5.5 percent to 12.9 percent of total state population; by 2010, the state's immigrant population rose still further to 19.2 percent. Florida had about 272,000 immigrants in 1960, 1.7 million in 1990, and 3.7 million in 2010. Florida's Hispanic population has also been increasing at a rapid pace, from about 405,000 in 1970 (when the U.S. Census first began reporting data on Hispanics) to 1.5 million in 1990, 2 million in 2000, and 4.2 million 2010. One final statistical measure emphasized the degree to which the demography of modern Florida has been altered by a half century of new immigration: 2010 census statistics reported that some 3.5 million Florida residents, or just over 19 percent of the state's population, spoke a language other than English at home. About half of those non-English speakers live in Miami-Dade County, where 71.9 percent of the residents conversed in native languages at home, primarily Spanish but also Haitian-Creole and several Asian languages. The remainder of the non-English speakers are distributed throughout the state, both in large metropolitan counties—Osceola, Broward, Orange, Palm Beach, and Hillsborough—where the foreign speakers ranged from 45 to 25 percent of residents, and in smaller agricultural counties—Hendry, Hardee, Collier, and De Soto—where 42 to 29 percent of the population used other languages at home. These demographic trends over several decades emphasized the degree to which Florida has become a center of new immigration.

The Latinization of Florida generally has been attributed to the massive exodus of Cuban exiles to south Florida since 1959. This is only partially true. Cubans did form a majority of all Florida Hispanics in 1970 and 1980, but by 1990 other Hispanics considerably outnumbered Cubans. Since 1970, the proportions of Mexicans, Puerto Ricans, and other Hispanics all grew more rapidly than Florida's Cuban population. For example, the number of Mexicans in Florida—about 20,000 in 1970—grew enormously to 150,000 in 1990 and 630,000 in 2010. The state's Puerto Rican population rose at a staggering rate, from 28,000 in 1970 to 848,000 in 2010. The other Hispanic category, which includes Central Americans, South Americans, and Caribbean Hispanics such as Dominicans, increased at an equally amazing pace, from 106,000 in 1970 to 1.5 million in 2010. At the county level, only in Miami-Dade and Monroe Counties did Cubans consistently outnumber other Hispanic groups. In Broward and Palm Beach Counties, Central and South Americans outnumbered other Latin groups by the time of the 1990 census, and over the next two decades the number of other Hispanic peoples increased faster than any other group. In other big, urban counties—Hillsborough, Pinellas, and Duval—other Hispanics dominated in the 1980s and 1990s, but by 2010 their numbers were equaled or surpassed by Puerto Ricans. Puerto Ricans also became the predominant Latin group in the three metro Orlando counties—Orange, Osceola, and Seminole. And in seven rural, agricultural counties in central Florida—Hardee, Hendry, Highlands, Collier, Okeechobee, DeSoto, and Glades—Mexicans predominated, and in most cases outnumbered the other three Latin groups combined, both in 1990 and 2010.

County-level U.S. census data, then, revealed two important and often overlooked demographic trends that began to emerge as early as the 1970s. First, these statistics documented the diffusion of the Hispanic population throughout the state. Second, they demonstrated the rapid diversification of Florida's Latin population, as groups other than Cubans came to predominate in areas outside the southeast corner of the state. For example, in the Orlando area, beginning in the 1980s Puerto Rican real estate developers embarked on a successful campaign to build for and attract Puerto Ricans, often retirees, from the New York City area and from Puerto Rico. Their efforts proved to be remarkably successful. By 2010, almost 848,000 Puerto Ricans resided in Florida, mostly in a broad, central Florida corridor along Interstate 4 from Deltona through Orlando and Kissimmee to Tampa. Dominican immigrants, many moving from New York City, increased the diversification of Hispanic population in the Miami, Tampa, and Orlando metro areas during the 1990s and after, and the 2010 census reported more than 172,000 Dominicans in Florida. In southwest Florida, the Cape Coral–Fort Myers metro area more than doubled its foreign-born population between 2000 and 2010, rising from just over 40,000 to more than 95,000, primarily a consequence of Hispanic migration. The latest census also reported that other Central and South American nationality groups had arrived in Florida in large numbers by 2010—300,000 Colombians, 107,000 Hondurans, 102,000 Venezuelans, 101,000 Peruvians, and tens of thousands of others from Argentina, Ecuador, Peru, El Salvador, Panama, and the rest of Latin America. Brazilians, Latin but not Hispanic, also established large ethnic communities in Florida in recent decades, especially in the three-county Miami metro area, but also in Orlando, Jacksonville, and the Tampa Bay area.

The Latinization process, moreover, has now extended to Florida's rural areas, where over several decades Hispanic immigrant workers have largely replaced black and white Americans in the farm labor force. For instance, in 2010, Mexicans comprised 43 percent of the population of Hardee County, an agricultural area once known as the cucumber capital of the world. Miami's Little Havana is well known as a center of Hispanic life and culture in Florida, but a visit to Wauchula, Bowling Green, or Zolfo Springs—Hardee County's chief towns—provides unmistakable visual and cultural evidence that the Latinization process has spread to the agricultural center of the state. The most popular holiday in Hardee County now may be Cinco de Mayo, a Mexican national holiday, during which Aztec music, dancing, and folk culture are celebrated by these new Floridians. In Indiantown, a small agricultural community in Martin County, the big holiday is the festival of San Miguel Acatan, the patron saint of a large colony of Maya Indians, exiles from civil war in Guatemala who have settled in Indiantown and nearby farm communities. By 2010, a Mayan diaspora of almost 84,000 resided in Florida, primarily in agricultural and farmworker communities stretching from Immokalee to Homestead. As these examples demonstrate, the Latinization of Florida has spread far beyond Miami's Little Havana, and the Hispanic newcomers to the state represent a broad spectrum of Caribbean, Central American, and Latin American peoples. Nicaraguan, Brazilian, and Dominican, Puerto Rican and Cuban, Aztec and Maya—these newcomers and others from south of the border represented the powerful impact of immigration and migration, forces that reshaped the social, cultural, and economic life of much of modern Florida over the past half century.

By the end of the twentieth century, new immigration streams of Mexican and Guatemalan farmworkers began to transform Florida's rural spaces. Here, in 1990, three generations of a Latino family watch American television at a laundromat in Greenacres, an unincorporated area of Palm Beach County. Photo by Raymond J. Mohl, from the personal collection of Raymond A. Mohl.

The ethnic transformation of modern Florida is not simply a consequence of Latino immigration, however. Mirroring national patterns, Asian immigrants emerged as another fast-growing foreign-born group in Florida as early as the 1980s. The 1990 census reported 152,000 Asians in Florida, almost triple the number in 1980, but by 2010, Florida's Asian population had surged to 455,000. When the census added Asians "in combination," that is, multiracial people with some Asian heritage, the total number of Asians or part Asians in Florida reached 571,244. As noted earlier, small colonies of Chinese and Japanese emerged in the late nineteenth century, but racial discrimination and immigration restriction limited Asian immigration until the post–World War II era. The more recent Asian immigration to the Sunshine State stemmed initially from U.S. military involvement in Asia and the Pacific region, involvement that brought war brides and military spouses, military employees, and refugees. Asian numbers in Florida remained small until after passage of immigration reform legislation in 1965 that abolished the national origins quota system and established new immigration preferences based on family reunification and professional skills in such fields as engineering, science, and medicine. This shift in immigration policy led to a rapid rise in the nation's Asian population from about 1.2 million in 1965 to 14.7 million in 2010. Most Asian immigrants entered the United States in California or New York, but over time a secondary internal migration brought rising numbers of Asian people to Florida, attracted by the growth prospects of one of the largest Sunbelt states and perhaps by warmer climate.

Patterns of Asian immigration to Florida have shifted over time. In 1970, the largest Asian nationality groups were Filipino, Japanese, and Chinese, their numbers ranging between about 3,000 and 5,000. By 2010, the dominant groups were Filipino, Asian Indians, Vietnamese, and Chinese, ranging in size between about 40,000 and 62,000. Six other Asian groups had a visible presence in Florida, with populations ranging between 7,000 and 19,700: Koreans, Pakistanis, Japanese, Thai, Iranians, and Bangladeshis. Asian immigrants have now settled primarily in the state's eight largest metropolitan counties, with the highest number in Broward and Orange Counties, each with more than 56,000 Asians. Since the 1950s, Filipinos have been the largest group in Jacksonville and Pensacola, largely due to their tradition of employment with the U.S. Navy. Asian Indians are by far the largest group in the Miami, Tampa, and Orlando metro areas, followed by Vietnamese and Chinese. Asian immigrants are very entrepreneurial, establishing businesses wherever they settle; many are professionals, engineers, computer scientists, physicians, nurses, and professors. Others found specific economic niches. For instance, as early as the 1990s, Indian entrepreneurial families owned and operated more than 400 of Florida's small hotels and motels. Asian immigrants retained their identity, languages, cultures, and foodways to a remarkable degree, while also adapting to modern American life. They established their own grocery stores, shopping centers, weekly newspapers, language schools, churches, and ethnic festivals and parades. Florida has Latinized over the past half century, but a sizeable Asian migration since the 1980s brought new forms of diversity to the Sunshine State.

Modern Florida's ethnic diversity has other roots, as well. By the 1990s, more than 120,000 Jamaicans resided in the three-county Miami metro area, clustering in places called "Jamaica Hill," "Beat Street," and "Little Jamaica" in Kendall, North Miami, Miramar, Plantation, Lauderdale Lakes, Lauderhill, Coral Sprints, West Palm Beach, and Boynton Beach. South Florida has the largest concentration of Jamaicans anywhere outside of Jamaica itself.

Canadian tourists—more than 700,000 by 2001—still descend on Florida every winter, Quebecois primarily to the Atlantic coastal areas and English-speaking Canadians primarily to the state's west coast from Tampa Bay to Naples; tens of thousands of other snowbirds from north of the border have purchased condominiums and mobile homes and become part-time or permanent Florida residents. The "Little Finland" of Lake Worth and Lantana has retained its cultural identity as one of the largest Finnish settlements beyond Scandinavia, partially through a recent direct migration of younger Finns to Florida. By 2010, however, Lake Worth's Finns shared residential space with growing numbers of Haitians, Mayans from Guatemala, and other Latinos. After a decade of civil war and ethnic cleansing in Yugoslavia during the 1990s, several thousand Bosnian Muslims found new homes in Florida, as many as 6,000 in Jacksonville, others in Miami, Orlando, and Tampa. U.S. census data in 2006 revealed almost 60,000 African immigrants residing in Florida, primarily in metro areas. East European Jews migrated in huge numbers from northern cities to Miami-Dade County in the postwar decades. By 2010, Florida had a Jewish population of 655,000, more than half of them concentrated in the three-county Miami metro area, including about 10,000 Latino Jews and smaller numbers of Soviet Jewish émigrés. Florida's big urban areas, it should be clear, are now more ethnically and culturally diverse than ever as a result of persistent but constantly shifting patterns of immigration and internal migration.

Thus, Florida has become a multicultural state with few parallels elsewhere. Early in its history, Florida had difficulty attracting the European immigrants who poured into the northeastern and midwestern cities. With its historic connections to the islands and nations to the south, however, Florida had already become an immigrant destination for Cubans and Bahamians in the late nineteenth century. But since the 1960s, with revolutions, coups, political violence, and social and economic upheavals in Cuba, Haiti, Nicaragua, Jamaica, Venezuela, Mexico, and elsewhere, Florida exerted its magnetic attraction for exiles, refugees, and immigrants from the Caribbean and Latin America. Wealthy businessmen and professionals from Venezuela, Argentina, and Brazil found themselves sharing immigrant status in Florida with peasant farmers and urban workers from Haiti, Mexico, and the Dominican Republic. Immigration reform in the 1960s also had an impact on Florida over time, especially noticeable by the 1990s in the rising numbers of Hispanic, Asian, African, and Middle Eastern immigrants. In addition, undocumented immigrants added considerably to Florida's ethnic and cultural mélange after the mid-1980s. In 2010, depending on the source, between 720,000 and 825,000 unauthorized immigrants were living, and many working, in Florida.

The arrival of overwhelming numbers of newcomers—legal and not legal—over a half century has been accompanied by increasingly vigorous debate and controversy. State and business officials sought new immigrants in the late nineteenth century to stimulate the Florida economy, but this positive stance toward immigration had been reversed by the 1990s and into the twenty-first century. Florida's political leaders and businessmen no longer yearned for new immigration. Instead, they demanded stronger federal enforcement of U.S. immigration laws. They wanted more federal financial assistance to cope with demands that exiles and refugees imposed on the state's schools and social services. Many native Floridians expressed concern about rising ethnic and racial tensions touched off by the heavy immigration of recent years. In the 1990s, mirroring national trends, anti-immigration groups such as Floridians for Immigration Control and the Save Our State Committee pushed legislation curbing social services and other benefits to unauthorized immigrants.

During the first decade of the twenty-first century, the immigration wars heated up again. New anti-immigrant groups sprouted locally—Citizens of Dade United in Miami, Floridians for Immigration Enforcement in Jupiter, Citizens Against Illegal Immigration in Fort Myers, Minuteman Civil Defense Corps in Haines City—all demanding tough laws authorizing police checks of immigration status during traffic stops and denying work, schooling, and health services to those without official documentation. Governor Rick Scott and the state legislature eventually backed away from such legislation because of the potentially negative impact on the state's big agricultural employers, international investors, and the Latin American tourist trade and business interests. Nevertheless, anti-immigrant sentiment persisted and remained politically volatile in the election year of 2012. Whatever the outcome of current immigration debates, Florida has been, and likely will remain, a center of dramatic demographic change for decades to come. Immigration has reshaped the state of Florida economically, culturally, politically, even linguistically. Immigration also brought to Florida an unmistakable cultural vitality, a new burst of energetic ethnic entrepreneurialism, a huge consumer market, and diverse political voices. The rise and embedded nature of multiculturalism in Florida has placed every big metro area and every small rural county on a new trajectory of twenty-first-century change.

Notes

1. *Florida Agriculturist*, 19 January 1881.
2. *Tallahassee Semi-Weekly Floridian*, 1 December 1865.
3. *Tallahassee Weekly Floridian*, 14 January 1873.
4. *Nassau Tribune*, 12 October 1977.
5. Ira De A. Reid, *The Negro Immigrant: His Background, Characteristics, and Social Adjustment, 1899–1937* (New York: Columbia University Press, 1939), 184.
6. *Miami Herald*, 16 August 1933.
7. Harry F. Guggenheim, *The United States and Cuba: A Study in International Relations* (New York: Macmillan, 1934), 176.
8. Felix Roberts Masud-Piloto, *With Open Arms: Cuban Migration to the United States* (Totowa, N.J.: Rowman and Littlefield, 1988), 2, 42.

Bibliography

Boswell, Thomas D., and James R. Curtis. *The Cuban-American Experience: Culture, Images, and Perspectives.* Totowa, N.J.: Rowman and Allanheld, 1983.

Burns, Allan F. *Maya in Exile: Guatemalans in Florida.* Philadelphia: Temple University Press, 1993.

Cruz, Arturo J., and Jaime Suchliki. *The Impact of Nicaraguans in Miami.* Coral Gables: Graduate School of International Studies, University of Miami, 1990.

Desrosiers-Lauzon, Godefroy. *Florida's Snowbirds: Spectacle, Mobility, and Community since 1945.* Montreal: McGill-Queens University Press, 2011.

Garcia, Maria Cristina. *Havana USA: Cuban Exiles and Cuban Americans in South Florida, 1959–1994.* Berkeley: University of California Press, 1996.

Greenbaum, Susan D. *More Than Black: Afro-Cubans in Tampa.* Gainesville: University Press of Florida, 2002.

Grenier, Guillermo J., and Alex Stepick. *Miami Now: Immigration, Ethnicity, and Social Change.* Gainesville: University Press of Florida, 1992.

Hahamovitch, Cindy. *The Fruits of Their Labor: Atlantic Coast Farmworkers and the Making of Migrant Poverty, 1870–1945.* Chapel Hill: University of North Carolina Press, 1967.

Miller, Jake C. *The Plight of Haitian Refugees.* New York: Praeger, 1984.

Mohl, Raymond A. "Asian Immigration to Florida." *Florida Historical Quarterly* 74 (Winter 1996):261–89.

———. "Black Immigrants: Bahamians in Early Twentieth-Century Miami." *Florida Historical Quarterly* 65 (January 1987):271–97.

———. "Miami: New Immigrant City." In *Searching for the Sunbelt: Historical Perspectives on a Region*, edited by Mohl, 148–75. Knoxville: University of Tennessee Press, 1990.

———. "On the Edge: Blacks and Hispanics in Metropolitan Miami since 1959." *Florida Historical Quarterly* 69 (July 1990):37–56.

Mormino, Gary R., and George E. Pozzetta. *The Immigrant World of Ybor City: Italians and Their Latin Neighbors in Tampa, 1880–1980.* Urbana: University of Illinois Press, 1987.

Portes, Alejandro, and Alex Stepick. *City on the Edge: The Transformation of Miami*. Berkeley: University of California Press, 1993.

Pozzetta, George E. "The Chinese Encounter with Florida, 1865–1920." *Chinese America* 2 (1991):43–58.

———. "Foreign Colonies in South Florida, 1865–1910." *Tequesta: The Journal of the Historical Association of Southern Florida* 34 (1974):45–56.

———. "Foreigners in Florida: A Study of Immigration Promotion, 1865–1910." *Florida Historical Quarterly* 52 (October 1974):164–80.

Shell-Weiss, Melanie. *Coming to Miami: A Social History*. Gainesville: University Press of Florida, 2009.

Stepick, Alex, Guillermo Grenier, Max Castro, and Marvin Dunn. *This Land Is Our Land: Immigrants and Power in Miami*. Berkeley: University of California Press, 2003.

25

Boom, Bust, and Uncertainty

A Social History of Modern Florida

RAYMOND A. MOHL AND GARY R. MORMINO

In an astonishingly brief span of 175 years, Florida has passed from Old South to New South to Sunbelt South. In the process, the state has experienced momentous changes. The population has grown dramatically, shifting markedly in composition and character along the way. Changing patterns of race and ethnicity, and of migration and immigration, have created a new multiracial and multicultural Florida. Small towns, barrier islands, orange groves, and farmland have sprouted into great cities, towering at the center and sprawling at the edges. Technology and development have wrought enormous transformations upon the land, reshaping and reordering the way Floridians live, work, and play. An economy formerly based almost exclusively on agriculture and tourism has crossed over into the postindustrial age; agriculture and tourism remain important, but Florida has also developed a highly diversified service economy. Once perceived by Americans as a balmy, dreamlike, semitropical paradise, Florida's newest image has projected fears stimulated by race riots, massive immigration, environmental destruction, and high crime rates. In virtually every aspect of life, vast changes in the post–World War II era have transformed the old Florida, creating a powerful new Sunbelt juggernaut.

Perhaps more than anything else, relentless growth has served as a catalyst for the emergence of modern Florida. When admitted to the Union in 1845, Florida boasted a population of only 69,000 residents. By contrast, Florida's population in 2013 approaches 20 million inhabitants. The fourth-largest state in the Union will soon succeed New York as the third-largest state. To put this growth in perspective, on a busy weekend, Orlando's Magic Kingdom now attracts more tourists than the number of people who resided in the entire state a century and a half ago. During some decades, population growth was simply spectacular: over 51 percent during the boom years of the 1920s, over 78 percent during a second boom period in the 1950s, and over 43 percent during the 1970s. And throughout the twentieth century, Florida's population has grown at a rate considerably faster than the rate of growth for the nation as a whole, usually two, three, or four times as rapidly.

When Floridians cheered the coming of statehood in 1845, few residents south of Tallahassee heard the huzzahs. If a metaphor could describe the state of the mid-nineteenth-century state, it would be as a frontier. For Florida, the term *frontier* meant both place and process: geographically, vast portions of the peninsula lay remote, forbidding, inaccessible, and unsettled; experientially, the frontier mind-set typified by Indian wars, open ranges, environmental disregard, and rampant individualism has endured into the twenty-first century. In many respects, as late as the 1920s, Florida remained the last great frontier in the eastern continental United States.

Until the 1920s, almost half of the state's small population resided in the northern tier of counties stretching from Jacksonville to Pensacola. South Florida—broadly defined as the vast area south of an imaginary line drawn between Tampa and Melbourne—remained virtually uninhabited. On the eve of the Civil War, only about 7,000 people had settled in south Florida (Key West excepted). Dade County, which then included also the future megacounties of Broward and Palm Beach, numbered a scant 83 persons in 1860. Even as late as 1900, less than 5 percent of the state's total population resided in south Florida. Despite rapid population growth in the first half of the twentieth century, not until the 1950s did Florida achieve a population density (51.1 persons per square mile) that exceeded that of the nation at large (50.7). So the image of Florida as a frontier, with vast open spaces and a violent gun culture, matches the reality of the state's settlement patterns well into the twentieth century.

The peopling of Florida necessitated dramatic shifts to the south from population centers in the Panhandle and northern Florida. As late as 1880, three of every four residents still resided in the northern part of the state, chiefly middle Florida, the region between the Apalachicola and Suwannee Rivers. The 1920s saw the inexorable population movement of new settlers southward. In 1930, following the Florida boom, six in ten Floridians resided in central and south Florida. Since World War II, the population buildup of the Gold and Gulf coasts, and the space in between, has been supercharged.

On the eve of statehood, a handful of sparsely populated towns had taken hold in Florida. While small in population and periodically wracked by virulent epidemics of yellow fever, antebellum port cities served as vital centers of commerce, communications, and culture. Size was disproportionate to influence, but visitors were not always impressed by Florida's future urban prospects. Writing about Florida in the mid-1850s, for example, British traveler James Stirling observed in *Letters from the Slave States* that "here, in this poor Slave State, all is silence and stagnation; no cities are rising on the riverbanks."[1]

There was little in Florida's history up to 1880 that hinted at the state's future as one of the most populous and heavily urbanized regions in the nation. Only 10 percent of Floridians were urban dwellers in 1880. With its population buoyed by an influx of Bahamian "Conchs" and Cubans, refugees of the Cuban Ten Years War, Key West with 9,890 inhabitants stood as Florida's largest city. Only Jacksonville and Pensacola boasted populations greater than 3,000 persons in 1880.

A century later, Florida's status as one of America's most urbanized states was well entrenched, with fully 90 percent of Floridians classified as urban dwellers. Miami, Tampa, and Jacksonville dominated Florida's urban profile for most of the twentieth century, but during the 1980s and after, cities such as Fort Pierce, Fort Myers, Bradenton, Sarasota, and Naples soared in population. During the 1980s, ten of America's twenty fastest-growing metropolitan areas were found in the Sunshine State—a number that offers some measure of the dramatic development of Florida since 1945. Growth continues to cluster along the coasts; only two of the fast-track metro areas—Orlando and Ocala—are located in the state's interior. Naples and Palm Coast, in particular, merit attention as new Florida boomtowns. Naples, one of Florida's most isolated locales, exploded in the 1980s as a new retirement haven and tourist center, coming a long way since it was described in 1929 in the *Florida Highways* magazine as "only a hamlet with two hotels."[2] Flagler County had long vied for the distinction of being the state's least-populated county. In 1920, Flagler boasted fewer than 2,500 residents. In 2010, Flagler approached 100,000 residents, three-quarters of them in the new town of Palm Coast. The relentless march of urbanization has had a tremendous impact on the creation of contemporary Florida, full of excitement, diversity, and danger.

No less dramatic than the sheer record of urban growth has been change in the composition of Florida's population. In temperament and profile,

Florida was a slave state in 1845. In every census taken between 1845 and 1880, African Americans comprised nearly half of the state's population. Not until the 1920s did the proportion of black residents fall below one-third. Historically, the greatest concentration of African Americans was in the Black Belt, or middle Florida. In Leon, Jefferson, Madison, and other northern counties, blacks outnumbered whites. Today, Gadsden remains the state's last black majority county.

The urbanization of south Florida dramatically altered the racial and demographic profile of the state. The decades following World War I are critical to understanding the roots of modern Florida. The "Great Migration" of African Americans affected Florida but in ways different from the rest of the South. An exodus, principally from the Black Belt, carried thousands of African Americans from Florida to more promising urban centers in the North. But unlike the South, which witnessed a hemorrhage of blacks and whites for the next half century, Florida actually attracted new black and white migrants. Whereas the number of blacks in Georgia and Alabama failed to increase between 1910 and 1950, in Florida the African American population actually doubled over the same forty-year period. During this sustained migration, African Americans from north Florida, Alabama, and especially Georgia sought new opportunities in the growing cities of Miami, Tampa, St. Petersburg, Jacksonville, and Orlando. During every decade between 1880 and 1960, Florida was the main destination of blacks migrating from Georgia. This migration has been largely unnoticed because of the overwhelming numbers of white migrants arriving in Florida simultaneously.

Adding to the ethnic and cultural diversity of a growing black population, substantial migration of blacks from the Bahamas to Key West and Miami occurred between the 1880s and 1930. In 1920, for instance, Miami's population of 29,500 included about 5,000 black immigrants from the Bahamas. Ironically, given the city's later immigration experience, the black islanders made up over 65 percent of Miami's foreign-born population. In 1920 and 1930, New York was the only American city with a larger population of black immigrants than Miami.

While black migration and immigration made Florida more culturally diverse, demographic changes were redefining modern Florida in other ways, ironically making it the least southern state in the Deep South. Changes came swiftly in the twentieth century. Today, Florida is often described as a state where everyone is from some other place. Such was not the case a century ago. In 1880, an astonishing two-thirds of the state's population was born in Florida. Large numbers of transplanted Georgians and Alabamians also resided in Florida, giving the state a southern demographic profile.

A half century later, the great demographic transition was under way. By 1930, half of Florida's residents were born somewhere else, an indication of the large migration of new residents from the Midwest and Northeast. The proportion of population native to Florida continued to dwindle, so that by 1980 only about one-third of Floridians claimed native status, a proportion that rose to 43 percent in 2010. In Naples, Bonita Springs, and Palm Coast, nativity ranges from 14 to 20 to 24 percent. The inclusion of 1 million "snow-birds"—who, according to the U.S. Census, are "non-permanent residents" who spend winters in sunshine—adds further to the demographic divide between native and transplant. But some of the interior rural counties of south Florida, such as Hardee, Hendry, Glades, and DeSoto, retain high proportions of Florida-born residents and thus differ markedly from their urbanized neighbors.

Florida's exploding growth in the twentieth century stemmed almost entirely from wave after new waves of migrants, not from high birth rates. Whereas a century earlier Florida's new births matched the high rates of other southern states, since the 1920s the state has registered the lowest birth rate of any southern state. Beginning after World War II, and especially in the century's last decades, commentators noted a salient theme in the demographic profiles of several counties, including Pinellas, Citrus, Sarasota, Charlotte, Hernando, and Flagler: annually, more deaths than births were being recorded. According to the 1990 census, the number of residents in Charlotte County aged zero to sixteen equaled those residents seventy-five and over. The aging of the Sunshine State has become one of modern Florida's most pronounced social trends. From Johnny Carson, who pitched Coral Springs real estate, to Jerry Seinfeld and Del Boca Vista, comics lampooned Florida as "God's Waiting Room."

Ironically, Florida's state song, written by Stephen Foster in the nineteenth century, is "Old Folks at Home." But the phenomenon of growing old in America is a recent trend. Relatively few Americans lived to enjoy retirement prior to the twentieth century. Florida's status as a haven and heaven for elderly residents stemmed from several political, social, and economic developments: improved medical care, a national Medicare program, Social Security, improved pension plans, and air-conditioning. Inflated housing values in the Midwest and Northeast provided retirement capital for those who packed up for the move to Florida. The pattern first became apparent by the 1940s and 1950s as tens of thousands of Jews from the Northeast retired to Miami and Miami Beach, while midwesterners chose St. Peters-burg. Postcards of senior citizens lounging on green benches identified St. Petersburg as America's "Sunshine City," a positive image of old age in America.

Geography is not destiny. There was nothing inevitable about bean fields and cattle ranches becoming Century Village and Sun City Center. Develop-ers provided new housing for retirees on a massive scale—high-rise, ocean-front condominiums and gated golf-course communities for the wealthy, sprawling tract houses for the middle classes, and enormous apartment complexes and mobile-home parks for the less well-to-do. Retirees often lived in age-restricted communities with names like Leisure City, Leisure-ville, Leisure Lakes, Golf Village, and Serenity.

The graying of Florida has come swiftly and dramatically. In 1880, Florida was a frontier state populated by predominantly young people; the median age of Floridians stood at eighteen. By 1990, the state's median age was thirty-six, the nation's highest, climbing to 40.7 in the 2010 census. Most striking, in 1890, about 2 percent of Floridians were older than sixty-five; by 2010 the figure was 17 percent. Today, Flagler, Charlotte, Highlands, Her-nando, Martin, Sumter, Citrus, and Sarasota Counties rank among the old-est counties in America, each having a median age of fifty and older. The image of Florida as a relaxing, sunshine-filled paradise for retirees was a powerful one. Throughout the five and a half decades after 1950, a thousand retirees were moving to Florida each week, representing a staggering trans-fer of financial capital and emotional commitment. The state's over-sixty-five population increased 70 percent during the 1970s and 40 percent during the 1980s. Florida's invisible economy rests on a pillar of Social Security and pension checks. The aging of the now-middle-aged baby-boom generation will have a powerful impact on Florida's future, as the first wave of that de-mographic cohort reached sixty-five in 2011.

The history of modern Florida can be viewed as a dizzying set of migra-tions involving individuals, families, and groups over time. White and black Georgians sought fresh starts during Reconstruction, the 1920s boom, and the flush times of World War II. Emigrants from the West Indies worked as spongers in Key West, laborers in Miami, and cigar makers in Ybor City. During World War II, temporary workers from Jamaica, Barbados, and the Bahamas picked tomatoes in Belle Glade, harvested potatoes at Hastings, and cut sugarcane at Okeechobee. In the postwar era, countless GIs who had trained at bases in Florida returned to pursue their tropical dreams. Huge numbers of northeastern Jews and Italian Americans trekked to Florida in the decades after depression and war. New migrations of Cubans, Haitians, and Nicaraguans have revolutionized the demographic profile of Miami-Dade County in the past three decades, with spillover effects on nearby Monroe, Broward, and Palm Beach Counties. Annually thousands of Finns make the winter trek from the northern Midwest and Canada to Lake Worth. Since the 1950s, Canadians have been wintering in Florida in astounding numbers. In 2010, 3 million Canadians visited the Sunshine State, a figure comprising almost 10 percent of the Great White North's entire population! The presence of the Maple Leaf flag and sounds of Canadian accents alter the dynamics of Dunedin and Hollywood. These multiple and ongoing migrations contribute to the difficult task of comprehending a common history in the peopling of Florida. Ironically, the diverse migration stories provide a unifying theme in their history.

The migrations have contributed to a firestorm of social change in Florida. Such population growth over a compressed period of time is unparalleled in the American South. On the eve of Pearl Harbor, Florida's population of 1.9 million ranked it the least-populated state in the South. Since 1940, Florida's population has grown more than ninefold. Between 1970 and 1990, as the nation's population grew by 21 percent, the South's population soared by 40 percent, much of that growth the result of surging gains in Texas and Florida. One can only imagine what Florida will be like in the year 2050, when, according to one projection, the state's population will hit 47 million!

The dazzling pace of population growth has produced cataclysmic and catalytic change in modern Florida. The ecological relationship of man and land, between human groups and the geographical environment, has become increasingly unbalanced and destructive. Over time, man and machine, relentless growth and development, have taken their toll, transforming Florida, altering and reshaping the landscape, and reconfiguring the ways Floridians lived and live. In 1845, Florida's sylvan forests, lush lands, and superabundant waters must have seemed limitless. More than 30,000 lakes, rivers, and springs graced the state. The last century has witnessed a concerted private/public effort to dredge, ditch, dike, and dam the waters. Curiously, for a state where visionaries often invoked the metaphor of Florida as a land of dreams, the evidence suggests that most developers and dream makers sought to transform the land into something else. Florida beaches became seawall fortresses. Lagoons became Venetian canals, complete with gondoliers.

The diverse ecosystem known as Florida was often found to be too hot,

For nearly five decades, since the publication of her 1947 classic *The Everglades: River of Grass*, Marjory Stoneman Douglas (*left*), shown in her Coconut Grove home, was the most eloquent and enduring defender of the Everglades, Florida's last frontier, and the greatest roadless wilderness in the United States. In 1993, in recognition of her environmental activism, she was awarded the Presidential Medal of Freedom. Marjorie Carr of Gainesville (*right*) founded Florida Defenders of the Environment in 1969 to oppose construction of the Cross-Florida Barge Canal, which, Carr argued, would both destroy a large part of the scenic and sensitive Ocklawaha River and threaten the underground freshwater aquifer. As a result of her efforts, on 17 December 1976, the Florida cabinet formally recommended to Congress that canal construction be halted, and that subsequently was done.

too wet, and too inaccessible. Developers and politicians dreamed no small dreams when it came to improving nature. A favorite parlor game asks Floridians to name the most ill-conceived, harebrained project in state history. Choices include the drainage of the Everglades, the planned Jet Port along the Tamiami Trail, the efforts to make Old Tampa Bay a freshwater lake, the straightening of the Kissimmee River, and the Cross State Barge Canal.

An examination of a map of the Florida peninsula explains the irresistible appeal of a cross-state canal. Napoleon Bonaparte, who appreciated the significance of distances, once asserted that Italy was too long to be a country. Likewise, Florida is a long state; as well, it is the largest state east of the Mississippi, boasting 65,758 square miles of landmass and 3,800 miles of tidal shoreline. The state capital, Tallahassee, lies only 20 miles from the

Georgia border but 500 miles from Miami. The creation of modern Florida has been in large measure a struggle to overcome the tyranny of distance.

Indeed, Florida has been transformed by new technologies that shortened distances, speeded development, and promoted tourism. In 1845, anyone wishing to traverse the peninsula faced daunting and generally uncomfortable options. One might travel by horseback or stagecoach in some areas, by canoe or sailboat in others, primitive means untouched by the transportation revolution unfolding in the northern states. By the time of the Civil War, steamboats were plying the Apalachicola and St. Johns Rivers, but Florida had only 400 miles of railroad track in place and remained last among the Confederate states in railroad mileage.

By the end of the century, however, railroads crisscrossed the peninsula, reaching Pensacola and even distant Miami. Beginning in 1880, a great surge in railroad construction began to open up new areas for settlement, tourism, and economic development. Total railroad mileage in Florida surpassed 3,500 in 1900, and it nearly doubled to about 6,000 miles by 1930. Great railroad magnates such as Henry M. Flagler and Henry B. Plant pushed Florida into the twentieth century. Flagler's transportation and hotel empires eventually extended from St. Augustine to Key West, leaving in its wake the new or rejuvenated cities of Daytona Beach, Palm Beach, West Palm Beach, and Miami. Before his death in 1913, Flagler pushed his railroad all the way to Key West, an engineering marvel of the time.

On Florida's west coast, the iron messiah made and unmade cities. Cedar Keys, in 1880 one of Florida's most promising cities, was connected by rail to Fernandina on the east coast and was blessed with rich nearby cedar forests, as well as lumber mills, fine wharfs, and steamship connections to New Orleans and Key West. Yet it was devastated by hurricanes and Henry Plant's decision to select Tampa as a rail hub for his growing empire. A village of only 720 residents in 1880, Tampa prospered with the coming of the railroad in 1884. Now linked by rail to Jacksonville, Tampa was becoming part of a complex modern economic and transportation system. Cigar manufacturers in Tampa, lumber companies in the Panhandle, commercial fishermen in Fernandina, cattlemen on the open range, orange growers in Polk County, and truck farmers in Dade County all connected to an expanding integrated system of railroads and steamships, markets and schedules. Pompano from Boca Ciega Bay could now be rushed to New York City's Fulton fish market, while refrigerated rail cars brought freshly slaughtered pork and beef quarters from the Chicago stockyards.

Technology pierced the Florida interior. The steamboat and then the railroad opened markets and spurred the growth of specialty exports: Sanford celery, Frostproof oranges, Zellwood corn, Apopka green beans, and Plant City strawberries. Yet technology could be capricious. Just as new developments such as the railroad and cotton processing doomed the once thriving seaports of Apalachicola and St. Marks, so new technologies such as electrification and the internal combustion engine threatened the primacy of the railroad. Where once cities relied upon "natural advantages"—a seaport, river, or crossroads—electrical generating plants with their spinoff technologies (streetcars and telephones) reorganized and reshaped American cities. Above all, the automobile brought a flurry of big changes to the Sunshine State. The motorcar altered the roadside landscape, introducing the familiar trinity of the gasoline station, diner, and motel. Introduced by Henry Ford in 1908, the Model T helped reduce distances, socially and geographically, between rural and urban Florida. Farmers and rural families drove to town on Saturdays, accentuating the importance of downtowns with their attendant attractions of department stores, movie theaters, and chain stores. The automobile also democratized tourism in the 1920s, enabling middle-class "tin can tourists" to share Sunshine State attractions and amenities that had been the exclusive domain of the wealthy.

The building of highways and roads to serve the automobile accelerated the development of modern Florida. In 1906, when it had fewer than 300 automobiles, the state had only a handful of paved highways. As one travel writer confessed in 1918, "it was an exceedingly troublesome matter to get an automobile down into the central part of the state."[3] Prior to 1916, road building in the United States was in the domain of county government. Given the travail of distances and the inequitable capacities of counties to pay for highway construction, road building in Florida in the nineteenth and early twentieth centuries was a haphazard and many-splintered thing. During the Progressive Era, a popular idea known as the Good Roads Movement swept through the South: Good roads spelled progress, promise, and prosperity. The crisis of World War I crystallized the national movement for efficient transportation. The federal government now enlisted state participation in road building, helping to subsidize state efforts. The famous Dixie Highway linking Florida with Chicago stands as a testimonial to newfound resources for road construction.

By the 1920s, Florida's Good Roads Movement could point to real accomplishments. Road builders began laying asphalt and bricks that connected the state's cities and linked them with highways leading north. By 1925, a

A cabbage farm at Hastings in 1947. Florida's second-ranked industry after tourism by midcentury was agriculture, which in 1950 contributed $401 million to the state's growing prosperity—an increase of 300 percent over 1935. The various soils of the peninsula and Panhandle produced 104 different commercial crops, more than were grown in any other state. Most farmers owned the farms they managed. Truck and vegetable crops, harvested by resident and migratory workers, were shipped in ever-increasing tonnage to northern winter markets. Sugarcane brought in $9 million in south Florida; tobacco was a leading field crop in the northern and western counties. Commercial ornamental horticulture was a new and thriving agribusiness, producing chrysanthemums, gladiolus, lilies, orchids, roses, cut green foliage, ferns, and potted foliage plants for interior decoration of Florida's and the nation's profusion of new homes. By the 1990s, agriculture would gross $6 billion a year.

half million tourists were arriving annually in Florida by automobile, and by 1930 Florida had more than 3,200 miles of paved highways. Even working-class Americans, driving their Fords and Chevys down the Dixie Highway or across the Tamiami Trail or (after 1938) along the Overseas Highway to Key West, could take their families on a Florida vacation by the seashore. As the state road department's official magazine, *Florida Highways*, noted enthusiastically in 1930, "Florida's magnificent system of highways is creating a somewhat nomadic tribe of tourists" who were "now roaming all over the state."[4] By 1950, over 1 million cars a year were entering Florida for tourism and recreation. The bus and the truck also contributed in important ways to stimulating tourist traffic and economic growth.

The construction of the Tamiami Trail illustrates the impact of modern transportation upon a region and culture. The dream of an east-west highway artery across southern Florida had existed for decades, but its implementation lay beyond the financial means of individual counties. Beginning in the late teens, and aided by the geopolitical lobbying of land developer Barron G. Collier and Miami business interests, the dream took hold. The Tamiami Trail was an engineering marvel of the time. When it was finished in 1927, cars and trucks could travel on modern roads from Tampa to Miami (hence the name Tamiami). Alas, progress wrought social costs. The Seminole Indians, who prior to the 1920s had lived in semi-isolation, now confronted modernity. Dugout canoes and subsistence living quickly surrendered to airboats, Model As, and the invented tradition of alligator wrestling. A tourist economy offered the Seminoles a new and different lifestyle. Hunters enjoyed easy access to the bounties of Big Cypress country and quickly depopulated the wildlife of the region. When Winchesters and Remingtons failed to kill, Fords and Chevrolets often added to the toll. The Tamiami Trail proved ruinous to the Florida panther, unaccustomed to on-beam prestolites, ironically developed by Carl Fisher, the father of Miami Beach.

Road building in the modern era has reconfigured transportation patterns, population settlement, and political campaigning. The Sunshine State Parkway (now called Florida's Turnpike) in the 1950s and early 1960s and the interstate highway system in the 1960s and after dramatically enhanced mobility in Florida. Interstate 95 on the east coast linked Miami and south Florida directly to northeastern states. Interstate 75 connected Tampa with the Midsouth and the Midwest. Interstate 10 pushed across the northern tier of the state from Jacksonville to Tallahassee and Pensacola and beyond to New Orleans. Interstate 4 traversed a theme-park corridor from Busch Gardens in Tampa through the Disney landscape of Orlando to Daytona Beach on the Atlantic coast. These new highways launched tourism to lofty new levels and opened up areas of the state to business and residential development. Typically, a new stretch of I-75 between Tampa and Naples propelled the incredible spurt of recent growth in southwest Florida, now the fastest-growing part of the state. Heavy truck traffic on the interstates further undermined the declining railroads, the technology that originally made Florida accessible. Today, campaigning along the I-4 corridor has become a new political ritual. Students of American politics contend that winning the vote along the I-4 corridor, a microcosm of the state and nation, is tantamount to election.

New expressways resulted in unintended and intended consequences. The new interstate highways severed Florida's major cities. Local and state politicians believed that federal highway construction could be a handmaiden to local urban renewal. Urban expressways tore through established neighborhoods and uprooted entire communities—especially African American communities. In Tampa, expressways bisected historic Latin neighborhoods. Daily rush-hour traffic jams in Tampa, Orlando, and Miami made these highways less like expressways than slow-moving parking lots. But the new auto arteries did trigger a rapid spatial reorganization of urban populations, as white residents moved to the suburbs and African Americans pushed out of redeveloped inner-city areas to newer, formerly white, "second ghetto" neighborhoods.

The automobile had still other consequences. Some observers have noted that new and dynamic business and commercial centers—configurations of urban life called "edge cities"—have sprouted distant from traditional downtowns. Miami, Orlando, and Tampa all have developed such edge cities, usually at interstate highway interchanges or near large international airports. In part, they evolved because the automobile promoted the decentralization of urban business and the deconcentration of city people. Older metropolitan areas such as New York, Chicago, and San Francisco developed with mass transit, so their building and population patterns reflected high levels of residential density. By contrast, Florida's metropolitan areas grew up in the automobile age and thus are settled out rather than up, revealing relatively low-density rates as well. Recent and expensive attempts to persuade Floridians to give up their automobiles, notably in Miami and Jacksonville, have not met with encouraging results. South Florida's Tri-Rail system, a commuter rail network linking West Palm Beach with Miami, and Miami's above-ground transit system known as Metrorail, attracted few regular riders; most urban Floridians prefer the privacy and flexibility of their own vehicles, even at the expense of daily traffic jams. The dream of high-speed rail in Florida seemed assured with the 2008 election of Barack Obama and the pledge to spend $2.4 billion in federal funds for the 85-mile Tampa-to-Orlando link. But newly elected Florida governor Rick Scott rejected the transportation stimulus funds in 2011, killing the project.

A year later, private investors at Florida East Coast Industries concocted a new high-speed rail plan, this time connecting Miami and Orlando, with future extensions to Tampa and Jacksonville. Lacking billions in taxpayer subsidies, the new plan seemed just another Florida pipe dream.

By the late twentieth century, commercial air transportation had come to rival the automobile in importance. Indeed, aviation technology has had a bigger impact on Florida than on most other states. During World War I, U.S. naval air stations were established in Pensacola, Miami, and Key West. Before the end of the decade, regularly scheduled air service carried passengers from Key West, Miami, and Palm Beach to Cuba and the Bahamas. In the 1920s, the U.S. Congress laid the foundations for the national air transportation industry by subsidizing airmail service. Aviation entrepreneurs in Florida quickly seized the opportunity, and soon three major airline companies emerged in the state: Pan American Airways and Eastern Airlines in Miami and National Airlines in St. Petersburg. By the 1930s, these and other airlines, using the newly developed DC-3 airliner, were carrying tens of thousands of passengers monthly to Florida from U.S. and Latin American cities. Increasingly after midcentury, commercial air travel supplanted rail and auto transportation as a mainstay of Florida's tourist economy.

The novelty and excitement of aviation had come to be an essential ingredient in Florida's national image by the 1930s. Beginning in 1929, Miami provided the annual setting for the All American Air Races, seen by millions on newsreels at movie theaters. By the 1930s, the *Miami Herald* was carrying a regular aviation column called "Wings Over Miami." Goodyear blimps based in Miami became a common sight in the air over south Florida's Atlantic coastal beaches during the 1930s and after. This consciousness of aviation's importance intensified during World War II, when the federal government, seduced by powerful congressmen and induced by Florida's good year-round flying weather, located air training bases all over the state.

Thus, Florida entered the postwar era with a heightened sense of the importance of air travel. Business and political leaders quickly came to realize that aviation stimulated tourism, economic activity, and population growth. The Miami International Airport emerged as one of the nation's leading airports in passengers and air freight, especially as a gateway to Latin America. Several airlines selected Miami as a center for aircraft overhaul and maintenance operations, with important spillover effects: by 1960, Eastern Airlines, with more than 7,000 workers, had become the leading employer in the Miami metropolitan area. By the 1980s, an estimated 160,000 workers, or about one-fifth of the Miami labor force, were directly or indirectly employed in airport and aviation activities. Major new airport expansion and construction projects since the 1970s highlighted the degree to which airports have become elaborate image-boosting entry points, much like the opulent urban railroad stations of the late nineteenth century.

Technology not only revolutionized the way we traveled, it affected profoundly the way we lived, worked, played, even slept. Air-conditioning has become so omnipresent that we forget how recently climate control arrived in Florida. We also take for granted the manifold changes resulting from this new technology. Floridians, of course, had always been keenly—and physically—aware of the importance of passive cooling. Southern architects and carpenters understood the science and culture of passive cooling: wide verandahs, high ceilings, cross-ventilation, louvered jalousies, the central breezeway, and fast-growing chinaberry trees to cast shade. The riddle of removing humidity went unsolved until a nineteenth-century Apalachicola physician experimented with a steam-driven ice-making machine. John Gorrie's hospital patients, stricken with yellow fever, improved in the mechanically produced chilled air, establishing an early precedent for twentieth-century air-conditioning.

In 1929, Willis Carrier introduced the modern, prototype air conditioner. Still, air-conditioning for most urban Floridians in the 1930s and 1940s meant a visit to the movie theater or department store. Trains and buses bringing travelers to Florida were air-conditioned by the end of the 1930s, and a few hotels had air-conditioned ballrooms by the early 1940s, but otherwise tourists had the privilege of sweating in the semitropical heat just as the Florida natives did. The end of World War II, however, with its rush of accumulated savings and applied technology, soon introduced affordable window air-conditioning units. Houses and apartments, motels and shops, began sprouting the boxy window units in the 1950s, and the new technology was cooling planes and cars by the end of the decade. Air-conditioning augured still another New South, celebrated by historian Raymond Arsenault as "the end of the long hot summer."[5]

Air-conditioning, however, created a gradual rather than a sudden impact on sweltering Florida summers. As late as 1960, only 18 percent of all Florida households had air-conditioning, and only a scant 2 percent of African American households. The decade of the 1960s ushered it in on a massive scale, as homes utilizing climate control increased to 60 percent by 1970, to 84 percent by 1980, and to over 90 percent in the 1990s. By 1980, moreover, almost half of Florida's African American households had adopted air-conditioning. Certainly, the ubiquitous whirring of the central air unit made Florida more attractive year-round to retirees.

Florida homes that once obeyed the environmental imperatives of a tropical climate—"hot air rises and water may"—took on new forms, materials, and functions. Low ceilings, concrete-block walls, and TV rooms replaced high ceilings, wooden walls, and screened Florida rooms. Air-conditioning permitted Floridians to orient lives around schedules no longer dependent upon summer afternoon storms or seasonal change. Schools, which once began classes in late September or October, now begin in late August—just as in Philadelphia and Chicago. Floridians, who like other southerners had historically maintained a close association with the land, now became more detached from the natural world, cruising in air-conditioned cars to climate-controlled malls and offices, to domed stadiums, to housing developments with disassociated names such as Cypress Bend or Panther Trace. Air-conditioning has allowed Floridians to keep their sunshine and "cool it" twelve months a year. Florida's fantastic trajectory of population growth in the decades after 1950 would almost certainly have flattened out without the introduction and widespread adoption of air-conditioning. Tourists, who once regularly abandoned Florida between June and December, found that a controlled temperature means no seasonal boundaries. Once a six-month industry, tourism became a year-round business.

Tourism first attracted attention in the years following the Civil War, when small numbers of winter visitors arrived in Fernandina and Jacksonville. Many found their way on steamships up the St. Johns River and along the crooked Ocklawaha, destination Silver Springs. But if the 1870s belonged to charming stern-wheelers and glass-bottomed boats, the 1880s and 1890s unleashed a decade of conspicuous consumption in the building of elaborate Florida hotels—the Ponce de Leon, the Royal Poinciana, the Belleview Biltmore, and the Royal Palm. The Gilded Age set had arrived in Florida, traveling the rails of Henry M. Flagler and Henry B. Plant.

The 1920s unveiled a new Florida with new forms of pleasure. New freedoms, generated by economic prosperity and inventive genius, created a national consumer culture. The symbols of the era—Ford Flivvers, Palm Beach, Coral Gables, Miami Beach, and the Tamiami Trail—underscored the interlocking destinies of tourism and economic growth. Tourism and real estate speculation supplied the oxygen for Florida's boom. "All of America's gold rushes," noted journalist Mark Sullivan in his classic *Our*

Times (1935), "all her oil booms, and her free-land stampedes, dwindled by comparison . . . with the torrent of migration pouring into Florida."[6]

The promise of Florida, the dreams of the good life under sunshine and palm, on golf course and sandy beach, melded into compelling and romantic images. Dreams could be packaged into residential lots, gated developments, and municipal campgrounds. Historically, American cities evolved by developing commerce, industry, and transportation, but Florida cities such as Daytona Beach and Sarasota, St. Petersburg and Miami Beach sold themselves, promoting their beaches, salt air, endless sunshine, and the Florida dream. St. Petersburg appealed to frugal, middle-class midwesterners, while Miami Beach attracted a nouveau riche crowd interested in fishing, golf, polo, jai alai, horse racing, and gambling.

Postwar Florida came to embody and in turn radiate the values of a new American culture: youth, speed, leisure, consumption, mobility, and affluence. Tourism figured prominently in this midcentury culture. Television enhanced the image of Florida as the Sunshine State. Most Americans were familiar with the Miami-based TV shows of Arthur Godfrey and Jackie Gleason, both of whom shared affection for the good life in the Sunbelt before that concept had been invented. Dozens of glamorous new hotels went up on Miami Beach in the 1950s, including the extravagant and glitzy beachfront Fontainebleau. The publicity machine, one journalistic account noted in 1964, was "like a huge ballyhoo generator that never shuts down. Its output voltage is always there, waiting to stun the unwary."[7] Not surprisingly, tourism began hitting new peaks in the postwar era. In 1933, officials estimated that about a million tourists arrived in Florida. By 1940, they numbered 2.8 million, and that number increased exponentially to 5 million in 1950, 20 million in 1980, 40 million in 1990, and 86 million in 2011. A $32 billion industry by the mid-1990s, tourism became, truly, the bedrock of Florida's economy.

These raw statistics provide sparse insight into the myriad meanings of a tourist economy and its consequences. In the halcyon 1950s, Florida's top tourist attractions were Marineland, near St. Augustine, and Cypress Gardens, along Highway 441. In 1956, Miami and Miami Beach sparkled as the crown jewels of tourism, attracting nearly one-quarter of the state's visitors. Mostly, tourists came to pre-1970 Florida to luxuriate in the state's natural beauty, however "natural" attractions such as Cypress Gardens were. The opening of Disney World in 1971, however, inaugurated a dramatic new chapter. By the 1980s, it had become the world's greatest tourist attraction,

A part of hotel row on Miami Beach in April 1959. The hundreds of white sun-splashed hotels, both art deco and contemporary, became Florida's best-known architectural features in the years before the erection of the rocket gantries at Cape Canaveral and the Magic Kingdom turrets at Disney World. Described as the American Riviera of the leisured masses, Miami Beach attracted visitors not only to a year-round balmy surf but to 500 swimming pools, elegant shops on Collins Avenue, and a myriad of restaurants, cocktail lounges, and show bars. Since the mid-1980s, the beach has enjoyed a second boom of tourism and night life.

and continues to draw more than 17 million tourists annually. Disney's fantasy landscape meshed perfectly with the modern culture of leisure and consumption. The surging growth of the Orlando area over the past forty years has been based largely on the appeal of Mickey Mouse, but Sea World, Disney's Epcot, Disney's Animal Kingdom, Disney's Hollywood Studios, and Universal Studios' Islands of Adventure lure an additional 50 million visitors annually. Theme parks and attractions created artificial worlds of elaborately contrived environments where tourists "experienced" Thunder Mountain but rarely appreciated the real Florida.

Retirement rivaled tourism as a driving force behind Florida's postwar growth. The same palm tree, golf course, and beach imagery that attracted tourists also brought retirees. Postwar guidebooks with irresistible titles paved the way. George and Jane Dusenbury's *How to Retire to Florida* (1947) typified practical advice sought by millions. A. Lowell Hunt's *Florida Today: New Land of Opportunity* (1950) informed readers that "you don't have to be rich" to retire to Florida, a message with an impact.[8] The construction industry boomed during the 1950s and 1960s, working overtime to provide tract houses and condominiums for new Floridians. Tin-can tourists with travel-trailers hitched behind their cars had a postwar counterpart: the mobile-home retirement village. Mobile homes were fast, easy, and cheap, although rarely mobile. By 1980, Florida had more mobile homes than any other state, and by the 1990s over 12 percent of Florida's population resided in 760,000 mobile homes. By 2010, the number of mobile homes had grown to 840,000, but hurricanes, new safety standards, and disappearing trailer parks have dulled their appeal.

A final aspect of Florida's amenities can be found in sports and recreation. In the late nineteenth century, fishing and hunting opportunities in Florida attracted wealthy adventurers from the United States and Europe. Alligator and bear hunting, camping and tarpon fishing formed the stuff of such first-person accounts as James A. Henshall's *Camping and Cruising in Florida* (1884) and Charles E. Whitehead's *The Camp-Fires of the Everglades, or Wild Sports in the South* (1891). Early-twentieth-century sporting activities became tamer—golf, tennis, polo, horse racing, yachting, and other recreations that appealed initially to the upper crust of Florida visitors. Horseshoe pits and shuffleboard courts at city parks appealed across classes. By the late twentieth century, golf and tennis had become democratized and almost ubiquitous; virtually every condominium and apartment complex around the state had its own tennis courts and swimming pools. Palm Beach County had more golf courses per capita than any other county in the nation, a ranking challenged by Lee and Collier Counties. But spectator sports now rival tennis and golf, suggesting that many Floridians prefer their recreation in more sedentary forms. Modern Florida has come to be defined by big-time college football (between 1980 and 2010, the University of Miami, Florida State University, and the University of Florida football teams achieved astounding levels of success), by professional football teams in Miami, Tampa, and Jacksonville, by the Miami Marlins and Tampa Bay Rays Major League Baseball teams, and by professional basketball and soccer franchises. The improbable presence of two professional ice hockey teams in Florida is a testament to Sunbelt technology, economics, and demographics.

Sports, retirement, and tourism have helped shape Florida's image and propelled its economy. But in the years after World War II, powerful new forces of change emerged. The war itself had a tremendous impact. Military training facilities, air bases, naval bases, and major shipyards sprouted all over the state. Service personnel and their families migrated to Florida, and many thousands returned to live when the war was over. Miami, Tampa, Jacksonville, and Pensacola especially benefitted from military investment and enormous military payrolls. Huge federal wartime expenditures in Florida and throughout the Sunbelt produced essential new infrastructure, supported local economies, and stimulated construction and service industries. By the 1980s, defense spending and military payrolls in Florida surpassed $15 billion annually. Underlying much of the nation's changing economic and urban pattern in the postwar era has been the redirection of federal resources through military and defense spending, and this "military remapping" of America had special salience for Florida in the second half of the twentieth century. With the end of the Cold War, however, the federal military-industrial complex, once so vital to Florida's defense industries and military bases, began to shrink. In 2011, NASA ended the three-decade-long U.S. space shuttle program, causing massive layoffs. The Kennedy Space Center's workforce has been drastically reduced to 8,500 workers, the smallest number in more than three decades.

In 1959, a Pratt and Whitney engineer monitors a jet engine test in Palm Beach County. The 1950s marked the beginning of a dramatic increase in the number of industries that took root in Florida. In addition to Pratt and Whitney, these included Martin Aircraft, Sperry Rand, IBM, Maxwell House, Anheuser-Busch, and Disney World. The last-named corporation opened the Magic Kingdom in 1971 and Epcot Center in 1982, which together would draw more visitors each year than Florida had residents.

No event in its history brought Florida more national and international notice than did the launch of Apollo XI from Cape Kennedy on 16 July 1969. The rocket and space vehicle enabled American astronauts Neil A. Armstrong (*left*) and Edwin E. Aldrin (*right*) to become the first humans to walk on the surface of the moon. At the center of this photograph, taken beforehand, with the launch pad in the background, is Michael Collins, pilot of the mission command module.

The postwar federal presence was important, but a series of powerful economic changes also shaped post-1950 Florida. Scholars have begun to sketch the full dimensions of a long-term structural transformation of the American economy that dates back to the 1950s—a process of "deindustrialization" that has resulted in the dismantling and abandoning of much of the nation's increasingly obsolete industrial infrastructure. Taking the place of the aging Rustbelt factory industries are the dynamic new industries of the postindustrial economy—the high-tech, computerized information businesses and the more fully developed (and low-paying) service economy. The new American economy grew up around services provided by government, educational agencies, and financial services companies; it was spurred also by health care and medical delivery, food service, travel and entertainment, and retailing and consumerism. Fast food, motel chains, and car rentals, sprawling malls and shopping centers, lawn service and office temps, rent-a-maid and rent-a-nurse—these are some of the businesses that have emerged at the low end of Florida's recent economy, paralleling but hardly supplanting an older low-paid service economy centered on restaurant staff, hotel maids, and migrant farmworkers.

A high end of the new service economy has emerged, as well. In the new information age, the high-tech and business service economy is no longer tied to older metropolitan centers of the Northeast or Midwest. With computer networks and other instantaneous communication, it has been possible for major corporations—and individuals with a laptop—to relocate to Tampa, Miami, Boca Raton, or Sanibel Island; costs are reduced for company and employees alike, and all benefit from the low taxes, sunny climate, and enhanced amenities. Florida's new economy includes high-tech and computer companies in the state's "Silicon Beach" area stretching along the Atlantic coast north from Miami and in the Cape Canaveral area. The wondrous technological innovation of the late twentieth century, the personal computer, was developed at IBM's massive facility in Boca Raton. Major international trade and banking operations have clustered in Miami and Coral Gables since the early 1970s. Miami is scarcely the Hong Kong of the West, but many business and civic leaders have aspired to enhance south Florida's place in the emerging global economy. In the late 1990s and into the new century, Florida governors invested heavily to bring biotech firms to the Jupiter Island area. Some critics question the investment and return. Florida must continue to adjust and cope with the new technologies and global economic networks that will shape the twenty-first century.

New technologies and economies have helped to create modern Florida, but issues involving race and immigration have generated a more powerful impact in shaping national and world images of the state. Florida, in fact, has had a long and troubled history in the area of race relations. In the past, the legitimacy of its role as a "real" southern state was the subject of frequent debate, but the history of race relations in Florida leaves little doubt as to the answer. Florida's color line, drawn in exacting constitutional detail and cemented in everyday custom, swept across geographical and time boundaries. Jim Crow practices found easy acceptance even in Florida cities without southern-born populations, such as St. Petersburg, Miami, and Palm Beach. In tourist cities, leaders stressed the importance of maintaining a strict color line and docile black communities, making sure that blacks would serve but not be seen. When in Florida, most northerners adapted easily to southern racial customs and segregation. In Miami, Gainesville, Sarasota, and other places, some northerners, outraged at the status quo, courageously joined and led the civil rights movement.

Lynching, of course, loomed as the ultimate test of keeping blacks in their place. Historically, white Floridians vigilantly used the noose and the torch to control economic power and enforce southern customs. Florida, not Alabama or Mississippi, led the South in lynchings in proportion to population. Vigilante justice was not confined to Jefferson, Levy, Marion, or Jackson Counties in rural north Florida; Hernando, Pasco, Citrus, Polk, Hillsborough, and DeSoto Counties recorded especially notorious acts of racial violence. Nor was the violence limited to isolated cases and individual victims. Attacks on entire black communities took place at Lake City, Ocoee, and Rosewood between 1912 and 1923. African Americans were not passive victims; rather, they fought back as at Rosewood, and organized boycotts of streetcars, as in Jacksonville and Pensacola between 1901 and 1905. In some cities, such as Miami and West Palm Beach, they joined Marcus Garvey's black nationalist Universal Negro Improvement Association in large numbers. Until the 1940s, poll taxes and white primaries largely kept them from the voting booth most of the time, but when possible (as in nonpartisan municipal elections in Miami), blacks turned out in force to exercise the franchise.

Enforcement of the Florida color line continued forcefully after World War II. In Miami, over a six-year period beginning in 1946, an active Ku Klux Klan regularly paraded, burned crosses, torched houses, and dynamited apartment complexes in an effort to keep blacks from moving into white neighborhoods. In 1951, in the small Brevard County town of Mims, the Klan dynamited the home of Harry T. Moore, a relentless civil rights activist and statewide leader of the NAACP, killing him and his wife. National magazines published articles in the 1950s with such titles as "The Truth about the Florida Race Troubles," "Florida: Dynamite Law Replaces Lynch Law," "Bigotry and Bombs in Florida," and "Bombing in Miami."[9] Big-city police departments in Miami, Tampa, and Jacksonville vigorously enforced the color line, often violently.

African American activism shaped the civil rights movement in Florida, even in the 1940s and 1950s before the national freedom struggle took off. A bus boycott in Tallahassee in 1956 inspired a wider civil rights movement in the state capital. Lunch-counter sit-ins led by the Miami branch of CORE in 1959 (a year before the more celebrated sit-ins in Greensboro, North Carolina) ultimately led to the desegregation of Miami's public accommodations and schools. But the civil rights movement was accompanied by racial conflict in the 1960s and after. Violent police behavior in the ghetto prompted Miami's Liberty City riot of 1980, and troubled police-community relations persisted in Miami and Tampa through the 1980s. Even as Florida became less southern, traditional patterns of race relations persisted. Urban uprisings in late-twentieth-century Miami and St. Petersburg and extensive media coverage of Florida's racial conflicts initiated new popular images of the state. Few were happy with either the broad outlines or the minute details of that image.

Immigration patterns since the mid-1960s have also dramatically recast Florida's image. The Cuban refugee exodus that began in 1959, episodic but relentless over time, has brought such tumult and change in south Florida that words such as "transformative" and "profound" seem inadequate. By the 1990s, close to 1 million Cuban exiles had made the journey across the Florida Straits. They and others have transformed Miami into the capital of the Caribbean and Latin America. The Cubans were followed by massive migrations of Haitians and Nicaraguans and smaller contingents from virtually every Caribbean and Latin American nation. These migrations remade Miami and eventually all of south Florida. The demographic and cultural changes have been phenomenal—in 2010, some 1.4 million residents of Miami-Dade County spoke Spanish, a figure outnumbering English speakers. Moreover, large numbers of upwardly mobile Cubans and Latinos have migrated northward to Broward and Palm Beach Counties, an ethnic version of white flight. The newcomers came in great numbers, and their communities were constantly being replenished by new waves of exiles and refugees. They maintained their old-country cultures to a great degree, developed their own brand of exile and ethnic politics, established and succeeded wildly with their own enclave economies, and competed vigorously with native Anglos and African Americans for economic and political power. The conflict between blacks and Hispanics has been especially notable, and African Americans generally believe that they have been "displaced from mainstream opportunities by the newly arrived immigrants."[10] Older patterns of assimilation seemed not to apply in south Florida, which has emerged as a new multicultural cauldron and perhaps as a model for what the state as a whole might become.

In 1980, in dramatic spasms of pathos and chaos, images of black Haitians washing ashore in South Florida splashed on evening newscasts. Some observers estimate that 50,000, perhaps 60,000, Haitians entered Florida in the exodus of the "boat people." If south Florida and immigration officials recoiled at the influx of black Haitians, Miami welcomed, at least initially, the first wave of 125,000 Marielitos from Cuba. For two decades, Cuban émigrés had been largely middle-class and white. Mariel changed the dynamics. Large numbers of poor and black Cubans—about one in five Marielitos—flooded Miami. Marielitos also included criminals and the mentally ill. To be sure, the experience was traumatizing—one book described Miami as a "city on the edge."[11] On Mariel's twenty-fifth anniversary, the *Miami Herald* concluded: "Mariel nudged Hispanics close to a numerical majority in Miami. It also laid the foundation for today's Cuban-American political dominance." In 2005, Maurice Ferre, who had been the city's embattled mayor in 1980, reflected: "Time heals a lot of things. The question is this: Are the Mariel Cubans net givers or net takers? They are by far net givers."[12]

In reality, multicultural change has spread far beyond Miami and south Florida to distant parts of the state. The Latinization of Florida has been well under way for decades, leaving almost no part of the state untouched. Large communities of Mexicans have settled in rural parts of central Florida, such as Hardee and Highlands Counties. Puerto Ricans, many of them migrants from New York, surpass all other Hispanic groups in metropolitan Orlando. Guatemalans and Salvadorans labor in agriculture and landscaping in north and south Florida. Political unrest and social anxieties in South America have brought large numbers of Venezuelans, Colombians, and Brazilians to south Florida. *Florida Trend's* 2012 "Floridian of the Year" was Brazil. Jamaicans, Dominicans, and other black islanders from the Caribbean have established large communities in Dade and Broward Counties. Vietnamese fishermen have become an economic force in Pensacola and the Panhandle coastal region. Asians, primarily from India, China, Korea, and the Philippines, make up Florida's fastest-growing immigrant group. Census officials struggle to create new categories for Chinese Jamaicans and Brazilian Cubans.

For decades, Sunbelt states such as Florida, California, and Texas have been on the edge of a global migration of workers and refugees from poorer and less-developed countries and regions. Given the instability of the Third World, especially Latin America and the Caribbean, Florida's future will be tied even more closely to geopolitics and national foreign policy. A new "Columbian exchange" has taken place—an exchange that is happening now on the streets, in the schools, in the workplace, in the supermarkets, even in politics in some places. Ethnically and socially, the new Florida has become more multicultural, more ethnically and linguistically diverse, more Catholic and Latin than the old, and ever more different from the rest of the South. In many ways, Florida offers a glimpse of what America will become. Reconciling increasing numbers of senior citizens with new immigrants and established citizens will be a great challenge. New tensions in race relations in the post–civil rights era and new waves of exiles and refugees from the south have unalterably transformed Florida and the way people at home and abroad perceive the Sunshine State.

Among Florida's other problems, the massive surge of immigrants has created ethnic and social tensions, especially in metropolitan Miami. Rioting and racial conflict have pockmarked Miami, Tampa, Jacksonville, and other Florida cities. By the 1980s, Florida had the highest crime rate in the nation, and for a time Miami had an unenviable reputation as the drug and murder capital of the United States—witness the popular imagery of "Cocaine Cowboys" and the film *Scarface* (1983). Crime, drug dealing, and random violence increasingly shape public images of Florida as "the lost paradise."[13] If Florida had a quaint charm and appeal in the late nineteenth century, little of that natural and innocent quality remains at the dawn of the twenty-first century.

The dizzying pace of new immigration and the challenges the immigrants pose suggest that big change has its costs. In fact, the rapid growth of Florida since midcentury should not be interpreted entirely as a success. Modern Florida may be a developer's dream, but it is an environmentalist's nightmare. Dense urban development along the Atlantic and Gulf coasts has destroyed much of the tropical allure of old Florida and left millions of residents vulnerable to hurricane damage. Urban sprawl has been gobbling up rich agricultural land in south Florida, and the builders and developers seem unstoppable. In central Florida, periodic freezes have damaged citrus crops and forced orange growers to move farther south, leaving abandoned grove lands to suburban Orlando and Polk County developers. Urban development has encroached on the edges of the Everglades for many decades, threatening the underground aquifer that serves as a water supply for 5 million people in south Florida. Overdevelopment in the Florida Keys has produced a polluted paradise, killing off remaining live coral reefs and threatening marine life. The paving of paradise continues unabated.

All of these problems have been magnified by a weakly developed public sector—a political and governmental system that routinely avoids important action addressing the state's social problems. The state legislature more often than not mimics the political gridlock that has characterized the nation's capital in recent decades. Political leaders seem more interested in low taxes than needed public investment in education, social services, infrastructure, growth management, or environmental protection. Boasting a relatively high per capita income, Florida has no income tax and relies almost entirely on sales taxes, tourist taxes, and a lottery to support state government activities and services. Few state leaders seem ashamed that Florida's support for higher education is eroding, or that the state's public schools are badly overcrowded and notoriously undersupported, or that Florida ranks high among the states in the number of prison inmates per capita. High social service demands, especially among the young and the elderly, are met minimally by governmental programs. In recent decades, the Sunshine State has cast some ominous shadows.

But still they came. Nothing, it seemed, could deflate or derail the Florida Boom. For decades, Cassandras and Jeremiahs had warned that Florida stood on the eve of destruction. The new century and millennium has challenged the most ardent boosters. Whipsawed by political storms and ballot-chasing lawyers in the 2000 presidential election, Florida was whiplashed by real storms and more lawsuits in 2004. In a span of forty-four days, four powerful hurricanes crisscrossed the state. The Sunshine State, quipped pundits, had become the Plywood State and the National Disaster State. The hurricanes wrought terrible havoc and destruction, but Charley, Frances, Ivan, and Jeanne curiously brought Floridians together in ways the state's geography and politics have not.

These were not the first hurricanes or even the most expensive hurricanes to slam Florida. In August 1992, Hurricane Andrew pummeled south Florida with the force of a Category 5 storm, leaving in its wake 65,000 homes destroyed, 175,000 people homeless, and insurance companies in shambles. Until Hurricane Katrina, which flooded New Orleans in 2005, Andrew was the costliest hurricane in American history: $26 billion in today's dollars. Hurricane Andrew's legacy is mixed: the good news is that the disaster forced new building codes with hurricane-resistant features; the bad news is that the storm also flattened the insurance business. Few Floridians have confidence that Citizens, the new state insurer, can survive the next disaster.

Still they came. Mere months later, after having been battered by Hurricane Ivan, property values escalated along Pensacola Bay. Overall, Florida's population surged, rising by 600,000 from 2000 to 2005. If Floridians had adopted a state conversation topic, it might have been the question: How much has my house appreciated? How much since last week? An amenities revolution saw houses soar in price and size. It was a flipper's paradise. Not even hurricanes, fast-buck artists, and naysayers could stop the boom.

In April 2006, the *Florida Trend* cover story was titled "1,060 New Floridians Every Day."[14] Reporters tracked the paths of newcomers and concluded that on a typical winter day, the state added 1,060 new residents. Such was not news. Floridians had been adding a thousand newcomers daily for decades, but these figures were revealing. In reality, fully 1,890 newcomers were arriving daily, but alarmingly, 946 Floridians were leaving. Few Floridians ever asked, and even fewer had answers for the question, "What will happen when a thousand newcomers stopped coming?" Floridians quickly found out when, months following the *Florida Trend* publication, the Great Recession shook Florida to its roots.

Few Floridians could recall the Florida Bust that pricked the Land Boom in 1926. History may not repeat itself, but in Florida it rhymes. "Under the blistering heat of this tropical Florida sun," observed a journalist, "there lie a thousand developments scattered about the State . . . with here and there a half-completed building, a former field office or a lonesome shack, marking the graves of the hopes of armies of investors a year ago."[15] The year was 1926! In 2009, George Packer took readers for a tour of the "ghost subdivisions" of Pasco County, a place that had grown from 20,000 residents in 1950 to a half million in 2008, and then crashed.[16]

In November 1925, Jacksonville newsboys hawked newspapers with the sensational headline: "Ponzi in Jax! Promises Comeback!" Indeed, Charles (Carlo) Ponzi, having been convicted for a financial pyramid scheme that gave his name to a crime, moved to Jacksonville (and later, Tampa), to recruit more suckers. In the Great Recession, Florida may have been the epicenter in American financial fraud schemes. Bernie Madoff wintered at his palatial home in Palm Beach, a city hit especially hard by the New Yorker's Ponzi crimes. His misdeeds devastated Florida retirees, banks, country clubs, and even charities.

The Great Recession has taken a toll. Floridians have had to learn a new glossary to understand the malaise: underwater/upside down/toxic/subprime mortgages, short sales, REITs (real estate investment trusts), robo-signings, and flipping. Journalists have lacerated the state and its follies in national publications. Provocative titles asked and exposed, "Is Florida the Sunset State?," "Is Florida Over?," "Florida, Despair and Foreclosures," and "The Ponzi State."[17] In Cape Coral—the largest city on the Gulf coast south of Tampa—tourists and speculators take foreclosure boat tours! Dateline

Leigh Acres, Twin Lakes, Orange Park, and Dundee reveal layers of fraud, tragedy, and hubris. The Great Recession has only worsened some alarming social and economic indicators. "We're first in the nation in mortgage fraud, second in foreclosures, last in high school graduation rates," writes Michael Grunwald in *Time* magazine. Grunwald concludes, "The question is whether it [Florida] will grow up."[18]

The question, "Will Florida ever grow up?" has been asked before. In 1943, the Miami writer and critic Philip Wylie challenged and pleaded with Floridians to change habits in a front-page *Miami Herald* article. "At the end of the war, there will be two courses open to us," contended Wylie. "We can seize the gigantic opportunities at hand and develop this unique region into a new heart of the new world—or we can go on being a tropical Coney Island." In words all too familiar to Floridians in 1886, 1926, or 2012, Wylie desperately wished for something better than a "tropical Coney Island." He complained, half optimistically, half pessimistically: "We haven't asked people to live here. We've asked them to visit." But in words resonant today, he reminded readers, "The original buildup of south Florida as a land of Oz collapsed with the boom."[19]

Today, Florida stands at a crossroads with new and profound challenges. Will we grow up? Can Florida become a model showing the nation how to manage growth, restore ecosystems, preserve water, and balance generations of diverse residents into a common cause? Will the challenge of global warming simply overwhelm a state with over a thousand miles of coastline or serve as a rallying cry? The state legislature seems determined to do everything possible to jump-start the growth machine by abolishing impact fees, cutting taxes, and eliminating laws that protect wetlands. Can Florida possibly maintain the pell-mell growth that added 16 million residents between 1945 and 2005? Will baby boomers rescue Florida by choosing to retire in Florida, or will they prefer new destinations with less sunshine but more amenities? Will age-restricted communities such as the Villages and Sun City Center be as alluring to boomers as they were to their parents? The 2010 census indicated that growth had drastically declined in the newly built, far-flung boomburbs. Floridians were returning to cities. What is the tipping point when future tourists and residents simply reject Florida because its roads are too congested, its lakes and rivers too polluted, and its infrastructure simply inadequate?

To rephrase the question: What will, what should, the next Florida dream be? The Florida dream will reinvent itself—it always has—but in what form? Born in the peaceful but anxious days after World War II, a new Florida dream emerged. Americans flocked by the millions to Florida, driven by the lure of easy living, low taxes, cheap housing, and better Februarys. Like California, its dream-state twin, Florida offered Americans eternal sunshine, saltwater breezes, but most importantly, the promise of a better life. For senior citizens—as well as Ponzi schemers—Florida was a place of second chances, a place where new designs of living unfolded for retirees. The Florida dream worked so well that aside from some mild hiccups, the economy and population added hundreds and sometimes thousands of newcomers daily, each of whom needed housing, sod, plumbers, and other necessities.

Florida today, like the rest of the United States, struggles with doubt and uncertainty. Global warming poses an ominous cloud over the state's future. Several major trends, each carrying the weight of history, have converged. The big changes that we have outlined—demographic revolution, technological innovation, shifting economic patterns, troubled race relations, and waves of new immigration—have brought us to our contemporary condition. And those same forces of change will still be at work shaping the Florida of tomorrow.

Notes

1. James Stirling, *Letters from the Slave States* (London: J. W. Parker, 1857), 227.

2. Frank F. Rogers, "The State of Florida and Its Highways," *Florida Highways* 6 (May 1929):5.

3. Nevin O. Winter, *Florida: The Land of Enchantment* (Boston: Page, 1918), 369.

4. "Florida Highways," *Florida Highways* 7 (March 1930):34.

5. Raymond Arsenault, "The End of the Long Hot Summer: The Air Conditioner and Southern Culture," *Journal of Southern History* 50 (November 1984):597–628.

6. Mark Sullivan, *Our Times*, 6 vols. (New York: Scribner's, 1926–35), 6:647.

7. June Cleo and Hank Mesouf, *Florida: Polluted Paradise* (Philadelphia: Chilton, 1964), 2.

8. A. Lowell Hunt, *Florida Today: New Land of Opportunity* (New York: Scribner's, 1950), 2.

9. Joe Alex Morris, "The Truth about the Florida Race Troubles," *Saturday Evening Post*, 21 June 1952, 24–25, 50, 55–58; William S. Fairfield, "Florida: Dynamite Law Replaces Lynch Law," *Reporter*, 5 August 1952, 31–34; "Bigotry and Bombs in Florida," *Southern Patriot* 10 (January 1952):1, 4; Nathan Perlmutter, "Bombing in Miami: Anti-Semitism and the Segregationists," *Commentary* 25 (June 1958): 498–503.

10. Frank Soler, "Thoughts from a Wounded Heart," *Miami Mensual* 5 (August 1985):11.

11. Alejandro Portes and Alex Stepick, *City on the Edge: The Transformation of Miami* (Berkeley: University of California Press, 1993).

12. *Miami Herald*, 3 April 2005.

13. Brian Duffy, "Florida, Paradise Lost," *U.S. News and World Report*, 11 October 1993, 40–53.

14. Mike Vogel, "Good Migrations," *Florida Trend* 48 (April 2006):26–31.

15. "Stake in the Weeds," *Los Angeles Times*, 27 July 1926.

16. George Packer, "The Ponzi State: Florida's Financial Disaster," *New Yorker*, 9 February 2009, 81.

17. Michael Grunwald, "Is Florida the Sunset State?" *Time*, 10 July 2008; Packer, "The Ponzi State," 80–93; Damien Cave, "Florida, Despair and Foreclosure," *New York Times*, 8 February 2009; "Is Florida Over?," *Wall Street Journal*, 29 September 2007.

18. Grunwald, "Is Florida the Sunset State?"

19. Philip Wylie, "True Greatness," *Miami Herald*, 2 December 1943.

Bibliography

Since the publication of the original essay in 1996, modern Florida has become a cottage industry for writers and historians. Some of the best new books include:

Braden, Susan R. *The Architecture of Leisure: The Florida Resort Hotels of Henry Flagler and Henry Plant*. Gainesville: University Press of Florida, 2002.

Colburn, David, and Lance DeHaven-Smith. *Florida Megatrends: Critical Issues in Florida*. Gainesville: University Press of Florida, 2002.

Davis, Jack E., and Raymond Arsenault, eds. *Paradise Lost? The Environmental History of Florida*. Gainesville: University Press of Florida, 2005.

Derr, Mark. *Some Kind of Paradise: A Chronicle of Man and the Land*. Gainesville: University Press of Florida, 1998.

Desrosiers-Lauzon, Godefroy. *Florida's Snowbirds: Spectacle, Mobility, and Community since 1945*. Montreal: McGill Queens University Press, 2011.

Dunn, Marvin. *Black Miami in the Twentieth Century*. Gainesville: University Press of Florida, 1997.

Foglesong, Richard E. *Married to the Mouse: Walt Disney and Orlando*. New Haven: Yale University Press, 2003.

Garcia, Maria Cristina. *Havana USA: Cuban Exiles and Cuban Americans in South Florida*. Berkeley: University of California Press, 1997.

Green, Ben. *Before His Time: The Untold Story of Harry T. Moore*. New York: Free Press, 1999.

Grunwald, Michael. *The Swamp: The Everglades, Florida, and the Politics of Paradise*. New York: Simon and Schuster, 2007.

Hahamovitch, Cindy. *The Fruits of Their Labor: Atlantic Coast Farmworkers and the Making of Migrant Poverty, 1875–1945*. Chapel Hill: University of North Carolina Press, 1997.

Mohl, Raymond A. *South of the South: Jewish Activists and the Civil Rights Movement in Miami, 1945–1960*. Gainesville: University Press of Florida, 2004.

Mormino, Gary R. *Land of Sunshine, State of Dreams: A Social History of Modern Florida*. Gainesville: University Press of Florida, 2005.

Noll, Steven, and David Tegeder. *The Ditch of Dreams: The Cross Florida Barge Canal and the Struggle for Florida's Future*. Gainesville: University Press of Florida, 2009.

Ortiz, Paul. *Emancipation Betrayed: The Hidden History of Black Organizing and White Violence in Florida from Reconstruction to the Bloody Election of 1920*. Berkeley: University of California Press, 2005.

Pittman, Craig, and Matthew Waite. *Paving Paradise: Florida's Vanishing Wetlands and the Failure of No Net Loss*. Gainesville: University Press of Florida, 2009.

Provenzo, Eugene, Jr., and Asterie Baker Provenzo. *In the Eye of Hurricane Andrew*. Gainesville: University Press of Florida, 2002.

Rabby, Glenda Alice. *The Pain and the Promise: The Struggle for Civil Rights in Tallahassee, Florida*. Athens: University of Georgia Press, 1999.

Revels, Tracy. *A History of Florida's Tourism*. Gainesville: University Press of Florida, 2011.

Roberts, Diane. *Dream State*. Gainesville: University Press of Florida, 2004.

Shell-Weiss, Melanie. *Coming to Miami: A Social History*. Gainesville: University Press of Florida, 2009.

West, Patsy. *The Enduring Seminoles: From Alligator Wrestling to Ecotourism*. Gainesville: University Press of Florida, 1998.

Ziewitz, Kathyn, and June Wiaz, *Green Empire: The St. Joe Company and the Remaking of Florida's Panhandle*. Gainesville: University Press of Florida, 2006.

Contributors

Amy Turner Bushnell, retired from the College of Charleston, is adjunct associate professor of history at Brown University and an invited research scholar at the John Carter Brown Library. She is the author of *The King's Coffer: Proprietors of the Spanish Florida Treasury, 1565–1702*, and *Situado and Sabana: Spain's Support System for the Presidio and Mission Provinces of Florida*, and the editor of *Establishing Exceptionalism: Historiography and the Colonial Americas*.

William S. Coker (1924–2002) was professor emeritus of history at the University of West Florida. He is the author or editor of fourteen books, including *Indian Traders of the Southeastern Spanish Borderlands: Panton, Leslie & Company, and John Forbes & Company, 1783–1847* (coauthored with Thomas D. Watson).

David R. Colburn is formerly provost and senior vice president at the University of Florida and has been a member of the University of Florida history faculty since 1972. He is the author of *Racial Crisis and Community Conflict: St. Augustine, Florida, 1877–1980*; coauthor of *Florida's Gubernatorial Politics in the Twentieth Century* (with Richard K. Scher); and coeditor of *The African American Heritage of Florida* (with Jane Landers).

Jack E. Davis is professor of environmental history at the University of Florida and the author or editor of several books, including *Race Against Time: Culture and Separation in Natchez Since 1930*, winner of the Charles S. Sydnor Award; and *An Everglades Providence: Marjory Stoneman Douglas and the American Environmental Century*, awarded the gold medal in nonfiction from the Florida Book Awards.

Robin F. A. Fabel is the Hollifield Professor of Southern History at Auburn University, Alabama. He is the author of *Bombast and Broadsides: The Lives of George Johnstone*, and *The Economy of British West Florida, 1763–1783*; and the editor of *Shipwreck and Adventures of M. Pierre Viaud*.

Michael Gannon is Distinguished Service Professor Emeritus of history at the University of Florida. He is the author or editor of six books on Florida history, four books on World War II subjects, and a play. In 2010, the Florida Humanities Council presented him with its first Florida Literary Lifetime Achievement Award. King Juan Carlos I of Spain awarded him the decoration Knight Commander of the Order of Isabel la Católica.

Thomas Graham is professor of history emeritus at Flagler College in St. Augustine, where he taught full-time for thirty-five years. He is the author of *The Awakening of St. Augustine* and is a past president and life member of the St. Augustine Historical Society. A native Floridian, he is a lineal descendant of Francisco Xavier Sanchez of St. Augustine.

John H. Hann (1926–2009) was site historian at San Luis Archaeological and Historic Site in Tallahassee and the author of *Apalachee: The Land between the Rivers, Missions to the Calusa*, and *A History of the Timucua Indians and Missions*.

Paul E. Hoffman is professor of history at Louisiana State University. He has written two award-winning books on early Florida: *A New Andalucia and a Way to the Orient* and *Florida's Frontiers* and is the author of *Spain and the Roanoke Voyages*.

Jane Landers is the Gertrude Conaway Vanderbilt Professor of History at Vanderbilt University. She is the author of *Black Society in Spanish Florida* and *Atlantic Creoles in the Age of Revolutions*; and editor of *Colonial Plantations and Economy in Florida* and *Against the Odds: Free Blacks in the Slave Societies of the Americas*. She coedited *The African American Heritage of Florida* with David Colburn, and *Slaves, Subjects, and Subversives: Blacks in Colonial Latin America* with Barry Robinson.

Eugene Lyon is director of the Center for Historic Research at Flagler College. The author of *The Enterprise of Florida* and *Richer than We Thought*, he is a frequent contributor to *National Geographic*.

Susan A. MacManus is Distinguished University Professor in the Department of Government and International Affairs at the University of South Florida. She is the author of *Young v. Old: Generational Combat in the 21st Century?* and *Targeting Senior Voters*. She is the coauthor of *Florida's Politics* (3rd ed.), with Aubrey Jewett, Thomas R. Dye, and David J. Bonanza; *Florida's Politics: Ten Media Markets, One Powerful State*, with Kevin Hill and Dario Moreno; and *Citrus, Sawmills, Critters, and Crackers: Life in Early Lutz and Central Pasco County*, with Elizabeth Riegler MacManus.

Jerald T. Milanich is curator emeritus in archaeology at the Florida Museum of Natural History, University of Florida. He is the author of *Archaeology of Precolumbian Florida* and *Florida Indians and the Invasion from Europe*; coauthor, with Susan Milbrath, of *First Encounters: Spanish Explorations in the Caribbean and the United States, 1492–1570*; and coauthor, with Charles Hudson, of *Hernando de Soto and the Indians of Florida*.

Amy M. Mitchell-Cook is associate professor of history at the University of West Florida. She is the author of several journal articles on maritime history and is currently finishing a manuscript on shipwreck narratives, "A Sea of Misadventures: Shipwreck and Survival in Early America."

Raymond A. Mohl is Distinguished Professor of History at the University of Alabama at Birmingham. He is the author, most recently, of *South of the South: Jewish Activists and the Civil Rights Movement in Miami, 1945–1960* and numerous scholarly articles on the racial and ethnic history of modern Florida, especially Miami.

Gary R. Mormino is the Frank E. Duckwall Emeritus Professor of History at the University of South Florida St. Petersburg. He is the coauthor, with George Pozzetta, of *The Immigrant World of Ybor City*, and coeditor, with Ann Henderson, of *Spanish Pathways to Florida, 1492–1992*.

Susan Richbourg Parker is executive director of the Saint Augustine Historical Society and specializes in the Spanish presence in the Southeast. She served as a historian and a historic preservation consultant with the Florida Department of State and taught at the University of Florida, University of South Florida, and University of North Florida. She has contributed chapters to *Signposts: New Directions in Southern Legal History, America's Hundred Years' War,* and *Colonial Plantations and Economy in Florida*.

George E. Pozzetta (1942–1994) was professor of history at the University of Florida for twenty-three years. A renowned authority on immigration history and ethnicity, he coauthored, with Gary R. Mormino, *The Immigrant World of Ybor City*.

Larry Eugene Rivers is professor of history at Valdosta State University in Valdosta, Georgia. He is the author of *Slavery in Florida: Territorial Days to Emancipation* and *Rebels and Runaways: Slave Resistance in Nineteenth-Century Florida*. He lives in Tallahassee, Florida.

William W. Rogers is retired Distinguished Teaching Professor of History at Florida State University. He is the author of *Outposts on the Gulf: A History of St. George's Island and Apalachicola from Early Times to World War II*; *The One-Gallused Rebellion: Agrarianism in Alabama, 1865–1896*; and other monographs in Florida, Alabama, and Georgia history.

Daniel L. Schafer is professor of history emeritus and university distinguished professor, the University of North Florida. He is the author of numerous journal articles on African American and Florida history, and *Anna Madgigine Jai Kingsley: African Princess, Florida Slave, Plantation Slaveowner*; *Thunder on the River: The Civil War in Northeast Florida*; *William Bartram and the Ghost Plantations of British East Florida*; and *Zephaniah Kingsley and the Atlantic World: Slave Trader, Plantation Owner, Emancipator*.

Della A. Scott-Ireton is associate director of the Florida Public Archaeology Network (www.flpublicarchaeology.org) and serves on the boards of the Advisory Council on Underwater Archaeology and the Society for Historical Archaeology. She is also a member of the Register of Professional Archaeologists and is appointed to the Marine Protected Areas Federal Advisory Committee. Her research interests include public interpretation of maritime cultural heritage, both on land and underwater.

Jerrell H. Shofner is retired professor of history at the University of Central Florida. The author of numerous books, including *Nor Is It Over Yet: Florida in the Era of Reconstruction, 1863–1877*, he became editor of the *Florida Historical Quarterly* in 1995.

Robert A. Taylor is professor of history and head of the Humanities and Communication Department at the Florida Institute of Technology. The author, coauthor, editor, or coeditor of seven books, Taylor's latest is *Florida: An Illustrated History*.

Brent R. Weisman is professor of anthropology at the University of South Florida. He is the author of *Unconquered People: Florida's Seminole and Miccosukee Indians*, and *Pioneer in Space and Time: John Mann Goggin and the Development of Florida Archaeology*.

Index

Page numbers in *italics* refer to illustrations.

AAA. *See* Agricultural Adjustment Act

Abolitionists, 240

Adams, John Quincy, 176, 220, 224, 228

Adams-Onís Treaty, 176, 220, 224, 228

Adelantado (conqueror and king's representative): La Florida's transition away from, 76–78; Menéndez de Avilés as, 57–73, 91, 93; Ponce de León as, 22

Aesthetics, natural, 369–70

AFL. *See* American Federation of Labor

African Americans: churches, 451–52; complicated present of, 466–67; Duval County, 446; Gainesville family portrait, *445*; Harlem Renaissance and Florida, 455, 456; Jacksonville, 446–49, 451–55, 457, 458, 464, 467; masonry and, 451; NAACP, 310, 344, 458, 461–64; overview of Florida state, 444–67; population, 445–46, 457–58, 472, 500; traveling of, 451. *See also* Blacks; Free blacks

Africans: in Americas, 179; British and, 171, 186–87; Native Americans and, 172, 174, 179–82, 184, 187, *188*, 190, 192, 202–4; in Second Spanish Period, 187–93; settlers and ecology, 41, 47, 52; Spain and, 179–80, 183; in Spanish Caribbean, 180, 181, 192–93; Spanish expeditions and, 179–82; Spanish Florida and, 122–24, 179–84, *185*, 186–93, 203–4; Spanish settlements and, 78, 122, 123, 174. *See also* Blacks; Free blacks

African slaves, 86; in British Florida, 186–87; British settlements and, 114, 150–51, 154, 186–87; Civil War impact on, 252–53; Native Americans and, 24, 204, 205; quarters, *226*; Saint-Domingue revolt, 191; Seminole Indians and, 187, *188*; Spain and, 179, 191; in Spanish Florida, 179–93; Spanish settlements and, 24, 78; U.S. and, 174, 175, 190, 192, 193, 203. *See also* Freedmen; Slavery

Agricultural Adjustment Act (AAA), 319, 325, 423

Agriculture, 366, 507; blacks and, 449–51, 454, 457; Civil War and, 250–52, 276; climate and, 50–51, 286; ecology and, 44, 48, 53n5; of European settlements, 48; in Great Depression, 319, 323–26; immigration and, 473–75; labor, 325, 338–40, 345, *478*, *480*; of Native Americans, 48, 109–10; New Deal for, 319, 323–26; in 1920s, 307; piedmont, 44, 53n5; precolumbian, 8, 11–14; quarantines (1929), 307–8; schools, 451; of Spanish settlements, 66–67, 70, 109–10, 168; during World War II, 338–40. *See also* Farmers; *specific agricultural topics*

Aguacaleyquen (village), 29

Air-conditioning, 511–12

Airplanes. *See* Aviation

Ais, 82

Ais Indians, 182

Alabama, 172, 204, 340

Alachua, 147, 238; precolumbian culture, 12–13

Alaminos, Antón de, 19–23, 357–58

Alcohol: coastal smuggling of, 408–9; Prohibition, 291, 292, 297, 298, 310n1, 316, 408–9

Aldrin, Edwin E., *517*

Alexander VI, 91

Alibama Indians, 140

All American Air Races, 510

Alvarado, Luis Moscoso de, 33

Amacano Indians, 92, 102

Ambrister, Robert Chrystie, 172

Amelia Island, 174, 176

American Federation of Labor (AFL), 319

American Revolution, 154–59, 186, 187, 397
American Scene, The (James), 368
Amos, Ernest, 300, 304–6, 308, 313, 315
Añasco, Juan de, 27–28
Andrews, Charles O., 316, 317
Andrews, Daniel, 378
Anhaica (town), 31–32
Animals. *See* Wildlife
Anti-Catholicism, 291–92
Anticorporation politics, 282, 287
AOA. *See* Armed Occupation Act
Apalachee Indians, 45, 86, 88, 125, 128, 146; La
    Florida missions and, 91, 92, 96, 98, 100–102,
    104–9, 112–15, 118; Spanish expeditions and,
    11, 24–25, 31–32
Apalachee province, 84–85, 88, 92, 96, 101–2,
    104, 107, 112, 128; Spanish expeditions in,
    24–25, 31–32
Apalachee Rebellion (1647), 86
Apalachicola (town, port), 247, 256, 376
Apalachicola Bay, 320
Apalachicola County, 320
Apalachicola Indians, 88, 114
Apalachicola province, 86, 88, 144
Apalachicola River, 144, 204, 228, 406
Apollo XI, *517*
Arbuthnot, Alexander, 172
Archaeology: map of sites, *5*; of precolum-
    bian cultures, 3–15, 355–57; of shipwrecks,
    394–97, 403, 405–6; Underwater Archaeo-
    logical Preserve, 402–5, 407–11, 413. *See also*
    Maritime heritage
Archaic period: early, 5–6, 390; late, 7–8, 11, 13,
    391; middle, 6, 390
Architecture, 361–62
Arkansas, 33
Armed Occupation Act (AOA), 231, 232, 366
Armistead, Walker K., 210
Armstrong, Neil A., *517*
Army Corps of Engineers, 371
Arpeika (Sam Jones) (Mikasukis medicine
    man), 208–10, 212–14
Arredondo, Antonio de, 120
Arriola, Andrés de, 130–33
Artists, 369–70
Asian immigration, 470, 488, 491–93
Askew, Reubin O'Donovan, 431, *432*, 436–37
Audubon, John James, 369
Audubon Society, 287

Automobiles, 291; social change from, 506–9;
    tourism by, 292, 301–2, 506–8. *See also* Roads
Aviation: airline companies, 510; airports,
    510–11; commercial air transportation, 510;
    during Great Depression, 328; history of
    Florida, 510–11; ship launched aircraft, *294*;
    social change from, 510–11; transportation
    development (1920s), 302; World War I
    training bases, 293; World War II and, 328,
    335, 336, 338, 349–50
Ayllón, Lucas Vázquez de, 23–24, 31, 180
Ayllón, Lucas Vázquez de (the younger), 56

Bahamas, 340, 358
Bahamians, 476–79, *478, 480,* 493
Bahía Santa María Filipina, 128, 129
Baker, Mary Lou, 346
Banking Act (1931), 313
Banks: Bank War, 235; failures, 305–6, 308, 313;
    Florida Territory, 234–36; in Great Depres-
    sion, 313, 317–18; in modern Florida, 518; in
    1920s, 303–6, 308
Barrier islands: Cedar Keys, 376–79, 505; ecol-
    ogy, 47, 53n8, 376–79; soils, 47
Bartram, William, 147, 368, 369, 370
Baton Rouge, 156, 157, 163, 169
Battle of New Orleans, 171, 220
Bay County, 336
Beaches: erosion and renourishment, 374;
    houses of refuge, 406, *407*; surf bathing,
    372, 373; tourism at, 372–74. *See also* Coasts;
    specific beaches
Bell, John, 241
Belle Glade: precolumbian culture, 13–15; veg-
    etable plant, 323
Bethune, Mary McLeod, *447*
Biassou, Jorge, 191
Bienville, Sieur de, 134–37
Big Bend, 377, 380
Big Cypress: Seminole Indians, 214, *215*, 367;
    Swamp, 209, 380
Billings, Liberty, 264, 266
Bimini, 19, 22
Binder Boys (real estate hucksters), 302, 303
Birds: Audubon and, 369; conservationist
    protection of, 287; plumes, 286–87
Black, Hugo, 460
Black Auxiliaries, 191
Blacks: agriculture and, 449–51, 454, 457;

Bahamian, 476–79, *480*; Black Auxiliaries, 191; Black Seminoles, 202–3; as Civil War soldiers, 254; Democrats and, 448–49, 462; discrimination against, 238, 262, 309, 453, 454, 457, 459–64; education and, 290, 308–9, 321–23, 446–48, 451–53, 460–61, 463; Hispanics and, 520; immigration and, 472–73, 476–79, 500; labor and, 382–83, 455, *457*; lynchings, 309, 420–21, 453–54, 459, 519; marriage to whites, 190; migrants, 343; migration within Florida and U.S., 343, 419–21, 454–56, 500; newspapers of, 458–59; in 1920s, 308–10, 457; police and, 459–60; politics and, 267, 273, 283, 284, 431, 448–49, 462, 464–65; protective leagues, 458; racial discrimination against, 238, 262, 309, 453, 454, 457, 459–64, 479; Reconstruction and, 261–68, *265*, 270, 271, 273, 274, 277, 416–17; schools and, 446–48, 451–53, 463; violence and, 268, 309, 420–21, 453–54, 459–60, 462–63, 465–66, 519–20; voting of, 265, 266, 268, 274, 284, 296, 317, 449, 459, 462, 464, 519; during World War I, 458–59; in World War II, 339, 343–45, 424. *See also* Africans; Free blacks; Race; Segregation
Black Seminoles, 202–3
Blake, Luther, 212
Bloxham, William D., 271, 277–79, 283, 288
Boca Grande Beach, *304*
Boca Raton, 299
Boca Ratones Indians, 14
Bonus Army, 315
Bosnian Muslim immigrants, 493
Bowlegs (Seminole chief), 204–6
Bowlegs, Billy. *See* Holata Micco
BP oil spill, 439–40
Braden, Hector, 225, 232
Branch, John, 224, 236
Brayton, Caleb Lyndon, 231–32
Breckenridge, John C., 241, 244
Brim, "Emperor" (Creek chief), 197, 200
British: Africans and, 171, 186–87; Caribbean, 183; conflicts with French, 110, 115, 125–26, 132, 133, 139, 141–42, 144, 157, 158; conflicts with Native Americans, 110, 114, 119–20, 122, 125–26, 139, 141, 144, 197–98; conflicts with Spanish, 72, 105–7, 110, 112–26, 132–34, 141–42, 144, 154–59, 162, 170–71, 184, 186, 187, 197; Cuba and, 126, 141, 144; French and

Indian War, 125–26, 139, 141, 144; Jamaica and, 86; La Florida and, 107, 110, 113, 156, 158–59, 164, 170; pirates, 35, 78, 83, 183; Protestants, 164; shipwrecks, 396–97; slavery in British Caribbean, 183; trade, 114, 124, 141, 168, 197, 201, 202, 205; U.S. conflicts with, 154–59, 170–72, 220
British Florida: acquisition of, 126, 137, 141, 186, 363; African slaves in, 186–87; American Revolution and, 154–59, 186, 187, 397; East Florida, 144, *145*, 147–50, 153–59, 162, 187; free blacks in, 186–87; maritime heritage of, 396–97; Native Americans and, 200–202; overview, 144–59; U.S. and, 154–59, 162; West Florida, 144, *145*, 146, 147–53, 155–58, 162
British settlements, 72, 362; African slaves in, 114, 150–51, 154, 186–87; Carolina, 114, 115, 118–22, 126, 184, 187, 197; Charleston, 86, 105, 114, 118, 120, 124–26, 155, 157, 158, 184; Georgia, 117, 120–26, 187, 197; Native Americans and, 105, 106, 110, 114, 118–22, 133, 137, 138, 141, 147, 152–54, 171, 197–99; Native American slaves and, 110, 114, 118, 197; Pensacola, 132, 141, *142*, 146, 148, 151, 155–57; Spanish settlements and, 72, 110, 114–26, 132, 137, 141, 142, 144, 146, 156, 158, 159, 184, 186, 197; St. Augustine, 126, 144, 146–59. *See also* British Florida
Brooke, George F., 229
Broome, James, 213
Brotherhood of Sleeping Car Porters, 310, 455, 457
Broward, Napoleon Bonaparte, 288–90, 453
Broward County, 216
Brown, Canter, 448–49
Brown, Thomas, 225, 236
Brown v. Board of Education of Topeka (1954), 425, 463
Bryan, William Jennings, 289, 298, 302
Bryant, Farris, 426
Buckman Act (1905), 290
Bureau of Indian Affairs, 215, 216
Burial: Christian, 108; mounds, 8, 9; Native American, 108; precolumbian, 6, 8, 9
Burns, Haydon, 426
Burt, Al, 370
Bush, George Herbert Walker, 335
Bush, John Ellis "Jeb," 438–39
Busk. *See* Green Corn Dance

Cabeza de Vaca, Alvar Núñez, 24–27

Caciques, cacicas (Indian chiefs), 61, 64, 65, 77, 80, 81, 86

Cades Pond precolumbian culture, 10–12

Cádiz, 67, 68

Caldwell, Millard, 339, 344, 423, 424, 453–54

California missions, 91, 93, 98

Call, Richard Keith, 208, *221*, 222–25, 234, 242, 245

Call, Wilkinson, 262, 282

Callava, José, 171, 172, 221

Callaway, Elvey E., 316

Caloosahatchee precolumbian culture, 14, 15

Caloosahatchee River, 15

Calusa Indians, *23*, 84, 94, 103, 126, 373; Carlos, 22, 61, 64–65; precolumbian, 354–57; Spanish living with, 359

Camp Blanding, 333, 334, 336

Canada, 144

Canadians: tourism of, 493; winter migration to Florida, 503

Cáncer de Barbastro, Fray Luis, 34

Canoes, prehistoric, *390*, 391

Cantero, Raoul G., III, 431

Cantino, Alberto, 18

Cape Canaveral, 82, 83, 350

Cape of the Currents (Cabo de las Corrientes), 21

Capone, Al, 298

Caribbean: Africans in Spanish, 180, 181, 192–93; British, 183; early map, 18–19, *20*; Spanish expeditions to, 180, 181

Carleton, Guy, 157, 158

Carlos (Calusa chief), 22, 61, 64–65

Carlos (Calusa village), 64, 94

Carlos II, 129, 133

Carlos IV, 166, 191

Carlos V, 22, 24, 26, 30

Carlton, Doyle E., 297, 306, 308, 313–16, 422

Carolina (British settlement), 114, 115, 118–22, 126, 184, 187, 197

Carr, Marjorie, 504

Carrera de Indias (Indies Run), 392

Carrère, John, 280

Carrier, Willis, 511

Carroll, Jennifer, 431

Carter, Jerry W., 316–17

Casa de Contratación (House of Trade), 58, 67

Casey, John, 213

Castile, 67

Castillo, Pedro del, 67

Castillo de San Marcos (St. Augustine fort), 87, 118, 120, 122–25, 144, 146; construction, 87, 114, 115; maps of, *113*, *116*, *117*. *See also* Fort St. Mark

Castro, Fidel, 481–82

Catholicism, 91; anti-Catholicism, 291–92; in Second Spanish Period, 164–66; of Spanish settlements, 63–65, 69, 79. *See also* Spanish missions

Cattle, 154, 227–29, 284–85; free roaming, 367; industry (1920s), 307–8, 450; ranches, 118–19, 183, 189, 218, 226, 233; running or droving, 50, 232, 233, 250, 251, 367–68; Spanish introduction into Florida, 362–63

Catts, Sidney J., 291–93, 296, 297, 420–21, 454–55

Cawthon, W. S., 309

CCC. *See* Civilian Conservation Corps

Cedar Keys, 376–79, 505

Central Florida, and climate, 365

Central ridge, 45

Cermak, Anton, 317

CERP. *See* Comprehensive Everglades Restoration Plan

Chacato Indians, 92, 102, 106

Chacato missions, 104

Chambers, et al. v. Florida, 460

Chambers, Isiah, 460, 461

Chandler, L. L., 340

Charles II, 114, 115, 184

Charles III, 156

Charles IV, 130

Charleston: British settlement of, 86, 105, 114, 118, 120, 124–26, 155, 157, 158, 184; during Civil War, 248, 250–51, 254–55

Charles V, 58, 76

Cheney, John E., 376

Chesapeake Bay, 71, 94

Chichimeca Indians, 76

Chickasaw Indians, 33, 147

Child labor, 291

Chiles, Lawton Mainor, Jr., 438

Chine Indians, 92, 102

Chinese immigration, 473

Chipley, William D., 282

Choctawhatchee Bay, 11

Choctaw Indians, 128, 137, 147, 152

Christianity: burials, 108. *See also* Catholicism; Protestants

Churches: African American, 451–52. *See also* Religion

Cigar manufacturing, 285, 475, *476*

Cinco de Mayo, 490

CIO. *See* Congress of Industrial Organization

Cities: distance between, 417; edge cities, 509; urban dwellers, 499, 509; World War II changes to, 340–41. *See also specific cities*

Citrus: frozen concentrate, 365–66; geographic history of, 364–65; grove, 363; growing areas, 364; oranges, 338, 363–64, 366; Spanish introduction into Florida, 363–64

Citrus industry, 286, 325, 326, 363; blacks in, 450–51; climate and, 364–65; freezes impact on, 281, 364, 365, 450, 522; land and, 365; production innovations, 365–66; during World War II, 338, 339

City of Hawkinsville (steamboat), 403, *404*

Civilian Conservation Corps (CCC), 319, 320, 324

Civil rights: activism, 461–65, 519–20; bus boycotts, 464; Civil Rights Act, 426; costs of gains, 465–66; Florida politics and, 425–27; NAACP and, 463–64; violence and, 520

Civil Rights Act (1964), 263, 426, 464

Civil War (1861–1865), 211; agriculture and, 250–52, 276; black soldiers, 254; Florida and, 244–56, 260, 360, 416; immigration need after, 472; impact of, 252–54; maritime heritage of, 399–402; naval blockade, 247–48, 399–401; shipwrecks, 402; slavery and, 236, 252–53; steam vessels, 401–2; vessels, 399. *See also* Confederate States of America; Secession

Civil Works Administration (CWA), 318–19

Clay County, 233, 234, 241, 333

Climate, 41; agriculture and, 50–51, 286; Central Florida and, 365; citrus industry and, 364–65; control, 511–12; development and, 365, 511–12; of earlier geologic age, 353–54; ecology and, 49–52; ENSO events, 50–51, 53n14; freezes, 281, 364, 365, 450, 522; Gulf Stream and, 364; of La Florida, 113; lightning strikes, 50, 368; overview, 354; precolumbian, 3–7; rainfall, 50–51, 368; of South Florida, 364. *See also* Ecology; Hurricanes

Climate change, 384

Clinch, Duncan L., 206, 207, 227

Coacoochee (Wildcat) (Seminole leader), 208–10

Coastal Construction Control Line, 361

Coastal plain: ecology, 42–45; soil, 44; Spanish settlements, 44

Coasts: ecology of, 42–45, 373–79; Gold Coast, 14, 347, 428; hurricanes and construction near, 360–62; settlements on, 375, 378; shipping along, 409; working waterfronts, 374. *See also* Beaches; Gulf coast

Cocoris, John, 376, 475

Coligney, Gaspard de, 55

Colleges, 309; blacks and, 447–48, 460, 463; early development of, 290–91; fraternities and sororities, 452–53; during Great Depression, 323; during World War II, 341, *342*, 349

Collins, John, 299

Collins, LeRoy, *425*, 425–26

Colonial settlements: ecology and, 42. *See also* European settlements

Columbus, Christopher, 18, 19, 357

Comprehensive Everglades Restoration Plan (CERP), 371

Compromise of 1877, 273

Computer companies, 518

Cone, Fred P., 313, 316, 322, 326, 328, 423

Confederate Impressment Act (1863), 251

Confederates, 360; in Reconstruction Florida, 261–62, 264, 268, 271

Confederate States of America: Florida in, 242–56, 260, 360, 416–17. *See also* Civil War; Secession

Congress of Industrial Organization (CIO), 319, 326

Conquest by Contract, 77, 89

Conquistadors, 76, 197, 357, 370. *See also* Adelantado; Spanish expeditions

Conservationists: bird protection by, 287; Everglades and, 290, 371–72; Muir, 377–79; projects of CCC, 319, 326

Conservative-Democrats, 271–73, 283

Constitution, U.S.: Fourteenth Amendment, 264; Eighteenth Amendment, 292; Nineteenth Amendment, 296; Twenty-First Amendment, 316

Constitutional Union Party, 241

Constitutions, Florida, 262, 264; of 1868, 266, 283; of 1885, 273–74, 283–84; of 1968, 427

Construction, 515; architecture design in, 361–62; Castillo de San Marcos, 87, 114, 115; hurricanes and coastal, 360–62; nature and, 360–62, 374; railroad, 239–40, 270–71, 276, 279–82, 285, 288, 300, 505; Tamiami Trail, 508. See also Development

Convict-leasing, 286, 382–83

Coolidge, Calvin, 297

Coosa, Georgia, 32, 35, 37

Coosa Indians, 37

Coppinger, José María, 175, 176

Coppinger, Polly, 206

Coral Gables, 299

Cornejo, Francisco de, 135–36

Cornwallis, Charles, 157

Corporations, 282, 287

Corsairs. See Pirates

Cortés, Hernán, 22, 24, 181

Cotton: plantations, 45, 186, 233; production, 44, 168, 225, 233–34, 238, 239, 261, 276, 381; slavery and, 186, 225, 238, 239

Cove of the Withlacoochee, 206, 208, 210

Cowkeeper (Creek/Seminole chief), 147, 199–202, 206

Crackers, 50, 149, 232, 233, 329, 454; architecture, 361, 362; cowboys (cowmen), 367

Craig, John A., 225, 232

Creek Indians, 124, 125, 126, 152–54, 167; conflicts, 105, 106, 115, 118, 119, 170, 172, 197–98, 200, 204, 208, 209, 220, 228; Cow Creek Seminole, 214, 215; Cowkeeper (chief), 147, 199–202, 206; Creek War, 170, 172, 209, 220, 228; "Emperor" Brim, 197, 200; Florida colonization (1716–1767), 199–200; Green Corn Dance, 196, 215; Long Warrior, 147; Lower Creeks, 88, 113, 198, 200; overview and origins, 195–99; Payne (chief), 202, 203, 206; period of enterprise (1767–1817), 201–3; pottery of, 200; Red Stick Creeks, 203, 206; Seminole Indians and, 147, 152, 154, 195–202, 204, 206, 208–10, 213–16, 229; settlements, 199–202. See also Seminole Indians

Crestview, 349

Crime, 522

Crist, Charles "Charlie" Joseph, Jr., 439–40

Crosby, Alfred, 362

Cross State Barge Canal, 504

Cuba: British and, 126, 141, 144; cigar manufacturing and, 285, 475, 476; early map, 20; exchange of La Florida for, 126, 141, 142, 144, 146; Havana, 22, 27, 28, 33, 35–38, 44, 56, 61, 63, 80, 83, 85, 87, 109, 118, 119, 125, 126, 141, 479; independence (1868), 285, 479; rebels, 288; Spanish, 62, 63, 73, 80, 83, 85, 87, 100, 104, 107, 109, 118, 119, 122, 123, 125, 126, 141, 144, 146, 176, 192, 202, 288; Spanish-American War, 288–89, 479; Spanish expeditions and, 18, 19, 23, 27, 28, 35, 37, 38, 61; Ten Years War, 475; trade, 85, 168, 202

Cuban Adjustment Act (1966), 485

Cuban Americans, 288; Florida politics and, 431, 433

Cuban Revolution (1933), 479

Cuban Revolution (1959), 481–82

Cubans: exiles, 479, 480, 482–87, 485, 489, 520; immigrants, 475–76, 479–89, 485, 493, 520, 521; Mariel boatlift, 435, 483, 485, 521. See also Hispanics

Culture: nature and, 384; postwar Florida and, 513. See also Precolumbian cultures

Cushing, Frank Hamilton, 355–57

CWA. See Civil Works Administration

Cypress trees, 379–81

Dade County: hurricane damage, 305; precolumbian, 14

Dania (Danish settlement), 474

Darling, John, 242

Dauphin (Massacre) Island, 130, 135, 139, 171

Davis, D. P. "Doc," 299

Davis, Edward D., 459

Davis, Jefferson, 212, 245

Davis, Mike, 374, 375, 377

Daytona, 373

DDT, 339

Deagan, Kathleen, 186

DeBary, Frederick, 270

DeLand, Henry, 276

Democrats, 236, 277, 283, 288, 416, 421; blacks and, 448–49, 462; Conservative-Democrats, 271–73, 283; in Great Depression, 315–17, 319, 320; Jacksonian Democratic Party, 235; in 1920s, 296–98, 426; one-party state period, 415, 418; progressive, 419; Reconstruction and, 268, 271–74, 282, 296; religion and, 291–92; slavery, secession and, 236–37,

240–42; whites as, 282, 296. *See also* Florida politics

Demographics: Florida population, 470, 481, 482, 488–93, 499–502; immigration, 481, 482, 488–93; migration changes to, 500–501

Denham, James M., 232

Depression: in 1890s, 288. *See also* Great Depression

Deptford precolumbian culture, 9

De Soto, Hernando: engraving of, *27*; La Florida and, 12, 26–37, 42, 44, 53n5, 181–82, 223; map of route through La Florida, *30*; Native Americans and, 28–34, 101; Spanish expeditions of, 12, 26–37, 42, 44, 53n5, 181–82

Developers: early (1877–1918), 276–94; railroad, 276, 279–82, 285, 287, 288, 289, 293, 505. *See also* Industry

Development: aviation transportation (1920s), 302; climate and, 365, 511–12; colleges' early, 290–91; ecology and, 503–4, 522; education's early, 290–91; environmental impact of, 522; Florida politics and, 419–21; hotel, 279–82; industry, 516–18; land, 277–79, 282, 283, 285, 289–90, 299–306, 365, 368–71, 417, 419, 524; Miami, 281, 364; modern Florida, 497–526; New Deal, 320–29; during 1920s, 299–306; Palm Beach, 281, 299; Panhandle early, 282; retirees and, 514–15; road, 291–93, 300, 302, 423, 506–9; Seminole Indians and modern tribalism, 215–19; Tampa early, 279, 280, 285, 505; technology, 505–12, 518; tourism and, 280–81, 512–15; transportation, 505–11; water and, 289–90, 365, 368–74; wetlands draining and, 289–90, 365, 368, 370–71; during World War II, 336, 338, 345, 348–49, 423, 515–16. *See also* Construction

Dickel, David, 5

Dickison, J. J., 268

Disease: influenza pandemic (1918), 293; La Florida and, 86, 112; La Florida missions and, 100, 105–7, 110, 112; Native Americans and, 16, 18, 83, 86, 100, 105–7, 110, 112, 119–20, 147, 197, 357; yellow fever, 287, 289

Disney, 373, 426, 516

Disney World, 513–14, 516

Disston, Hamilton, 278–79, 283, 370

Divorce law, 282

Dixie Highway, 292

Dobyns, Henry, 100, 101

Doctrinas (mission centers), 80, 83, 85, 88, 95, 98. *See also* Spanish missions

Dominican friars, 24, 34, 37

Donation Act (1824), 366

Doran, Glen, 5

Doughy, H. R., 304

Douglas, Marjory Stoneman, *504*

Douglas, Stephen, 240–41

Downing, Charles, 224

Dredges, 278, *278*, 282, 288, 289, 374

Drew, George F., 272, 273, 277

Dunn, Marvin, 462

DuPont, Alfred I., 314, 325

Durnford, Elias, 148, 155

Duval, William P., 222, *223*, 224, 228, 229, 366

Duval County, 222, 225–26, 233–34, 238, 241, 242; African Americans in, 446

Duvalier, Francois "Papa Doc," 484

Dyke, Charles E., 266

East Florida: British, 144, *145*, 147–50, 153–59, 162, 187; Florida Territory, 220, 222, 224–28, 232, 235, 237, 238; Spanish, 162–68, 173–76, 220, 222

Ecology: African settlers and, 41, 47, 52; agriculture and, 44, 48, 53n5; barrier islands, 47, 53n8, 376–79; of Calusa Indians, 354–55; central ridge, 45; climate and, 49–52; coastal, 42–45, 373–79; colonial settlements and, 42; development impact on, 503–4, 522; of earlier geologic age, 353–54; early 19th-century period and, 42; European settlements and, 41, 47–51, 52; Florida, 353–84; of Georgia, 42, 43, 45, 47–51; inhabitants reactions to, 41; La Florida, 41–44, 48; Native American settlements and, 41, 47–50, 52, 368; overview, 41–52, 353–54; peninsular Florida, 41, 44–45, *46*, 47–52; piedmont, 43, 44; population growth and, 503; rivers, 48–49; settlements and, 48, 368–70; soil, 41, 43–45, *46*, 47, 52n3; southern uplands, 45; Spanish settlements and, 44, 358, 362–64; tropical storms, 51–52. *See also* Climate

Economy: diversity of Florida, 417–18; Great Recession, 524–25; new, 517–18; service, 518; World War II boom, 336, 338. *See also* Development; Industry

Edge cities, 509

Education: blacks and, 290, 308–9, 321–23, 446–48, 451–53, 460–61, 463; early development of, 290–91; during Great Depression, 321–23; New Deal for, 322–23; race and, 290, 308–9, 321–23; segregation, 308–9, 463; teaching evolution, 298; women's, 290, 309, 323, 341, *342*. *See also* Schools
Eighteenth Amendment, 292
Elderly: migration of, 354, 501–2; retirees and aging of Florida, 501–2
El Niño-La Niña Southern Oscillation (ENSO), 51–52, 53n14
Emancipation: slavery, 242; women's, 346
Emerson, Ralph Waldo, 354
English. *See* British
Environment: DDT and, 339; development impact on, 522; exploitation and damage to, 384, 522; legislation (1970s), 371; lumber industry and destruction of, 379, 380, 381; under New Deal, 326; turpentine production and destruction of, 383. *See also* Climate; Conservationists; Ecology; Nature
Environmentalists, *504*; white, 383
Escambia County, 461
Espinosa families, 122, 124
Ethnicity: Florida history of immigration and, 470–94, 520–22. *See also* Race
European expeditions: maritime heritage of, 391–95; Native Americans and, 18–38, 197. *See also* French; Spanish expeditions
European settlements, 1; agriculture of, 48; ecology and, 41, 47–51, 52; first, 24; inhabitants' surnames, *68*; maritime heritage of, 391–95; Native Americans and, 7, 9, 16, 51, 53n11; nature and, 362, 368; near rivers, 49. *See also* British settlements; French settlements; Spanish settlements
Everglades, 14, 47, 49, 287; Army Corps of Engineers project, 371; CERP, 371; conservationists and, 290, 371–72; draining for settlements, 289–90, 370–71; environmentalist, *504*; hurricane (1928) impact on, 371; New Deal programs for, 324; Seminole Indians and, 201, 214, 216, 217, 367. *See also* Wetlands
Everglades National Park, 216, 217
Everglades: River of Grass, The (Douglas), 504
Evolution, teaching, 298
Extremadura, 67, 68

Faber, Eberhard, 378
Farmers, *507*; Farmers Alliance, 288; Grange, 287–88; in Great Depression, 325. *See also* Agriculture
Farmers Alliance, 288
Farrey, John J., 361
FDIC. *See* Federal Deposit Insurance Corporation
FECR. *See* Florida East Coast Railway
Federal Deposit Insurance Corporation (FDIC), 318, 320
Federal Emergency Relief Administration (FERA), 318, 320, 324, 326
Federal Theatre Project, 319, 326
Federal Writers' Project, 319, 326
Felipe II, 35, 38, 55
FERA. *See* Federal Emergency Relief Administration
Fernando II, 19
Fernando VII, 170, 176
Finegan, Joseph, 261
Finnish immigrants, 493
Fisher, Carl G., 299
Fishing: Gulf of Mexico, 374, 375, 379; industry, 285, 325, 374, 379, 398, 405–6; mullet, 375–76, 378; precolumbian, 356, 374–75; recreational, 515; trade and, 374–75; vessels, 405–6. *See also* Marine life
Flagler, Henry M., 279–82, 327, 372, 505
Fleming, Francis P., 287
Fletcher, Duncan U., 296, 297, 308, 316
Floods, 371
Flora. *See* Plants
Florida: dream, 525–26; as independent country, 245; maps, *198*
Florida East Coast Railway (FECR), 474, 476
Florida Forest Service, 324
Florida Keys, 358
Floridan Aquifer, 369, 370
Floridanos, 78, 84–87, 112, 126
Florida politics: civil rights and, 425–27; constitution and legislative shake-up (1968–1969), 427; Cuban Americans and, 431, 433; development in, 419–21; divisions and issues (1960s–2010s), 435–41; early twentieth century, 419–21; in 1800s, 416–17; Florida's unique attributes and, 417–18; future change, 441; governors (1960s–2010s), 435–41; Great Depression and, 313–29,

422–23; Hispanics and, 431–32; history of, 415–41; House partisan makeup from Florida (1980–2010), *429*; imported politics, 427, *428*; minorities in, 428, *430*, 431–32; north, 418; one-party Democratic state period of, 418; overview, 415–16; political battleground in, 415–16; population growth (1960s–2010s) impact on, 435–41; race and, 419–21, 424–28, *430*, 448–49; Republican's growing strength (1960s), 432–35; segregation in, 419, 421, 424–27; two-party state development, 427–28, *429*, *430*; World War II and, 423–24. *See also* Constitutions, Florida; Governors, Florida; Legislature, Florida; Politics

Florida Possession (1812) and Territory (1822–1845): banks, 234–36; capital, 222; constitution (1839), 236; East Florida, 220, 222, 224–28, 232, 235, 237, 238; free blacks in, 192, 237; Jackson as governor of, 220–22, 224, 228–30; land transactions, 228, 234–35; maritime heritage of statehood and, 397–99; Middle Florida, 225, 228, 231, 232, 234, 238; "Nucleus" elites, 222, 234, 235–36; overview, 220–38; Pensacola in, 220–22, 224, 225, 228, 234, 238; Seminole Indians and, 206–12, 227–32, 235; Seminole Wars and, 202, 203, 206–12, 230; settlements, 231–34; slavery in, 225–29, 231–38; St. Augustine in, 220, 222, 226–29, 234, 237–38; Tallahassee in, 223–24, 227, 228, 234, 238; trade, 398; West Florida, 220, 222, 225, 228, 231

Florida state: modern challenges, 525–26; statehood (1845), 224, 235, 236–42, 498, 499. *See also* Modern Florida; *specific Florida state topics*

Florida State College for Women, 290, 309, 323, 341, *342*, 349

Florida State Teachers Association, 461

Florida State University, 5, 290, 349

Florida Straits, 358

Florida Supreme Court, 431, 453, 460, 463, 465, 466

Fontaneda, Hernando d'Escalante, 61, 359

Forbes, James Grant, 228

Forbes, John, 166–69, 228

Fort Caroline, 56, *57*, 59–60. *See also* San Mateo

Fort Center site (Glades County), 14, *15*

Fort Diego, 121, *122*, 123

Fort Lauderdale, 347

Fort Mose, 122–23, *187*, 202

Fort Myers, 361

Fort Myers–Fort Pierce Inlet line, 47, 48

Fort Pickens, 246, 360

Fort Pierce, 231, 232, 334

Fort San Carlos de Austria, *130*, 130–31, 134, 135

Fort San Carlos de Barrancas, 171, 172

Fort San Miguel, 138–39, *146*

Fort Santa Lucía, 61

Fort Scott, 204

Fort St. Mark, 146, 148. *See also* Castillo de San Marcos

Fort Sumter, 246, 360

Fort Walton precolumbian culture, 11, 12

Foster, John, 262, 263, 264

Foster, Stephen, 501

Fountain of Youth, 19, 363, 370

Fountains, 369

Fourteenth Amendment, 264

France: Atlantic policy, 55; French and Indian War, 125–26, 139, 141, 144; internal conflicts, 55; La Florida and, 35, 38, 43, 55, 359–60; land sales to U.S., 169; U.S. and, 169

Franciscan missionaries, 86, 105, 109, 114, 124, 133, 166; mission names and locations, *97*, *99*; Native Americans and, 78, 80, 84, 102, 103; overview, 91, 93–96, 98, 100, 107–8; rations, 85

Franck, Jaime, 130, 131

Frank, Neil, 359

Franklin County, 320

Free blacks: in British Florida, 186–87; in Florida state, 238–40; in Florida Territory, 192, 237; Haiti government of, 191, 238; Seminole and, 192; slavery and, 239; in Spanish Florida, 122–24, 183, 189–92; women, 190. *See also* Africans; Freedmen

Freedmen: Reconstruction and, 260–64, 266, 268, 271; Spanish Florida and, 184, 186

Freedmen's Bureau, 260, 261, 263, 268

Freezes: citrus industry and, 281, 364, 365, 450, 522; Great Freeze (1894–1895), 281, 364, 365, 450

French: conflicts with British, 110, 115, 125–26, 132, 133, 139, 141–42, 144, 157, 158; conflicts with Spanish, 55, 58–61, 64, 96, 110, 114–15, 130–36, 142, 169, 170, 173, 176, 191, 359–60, 372; Native American conflicts with, 197–98; pirates, 35, 82, 183; Protestants, 63

French and Indian War, 125–26, 139, 141, 144

French expeditions, 114–15; Native Americans and, 56; to New France, 55–57; to Pensacola Bay, 115, 129–32

French settlements: Fort Caroline, 56, 57, 59–60; Louisiana, 115, 132–33, 140, 141, 142, 169; in Mobile, 108, 118, 130, 133–37, 146; Native Americans and, 56, 64, 81, 108, 115, 118–19, 125, 132, 140, 197–98; in Pensacola Bay, 130, 132–35; Spanish settlements and, 55–61, 115, 128–37, 140, 141–42, 359–60; trade, 115, 132, 134, 137, 140

Freshwater, 48; Floridan Aquifer, 369, 370; settlements near, 368–69, 372; springs or fountains, 369, 370

Freshwater Timucua Indians, 94–95, 100–101

Friars, 94. See also Franciscan missionaries

Frontier, 498

Fuller, Walter, 306

Fundamentalists, 298–99

Gadsden, James, 225, 229, 230

Gaines, Edmund Pendleton, 204, 206–7, 366

Gainesville, 4, 29, 96, 101; African American family portrait, 445

Gálvez, Bernardo de, 155–56, 157

Gamble, Robert, 225, 231, 232, 266

Gambling, 299, 314

Gandy, George S., 299

Gárrido, Juan, 180, 181

Garvey, Marvin, 479

Gayoso de Lemos, Manuel, 165

Geography: areas, 103–4; of Florida, 58, 103–4, 323, 364–66, 389, 411, 417, 418, 504–5; history of citrus, 364–65

George III, 148, 151, 156, 187

Georges Valentine (ship), 407

Georgia, 13, 24, 172, 340; British East Florida and, 154, 156; as British settlement, 117, 120–26, 187, 197; coast, 43, 61, 96, 98, 100, 105, 112, 114; ecology of, 42, 43, 45, 47–51; La Florida and, 31–32, 35, 81, 82, 92, 98, 100, 102, 103, 105, 112, 114, 117, 120–26, 173; missions, 103, 105; Patriot War, 173–74, 188, 191; Santa Elena settlement, 35, 37–38, 53n11, 62, 65, 66, 69, 70, 72, 73, 78; as U.S. state, 190, 191, 202–5

Germans: prisoners of war, 335–36, 344; World War II attacks off Florida coast, 335, 337, 341

Gibbs, Jonathan C., 266, 267

Gilchrist, Albert, 290

Gilmore, Quincy A., 255

Glades County, 14

Gleason, William H., 265, 266, 268

Gold Coast, 14, 347, 428

González [Ponce] de León, Juan, 19, 180

Good Roads Movement, 506

Gore, Al, 434

Gorrie, John, 511

Governors, Florida: overview (1960s to 1970s), 435–41. See also Florida politics; specific governors

Governor Stone (coastal schooner), 408, 409

Gracia Real de Santa Teresa de Mose. See Mose

Graham, Daniel Robert "Bob," 437, 465

Grange, 287–88

Grant, James, 148–53, 149, 155, 158, 159, 269

Grant, Ulysses S., 256, 263–64, 270

Great Depression (1929), 307–8; agriculture in, 319, 323–26; aviation during, 328; banks in, 313, 317–18; colleges during, 323; Democrats in, 315–17, 319, 320; education during, 321–23; farmers, 325; Florida politics in, 313–29, 422–23; New Deal, 313, 315, 316, 318–21, 325–27, 329, 336, 460–61; overview, 313–30; Republicans in, 315–17, 319; Seminole Indians and, 321, 322; tourism, 328; World War II and, 329, 336

Great Recession, 524–25

Greeks: immigration, 376, 475; sponge divers, 376, 475

Green Corn Dance (busk), 196, 203, 215, 218

Griffin, Noah, 461

Growth Management Act (1985), 437

Grunwald, Michael, 525

Guale Indians, 88; La Florida missions and, 94–96, 98, 100, 103, 105–7, 112, 114; revolts of, 82, 95–96, 98, 180

Guale province, 70, 82, 88, 94

Guale Uprising (1597), 82, 95–96, 98

Guardians of Liberty, 292

Guatari, 65

Guggenheim, Harry, 480

Gulf coast, 144; Big Bend, 377, 380; ecology of, 373–79; precolumbian, 9, 10, 11, 13; sponges, 285, 376

Gulf of Mexico, 144; BP oil spill, 439–40; fishing, 374, 375, 379; working waterfronts, 374

Gulf Stream (Florida Current), 21, 358, 364
Gunther, John, 349

Haiti: "boat people," 521; exiled immigrants, 484–88, 493, 521; free black government, 191, 238; Saint-Domingue slave revolt, 191
Half Moon (racing yacht), 408, *410*
Hann, John, 119
Hardee, Cary A., 296–97, 315, 421
Harlem Renaissance, 455, 456
Harrison, William Henry, 224
Hart, Hubbard, 268, 270
Hart, Isaiah David, 227
Hart, Ossian B., 264, 271
Hastings, Thomas, 280
Hatchett, Joseph, 431, 465, *466*
Havana. *See* Cuba
Hawkins, Virgil, 463
Hayes, Rutherford, 272, 273
Health: county departments of, 321; State Board of Public Health, 287, 321
Hedges, John, 144, 146
Hernández, Joseph M., 224
Herrera y Tordesillas, Antonio de, 19, 20, 21
Hillsborough County settlement, 232
Hiroshima, 348
Hispanics, *491*; blacks and, 520; Civil War and, 253; Florida politics and, 431–32; immigrants, 481, 483, 488–90, 493, 521. *See also* Cubans
Hispaniola, 180, 181, 183, 191
Hoffman, Paul E., 180
Holata Micco (Billy Bowlegs) (Seminole chief), 209, 210, 212–14
Holland, Spessard L, 317, 339, 423
Hoover, Herbert, 297, 307, 314–15
Hoovervilles, 315
Hopkins, Edward, 241
Hotel Alcazar, 280
Hotel Ponce de Leon, 280, *281*
Hotels: early development of, 279–82, 513; Miami Beach, 513, *514*; World War II training in, 333–34
Houses of refuge, 406–7; Gilbert's Bar, *407*
Housing, 523–25; mobile homes, 515. *See also* Architecture
"Hundred Days" session (1933), 318
Hunter-gatherers, 3–16, 389–90
Hunting, recreational, 515

Hurricanes, 51, 378, 379; coastal construction and, 360–62; Dade County damage, *305*; modern Florida, 523; 1926, 303, 305, 361; 1928, 306, 371; 1935, 327; 1947, 371; overview, 359; Spanish expeditions and, 359–60; Spanish settlements and, 36, 83, 138, 140, 359–61
Hurston, Zora Neale, 310, 381, 382, 450, 455, *456*

Iberia, 30
Iberian New World, 66
Iberian peninsula, 66
D'Iberville, Sieur. *See* Le Moyne d'Iberville, Pierre
Ickes, Harold L., 318
Immigration: agriculture and, 473–75; Asian, 470, 488, 491–93; Bahamian, 476–79, *478*, *480*, 493; blacks and, 472–73, 476–79, 500; Cuban, 475–76, 479–89, *485*, 493, 520, 521; debates and controversy over, 494; demographics, 481, 482, 488–93; Florida history of ethnicity and, 470–94, 520–22; foreign, 472–73; Haiti exiles, 484–88, 493, 521; Hispanic, 481, 483, 488–90, 493, 521; Italian, 471–73, 475–76, 479–81; Latin, 475, 479, 480, 489–90; need after Civil War, 472; Nicaraguan exiles, 486–88, 490, 493; population and, 471, 472, 481–82, 488–93; race and, 473, 522; racial discrimination and, 479; railroads and, 474–75; settlements, 471, 473–75; World War II temporary, 340. *See also* Migration
Immigration and Naturalization Service, U.S. (INS), 485
Independent Order of Odd Fellows, 452, 458, 459
Independents, 282–83, 287
Indian Claims Commission, 217
Indian Removal Law (1830), 228
Indian River, 71, 231, 232, 287
Indians. *See* Native Americans
Industry: cattle (1920s), 307–8, 450; development, 516–18; fishing, 285, 325, 374, 379, 398, 405–6; motel, 302; phosphate, 284; pulp paper, 324–25; salvaging, 358–59, 398; World War II shipbuilding, 336, 338. *See also* Development; *specific industries*
Influenza pandemic (1918), 293
Innerarity, James, 170
INS. *See* Immigration and Naturalization Service, U.S.

Iowa, 236
Italian immigration, 471–73, 475–76, 481

Jacan Indians, 71
Jackson, Andrew, 235; in Creek War, 170, 220, 228; engraving, *171*; as Florida Territory governor, 220–22, 224, 228–30; Native Americans and, 171, 172, 192, 204–5, 207, 230; as president, 228; Spanish Florida and, 171, 172, 176, 220; in War of 1812, 170, 171
Jackson, David H., Jr., 454
Jackson County, 222, 225
Jacksonian Democratic Party, 235
Jacksonville, 8, 154, 171, 173, 227, 233, 234, 287, 293, 368, 406; African Americans, 446–49, 451–55, 457, 458, 464, 467; during Civil War, 255, 256; fire destruction (1901), 285; during Reconstruction, 268; during World War II, 333, 334, 335, 338, 340, 343, 347
Jacksonville Naval Air Station, 293
Jamaica, 86, 113, 156, 158, 340, 492
James, Daniel "Chappie," *432*
James, Henry, 368
Japanese colony, *474*, 475
Jefferson, Thomas, 190, 225
Jefferson County, 225, 236, 238
Jennings, William S., 289
Jesuit missionaries, 63–65, 71, 93–95
Jesup, Thomas S., 208, 209
Jewish immigrants, 493
Jim Crow discrimination, 309, 453, 454, 464
John Gorrie Bridge, 320
Johns, Charlie, 464
Johnson, Andrew, 260–64
Johnson, Cassandra Y., 383
Johnson, Elisha, 271
Johnson, James Weldon, 310, 455, 458
Johnstone, George, 148–49, *149*, 152, 153
Jones, B. Calvin, 32
Jones, Maxine D., 451
Jones, Sam. *See* Arpeika
Jordán de Reina, Juan, 128–30
Jororo Indians, 103, 106
Juan Ponce. *See* Ponce de León, Juan

Keith, Richard, 245
Kelly, Colin Purdie, Jr., 332
Key, V. O., Jr., 418
Key Biscayne, 21

Key Marco site, 14
Key West, 21, 285, 293, 326–27, 358, 376; immigration, 475–77, 479, 480; during World War II, 340–41
King, Martin Luther, Jr., 464
Kingsley, Zephaniah, 189, 226, 238
Kirk, Claude Roy, Jr., 436, 465–66
Kissimmee (town), 278
Kissimmee River, 14, 278
Knott, William V., 291, 292
Knotts, Armonis F., 315
Ku Klux Klan, 462; violence, 268, 309, 453, 459–60, 463, 519

Labor: agriculture, 325, 338–40, 345, *478*, *480*; blacks and, 382–83, 455, *457*; child, 291; convict-leasing, 286, 382–83; disputes, 294; lumber industry exploitation of, 285, 326, 382–83; migrant, 325, 476; New Deal for, 319, 325; strikes, 294, 303; unions, 310, 319, 455, 457; during World War I, 293, 294; during World War II, 339–40, 345
Labor levy. *See* Repartimientos
La Florida: British and, 107, 110, 113, 156, 158–59, 164, 170; climate of, 113; decline of, 112; de Soto and, 12, 26–37, 42, 44, 53n5, 181–82, 223; discovery by Spanish, 1, 20–21, 73; disease and, 86, 112; ecology, 41–44, 48; exchange of Cuba for, 126, 141, 142, 144, 146; France and, 35, 38, 43, 55, 359–60; Georgia and, 31–32, 35, 81, 82, 92, 98, 100, 102, 103, 105, 112, 114, 117, 120–26; map of de Soto route through, *30*; Menéndez de Avilés as adelantado of, 57–73, 91, 93; naming of, 20, 23; Native American pacification in, 77, 81–82, 84, 89; pirates and, 113, 183; Ponce de León and, 1, 18–23, 26, 34, 180, 181, 355, 357, 363, 393; region boundaries, *30*, 41–43; rivers, 48–49; settlement and exploration sites, *62*; situado of, 77, 80, 82, 84–86; society in 16th century, 67, 69–73; soldiers and settlers in, 92; Spanish expeditions in, 1, 20–38, 43, 44, 180–82, 357, 372; states included in, 42; subsidy from Spain, 70–71; threats and defense of, 86–88, 105, 106, 112–26; trade, 42, 49, 70, 85, 86, 88, 124–26, 132, 134, 137, 140, 141, 166–68, 174, 202, 205, 397; transition from adelantado to royal colony, 76–78. *See also* Spanish Florida; Spanish settlements

La Florida mission provinces, 77, 80–81, 84, 96, 98; listing and statistics on, 103–4

La Florida missions, 42, 49; disease and, 100, 105–7, 110, 112; doctrinas, 80, 83, 85, 88, 95, 98; Jesuit missionaries, 63–65, 71, 93–95; La Florida situado and, 77, 80; listing and statistics on, 103–4; loss of, 83, 105, 118, 119; Menéndez de Avilés and, 93; mission church, 102; Native Americans and, 63–65, 71, 76–78, 80, 82–84, 89, 91–110, 112–14, 118–20, 122, 124–26, 129, 197; Native American settlements and, 98, 107–9; other Spanish missions compared to, 93, 98; overview, 91–110; Pensacola, 106, 133–34; Spanish presidios and, 77, 87; St. Augustine and, 80, 86–88, 95, 97, 98, 105–7. See also Franciscan missionaries; Spanish missions

La Florida revolts, 102, 103, 124; Apalachee Rebellion (1647), 86; of Guale Indians, 82, 95–96, 98, 180; overview, 82–83; of Timucua Indians, 82–83, 86, 113

LaGuardia, Fiorello, 310n1

Lake Jackson Mounds, 11, 12

Lake Mayaimi, 13

Lake Monroe, 270, 276

Lake Okeechobee, 13, 15, 214, 278, 289, 306, 324, 371

Land: auction (1920s), 301; boom and bust (1920s), 299–306, 328, 524; citrus industry and, 365; development, 277–79, 282, 283, 285, 289–90, 299–306, 365, 368–71, 417, 419, 524; Indian reservations, 199, 205, 206, 211, 212, 214–18, 228–32, 366, 367; Louisiana Purchase, 169; under New Deal, 326; real estate, 364, 365; sales from France to U.S., 169; transactions in Florida Territory, 228, 234–35; transfers between Native Americans and U.S., 168, 216–17, 227–33; transfers between Spanish Florida and U.S., 168–72, 176, 187, 192, 202, 205, 220, 224, 227–28; transfers during Reconstruction, 261. See also Agriculture; Soil; Wetlands

Landon, Alfred M., 316

Lanier, Sidney, 369, 370

La Salle, Sieur de, 128

Latino. See Hispanics

Latins, 475, 479, 480, 489–90; Latinization of Florida, 521. See also Cubans; Italian immigration; Spanish

Laudonnière, René de, 56, 57, 59

Law: divorce, 282; Florida Supreme Court, 431, 453, 460, 463, 465, 466; New Deal, 318; racial discrimination lawsuits, 461, 463; U.S. Supreme Court, 309, 345, 425, 426, 460, 462, 463, 465. See also specific laws

Lee, John M., 315, 318

Lee, Robert E., 247, 256

Legislative Reorganization Act (1969), 427

Legislature, Florida: House partisan makeup (1980–2010), 430; minority membership (1966–2010), 430; minority pathbreakers, 431–32; Senate partisan makeup (1980–2010), 429; shake-up (1968–1969), 427; women's membership (1929–2010), 430. See also Florida politics

Le Maire, François, 133–34

Le Moyne d'Iberville, Pierre, 115, 129

Levy, Moses Elias, 227

Lightning strikes, 50, 368

Lincoln, Abraham, 241, 244–46, 255, 260, 261, 268, 360

Little Haiti, 486, 487

Little Havana, 480, 483, 484, 488, 490

Little Ice Age (LIA), 53n14

Long, Ellen Call, 272

Longleaf pine trees, 381, 383

Long Warrior (Creek Indian), 147

Loomis, Gustavus, 214

Louisiana: as French settlement, 115, 132–33, 140, 141, 142, 169; as Spanish settlement, 141, 142, 156; as U.S. state, 169

Louisiana Purchase, 169

Lovel, Leo, 367, 375, 383–84

Lumber industry, 234, 285, 324–26, 398; cedar and pencil manufacturing, 378–79; cypress and, 379–81; environmental destruction of, 379, 380, 381; labor exploitation by, 285, 326, 382–83; pine, 378–82; shipping, 403

Luna y Arellano, Tristán de, 35–38, 128, 360, 393, 394

Lyman, Phineas, 151–52, 155

Lyman, Thaddeus, 155

Lynchings, 309, 420–21, 453–54, 459, 519

Lyon, Eugene, 44, 92, 95

Mabila natives, 32

MacGregor, Gregor, 176

MacKay, Buddy, 438

Macomb, Alexander, 209–10, 211
Madison, James, 174
Madoff, Bernie, 524
Mahon, John K., 230
Mallory, Stephen R., 245–46, 291
Manasota precolumbian culture, 11
Manatee River, 232
Manchac, 151, 156, 175
Maple Leaf (Civil War vessel), 401–2
Maps: archaeological sites, *5*; Caribbean, 18–19,
    20; Cuba early, *20*; de Soto route through
    La Florida, *30*; Florida, *198*; Pensacola, *30*,
    131, *142*, *146*; Spanish expeditions, 18–19, *62*;
    Spanish settlements, *62*; St. Augustine, *81*,
    117, *187*
Mariel boatlift, 435, 483, *485*, 521
Marine life: mullet, 375–76, 378; sea turtles, 378;
    sponges, 285, 376, 475. *See also* Fishing
Marion County, 29; precolumbian, 12–13
Maritime Florida. *See specific maritime topics*
Maritime heritage: British Florida, 396–97;
    Civil War, 399–402; European contact and
    colonization, 391–95; Florida Territory and
    statehood, 397–99; maritime archaeology
    and underwater cultural heritage, 412–13;
    modern maritime Florida, 407–11; prehis-
    toric Florida, 389–91; Reconstruction and
    maritime industry, 402–7; Second Spanish
    Period, 396–97; Spanish Florida, 391–97; into
    twenty-first century, 411–12
Maritime industries: maritime heritage of,
    402–7; railroads and, 406; shipping and
    infrastructure, 406. *See also* Fishing; Lumber
    industry
Maroons, 202–3
Márquez Cabrera, Juan, 87
Marshall, Thurgood, 344
Martí, José, 288
Martin, John W., 297, 303, 304, 315, 316
Martínez, Bartolomé, 72–73
Martínez, Pedro, 64
Martinez, Robert "Bob," 431, 437–38
Martyr, Peter, 18–19, 20
Marvin, William, 236, 262
Masonry, 451
Masot, José, 172
Matanzas (place of slaughter), 60–61, 372
Mathews, George, 174
Mayaca Indians, 92, 100, 102–3, 106

Mayo, Nathan, 325
McCall, George A., 366, 379–80
McCall, Willis, 463
McCarty, Dan, 424
McCook, Edward, 260
McDaniel, Josh, 383
McGehee, John C., 241
McGill, S. D., 460, 461
McGillivray, Alexander, 167, 202
McIntosh, John, 191–92, 227
McIntosh, McQueen, 266
McLeod, Ferdinand, 262
McPhee, John, 363
Menéndez, Francisco, 122, 184, 186
Menéndez de Avilés, Pedro, 37, 38, 44, 84;
    as adelantado of La Florida, 57–73, 91, 93;
    engraving of, *60*; La Florida missions and,
    93; Native Americans and, 59, 62–64, 71–72,
    93, 94–95, 357; San Mateo and, 57, 60, 61;
    Spanish settlements and, 57–73, 182, 359–60,
    372, 393–94; St. Augustine and, 59–62, 67,
    69, 70, 73, 182, 394; Timucua Indians and, 59,
    62–64, 72
Menéndez Marqués, Pedro, 61, 71, 72, 87
Menéndez Marqués family, 87
Merrick, George E., 299
Mexican War, 211
México. *See* New Spain
Miami, 459, 462, 466; based television, 513;
    development, 281, 364; immigration, 477–90,
    492–94; Little Haiti, 486, *487*; Little Havana,
    480, 483, *484*, 488, 490; during World War
    II, 334–36, 338, 340, 341, 343, 345–49
Miami Beach, 361; creation of, 299; hotels, 513,
    514; World War II trainees in, *334*
Miami Beach Lions Club, *330*
Miami-Dade County, 481, 483, 484, 487, 488,
    493
Miami Herald, 302
Miami International Airport, 510
Miami News, 302
Micanopy (Seminole chief), 206, 208, 209
Miccosukee Indians, 1, 45, 47, 195, 199, 203, 204,
    214, 217, 218. *See also* Seminole Indians
Middle Florida, 209; Florida Territory, 225, 228,
    231, 232, 234, 238. *See also* Panhandle
Migrants: black, 343; labor of, 325, 476; World
    War II, 340
Migration: of blacks within Florida and U.S.,

343, 419–21, 454–56, 500; booming and great migrations, 343, 419–21, 454–56, 475, 500, 513, 523–24; Canadian winter, 503; demographic changes from, 500–501; of elderly, 354, 501–2; historical overview of Florida, 502–3; 1920s, 300–301; social change and, 503. *See also* Immigration

Mikasuki Indians, 204, 214, 253

Military: spending, 516; World War II installations, 333–35, 349

Milton, John, 241, 246–47, 256, 260

Minorities: in Florida politics, 428, *430*, 431–32; political pathbreakers, 431–32. *See also* Race

Miranda, Catalina Menéndez de, 71, 72

Miranda, Hernando de, 71, 72

Missionaries: Jesuit, 63–65, 71, 93–95; Seminole Indians and, 216. *See also* Franciscan missionaries

Mission provinces. *See* La Florida mission provinces

Missions. *See* Spanish missions

Mississippi River, 33, 144, 151, 155, 156, 169

Mitchell, David, 191

Mizner, Addison, 299, 362

Mobile, 156, 157, 169–72; French settlement in, 108, 118, 130, 133–37, 146, 163

Mobile Bay, 133, 135

Mobile homes, 515

Mocama Indians, 56, 62, 95, 96, 105, 106

Modern Florida: challenges, 525–26; social history and development of, 497–526

Monkey Laws, 298

Monroe, James, 191, 192, 205, 220, 221

Monroe, John, 213

Monroe County, 216; precolumbian, 14

Montesinos, Antonio de, 24, 34

Montiano, Manuel de, 122–24, 187

Moore, Harry T., 424, 461, 462, 463

Moore, James, 105, 115, 116, 118, 125

Morehouse, Ward, 333

Mormino, Gary, 372

Morton, Jackson, 236, 241

Mose, 122, 184, *187*

Moseley, William D., 236

Motel industry, 302

Moultrie, John, 153, 154, 156, 158–59

Mounds: burial, 8, 9; of precolumbian cultures, 8–11, 13–15, 195–96, 356–57, 377

Mowat, Charles, 158

Muir, Helen, 334, 346, 348

Muir, John, 377–79, 381

Mullet, 375–76, 378

Mullin, Michael, 183

Murphy Act (1937), 328

Mustin, Henry C., 294

Mutinies, 24, 37, 56, 61, 69

NAACP. *See* National Association for the Advancement of Colored People

Narváez, Pánfilo de, 24–28, 181

Natchez, 144, 151, 155–57, 163, 165, 169

National Association for the Advancement of Colored People (NAACP), 310, 344, 458; civil rights and, 463–64; Florida State Conference of Branches, 461–62

National Labor Relations Act (NLRA), 319

National Recovery Administration (NRA), 319

National Social Security Act (1935), 319, 321

National Youth Association (NYA), 319, 323

Native Americans, 363; Africans and, 172, 174, 179–82, 184, 187, *188*, 190, 192, 202–4; African slaves and, 24, 204, 205; agriculture of, 48, 109–10; British Florida and, 200–201; British settlements and, 105, 106, 110, 114, 118–22, 133, 137, 138, 141, 147, 152–54, 171, 197–99; burials of, 108; caciques and cacicas, 61, 64, 65, 77, 80, 81, 86; Civil War and, 253; conflicts with British, 110, 114, 119–20, 122, 125–26, 139, 141, 144, 197–98; conflicts with U.S., 171, 172, 174–76, 188, 192, 202–15, 220, 366–67; conflict with Spanish, 64–65, 71–72, 77, 82–86, 88, 95–96, 105–6, 113, 114, 118–19, 124–26, 133, 135, 137–40, 191, 197–98, 200, 355, 357, 359, 372; Conquest by Contract, 77, 89; de Soto and, 28–34, 101; disease and, 16, 18, 83, 86, 100, 105–7, 110, 112, 119–20, 147, 197, 357; European expeditions and, 18–38, 197; European settlements and, 7, 9, 16, 51, 53n11; French and Indian War, 125–26, 139, 141, 144; French conflicts with, 197–98; French expeditions and, 56; French settlements and, 56, 64, 81, 108, 115, 118–19, 125, 132, 140, 197–98; Jackson and, 171, 172, 192, 204–5, 207, 230; La Florida missions and, 63–65, 71, 76–78, 80, 82–84, 89, 91–110, 112–14, 118–20, 122, 124–26, 129, 197; land transfers, 168, 216–17, 227–32; marriage to Spanish, 78; Menéndez de Avilés and, 59, 62–64, 71–72, 93, 94–95, 357;

Native Americans—*continued*
nature and, 384; New Deal for, 321;
pacification in La Florida, 77, 81–82, 84,
89; Pensacola Bay and, 128, 129, 133, 135,
137–40; precolumbian cultures, 3–16, 195–96;
repartimientos and, 63, 82, 85, 93, 107,
112–13; Republic of Indians, 76, 77, 78, 82, 89;
reservations, 199, 205, 206, 211, 212, 214–18,
228–32, 366, 367, 378; Sabana System, 82;
slaves and British settlements, 110, 114, 118,
197; society of, 108–9; Spanish expeditions
and, 18, 21–26, 28–35, 37, 61, 64, 197, 357,
358, 359, 372; Spanish presidios and, 76–82,
80–82, 85–89; Spanish settlements and, 59,
61–65, 70–72, 167–68, 172, 174, 176, 179, 182,
184, 187, 191, 192, 197–200, 202; tourism and,
373; trade, 114, 115, 132, 140, 167–68, 197,
200–202, 205, 397; tribal conflicts, 21, 114,
138, 140, 212; U.S. and, 168, 171, 172, 174–76,
188, 192, 202–19, 220. *See also* Precolumbian
cultures; *specific Indian topics*
Native American settlements: Creek Indians,
199–202; ecology and, 41, 47–50, 52, 368; La
Florida missions and, 98, 107–9; near rivers,
49; Seminole Indians, 214
Native American uprisings: Yamasee War, 106.
See also La Florida revolts
Nature: aesthetics of, 369–70; architecture design and, 361–62; construction and, 360–62,
374; culture and, 384; detachment from,
512; European settlements and, 362, 368;
exploitation and destruction of, 384; Florida,
353–84; historical agency of, 353; Native
Americans and, 384; precolumbian cultures
and, 354–57; purpose and richness, 379;
Spanish expeditions and, 357–58; tourism
and, 370. *See also* Climate; Conservationists;
Ecology; Environment; Plants; Wilderness;
Wildlife
Neamathla (Seminole chief), 204, 223
Negro Fort, 172, 204
New Deal: agriculture, 319, 323–26; development under, 320–29; education, 322–23; environment under, 326; Everglade programs,
324; Great Depression, 313, 315, 316, 318–21,
325–27, 329, 336, 460–61; labor, 319, 325;
land under, 326; laws, 318; Native American,
321; programs, 318–27, 423; race and, 460–61;
Second, 319

New France (Nouvelle France), 55–57
New Laws of 1542, 30, 34
New Orleans, 137, 144, 149, 155, 170, 172; Battle
of, 171, 220
New Smyrna, 471
New Spain (México), 24, 33, 35, 36, 58, 59, 76,
77, 113, 133; Pensacola and, 128–32, 134, 137,
138, 140
Newton, John, 260
New World, 18; Iberian, 66; shipbuilding,
394–95; Spanish, 19, 26, 30, 64, 91; vessels,
392
Nicaraguan immigrants, 486–88, 490, 493
1920s: agriculture, 307; aviation transportation
development (1920s), 302; banks in, 303–6,
308; blacks in, 308–10, 457; cattle industry,
307–8, 450; Democrats, 296–98, 426;
development during, 299–306; land boom
and bust, 299–306; migration, 300–301;
overview, 296–310; politics, 296–99, 426;
prison reform, 308; race in, 309; religion in,
298–99; Republicans in, 296–97; tourism,
301, 306. *See* Great Depression
Nineteenth Amendment, 296
Nininger, Alexander Ramsey, Jr., 332
NLRA. *See* National Labor Relations Act
Noble, James, 141
Nombre de Dios (mission), 95, 100, 120, 124
North Florida: politics, 418; settlement, 498
Noyan, Chevalier de, 135
NRA. *See* National Recovery Administration
"Nucleus" elites, 222, 234, 235–36
NYA. *See* National Youth Association

Obama, Barack, 467, 509
"Ocala Demands," 288
Ocala Forest, 285
Ocale province, 29
Ochuse, *30*, 35–38. *See also* Pensacola Bay
Ocklawaha River, *269*, 270, 370, 504
Ocoee riots, 459
Odum, Howard, 380–81
Ogilvie, Francis, 146–47
Oglethorpe, James Edward, 117, 120–24, *121*,
186
"Old Folks at Home," 501
Olmos, Alonso de, 69–70, 71
Olustee campaign, 254–55
Onís, Luis de, 172, 176, 220, 224, 228

Operation Drumbeat, 335

Oranges, 363–64; frozen concentrated juice, 338, 366. *See also* Citrus

Orlando, 278, 299, 514

Ormond, 373

Ortíz, Juan, 28

Ortiz Parrilla, Diego, 140–41

Osborn, Thomas W., 265, 268

Osceola (Seminole leader), 206, *207*, 208–9

Otulke Thlocco (Seminole prophet), 208, 209, 210

Pacara Indians, 92, 102

Pacification, 77, 81–82, 84, 89

Paisley, Clifton, 224

Paleoindians (hunter-gatherers), 3–16, 389–90

Palm Beach, 306; development, 281, 299

Palm Beach County, 216

Palmetto Leaves (Stowe), 353

Panhandle, 144; early development, 282; precolumbian cultures, 4, 8, 9, 11. *See also* Middle Florida; Pensacola

Panton, William, 166–69, 189

Panzacola (Pansacola), 128–29, *163*. *See also* Pensacola

Panzacola Indians, 128

Pardo, Juan, 44, 62, 65–66, 84

Parish Registers document, *79*

Passive cooling, 511

Patriot War (1812), 173–74, 188, 191, 192

Payne (Creek chief), 202, 203, 206

Payne, Jesse, 344

Peace River, 284

Pearl Harbor, 332

Pearl River, 128, 169

Peeler, Anderson J., 262

Pelican Island Wildlife Refuge, 287

Pena, Diego, 198

Pencil manufacturing, 378–79

Peninsular Florida, 4, 8, 42; ecology, 41, 44–45, *46*, 47–52; soil types, 52n3

Peninsular War, 169, 170, 176

Pensacola: British settlement in, 132, 141, *142*, 146, 148, 151, 155–57; in Florida state, 239–40, 242; in Florida Territory, 220–22, 224, 225, 228, 234, 238; Fort San Miguel, 138–39, *146*; La Florida missions in, 106, 133–34; maps, *30, 131, 142, 146*; New Spain and, 128–32, 134, 137, 138, 140; overview (1686–1763), 128–42; as Panzacola or Pansacola, 128; precolumbian culture, 11; Spanish presidios, *131*, 132–42, *139*; Spanish settlement in, *30*, 35–38, 115, 128–42, 360, 393, 394; Spanish West Florida, 162, *163*, 164, 165, 167, 169–72, 176; during World War II, 332, 335, 338, 340, 346

Pensacola Bay, *139, 142, 163*; Fort San Carlos de Austria, *130*, 130–31, 134, 135; French expeditions to, 115, 129–32; French settlement in, 130, 132–35; Luna settlement in, 35–38, 128; Native Americans and, 128, 129, 133, 135, 137–40; as Ochuse, *30*, 35–38; overview (1686–1763), 128–31, 133, 135, 136, 139; Spanish expeditions to, 128–29, 393; Spanish presidios of, *131*, 132

Pensacola Naval Air Station, 293

Pepper, Claude, 316, 320, 333, *422*

Perdido River, 43, 133, 169

Perry, Edward A., 273, 283

Perry, Madison S., 241, 244

Petteway, Raleigh W., 316

Pez, Andrés de, 129

Phagan, John, 229

Philip (Calusa chief), 65

Philip II, 44, 56, 57, 59, 71, 76, 78

Philippines, 332, 339

Philip V, 115

Phosphate industry, 284

Piedmont, 42; agriculture, 44, 53n5; ecology, 43, 44; soils, 44

Pineda, Alonzo Alvarez de, 22

Pine trees: longleaf, 381, 383; lumber industry, 378–82; pine sap tapping and turpentine, 285, *286*, 326, 381–83

Pioneers, 224, 232, 276, 279, 281

Pirates: British, 35, 78, 83, 183; French, 35, 82, 183; La Florida and, 113, 183; shipwrecks and, 395; Spanish missions and, 105; Spanish settlements and, 83–85, 88, 183; threats to trade, 35

Piritiriba, 116, 119

Pius V, 69

Plant, Henry Bradley, 279–82, 288, 372, 505

Plantations, cotton, 45, 186, 233

Plants, 368; overview, 354. *See also* Trees

Pleistocene era, 3, 5, 7

Plume birds, 286–87

Politics: anticorporation, 282, 287; blacks and, 267, 273, 283, 284, 431, 448–49, 462, 464–65; in 1920s, 296–99, 426; problems in modern Florida, 522–23; progressive, 288–92; religion and, 291–92, 297; women in, 346; World War II, 333, 345, 346. *See also* Florida politics; *specific political topics*

Poll tax, 284, 296, 317, 449, 462

Ponce de León, Juan, 16, 18, 38n1; as adelantado, 22; Bimini and, 19, 22; Calusa natives and, 22, *23*; La Florida and, 1, 18–23, 26, 34, 180, 181, 355, 357, 363, 393; Spanish expeditions of, 1, 18–23, 26, 34, 180, 181, 355, 357, 358, 363

Ponzi, Charles (Carlo), 524

Pope, Frank, 283

Pope, John, 264

Popham, William Lee, 299–300

Population, Florida: African American, 445–46, 457–58, 472, 500; demographics, 470, 481, 482, 488–93, 499–502; ecology and growth of, 503; growth impact on politics, 427–28, *429*, *430*, 435–41; history of, 497–503; immigration and, 471, 472, 481–82, 488–93; percentages by race, *428*; retirees and aging of, 501–2; shift, 428

Port Royal, 56

Potano Indians, 13, 29, 96, 98, 101, 105

Potter, Marcellus, 459

Potter, Mary Ellen Davis, 459

Pottery: Creek Indian, 200; precolumbian, 7, 9, 11

Powell, William, 206

Pratt and Whitney engineer, *516*

Preble, George Henry, 367

Precolumbian cultures: archaeology of, 3–15, 355–57; Archaic period, 5–8, 11, 13, 390–91; Calusa, 354–57; fishing, 356, 374–75; mounds of, 8–11, 13–15, 195–96, 356–57, 377; nature and, 354–57; overview, 3–16; Paleoindians, 3–7, 389–90. *See also specific precolumbian cultures*

Prehistoric Florida: canoes, *390*; maritime heritage, 389–91. *See also* Precolumbian cultures

Presidential election (2000), 434

Presidios, 76. *See also* Spanish presidios

Prevost, Augustin, 141, 146–47, 155

Prisons: convict-leasing, 286, 382–83; reform (1920s), 308; World War II, 335–36

Proctor, Samuel, 453

Progressives, 288–92, 419, 420, 506

Prohibition, 291, 292, 297, 298, 310n1, 316; coastal alcohol smuggling, 408–9

Prohibition Party, 292

The Prophet. *See* Otulke Thlocco

Prostitution, 346–47

Protestants: British, 164; French, 63; politics and, 291–92; Spanish Florida, 165, 166

Public Works Administration (PWA), 318, 320

Pulp paper industry, 324–25

PWA. *See* Public Works Administration

Quadruple Alliance, 134

Queen Anne's War (War of the Spanish Succession), 115, 133, 134

Race: education and, 290, 308–9, 321–23; Florida politics and, 419–21, 424–28, *430*, 448–49; history of modern Florida, 518–20; immigration and, 473, 522; labor disputes and, 294; New Deal and, 460–61; in 1920s, 309; population percentages in Florida, *427*; Reconstruction and, 261–62, 264–68, *265*, 270, 271, 273, 274, 416–17; wilderness and, 383; World War II and, 339, 342–45, 424. *See also* Blacks; Minorities; Segregation; Whites

Racial discrimination: against blacks, 238, 262, 309, 453, 454, 457, 459–64, 479; against immigrants, 479; Jim Crow, 309, 453, 454, 464; lawsuits against, 461, 463. *See also* Civil rights

Racing, 299, 314

Railroads: construction, 239–40, 270–71, 276, 279–82, 285, 288, 300, 505; developers, 276, 279–82, 285, 287, 288, 289, 293, 505; high-speed rail, 509–10; immigration and, 474–75; maritime industries and, 406; strike (1925), 303

Rainfall, 50–51, 368

Randolph, Philip, 310, 455, *457*

Rather, Dan, 441n2

Rawlings, Marjorie Kinnan, *329*

Real estate, 364, 365. *See also* Land

Rebolledo, Diego de, 86, 113

Reconquista, 30

Reconstruction (1865–1868): blacks and, 261–68, *265*, 270, 271, 273, 274, 277, 416–17; Confederates in, 261–62, 264, 268, 271; Democrats and, 268, 271–74, 282, 296; Florida and, 260–74, 416–17; freedmen and, 260–64, 266, 268, 271; Jacksonville during, 268; Johnson's, 260–64; land transfers, 261; maritime heritage of, 402–7; race and, 261–62, 264–68, *265*, 270, 271, 273, 274, 416–17; Republicans and, 264–68, 270–74, 282, 296; steam vessels, 402–3, *404*; Tallahassee during, 266, 273, *274*; tourism during, 268, 270; Unionists in, 261–63, 271, 272; whites and, 261, 262, 264–66, 271, 282

Reconstruction Finance Corporation, 315

Recreation, 515

Reed, Harrison, 261, 266, 267, 268, 270–71, 273

Reed, Walter, 289

Reid, Robert R., 236

Religion: in 1920s, 298–99; politics and, 291–92, 297; teaching evolution and, 298. *See also* Churches; *specific religious groups*

Repartimientos (native labor levy), 63, 82, 85, 93, 107, 112–13

Republicans, 241, 283, 288, 415, 416, 418, 426; blacks and, 448–49; emancipation and, 242; in Great Depression, 315–17, 319; growing strength (1960s), 432–35; in 1920s, 296–97; Reconstruction and, 264–68, 270–74, 282, 296. *See also* Florida politics

Republic of Indians, 76, 77, 78, 82, 89

Republic of Spaniards, 76, 77, 78, 89

Republic of West Florida, 169

Reservations, 199, 205, 206, 211, 212, 214–18, 228–32, 366, 367, 378

Retirees: aging of Florida population, 501–2; development and, 514–15

Revolts: Saint-Domingue slave, 191. *See also* La Florida revolts

Ribaut, Jean (Ribault), 56, 57, 59–61, 64, 359–60, 364

Rice, Ron, 373

Richard, Francis, 226

Richards, Daniel, 264, 266

Rivera y Villalón, Pedro de, 138

River May. *See* St. Johns river

Rivers: connections, 49; La Florida, 48–49; natural moats defenses of, 53n11; settlements near, 49, 368–69; trade and, 49. *See also specific rivers*

Roads: development of, 291–93, 300, 302, 423, 506–9; expressway consequences, 509; Good Roads Movement, 506; state road

department, 302; transportation patterns and building, 508–9. *See also* Automobiles

Robinson, Joseph T., 297

Rockefeller, John D., 279

Rockledge, 270

Rogel, Juan, 65

Rojas y Borja, Luis de, 83, 84

Román de Castilla y Lugo, Miguel, 139–41

Roosevelt, Franklin D., 315–18, 320, 329, 336, 342, 460

Roosevelt, Theodore, 285, 287, 288, 444–45

Rosewood, 309, 421, 459

Royal Palm Park, 287

Rum runners, 408–9

Rural Electrification Administration, 323

Sabacola Indians, 92

Sabana System, 82

Safety Harbor precolumbian culture, 13

Saint-Domingue slave revolt, 191

Salazar y Vallecilla, Benito Ruíz de, 86

Salt production, 248–50, 378

Salvaging: industry, 358–59, 398; Spanish, 395

Sammis, John, 261

San Carlos Bay, 14, 21, 22, *23*, 28

Sánchez, Edimboro, 189, 192

Sánchez, Francisco Xavier, 126, 189, 226

Sánchez families, 121–22, 124, 126

Sanderson, John, 242

Sanford (town), 270

Sanford, Henry S., 270, 272, 276, 473

San Juan (mission), 95, 100

San Juan de Aspalaga (village), 128

San Juan del Puerto (town), 83, 95, 116, 119

San Luis, 85, 86, 118

San Luis de Talimali (mission church), *102*

San Marcos de Apalachee, 172

San Mateo (St. Matthew), 57, 60, 61. *See also* Fort Caroline

San Miguel de Gualdape, 24, 180

San Pedro (mission), 95, 100

Santa Elena (Georgia), 35, 37–38, 53n11, 62, 65, 66, 69, 70, 72, 73, 78

Santaluces, 14

Santa María de Galve (village), *130*

Santa Rosa Island, 129, 130, 134, 136–38, *139*, 246

Santa Rosa-Swift Creek precolumbian culture, 9

Saturiwa, *10*

Sauer, Carl, 358

Saunders, Robert, 463, 464

Savannah, 155, 157, 158

Savannah River, 48, 92, 114

Schools: agriculture, 451; blacks and, 446–48, 451–53, 463. *See also* Colleges

Scott, Richard "Rick" Lynn, 440–41, 509

Scott, Winfield, 206, 207, 211

Scuba diving, 413

Sea life. *See* Marine life

Searles, Robert, 86, 113

Sea turtles, 378

Secession: Democrats, and, 236–37, 240–42; Florida and, 236–37, 240–42, 244–47, 360; slavery and, 236–37, 240–42, 244–47. *See also* Civil War; Confederate States of America

Second Spanish Period, 205, 364, 375; Africans in, 187–93; maritime heritage of, 396–97; overview, 162–76

Segregation, 284, 453, 464, 465; desegregation, 426; education, 308–9, 463; Florida politics and, 419, 421, 424–27; World War II, 343–45

Seminole Indians, 1, 152, 154, 190, 192; African slaves and, 187, *188*; Big Cypress, 214, *215*, 367; Black Seminoles, 202–3; Bowlegs (chief), 204–6; chickee, 214, *215*; as cimmarones, 195; Civil War and, 253; Coacoochee, 208–10; conflicts, 47, 174, 175; Cow Creek Seminole, 214, 215; Creek Indians and, 147, 152, 154, 195–202, 204, 206, 208–10, 213–16, 229; enterprise period (1767–1817), 201–3; Everglades and, 201, 214, 216, 217, 367; Florida colonization (1716–1767), 199–200; Florida state and, 212–19, 239, 240, 508; Florida Territory and, 206–12, 227–32, 235; Great Depression and, 321, *322*; Green Corn Dance, 203, 215, 218; Holata Micco (chief), 206, 209, 210, 212–14; Hollywood, Florida, 214, 216–18; isolation (1858–1880), 214–15; Micanopy (chief), 206, 208, 209; missionaries and, 216; modern tribalism development, 215–19; Neamathla (chief), 204, 223; Osceola, 206, *207*, 208–9; Otulke Thlocco, 208, 209; overview and origins, 195–99; reservations, 199, 205, 206, 211, 212, 214–18, 228–32, 366, 367, 378; settlements, 176, 214; Tamiami Trail, 214, 216, 217; white encroachment on, 206, 208–15, 366. *See also* Creek Indians; Miccosukee Indians

Seminole Wars, 192; First (1817–1818), 47, 171, 203–5, 220; Florida Territory and, 202, 203, 206–12, 230; Second (1835–1842), 202, 203, 206–11, 230, 231, 366–67; Third, 212–14, 230; warfare and revitalization, 203

Serres, Dominic, 137

Service economy, 518

Settlements: coastal, 375, 378; ecology and, 48, 368–71; Everglades draining for, 289–90, 370–71; historical shifts in, 498; immigration and, 471, 473–74; near freshwater, 368–69, 372; near rivers, 368–69; white, 206, 208–15, 366, 368. *See also* Colonial settlements; Native American settlements

Seven Years' War, 125–26. *See also* French and Indian War

Seymour, Truman A., 255

Shield's Cove, 405

Shipbuilding, 399; industry in World War II, 336, 338; New World, 394–95

Shipping: coastal, 409; goods, 398–99, 403; lumber industry, 403; maritime industries, 406; World War II, 409, 411

Ships: careening grounds, 396–97; Civil War naval blockade, 247–48, 399–401; Spanish, 394–95. *See also* Vessels

Shipwrecks: archaeology of, 394–97, 403, 405–6; British, 396–97; Civil War, 402; houses of refuge, 406, *407*; Spanish, 394–95; World War II sunken ships, 411

Shofner, Jerrell, 265

Sholtz, Dave, 313, 315–18, 327–28, 423

Sigüenza y Góngora, Carlos de, 129

Sikes, Robert "He-Coon," 333, 349

Silas, Lawrence, 450

Silver, 76, 77

Silver Springs, 370

Simmons, William H., 222

Simpson, Charles Torrey, 384

Situado, 77, 80, 82, 84–86

Slavery, 86, 444; abolitionists, 240; in British Caribbean, 183; British settlements and Native American, 110, 114, 118, 197; Civil War and, 236, 252–53; cotton and, 186, 225, 238, *239*; Democrats and, 236–37, 240–42; emancipation, 242; in Florida state, 238–42, 276; in Florida Territory, 225–29, 231–38; free blacks and, 239; rebellions, 240; secession and, 236–37, 240–42, 244–47; in South, 244;

Spanish expeditions and, 18, 22–23. *See also* African slaves; Freedmen

Slemmer, Adam J., 246

Smacks, 405–6

Smith, Alfred E., 297

Smith, Stanley, 216

Smith v. Allwright, 345, 462

Social change: from automobiles, 506–9; from aviation, 510–11; from migrations, 503

Social history, of modern Florida, 497–526

Socialists, 296, 297

Social Security, 319

Soil: barrier islands, 47; central ridge, 45; coastal plain, 44; Native American settlements and, 47–49; overview, 41, 43–45, *46*, 47, 52n3; peninsular Florida, 52n3; piedmont, 44; southern uplands, 45; types, 43–45, *46*, 47, 52n3. *See also* Agriculture; Land

Solomon, Samuel B., 462

Somoza, Anastasio, 486

South, 256; slavery in, 244. *See also* Confederate States of America

South, Stanley, 69, 70

South Carolina, 105, 106, 126, 156, 246

Southern uplands ecology, 45

South Florida: climate of, 364; settlement, 498

Space program, 516, *517*

Spain: Africans and, 179–80, 183; African slaves and, 179, 191; constitution (1812), 169–70; subsidy to La Florida, 70–71; U.S. and, 162, 169, 220–21, 228

Spanish: conflicts with British, 72, 105–7, 110, 112–26, 132–34, 141–42, 144, 154–59, 162, 170–71, 184, 186, 187, 197; conflicts with French, 55, 58–61, 64, 96, 110, 114–15, 130–36, 142, 169, 170, 173, 176, 191, 359–60, 372; conflicts with U.S., 171–76, 188, 191–92, 202, 204–5, 220; conflict with Native Americans, 64–65, 71–72, 77, 82–86, 88, 95–96, 105–6, 113, 114, 118–19, 124–26, 133, 135, 137–40, 191, 197–98, 200, 355, 357, 359, 372; immigration into Florida state, 475–76; living with Calusa Indians, 359; marriage to Native Americans, 78; salvaging, 395; ships, 394–95

Spanish-American War (1898), 288–89, 479

Spanish Caribbean, and Africans, 180, 181, 192–93

Spanish expeditions: Africans and, 179–82; to Caribbean, 180, 181; Cuba and, 18, 19, 23, 27, 28, 35, 37, 38, 61; of de Soto, 12, 26–37, 42, 44, 53n5, 181–82; discovery of La Florida, 1, 20–21, 73; hurricanes and, 359–60; La Florida and, 1, 20–38, 43, 44, 180–82, 357, 372; map of sites, *62*; maps of, 18–19; Native Americans and, 18, 21–26, 28–35, 37, 61, 197, 357, 358, 359, 372; nature and, 357–58; overview, 18–38; to Pensacola Bay, 128–29, 393; of Ponce de León, 1, 18–23, 26, 34, 180, 181, 355, 357, 358, 363; precolumbian cultures and, 11, 13; slavery and, 18, 22–23

Spanish Florida, 42, 391; Africans in, 122–24, 179–84, *185*, 186–93, 203–4; African slaves in, 179–93; East Florida, 162–68, 173–76, 220, 222; free blacks in, 122–24, 183, 189–92; freedmen in, 184, 186; land transfers, 168–72, 176, 187, 192, 202, 205, 220, 224, 227–28; maritime heritage of, 391–97; Patriot War, 173–74, 188, 191, 192; Protestants, 165, 166; Second Spanish Period, 162–76, 187–93, 205, 364, 375; Spanish constitution in, 169–70; U.S. and, 162, 163, 168–76, 187, 188, 191, 192, 202, 205; West Florida, 162–69, 172, 176, 220, 222. *See also* La Florida

Spanish missions: California, 91, 93, 98; La Florida missions compared to other, 93, 98; pirates and, 105; Second Spanish Period and, 166; in Spanish New World, 91. *See also* La Florida missions; *specific missions*

Spanish New World, 19, 26, 30, 64; Spanish missions in, 91. *See also* La Florida

Spanish presidios, 78; La Florida missions and, 77, 87; La Florida situado and, 77, 80, 82, 84–86; Native Americans and, 76–82, 80–82, 85–89; overview, 76–77; Pensacola Bay, *131*, 132–42, *139*; Republic of Spaniards, 76, 77, 78, 89; Sabana System and, 82; silver and, 76, 77; St. Augustine, 78, 80–81, 83–86. *See also* Spanish settlements

Spanish settlements, 43; Africans and, 78, 122, 123, 174; African slaves in, 24, 78; agriculture of, 66–67, 70, 109–10, 168; British settlements and, 72, 110, 114–26, 132, 137, 141, 142, 144, 146, 156, 158, 159, 184, 186, 197; Catholicism of, 63–65, 69, 79; coastal plain, 44; Conquest by Contract, 77, 89; ecology and, 44, 358, 362–64; first, 22–25, *30*, 33, 35–38; French settlements and, 55–61, 115, 128–37, 140,

Spanish settlements—*continued*
141–42, 359–60; hurricanes and, 36, 83, 138,
140, 359–61; inhabitants' surnames, *68*; map
of, *62*; Menéndez de Avilés and, 57–73, 182,
359–60, 372, 393–94; mutinies, 24, 37, 56,
61, 69; Native Americans and, 59, 61–65,
70–72, 167–68, 172, 174, 176, 179, 182, 184, 187,
191, 192, 197–200, 202; Philip II and, 76, 78;
pirates and, 83–85, 88, 183; rivers and, 49. *See
also* La Florida; Spanish missions; Spanish
presidios; *specific Spanish settlements*
Spencer, Lucian, 216
Sponges, 285, 376, 475
Sports, 515
Sprague, John T., 266, 366
Springs, 369; Silver Springs, 370
Starke (town), 333
State Board of Public Health, 287, 321
State Board of Public Welfare, 314, 319
State Racing Commission, 314
St. Augustine, 56; British settlement of, 126, 144,
146–59; Castillo de San Marcos stone fort, 87,
88, 105, *113*, 114, 115, *116*, *117*, 118, 120, 122–25,
144, 146; church, *167*; defense of, 86–88, 105,
106, 112–26; in Florida state, 239, 279–81;
in Florida Territory, 220, 222, 226–29, 234,
237–38; Fort St. Mark, 146, 148; Governor's
House, *148*; hotels, 281; La Florida missions
and, 80, 86–88, 95, *97*, 98, 105–7; maps, *81*,
117, *187*; Menéndez de Avilés and, 59–62, 67,
69, 70, 73, 182, 394; nationalities of inhabitants of, 78; Parish Registers document, *79*; as
penal colony, 78; as seaside presidio, 78, 80;
Spanish East Florida, 162, 164, 166, 167, 170,
174, *175*, 176; as Spanish presidio, 78, 80–81,
83–86; Spanish settlement of, 1, 24, 44, 51, 52,
53n11, 59–62, 67, 69, 70, 73, 78–88, 95, *97*, 98,
105–7, 112–26, 129, 182–84, 186, *187*, 188, 190,
191, 197, 394
Steam vessels, 268, *269*, 270, 398–99, 505; *City
of Hawkinsville* steamboat, 403, *404*; Civil
War, 401–2; Reconstruction, 402–3, *404*;
tourism and, 402
Stearns, Marcellus L., 271, 272
Steele, Charles Kenzie, 464
Stickney, Lyman, 261
St. Johns: missions, 103; precolumbian culture,
8–9
St. Johns River, 49, 53n11, 56, 57, 100, 121, 124,

174, 227, 234, 268–70, 353; overview, 364;
precolumbian inhabitants along, 6–10
St. Joseph, 235–36
St. Marks, 25, 200, 204; fort, 119, 120, 125, 126;
river, 48, 49, 115, 116, 125
St. Marys River, 49, 144, 174, 175
Stowe, Harriet Beecher, 268, 343, 363, 364, 402
Strikes, labor, 294, 303
Stuart, John, 152–54, 156, 201
Sturkie Resolution, 291, 292
Sugar production, 231, 324, 325, 339
Sullivan, Mark, 512
Summerlin, Jacob, 232, *233*
Suntan lotions, 373
Supreme Court, U.S., 309, 345, 425, 426, 460,
462, 463, 465
Surruque, 82
Suwannee River, 31, 49, 84, 96, 172, 369, 378
Suwannee Valley precolumbian culture, 12, 13
Swamp Land Act (1850), 368, 369
Swamps: cypress in, 379–80. *See also* Wetlands
Swanson, Thomas E., 316
Swift Creek precolumbian culture, 9, 11

Tabert, Martin, 308
Talapoosa Indians, 137
Tallahassee, 125, 283; Capitol, *274*; during
Civil War, 242–45, 256; in Florida Territory,
223–24, 227, 228, 234, 238; during Recon-
struction, 266, 273, *274*; during World War
II, 341–43, 345, 347
Tallahassee Hills, 45
Tama Indians, 92, 102
Tamiami Trail (U.S. 41), 214, 216, 217; construc-
tion, 508
Tampa, 288, 336, 475; early development, 279,
280, 285, 505; immigration, 475–76, 479,
480, 481, 489, 490, 492, 493
Tampa Bay, 279; precolumbian, 6, 7, 10, 11, 13;
Spanish expeditions and, 28, 31, 32
Tampa Bay Hotel, 279, *280*, 288
Tampa Bulletin, 459
Tarpon (coastal steamer), 409
Tarpon Springs, 376, 475
Taylor, Zachary, 208–9
Taylor County, 321
Technology: computer companies, 518; develop-
ments, 505–12, 518; high-tech and business
service economy, 518

Television: advent (1949), 349; Miami-based, 513

Tennessee, 203

Ten Thousand Island region, 14

Tequesta natives, 14, 94

Territory of Florida. *See* Florida Possession (1812) and Territory (1822–1845)

Texas, 176

Theme parks, 513–14

Thomas, Norman, 297

Thompson, George F., 268

Tibbets, Enola Gay, 348

Tibbets, Paul, Jr., 348

Tilden, Samuel, 272

Timber. *See* Lumber industry

Timucua Indians, 12, 13, 16, 25, 29, 45, 48, 147, 364; French settlements and, 56, 64, 81; Freshwater, 94–95, 100–101; La Florida missions and, 92, 94–96, 100–101, 103–9, 112–15; Menéndez de Avilés and, 59, 62–64, 72; revolt of, 82–83, 86, 113; Saltwater, 94–95, 100–101

Timucua province, 84

"Tin Can Tourists of the World," 301

Tobacco, 166, 285

Tocobaga Indians, 13, 84, 102

Tolomato Indians, 98

Tonyn, Patrick, *153*, 153–54, 156, 158–59

Torres y Ayala, Laureano, 88, 128, 129

Tourism, 293, 364; by automobiles, 292, 301–2, 506–8; at beaches, 372–74; of Canadians, 493; development and, 280–81, 512–15; Great Depression, 328; Native Americans and, 373; nature and, 370; 1920s, 301, 306; Reconstruction, 268, 270; steam vessels and, 402; World War II, 338, 341, 347

Towns: World War II impact on small, 341, 349. *See also* Cities; *specific towns*

Trade: British, 114, 124, 141, 168, 197, 201, 205; Cuba, 85, 168, 202; fishing and, 374–75; Florida state, 403; Florida Territory, 398; French settlements, 115, 132, 134, 137, 140; La Florida, 42, 49, 70, 85, 86, 88, 124–26, 132, 134, 137, 140, 141, 166–68, 174, 202, 205, 397; Native Americans, 114, 115, 132, 140, 167–68, 197, 200–202, 205, 397; pirate threats to, 35; precolumbian, 9, 11; rivers and, 49; U.S., 168, 174

Trammell, Park, 297, 316, 420

Transportation: commercial air, 510; development of aviation (1920s), 302; historical development of Florida, 505–11; patterns and road building, 508–9. *See also* Automobiles; Aviation; Railroads

Travel: of African Americans, 451. *See also* Tourism

Travels, The (Bartram), 368

Treaty of Fort Gibson, 229, 230

Treaty of Madrid, 120

Treaty of Moultrie Creek (1823), 206, 230

Treaty of Paris, 126, 158

Treaty of Payne's Landing (1832), 229, 230

Treaty of Tordesillas (1494), 391

Treaty of Versailles, 162

Trees: cypress, 379–81; pine, 285, *286*, 326, 378–83. *See also* Lumber industry

Tropical storms, 51–52

Turnbull, Andrew, 53n8, 151, 471

Turpentine: camps, 285, 326, 382, 383; production, 285, 326, 381–83

Tuttle, Julia, 281

Twenty-First Amendment, 316

Twiggs, David, 212

Tyler, John, 236

Underwater Archaeological Preserve, 402–5, 407–11, 413

Unionists: in Civil War Florida, 245, 247, 254, 256; in Reconstruction Florida, 261–63, 271, 272

Unions: Brotherhood of Sleeping Car Porters, 310, 455, 457; New Deal for, 319

United States (U.S.) : African slaves and, 174, 175, 190, 192, 193, 203; black migration within Florida and, 343, 419–21, 454–56, 500; British conflicts with, 154–59, 170–72, 220; British Florida and, 154–59, 162; conflicts with Native Americans, 171, 172, 174–76, 188, 192, 202–15, 220, 366–67; France and, 169; land transfers, 168–72, 176, 187, 192, 202, 205, 216–17, 220, 224, 227–32; Native Americans and, 168, 171, 172, 174–76, 188, 192, 202–19, 220; Patriot War, 173–74, 188, 191, 192; Spain and, 162, 169, 220–21, 228; Spanish conflicts with, 171–76, 188, 191–92, 202, 204–5, 220; Spanish Florida and, 162, 163, 168–76, 187, 188, 191, 192, 202, 205; trade, 168, 174. *See also* American Revolution; *specific U.S. states*

Universal Negro Improvement Association, 479
University of Florida, 291, 309, 323, 463
U.S. Department of Agriculture (USDA), 339–40
Utina Indians, 96, 98, 101, 105

Valdés, Pedro de, 61
Van Buren, Martin, 224
Velasco, Diego de, 69–70
Velasco, Luis de, 35, 38, 42
Veracruz, 34, 37, 131, 135, 139
Vessels: canoes, 390; Civil War, 399; fishing, 405–6; Mariel boatlift, 485; of New World, 392; prehistoric, 390, 391; rum runner, 408. See also Ships
Vickers, Raymond B., 308
Villafañe, Ángel de, 37–38
Violence: blacks and, 268, 309, 420–21, 453–54, 459–60, 462–63, 465–66, 519–20; civil rights and, 520; Ku Klux Klan, 268, 309, 453, 459–60, 463, 519; lynchings, 309, 420–21, 453–54, 459, 519
Virginia, 247
V-J Day, 348
Voting: of blacks, 265, 266, 268, 274, 284, 296, 317, 449, 459, 462, 464, 519; Florida party registration (1972–2012), 434; poll tax, 284, 296, 317, 449, 462; in presidential election (2000), 434; Voting Rights Act, 426; white primary system, 449; of whites, 284; of women, 296, 317
Voting Rights Act (1965), 426, 431, 464

Walker, David, 262, 263
Wallace, John, 446
Walls, Josiah T., 267
Walt Disney World, 373
War of 1812, 168, 170–72, 203, 204
War of Austrian Succession, 121
War of Jenkins' Ear, 121
War of the Quadruple Alliance, 134
War of the Spanish Succession (Queen Anne's War), 115, 133, 134
Warren, Christopher, 365
Warren, Fuller, 317, 423, 424, 462
Washington, Booker T., 454
Washington, George, 157
Water, 4, 353, 355; development and, 289–90,
365, 368–74; floods and flood control, 371. See also Freshwater; Rivers; Wetlands
Waterbury, Jean Parker, 126
Watson, J. Tom, 315
Wauchope, Alejandro, 136–37
Weather. See Climate
Wedgworth, Herman Hamilton, 323
Weeden Island cultures, 9–13
Welfare: programs, 327–28; State Board of Public Welfare, 314, 319
Westcott, James D., 236, 266
West Florida: British, 144, 145, 146, 147–53, 155–58, 162; Florida Territory, 220, 222, 225, 228, 231; Republic of West Florida, 169; Spanish, 162–69, 172, 176, 220, 222
Westoes Indians, 114
Wetlands: development and draining of, 289–90, 365, 368, 370–71. See also Everglades; Swamps
Whigs, 224, 234, 235, 241, 242
White, Joseph M., 224
White, Pleasant W., 251
Whitehair, Francis P., 317
Whites: Democrats, 282, 296; encroachment on Seminole Indians, 206, 208–15, 366; environmentalists, 383; marriage to blacks, 190; primary system, 449; Reconstruction and, 261, 262, 264–66, 271, 282; settlements, 206, 208–15, 366, 368; voting of, 284. See also Race
Wildcat. See Coacoochee
Wilderness, 353; race and, 383
Wildlife, 353, 368; overview, 354. See also Birds; Marine life
Williams, John Lee, 222
Willing, James, 155
Willkie, Wendell L., 316
Wilson, Woodrow, 293
Windover Pond site (Brevard County), 5–6
Withlacoochee River, 29, 229; Cove of, 206, 208, 210
Witten, Judy, 187–88
Witten, Prince, 187–89, 191, 192
Women: Civil War impact on, 252; education of, 290, 309, 323, 341, 342; emancipation, 346; free black, 190; pay inequality of, 309; in politics, 346; voting of, 296, 317; in World War II, 345–47

Works Progress Administration (WPA), 319, 320, 322, 324–26, 376
World War I, 293–94; blacks in, 458–59
World War II, 320; agriculture during, 338–40; aviation and, 328, 335, 336, 338, 349–50; blacks in, 339, 343–45, 424; changes to cities, 340–41; citrus industry during, 338, 339; colleges during, 341, *342*, 349; development during, 336, 338, 345, 348–49, 423, 515–16; economic boom, 336, 338; Florida politics and, 423–24; German attacks off Florida coast, 335, *337*, 341; GIs at USO club, *344*; Great Depression and, 329, 336; Jacksonville during, 333, 334, 335, 338, 340, 343, 347; Key West during, 340–41; labor during, 339–40, 345; Miami during, 334–36, 338, 340, 341, 343, 345–49; migrants, 340; military installations, 333–35, 349; overview, 332–50; Pensacola during, 332, 335, 338, 340, 346; politics, 333, 345, 346; prisons, 335–36; race and, 339, 342–45, 424; recruits, *334*, 335; segregation, 343–45; shipbuilding industry, 336, 338; shipping, 409, 411; small town impact, 341, 349; sunken ships, 411; Tallahassee during, 341–43, 345, 347; tourism, 338, 341, 347; trainees in Miami Beach, *334*; training

in hotels, 333–34; V-J Day, 348; women in, 345–47
Worth, William Jenkins, 210–11
WPA. *See* Works Progress Administration
Writers, 369–70
Wylie, Philip, 348, 525

Yamasee Indians, 92, 122, 140, 146, 197; conflicts, 106, 107, 114, 118–20, 122, 198; Yamasee War, 106, 198
Yamato (Japanese colony), *474*, 475
Ybor, Vincent, 285, 475
Ybor City, 285, 475
Yeats, David, 158, 159
Yellow fever, 287, 289
Yonge, Henry, 225
Young, Joseph W., 299
Yuchi Indians, 195
Yulee, David Levy, 227, 236, *237*, 239, 240, 378
Yustaga, 84, 86, 98, 105
Yustaga Indians, 96, 100, 101, 105

Zangara, Guiseppe, 317
Zéspedes, Manuel de, 140, 159, 202
Zúñiga y Zerda, Joseph, 116, 119